Legal and Political Reforms in Sa'udi Arabia

The fractious relationship between the United States and Sa'udi Arabia has long been a central concern in Washington. In the aftermath of 9/11 and amongst ongoing wars, the United States confronts an acute dilemma: how to cooperate with Riyadh against terrorism whilst confronting anti-Americanism in the kingdom.

Using information gathered from extensive interviews with a plethora of officials, this book aims to analyze Sa'udi domestic reforms. It addresses the significant deficiency of information on such diverse matters as the judiciary and ongoing national dialogues, and provides alternative understandings of what motivates Sa'udi policy makers.

How these reforms may impact on future Sa'udi decision-making will surely generate a slew of policy concerns for the United States and other powers. This study consequently offers several clarifications and solutions and should be of interest to anyone seeking a new perspective on the motivation behind legal and political reforms in Sa'udi Arabia, and on the effects of these reforms beyond the Middle East.

Joseph A. Kéchichian is the CEO of Kéchichian & Associates, LLC, a consulting partnership that provides analysis on the Arabian/Persian Gulf region, specializing in the domestic and regional concerns of Bahrain, Iran, Iraq, Kuwait, Oman, Qatar, Sa'udi Arabia, the United Arab Emirates and Yemen. He is also a syndicated columnist based at *Gulf News* in Dubai since 2003. Between 2006 and 2011, he served as the Honorary Consul of the Sultanate of Oman in Los Angeles, California.

Legal and Political Reforms in Sa'udi Arabia

Joseph A. Kéchichian

Routledge
Taylor & Francis Group
LONDON AND NEW YORK

First published 2013
by Routledge
2 Park Square, Milton Park, Abingdon, Oxon OX14 4RN

Simultaneously published in the USA and Canada
by Routledge
711 Third Avenue, New York, NY 10017

Routledge is an imprint of the Taylor & Francis Group, an informa business

© 2013 Joseph A. Kéchichian

The right of Joseph A. Kéchichian to be identified as author of this work has been asserted by him in accordance with sections 77 and 78 of the Copyright, Designs and Patents Act 1988.

All rights reserved. No part of this book may be reprinted or reproduced or utilised in any form or by any electronic, mechanical, or other means, now known or hereafter invented, including photocopying and recording, or in any information storage or retrieval system, without permission in writing from the publishers.

Trademark notice: Product or corporate names may be trademarks or registered trademarks, and are used only for identification and explanation without intent to infringe.

British Library Cataloguing in Publication Data
A catalogue record for this book is available from the British Library

Library of Congress Cataloging in Publication Data
Kéchichian, Joseph A.
Legal and political reforms in Saudi Arabia / Joseph A. Kéchichian.
p. cm.
Includes bibliographical references and index.
1. Constitutional law–Saudi Arabia. 2. Law reform–Saudi Arabia. 3. Saudi Arabia–Politics and government–21st century. I. Title.
KMT2050.K43 2012
320.9538–dc23
2012019415

ISBN 978-0-415-63018-4 (hbk)
ISBN 978-0-415-63019-1 (pbk)
ISBN 978-0-203-08120-4 (ebk)

Typeset in Times
by Taylor & Francis Books

 Printed and bound in Great Britain by the MPG Books Group

For Thérèse, Jean, and Jeanette, who were there at the beginning.

Contents

About the author — x
Acknowledgements — xii
A note on transliteration — xiv

Introduction — 1
   Critical legal concerns 2
   A transformation of the judiciary 7
   National dialogues 9
   Political participation and municipal elections 10
   Succession and the Allegiance Commission 11
   The United States and Saʻudi Arabia 13
   Existential challenges 15
   Methodological approach 16

1 Reforms within the judiciary — 19
   Reforming the judiciary in Saʻudi Arabia 20
   The judiciary and social concerns 31
   The non-establishment 'Ulamah 34
   The status of women 43
   The judiciary and political concerns 51
   The war on terrorism 55
   Conclusion 59

2 National and international dialogues — 62
   Constitutional continuum in Saʻudi Arabia 64
   The Basic Law of Government and national dialogues 69
   King 'Abdul 'Aziz Center for National Dialogue 71
   National meetings 73
   The Saʻudi view of national dialogues 97
   A meaningful Vatican summit 99

Interfaith dialogues   101
Conclusion: another call for co-existence   106

3   **Political participation and municipal elections**   109
Political participation in a tribal environment   110
Majlis Al-Shurah under King 'Abdallah   121
An assessment of the 2005 elections   125
Conclusion: consequences of legislative changes for the monarchy   129

4   **Political reforms and the succession dilemma**   131
'Abdallah bin 'Abdul 'Aziz Al Sa'ud and the 1992 edict   133
'Abdallah after 2005   135
'Abdallah bin 'Abdul 'Aziz and succession   137
Composition of the Commission   140
Allegiance Commission responsibilities   141
Mode of operation   143
The Second Deputy Prime Minister   146
Nayif bin 'Abdul 'Aziz   146
Talal bin 'Abdul 'Aziz questions succession strategy   150
Calls for the establishment of political parties   154
Succession dilemma for Al Sa'ud   156

5   **Reforms and the petition industry**   159
Supplication to rulers   161
Petition traditions before 1979   163
Juhayman 'Utaybi and his "Letters"   165
Militant fundamentalism before 1991   167
Letters and memoranda   169
Petitions after 1992   174
Political petitions after 9/11   174
Political petitions under 'Abdallah   177
Conclusion   184

6   **Sa'udi Arabia and the United States**   188
The Sa'udi–American divorce   189
American views of post-2005 Sa'udi reforms   191
Legal and religious reforms   192
Women's emancipation   195
Scientific education   196
Socio-political dialogues and elections   197
Succession concerns   199
Security ties with US   203

The American–Saʻudi re-engagement 206
Conclusion 209

7 Conclusion   **212**
  Key social changes affecting women 214
  Legal challenges and reforms 217
  Gradual reforms 219

Appendices
  1 *Interviews 221*
  2 *Consent to Establish the King ʻAbdul ʻAziz Center for National Dialogue 222*
  3 *King ʻAbdallah's opening speech in Madrid 224*
  4 *The Madrid Declaration 226*
  5 *Saʻudi Arabia: excerpts from the 1992 Basic Law 230*
  6 *Saʻudi Arabia: Allegiance Law of Succession 231*
  7 *Saʻudi Arabia: Bylaws of the Allegiance Commission 237*
  8 *Partners in One Nation 242*
  9 *"Secular" Petition to King Fahd December 1990 248*
  10 *"Religious" Petition to King Fahd February 1991 254*
  11 *A Vision for the Present and Future of the Nation 257*
  12 *In Defense of the Nation 262*
  13 *A Deviant Junta has Taken Hold of the Saʻudi Media and is Endangering Islamic Society and Its Values 271*
  14 *2007 Saudi Women Petition for Driving Right 274*
  15 *Saʻudi Activists Petition King for Reforms 275*
  16 *A Declaration of National Reform 283*

Notes   288
Bibliography   328
Index   336

About the author

Dr. Joseph A. Kéchichian is the CEO of Kéchichian & Associates, LLC, a consulting partnership that provides analysis on the Arabian/Persian Gulf region, specializing in the domestic and regional concerns of Bahrain, Iran, Iraq, Kuwait, Oman, Qatar, Sa'udi Arabia, the United Arab Emirates, and Yemen. He is also a syndicated columnist based at *Gulf News* in Dubai since 2003 (with Arabic translations simultaneously published in the Muscat, Oman daily *'Uman*). Between 2006 and 2011, he served as the Honorary Consul of the Sultanate of Oman in Los Angeles, California.

Dr. Kéchichian received a doctorate in Foreign Affairs from the University of Virginia in 1985, where he also taught (1986–88) and assumed the assistant deanship in international studies (1988–89). In the summer of 1989, he was a Hoover Fellow at Stanford University (under the US State Department Title VIII Program) and, between 1990 and 1996, he was an Associate Political Scientist at the Santa Monica-based RAND Corporation, as well as a lecturer at the University of California in Los Angeles (UCLA).

Between 1998 and 2001, Kéchichian was a fellow at UCLA's Gustav E. von Grunebaum Center for Near Eastern Studies, where he held a Smith Richardson Foundation grant (1998–99) to write *Succession in Saudi Arabia* [New York: Palgrave (2001)], which was translated into Arabic as *Al-Khilafah fil-'Arabiyyah al-Sa'udiyyah* in 2002, and reprinted in a 2nd edition in 2003 [Beirut and London: Dar Al Saqi]. In 2003–4 he held a Davenport fellowship at Pepperdine University in Malibu, California, to produce *Power and Succession in Arab Monarchies* (also on a Smith Richardson Foundation grant) [Boulder, Colorado: Lynne Rienner Publishers (2008)], which was translated into Arabic as *Al-Sultah wa-Ta'aqub al-Hukm fil-Mamalikah al-'Arabiyyah*, 2 volumes [Beirut and London: Riad El-Rayyes Books (2012)].

Kéchichian published *Political Participation and Stability in the Sultanate of Oman* [Dubai: Gulf Research Center (2005)], *Oman and the World: The Emergence of an Independent Foreign Policy* [Santa Monica: RAND (1995)], and edited *A Century in Thirty Years: Shaykh Zayed and the United Arab Emirates* [Washington, DC: The Middle East Policy Council (2000)], as well as *Iran, Iraq, and the Arab Gulf States* [New York: Palgrave (2001)]. In 2003, he co-authored (with R. Hrair Dekmejian) *The Just Prince: A Manual of*

Leadership [London: Saqi Books], which includes a full translation of the *Sulwan al-Muta'* by Muhammad Ibn Zafar al-Siqilli, which appeared in Turkish as *Adil Hükümdar* (translated by Baris Dogru) [Istanbul: Kirmizi Kedi Yayenevi] in 2009. His most recent contribution was *Faysal: Saudi Arabia's King for All Seasons* [Gainesville, Florida: University Press of Florida (2008)], which was translated into Arabic as *Faysal: Al-Malik wal-Dawlah* [Beirut: Dar al-'Arabiyyah lil-Mawsu'at (2012)].

The author of over a dozen book chapters, close to fifty peer-reviewed academic essays, and over 300 book reviews, Kéchichian's latest study is *Qaboos: A Ruler who Revived the Sultanate Of Oman* [forthcoming].

Acknowledgements

The first decade of the 20th century was difficult for young Sa'udis who, more often than not, were better plugged into the rest of the world than most of their global counterparts. Savvy travelers who frequently vacationed with their families in Europe or Asia, most were bombarded with negative interpretations of their country. An undeniable generational gap between the vast majority of the population and the kingdom's leadership allegedly prevented the latter from recognizing socio-economic needs that, presumably, preoccupied scores of young men and women eager to make whatever contributions they could to their societies. Expert opinion concluded that most were not allowed to contemplate such contributions, much less implement them.

The idea for this book must be attributed to a young Jiddah university student who challenged me to observe and analyze the many reform programs under way in her country and, in her inimical words, "see for yourself whether King 'Abdallah bin 'Abdul 'Aziz is a reformer or not." To be sure, the octogenarian monarch was in a hurry to introduce as many changes as possible, which was uncharacteristic of Arabian Peninsula rulers. After 2005, a series of announcements were made at a dizzying pace, often to address sensitive questions that were either raised by Sa'udis anxious to see genuine reforms or were the result of spillover effects of epochal proportions elsewhere in the Arab and Muslim worlds. In response, the king tackled taboo topics, including legal matters, a subject heretofore reserved for esoteric studies that delved into religious texts far more than political ones. Given the nature of *Shari'ah* law and the role it played in Sa'udi society, this was entirely understandable, though one could not possibly fathom the scope of these reforms without gaining some insights into the religious texts under discussion. Although my young interlocutor's challenge was daunting, my class notes – and scores of textbooks – from Professor 'Abdul 'Aziz Sachedina's magisterial courses on *Usul al-Fiqh* at the University of Virginia, proved to be invaluable. Little did I know how valuable his year-long seminars in 1982–83 would be, and I wish to extend my profound gratitude to this immensely gifted scholar.

Professor Robert E. Looney, who taught me how to solve analytical problems, deserves special praise. Over the years he graciously devoted some of his valuable time whenever I called on him for advice (which was often), and it is a real pleasure to recognize his contributions towards my intellectual development.

Dozens of individuals in the Kingdom of Sa'udi Arabia welcomed me into their offices and homes to answer scores of questions on a variety of subjects during repeated visits to the country. Although 48 personal interviews were conducted for this project, only 16 were on the record, which is the reason why 32 names were left off my list (appendix 1). I thank those who agreed to be quoted, as well as those who requested anonymity. It was difficult to determine whether off-the-record conversations were any different, or franker, but I respected everyone's preferences.

The Smith Richardson Foundation in Westport, Connecticut once again found merit in my proposal, and awarded me a grant to embark on this project. The Foundation's *International Security and Foreign Policy Program*, whose goal is to assist the US policy community develop "effective national security strategies and foreign policies," supported projects that assisted in identifying, protecting, and advancing American interests and values overseas. Allan Song, the Senior Program Officer, encouraged me to apply for the grant, and I wish to formally acknowledge the Foundation's consistent attention to the Gulf region in general, and Sa'udi Arabia in particular, given that the region and the countries around the Persian Gulf are vital US national security interests. Paula Landesberg, the Administrative Associate, and Dale Stewart, the Foundation's Records Coordinator, proved to be congenial colleagues. Under the able leadership of the Senior Vice President, Dr. Marin Strmecki, the Foundation approved timely extensions to complete this work and to secure its publication. Dale also coordinated the grant's various requirements at the Middle East Institute (MEI) in Washington, D.C.

At MEI, President Wendy Chamberlin welcomed me as a Non-Resident Fellow in 2009–11 when the bulk of the book was composed, and I thank this talented former ambassador who served our nation with distinction. As a long-term member of this noble institution, I value and cherish my association with one of our nation's premier centers, whose focus on the Middle East in general, and on the Arab world in particular, is legendary. I also thank Michael Ryan, now a Senior Fellow at The Jamestown Foundation, who shepherded the grant at MEI in his capacity as Senior Vice President.

Finally, I thank the publications teams at Routledge in London, starting with Cathy Hartley and Joe Whiting for accepting the manuscript, and Kathryn Rylance for shepherding it through various editorial stages. Andrew Watts, my production editor, deserves special accolades for his coordination skills as the manuscript moved from one station to the next. Peter Rozum Murray, my copy editor, must receive special recognition. He attended to every detail, caught embarrassing mistakes, and otherwise was diligent with the final text. As publishing teams go, the one at Routledge stood out, and I am grateful for their meticulousness.

A note on transliteration

A modified version of the Library of Congress transliteration system has been adopted throughout this book. However, the style used by the *International Journal of Middle East Studies* has been relied upon in rendering Arabic words and names. For practical purposes, all diacritical marks for long vowels and velarized consonants have been eliminated, except for the *hamza* (') and the *ayn* ('). Thus, a name that is commonly rendered in English as Mohammed, becomes Muhammad, and Mecca becomes Makkah. Regrettably, there are still numerous references to Mecca or Sheik, which need attention if for no other reason than consistency. In modern Arabic, even when using standard pronunciation, the feminine *-ah* is often ignored, with the *-h* usually silent and not recorded. Consequently, we see it as *-a*, like in *fatwa, Shia, Sharia*, or even *Ulama*. Strangely, however, the *-h* is kept in other circumstances, including Riyadh or Jiddah or even Shaikh when it is not written as Sheikh. Throughout this book, an effort has been made to be both consistent and accurate, which is why the *-h* is recorded in all instances. Therefore, all transliterated words that qualify include the silent *-h*, as in *fatwah, 'Ulamah, Shari'ah, Shaykh*, and *Shurah*. Although special care has been devoted to standardizing the spellings of as many transliterated words as possible, there are—inevitably—a few inconsistencies that, I trust, readers will understand.

An effort was made to clarify family names as well. When referring to the proper appellation of ruling families, the Arabic word *Al*, which means "family," precedes the name of the eponymous founder. In Sa'udi Arabia, the founder imparted his name to the family, thus the Al Sa'ud. A lower case *al-* often refers to a sub-branch of the ruling family. For instance, Sa'ud al-Faysal is the son of the late King Faysal bin 'Abdul 'Aziz Al Sa'ud. Furthermore, although the transliteration of *'Abd* (servant or slave in Arabic) is rendered as *'Abdul*, I am aware that the *-ul* (*-al*) is really the article of the succeeding word, as in 'Abdul Allah, and that together they mean "servant of God." In that regard the family of Muhammad 'Abdul Wahhab is not simply Al Shaykh, but Al al-Shaykh, or "House of the Shaykh," as his descendents are called. Yet, I use 'Abdallah rather that 'Abdullah throughout this text because it comes as close as possible to Library of Congress and *International Journal of Middle East Studies* protocols.

Finally, while I use the common English spellings for proper names whenever known, as well as for names of countries, I include the *hamza* or *ayn* as applicable. Thus Sa'udi Arabia rather than Al-Mamlakat al-'Arabiyyah al-Sa'udiyyah. Arabic speakers will know the correct reference for transliterated words throughout the text and understand how difficult transliteration can be. I urge patience and understanding, as well as forgiveness wherever I digressed.

Introduction

Over a single week in late 2007, the Custodian of the Two Holy Mosques, King 'Abdallah bin 'Abdul 'Aziz, authorized the establishment of a High Court, issued by-laws for his 2006 succession edict that named its permanent members, and ordered his foreign minister to take necessary steps to counter the rise of the kingdom's regional hegemonic foe. 'Abdallah affirmed his will to power, husbanded new reforms that aimed to refurbish vital institutions, and strengthened the Al Sa'ud ruling family.[1] Though critics dismissed these measures as cosmetic steps that failed to introduce genuine reforms in the Sa'udi body politic, the monarch's initiatives were anything but superficial, as painstakingly explained by the patient ruler. To be sure, while every sovereign articulates a "will to power," Riyadh perceived its various political and religious institutions as the vehicles for the kingdom's *raison d'état*, which first emerged in 1932 under 'Abdul 'Aziz bin 'Abdul Rahman – erroneously referred to Ibn Sa'ud – and was honed into an art form by Faysal bin 'Abdul 'Aziz. Although the founder articulated a "Sa'udi" identity, this will to power was severely tested under Faysal, who confronted an ideological challenge from Egypt and family members who objected to his austerity measures.[2] Successive rulers secured the survival of the regime, linked the latter to order, and ensured the triumph of Al Sa'ud ideology. Faysal sharpened the parameters through which ideology was understood, and envisaged a logically constructed view of social and political life containing elements of myth and symbolism, which were used to communicate his message in simplified form. For him, as for 'Abdallah in 2012, ideology was a lens through which the world was viewed to develop positive judgments that could be relied upon to form subjective assessments. 'Abdallah thus identified what he considered to be deleterious behavior, recognized values and outcomes worth striving for, and adopted normative parameters to help him govern effectively. His "will to power" was the sum total of his assessments, as well as the proper allocation of resources throughout the social strata, to enhance rulership and authority and, by implication, to guarantee the regime's legitimacy.[3] How well 'Abdallah managed his manifold domestic concerns, and successfully moved political markers, illustrated his preoccupations as they revealed the many internal challenges facing Riyadh.[4]

Critical legal concerns

The first critical step taken by 'Abdallah a few years after his accession was the establishment of an independent judiciary. In fact, this move was neither a spontaneous decision, nor a reaction to the slew of clashes that had occurred between the kingdom's clerics and members of the intelligentsia throughout the past two decades. Still, what prompted the king to finally launch his long-term plan were several egregious cases that mobilized public opinion.

One of the key events that prompted action was the September 2007 petition to King 'Abdallah, which urged him to release nine advocates who were held for at least seven months without a trial, ostensibly because they called for the establishment of a constitutional monarchy. According to Muhammad bin Hudayjan al-Harbi, one of the signatories, at least 50 reformists signed the petition at the time. Ironically, this particular plea was mailed to the ruler rather than hand-delivered in an audience, as custom would require, because many of the signatories deemed that they were not welcome at Court. Remarkably, the petition was widely circulated and debated, which highlighted both the crackdown on reformists and, more important, Riyadh's awareness of its consequences.[5] Importantly, the ten-page document carried cellular telephone numbers in addition to names, which illustrated how emboldened many felt, aware that their actions might guarantee reprisals. It was the dawn of a new era, long before Arab youth revolted throughout the region, starting in late 2010 and early 2011.

Whether these petitioners were energized by a senior member of the ruling family, HRH Talal bin 'Abdul 'Aziz, and his call to establish a political party, which would presumably be open to reformists, was difficult to determine. Suffice it to say that activists supported Prince Talal's oft-repeated ideas. In the event, the nine detainees, all prominent lawyers who were first arrested in February 2007, faced serious charges.[6] According to interior ministry officials, the "Riyadh 9" were allegedly involved in funding terrorist groups, or were mulling the formation of an Islamic political party. Since the nine did not appear in a court of law to answer charges, observers believed that they were arrested for contemplating the creation of a political party that, under current regulations, is banned in Sa'udi Arabia. The petition on their behalf confirmed this assertion because it read that all nine were "examining ideas pertaining to civil society mechanisms, such as an 'Islamic national charter' or an 'Islamic constitution party' and a 'committee for freedoms and basic rights' that would be proposed to a number of reformists." The guilt-by-association charge – funding terrorists – was rejected *in toto* as the document contended that the real purpose of these detentions was to "tarnish [the image of] proponents of a civil society."[7] In the event, the petition urged King 'Abdallah to free all nine activists, or to ensure that they get a public trial as stipulated by Sa'udi law. The very idea of asking citizens be granted a trial was new and clearly upset the proverbial apple-cart as conservative officials seldom appreciated being asked how to interpret the law. 'Abdallah surprised many when he ordered that 'Isam Basrawi, one of the nine advocates of a constitutional monarchy, be freed in late September, although he may have been released for health reasons.[8]

This decision was not the only step taken by the ruler. In what must have been the toughest judgment since he acceded to the throne, 'Abdallah warned Sa'udi clerics not to exploit their privileges for political ends, a message whose tone and content recalled the founder's fury at religious figures who challenged his authority.[9] An oft-reported oral tradition alleged that the founder king stopped Shaykh Ibn Nimr's Friday *khutbah* (sermon) in a Riyadh mosque when the latter recited several Qur'anic verses to discourage cooperation with non-Muslims. 'Abdul 'Aziz's fury against the Shaykh became a true legend that encouraged the "live and let live" philosophical preferences of the Al Sa'ud, who understood, perhaps more than the preacher in the 1930s – as well as more recent equivalents – the need to seek and receive sorely needed developmental assistance. In recent years, Riyadh insisted that some imams were manipulating their privileged platforms to rant against issues to which they were not privy, and called for self-restraint. Speaking with the ruler's blessing, one of the kingdom's leading clerics, Shaykh Salih Al Luhaydan, publicly warned against the transformation of prayer into political speech. In Luhaydan's own words: "There are imams who digress from prayer to the point where it becomes a news bulletin. [Our prayers are] not an occasion to mention friends and enemies," he opined.[10] Another influential cleric, Shaykh Salih Al Sadlan – a leading faculty member at the Imam Muhammad bin-Sa'ud Islamic University in Riyadh – chimed in with an even stronger criticism, maintaining that some imams were transforming their pulpits into the "United Nations Organization." In fact, many imams were probably taking advantage of their positions to pray for Muslim "victories" in Chechnya, Afghanistan, Iraq, Somalia and other countries going through crises, which did not please the monarch.[11]

Remarkably, this warning was just the tip of the iceberg, as observers felt the palace's growing anger. In a major blow to the Islamist ideology espoused by extremists like 'Usamah bin Ladin and his followers, Riyadh managed to persuade a leading opposition figure, Shaykh Salman bin Fahd Al-Awdah, to criticize those who injured Islam. "We as scholars of Islam reject what Osama does," Al-Awdah wrote in an open letter posted on his website, www.islamtoday.com, and he questioned the validity of the reliance on violence. "What have we gained from the destruction of a whole country such as Iraq and Afghanistan," asked the popular cleric, and "who benefits from turning countries like Sa'udi Arabia, Algeria, and Morocco into insecure places?"[12]

In the event, this was a significant victory for the Al Sa'ud because al-Awdah was never part of the official religious establishment, and though he switched sides, his core beliefs were always suspect. Still, because of his reputation, his views were perceived by a vast majority, especially among younger Sa'udis, as being relatively objective.[13] Indeed, the scholar did not mince his words and repeatedly asked: "Brother Osama. How many wars and how much bloodshed have occurred in the name of Al-Qaeda? How many innocents, old men, children are killed in the name of Al-Qaeda? Are you happy to meet God carrying this heavy burden on your shoulders?" Those who heard Al-Awdah were awed by his straightforward tone, blaming the Al-Qa'idah leader for what no one else dared utter: namely, a lust for power. Amazingly, and furthermore, Al-Awdah made a direct linkage with the tragic events of 9/11 when he declared: "The attacks of September 11 resulted in the deaths of thousands of human beings. Unknown callers to Islam (missionaries) are by far better. They help tens of thousands become Muslims without shedding blood."[14] Whether the Al-Awdah essay was planned with the blessings of the kingdom's religious and civilian authorities were difficult to determine, although repeated inquiries indicated that he was not coached. Still, in a carefully vetted system where little occurs haphazardly, Al-Awdah was probably privy to what was about to happen to the clerical establishment. An astute Al-Awdah could well have taken preventive measures, or he may have finally realized that Islam's peaceful attributes deserved far more attention than extremists granted it. As it happened, Al-Awdah rejected violence and expressed his sorrow over the negative image that certain extremist actions imposed on Islam, which was, at least from King 'Abdallah's perspective, a good omen for the country. The monarch was satisfied by such contributions but gave strict instructions to pursue criminals who refused to repent.

Starting in 2004, Sa'udi authorities led by Muhammad bin Nayif, the Deputy Interior Minister for Security Affairs, spread a broad canvas and arrested 3,200 individuals charged with embracing the *takfir* ideology (accusing Muslims who disagreed as being infidels).[15] This was a major sweep, but what was unique this time around was the lengthy counseling that followed. Most detainees, who included clerics, were subjected to heavy psychoanalysis. A Counseling Committee composed of about 100 "Ministry of Interior" and "Ministry of Islamic Affairs, Endowments, Call and Guidance personnel" – religious scholars, preachers, specialists in religious doctrine and law, psychologists and social workers – reformed detainees. According to Muhammad Al-Nujaimi, a member of the Counseling Committee and professor of comparative jurisprudence at the King Fahd Security College, thousands of meetings were held to counsel extremists what *Shari'ah* [Islamic] law actually stipulated. "The suspects were largely confused about the meaning of *jihad*, which led to their believing in committing blind violence," Al-Nujaimi asserted.[16] "They also viewed that the present Muslim rulers, scholars and public were infidels, and therefore demanded the establishment of a single Islamic state," which was neither acceptable nor doable.[17]

There was no doubt that this was an exercise in deprogramming. For Al-Nujaimi, individuals were released – and 1,500 were "healthy" enough to return home by late 2007 – "after several graded sessions with the committee," convinced them "of their misguided vision, [as] they renounced their erroneous ideologies, including the concept of driving out all infidels from the Arabian Peninsula." King 'Abdallah's will to power required that those subjected to these counseling sessions understood and accepted "the concept of obedience to a ruler, loyalty, conditions for *bay'ah* (declaration of allegiance to a ruler) and the mistaken concept of murder and violence without guilt."[18] Slowly but surely, Islamist clerics were rehabilitated, as hundreds turned away from extremism. Interestingly, popular opposition to many excesses helped Riyadh accelerate its rehabilitative initiatives, relying on public opinion to mobilize support. In fact, prevalent anger was no longer simply a matter of anecdotal occurrences, as disproportionate reactions became frequent. In September 2007, two Sa'udi women called members of the Commission for the Promotion of Virtue and the Prevention of Vice "terrorists," allegedly because they were stopped for not conforming to the kingdom's public dress code. What was remarkable about this incident was the courage of the women, one of whom sprayed the *mutawa'in* – the dreaded religious police – with pepper spray while the other filmed the incident that occurred in the Eastern Province city of Al-Khobar. According to a Commission spokesperson, two officers "were attacked, cursed and sworn at by two women, who were blatantly dolled up," meaning the women were wearing makeup. Although the women apologized for "attacking" *mutawa'in* officers, signed a statement recognizing their infringements, and were promptly released, the mere fact that Commission members saw the women's faces meant that the latter were not veiled. Other incidents in the far more liberal city of Jiddah preoccupied *mutawa'in* who worked in earnest to prevent the mixing of the sexes. Few contemplated that such reactions would ever be recorded in Sa'udi Arabia.[19] Over the course of several visits to the kingdom, it was now possible to confirm that Sa'udi women, not their expatriate counterparts, moved about without a *niqab* (face veil). Although more frequent in Jiddah than elsewhere, Sa'udi women walked along the *corniche*, or shopped in various malls, uncovered. Moreover, it was also possible to see Sa'udi women in Ta'if and Abhah with exposed faces, although less so in Riyadh.[20] While *mutawa'in* patrols diminished in frequency, they were still visible, as were emboldened women who went about their businesses. Members of the ruling family, including the monarch, followed periodic incidents vigilantly and while most interlocutors restrained themselves to the utmost, discussions held in majlis settings often covered details, especially what was seldom revealed in the press.[21] Nevertheless, the straw that broke the proverbial camel's back, and which led 'Abdallah to action, was the horrible case of the so-called "Qatif Girl."[22]

According to a well-placed source, King 'Abdallah was furious when he heard of the case, and turned his wrath in private against clerics who appeared to be taking the law into their hands. In the case of the "Qatif Girl," a couple was raped by a gang, with the young woman sentenced to 200 lashes and six months in prison because she was found guilty of being in "isolation" with a man in a automobile vehicle. 'Abdallah deemed that the victim had been subjected to "a brutal crime" and issued a full pardon. Importantly, Justice Minister 'Abdallah Al al-Shaykh read the exoneration on television and, in the ruler's own words: "A mistake in pardoning is less than a mistake in punishment, according to Islamic jurists. As no final ruling was issued by the court, besides a *Ta'azir* ruling [a ruling based on an interpretation of *Shari'ah* by a judge or panel of judges], we are allowed to pardon her." The King would simply not allow the court to carry out its excessive sentence of 200 lashes and prison term because the woman was deemed to be a victim and because the man with whom she was in "isolation" was in fact her fiancé. The pardon further ordered the suspension of the trial against both defendants as well as a full pursuit of the seven young men accused of rape.

Although the monarch uttered supportive words towards independent justices, his pardon nevertheless sent a warning to those who failed to protect victims, which was an incredibly novel idea. A day after the pardon, members of the "Sa'udi Women's Association," issued a statement thanking 'Abdallah "for recognizing the brutal nature of the crime and reversing the decision to punish the rape victim." The statement further requested that Riyadh issue legislation to protect "women from abuse and family oppression."[23] While no such legislation has appeared to date, the monarch was on a roll, asserting his will to power and sending clear warnings to the religious establishment. Developments between 2008 and 2012 further illustrated Riyadh's intent and while several clerics were unhappy with the pace of change, most reluctantly accepted the ruler's decrees. In fact, Riyadh tightened its grip an extra notch by introducing a specific royal order that defined who was authorized to issue religious interpretations, best illustrated by the Summer 2010 injunction to curtail the issuance of religious decrees to qualified members.[24] Nevertheless, in 2007 the Sa'udi government was probably responding to pleas issued by local and international human rights organizations, and the "Qatif Girl" case demonstrated that the monarch was monitoring the matter rather closely. Moreover, like his father, 'Abdallah bin 'Abdul 'Aziz was keen to set specific parameters on judicial matters. According to reliable sources, the monarch winced when told that "one of the judges of the High Court openly expressed his desire to see the rape victims and the rapists executed" in this case, horrified that respected members of the community could think and speak in such a degrading fashion. Therefore, it came as no surprise that he rejected the clerical verdict rendered in this case for being unjust and, like his father, took it upon himself to bestow true and fair justice.

Yet, to placate powerful clerics and to further channel challenges emanating from conservative clergymen, 'Abdallah allocated SR7b (US$2.8b) to develop the judiciary and Grievances Board laws, to prepare a new cadre of qualified judges. Modern facilities, court buildings and other requirements were envisaged to alter the medieval image of the judiciary. In fact, the new regulations foresaw the transfer of judiciary privileges from the Supreme Judiciary Council (SJC) to the Supreme Court, leaving the function of the SJC confined to the employment affairs of judges. This was classic 'Abdallah, who recognized clerical rights but worked in earnest to modernize them. Towards that end, his latest call stipulated the establishment of seven grades for the judiciary, including the Supreme Court, which was responsible for monitoring the application of verdicts under *Shari'ah* as well as all royal decrees. The Supreme Court, which would be the equivalent of a Western-style Supreme Court, would thus rule on appeals, criminal prosecutions, personal affairs, and commercial and labor cases. What 'Abdallah was clearly doing was empowering an institution to stand as "an independent demonstrative judiciary reporting directly to the King," whose magistrates enjoyed guarantees, stipulated in the emergent judiciary system.[25] No one was immune to these methods as an unnamed imam in Ha'il found out in early 2008. Spewing anti-Western sermons from the pulpit, the imam was sentenced to seven months in jail and 150 lashes. Riyadh balked at various pleas to release him after the overzealous cleric issued death threats to a government official.[26]

While the October 2, 2007 announcements – to create an independent High Court as well as a Grievances Board – mandated that the two bodies to supervise the implementation of *Shari'ah* and laws enacted by the king, they buttressed the authority of trained judges to reach relatively free decisions. In fact, the new High Court was empowered to do much more than evaluate rulings, or uphold verdicts issued by appeals courts. Once fully realized, plainly defined directives required that adjudicators apply fair and uniform measures across the board, precisely to eliminate current fluctuations due to varying and sometimes contradictory interpretations. This was a major step forward, and while the Supreme Judiciary Council was authorized to oversee administrative aspects of the bench, including the appointment of magistrates, another feature required that judges undergo periodic training. This truly unique novelty was astonishing in a country that experienced a severe shortage of magistrates, where fewer than 50 men adjudicated over 80,000 cases per year. Thus, the challenge was to provide adequate training to judges and attorneys not only in the law itself, but also in the sorely needed accountability process.[27] Nevertheless, the mere fact that significant resources were earmarked for such projects illustrated the ruler's intentions, clearly motivated by the quest for proficiency.

A transformation of the judiciary

The Sa'udi judicial system has often been criticized for its failure to administer justice, largely due to inadequate legal procedures, red tape and rigid interpretation of *Shari'ah* law by appointed judges. The mere fact that King 'Abdallah tackled this critical issue illustrated his grave concerns with the rule of law. Indeed, among the many reforms that were introduced in recent years, none were as significant as legal transformations, especially as these were ill understood because so few experts addressed fundamental changes under way within the country's judiciary. Many legal experts have pointed out that the problem with the current system was qualitative as well as quantitative. Courts were overburdened, and there was an acute shortage of judges, which overwhelmed the system: courts simply took years to rule on simple cases of divorce or family disputes. Furthermore, bureaucracy and red tape created unnecessary delays, which frustrated litigants caught in the whirlwind of judicial inefficiency. As reported above, 'Abdallah announced a major project to reform the judicial system, and allocated SR7 billion (approximately $2.8b) to upgrade courts and train judges in an attempt to reform the entire judiciary.[28] Planned changes included establishing special criminal courts and family courts, along with courts for issues related to traffic, the economy, business and sports. In fact, the Ministry of Justice defined the new jobs that would be available with the start of the specialized courts in 2008, concentrating on legal training to guarantee more qualified judges and lawyers.

Still, Muslim scholars believed that more drastic measures were necessary to achieve successful reforms. "To reform the judiciary, we need to reform the *Shari'ah* colleges first and upgrade the level of these institutions," declared Dr. Tarek Al-Suwaidan, a prominent scholar. "There should be a more advanced curriculum, and the teaching standards should be enhanced," he underscored.[29] While the cleric recognized that the poor quality of education in these very important institutions was a handicap, he urged the creation of well-rounded Muslim scholars and judges familiar with international law and educated on aspects of modern-day needs and concerns. According to Dr. Al-Suwaidan, students who planned to join *Shari'ah* colleges ought to have at least a bachelor's degree in business, law or other specialized fields, to make them more knowledgeable and guarantee a higher standard of qualification.[30] An equally critical focus emphasized that *Shari'ah* law graduates should be well versed in current commercial laws and familiar with cyberspace crime, copyright violations, or labor issues, as well. Indeed, the inadequacy of current judges and their narrow breadth of knowledge may well have created many grievances and denied both nationals and expatriates their right to fair trials and legal representation in the kingdom. How to transform such a system was a gargantuan challenge. Simply stated, it was forcefully argued that judges could no longer ignore contemporary advancements, either through ignorance or tunnel vision, because doing so jeopardized the very relevance of *Shari'ah* law in a modern world. It was such a lack of knowledge that infuriated King 'Abdallah in the "Qatif Girl" rape case that sentenced the victim to a prison term.

What were, consequently, the debates that propelled Sa'udis to demand changes in the judiciary? Was Sa'udi society as a whole embarrassed by its legal system when this case surfaced? What were the pressures on the executive to reform a system that rendered verdicts that failed to distinguish victims from criminals? Indeed, the Sa'udi National Society for Human Rights forcefully raised these questions in 2007, when it published a report that strongly criticized the judicial system, accusing clerics of failing to serve justice.[31] The report outlined many human rights violations, among them rampant discrimination against women (essentially sanctioning domestic violence), awful conditions in Sa'udi prisons, and the maltreatment of non-Sa'udis working and living in the kingdom. It further railed against the actions of the *Hay'at al-Amr bil-Ma'ruf wal-Nahi 'an anl-Munkar* [Commission for the Promotion of Virtue and Prevention of Vice] in its dealings with law-abiding citizens. "We need to establish civic courts administered by judges who have graduated from law colleges with degrees obtained from abroad," said Kamel Ahmad Al-Shamsi, a Sa'udi legal expert.[32] "We need to use the expertise of other, more advanced Arab countries in civic law and sign contracts with cadres who can serve as consultants and judges," he confessed, highlighting the overall awareness that urgent actions were necessary. Sa'udi judges, many of whom insisted that students should learn through apprenticeships or with scholars who traced their learning to Islam's roots, did not share these courageous perspectives. Naturally, qualified law professors wished to update various legal institutions, and this difference was the principal reason behind the lack of a globally accepted qualification of a *Shari'ah* scholar and the absence of globally accepted standards for *Shari'ah* rules. In fact, *Shari'ah* rules continued to be subject to different interpretations from different Muslim scholars who were reluctant to codify *Shari'ah* laws, and there was a lack of consensus on many issues that remained of major concern to Muslims in general and Sa'udis in particular. Moreover, what was of some significance was the Sa'udi awareness that the time to address these grave shortcomings was limited, and that further indecision, or acquiescence to the status quo, would not be in Sa'udi interests. That is why special efforts were made to articulate a sense of urgency.[33]

Reforming the legal system and training qualified judges, therefore, would not be easy, even though King 'Abdallah made it a top priority. It was essential for Sa'udi scholars to be connected with the needs and concerns of the international Muslim community, he reasoned, as he encouraged senior legal advisors to think of how *Shari'ah* could be codified to better serve Sa'udis and all Muslims. It was essential not only to outline the rights and duties of citizens and expatriates alike, the monarch informed his advisors, but also to define the responsibilities and limits of all religious officials.[34] This latter initiative was revolutionary, to say the least, even if its repercussions were unclear. 'Abdallah insisted that no one should be above the law – not judges, not members of the Commission for the Promotion of Virtue and Prevention of Vice, not the wealthy, not even religious scholars. It was uncertain whether such a sweep included the ruling family, but the mere fact that a debate to urgently reform the judiciary was now open in the kingdom was worthy of attention.

National dialogues

An equally important recent development that affirmed 'Abdallah's "will to power" was the decision to encourage a national dialogue on different social issues.[35] As discussed at some length in Chapter 2, a series of major national gatherings occurred over a relatively short period of time, which illustrated how rich these debates were. In the event, they showcased both the society's cultural strengths, as well as those shortcomings that needed attention at this stage in the country's development. They certainly allowed many to display intellectual and managerial experiences that were documented for the benefit of all citizens.[36]

To date, the eight National dialogues illustrated what it actually entailed to engage in such efforts, either to create positive changes or resisting them.[37] Sa'udis discovered how difficult it was to achieve change, especially when the environment was not habituated to welcoming them. Nevertheless, what these dialogues demonstrated was that preparing for reform was time consuming, and that dialogue could not become a competition where potential winners and probable losers clashed. Rather, the public was exposed to ideas, projects, and various recommendations to assess their worth. Opening channels of communication and creating opportunities for participation were novel methodologies that shocked television viewers. Many quickly learned that dialogue did not mean one-way communication. In rarely seen public social exercises, Sa'udis heard how ambiguities meant lack of clarity, and how the latter prevented reforms. They paid attention to speakers who clarified objectives, defended ideas no matter how complex, and focused on the subject matter rather than repeating stale personality-driven prose. The initial national dialogue experience taught citizens that those who resisted change backed off when they understood what the debate was all about. As the frequency of the debates increased, many learned from shared experiences, some accustomed themselves to listening, while others understood the substances of key debates. A few even had the courage to admit miscalculations, and apologized for their persistence, instead of resisting. The first eight dialogues allowed thousands of Sa'udis to participate – while millions watched on television – and for Riyadh to raise the bar by broadcasting such fare and illustrating a level of transparency in the type of conversations under way. King 'Abdallah was anxious to further empower the fora as the latter identified specific socio-economic shortcomings that could only be tackled with public support. The dialogues stood as pillars of 'Abdallah's will to power to further demonstrate that the best decisions were based on national consensus.

Political participation and municipal elections

To be sure, national dialogues set the tone for fundamental changes facing Sa'udi Arabia, but so did the much promised yet perpetually postponed municipal elections. As discussed in detail in Chapter 3, the concrete and natural next step was the introduction of electoral processes, which was unhurriedly laid out in Riyadh on February 10, 2005, followed by the Eastern Province, as well as several southern provinces in early March 2005. These municipal elections concluded following plebiscites in the West and North in April 2005. Remarkably, but not surprisingly, the relatively well-attended elections (75% turnout for registered voters in Riyadh, for example) proved far more popular than anticipated. Yet, conservative, pro-clerical candidates won the most seats, illustrating the intricacies of democratization.[38] Although half of the 178 municipal posts would eventually be appointed by government minions, a significant precedent was established when ordinary Sa'udis flocked to polling stations, leading observers to foresee universal suffrage elections to the *Majlis al-Shurah* [Consultative Council] before long. Irrespective of future initiatives, Al Sa'ud leaders responded to public demands by accepting the idea of political participation, even if the process was not entirely transparent.[39] In fact, Riyadh managed a series of contradictory initiatives throughout 2004, which highlighted confusion in devising political, economic, and social reforms. For example, it authorized key dialogues, yet jailed a group of reformists in March 2004 without addressing any of their grievances. Strangely, reformists – not dissidents – called for the establishment of a constitutional monarchy that, at its very core, supported Al Sa'ud authority.[40] Whether the balancing act was necessary to maintain public order was debatable, although Riyadh was certainly emboldened by numerous arrests of *Jihadist* elements. In a lucid message, the Cabinet issued a September 2004 ban forbidding all government employees, including academics (given that all universities fell under "State" regulations), from questioning policies enunciated by the Al Sa'ud. Reforms would certainly be introduced, but only on a carefully laid out timetable, free of what certain officials perceived as foreign interferences in internal Sa'udi affairs.

Succession and the Allegiance Commission

'Abdallah reaffirmed his will to power on October 8, 2007 with an 18-article decree that provided by-laws to the 2006 Succession edict, which regulated political succession.[41] Although the 25-article "Allegiance Law of Succession" replaced the informal family gathering that selected and approved successors, it lacked critical operational features, which was probably intentional. In fact, while secret deliberations were not excluded in this latest imprimatur, the Commission was now equipped with clear regulations to rationalize the procedure.

In a surprise move, 'Abdallah addressed his brothers, sons, and nephews in a remarkable talk that centered on service to the nation and to Islam.[42] He reiterated his belief that the Al Sa'ud ruling family was of the "nation and the people are from us, and we all share the honor of belonging to this country."[43] The discourse was spontaneous, reminiscent of impromptu talks that the late King Faysal bin 'Abdul 'Aziz was famous for, as 'Abdallah called on the *'Ulamah* "of wisdom, thought and creed" to rally around the throne because the Al Sa'ud respected them. He further urged his brothers, sons and nephews, "to become God fearing people and to enhance the pillars of justice, to close ranks, settle differences through discussion and dialogue, and never allow anyone to interfere in the family's affairs."[44] Most in attendance were stunned at this level of attention in preliminary remarks and anticipated a major declaration. As discussed in some detail in Chapter Four, 'Abdallah did not disappoint.

Speaking to all the surviving sons of the founder, 'Abdul 'Aziz bin 'Abdul Rahman, who were led into the Majlis by Prince Mish'al, then Heir Apparent Sultan, as well as dozens of grandsons, the monarch issued a breadth-taking order that identified the membership of his "Allegiance Commission," which encompassed every son of the founder or, in case of a death, a single grandson chosen by family-members of the sub-branch. Remarkably, the royal decree placed 35 specific names around the decision-making table, where the next ruler was to be chosen. Although the monarch and his heir apparent were naturally absent from this list, their respective eldest sons were part of the group, which was divided more or less evenly between sons and grandsons. All vowed before the ruler, pledging to "God Almighty to remain loyal to Religion, King and Country, not to divulge any of the state's secrets, to preserve its interests and systems, to work for the unity of the ruling family as well as the national unity, and to perform duties sincerely, honestly and justly." The Sa'udi monarch named Mish'al bin 'Abdul 'Aziz, a former deputy defense minister and Governor of Makkah, chairman of the Commission. Its task was to select future kings and heir apparents as the closed room conclave between a handful of senior men literally vanished. It took more than a year from the initial announcement on October 7, 2007 for the Commission to be formed and its members appointed, but it was nevertheless a major development, as it regulated the super sensitive question of succession that recurred at the death of every king.

Interestingly, and as elaborated below, 'Abdallah first issued the institution's bylaws, which explained how the process would actually work. He did this before choosing its members, perhaps to allow for the idea to sink in, itself an innovation. Nevertheless, it was apparent that the reliance on a growing number of grandsons confirmed that an institutionalization process was under way, because members of this second generation lacked their predecessors' indispensable experiences in Royal Court procedures. What the non-conformist monarch was clearly aiming for, consequently, may be summarized as follows: after Sultan bin 'Abdul 'Aziz, and upon the death of a monarch, it was up to the Commission to quickly gather to choose a ruler and to confirm the latter's heir apparent, who must be designated within ten days of the ruler's accession to the throne. Failure to do so would mean accepting the Consultative Council's alternative choice. This did not mean that family enclaves could not be held. Rather, given the fact that many Commission members were also senior family members, the preference was to institutionalize the process, instead of leaving the decision to a handful of men. Still, while the statute further confirmed that the king must approve Council decisions, it was not clear what procedures would be followed if the king contested the Commission's selections. This major stumbling block notwithstanding, what King 'Abdallah was doing was to slowly place his own mark on the Sa'udi monarchy, by refining the "Allegiance Law." Although the powers of the monarch were not questioned in this law, his careful stewardship illustrated the ruler's meticulous approach, along with insights into his fundamental preferences.

The United States and Sa'udi Arabia

In one of the better recent studies on Sa'udi Arabia, Nathan Citino brilliantly demonstrated how inexpensive Middle Eastern oil "was the life blood of the global economy after 1945," which required "Anglo-American allies jointly [to] pursue strategic planning" and to solve oil crises through military intervention.[45] Drawing on recently declassified government reports, Citino's study elucidated the opposition that this approach engendered. Not surprisingly, long subjugated Arab societies unfurled revolutionary nationalism against Western colonialism, and the Eisenhower Administration proved incapable of accommodating the new realities of Arab politics. Though the seeds of such opposition had been planted long before the early 1950s, it was at that time that Washington willingly assumed the leadership mantle of the Middle East from Britain. Eisenhower's policies guaranteed that Sa'udi oil revenues would be methodically re-invested in the United States through various weapons programs. Under the circumstances, and though American interests might have required that Washington focus narrowly on safeguarding the area's oil resources, Arab interests did not require Arab governments to do so.

Yet, the failures of Arab nationalism were legend, starting with the inability to create wealth that would enable the entire region to join the ranks of the developed world. Citino masterfully analyzed how OPEC (the Organization of Petroleum Exporting Countries), which was established to protect oil-producing countries' income, failed to develop regional development institutions. Such shortcomings notwithstanding, successive Sa'udi rulers protected oil revenues, especially from secular Arab nationalists. Citino showed how oil income, which spiked after the 1973 Arab–Israeli War, enriched Gulf states and some of their citizens, but delayed political reforms even when ideas for such modifications originated within the ruling families. It must also be noted that while the kingdom and its neighboring Shaykhdoms eventually embarked on a slow development path, it was critical to point out that this was not a priority at the time. Eisenhower championed anti-colonialism and appeared to rebuke his erstwhile British allies, but his administration, along with its successors, strengthened the emerging American empire. In some ways, American involvement in Sa'udi Arabia was no different from that of its predecessor, Great Britain. However, the U.S. military presence in Sa'udi Arabia was much larger and more extensive than Britain's, which was understandable given the two countries' relative sizes. In fact, the United States established military bases in the kingdom, sponsored specific defense schemes, and invested in a long-term military alliance with the Al Sa'ud. It may thus be accurate to state that it was only a matter of time before military coups elsewhere in the Middle East, the Iranian Revolution, the Iraqi invasion of Kuwait, and Baghdad's access to significant quantities of weapons of mass destruction, would necessitate a substantial American military presence in Sa'udi Arabia (and elsewhere in the Gulf) on a more or less permanent basis.

Of course, Sa'udi Arabia was ill equipped to maintain and nurture its nascent alliance with the United States, assume the mantle of an emerging state, and keep its house in order all at once. Accordingly, that the Sa'udis could manage all three of these tasks for close to eight decades is no small accomplishment. Where Sa'udi officials encountered their greatest challenge was in reconciling the security alliance with Washington and the domestic political alliance with the religious establishment. It was worth recalling that the United States preferred to have a strong Unitarian (*Wahhabi*) Sa'udi regime in charge of Islam's holiest shrines – not the radical variety that was prevalent elsewhere. For years, Washington encouraged Riyadh to champion moderation in Muslim affairs, and for years, those policies paid off handsomely, including when President Ronald Reagan identified the Afghan *mujahhidin* as freedom fighters, or when Riyadh was asked to provide financial assistance to such adventures as the Iran-Contra rebellion.[46] In the words of an astute observer, who discussed the "illusion of security" that surrounded the kingdom, this predicament evolved during the past few decades.[47] J. E. Peterson, a seasoned historian and shrewd analyst, recognized that both Sa'udi Arabia and the United States were caught in a "special relationship" that required periodic adjustments. Yet, he also recognized that neither side could abandon the other, which was as elegant a conclusion as any, and one that was certainly worthy of some reflection. Others advanced similar arguments. One posed such eye-opening questions as whether the entire Sa'udi society ought to be treated as if it were composed of terrorists, or whether the George W. Bush Administration's many post-9/11 actions fulfilled what 'Usamah bin Laden wanted?[48] For Anthony Cordesman, the author of several valuable studies on the kingdom, Sa'udi policy hovered around the ability, as well as a willingness, to increase oil production at short notice.[49] This, he correctly argued, stabilized world markets. The Al Sa'ud might have failed in certain areas, but they always kept their end of the energy-for-security bargain. Cordesman, a leading military expert on the region, was no apologist, but emphasized those aspects of Sa'udi policy that fell short. Specifically, he blamed Riyadh for retreating into denial of a terrorist threat, cajoled the Al Sa'ud for operating a lackadaisical internal security system, and called for bolder policies that would deny religious extremists from gaining influence. Anthony Cave Brown was equally sharp as he advanced more or less similar arguments, confirming through a detailed assessment of the Sa'udi–American oil compact that Riyadh never failed to fulfill its obligations, notwithstanding the 1973–74 oil embargo.[50] Oil was and remains at the heart of Sa'udi–American ties, and little would probably alter the anchor on which every aspect of the relationship was built, at least for the foreseeable future.[51]

In the post-9/11 environment, however, undeniable domestic pressures, both in the United States and in Sa'udi Arabia, meant that leaders engaged in serious reconsiderations. It was not entirely clear how the many policy changes would alter the nearly eight-decades-old compact, although few harbored illusions that serious changes were planned, with grave consequences for both countries. Some of these concerns are addressed in the last chapter of this book to better ascertain whether the time was finally right to renew the existing oil for security alliance or devise and implement a fresh one. Whether King 'Abdallah bin 'Abdul 'Aziz will be the monarch who will renew the alliance or usher in a new one is impossible to determine. Chances are excellent that his successor will pursue reforms currently under implementation, since Riyadh can hardly abandon the progress achieved at a time when its regional and international leadership roles are so critical and confronted with a slew of challenges.[52] Inasmuch as 'Abdallah is fully immersed in transforming his country, the relationship with Washington must, therefore, remain at the very top of the agenda, irrespective of all other considerations. Simply stated, no Sa'udi monarch can neglect this key relationship, and neither the current ruler nor his successor will venture to fundamentally alter it, even if inevitable adjustments may be necessary.

Existential challenges

As if the challenges facing Riyadh, and the various measures agreed to by the ruler were not stunning enough, Prince Talal bin 'Abdul 'Aziz, most probably with the king's full approval, has repeatedly proposed forming a political party in Sa'udi Arabia. This was a calculated declaration by a trusted brother who no longer challenged family concord. In fact, Talal believed that political reforms were in the best interests of the ruling establishment, even if others preferred a slower pace. 'Abdallah recognized that genuine sociopolitical reforms were long overdue and seemed to be working in earnest to address them. Should a political party be established, chances were excellent that it would be led by an Al Sa'ud steeped in established traditions, to further guide whatever reforms were implemented. The ultimate challenge for Riyadh, however, was whether the Al Sa'ud were able to keep up with the reformist ruler since reorganizations by themselves were not enough. Rather, as societies equip their citizens with the wherewithal to govern them, and train legal minds were empowered to look after their interests – both the general public as well as each individual – it behooves the ruling establishment to correctly interpret their "will to power." 'Abdallah's ultimate challenge was to affirm his own will, as well as to acculturate putative successors to appreciate the limits of power. This was critical as the ruler forged ahead with inclusive political institutions that added value to citizens at large. These are not easy propositions under the best of circumstances, but certainly they are within the realm of the possible in Riyadh because of the monarch's foresight, dedication, and impeccable credentials.

Reform preferences notwithstanding, the gravest immediate challenges were the many uncertainties, variables, wild cards, and obstacles associated with the king's raft of initiatives, all of which originated in the ruling Al Sa'ud family. When the police stormed homes, arrested prominent reformists, including lawyers, doctors, academics, and judges, and did not bother to charge them with any crimes, the monarch's own record was compromised.⁵³ After his accession in 2005, and to placate such perceptions, 'Abdallah promised permanent change. He thus introduced key steps to restore his citizens' dignity even if average Sa'udis demanded a lot more. That he slowed down was somewhat natural, although 'Abdallah's "will to power" was strong enough to withstand internal criticisms from extremist Sa'udis who wished to disrupt his momentum. Equally important were the many petitions issued as pleas for faster reforms, and while the monarch may well be convinced that those who were calling for change were speaking out as genuine citizens, he could not simply dismiss the latter's positive calls. Admittedly, the ruler's task was difficult, but it was essential that he appeared to dictate the pace of change. Were 'Abdallah to support the more conservative elements within the ruling family, who would prefer to nip such plans in the bud, the monarch's carefully designed scheme would not survive long. Indeed, while political dissent was still frowned upon in the kingdom, 'Abdallah's very rule was premised on change, which could not be reversed without inflicting permanent damage. Many Sa'udis harbored high hopes that he would not drop the baton, especially since he routinely demonstrated that he could deliver. His greatest challenge, therefore, came from the ruling family itself, which the monarch was forced to tame with utmost care. Ultimately, 'Abdallah's "will to power" required that he harness and unite the energies of both liberal and Islamist reformists both within society at large, as well as inside the ruling family, if genuine socio-political reforms were to succeed and establish permanent foundations that would withstand the tests of time.

Methodological approach

The Kingdom of Sa'udi Arabia was, to say the least, in the docket for many in the United States. From angry officials to a bewildered and weary population, from ill-informed media personalities to biased think tank analysts and an assortment of instant experts who mushroomed in the aftermath of the tragic attacks of September 2001, everyone reached more or less the verdict that Sa'udi Arabia was guilty on the following counts: of religious fundamentalism and intolerance, of abetting terrorists and, worst of all, of generating and spreading anti-Americanism.⁵⁴ Can Riyadh be exonerated, or – for that matter – does it deserve to be? Less sanguine "Sa'udiologues" were pondering whether the Al Sa'ud ruling family could survive this onslaught.⁵⁵ They were also pondering whether Unitarian (*Wahhabi*) religious leaders could finally address specific indictments – ranging from ending their alleged support of terrorists, whose only objective was to incite violence on a mass scale, to introducing urgently needed reforms in the education system – and whether the few existing institutions throughout the kingdom would survive. Indeed, even among seasoned academics, it was open season on everything Sa'udi. Among recent studies, several offered rich information and analysis, and each clarified specific issues. Some elucidated obscure points, while others raised

Introduction 17

immensely critical questions, and presented the reader with an opportunity to think critically about Sa'udi Arabia – its government, leading religious and secular officials and, ultimately, its people.

This study aims high and embarks on a subject area where few have ventured. As discussed above, the number of books published on the kingdom during the past few years reached into the hundreds, as scores of writers, both specialists as well as instant experts with a motive to benefit from market conditions, offered a variety of interpretations on what went wrong.[56] Though most of these contributions cover familiar ground, few if any examine discussions of reforms, and when they did, they seldom focused on legal questions, which necessitated both intimate knowledge of that society as well as privileged access to decision-makers.[57] Simply stated, it was the accumulated value of contacts established during the past few decades that ensured renewed access to familiar representatives of the Sa'udi intelligentsia and government officials, and which facilitated this research effort. Naturally, given the nature of this subject, a variety of jurists were tapped to better understand the many changes under way in the kingdom. Regrettably, most did not wish to be identified by name, which necessitated multiple entreaties to verify specific pieces of information. The vast majority of the interviews conducted for this book proved to be extremely valuable even if the "anonymous" variety posed a serious dilemma. In fact, because of the sensitive nature of my questions, wondering about the judiciary and succession matters in particular, it would have been nearly impossible to compose this book without numerous interviews. During several extended visits to Sa'udi Arabia between 2009 and late 2011, a total of 48 officials were interviewed for this book, but only those who consented to speak on the record are quoted in the pages that follow.[58] All others – by my count, 32 individuals – insisted on speaking off the record. Such anonymous interviews have no value in an academic book that attempts to elucidate, though readers familiar with Sa'udi Arabia will know how to separate the wheat from the chaff by reading between the lines. When a fact could be verified from published material, the citation was used to buttress any analysis that followed, with the un-attributable source discarded. Those who prefer to focus on what is clearer and unambiguous will be disappointed but, regrettably, also oblivious to the kingdom's multi-faceted political realities that still prevent many from speaking on the record. To mitigate such criticisms, I have done my best to be both accurate and analytical without falling into excessive speculation, even if some was inevitable.

There are at least three sets of questions to tackle in studying political reforms in Sa'udi Arabia: changes within the judiciary; ongoing "National Dialogue" fora; and internal royal family dynamics pushing for the establishment of political parties. How well we understand the many permutations within these three communities is important and forms the background that compelled this investigation. First, and as discussed above, after his accession to the throne in 2005, King 'Abdallah established an independent judiciary in a move that was neither spontaneous nor a reaction to the many clashes that occurred between clerics and members of the intelligentsia. The monarch imposed a massive reeducation campaign on thousands of clerics, forced the religious community to cooperate with the "State," and launched a long-term plan to address arbitrary arrests and condemnations. One of the most critical questions to investigate is to know whether the ruler's warnings – for example, for clerics not to exploit their privileges for political ends – will be heeded. Who are the monarch's allies against the clerical establishment? Will those who see their functions confined only to judicial employment affairs accept transfers of authority from the Supreme Judiciary Council to the new Supreme Court? How will they react to this sharp diminution of influence? Second, 'Abdallah encouraged national dialogues on different social issues during the past few years, and a series of major events illustrated how rich these debates were. They showcased the society's cultural strengths as well as shortcomings that needed attention. What was remarkable about these dialogue sessions, in addition to discussing controversial topics like women's rights and relationships with "others" [meaning non-Sa'udis and non-Muslims], was their open display of intellectual exchanges. These televised debates were not the stale variety delivered against musical backgrounds by Mozart or Vivaldi, both of whom receive more airtime on Sa'udi television than in their native lands. Rather, they were vivacious exchanges, often heated, about what Sa'udis cared about. Yet, after eight dialogues, the question that needs attention is whether these events can actually be instruments for political change, and whether they will, in fact, introduce sorely needed improvements. Can conservative Sa'udi Arabia tolerate such discourses especially when inevitable follow-up steps introduce genuine changes that will undoubtedly erode entrenched interests? Ultimately, and this much is fair to ask, will the dialogues continue without ruling family backing? In the negative, what will they have to be replaced with? Finally, and as stated above, the gravest immediate challenges are the many uncertainties, variables, wild cards, or obstacles associated with the monarch's raft of initiatives, all of which originated in the ruling Al Sa'ud family. How will 'Abdallah manage against such odds, and what can his successor do to build on his legacy?

1 Reforms within the judiciary

To say that Sa'udi Arabia is undergoing extreme renovation of its vital institutions would be an understatement. With repeated and swift royal decrees after his accession to the throne in 2005, the Custodian of the Two Holy Mosques, 'Abdallah bin 'Abdul 'Aziz, has proposed a variety of changes and continues to be more creative than many assume. In 2007, for example, the monarch established an independent Supreme Court and provided bylaws for his 2006 Succession edict. Because Sa'udis professed that the kingdom followed scriptures, going so far as to claim that their constitution was the Holy Qur'an, and because of the 1744 politico-religious alliance between the Al Sa'ud and the Al Shaykh, the very idea of reforms within the judiciary was problematic.[1] Inasmuch as most socio-political issues were addressed within fundamental religious parameters, it is legitimate to inquire how the ruler's reforms, which were clearly moving the kingdom's political markers, would dramatically affect the lives of Sa'udi citizens and expatriate workers toiling in the country.

While the October 2, 2007 announcements – to create an independent Supreme Court as well as a Grievances Board – mandated the two bodies to supervise the implementation of *Shari'ah* and laws enacted by the king, they buttressed the authority of judges to reach relatively free decisions. In fact, the new Supreme Court (SC), which replaced the Supreme Judiciary Council (SJC), was empowered to do more than evaluate rulings or uphold verdicts issued by appeals courts. Once fully realized, plainly defined directives required that adjudicators apply fair and uniform measures across the board, precisely to eliminate current fluctuations due to varying and sometimes contradictory interpretations.

This was a major step forward, and while the SJC was authorized to oversee administrative aspects of the judiciary, including the appointment of magistrates, new features within the contemplated SC required that judges – who ruled under *Shari'ah* and relied on *ijma'* (consensus) and *qiyas* (analogy) – undergo periodic training, which was a revolutionary idea indeed. Moreover, the new SC was to sit at the top of a truly independent body, if that was possible to fathom, with appeal benches that reviewed verdicts by first-degree courts that, in turn, retained some distance from criminal, personal affairs, commercial and labor canons. At the time these announcements were made, the Sa'udi monarch allocated 7 billion Sa'udi Riyals (approximately US$2.8 billion) to train qualified cadres and to build a sophisticated legal infrastructure, including law schools housed in separate edifices. Equally important, the royal decrees called for a streamlined process to absorb legal findings under *Shari'ah*, which necessitated trained and highly capable prosecutors. Yet, with a severe shortage of magistrates – less than 50 throughout the kingdom adjudicating over 80,000 cases per year in 2007 – the challenge was to provide adequate training to judges and attorneys not only in the law itself, but also in the sorely needed accountability process. Nevertheless, the mere fact that significant resources were earmarked for such projects illustrated the ruler's intentions, clearly motivated by the quest for proficiency.

As discussed throughout this study, King 'Abdallah bin 'Abdul 'Aziz recognized that genuine sociopolitical reforms were long overdue and seemed to be working in earnest to address them. In this chapter, an effort is made to address new judiciary laws, along with an investigation as to whether Riyadh managed to keep up with the reformist ruler since the 2007 reorganizations. To be sure, while a society must be equipped to govern itself, and must train legal minds that will look after the interests of both the general public as well as each individual, *these are long-term propositions that require persistence*. Sa'udi society is no exception. Indeed, it remains to be determined whether Al Sa'ud leaders can acculturate themselves to produce successors who can appreciate the limits of power, and whether they can forge ahead with inclusive political institutions that may add value to citizens at large. Likewise, and with respect to the judiciary, it is critical to understand whether the clergy who handled the law in Sa'udi Arabia were ready to share doctrinal responsibilities with officials appointed by the State to administer justice.

To better address these questions, this chapter is divided into three sections, all focusing on changes in the country's legal framework. It first concentrates on the actual reform mechanisms within the judiciary, emphasizing economic requirements, as well as the establishment of an independent Supreme Court. This is followed by an examination – concentrating on education, including its religious variety, as well as the status of women – of the primary social functions that involve legal authorities in a country where the very idea of separation of powers is still a work in progress. Finally, the context, and the key political repercussions, of judiciary involvements are scrutinized, highlighting the war on terrorism and political violence. An understanding of how Al Sa'ud leaders have dealt with, and are handling, the kingdom's various judicial affairs will identify and confirm whether proposed reforms are, in fact, genuine.

Reforming the judiciary in Sa'udi Arabia

While the political reforms of the 1990s, including the adoption of a Basic Law, expanded some of the checks and balances that existed in the kingdom, key royal orders were issued to improve the tacit 1744 Al Sa'ud–Al Shaykh Alliance.[2]

If the Al Sa'ud forged a legitimizing institution by aligning themselves with the Al Shaykh, they nevertheless adhered to a sophisticated constitutional mechanism that rested on *Shari'ah* law. Moreover, and beyond founding society on religious precepts, the Al Sa'ud mixed Islamic law with tribal instruments that guaranteed loyalty. By emphasizing *Shurah* (consultation) and implementing *bay'ah* (allegiance), both of which were backed by Scriptures, the Al Sa'ud preserved traditions that strengthened kingship. As discussed in some detail in Chapter Four, the 1992 Basic Law introduced provisions regulating the succession process.[3] Yet, 'Abdallah bin 'Abdul 'Aziz was not only reforming the critical succession procedures in place, but embarked on extensive reform plans that addressed "key areas of good governance, political reform, women's rights, judicial reform, economic reform and educational reform."[4] Of course, such initiatives meant that Riyadh tinkered with the country's constitutional and administrative practices, even going so far as introducing an evolutionary *modus operandi* that was uncharacteristic and, potentially, challenging if the clergy opposed Al Sa'ud reforms.

Critics of the kingdom asserted that Sa'udi Arabia stood at "the forefront of spreading the radical *Wahhabi* message throughout the Muslim world" through "the Islamic World League (Rabitat al-'Alam al-Islami), the World Association of Muslim Youth, and the World Association of Mosques." Apparently, these institutions were "notorious for their support of radical and terrorist organizations throughout the world, and for spreading texts that indoctrinate Muslims to intolerance of non-Muslims."[5] This was, of course, a narrow reading of the kingdom's complex religious institutions and the legitimizing roles they played in fostering harmony. Because all three Sa'udi monarchies were based on an alliance between two collegial establishments that withstood the test of time, it was imperative for these two conventional poles of authority to act in relative harmony. Doing otherwise would only mean perpetual clashes that, in a tribal environment, presaged bloody conflict even if Makkah was not "a center of Islamic learning" after the ninth century. Still, to claim that *Wahhabi 'Ulamah* (Islamic scholars) "were not there before the state," which is to say that they had not successfully established "old and respected" establishments like al-Azhar in Cairo, was excessively harsh.[6]

Rather, and over the centuries, Al Sa'ud rulers cultivated religious leaders and attempted to prevail over them long before the kingdom was formally declared in 1932 in its current geographical setting. Moreover, to assert that the importance or value of the religious establishment increased after the 1973–74 oil booms, is also inaccurate. In fact, the founder of the kingdom, 'Abdul 'Aziz bin 'Abdul Rahman understood the intrinsic value of clerics for the regime around the turn of the century. He cajoled many to join him during the unification battles that ensued. Throughout history, but especially in times of turmoil, Sa'udi rulers perceived the clerical establishment as an asset. In the late 1950s and early 1960s, Faysal bin 'Abdul 'Aziz relied on, and received, the necessary blessings of senior religious figures to usher in his rule. Khalid bin 'Abdul 'Aziz needed, and relied on, critical fatwahs to dislodge dissidents who attacked and occupied the Grand Mosque in Makkah in 1979. Fahd bin 'Abdul 'Aziz sought and received a legal imprimatur to legitimize the deployment of UN-sanctioned and US-led foreign coalition troops in the 1991 War for Kuwait. All of these events and many more enhanced the political power of the religious establishment, even if a variety of opinions, especially dissenting voices, emerged from time to time. Consequently, it would be nearly impossible to separate vested clerical interests in Sa'udi Arabia from those of the ruling family, even if the Al Sa'ud enjoy a *primus inter pares* (first among equals) advantage. In fact, it was remarkable to note the extent to which the Al Sa'ud shared common perceptions with senior clerics, many of whom held similar perspectives on vital concerns on many global concerns. A few radicalized Shaykhs notwithstanding, the vast majority of clerics did not support the creation of an Islamic government along the Iranian model, not only because most were financially beholden to the Al Sa'ud, but also because they sincerely believed in the authenticity of their alliance. Likewise, and despite periodic anomalies emanating from Shaykhs with bizarre inclinations, senior ruling family members fully understood that Sa'udi Arabia without the religious legitimacy of the *Wahhabi* establishment would not, perhaps even could not, assert its authenticity. Few concerns ranked as high as the putative alternative to the Al Sa'ud-Al Shaykh alliance, whether a theocracy modeled after the Islamic Revolution in Iran, or a Westernized democracy that would upset the norms of the traditional society.

An evolving alliance

When Shaykh Muhammad Ibn 'Abdul Wahhab, the founder of the *Muwahhidun* (Unitarian) movement died in 1792, the *wali al-amr* (political leader), Muhammad Ibn Sa'ud, assumed the title of imam, too. A precedent was established, whereby Sa'udi political leaders could also be recognized as imams, which improved their religious authority by granting them judicial and administrative privileges, even if they were not *muftis* (jurists). In 1924, that is, after the founder conquered the Hijaz and became ruler over Makkah and Madinah, he assumed the title of *Khadim al-Haramayn* (Custodian of the Two Holy Mosques), which was a title used by Ottoman Sultans.[7] To his credit, the founder ruler strengthened the alliance through intermarriage, which brought the two families even closer together. In fact, the late King Faysal's mother, Tarfah bint Al Shaykh, the daughter of an Al Shaykh judge who was a direct descendant of Ibn 'Abdul-Wahhab, "was the critical link that legitimized the military–religious alliance."[8] Through such relationships, which continued over the decades, the Al Shaykh confirmed their part of the pact, not only as religious authorities but also from their active participation in the creation of the ruling elite. Ever since 'Abdul 'Aziz bin 'Abdul Rahman, successive Sa'udi monarchs entrusted the religious ministries and the post of the Grand Mufti to Al Shaykh family members. While learned men from other families occupied key posts, too, the Al Shaykh received preferential treatment, if for no other reason than to maintain the harmony of the alliance. Honoring the terms of the 1744 pact was, consequently, an existential issue that could not be breached, except under extraordinary circumstances. Naturally, as responsibilities increased and non-Al Shaykh clerics stepped forward, many individuals were brought into the system, but almost always under the overarching control of the Al Sa'uds and the Al Shaykhs acting in unison to preserve and protect core interests as well as the kingdom. Shaykh Salih al-Lahidan, for example, became the chairman of the Higher Council of *Qadis* and a member of the *Hay'at Kibar al-'Ulamah* (Board of Senior *'Ulamah*) (BSU). Shaykh 'Abdallah bin Muhammad al-Lahidan was put in charge of religious affairs, endowments, and *da'wah* in the eastern region. Others received equally important posts and titles.

With changing times, Riyadh invested in religious affairs by building theology schools that rekindled Islamic scholarship in Makkah and Madinah that, in turn, tied them to the Sa'udi regime. In turn, the *'Ulamah* flexed their political muscles as early as 1973, when several officials implored King Faysal to enforce the oil embargo against the United States and The Netherlands, two countries that extended military assistance to Israel during the October Arab–Israeli War. As discussed elsewhere, the first major crisis that threatened to upset the 1744 Al Sa'ud–Al Shaykh balance of power occurred in November 1979, when Juhayman al-'Utaybi and his followers occupied the Makkah Mosque.[9] This epochal event, which followed the February 1979 Islamic Revolution in Iran, as well as the open rebellion of Shi'ah communities in the oil-rich eastern province of the kingdom, placed the ruling family in a particularly awkward position. For the first time in contemporary affairs, King Khalid literally asked for, and received, the support of the *'Ulamah* on what was essentially a defining political concern. Few anticipated the actual use of force inside the Holy Haram and, naturally, Riyadh could not act with impunity without the all too critical religious imprimatur that condoned a reliance on the military to dislodge rebels. In the event, a new religio-political order emerged, which granted clerics additional powers after decades when their influence was on the wane.

More than a decade later, King Fahd called on the Senior Council of *'Ulamah* for a fatwah that legitimized the deployment of coalition troops on Sa'udi soil during the 1991 War for Kuwait.[10] As one observer saw things, Fahd felt threatened by the Iraqi invasion and, to mitigate putative action against the kingdom, "decided to re-empower and co-opt domestic critics and promote religiosity."[11] Whether the *'Ulamah* were coerced to become leading actors within the power structure of the country, or whether their politicization was a necessary step, is a debatable point. What is less so was the anxious participation of senior clerics as essential partners of the regime, which, for all practical purposes, meant that fringe elements would be further isolated if they considered themselves to be part of the opposition.

This was a departure from earlier behavior because the rise of so-called *Sahwah 'Ulamah* in the late 1980s and early 1990s hindered Riyadh's concerted efforts to centralize religious institutions. After the 1990 Iraqi occupation of Kuwait, however, King Fahd embarked on various institutional changes including the establishment of the *Majlis al-Shurah*, the appointment of new clerics to the BSU; the nomination of a new Grand Mufti; along with structural changes within the religious ministries. More important, Fahd created two new bodies in October 1994, the Supreme Council of Islamic Affairs (*al-Majlis al-A'lah li-Shu'un al-Islamiyyah*) and the Council for Islamic Mission and Guidance (*al-Majlis lil-Da'wah wal-Irshad*).[12] These were, clearly, successful models of co-optation that also allowed the *'Ulamah* to exercise their enhanced roles in the decision-making process.

The newfound status of the *'Ulamah* galvanized the latter to take more forceful positions in domestic and foreign affairs as the Grand Mufti of the Kingdom, Shaykh 'Abdul 'Aziz Ibn Baz and Shaykh Muhammad al-'Uthaymin, along with other establishment clergymen, supported petitions by non-establishment *'Ulamah* that called on Riyadh to undertake far-reaching reforms. Several petitions, which are analyzed in Chapter 5, criticized the dependence of the State on major Western powers, cleverly expressed through letters to the king presented under the guise of *nasihah* (advice), which the BSU boldly discussed.[13] In 1994, the BSU relied on its renewed popularity to encourage Muslims to "actively participate" in the UN Conference on Population and Development, and to express themselves on a variety of issues, even if few bothered to familiarize themselves with its objectives. At the time, the opportunity was too useful to ignore, and BSU officials relied on the regime-controlled Muslim World League to label the conference "an insult to Islam." Needless to say, Riyadh was directed to boycott the conference, which promptly caused the government to cancel its participation, further illustrating the rising power of the clergy.

Throughout the 1990s, such self-assertion by establishment clerics occasionally ignited conflicts between them and the Al Sa'ud, which further polarized decision-makers. For example, in the wake of the 1990 Iraqi invasion of Kuwait and the 1991 war that followed, a five-member committee, headed by Shaykh Ibn Baz, was established to examine the functioning of the preachers (*du'at*). Following the findings of this committee, hundreds of preachers were sacked, in most cases allegedly because they were critical of King Fahd's decisions.[14] In January 1992, Riyadh dismissed the preacher of King Sa'ud University Mosque because he, ostensibly, refused to endorse the Madrid peace process supported by the leadership. Authorities arrested several preachers and imams who criticized Sa'udi support for direct negotiations between Israel and the Arabs.[15] A few months later, the monarch asked the BSU to condemn a memorandum of grievances of the non-establishment *'Ulamah* that opposed the monopoly on religion granted to them, which drew a written statement from Shaykh Ibn Baz and other BSU members that was highly critical of Riyadh. An official spokesperson denied reports on disagreements between the Al Sa'ud and senior clerics, although in November 1992, the king nominated ten new *'Ulamah* to the BSU and later removed seven others.[16] Notwithstanding this hiccup, Shaykh Ibn Baz issued a fatwah that encouraged the peace process with Israel in 1994, further illustrating his allegiance to Riyadh and its policy preferences.[17] This was not a fluke but a carefully vetted process that underscored the power of the ruling family, no matter how "independent" minded the clergy was. Indeed, and particularly after 9/11, the religious establishment usually conformed to Al Sa'ud preferences and tended to adopt policies cleared at the Palace. Which party prevailed over the other depended on the issue, though the Al Sa'ud looked after the clergy with tender loving care.

Consequently, after the early 1990s, observers detected a greater sense of harmony between the government and the religious establishment. In fact, the trauma of the 1990 Iraqi invasion of Kuwait, followed by a devastating war and, more importantly, the cataclysmic developments in the aftermath of 9/11, clarified the many dangers faced by the kingdom, which persuaded clergymen to rally behind the throne. Rather than retire to the age-old formula of appeasement of the clergy, by backing down whenever a possible conflict loomed over the horizon, the Al Sa'ud embarked on a fundamental reform path that literally altered existing power relationships in the 1744 alliance. Riyadh was no longer willing to simply accommodate the clergy but insisted that the *'Ulamah* understand and support the interests of the entire country. No longer were the Al Sa'ud resigned to the predominance of the clergy in domestic and major foreign matters. It was time to introduce fundamental reforms in the judiciary, too, if the country were to distance itself from existential dilemmas. What were the legal challenges that faced the ruling family, and who were the principal actors that were, presumably, candidates for suitable reforms?

The legal system

Sa'udi Arabia's 1992 Basic Law provided specific definitions of each state authority, including the executive, legislative, and judiciary. While the system did not envisage a Jeffersonian separation of powers between the legislative and executive branches, all three branches enjoyed undeniable powers, which reinforced existing understandings.[18] The executive branch, for example, empowered the monarch and buttressed his Council of Ministers to rule over a vast bureaucracy that, in turn, reached every citizen throughout the country. Naturally, the monarch was an absolute ruler who retained ultimate authority over every aspect of the government. Moreover, he acted as the reference point for officials, whether civilian or military, and an equally critical point worthy of emphasis is that the king enjoyed a key role within the religious establishment as the *enforcer* of *Shari'ah* Law.[19] He alone was responsible for "the policy of the nation in accordance with the provisions of Islam" (Article 55) and oversaw the implementation of *Shari'ah*. According to the law, the ruler was empowered to appoint "Councils" or "Committees" to deal with particular issues that fell within the functions of the Council of Ministers, since the latter implemented the policies of the state. In such instances, the competencies of each Council, their composition, and the nature of whatever decisions they reached were defined by their respective decrees.[20] King 'Abdallah's excessive reliance on such committees irritated many members of the Sa'udi intelligentsia though few could find fault with the work undertaken by the Supreme Council of Higher Education, the Supreme Council of Islamic Affairs, the National Security Council, and the Higher Committee for Administrative Reform, to name but a few of these specialized organizations that functioned under the direct supervision of the monarch. While it is fair to criticize any ruler, and the Sa'udi king is no exception, such disapproval required a level of balancing, especially when an entire corpus of activities were placed under the analytical microscope.

The legislative branch

Unlike the executive branch, Sa'udi Arabia's legislative record was not particularly stellar, given concrete limitations imposed on the *Majlis al-Shurah*. Still, because *Shari'ah* law formed the basis of the country's legal system, and while the Basic Law used the term "regulatory authority" to refer to the legislative authority, the institution was caught in an existential dilemma. Inasmuch as the *Majlis* enjoyed the right to debate and vote on statutory laws and regulations, and even to approve international treaties, agreements, regulations and concessions, an intrinsic and nearly impossible quandary confronted *Majlis* members. How could they legislate when, under *Shari'ah*, only God enjoyed such power? In other words, and according to a savvy observer, the very word "legislation, which represents secular law" could not be "used in the kingdom." Consequently, "legislative authority [was to be] shared by the King, the Council of Ministers, and the Consultative Council (*Majlis al-Shurah*)."[21] As the enforcer of divine law, therefore, the monarch enjoyed broad discretion over matters of public interest, which were better known as *al-Siyasah al-Shari'yyah* [Islamic public policy].[22] The Basic Law thus granted the ruler ultimate legislative authority, which was supplemented by an absolute right to "repeal, enact, or amend any laws and regulations by Royal Order."[23] Unsurprisingly, successive monarchs relied on these privileges to govern through royal decrees over the years, even if such authority infringed on clerical privileges. In the words of an astute observer, "Saudi Arabia has never been subjected to a system of law administered by a central authority that exclude[d] or marginalize[d] the preeminence of Shari'a," that is, until 1992.[24]

After 1992, specifically after King Fahd created the *Majlis al-Shurah*, the institution stood as the crucible for a potential legislative body that may, eventually, exercise more powers. While its oversight functions were precisely what observers derided, arguing that the Council was nothing more than a rubber-stamp organization that gave citizens the illusion of direct participation, some scrutiny and accountability became the norm. This was perhaps not what its creators contemplated as deferential *Majlis* members learned how to raise pertinent questions without violating local norms. To be sure, and although the traditions-bound organization produced little or no serious work on the dockets, a few tangential years later and gradually an institutional memory emerged. Fostering such confidence for an appointed establishment was not easy, but serious steps were taken to achieve declared goals. Suffice it to say that the *Majlis al-Shurah*, discussed in more detail in Chapter 3, embarked on a legislative process that aimed, in time, to foster a truly independent body.

Its limited powers notwithstanding, the *Majlis al-Shurah* stood as the most visible legislative institution for Riyadh, although several major advisory authorities assisted the Al Sa'ud to apply *Shari'ah* law.

The judicial branch

Before King 'Abdallah promulgated the new Law of the Judiciary in 2007, the Sa'udi court system was composed of a Supreme Judicial Council, the *Shari'ah* Review Court (*mahkamat al-tamyiz*), which resembled an appeals court, and First-Instance Courts (General Courts and Summary Courts).[25] In addition, an administrative judicial body known as the Board of Grievances, which stood alongside the Courts System and was affiliated directly with the Palace, exercised some legal powers. This board carried out specific appeals functions through several layers of authority, including the Board of Appeal Circuits, Circuits of Appeals, and First-Instance Circuits. In turn, each of these institutions enjoyed jurisdiction over cases brought before each one of them in accordance with *Shari'ah*. Moreover, the legal system included several administrative committees that adjudicated civil, commercial, administrative and criminal cases.

On 1 October 2007, 'Abdallah issued his epochal Royal Decree (M/78-19/09/1428H), which was intended to overhaul the country's judiciary. The choice of the word "overhaul" is somewhat problematic since inherent contradictions existed between what the monarch proposed, and what the new Law of the Judiciary anticipated, in terms of implementable changes. The most important novelty was the establishment of a Supreme Court, which was slated to take over the functions of the Supreme Judiciary Council as the highest judicial authority in the kingdom. Under the new regulation, the existing Courts of Appeals were abolished, replaced with new Courts of Appeals in the kingdom's provinces. These were authorized to exercise their respective jurisdictions through Labor, Commercial, Criminal Circuits, Personal Status, and Civil Circuits. Moreover, First-Degree Courts were established in various parts of the country, according to local needs. Likewise, their jurisdictions were lined up through specialized Criminal, Commercial, Labor, Personal Status, and General Courts. Several of these courts were foreseen to oversee disputes that were previously addressed by special administrative committees, although none of them were identified in late 2012.

Justices and other senior personnel

In the past, the Board of Senior *'Ulamah* headed the religious authority in the kingdom. It was the official body comprised of the most senior scholars, oscillating between thirty and forty members at any given time, who were empowered to issue religious decrees (fatwahs) on a variety of concerns either submitted to it by the government or other religious figures. Importantly, while the 1992 Basic Law recognized the Holy Qur'an and the Sunnah of the Prophet as the ultimate sources of authority, it also and specifically acknowledged the existence of the Board. Article 45 stated that the "Law shall specify the hierarchical organizations for the composition of the Board of Senior *'Ulamah*, the Research Administration of Religious Affairs, and the Office of the Mufti, together with their jurisdictions."[26] Although not part of the legislative authority, the Board of Senior *'Ulamah* participated in the legislative process responsible for enacting statutory laws for as long as anyone could remember and, in certain instances, its contributions were crucial to gaining public support. To be sure, there were similar bodies throughout the different regions of the country, but these tended to be affiliated with academic institutions and would chiefly be used for consultations by local judges (*qadis*). Among the latter were the Islamic Fiqh Academy at the Muslim World League, located in Makkah, and the International Islamic Fiqh Academy affiliated with the Organization of the Islamic Cooperation in Jiddah.

It is valuable to note also how the 2007 law offered to address problems among jurists, which was heretofore a more-or-less internal matter, to which only the clerical establishment was privy. According to the latest reorganization, the Board of Grievances would henceforth follow a new order: seniority would be held by the High Administrative Court, followed by the Administrative Courts of Appeals and, lastly, the Administrative Courts themselves. According to the king's wishes, a High Administrative Court would thus be established to look into cases objecting to the rulings issued by Administrative Appeal Courts, a major novelty in the kingdom. Moreover, the law envisaged the creation of Administrative Courts to look into cases related to the rights of employees toiling within the judiciary, along with putative examinations of administrative decisions, compensations, contracts, disciplinary actions and requests for the implementation of foreign rules, as necessary. King 'Abdallah approved these difficult functional approaches to the legal system, perhaps cognizant that most of them would need to go through long transition periods, as participants learned how to organize themselves and gradually transform the existing system into a modern institution. Although few publicly questioned the qualifications and performances of most individuals affiliated with the judiciary, most Sa'udis demanded better results, starting with more sophisticated training for judges who were overwhelmed by modernizing requirements. It may indeed be accurate to state that the monarch's efforts ensured the long-term independence and impartiality of judges, provided the latter adopted safeguards, which resulted in fair contributions to society.

The Sa'udi judicial system reorganized

When 'Abdallah bin 'Abdul 'Aziz allocated nearly $2.8bn to overhaul the kingdom's judicial system and upgrade its court facilities, ostensibly to streamline the legal process that remained a perennial source of dissatisfaction for many, few perceived the move as a serious proposition. Most concluded that the very idea of modernizing the Saʻudi legal system was imaginary at best, a futile effort at worst. Critics contended that spending a couple of billion dollars would not be effective as long as the ideological foundations, on which the entire legal premise of the country was based, were embedded in *Shariʻah* law.

Inasmuch as ʻAbdallah was an innovator, his move to reinforce the standing of the country's courts and, more important, to introduce the idea that judges ought to make their rulings free from outside influence, stood out. His desire to overhaul – when the term itself was revolutionary – from the top down was equally bold. To be sure, the monarch's proposals were meant to expedite ongoing economic reform measures, even if the creation of a supreme court was bound to have far reaching consequences, including a marked improvement in civil liberties.

It was important to note that while Riyadh's schemes reflected a need to streamline the kingdom's growing economy, not all of the changes were directly related to Saʻudi interactions with the outside world. In fact, most civil proceedings that involved claims against the government, as well as enforcement of foreign judgments, were time consuming and problematic, not because they were heard by special administrative tribunals, like the Commission for the Settlement of Labor Disputes or the Board of Grievances, but because these institutions were burdened by heavy bureaucratic treatment. Beyond the intricacies of the laws themselves, disputes were handled by Ministry of Commerce and Industry committees, or Ministry of Labor subordinates, which earned poor reputations for notorious rulings that seldom handled commercial disputes fairly. Labor challenges were rarely adjudicated with any degree of impartiality. In short, whimsical bureaucrats tended to err on the side of the impossible, which prevented the development of fair and relatively transparent commercial settlements. Under the new law, independent commercial courts would henceforth be responsible for resolving what disputes that may arise in a more-or-less impartial way, delivering judgment on the merits of a case, rather than tailor their putative decisions to the narrower institutional interests of a particular ministry.

In fact, with the creation of independent commercial courts, as well as appropriate appeals tribunals, domestic and foreign investors in Saʻudi Arabia would presumably receive a far more expeditious enforcement of contracts. Undeniably, the purpose of these reforms was precisely to ensure that everyone operated within a sound investment climate, to protect businesses from the vagaries of periodic disputes. Equally important, ʻAbdallah insisted that these technical courts be staffed by specially trained magistrates with knowledge or even expertise in commercial affairs, because he wished to unburden the religious courts that were saddled with such responsibilities until now. In the words of a leading observer:

In the age of global trade developments, and overriding concerns about government transparency and legal accountability, it is becoming increasingly untenable that multi-billion dollar transactions would be vulnerable to the particular views a specific judge may apply when judicially reviewing such transactions. This vulnerability is particularly noteworthy when leading members of the Saudi Shari'a establishment, i.e. the *ulama*, themselves admit that not all Saudi judges are qualified to exercise *ijtihad* in adjudicating disputes brought to Shari'a courts. The *ulama* voicing these concerns, as well as many in the legal community, advocate the codification of the rules of Shari'a. But many *ulama* are resistant to these calls."[27]

To his immense credit, the monarch appreciated the value of his religious judges, but understood that the brightest among them could not possibly display universal proficiency on every subject. Naturally, neither the talent of commercial magistrates nor their training would be accomplished immediately, but Riyadh was determined to embark on a long-term overhaul of its legal institutions, including bankruptcy legislation, shareholder protection, as well as the various regulations that governed access to lines of credit. 'Abdallah was aware that legal reforms were interconnected, which necessitated carefully studied adaptations of the financial sector, working and interacting with both commercial and industrial activities. His challenge was to introduce meaningful improvements in these areas without upsetting existing institutions that legitimized Al Sa'ud rule. Nevertheless, the ruler was cognizant that the time was ripe to take a dramatic step towards that goal, which was the introduction of a Supreme Court worthy of the name.

The Supreme Court

To maintain relative harmony, 'Abdallah abolished the Supreme Judicial Council (SJC) in 2007, as he envisaged a functioning replacement that would become the kingdom's highest legal tribunal. It may be useful to repeat that while the 1975 Law of the Judiciary (especially Article 5) identified the Supreme Judicial Council as the highest legal authority in the kingdom, the institution was no longer efficient. Composed of eleven members, the SJC was staffed by five judges who constituted a Permanent Panel of the Council, which acted as its own embedded Appellate Court.[28] These magistrates were full-time members but were seconded by another five part-time *qadis*, which included the Chief of the Appellate Court or his deputy, the Deputy Minister of Justice, and the three members with the longest time in service as Chief Judges of the General Courts in Makkah, Madinah, Riyadh, Jiddah, Dammam and/or Jizan. In addition to these ten men, a Chairman appointed by the monarch convened panelists on an as-needed basis, which expedited matters. SJC duties encompassed a host of additional activities, ranging from administrative, legislative, consultative, and judicial functions. Of course, because the SJC supervised most courts, administered employment-related affairs of the judiciary, and assumed the burden of rendering judgments on religious, social, commercial and a myriad topics, these responsibilities made it nearly impossible for the organization to function with any degree of effectiveness. How could magistrates render fair rulings on major criminal cases, including those involving death sentences, while simultaneously opining on general *Shari'ah* principles? How could magistrates exercise the autonomy granted them under *Shari'ah* law while remaining subservient to state regulations?

It was precisely to address these fundamental questions that the ruler embarked on the creation of a Supreme Court, whose writ was narrower, and that would address administrative matters that concentrated on the selection of judges, the setting up of tribunals and other specialist courts, all to implement the king's recommendations. Indeed, the envisaged body was not meant to be a *supra*-national institution that would act as a co-equal branch to the executive – as is the case of the US Supreme Court or the British High Court of Justice – but a body that would expedite the kingdom's affairs. In fact, what 'Abdallah foresaw was a high court that would in a first instance examine cases involving administrative appeals rulings, and secondarily to handle disputes involving the rights of employees, compensation, contracts, disciplinary issues, administrative decisions and the implementation of foreign regulations. A separate Board of Grievances was created to henceforth supervise administrative disputes involving government departments, to act as an independent body and be directly answerable to the king.[29]

Second, as also envisaged by the ruler, the Supreme Court was to focus on selected cases that required national attention. While still not fully defined, the reformist 'Abdallah apparently recommended that the Supreme Court devise an official website to publish Islamic legal rulings, or fatwahs, to ensure that these – and only these – are recognized by all scholars who must rely on precedent. There was, in other words, a prominent guidance role for the Supreme Court that did not exist in the case of the SJC. What remained to be determined, however, was the interaction – or clash, as the case may be – between members of the Supreme Court and the Board of Senior *'Ulamah*, many of whom balked at their gradual loss of influence on legal matters. It was therefore essential for Riyadh to ensure that the Supreme Court would eventually grow to become the institution that upheld all laws in Sa'udi Arabia, without questioning the *'Ulamah*'s professionalism that, obviously, was not a given. It was hoped that over time, a reformed legal system would eliminate arbitrary judgments, and while the codification of laws could not be automatic (as it will remain under *Shari'ah*), King 'Abdallah's vision surely strengthened the monarchy rather than weakened it.[30]

The judiciary and social concerns

Because all legal questions were interpreted through religious rulings in Sa'udi Arabia, the very idea of "reforms," even if putative, surprised secularists as being an imaginary concept at best. Most pointed to Riyadh's willingness to throw money at any given problem as a perfect illustration of what needs to change first, but while disbursing large sums of riyals to address fundamental social problems might not necessarily solve then, intrinsic shortcomings cannot possibly be resolved if bold measures were not adopted. Yet, by taking the initiative, the monarch embarked on a series of sweeping legal changes that intended to reform existing *institutions*, focus on the ills embedded in the country's education system, and affect the status of women in this segregated society.

The religious establishment

Because the kingdom's religious establishment exercised authority on several levels, it was important to first provide a brief description of its leading institutions, before tackling any reform initiatives introduced after 2007. At the top of these established bodies was the

1. *Hay'at Kibar al-'Ulamah* or the Board of Senior *'Ulamah* (BSU), which issues fatwahs on major public concerns. The BSU was established in 1971 and headed by the Grand Mufti. By virtue of its privileges, it was the top Sa'udi religious institution, whose pronouncements were seldom challenged.
2. This was followed by the *Lajnah al-Da'imah lil-Buhuth al-'Ilmiyyah wal-Ifta'* or the Permanent Committee for Scientific Research and Legal Opinion (CRLO). Importantly, this committee was responsible for conducting research, administering private rulings, and providing bureaucratic support for the BSU.
3. The Grand Mufti, in his capacity as the chairman of both the BSU and the CRLO, maintained an independent office that enjoyed specific immunity and many privileges.
4. In turn, the *Majlis al-A'lah lil-Shu'un al-Islamiyyah* or the Supreme Council of Islamic Affairs, along with the *Majlis lil-Da'wah wal-Irshad* or the Council for Islamic Mission and Guidance, both of which were created in October 1994, completed the top hierarchy.

Interestingly, the defense minister and the minister for Islamic Affairs, Religious Guidance, and Endowments were respectively nominated as the heads of the two 1994 Councils in what was a clear effort to streamline the influence of the state on the legal system. Whether the Al Sa'ud concluded that it was necessary to better guide Sa'udis abroad, or whether to impose more systematic norms at home, was impossible to determine. Suffice it to say that moral behavior and the proper conduct of mosque functionaries concerned senior leaders who wished to regulate or attempt to regulate mosque activities. Naturally, these initiatives were specifically meant to bypass existing mechanisms and, in a not too subtle way, curtail the authority of *'Ulamah* who failed to implement strict regulations.[31]

By virtue of their positions and privileges, several dozen *'Ulamah* who were members of these organizations – and who were consequently the most influential religious figures in the kingdom, even if all were officially state employees – were the group that the monarch determined needed attention. In addition, thousands of other religious scholars held various positions in a multitude of agencies, also supported by Riyadh. While an exhaustive list of offices with which clerics were associated was nearly impossible to draw up, the following ought to provide a fairly solid illustration:

1 The Ministry of Pilgrimage (*Hajj*) and Endowments *[Awqaf]*, which dealt with both *da'wah* and *irshad* (outreach and guidance);
2 The *Hay'at al-Amr bil Ma'ruf wal-Nahi 'an al-Munkar* or the Commission for the Promotion of Virtue and the Prevention of Vice – (pejoratively known as the *mutawwiyyah*), which enforced fatwahs and punished those who did not fulfill their religious obligations;
3 The Muslim World League, a government body for spreading Unitarian (*Wahhabi*) doctrine among Muslims throughout the world;
4 The Higher Council of *Qadis* (judges);
5 The *muftis* of the Grand Mosques in Makkah and Madinah (and their extensive staffs);
6 The *Shari'ah* (religious) courts where all judges and attorneys were vetted;
7 Imams and Khutab in mosques to lead worship services and deliver sermons during the Friday or Eid prayers;
8 Staffing at Islamic universities, which were officially subordinate to the Education Ministry but, in reality, followed the Grand Mufti's instructions; and,
9 The Education Ministry, with local schoolmasters and teachers routinely vetted to ensure proper guidance.[32]

Although difficult to ascertain, the total number of *'Ulamah* in the kingdom probably did not exceed 1,000, even if an estimated 18,000 imams increased that figure somewhat, which made any reform initiative problematic if introduced by fiat and without proper consultations. When one included family members who enjoyed equal privileges, the more realistic figure of 80,000 people ought to be considered, even if these were guesstimates.[33] Of course, less than fifty *'Ulamah* enjoyed critical decision-making *rights*, even fewer had the ability to challenge political elites. The monarch routinely received senior clerics into his *majlis* and listened to their views, though he did not refrain from criticizing them either. On March 11, 2011, for example, the ruler provided generous stipends to the clerical class, but a few months later, he scolded them for failing to provide definitive statements on terrorism.[34] In early 2012, King 'Abdallah dismissed Shaykh 'Abdul 'Aziz bin Huma'yn al-Huma'yn, the head of the Commission for the Promotion of Virtue and the Prevention of Vice, and replaced him with Shaykh 'Abdul Latif bin 'Abdul 'Aziz bin 'Abdul Rahman Al Shaykh.[35] 'Abdallah "ordered him and his fellow colleagues to be lenient when dealing with people and to show good will and respect to them," which was telling in more ways than one.[36]

Periodic admonishments notwithstanding, the clergy enjoyed genuine political influence, as senior clerics, who were increasingly drawn from the Najd region instead of the Hijaz, served with Al Sa'ud consent.[37] Most fit the definition of moderate establishment *'Ulamah*, although sensational reportage on extreme positions frequently made the headlines. As discussed below, conditions pertaining to women received plenty of attention, but this did not mean that clerics were all obtuse in their views. For example, in a rare and unprecedented statement on Sa'udi television in June 2004, Dr. Muhammad bin Suleiman Al-Mani'i opined during a talk show that "Islamic law prohibited raising a weapon against any lover of peace, a merchant, or anyone who entered (the country) on a work contract."[38] He specifically used the word *dhimmi*, those who enjoyed a protected status and from whom certain responsibilities were taken, which is how Jews and Christians are referred to in Scriptures as people of the book. He further clarified that *Shari'ah* permitted one to raise a weapon only against whoever aimed a weapon at a Muslim in order to fight him. This was a cathartic moment as the cleric explained why it was important for Muslims to treat non-Muslims with dignity and respect, since such behavior might encourage the latter to eventually convert to Islam. Another cleric, Shaykh Salih al-Sidlan, stated in his weekly religious ruling show on Sa'udi television that terrorists distorted Islam by killing both infidels and the Muslims who were near them. In unabashed language, the Shaykh condemned those responsible for the terror attacks in the kingdom, accusing perpetrators of deviancy.[39] Another unusually moderate comment was made by Shaykh 'Abd al-Muhsin al-'Ubaykan, a member of the *Shurah* Council, who stated in a meeting with young Sa'udis that he was against the call to join *jihad* in Iraq because it might cause *fitnah* (strife) within the community. He affirmed that the call to *jihad* deviated from the basic precept that *jihad* was a decision that had to be made by the ruler (*wali al-'amr*) himself, and not by anyone else.[40]

These declarations illustrated how complex the debate among so-called moderate clerics became, with most struggling to stay ahead of systematic attacks on their credibility.[41] Extremists regularly attacked clergymen close to the Al Sa'ud, labeling them apostates, which was both insulting as well as injurious. Most wished to guide the debate, and whether they themselves were targeted for moderate positions, or whether the government persuaded them to promote non-violence, was at the heart of concerns facing the clerical establishment. In the event, the legal discourse was tested by non-establishment scholars who enflamed passions, with most seldom displaying any shyness about voicing their convoluted opinions. Who were the leading *'Ulamah* that fit the category of non-establishment clergymen, and what were their demands?

The non-establishment *'Ulamah*

Non-establishment *'Ulamah* may be categorized geographically, ideologically, and sociologically. Geographically, Najdi "neo-Salafi" groups, which were oriented to a strict interpretation of *Shari'ah*, began to chafe in the 1990s at the Hijazi predominance and to reject the rulings of Hijazi scholars. During the first decade of the twenty-first century, Hijazi *'Ulamah* represented the large proportion of radical Shaykhs who opposed what many amongst them perceived as an outright takeover, objecting to their Najdi counterparts' open compliance with Al Sa'ud directives. Still, the list of outlawed scholars consisted of *'Ulamah* from diverse regional and tribal origins, and from rich and poor families alike. In fact, it was difficult to draw clear patterns, since urbanization probably played a key role in whatever banishments occurred. This indicated that the geographical categorization was not as relevant as it may have been at an earlier time, though those who opposed establishment norms were adamant in rejecting subservience to the Al Sa'ud.

On the ideological level, however, non-establishment *'Ulamah* could be better identified. In fact, scholars who belonged to the *Sahwah al-Islamiyyah*, or "Islamic Awakening," were the easiest Shaykhs to recognize. The *Sahwah* emerged in the 1980s, first because its leadings members opposed establishment scholars who were perceived as corrupted elements, and, second, because most were far better educated than entrenched Shaykhs. A year after Juhayman al-'Utaybi took over the Makkah Mosque, several Sahwists started to mobilize, anxious to redraw the parameters of religious discourse in the country.[42] Ironically, even if none of them held official positions, most benefited from Riyadh's generous support of all religious institutions. Moreover, their influence grew dramatically in the aftermath of the War for Kuwait (1990–91), when leading Sahwists criticized the Al Sa'ud for inviting foreign troops to defend the kingdom. Of particular interest among this group of *'Ulamah* were two of the Sahwah's most prominent and remarkable members, Salman al-'Awdah and Safar al-Hawali, both of whom were considered hard-line supporters of al-Qa'idah.[43] Both men were arrested and jailed in September 1994, together with approximately a thousand of their supporters, and spent two years in prison. Shaykh 'Abd al-'Aziz bin Baz, the blind but charismatic Grand Mufti, issued a fatwah that justified their arrest, though many of the *'Ulamah* were hesitant to denounce the *Sahwah*, probably because they identified with their preachings.

A second group of non-establishment *'Ulamah* were the so-called *wasatiyyun*, modernizing intellectuals who sometimes referred to themselves as *tanawiriyyun* (enlighteners), *islahiyyun* (reformers), or *'aqlaniyyun* (rationalists). Most *wasatiyyun* members were former *Sahwah* Shaykhs such as 'Abd al-'Aziz al-Qasim, who was one of the fifty-two *'Ulamah* who signed the 1991 "Letter of Demands" to King Fahd. Al-Qasim was a prominent figure in the *Lajnat al-Difa' 'an al-Huquq al-Shar'iyyah* [Committee for the Defense of Legitimate Rights (CDLR)], the banned organization led by Dr. Muhammad al-Mas'ari, who was briefly arrested in 1997 but released several weeks later.[44] Since that time, al-Qasim became an advocate of *ijtihad*, democratization and Sa'udi nationalism, even if his liberal thoughts did not extend to women's rights. Al-Qasim considered *jihad* to be a fundamental pillar of Islam and not the sole prerogative of the ruler, which prompted him to take increasingly antiestablishment positions, including opposition to clergymen he perceived to be subservient. *Wasatiyyun* Shaykhs saw their ranks expand with 'Abdallah al-Hamid, a former Sahwah scholar from Buraydah, who proposed a return to *ijtihad* and what he called "innovative Salafiyyah," claiming that the true *Salafiyyah* was imaginative, able to bridge the gap between the text and the real world.[45] An equally forceful voice was that of Hasan al-Maliki, another former Salafi scholar who was a critic of Sa'udi historiography and the educational curriculum, and who was dismissed from his government post for his iconoclastic views. It was useful to underscore, as one Western observer concluded, that the common denominator among all of the *wasatiyyun* was their call for a rationalist review of *Wahhabi* doctrine, which presented something of a problem for the establishment.[46]

The third group of non-establishment *'Ulamah* were the so-called *takfiris*, who were mostly militants who labeled government officials and establishment clergymen as apostates. This was a serious charge, since declaring a Muslim a *kafir* (apostate) was tantamount to a condemnatory sentence, with very grave consequences. Among the more prominent *takfiri* Shaykhs were Nasir al-Fahad, 'Ali al-Khudayr, and Ahmad al-Khalidi, who were inspired by earlier writings of such prominent *Wahhabi* writers as Muhammad bin 'Abd al-Wahhab, Muhammad al-Qahtani, Muhammad bin Ibrahim Al-Shaykh and Humud bin 'Uqlah al-Shu'aybi.[47] Al-Fahad, al-Khudayr, and al-Khalidi were arrested in 2003, allegedly because they authorized the terrorist attacks in the residential compounds that devastated Sa'udi Arabia.[48] As a result of a major military campaign against them, most of these *takfiri* Shaykhs, along with scores of supporters, were killed in clashes with Sa'udi security forces. Many more were on the run and remained "wanted" by the state. To its credit, Riyadh managed to isolate *takfiris* within society, even if it could not eliminate the ideological trend, since a significant group of popular preachers sympathized with their rhetoric. That was the primary reason why ministry of interior patrols routinely canvass mosques throughout the kingdom, to identify any *'alim* who may harbor extremist sentiments, enroll them in carefully designed rehabilitation programs and, most importantly, deny them platforms to spread any non-establishment ideas.

Nevertheless, and inasmuch as schools and universities graduated a large number of young men with non-marketable skills, what to do with those who could not find suitable employment remained the existential question for the Al Sa'ud. Many young graduates were frustrated with their personal situations, which prompted some to rely on tangential religious knowledge to gain public and political status, especially among less educated and equally embittered populations that likewise suffered from unemployment. Riyadh faced the challenge of channeling non-establishment clergymen into appropriate positions, empowering them with sound religious knowledge, while insisting that they forego extremism and violence. It is fair to wonder how useful were legal reforms, if religious institutions continued to produce a disproportionately high number of graduates who could not find suitable employment. Was the adoption of new legal reforms sufficient, when the kingdom's education system was irredeemably hampered by severe religious constraints that focused on rote learning? Could the monarch's bold steps on the legal front succeed without a commensurate push in the religious education curriculum?

Religious education in the kingdom

Although the need to address some of the issues related to legal and religious reforms has received the attention of Sa'udi officials since 2001, critics saw little change in their assessments.[49] In his erudite volume, Dore Gold, a former Israeli ambassador to the United Nations, asserted that Sa'udi Arabia financed terrorism for decades and, more importantly, that Sa'udi religious authorities indoctrinated their impressionable flock with visceral hatred of the United States. His thoroughly researched study provided numerous examples of religious writings that were anti-Christian and anti-Jewish – perhaps even anti-Semitic, although that latter charge was egregious given that Muslims were also Semites. Indeed, for some Sa'udis, the Christian world was still engaged in crusades against Muslims, and Christians and Jews were nothing more than infidels or polytheists who, therefore, are not protected peoples.

Two specific issues raised by critics deserved special attention at this juncture: the bases on which Sa'udi education rested and the alleged Sa'udi financing of terrorist groups. It was a fact that Sa'udi education failed the kingdom. Sadly, Riyadh could not rely on its own institutions to equip the country's fledgling industries, commercial enterprises, and other private sector needs. Instead, the curriculum emphasized religious indoctrination, with many unskilled graduates who yearly filled the ranks of the unemployed. Yet, it was also critical to ask whether a country's cultural environment was easily replaced or rapidly altered. As Eleanor Abdella Doumato illustrated, most of what passed for hate was, in fact, fueled by fear and an overall defensive interpretation.[50] While it was fashionable to blame the co-founder of the 1744 alliance for these ills, Muhammad 'Abdul Wahhab called on Muslims to return to Islam's original teachings at a time when most believers had deviated to worshiping idols and to venerating saints. That his methods were harsh was undeniable, but to impugn his teachings by asserting that they promoted hatred of Christians and Jews was facile. In the harsh conditions of the Arabian Peninsula, where life was often tested, it was 'Abdul Wahhab who saved his people. Not only did his association with Muhammad Al Sa'ud ensure tribal unity where none had existed for hundreds of years, it may also be said that the burden of preserving existing traditions could not have been better served.[51]

How contemporary Sa'udi leaders addressed the new requirements of their educational institutions, updated their textbooks, and removed the fear that many authors instilled in themselves and in their children, is yet to be determined. In this respect, one recommendation advanced by critics, namely, that Western diplomats – and, one may add, not just diplomats – should monitor

Sa'udi textbooks, speech, and other discourse both to hold them accountable and to assist them, was very pertinent.[52]

The second major issue, this one dealing with alleged financial support to terrorist groups, has been treated at length by several writers, including by Antoine Basbous and Stéphane Marchand in two outstanding recent books.[53] Both authors "documented" various financial transactions between different Sa'udis and known terrorists, their supporters, and organizations. Others relied on American (and Israeli) intelligence sources, to document how certain Al Sa'ud princes paid 'Usamah bin Ladin and his al-Qa'idah organization – essentially to buy protection. According to these sources, bin Ladin promised to refrain from conducting operations in Sa'udi Arabia proper, if Riyadh limited its response to al-Qa'idah activities elsewhere. Few disputed that certain Sa'udis provided financial support to al-Qa'idah. However, to conclude that the Kingdom of Sa'udi Arabia had "gone to the dark side" by 1996 fit better into the screenplay of a science fiction film like *Star Wars* than into a judicious analysis of the connection between Sa'udi Arabia and terrorism.[54] Although there were undoubtedly Sa'udis, including princes and preachers, who supported extremists, the Sa'udi state did not sanction such behavior and there was no evidence that linked the state with any such financial disbursements. On the contrary, Riyadh focused on the means to identify, apprehend, rehabilitate, and, when all else failed, imprison extremists. It did not bargain with its security even if the state took timid steps in addressing intrinsic problems. King 'Abdallah pushed for legal reforms but did not link alterations on that front with necessary changes within the field of religious education. What else could have been done to give legal and political reforms new life?

This is not an easy question to answer since religious education in the kingdom remained unchanged for several centuries. From a jurisprudence aspect, pious teaching and learning consisted of nothing more than sectarian texts devoid of serious evidence. Most of the manuscripts used in religious institutions were written hundreds of years ago, whose contents were memorized verbatim by students expected to adjust to contemporary circumstances. For example, while students studied and committed to memory the *Za'ad al-Mustaqni'* in Hanbali jurisprudence, the *Mukhtasar Khalil* in Maliki jurisprudence, the *Al-Taqrib* by Abu-Shujah in Shafi'i jurisprudence, or the *Mukhtasar al-Quduri* in Hanafi jurisprudence, one wondered how relevant each one was to the twenty-first century?[55]

For one commentator, "these texts were written with extreme brevity in words, puzzling sentences, and a reduction of meaning."[56] Dr. al-Qarni, a well-known Sa'udi scholar, concluded that these texts lacked solid references to the Holy Scriptures and were often assumed to be definitive. Indeed, such interpretations contained value as long as they were used for deduction using *Shari'ah* evidence, and not the other way around. Moreover, jurisprudence opinions could not be categorical, which meant that if an interpretation was false, sectarian fanaticisms resulted. The erudite al-Qarni provided the following evidence to buttress his analysis. In the *Za'ad al-Mustanqi'*, for example, one reads: "The water is of three categories," which is wrong, since there are only two categories (clean or dirty). It continued: "If clean clothes are suspected of being mixed with dirty ones, then you perform a number of prayers equal to the number of the clothes plus one," which literally forced a follower of Hanbali jurisprudence to perform 21 prayers, if one had 20 items of clothing. Rather, according to al-Qarni, what was required was far simpler: to "ascertain whether any of the items were dirty before embarking on a ritual. True believers ought not let their minds wonder into tangential investigations but remain true to the teachings of the Holy Qur'an and the *Hadith* instead of wallowing in ambiguity."[57] Inasmuch as learned scholars were preoccupied with such minutiae, one wondered what kind of education was necessary to introduce real reforms, especially the kinds that society demanded in the twenty-first century. Indeed, this was one of the greatest challenges that faced Muslim jurisprudence today: the need to clarify for believers why they should concern themselves with puzzling sentences written by leading *fuqahah* (experts in Muslim jurisprudence, plural of *faqih*) who lived in earlier periods and whose interpretations were hardly relevant today. Why should a believer bend over backwards to explain what was meant by convoluted sentences produced under wholly different circumstances? Who would be qualified to separate intelligent prose from the confused? Reforming jurisprudence, therefore, necessitated the establishment of careful distances between such scholarly works and the Scriptures. Al-Qarni and younger scholars from this generation wished to rely on the Qur'an, since they believed that it included "guidance, enlightenment, comprehensive explanations, and sufficient answers," which did not require legal summersaults.[58] Moreover, reformists were justifiably irritated by additional misinterpretations, doubting whether some *fuqahah* issued fatwahs without distinguishing between a correct and a weak *Hadith*.[59] Often, they did not bother to provide solid evidence, and only memorized jurisprudential texts that served their purposes. Unsurprisingly, this is a hugely controversial issue since Muslim scholars take their interpretation responsibilities seriously, within specifically delineated schools of law. How a Sunni Muslim who belonged to the Hanbali School interpreted a concern vis-à-vis his Maliki, Shafi'i, and Hanafi counterparts, mattered. How all four projected those interpretations vis-à-vis the Shi'ah Ja'afari School was also critical. Still, under King 'Abdallah's reform initiatives, men like al-Qarni were called upon to reform their legal education methods so that students could study the jurisprudence of the Holy Qur'an and the *Sunnah*, devising laws that would be true to the faith while adapting to the times. In a strange way, it may be accurate to state that the monarch threw a gauntlet down before the scholars, challenging them to practice law just like previous imams, men of the caliber of Ibn Taymiyyah, Ibn 'Abdul Bar, Ibn 'Abdul Wahhab, Al-Sana'ani, Al-Shawkani, and others did, by relying on *Hadith* without abdicating their own intellectual prowess.[60]

Although this test was a product of the times, it was also a reality check, for today's jurisprudence is no longer limited to certain subjects. If traditional scholars learned philosophy, logic, and grammar to complete their education, contemporary requirements were far more demanding. Like all students at the intermediate and secondary stages, Muslim children who grew up to embark on a religious career were exposed to religion, mathematics, algebra, geometry, physics, chemistry, biology, English language, literature, grammar, culture, history, geography, and several other subjects. Even if a select few continued their specialized education by enrolling in advanced logic courses, for example, most were overwhelmed by the amount of knowledge to be acquired. Regrettably, few mastered languages other than Arabic, and even fewer were versed in scientific subjects, although international exposure was now routine and a thorough knowledge of scientific subjects a necessity, if for no other reason than to render sound religious judgments. In any case, few Muslim scholars in the twenty-first century mastered physics, or chemistry, or enjoyed a healthy familiarity with biology, even if many were called upon to render opinions on celestial affairs, environmental questions, or heath issues related to sexuality. Obviously, excelling in tenth century algebra is somewhat irrelevant to the study of celestial mechanics in the twenty-first. In short, it was problematic when contemporary knowledge, in such diverse subjects as geometry, arithmetic, geography, or any number of other subject matters, overwhelmed scholars caught in what one learned man labeled "the curricula [that] became a 'quagmire'," which added to the heavy burden of balancing these studies with *Shari'ah* law.[61] No wonder that so few *fuqahah* practice today, since such a title required one to be an outstanding interpreter, a prominent writer, as well as a brilliant grammarian, in addition to mastering a variety of scientific subjects. This was the ultimate challenge that faced reformists whose task was to update jurisprudence without losing its essence.

In fact, while the judicial system failed to administer justice because of inadequate legal procedures, red tape, and a rigid interpretation of *Shari'ah* law, the primary reason for the stalemate was not courts being overburdened or the acute shortage of judges – although these significantly contributed to the overall malaise – but the core education problems within the judiciary. Leading Muslim scholars believed that drastic measures were necessary to improve conditions, especially in terms of the actual training jurists enjoyed, which was in need of a major overhaul. To reform the judiciary, declared Tarek Al-Suwaidan, a prominent Muslim scholar, Sa'udi Arabia was better off if it first focused on the curriculum and the teaching standards at *Shari'ah* colleges.[62] In the words of a leading observer of the kingdom,

> the reason behind the poor quality of education in these very important institutions is the poor academic standards of their students. The students who enroll in these colleges are the ones who graduate from school with poor or average grades; therefore, they are not usually the brightest. Furthermore, their studies are mostly confined to subjects related to Islamic jurisprudence.[63]

This was as clear a diagnosis of the problem as any, which called for the "creation of well-rounded Muslim scholars and judges familiar with international law, educated on aspects of modern-day needs and concerns." In fact, Sa'udi scholars understood that the time was long overdue for students who joined *Shari'ah* colleges to have more than a basic secondary education. If institutions of higher learning admitted graduates with at least a bachelor's degree in business, law, or any other specialized field, it was far more likely that their putative religious diplomas could only be enhanced beyond standardized qualifications. *Shari'ah* graduates were increasingly expected to be well-versed in current commercial laws and be familiar with cyberspace crime, copyright violations, or labor issues, to name just a few areas of relevance to contemporary affairs, if their potential "opinions" were to be germane. King 'Abdallah and his advisors probably concluded that this was what the country needed because they also knew that current judges were inadequately prepared to render such pronouncements. Regrettably, the narrow breadth of knowledge that was all too prevalent among the clergy meant that most believers were probably better trained than the doctors of law, which meant that grievances increased and justice was denied.

In the words of Samar Fatany:

> When the Prophet (peace be upon him) spoke more than 1,400 years ago, he tailored his words to the people of that time and addressed the issues of those days in terms understandable to much simpler people in much simpler times. In a world made smaller by transportation and telecommunications networks and a world of great cities and global commerce, it is incumbent upon the keepers of Shariah law to ensure the relevance of its interpretation in the daily lives of the millions of adherents to Islam today.[64]

Fatany quoted Kamel Ahmad Al-Shamsi, a Sa'udi legal expert, in her essay, who called for the establishment of "civic courts administered by judges who have graduated from law colleges with degrees obtained from abroad ... We need to use the expertise of other, more advanced Arab countries in civic law and sign contracts with cadres who can serve as consultants and judges," concluded Al-Shamsi, which was a view shared by more liberal elites. Still, this was far easier said than done, given the kingdom's very strict traditional and tribal norms. Establishment *qadis* insisted that students should learn through apprenticeships and with scholars who can trace their learning to Islam's roots – not from qualified law professors. How could Riyadh alter such penchants when it faced a generational gap, along with tested preferences among established clerics for whom *Shari'ah* rules were in no need of any changes? How could the foresightful monarch encourage scholars to codify *Shari'ah* so that Muslims everywhere could understand what rules and regulations existed and how to submit to them?[65] To his credit, the Sa'udi ruler opened a reform spigot that will be next to impossible to shut off, even if critics seldom missed an opportunity to lament the clergy's mendacious responses.

Indeed, while it might take years to retrain legal experts, the Muslim world will surely witness major transformations of its jurisprudence during the course of the next few decades. For it will be nearly impossible to close the knowledge gap unless religious scholars adapt and contribute toward the advancement of their societies.

Again, this was neither a given nor a certain outcome, although many were aware of the major hurdles that need to be crossed. For example, in the field of Islamic banking, and according to *Shari'ah* scholar Shaykh Nizam Yaquby, "there were roughly 50 to 60 scholars in the world qualified to advise banks on Islamic Law, and as many as ten times more [we]re required to serve in the Middle East alone." It was, therefore, "essential to train more scholars for Islamic bank supervision to keep up with the global demand," especially as the Kingdom of Sa'udi Arabia was poised to occupy a far larger role in international financial affairs. According to the London-based Chartered Institute of Management Accountants: "The rapid growth of Islamic banking had fueled a need for Muslim financial experts. However, scholars must be experts in Islamic Law and Islamic banking and, at the same time, have a thorough knowledge of conventional laws and banking systems, which requires a high standard of English."[66]

King 'Abdallah probably knew that reforming the legal system and training more judges were not easy proposition in Sa'udi Arabia, and despite sustained criticisms, he made the transformations his priority. It was essential, he concluded, that Muslim and especially Sa'udi scholars distance themselves from obscurantism. More important, it was necessary for them to integrate the global community of men and women to resolve problems at the local, regional, and international levels. Likewise it was indispensable for *fuqahah* to concern themselves with rapidly evolving conditions that affected the Muslim world and humanity at large. According to several ranking members of the Al Sa'ud ruling family, the monarch was aware that his legal reforms, coupled with intrinsic political transformations, required major modifications of *Shari'ah* law, which was neither easy nor automatic. Nevertheless, he apparently chose to push hard on this front, because he understood that religious officials needed to become part of the solution. Simply stated, 'Abdallah was keenly aware that a majority of Sa'udis rejected excesses that *qadis* or members of the Commission for the Promotion of Virtue and Prevention of Vice were inclined towards, considering themselves to be above the law simply because they interpreted it. Scholarship did not translate into *supra*-legality, the ruler reasoned, which meant that the monarchy's very survival was at stake unless drastic measures were tackled in the sacrosanct religious education field. What was the role of the establishment in the country's education system, and were practitioners ready to heed the Palace's call?

The role of the Sa'udi Islamic establishment in education

"Thirty to forty percent of the curriculum [in Sa'udi general education establishments] focused on religious doctrine," opined a leading report on the

Muslim world.[67] Reportedly, more than seventy percent of the curriculum in the four "secular" universities involved religious studies and Arab and Islamic history, which led analysts to conclude that religious studies held a central place even in educational programs for science, geography, and similar subjects. What many authors who focused on this topic implied was that the Sa'udi education system was an incubator that produced radicalization, coloring the attitudes of average citizens toward non-Muslims.[68] Critics asserted that the Sa'udi curriculum included negative portrayals of Christians and Jews that displayed a high level of intolerance towards non-*Wahhabis*, coupled with support for *jihad* against perceived enemies of Islam. Moreover, they also asserted, the general education called for the need to empower Muslims militarily to conduct this putative *jihad*, reject Shi'ahs or consider them to be *takfiris*, denounce democracy allegedly because it arrogates lawmaking to man instead of God, as well as the ultimate sin that separated powers. The list was long and inelegant.[69]

Whatever inconsistencies existed in the curriculum, especially towards other Muslims, and because of very strong external pressure to alter the tone as well as content of what passed for scholarly work, Riyadh launched a series of reforms in this area starting in 2003. Hostility towards the West in general and calls for *jihad* were substantially curtailed. Sa'udi teachers were given advanced training to impart a fairer interpretation, which was not an easy task because of entrenched mentalities, even if ministerial directives were adamant. In fact, senior members within the religious establishment opposed these reforms, and while Riyadh could not simply ignore '*Ulamah* objections, it nevertheless purged much of the offending texts. 'Abdallah kept his promise and overrode protestations, which in effect further reduced the influence of the religious establishment where it mattered most, namely in the social and educational levels, which resulted in the dismissal of approximately 2,000 preachers after the tragic events of September 11, 2001.[70] The monarch was pleased with many of these changes even when criticisms persisted. Nevertheless, 'Abdallah knew that concerns dealing with women, and how the law interpreted the many challenges that emerged in the kingdom, were the determinant factors in social reforms.

The status of women

Samar Fatany probably said it best when she asked: "What do we tell our own people or the world, for that matter, about how we value the rights of women when her brothers can order her to divorce because they don't approve of the husband their late father chose?" Fatany, a leading social commentator in Jiddah, reacted to a case where several brothers of a young woman who married someone she loved and with whom she started a family, contended that "she had shamed her tribe," which is why they wanted a divorce. "We as a people," Fatany concluded, "should be ashamed of a legal system where such a case could be initiated, where a family could be broken up and a mother and her children could be forced to live in a shelter."[71] This was one of several bizarre cases that filled the dockets in Sa'udi Arabia and were part of why King 'Abdallah wished to introduce dramatic reforms into the system. Many similar occurrences surfaced from time to time, which highlighted serious problems within the segregated society, and which inevitably shocked the entire country. In one instance, a judge denied a mother's petition to gain custody of a child from her abusive husband, only to discover that the father eventually beat his child to death. In another instance, and as discussed above, the case of the Qatif Girl mobilized even the Palace after an engaged couple was raped by several young men and which drew the ire of the judiciary – except by blaming the victims as much as the culprits.

In time, the frequency of such developments prompted the Sa'udi National Society for Human Rights to publish a complete report, which strongly criticized the judicial system for failing to serve justice.[72] The voluminous account included over 200 pages of minute detail whose publication could not have been possibly authorized without strong backing from the monarch. It outlined many human rights violations and focused on rampant discrimination against women. In a conservative society like that in Sa'udi Arabia, discussing domestic violence was rare, and suggesting that judges overlooked grievances and were, consequently, partially responsible for such wanton violence, was even more uncommon. Moreover, it was clear that the ruler wished to highlight this scourge by authorizing publication, to further draw attention to the bane. Other sensitive topics were also addressed, including the awful conditions in Sa'udi prisons, as well as routine abuses inflicted on the most vulnerable expatriate workers toiling as domestics in Sa'udi homes. Still, what really shocked in the report was its unabashed disapproval of actions attributed to the Commission for the Promotion of Virtue and Prevention of Vice. According to the report, it was time for authorities pretending to apply *Shari'ah* law to learn how to deal with law-abiding citizens, which eventually prompted the monarch to call on its new leader to change the institution's ways.[73]

Whether the Sa'udi monarch intended to force the issue of how woman were treated in society was a nearly impossible question to settle. There were, nevertheless, specific signs that he wished to sensitize the religious establishment to excesses. Indeed, while progress on this front crawled, it was rather obvious where 'Abdallah stood even if it was a mistake to assume that the ruler was a closet liberal. He fit no such categorization though it was fair to assume that he was a reformer – a conservative reformer. On the question of women, however, 'Abdallah meant what he said and what he did. Beyond periodic feuds between some of the most influential *Salafi* Shaykhs and the monarch, Riyadh abhorred radical clergymen whose behavior was nothing short of arrogant, because they highjacked the tone and substance of debates. When the influential Shaykh 'Abdul Rahman bin Nasir al-Barrak, who advocated strict segregation of the sexes, issued a fatwah that declared any individual "condoning the mixing of the sexes in the workplace or in the educational arena should be killed," the king was furious.[74] "Anyone who accepts that his daughter, sister or wife works with men or attends mixed-gender schooling cares little about his honor and this is a type of pimping," wrote al-Barrak, which naturally drew fire from a Riyadh judge, Shaykh 'Isa al-Ghayth, who accused him of "raising discord" and "inciting brother against brother."[75]

Not surprisingly, the extremist fatwah received widespread attention, including an acerbic comment by Maureen Dowd in the *New York Times* who happened to be in Riyadh at the time the edict was issued. The gifted Dowd asked the Foreign Minister, Prince Sa'ud al-Faysal, whether the "pugnacious cleric, [who] shocked Saudis by issuing a fatwa against those who facilitate the mixing of men and women," was not also targeting the king himself.[76] Sa'ud apparently dismissed the assertion, declaring: "I think the trend for reform is set, and there is no looking back. Clerics who every now and then come with statements in the opposite direction are releasing frustration rather than believing that they can stop the trend and turn back the clock." This was certainly an accurate assessment, though frustration was a combustible element that gained momentum in the kingdom after the 2009 inauguration of a state-of-the-art, $10 billion university near Jiddah, the King 'Abdallah University of Science and Technology (KAUST), that was the country's first mixed institution of higher learning.[77] At the time, the ruler sacked a "senior cleric who demanded that religious scholars vet the curriculum at the new $10bn co-educational international science university," which coincidentally occurred just after the king appointed Nura al-Fayiz as the country's first woman deputy cabinet minister.[78]

Still, the level-headed and immensely foresightful 'Abdallah was not amused by Shaykh al-Barrak's fatwah and ordered, albeit for a period of a few months only, that the "learned man's" website be shut down. In the words of an Al Sa'ud princess who related the monarch's furious reaction, "this was the level of material that our ruler has to deal with, which is why change occurs at a crawl in this country."[79]

According to Raouf Ebeid, the "King obviously understood the old adage, 'a picture is worth a thousand words,' when he decided to stand behind the mixing of the sexes in an unprecedented open display – complete with photo-op."[80] On 5 May 2010, the monarch and his brother Heir Apparent Sultan bin 'Abdul 'Aziz – whose presence strongly implied a pointer to future policies – appeared in an unusual group photograph flanked by 40 women mostly with their faces bare, though wearing modest *abayas*. Not only was this a novelty, but it also occurred in the southern city of Najran, as participants gathered for the April 8–10, 2010 National Dialogue Forum (see Chapter 2). The photograph directly challenged existing norms because the two men in the snap were obviously not related to the women. Consequently, it may be safe to note that *Shari'ah* law as practiced in the country was amended, since the women appeared without their male guardians. The reactions to the publication of the photograph were ecstatic and came a few weeks after the Palace intervened with the Commission for the Promotion of Virtue and Prevention of Vice to reverse a decision to sack Shaykh Ahmad al-Ghamdi, its head for the Makkah region, because the cleric had earlier questioned whether Islam in fact required gender segregation. Ghamdi's swift reinstatement was not an accident and indicated a renewed confidence by the palace in reformist ideas, as was the photograph with the women attending the National Dialogue Conference. Clearly, the photo was a symbolic message sent to the nation that the time was right for women to be recognized and, in a sublime touch, "all the women in the picture got a pleasant surprise when they received an official copy" before its public release.[81] "I think this is a great picture and everyone is talking about it," said Maha Muneef, a prominent physician and government adviser, who continued: "This is a picture that sent a message that it is OK to work with women … and that there's nothing wrong with that."[82] Several of the women present spoke of the rare opportunity. "It was not surprising at all," said Sa'udi poet Nimah Nawwab: "The Custodian of the Two Holy Mosques King Abdullah made women part of the civil society delegation to India during his 2006 visit to that country. That picture was also prominently displayed in our media." Manal Faysal Al Sharif, who headed the women's section at the Jiddah-based *Okaz* newspaper, which also published the photo on its front page, stated that the publication of this and other such photographs indicated women were being recognized as partners in the progress of the nation: "Slowly and surely, their contributions are being recognized. And so naturally, we are happy." Economic researcher and writer 'Abdallah al-'Alami was among those who were delighted with the way newspapers treated the photograph. "I saw it in *Okaz* first," he opined, "and then I wrote to some of the women in the picture congratulating them. They were obviously very excited about it. I was happy for them as Saudi women have been oppressed and humiliated enough in the past, and it is about time to recognize their achievements."[83]

This was not the only example of dramatic changes ushered in by the ruler in the aftermath of the disastrous Shaykh 'Abdul Rahman bin Nasir Al-Barrak fatwah. On 21 March 2010, King 'Abdallah received Shaykhah Mawzah bint Nasir al-Misnad, the wife of the Amir of Qatar Shaykh Hamad bin Khalifah Al Thani, and Chairperson of the Qatar Foundation for Education, Science and Community Development, in his Riyadh Palace. The Qatari first lady was obviously a married woman, well known for her impeccable fashion, as well as high visibility social commitments around the world despite her Unitarian (*Wahhabi*) affiliation. The Shaykhah traveled to the kingdom unaccompanied by her husband, apparently was there to discuss educational and social issues related to the Gulf region, and did not mind being photographed with the Sa'udi monarch while her face was uncovered. In a widely distributed photograph showing her in conversation with the king, she even took the liberty to sit with her legs crossed, which highlighted a seldom seen level of comfort at such gatherings in the Gulf region. It was, to put it mildly, a historic meeting, far more meaningful than many assumed and served the status of women in the Gulf very well. By welcoming Shaykhah Mawzah in his office, King 'Abdallah telegraphed to conservative members of his society that the times were changing and that everyone was to play a role in advancing overall conditions. No longer was he willing to play the two-steps forward, one-step

Figure 1.1 Shaykhah Mawzah bint Nasr al-Misnad and King 'Abdallah bin 'Abdul 'Aziz Al Sa'ud in Riyadh, photograph posted on the webpage of the Royal Embassy of Sa'udi Arabia, Washington, D.C., at http://www.saudiembassy.net/latest_news/news03211001.aspx.

back game that was practiced with a vengeance, when every Gulf country needed its citizens – all of its citizens – to contribute.

In March 2010, a Sa'udi woman poet, Hassah Hilal (known as "Rimayyah"), participated in a popular TV program in Abu Dhabi that further highlighted the dilemma facing *Shari'ah* law in Sa'udi Arabia. On the *Millionaire Poetry Competition* show, Rimayyah surprised the audience and most watchers, as she delivered a brilliant poem that was a blistering attack on Muslim clerics, especially Shaykh al-Barrak, whose fatwahs incited hatred and violence. Fully covered from head to toe in accordance with *Shari'ah* law, Rimayyah challenged Shaykh al-Barrak and others, explaining that she "totally refused the chaotic atmosphere represented by the increasing number of fatwahs that called for bloodshed or were pronounced to achieve personal gains."[84] Importantly, the judges acknowledged that the poem represented an important contribution to society and Rimayyah advanced to the next stage. Sadly, the poem drew the ire of Islamists who literally called for her death, which prompted the young woman to declare: "my poem is to protect our nation from these radicals who have made out of us 'a country feared by the rest of the world'." She also called for women to speak up and fight those who want to marginalize women and stifle their voices.[85] Her poem, which earned her well-deserved fame, read in part:

> I saw evil stalking from the eyes of their fatwahs
> In an era when they contaminated the *halal* with the *haram*

I've uncovered the face of the truth
Revealing the monster hidden behind the mask
A savage, resentful, barbaric, blinded mind
Wearing a cloak of death under a tightened belt
Howling and terrifying the populace through brutal politics
Preying on every soul yearning for peace
The voice of the truth seeks refuge, and rightness is dying in isolation
In the pursuit of self-interest the one who speaks freely is disgraced ... [86]

Though she came in third in the 2010 competition, Hassah Hilal made her point, which was to sensitize Sa'udi society to ongoing developments that touched on discrimination and arbitrary decisions. The fact that she also took home over $800,000 in prize money was certainly worth her effort, even if her claim to fame was probably far more important. Indeed, by relying on a popular forum, and obeying established norms, she certainly awakened dormant voices that could no longer make such a plea. Inasmuch as legal opinions delivered by Shaykhs like al-Barrak further isolated the clergy, a prominent Islamist writer, Yasir al-Za'atrah, warned radical elements in the kingdom to re-evaluate their zeal. Speaking on *Al-Jazeera* television in mid-March 2010, al-Za'atrah pointed to Western opinion pieces – like Maureen Dowd's – criticizing the conditions to which women were submitted and, more important, to the reactions they solicited from senior officials – in this case the foreign minister – as evidence of liberal biases. In other words, al-Za'atrah contended that the more conservative voices opted for what many saw as extreme positions, while government officials invariably fall back on liberal views. This, he concluded, was not in the clergy's long-term interests, since a putative liberal trend would change the balance of power in the kingdom. That was why, al-Za'atrah affirmed, moderate religious figures ought to speak out against conservative figures, especially since so few of them were familiar with decisive Western perspectives.[87] He believed that rigid fatwahs, such as the one delivered by Al-Barrak, were not helping the religious cause they both championed. Therefore, and to mitigate further ostracisms, al-Za'atrah urged moderate clerics to step-up and make their voices heard. Ironically, the erudite al-Za'atrah quoted a passage from Christian Scriptures, which probably infuriated some watching the program, and affirmed that Muslims should "render unto Caesar what belonged to Caesar and to God what belonged to God." While such a quotation was akin to throwing gasoline on a fire, the Jericho, Palestine born journalist who sympathized with conservative sentiments, understood that making an allegation that equated Sa'udi liberals with their Christian counterparts certainly negated any progress they could hope to accomplish. Al-Za'atrah's exercise was thus a solid illustration of the raging battles between liberal and radical opinions, which the Al Sa'ud, led by King 'Abdallah, were asked to address and resolve.

How the monarch analyzed and ruled over controversies that emerged with the rapidly changing status of women in the kingdom was of utmost importance.

Reforms within the judiciary 49

As a bellwether of social trends in the country, this concern preoccupied senior members of the ruling family for essentially three reasons, which were all inter-related. First, because a younger generation of educated women wished to make useful contributions to society in ways that their mothers and grandmothers seldom dreamed of doing. Second, because the kingdom was no longer segregated from the rest of the Muslim world – and the world at large – as millions of women, including millions of Muslim women elsewhere, managed to add value without breaching *Shari'ah* law. Third, because Sa'udi clerics could no longer justify policies that neglected, *inter alia*, potential female contributions to *Shari'ah* law. This last point was especially important since several scholars suggested that the top religious organization in the kingdom, the Board of Senior *'Ulamah*, should ideally include women, positing that the Prophet treated women as women – and not only as mothers, or sisters or daughters in Islam.[88]

When the recommendations were first made in 2008 to invite women to join, leading members of the Board rejected the idea, though most realized that King 'Abdallah, or one of his successors, would eventually appoint women to the Board of Senior *'Ulamah*. In 2012, the Board consisted of 17 scholars, all of whom were appointed by Royal decrees to serve for renewable four-year terms. In other words, and this is critical to underscore, the country's *'Ulamah* served Riyadh in an advisory capacity even if their writ was to opine on *Shari'ah* law. By rejecting a mere recommendation to include a few women on the Board, which would not have been made without the monarch's knowledge and approval, the more conservative Shaykhs wished to signal to the Al Sa'ud that they should not venture on this path. How the king responded was telling even if 'Abdallah managed to swing back and forth and postponed the decision to move on this front.

The 2008 controversy, which erupted after initial reform plans were introduced to update the judiciary, concentrated on two leading *'Ulamah*, Shaykhs Qays bin Muhammad bin 'Abdul Latif Al Mubarak and 'Abdul Rahman Al-Zunaydih, even if others chimed into the debate and made their voices heard.[89] The two scholars, who signed the "How Can We Co-Exist" pamphlet that responded to a paper prepared by the Institute for American Values entitled "What We're Fighting For," and which was signed by sixty American intellectuals searching for a dialogue between the West and the Muslim world, suggested that women should be included among their ranks.[90] Inasmuch as their argument on the inclusion of women on the Board was meant to assist women who submitted questions to the religious body, the intention was to reduce overall embarrassment, and not necessarily to upset the existing balance of power. In fact, the reformist Al Mubarak believed that men and women should intermingle in scholarly meetings, "arguing that at the time of the prophet women and men were permitted to listen and discuss issues together," which was not a controversial issue then and ought not be one today.[91] For his part, Al Zunaydih, a prolific writer in his own right, likewise emphasized that female members would fulfill an important role in understanding and responding to female audiences, if given an opportunity to participate and contribute.[92]

It was not long after these suggestions were advanced that a leading member of the Board, Shaykh 'Abdallah bin Sulayman bin Mani' unleashed his fury, avowing that the Board was part of the *Imamah al-Kubrah* [The Highest Imamate] in the land and, as such, could not possibly include women because the Prophet Muhammad declared that "no People shall succeed if ruled by a woman."[93] This quotation from a widely quoted *Hadith* attributed to three separate sources: al-Bukharih, al-Tirmidhih, and al-Nassa'ih, and was always used by scholars who not only claimed that it was prohibited for women to take part in general guardianship and public affairs, but who insisted on its literal interpretation.[94] The circumstances under which this *Hadith* was attributed were political and not necessarily related to gender. When visitors from Persia arrived into Madinah to see the Prophet Muhammad, he asked them: "Who is in charge of Persia?" According to al-Bukharih, one of them replied: "A woman," to which the Prophet retorted: "No people shall succeed if they put their affairs under the authority of a woman." Some scholars believed then and continue to refer to the saying as a unique political prophecy that witnessed the termination of the Persian sovereign, and that applied at the time only, which meant that it could not be generalized. According to this view, the declaration was prophetic in another way since it came to be fulfilled a few years later, which ended its veracity. Consequently, one could not extrapolate a general policy that prohibited women from taking charge of political affairs from a prophecy that was consummated in a specific event. Whether this interpretation is valid today is open for debate, even if Al Sa'ud officials seldom raised it in their assessments. For if the purpose of this quotation was to exclude women from occupying the highest leadership position in the land, the criticisms would have been tolerated by the ruling family, which was still experimenting with the idea. If, on the other hand, Bin Mani' wished to arrogate to himself and, by extension, to other members of the *Hay'at Kibar al-'Ulamah*, powers that were equal to those of the monarch, then the rejections posed serious problems. In the event, the Board was important for Riyadh but not as important as the monarchy that ruled the kingdom, which was telegraphed to one and all. Sa'udi Arabia was a monarchy, and lest zealous preachers neglected to note that fact, the Al Sa'ud were anxious to reiterate it for one and all. Whatever objections were advanced to appointing women judges – for example, child-bearing responsibilities or similar obligations – women would be able to fulfill duties assigned by the monarch if the latter deemed such appointments to be in the best interests of the kingdom. Bin Mani''s "highest imamate" argument, which placed the Board's powers on a par with those enjoyed by the king, were categorically rejected, and that underscored intrinsic disputes between the religious establishment and younger members of the ruling family, who concluded that Sa'udi Arabia needed women as much as men.[95] When the king tabled the recommendation, Bin Mani' then suggested that women could act as advisors, which was a concession of sorts. The very idea of women justices acting as advisors during an interim period appealed to judges and 'Ulamah, including 'Abdul Muhsin Al Ubaykan, a senior advisor to the Minister of Justice and one of the country's leading religious authorities. Such support implied that women were able to perform judiciary responsibilities that undercut arguments advanced by the more conservative figures, who obviously wished to preserve this privilege, rather than enlarge the circle of authority adjudicating *Shari'ah* law. Still, it was logical to assume that, over time, the new Supreme Court could possibly include women justices. Although local tribal traditions prevented such appointments in the past, there was nothing in Islam that prevented qualified women from dispensing advice and guidance, and this was something that motivated the Al Sa'ud to ponder their options on the matter. In fact, the very word *Ifta'*, from which the word fatwah originated, meant dispensing religious legal opinion, and it was critical to note that, while *muftis* were traditionally men not just on the Arabian Peninsula but throughout Muslim societies, there were no religious prohibitions on women fulfilling such roles. A potential *muti'ah* (woman jurist) could contribute to society, and it was up to the monarch in the case of Sa'udi Arabia, in consultation with senior '*Ulamah*, to gradually acculturate society's most entrenched positions to alter their ways. When one considered that the Sa'udi judiciary was still engaged in this most basic wrangle – over the putative roles of women – one could not be optimistic. Yet, challenging beliefs and pitting different segments of society against each other were entirely different propositions for the Al Sa'ud. While King 'Abdallah and his potential successors strongly believed in gradual reforms, they were not interested in starting social wars among various segments of the population. Nevertheless, because of Riyadh's methodical approaches, chances were excellent that the concentration of religious powers entrusted into the hands of a few at the beginning of the twenty-first century, which was the result of the 1744 Al Sa'ud-Al Shaykh alliance, would not possibly remain so forever. Consequently, it was entirely logical to assume that fundamental changes would be introduced over time, especially with respect to the judiciary. Controversies aside, it was also clear that the Al Sa'ud were anxious to engage in healthy debates to educate their growing population, instead of contemplating an erosion of such influences.

The judiciary and political concerns

If the confidence levels in establishment '*Ulamah* declined steadily after the epochal 1979 Makkah mosque takeover, the Grand Mufti, Shaykh 'Abdul 'Aziz bin Baz, continued to enjoy the respect of the Sa'udi ruler and, equally important, the support of rank and file '*Ulamah*. The charismatic Bin Baz lent his own credibility to that of the *ifta'* institution, which he headed, but his shocking commentaries on various socio-political concerns, which ranged from a claim that the earth was flat, to his equally comical concerns with a woman's menstrual cycle, tarnished his reputation. Shaykh bin Baz passed away on May 13, 1999 and was succeeded by 'Abdul 'Aziz bin 'Abdallah bin 'Abdul Latif Al al-Shaykh who, in the tradition of Al Shaykh scholars, worked diligently to restore the credibility of the religious establishment. If tacit support for controversial policies (especially from an Islamic point of view) offered by establishment clergymen to Riyadh weakened their status in the eyes of the populace at large, and in certain cases presented them as "collaborators" of the regime, religious authorities encountered formidable competition in-house, too. As discussed above, non-establishment *Ulamah*, particularly those associated with the *Sahwah* steadily gnawed at whatever trustworthiness many pretended to possess and impart. Shaykh Safar al-Hawali, a lecturer and later the head of the religious department at the Islamic University in Madinah, Shaykh Salman al-'Awdah, a lecturer in religious studies at the Imam Muhammad University in Buraydah, and others, gradually strengthened their positions by delivering a hopeful message. Most displayed hostility toward Western values even if their primary targets were all local figures. Many relied on modern media methods and outlets to erode the positions of establishment *Ulamah*, and through the latter, the power of the Al Sa'ud. Access to the Internet, radio and television, newspapers and magazines, as well as audio and videocassettes and CDs, radically transformed how preachers reached their publics. Several Shaykhs, including al-Hawali and al-'Awdah even fell back on the institution of the fatwah, which was a more or less exclusive tool in the hands of establishment clergymen. It is therefore safe to assert that a schism emerged within the clergy, with establishment figures adrift, especially with respect to the all-critical-ability to control the numbers and contents of speeches and fatwahs. It was within such a context that King 'Abdallah bin 'Abdul 'Aziz Al Sa'ud issued his key legal reforms both to update the system, as well as restore the critical role of the religious establishment in the pivotal 1744 alliance between the Al Sa'ud ruling family and the Al Shaykh religious dynasty.

The struggle for Islamic primacy in Sa'udi Arabia

Although public demands for a more effective participation motivated the government to embark on significant "National Dialogue" initiatives, consensus on political, religious, and economic reforms was still at its early stages. Riyadh registered popular calls and paid close attention to *Sahwah 'Ulamah*, allowing them to articulate grievances, while attempting to steer the debate within carefully established boundaries. It was within such a context that Shaykh Salman al-'Awdah was allowed to express his views freely in the newspaper *Al-Jazeerah*, for example, while a reconciliation of sorts was allowed to blossom between senior members of the ruling family and the more vocal critics of the government.[96] While prescience moderated most *Sahwists*, whose post-9/11 defense of the kingdom was truly appreciated by the Al Sa'ud, strident contributions battered establishment clergymen. This further weakened the positions of the clergy, which prompted critics to assume that Riyadh had embarked on a systematic policy to replace one group by another.[97] For no matter how creative these measures might have been, the tactic succeeded in rallying Sa'udis around the throne, especially in the aftermath of the May 2003 terrorist attacks in Riyadh. If Shaykhs Safar al-Hawali and Salman al-'Awdah played major roles in tantalizing the regime throughout the 1980s, their efforts to combat so-called "radicals" during the first decade of the twenty-first century, proved to be diametrically different. Shaykh al-Hawali in particular mediated between the government and outlawed al-Qa'idah members that resulted in a few wanted dissidents surrendering themselves to authorities, at the Shaykh's residence in Jiddah.[98]

Following this successful first step, several dozen non-establishment *Ulamah* met with 'Abdallah bin 'Abdul 'Aziz and agreed to denounce terrorist activities in Sa'udi Arabia, which was a major coup for the then Heir Apparent. Al-Hawali even rejected a call from Sa'ad al-Faqih, the head of the London-based Movement for Islamic Reform in Arabia (MIRA), for demonstrations in the kingdom, arguing that genuine reforms were required according to *Shari'ah*. This last point was critical since the Hanbali interpretation of *Shari'ah*, as it was practiced in the kingdom, called for believers to support secular authorities.[99] From the *Sahwah* point of view, however, it was clear that a desire to see the kingdom survive and for violent elements to weaken was taking on greater importance. To their credit, the Al Sa'ud understood how to reward a portion of the *Sahwists* by allowing key Shaykhs to enjoy public fora and publicizing them in official media outlets, all to better isolate and defeat extremists. Paradoxically, Riyadh's policy led to a decline in the status of establishment *Ulamah*, while at the same time upgrading that of their rivals, the non-establishment *Ulamah*, although the Al Sa'ud knew that the greater danger stemmed from terrorists struggling to impose their narrow interpretations of Islam on the population. If post-*Sahwah* clerics built their credibility as government opponents, then that was a risk worth taking, especially when younger Al Sa'ud family members no longer perceived the "official religious establishment" as being indispensable.[100] Moreover, by accepting *Sahwists* as genuine scholars with whom establishment clerics disagreed on the nature of the Sa'udi state, they validated Al Sa'ud displeasure.[101] Even denying the legitimacy of both the *Wasatiyyun* and the *Takfiris* was not enough to appease those who rejected positions that were deemed to be unclear by one side or the other. To their credit, *Sahwist* Shaykhs declared *Wasatiyyun* as slanderers of forefathers (the original "*salaf*"), which was an opinion that earned Al Sa'ud approval. Likewise, most *Sahwists* confronted the reality that Muslims who withheld judgment and/or condemned *Takfiris* opened pandora's box, since the struggle for primacy in the political sense raised doubts about the legitimacy of the ruling family. Key leaders quickly distanced themselves from such interpretations, appreciating the power of the establishment, as well as the necessity to adjust to the nuances of the 1744 Al Sa'ud-Al Shaykh alliance. Consequently, how *Sahwists* positioned themselves in the triangular equation between the ruling family and establishment clerics, determined their fate, which, to their credit, was crowned with relative success. On the home front, at least, Riyadh expertly co-opted leading *Sahwists*, without formally abandoning pro-government clerics.

Still, while the *Sahwist* cooptation was somewhat successful, Sa'udi officials concluded that Shi'ah Islam posed a more imminent threat. In the wake of the May 2003 Riyadh terrorist attacks, Shaykh Salih al-Fawzan, a member of the Board of Senior *'Ulamah*, likened Shi'ahs to three religiously reprehensible categories from Islamic history.[102]

- The *Khawarij* (those who rejected the authority of the last Rashidun Caliph 'Ali ibn 'Abi Talib), justified violence against other Muslims, and who were behind several murders among the early caliphs;
- The *Munafiqun* (hypocrites), which referred to those who "lurked in the midst" of believers and wanted to harm Islam; and,
- The Vandals who sought protection with the *Mushrikun* (polytheists) after they fled Muslim lands.

Even if these categorizations were harsh, Riyadh's focus was on the domestic front, as the Al Sa'ud were not necessarily eager to compel *Sahwists* to change their positions on *jihad* in general and *jihad* acts in Palestine and Iraq in particular. When Safar al-Hawali justified 9/11 as a response to the missile attacks against al-Qa'idah in the aftermath of the 1998 US Embassy bombings in Kenya and Tanzania, the Al Sa'ud allowed him and other *Sahwists* some latitude in this regard.[103] The logic was impeccable, as such venting helped defuse internal tensions in Sa'udi Arabia among an increasingly dejected population. Still, several *Sahwah 'Ulamah* differed with the regime on the issue of *jihad* in Iraq, as Shaykhs al-'Awdah, al-Hawali and others, called for *jihad* against Washington and its allies, lambasted the regime for offering assistance and military aid to the allies in their war against Iraq. The "scholars" accused the West of heresy and apostasy (*riddah*), although this was both facile, as well as largely tangential.[104] A few months later, and at the height of fierce battles in Iraq, most notably in Fallujah, Shaykhs al-'Awdah and al-Hawali – along with twenty-six Sa'udi *'Ulamah* – signed their "open letter to the Iraqi people," as they called on the hapless population to join a defensive *jihad* against US military occupation. It was a classic armchair command-and-control initiative that highlighted how low the *Sahwist* discourse had reached.[105] These examples shed further light on the position of the Sa'udi establishment *'Ulamah* and how they handled radical anti-Western tendencies in their midst. By taking on more moderate tones and by allowing *Sahwists* to espouse radical positions, establishment *'Ulamah* appeared to balance their rhetoric with pro-government stances, just as the latter tended to play extremist elements against committed allies. In fact, Al Sa'ud skills in managing these powerful forces were legendary and became apparent after the 9/11 attacks, when Riyadh put significant pressure on establishment *'Ulamah* to temper provocative and anti-Western rhetoric.[106]

The war on terrorism

Naturally, leading scholars were caught in a quandary: either acquiesce to Al Sa'ud demands, which would further exacerbate their steady marginalization; or stand by the government to protect and preserve their interests. Anecdotal evidence of a few maverick scholars notwithstanding, establishment *Ulamah* irrevocably sided with the monarchy, aware that the kingdom was in a more-or-less permanent relationship with the United States. That was why senior clerics quickly echoed the government's condemnations immediately after 9/11 and published specific statements denying any religious justification for the deadly assaults that literally shook the world.[107] Shaykh 'Abdul 'Aziz Al al-Shaykh, the Grand Mufti of Sa'udi Arabia and Chairman of the Board of Senior *Ulamah*, was not the only scholar who voiced his revulsion. The Chief Justice of the Supreme Judiciary Council, Shaykh Salih al-Luhaydan, declared on September 14, 2001 that the attacks were "shameless evils, which are not justified by any sane logic, nor by the religion of Islam."[108] Whether this was deemed sufficiently contrite was debatable, which prompted the learned man to reiterate on September 18, 2001: "Islam forbids such attacks and aggression upon the innocent." Several scholars issued additional condemnations, all of which were carefully guided by government officials, aware of the negative consequences that mild declarations would generate. Indeed, declarations attributed to Prince Nayif bin 'Abdul 'Aziz Al Sa'ud, for example, were particularly difficult to understand and subject to wild misinterpretations. Indeed, in November 2002, the Interior Minister opined that was "impossible that 19 youths ... carried out the operation of September 11, or that bin Ladin or Al Qa'ida ... did that alone. ... I think [the Zionists were] behind these events."[109] This was classic Nayif bin 'Abdul 'Aziz speaking simultaneously to several audiences, which, inevitably, raised eyebrows. It would not be long before the Interior Minister would confront his nemesis on the home front.

For no matter how convoluted such commentary appeared to be after 9/11, the kingdom's attitude towards terrorism changed dramatically after the May 13, 2003 attacks on several compounds – one owned by the London-based MBI International and Partners subsidiary, another at the Al Hamrah Oasis Village, as well as the Vinnell Corporation Compound – that housed large numbers of Americans, Westerners, and non-Sa'udi Arabs. A total of 35 individuals were killed that day, while over 160 were wounded, some quite seriously. Al Sa'ud leaders were flabbergasted and vowed to engage the war on terrorism with renewed vigor. For several years after these major assaults, an assassination attempt on the Deputy Minister of the Interior in charge of Counter-Terrorism, Prince Muhammad bin Nayif, sealed the ruling family's determination to crush its homegrown terrorists. In fact, the August 27, 2009 attack on the son of the Interior Minister was so diabolical, and potentially so catastrophic for the Al Sa'ud, that King 'Abdallah visited the young prince's hospital bed to ensure that the architect of the country's counter-terrorism policies received all the support he needed. Ironically, the would-be assassin,

'Abdallah Hasan Talih 'Asiri, contacted the assistant minister of the interior for security affairs and gained access to the latter's home. In what was a largely unclear development, the murderer gained the prince's confidence, passed through checkpoints at two airports, in Najran near the Yemeni border as well as Jiddah, before boarding a private jet with his explosives. Though 'Asiri was on a suicide mission, Sa'udi authorities concluded that he would have a place in the kingdom's counter-terrorism program, which recorded significant successes. How did this attack on a key official alter the country's war against *takfiris* (apostates)?

According to an official statement, as well as a transcript of a phone conversation between the prince and 'Asiri that was released by the Interior Ministry and aired on Sa'udi television, Muhammad bin Nayif agreed to meet the dissident ostensibly to negotiate an amnesty agreement for him and several repentant militants. In a tone that was amazingly serene, Prince Muhammad inquired about 'Asiri's brother, Ibrahim, and their parents. In what must be an exceptionally tolerant mindset, the official wished the rebel a Ramadan Mubarak, which illustrated the level of confidence that Prince Muhammad had in his rehabilitation program.[110] During their telephone conversation, 'Asiri sounded remorseful, asking God to "bless all [and] make things easier." The Sa'udi leader reassured him, insisting: "Things will always be fine, as long as man bears God in his mind." The rebel then offered to "brief" the prince who, in turn, sought reassurances about several individuals. Muhammad bin Nayif cautioned 'Asiri to be wary of "evil people [who] would like to exploit everyone." "Rely on God," he told him "and come back to your homeland," and counseled him to bring along his "brothers ... before they [were] led astray by evil people."[111] Towards the end of the conversation, 'Asiri anticipated tribulations, and wondered aloud whether the prince would forgive him. "You don't have to talk to me about forgiveness," answered Muhammad bin Nayif, because "you are our son. All we want is your return to the fold before they exploit you."

Irrespective of any post-bombing bragging by al-Qa'idah, which focused on the suicide rebel's skills to pass security checkpoints, board a private aircraft, and blow himself up amongst the prince's guards, the daring act succeeded because the Deputy Minister of Interior wanted it to occur. This was part of a long-term program to recuperate those within society that strayed from the path of righteousness, relied on violence to solve problems, and embarked on a sustained campaign to spread havoc. In the few short years since Sa'udi Arabia adopted a multi-pronged policy to deal with easily persuaded youths, significant gains were achieved that resulted either in bloody clashes, or in the surrender of many who entered treatment camps. To be sure, 'Asiri was shameless as he pretended to seek forgiveness. Yet, by abusing God's name for false purposes, 'Asiri and his supporters abdicated any rights to speak in the name of the Creator. In the telephone conversation, 'Asiri told Prince Muhammad: "We love you for the sake of God, and God willing, we hope the situation will be resolved." How could any believer fake such sincerity and still be one?

If 'Asiri blew himself up believing in martyrdom, because the Scriptures allegedly command him to slay infidels or non-believers, one wondered what kind of nonsense this was. In the event, it was important to remind these perplexed characters that the Holy Qur'an did not prescribe murder. Simply stated, God did not endorse assassination, and anyone who believed such gobbledygook needed serious psychiatric attention. On the contrary, God was merciful and admonished all believers to be forgiving of themselves and of each other. Still, given all that occurred in the kingdom during the past few years, it was fair to ask whether the Sa'udi rehabilitation program was successful?

Like leading Western powers and most Arab governments, Riyadh dealt with security concerns with sternness, but quickly realized that a reliance on a framework that emphasized religious values was critical if it were to ever redress genuine grievances. Consequently, it sought to reform the behavior of its ideologically misguided subjects, and adopted a counseling program that aimed to forgive those who acknowledged their errors.[112] It was within this framework of tolerance that one needed to assess Muhammad bin Nayif's actions before and after the attacks that targeted him. His plea with 'Asiri to "return home," help the latter's parents end their "suffering," and pledge to "talk frankly," were all signs of strength rather than weakness. Nevertheless, the challenge was not to abandon any of these tested and effective measures, as authorities reassessed how to deal with perennial liars. In fact, extremists on the Arabian Peninsula adopted cross-border tactics after their effectiveness in Sa'udi Arabia declined, and while Muhammad bin Nayif won several battles of ideas, it behooves authorities not to forego past successes. For no matter how justified Riyadh would be to retaliate against attacks on civilians or assassination attempts on government officials, the most effective ways to eliminate deviancy was still through steadfastness, and by relying on one's core values.

Political violence

Following the terrorist attacks in Sa'udi Arabia, the establishment *'Ulamah* were again mobilized to defend the regime, and condemn their perpetrators. Various statements and fatwahs determined that these acts were in contradiction with *Shari'ah* law since they damaged the interests of the Muslim nation; were directed against "protected" non-Muslims, both *dhimmis* (non-Muslims living in a Muslim country) and *musta'mins* (those who entered the country with assurances of safety). Such interpretations led Shaykh Salih al-Fawzan to identify the perpetrators of the May 2003 terrorist attacks as *Khawarij*. For his part, Shaykh 'Abd al-Rahman al-Sudays, the Imam of the Grand Mosque in Makkah, called for the perpetrators to be nipped in the bud "in order to preserve the nation against trials and strife (*fitna*)."[113] Once many of these alleged terrorists were arrested, however, Sa'udi authorities faced the dilemma of charging them with crimes and trying them in a court of law. While the first duty of the state was to apprehend perpetrators, it was imperative to empower the judiciary with the tools to apply the laws of the land, especially if the ultimate objective was to depoliticize terrorism – if that were possible. With *Shari'ah* as the law of the land, Riyadh entrusted the judiciary with the immense task of trying a first batch of 330 al-Qa'idah members, with the first verdicts issued in July 2009.[114] Charged with a range of terrorism-related indictments, most of the defendants were in the government-sponsored Munasahah rehabilitation program that aimed to alleviate some of the judiciary's responsibilities. Muslim scholars, who made decisive recommendations to a panel of judges determining the fate of the accused, assisted psychologists, social workers, and academics to better analyze various options – imprisonment or rehabilitation. A team of over 100 operated the "treatment programs," which aimed to salvage those that could be, before being transferred to the judiciary. To a certain extent, and judging by the number of young men who were indeed rehabilitated, the program was successful. Those who could not be rehabilitated, and held on to *Jihadist* ideologies or al-Qa'idah "philosophy" – the 330 convicted – were tried in *Shari'ah* courts. Although complete details were not available, one of the clerics who participated in the Munasahah program, Shaykh Muhammad al-Najimi, a member of the Islamic Fiqh Academy, revealed that a very small percentage of those who were freed were recidivists. In fact, the Munasahah program received a certificate from the American "Secretary of State in recognition of its role in analyzing and fighting against terrorist ideology," which was particularly satisfying to al-Najimi.[115] Admittedly, and despite relative successes in convicting terrorists who could not be rehabilitated, Sa'udi Arabia adopted new anti-terrorism laws, which was heavily criticized by human rights groups when they were first leaked to the BBC.[116] A few weeks after the draft that was published, a spokesman for the Sa'udi *Shurah* Council, Muhammad Al-Muhannah, announced that the text was under revision.[117] According to press reports, necessary changes were made to ensure that the text was compatible with *Shari'ah* and that it did "not violate citizens' rights or the country's existing laws."[118]

For its part, Amnesty International, which published a draft of the Penal Law for Terrorism Crimes and Financing Terrorism on its website, declared on July 22, 2011 that Sa'udi authorities could use the law to stifle dissent and pro-democracy protests in the monarchy, although the draft law, in the version leaked to Amnesty, identified threats to "national unity" or "harming the reputation of the state or its position," as potential terrorist crimes. What remained unclear were the various stipulations regarding minimum ten-year jail sentences for questioning the integrity of the king or heir apparent. According to a Sa'udi activist, Walid Abul Khayr, authorities were considering amendments to the draft to alter these specific charges. It remained to be determined whether the Ministry of Interior would force an adoption of this law, even after it was amended, without judicial authorization or oversight.

Conclusion

Reforming the judiciary in the Kingdom of Sa'udi Arabia was never going to be an easy proposition. As discussed above, and in response to disputed religious opinions and court rulings issued largely by clergymen who were entrusted with *Shari'ah* law, King 'Abdallah finally intervened to ensure that none of the more outrageous legal opinions and rulings issued from time to time were implemented. In one particularly egregious case, Riyadh curtailed media access to their authors because the issue pertained to retribution, which drew the ire of Amnesty International along with significant negative publicity.[119] In another case, perennial and embarrassing gender mixing surfaced, albeit in a comical way.[120] In a third instance, the controversy was over the employment of women, which was deemed controversial at a time when unemployment was still quite high in the country.[121] What really irritated clerics, however, was Riyadh's declarations over Friday sermons, long considered to be a privileged fiefdom but that mobilized young and old alike.[122] The Ministry of Islamic Endowments, *Da'wah*, and Guidance Affairs, further curtailing clerical powers, ordered clergymen to keep their Friday sermons short and smart. Through such measures, the monarch gained the upper hand in his battle to push through sweeping legal reforms and codification of Sa'udi law, although most clergymen failed to recognize that the monarch's legal reform offered them an opportunity to consolidate their non-negligible influence. Many more were intent on scoring against the State, which literally undermined the clergy's public credibility and, ultimately, signaled the decline of clerical power in Sa'udi Arabia. By rejecting popular Al Sa'ud initiatives, the clergy run the risk of marginalization, which could only enhance the ruling family's legitimacy that would go beyond their historical reliance on religion to buttress a secure power base. Moreover, and irrespective of internal criticisms, Riyadh moved on key social levels, which finally addressed human rights standards. The latter were not particularly strong and the aging ruler was loath to let another generation pass without significant improvements on this front.

To better address his concerns, 'Abdallah bin 'Abdul 'Aziz thus embarked on a restructuring of the court system, after he persuaded the country's senior religious leaders to endorse his reforms and codification proposals. Importantly, and as discussed above, the monarch decreed that only members of the Board of Senior Islamic Scholars were authorized to issue fatwahs in a bid to halt religious rulings that routinely embarrassed the kingdom. It was a given that 'Abdallah's reforms would thus obligate establishment *'Ulamah* to obey codified rules and regulations that would be uniformly applied across the country. By firing Ibrahim al-Ghayth, the head of the Commission for the Promotion of Virtue and the Prevention of Vice, the so-called *mutawa'in* or religious police, 'Abdallah reminded his subjects that Sa'udis desired uniformity in the application of laws. Gayth's successor, 'Abdul 'Aziz bin Humayn declared that it was his duty to implement the monarch's agenda, pledging "to achieve the aspirations of the rulers."[123] This critical February 2009 step was a clear departure from previous defiant statements by those who clearly exceeded their power. More important, the ruler concluded that some of these enforcers of public morality lacked the intelligence and tact to treat people with respect, as he decided to deny them additional privileges. Indeed, by forcing the *mutawa'in* to recognize basic freedoms, 'Abdallah signaled that he wanted a commission that connected with society instead of living in isolation from it, or orbiting above the law. Remarkably, and in what was a record demotion less than three years after his appointment, the monarch replaced 'Abdul 'Aziz bin Humayn with 'Abdul Latif Al al-Shaykh, admonishing the latter "to treat citizens and foreigners with respect and leniency."[124] Interestingly, Shaykh 'Abdul Latif Al al-Shaykh espoused a moderate stand on contemporary issues, concluding that that hard-line approach to *ikhtilat* (mixing in public places) was unjustified as well as counterproductive. In June 2010, the Shaykh opined that gender "mixing was permissible under certain conditions," and he also favored a ban on the marriage of minor girls. He believed that what was forbidden was *khulwah* (a man and woman meeting in seclusion) and not *ikhtilat*, affirming "the wisdom behind the ban on *khulwah* or undesirable gender mixing [was] to avoid

Figure 1.2 Shaykh 'Abdul Latif Al al-Shaykh, Courtesy *Arab News, January 2012* at http://arabnews.com/saudiarabia/article563051.ece.

creating situations that might lead to sin." Moreover, he demanded believers to "adhere to the decisions of rulers seeking welfare of citizens," which was certainly welcome at the Palace.[125]

Because religious authorities committed several grave errors, which weakened their respective positions vis-à-vis the establishment, the insightful monarch was determined to act. In 2002, *mutawa'in* guards refused to let firemen to enter a girls' school in Makkah where 15 children were killed, and in 2007, they nonchalantly dismissed the 'Qatif Girl' rapists case by inflicting heavy sentences on both criminals as well as victims. Needless to say, such episodes disturbed ordinary citizens. Many concluded that their religious leaders, who applied what passed for judicial authority in the kingdom, neglected their duties to uphold the law and preserve life itself. 'Abdallah shared his public's revulsion at such misinterpretations and vowed to rectify perceived shortcomings, aware that only serious legal reforms would prevent future repetitions. Several years into his rule, the monarch demonstrated a knack for significant changes, first with his 2007 Succession Law and then with dramatic shifts in the judiciary. Neither of these steps were meant to upset the 1744 alliance between the Al Sa'ud and the Al Shaykh, which formed the cornerstone of the kingdom's legitimacy, and which would not be subjected to any cataclysmic tests. Rather, the Sa'udi ruler intended to strengthen that critical alliance by interjecting fresh reforms, not to eliminate any party or group, but to open the doors for gradual transformations required by time.

With an impeccable "will to power," 'Abdallah thus embarked on a multi-pronged program, which addressed the need for serious legal reforms, promote national dialogues, as well as hold municipal elections as a precursor for parliamentary consultations at a later stage. In short, his decisions foretold the king's preferences for a dynamic monarchy, based on an independent judiciary that would apply a living *Shari'ah*, updated by scholars who married religious requirements with the interests of the State.

2 National and international dialogues

Amidst the clamor for reforms that came in various petitions to the ruler, King 'Abdallah bin 'Abdul 'Aziz Al Sa'ud and his advisors took the January 2003 "Vision" appeal to organize national dialogues among members of the intelligentsia, to heart. As discussed below, the first domestic dialogue, which brought together approximately fifty religious leaders in June 2003, was a timid affair. Attendees gathered over four days to debate issues of concern, and they published an official communiqué that supported Riyadh. In it, the country's leading *'Ulamah* agreed that only a legitimate ruler can declare *jihad*, though they took it upon themselves to explain what the "struggle" meant to young adherents precisely to prevent them from embarking on ill-conceived interpretations of holy war. The first National Meeting for Intellectual Dialogue was held in the monarch's presence, and his opening statement set the tone, as 'Abdallah urged Sa'udis to "respect the opinions of others." The king used this forum to warn militants and, in an oblique way, cajoled doctors of law to moderate their views especially if any of them entertained sympathies towards deviancy.

Although the monarch was often criticized for appointing many committees, which presumably encouraged corruption and enriched those who sat on them, 'Abdallah's preference for instituting new mechanisms for dialogue did not fall in such a category. There was, to be sure, a decree to establish the King 'Abdul 'Aziz Center for National Dialogue, duly issued on August 4, 2003, that authorized construction work for a new center as well as the composition of specialized committees. More importantly, speaking for the incapacitated King Fahd, then Heir Apparent 'Abdallah set the tone by insisting that those engaged in dialogue would include "the elite of [Sa'udi] society from different persuasions and schools of thought," which was a direct reference to the much maligned Sa'udi *Shi'ahs*, whose members were considered heretics by doctrinaire Sunni*s*. He wisely perceived the long-term benefits of such discourses, especially as the ideal mechanism to fight "extremism and fanaticism," and hoped that future debates would "create a healthy and clean environment, which promotes enlightened attitude and rejects terrorism and terrorist ideologies."[1] He beseeched those present to emulate early *mu'minins* [believers], who "considered abusing a fellow Muslim an act of deviation and killing him outright apostasy," which was presumably a direction he did not wish his people to follow. In short, 'Abdallah's dream was for dialogue to follow a right path, fully ingrained in Islamic and Sa'udi traditions. What were his advocacy planks and how did he envision the tool of dialogue best serving his quest for reforms? Was 'Abdallah promoting tolerance at this early phase? How was this theme of tolerance shaping his views? Beyond the king's strong June 2006 pronouncement in the conformist city of Buraydah, where he addressed a group of ultra-conservative representatives, how did he react when many so-called liberals were referred to as "hypocrites" or, even worse, "secularists"?[2] Was it sufficient when he cajoled conservatives that such epithets were extremely divisive and harmful to national unity? How effective was he in including non-traditionalists in the enlarged sphere of debates? Did any of his national dialogue directives contradict established bureaucratic mechanisms in place?

This chapter will first examine the kingdom's established mechanisms for dialogue, including the critical roles played by the Council of Ministers and other government offices, before describing the King 'Abdul 'Aziz Center for National Dialogue (KACND) itself. It will also investigate the first eight "national dialogues" to date, and offer appraisals of their effectiveness, if any, in furthering King 'Abdallah's main objective. The monarch defined success as "peace, security and prosperity," and affirmed that this would occur when Sa'udis adhered to faith and unity. In his inimitable words: "We will have no life without Islam and we will have no greatness without the unity of our motherland. We will not permit anyone, no matter who he is, to tamper with the principles of our faith and in same manner we will not let anyone undermine the unity of our homeland no matter whoever he may be." 'Abdallah continued:

> This homeland, which has the honor of serving the two holy Harams [Mosques], and to which the hearts of Muslims from all over the world are attached, is not prepared to accommodate any idea even with slightest variation with the basic tenets of Islam. In the same manner, this homeland will not accept any ideology that is based on misinterpreting Islamic teachings, and which use misleading emblems to justify its evil scheme of sowing terror and declaring practicing Muslims as apostates. The Sa'udi people will not accept any substitute for a moderate belief, which rejects fanaticism as it rejects moral degeneration and permissiveness.[3]

Given the monarch's admonitions, how have reforms envisaged and channeled through the national dialogues, helped achieve these objectives? To better evaluate the institutionalization of dialogue, and because the Sa'udi monarch enlarged his various efforts to include international exchanges of ideas, the chapter will also provide an assessment of 'Abdallah's support for interfaith discussions held in July 2008 in Madrid, at the three-day international conference of religious leaders co-sponsored with Spain. This outreach initiative was meant to defuse interfaith tensions, improve Islam's image, and restore respect for religious values. Was this a mechanism to strengthen Riyadh's hand against extremist elements at home? Has it achieved any breakthroughs in the wide array of mutual grievances roiling relations between Muslims and Westerners, or was this a mere exercise, even if the Sa'udi monarch described the very idea of this gathering as something that had "obsessed" him for several years?[4]

Inasmuch as national and international dialogues played critical roles in the ruler's reform agenda, and to place these measures within the larger constitutional contexts of contemporary Sa'udi affairs that dealt with stability and security, the chapter first examines the kingdom's constitutional continuum, followed by a description and analysis of the King 'Abdul 'Aziz Center for National Dialogue, the eight topic-driven dialogues themselves, as well as the 2008 Madrid Assembly. Importantly, the sum total of these institutional efforts affirmed the monarch's long-term objectives to acculturate his nation to the very idea of dialogue, to further ingrain tolerance among a wary population that seldom enjoyed the benefit of mutual and peaceful coexistence. Doing so was a necessity at a time when ideas flourished and nations competed in many socio-cultural spheres. It was also a concrete illustration of the reforms that King 'Abdallah bin 'Abdul 'Aziz wished to introduce to Sa'udi Arabia.

Constitutional continuum in Sa'udi Arabia

Although the first Sa'udi monarchs weathered various crises, the gravest challenges that confronted the Al Sa'ud pertained to constitutional markers, because the founder considered the Holy Scriptures to be a valid "Constitution." As later developments illustrated, the ruling family anchored its legitimacy in various permutations of this dictum, especially as it motivated and protected contenders to power.

Having successfully extended his rule throughout most of Arabia, 'Abdul 'Aziz bin 'Abdul Rahman Al Sa'ud took the title of King of the Hijaz and announced, on August 31, 1926, the adoption of a Constitution. The latter stipulated that the kingdom was a monarchical constitutional Islamic state whose capital would be Makkah.[5] This document placed no limits on the monarch's authority, except to confine his rule to be compatible with *Shari'ah*. In addition, the 1926 constitution introduced the concept of succession in calling for the appointment of an heir apparent who would assist the ruler, and who would seek the cooperation of as many administrators as necessary to direct the affairs of the country. Finally, this first modern constitution called for the establishment of a Consultative Council, which would meet once a week and debate pertinent questions on the agenda prepared by the heir apparent.[6] This was the first attempt to institutionalize consultation in contemporary Sa'udi Arabia, even though the practice was widespread among Arabia's tribal communities.[7] In the event, this constitution was never fully implemented, but served as a basis for future permutations. On September 18, 1932, the name of the country was changed to "The Kingdom of Sa'udi Arabia," and while a new heir apparent was named as successor, the country was essentially ruled by decree until 1953, as the Council of Ministers executed the ruler's domestic and foreign policies. Originally, there were two ministries: Finance and Foreign Affairs, and in 1944 a Ministry of Defense was duly established. With additional revenues generated through the sale of petroleum, Sa'udi Arabia earned $160 million in 1953, leading 'Abdul 'Aziz to expand various government functions.[8]

Approximately one month prior to his death, 'Abdul 'Aziz promulgated a decree establishing a new Council of Ministers, as Heir Apparent Sa'ud was named Prime Minister. Still, the Council convened its first session on March 7, 1954 in Riyadh, which was after the founder passed away. One of the new ruler's first decrees, issued on March 26, 1954, defined the statutes that governed the Council that was expected to supervise the implementation of domestic and foreign policy initiatives, approve budgets, authorize the foreign minister to sign treaties and international agreements, and grant oil concessions as necessary. Significantly, the monarch, who was also his own Prime Minister, presided over Council meetings even if he could not vote. This was a technical matter with little importance since all Council decisions were subject to the ruler's approval.[9] The March 26 decree further provided for the establishment of a secretariat-general, an audit office, a grievances post, and a group of technical experts who were attached to the Council.[10] These new positions formed the Cabinet of the Council of Ministers, and were part of what the Viceroy of the Hijaz, Prince Faysal, was doing, as he sought to delegate administrative powers to qualified individuals. Parenthetically, King Sa'ud, in his capacity as Prime Minister, presided only over the first Council meeting. Faysal chaired all succeeding meetings after he became Prime Minister.

With respect to internal reforms, and largely at the insistence of senior family members, Sa'ud issued another critical decree on March 23, 1958, which gave Faysal full authority over foreign affairs, internal policy, and finance. When this authorization was deemed insufficient to resolve the political crisis that mired the Al Sa'ud, Sa'ud bin 'Abdul 'Aziz promulgated yet another decree (May 11, 1958) that expanded the prerogatives of the Council of Ministers. It was this measure that transformed the Council "from a purely advisory [institution] into a formal policy-making body with both executive and legislative powers under Faysal."[11] Although the king retained a veto power, the Council was in effect given legislative and executive privileges, which established the framework for future constitutional changes. While the May 11, 1958 decree was not a formal constitution, its 50 paragraphs could, indeed, be classified as constitutional articles.[12]

Many differences separated Sa'ud and Faysal, including political developments related to the appropriation of authority within the Council of Ministers, which enlarged the gap that existed between the two brothers. Regrettably, poor management of the kingdom's limited resources threatened the country with bankruptcy, which compelled senior princes to trust the administration of the state to the more capable Faysal who, in turn, instituted strict spending limits. Faysal introduced severe austerity measures that were unpopular among Sa'ud's supporters. The latter pressured the monarch to force his brother's resignation on December 19, 1960. Two days later, Sa'ud formed his own cabinet, which included six "liberal" princes including Talal bin 'Abdul 'Aziz and 'Abdallah Tariqi, who was then Director-General of the Department of Petroleum and Mineral Resources.[13] In many ways, what the so-called "Free Princes" called for was an enlarged dialogue, precisely to tackle the country's key concerns even if the methods backfired.[14]

Influenced by Egyptian President Nasir's pan-Arab calls, the new team in Riyadh began working on a constitutional project, which pretended to create a national assembly for Sa'udi Arabia. The zeal of liberal princes was not new and in fact may have started in 1958 with the transfer of all executive powers to Faysal. At the time, Tariqi claimed "exultantly: we in Sa'udi Arabia have just taken a step forward to a constitution. Eventually this country will become a constitutional monarchy."[15] The young technocrat, who proved himself a staunch nationalist during negotiations with oil companies and other founding members of the Organization of Petroleum Exporting Countries, ignited the flame of political participation. Yet, it was Talal bin 'Abdul 'Aziz who provided detailed constitutional proposals that led Sa'ud to break his ties with "progressive" ministers and entrust, once again, the Premiership and Foreign Ministry to Faysal on March 15, 1962. Although these concerns were chiefly discussed within strictly confined Al Sa'ud quarters, they nevertheless raised sensitive topics, which were seldom broached before.

Relations between the two brothers worsened over the Yemen conflict that pitted Sa'ud, favoring a military intervention on behalf of Imam Badr, against Faysal, who considered the Sa'udi Army too weak to confront the Egyptian military. Within his own camp, Faysal was criticized for not showing firmness towards Washington, which had adopted an ambiguous attitude towards Nasir's Yemeni policies while extending lukewarm support to Riyadh. Deteriorating relations between Sa'ud and Faysal led the latter to call on the Council of Ministers and the *'Ulamah* to hear his grievances. On March 30, 1964, the struggle for power ended, with the clerics introducing a bizarre solution. They declared that Sa'ud was "unable to carry out the affairs of the state," because of his "state of health" and "current circumstances," but would remain king and still have "the right to respect and reverence." The *'Ulamah* further stated that Faysal would "carry out all the internal and external affairs of the King, without referring back to the King in this regard."[16] On April 1, Khalid bin 'Abdul 'Aziz, the deputy Prime Minister and a future king in his own right, who presided over a sensitive period in the history of contemporary Sa'udi Arabia, notified senior ministers of the decision and asked them to approve it by signing the fatwah duly issued by the country's religious establishment. Sa'ud would reign but no longer govern.[17]

Such a situation could not go on without creating unnecessary disputes within the ruling family, especially since several members disapproved of Faysal's brilliant internal diplomatic maneuvers. Others concluded that the heir apparent was not empowered to exercise full authority as long as the monarch reigned. Not surprisingly, what transpired throughout the following months was managed chaos, as the country's – as well as the family's – interests were severely affected by top-level disagreements. By early November 1964, Faysal was ready to end the discord that ensued, as the Council of Ministers and the 'Ulamah were summoned to make a final decision. A verdict was brokered to depose Sa'ud and to proclaim Faysal King.[18] Consequently, the statutes of the Council of Ministers were duly revised on November 18, 1964, allowing the monarch to resume direct control of the Council's Presidency – a provision that remained applicable ever since. In fact, the Council was the only effective political institution in Sa'udi Arabia, although a draft constitution first drawn up in 1960 – and which called for the establishment of an independent national assembly – lingered.

On March 25, 1975, King Faysal was assassinated by his nephew Faysal bin Musa'id bin 'Abdul 'Aziz. Within a few hours, the Al Sa'ud named Khalid to succeed his brother and proclaimed him monarch. In turn, Khalid appointed Fahd his heir, and increased the latter's powers by naming him both first deputy Prime Minister as well as Interior Minister – a position he had held since 1962.[19] This reshuffling of the cabinet restored the balance within the ruling family, with Fahd representing the powerful Sudayri clan. Perhaps the gravest event in contemporary Sa'udi affairs occurred in 1979 with the attempted takeover of the Makkah Holy Mosque. That ordeal, in Islam's holiest shrine, created significant tension in the kingdom and forced Khalid to widen his rule by providing a channel for dissent.[20] It was clear, nevertheless, that without the assistance of religious authorities, the Sa'udi government would not have been able to isolate and defeat the rebellion.[21] The occupation of the Makkah Mosque revealed that there was organized opposition to the Al Sa'ud. This was particularly embarrassing since the attack occurred in a sacred city, revered by Muslims and entrusted to the Sa'udi ruling family. By early 1980, several steps were taken to ensure the security of the Holy places, as lackadaisical officials were demoted from office. Significant additional changes occurred within the ruling family that, noticeably, altered the existing balance of power at the time. King Khalid's position was reinforced at the expense of both Princes Fahd and 'Abdallah, while another victor was the kingdom's chief *mufti*, whose political strength added value to his already substantial religious authority. It was Shaykh 'Abdul 'Aziz bin Baz who "legitimized" the government's military actions after he issued an unambiguous fatwah that permitted the use of deadly force within the Holy Haram.[22]

The most significant political change, however, was heir apparent Fahd's 1980 pronouncement that the kingdom needed to develop new institutional structures. Fahd proposed that a new, 50- to 70-member Consultative Council, could begin its deliberations by approving a "charter" for the Government that would supplement the Qur'an as the kingdom's Constitution. For several reasons, including disturbances in the Eastern Province involving the Shi'ah minority population (perhaps influenced by Ayatollah Khomeini in Iran), these pronouncements were not formally implemented. On several occasions in 1982 and 1983, now King Fahd announced that a Consultative Council would be formed, and that a basic charter would be promulgated.[23] Such proclamations, calling for a modernization of royal institutions, were not new and had already been made on several previous occasions by Faysal and other members of the Al Sa'ud. Yet, what lacked was the urgency to act, certainly prompted by internal and regional developments. Change would come to the kingdom but these would be slow and, with respect to the all too important succession question, family debates would not always be incident-free.

Throughout the 1980s, King Fahd and Heir Apparent 'Abdallah shared governing responsibilities, the former concentrating on international concerns and the latter on regional, especially Arab, affairs. To a certain degree, this pattern of specialization reinforced underlying differences in orientation, with Fahd and 'Abdallah each viewing foreign policy issues from the perspective of their different capabilities. As a result, Fahd was labeled "pro-American" and 'Abdallah "pro-Arab."[24] In reality, these labels were greatly exaggerated because 'Abdallah was never "anti-American" and Fahd was seldom "anti-Arab." Both agreed with the vast majority of the Al Sa'ud family on the strategic necessity of good relations with major powers, including the United States and key Arab states like Egypt and Syria. Moreover, this conviction did not mean that periodic disagreements did not exist, as in the aftermath of the Camp David Accords, when then Heir Apparent Fahd argued for milder sanctions against Egypt while Prince 'Abdallah was inclined to support the Arab consensus against Cairo. At other times, both Fahd and 'Abdallah agreed, as in 1987, for example, when Riyadh requested that Washington recall Ambassador Hume Horan after a rather ugly incident that infuriated both men.[25]

The division of labor, at least for most of the 1980s and 1990s, was not always fluid, however. At times, differences on domestic issues appeared to be more pronounced than any alleged variations on foreign concerns. Both Fahd and 'Abdallah agreed on maintaining the dominance of the ruling family in internal affairs but shared distinct perspectives on how this could be achieved. These variances, in turn, were directly related to their corresponding political bases. With close ties to key tribes and conservative religious leaders, 'Abdallah favored a more cautious pace of economic development, arguing that overtly rapid development posed a threat to Sa'udi values and stability. While it was unlikely that he wished to turn back the clock, modernization presented a major challenge to the kingdom, especially after oil prices collapsed in the mid-1980s. Reduced income immediately translated into a weakening of his traditional base, as the recruiting process in the National Guard shrank. By contrast, Fahd favored a more "progressive" approach, seeking a rapid rate of development and implementation of social reforms. As Minister of Education in the 1950s, for example, Fahd had pushed for the education of women. Both as Heir Apparent and as monarch, he also favored the adoption of ambitious development strategies. In this perspective, his full brothers Sultan and Nayif, who reportedly believed that failure to provide material benefits to their constituency presented the greatest threat to internal stability, joined him. Naturally, additional expenditures for military and internal security operations translated into strengthened power bases for both.

These permutations notwithstanding, the superlative source of disagreement between Fahd and 'Abdallah throughout the 1980s centered on the question of political reforms. King Fahd repeatedly pushed for the rapid adoption of a Basic Law as well as the establishment of the long delayed *Majlis al-Shurah*.[26] 'Abdallah, on the other hand, made no public allusions to either before 1990. Of course, promises of basic political reforms were almost always associated with internal events that rocked the stability of the ruling family, including the epochal 1979 Makkah Mosque takeover. From Fahd's perspectives, these pronouncements could well have been designed to appease internal opposition. Nonetheless, the monarch's endorsement of such reforms pulled the loyalties of various disenfranchised groups, while 'Abdallah's lukewarm position alienated others. Yet, one of the most serious obstacles to the establishment of a Basic Law in the 1980s was the proposed solution to the succession issue, which is discussed in some detail in Chapter 4, below.[27]

In the event, and following the 1991 War for Kuwait, the Al Sa'ud ruling family became sensitive to both domestic and international pressures, calling for liberalizing reforms. For the first time in decades, dynastic succession in Sa'udi Arabia turned into a topic of discussion and analysis, due in large part to the vast influx of Western military personnel into the country. In addition to providing detailed coverage of the 1991 War for Kuwait, which became the first televised conflict in memory, the world's media focused on the cultural and ideological peculiarities of a closed society, encouraging Sa'udi traditionalists and more liberal elements alike to voice their opinions. To be sure, Fahd often spoke of reforms throughout the 1980s – even funding the construction of a building to house a consultative body (which remained empty for several years) – no changes were introduced before 1992. Against a new trend of open challenges, however, the ruler hinted that he was ready to nominate 60 leading citizens to a *Majlis al-Shurah*, though even this minor pledge was delayed. In this endeavor, and true to Al Sa'ud traditions, heir apparent 'Abdallah supported King Fahd as he rallied behind his monarch to ward off opposition (see Chapter 3 for a full discussion of the *Majlis*).

The Basic Law of Government and the national dialogues

On March 1, 1992, Fahd bin 'Abdul 'Aziz addressed his subjects on television and issued several key documents, including the Basic Law of Government, the statutes governing the newly created *Majlis al-Shurah*, and the Law of the Provinces.[28] This was, by any measure, a momentous step forward because an institutionalization process was clearly established. Even if the monarch's decision was propelled by the rising tide of internal opposition, as well as the repercussions of the War for Kuwait, significant and permanent changes were under way though assessing their consequences at the time was nearly impossible. The *majlis* came to be engaged in mildly useful discussions and, in one of Fahd's last decisions before his death in 2005, was expanded from 120 to 150 members, further indicating its growing popularity among Sa'udi elites.[29]

As discussed in Chapter 3, the Basic Law of Government was divided into nine main sections, dealing with the general principles of the state, the law of government, the values of Sa'udi society, the country's economic principles, the various rights and duties of citizens, the authority of the state, financial affairs, auditing authorities, and general provisions. Consequently, the contemporary history of the kingdom illustrated that Sa'udis experienced major disruptions in their socio-political lives, ranging from the assassination of a monarch to the violent takeover of the Grand Mosque in Makkah. Two regional wars spilled over into the country's security and stability prerogatives, creating serious tensions within the religious establishment, and dividing Sa'udis between conservatives and liberals. In fact, the 2003 American-led War for Iraq sent shock waves throughout the Gulf region, but especially in Sa'udi Arabia, because of fears that the kingdom's custodianship of the two holy mosques in Makkah and Madinah would be jeopardized as critics charged that Sa'udi acquiescence to Washington was akin to outright backing and contrary to Arab and Muslim interests. Riyadh remained exquisitely conscious of its responsibilities to the Muslim world but especially towards its Sunni adherents. Yet, the desire for political reforms did not necessarily spread through the ultra-conservative ruling family. Rather, public discourse took on a new dimension – in the form of the petition – which redefined how Sa'udis accessed authority (see Chapter 5). A slew of rather sophisticated supplications, addressed to the monarch and the Heir Apparent, became both frequent and public. Since early 2003, prominent Sa'udi reformers, led by 'Abdallah al-Hamed, argued that the best way to counter the spread of Muslim extremist thoughts was to transform the kingdom into a constitutional monarchy.[30] Al-Hamed, along with Matruk al-Faleh and 'Ali al-Dumayni, as well as thirteen other activists, were promptly arrested in March 2004, although only the three named individuals were still in custody by mid-2005 when a new monarch addressed their fate.[31] Remarkably, Sa'udi reformists adopted peaceful steps, with an attitude bordering on the reverential towards the ruling family. Although their demands were nothing short of spectacular – challenging the ruler's absolute power – 'Abdallah bin 'Abdul 'Aziz deemed it necessary to meet with leading petition signatories, and authorized well-thought-out dialogues as a partial rejoinder. By early 2004, a year before 'Abdallah became absolute ruler, the die was cast, which added pressure on the ruling Al Sa'ud to address serious concerns raised in several petitions. Indeed, the need for urgent dialogues among Sa'udis could no longer be postponed, with a stark choice to either conduct them as openly as possible or be subjected to unforeseen consequences. 'Abdallah, who was never known as someone who rushed into swift decisions, chose to meet the challenge head on.

King 'Abdul 'Aziz Center for National Dialogue

"I have no doubt that the foundation of the King 'Abdul 'Aziz Center for National Dialogue," affirmed 'Abdallah bin 'Abdul 'Aziz, "and the continuation of dialogue under its aegis will be – by the Grace of God – an historical achievement contributing to the development of a channel for responsible expression. This, in turn, will play an important role in the battle against prejudice, excess and extremism, and bring about an appropriate atmosphere from which wise positions and enlightened opinions will proceed."[32] On August 4, 2003, a decree issued by King Fahd formally created the King 'Abdul 'Aziz Center for National Dialogue (KACND) to spread a culture of dialogue and, following the expressed wishes of the Heir Apparent, to create a new norm for Sa'udis to speak with each other both as individual citizens and as members of extended families. It was, in a specific way, a new mechanism to rekindle the very idea of *Majlis* for the largely urbanized population that was gradually updating its traditional tools. Proponents wished to adhere to, and to take pride in, Islam, which was expected to further strengthen the concept and values of good citizenship as well as reinforce the security and unity of the nation. As described by 'Abdallah, the philosophy of the center was to foster a relatively sophisticated environment, whose ultimate goals included national unity, the dissemination of a peaceful culture of dialogue and the conduct of such discourse in a tolerant climate. Through the center, Riyadh aimed to create a fresh inclusive environment, with eight specific goals:

1. To strengthen the concept of dialogue and its associated behavioral patterns within Sa'udi society, so that it may become a lifestyle and a methodology for dealing with different issues.
2. To broaden the participation of individuals and groups in national dialogue, and to consolidate the role of institutions of Sa'udi society to achieve justice, equality and freedom of expression within the framework of Islamic *Shari'ah*.
3. To confirm national unity perceived within the framework of Islamic *Shari'ah*, and to deepen it through constructive intellectual dialogue.
4. To take part in fashioning proper Islamic dialogue based upon the middle road and moderation both within Sa'udi society as well as outside.
5. To give national dialogue an active role in coordination with the relevant institutions.
6. To deal with issues of national importance – social, cultural, economic, educational, etc. – through the channels of dialogue.
7. To crystallize a strategic vision for national dialogue, and to ensure that its recommendations are implemented; and
8. To strengthen the channels of communication and intellectual dialogue with individuals and institutions in Sa'udi society.[33]

Given the lofty nature of these objectives, KACND officials devised linguistically clear and uncomplicated vocabulary, to define what they meant by dialogue. Special definitions were drawn up and distributed to participants. Indeed, the linguistic meaning of dialogue was defined as a reply, debate, or review, according to well-established norms.[34] References drawn from the massive 20-volume comprehensive dictionary of the Arabic language, composed by the Tunis-born Shi'ah scholar Ibn Manzur, which had withstood the test of time, affirmed the root of the Arabic word for dialogue as: "to desist from something ... decrease after increase because he moved from one condition to another." Ibn Manzur explained: "dialogue was a process of engaging in mutual response, and that those involved in dialogue were replying to each other ... dialogue was therefore mutual review of what was said in discourse."[35] For KACND officials, consequently, dialogue was further defined as a form of discourse between two individuals or groups, in which each side enjoyed an equal opportunity to speak, with neither side monopolizing the discussion. It was critical to characterize dialogue to be conducted in an atmosphere of calm, far removed from the fanatical argumentation that dominated passionate socio-political questions throughout the Arab world. An example of the ideal dialogue contemplated by officials devising the institution was conversation between two friends, or colleagues in a workplace, or a group of people in an assembly. Relying on such a definition, guidelines identified synonyms for dialogue, falling back on disputation,[36] argumentation,[37] dispute,[38] and debate.[39]

There were, of course, several other definitions but these choices highlighted the importance attached to clearer nomenclature, and while such attention appeared to be pedantic work to outside observers, it may be worth underscoring that few Sa'udis had any experience in institutional dialogues outside traditional *majlis* conversations. The goal of specific argumentation was therefore underscored by a desire to eliminate doubts or unsound countervailing opinions. Both sides were encouraged to arrive at the truth, each elucidating to the other what might be hidden, relying on analogical reasoning (*qiyas*). Naturally, KACND officials did not invent this basic human need, which was certainly practiced among traditional Arabian societies for millennia, though contemporary social imbalances necessitated a reappraisal. In fact, it was safe to assume that constructive dialogue to serve national interests, took precedence over narrowly defined tribal affinities. The search for equilibrium between staunchly independent Sa'udis and the necessities of political consensus certainly influenced, perhaps even shaped, whatever dialogue might have been contemplated.

Equally important was the balance between entrenched tribal norms and the informational preferences that urbanized and increasingly educated Sa'udis demanded. While it was possible to persuade elders with a sophisticated *majlis* harangue, younger Sa'udis preferred scientific conferences, meetings, and symposia, where issues received full airings away from normative pressures. Often, well-informed citizens sought to benefit from research and independent investigations, in fora where contrary views were discussed with the ultimate goal of elucidating any and all options.[40] Thus, dialogue participants were encouraged to prepare intelligent strategies, wait for their turns to speak, listen as needed, emphasize the opinion rather than the person making the point, choosing the appropriate moment to speak, smile while debating, and otherwise engage in ethical behavior.[41] There were even recommendations made as to the tone of one's voice, as loud deliveries were frowned upon, since such techniques were often proven to be counter-productive. Not only were speakers asked to be polite, well prepared, and tolerant, they were also guided to add value to the overall conversation that presumably served the nation – which they quickly understood. Remarkably, and rather than perceive these draconian measures to define every nomenclature permutation as little more than condescension, Sa'udis welcomed the guidance, as most were anxious to get on with the tasks ahead.

National meetings

Starting in December 2003, several national dialogue rounds were held to discuss, at times with unabashed frankness, sensitive questions. Before assessing in some detail the eight major dialogues to date, it was important to place their results in the larger context of socio-political reforms in the kingdom, especially as Sa'udis seldom debated sensitive topics like gender matters, municipal elections, religious differences, and education concerns openly, which were some of the subjects that concerned citizens and whose lingering irresolution caused or at least contributed to the rise of extremist interpretations and actions.[42] While the first gathering focused on national unity, it was the second dialogue that drew significant attention, ostensibly because the 2004 National Dialogue on Women – held in Madinah, the city that first took in the Prophet Muhammad as a political refugee – electrified audiences. Few Sa'udis could remember holding such debates in their lifetimes. When the monarch was urged to "assign a body to study a public-transport system for women to facilitate mobility," most dismissed the exercise for its futility. To be sure, this tame request failed to resolve a fundamental contention – to allow women the right to drive. – Yet, the mere fact that it was made at all was correctly interpreted by beady-eyed observers as a remarkable feat. Beyond arcane social norms, 19 fresh recommendations on ways to improve women's lives in the country were prepared for the ruler by dialogue participants.[43] Because Sa'udi women were still not allowed to mingle freely while uncovered, organizers limited their demands for what could be realistically accomplished. Remarkably, and although a Sa'udi woman was not permitted to drive, sail a boat, or fly a plane, none of the country's existing regulations prevented Ms. Hanadi Hindi, who trained for a pilot's license in Jordan, from signing a contract with billionaire Prince Al Walid bin Talal bin 'Abdul 'Aziz in January 2005. Ms. Hindi joined the businessman's roster of private pilots thereby directly challenging the country's ultra-conservative clerics.[44] This was a singular step for an energetic woman but also a giant leap for Sa'udi society.

Likewise, dialogue participants debated divorce laws and the super sensitive question of child custody. Al Sa'ud leaders purposefully aimed to introduce real reforms in this area of *Shari'ah*, after one of the kingdom's most popular television personalities, Rania al-Baz, gained immense sympathy for her tragic case. Al-Baz, who was severely beaten by her husband, and against family counsel, invited photographers into her hospital room to record her injuries. She spoke out in public and filed for divorce in which she asked for her children's custody. She was granted a quick annulment and, surprisingly, won custody of her children even if a father routinely received custodianship after juveniles reached the age of 7 under Islamic law. Al-Baz also formed a support group to publicize abuse cases in the kingdom, which was truly a novel solution even if various women's organizations addressed such concerns in strict confidence.[45]

To be sure, this custody victory was the result of a *cause célèbre* but, once enacted, several National Dialogue recommendations concerning women necessitated fresh perspectives. Al Sa'ud reformists understood that the creation of special courts to adjudicate similar cases, along with the establishment of additional women's-only courts, ruffled feathers. Naturally, all judges would still be religious men during an interim period – presumably until such time as women magistrates could be trained to assume such burdens – but the Al Sa'ud signaled that they expected establishment figures entrusted with interpreting the law to become "more aware" of women as human beings. Still, skeptical voices wondered whether this dialogue would expand to eventually empower the kingdom's healthy and expanding women student body population, estimated at 55% of all university attendees whose life expectancy was 72 years in 2011, to assume unusual burdens of responsibility. In 2005, Sa'udi women made up 6% of the workforce – a figure expected to increase dramatically over the coming few decades – but, for the first time in history, the epoch-making dialogue allowed taboo social subjects from being aired more or less openly, which was also unprecedented.

It may be worth noting that the first few dialogues touched upon critical internal questions that certainly deserved the attention of senior Al Sa'ud leaders. Understandably, little was said about the kingdom's equally crucial ties with the rest of the Muslim world as well as the world at large. By April 2005, however, the KACND announced that the Fifth forum, to be held in December 2005 in the city of Abhah, located in Asir Province close to the Yemeni border, would cover a unique theme that went beyond core domestic concerns, although its purpose was certainly to awaken hidden issues seldom discussed in the conservative country. The proposed conference, appropriately titled, "Our Relations with Others: A Collective National Vision for Dealing with World Cultures," aimed high.[46] Even if overtly ambitious, the effort was certainly remarkable given that Sa'udi Arabia has had its share of very difficult ties with many Muslim and Western societies. In the event, the discussions ranged from diversity inside and outside Sa'udi Arabia, to the role of women and the Sa'udi view of foreigners, issues considered taboo only a few years ago. The fact that Sa'udis were looking at themselves and their relations with the rest of the world was certainly fresh and healthy. Moreover, by confronting the challenges inherent in this process, perhaps even by discussing them in a calm and informed manner, the interchanges helped participants and all watchers – as these were the first dialogues broadcast on television – make necessary adjustments. Critics objected that "the concept for 'Us and Others' [wa]s completely false, [since] modern travel and communications have shrunk the globe."[47] Yet, others recognized that "Islam unite[d] Saudis with the hundreds of millions of Muslim throughout the world," but that much more could be done to promote cultural exchanges. Sa'udis concluded that recognition of differences did not threaten social harmony, that ingrained and largely negative attitudes towards expatriate workers necessitated complete reappraisals, and civility actually enriched the existing diversity. At the conclusion of the gathering, King 'Abdallah embraced several participants as he received their recommendations, pledging to devote appropriate resources to implement them.[48] It was a cathartic experience that highlighted the level of awareness at the very top of the country's hierarchy. Importantly, the astute monarch surprised many with future dialogue topics, with his visionary co-sponsorship of a multi-faiths dialogue in Madrid, Spain. Although that occurred a few years into the ongoing dialogue exercises, what was amply clear was the overall trend espoused by Riyadh: Sa'udi society would adapt and distance itself from monolithic concepts, and would do so at its own pace, slowly but surely. While critics objected to the pace at which dialogue was encouraged, and while many of the recommendations reached at various sessions scuttled themselves in the country's bureaucratic mazes, the overall direction was crystal clear: Sa'udi society would address its concerns with courage even if it failed to implement every single proposal. Difficult subjects were chosen not because little would or could be realistically changed in the short term, but because Al Sa'ud leaders contemplated the fate of the country, as well as that of the monarchy, through the prism of grandiose challenges. To date, each of the themes identified for discussion confirmed this assertion, which illustrated the ruler's overall confidence in tackling them as well as negative consequences for the country in case the Al Sa'ud chose to ignore them.

First national meeting: intellectual dialogue

Given its importance, the first meeting was bound to focus on a major theme, and organizers did not disappoint. On July 15, 2003, and under the patronage of the monarch, then Heir Apparent 'Abdallah bin 'Abdul 'Aziz opened the inaugural national dialogue, which was held at the meeting hall of the King 'Abdul 'Aziz Public Library in Riyadh. The four-day event allowed the kingdom's leading *'Ulamah* to gather for the historic event, along with intellectuals representing diverse opinions. While the scientific title of the conference was "International Relations and Treaties and the Effect of the Way they are Understood on National Unity," the gathering was a polite confrontation on national unity, which was a loaded agenda item, to say the least. Indeed, the idea itself was a response to new challenges that targeted the country's national security, especially after the May 2003 bombings in Riyadh that shook the country to its core. In the event, and during the four-day meeting, various discussions were held by a number of speakers, concentrating on two main themes: national unity and the role of the *'Ulamah* in cementing it.

Under the first theme, participants broached the topic from a religious point of view, focusing on basic *Shari'ah* law concepts that buttressed unity. Likewise, the pioneering roles of the *'Ulamah* in ensnaring nationwide cohesion was tackled from a well-understood angle, even if divisions existed within the ranks. Participants were called upon to debate the rise of extremism in the kingdom and to condemn whenever possible those unfortunate practices that excused deviancy. Inasmuch as intellectuals who confronted religious scholars raised these questions, the novelty was uniquely Sa'udi, since few senior Shaykhs could avoid the basic tenets of religion and the effects of deviating from accepted practices on society. In other words, Riyadh challenged the *'Ulamah* to assess whether religious extremism was something to be tolerated in the name of religion, if and when such freedoms threatened national unity. To alleviate some of the pressures that were palpable during the meetings, a variety of other topics were raised too, including the diversity of views among diverse sections of society, the rights of women, their obligations and their place in the society, freedom of expression, contemporary fatwahs (edicts), the ways and means for linking them with realities on the ground, among others. Presumably, all of these themes touched on national unity, even if the main attention was on clerics and the roles they played in securing concord. In a "two steps forward, one step back" mechanism, Riyadh enlarged the discussions with a second theme that concentrated on Islam and its international relations. Several speakers tabled ideas on how best to present Islam to both Muslims and non-Muslims around the world, identifying those aspects of ties that bound Sa'udis to others. Common interests between the kingdom and leading nation-states were broached as participants exchanged views on how to deal with non-Muslims according to strict injunctions revealed in the Holy Qur'an. There was even a brief assessment of *jihad* (holy war), what *Shari'ah* said about it, and how the rest of humanity perceived it.

At the conclusion of the first dialogue, seven major recommendations were issued, which highlighted some of the rich debates that occurred among invited participants. Attendees affirmed the following:

1 The realization of the dangers encircling Sa'udi Arabia and the vicious attacks on its religious beliefs and national unity, the awareness of the resultant tribal, regional, or intellectual discord and dissension, which could have an adverse effect upon the bonds of solidarity, cohesion, and brotherly relations in the common homeland;
2 The realization that the existence of intellectual differences and a diversity of belief were facts Sa'udis could observe in their lives. Moreover, aspects

of human nature, which could be taken advantage of in laying the groundwork for a strategy of interaction through dialogue, exhortation, and counsel, were to be employed in a manner that served the goals of the kingdom and its *Shari'ah*-based principles and values;
3 That care and thought should be focused on the issue of Islamic discourse both within and without the kingdom, so as to affirm the kingdom's adherence to its Islamic creed, its ties with the Islamic world and its national unity, all within a framework characterized by moderation and adoption of the middle ground;
4 That scholarly developments addressed at this meeting, and expansion of the circle of participation to encompass full examination of diverse topics, should be encouraged. This would be accomplished through the establishment of a Center for National Dialogue that would be charged with the organization of meetings and the preparation of studies and research. It was the desire of the participants that this center be established under the auspices of His Royal Highness Prince 'Abdallah bin 'Abdul 'Aziz, who was then Heir Apparent;
5 Preservation of Sa'udi national unity, on the basis of correct Islamic doctrine and *Shari'ah*-based constants, from which the state derived its basic system, and society derived its personality. Through such means, which were implicit in the oath of allegiance, obedience in all that was virtuous was to be deepened to strengthen the cohesion of the group, avoid dissension and division, and thereby to bring about true security in all its concrete and abstract meanings;
6 Affirmation of the importance of dialogue as a means for the expression of opinion and as a way of life, so as to realize coexistence through a comprehensive methodology which firmly adhered to *Shari'ah*-based principles and constants;
7 Differences and intellectual diversity were universally observed historical facts that were impossible to ignore or bypass. Implementing the methodology of the Holy Qur'an in judging opinions, objects, and people, reduced the possible negative effects of this diversity. This comprised the examination of objective truth, justice, coexistence with differences, differentiation between constants and opinions in the realm of diversity and difference, and definition of the Qur'an and *Sunnah* as points of reference.[49]

As these recommendations attested, the overall message from this first experiment focused on encouraging contacts among young people with differing viewpoints, as serious efforts were exerted to acquaint all parties with the culture of dialogue. Attendees concluded that various groups and organizations ought to dedicate their efforts to the welfare of young people to whom a great deal of attention must be devoted in both cultural and social spheres. They were persuaded that more cultural centers, including literary clubs and libraries, ought to be established in different parts of the country with the aim of helping young people acquire better knowledge of society and, more important, deny potential recruiters from appropriating them for terrorism. Interestingly, special attention was devoted to young Sa'udis and the need to encourage them to take part in voluntary service to acculturate them with the life of a united nation and with their responsibilities towards it. This too was certainly a novel approach, couched in cultural programs, though the intentions could not be clearer: draw young citizens towards the state and its institutions – away from untraditional norms. This was deemed crucial as participants reached various assessments, including one that called on society to assume responsibility towards its youths, so that few young people could ever be recruited for mischief. Participants argued that no one should neglect the consequences of their putatively anti-Sa'udi actions, and while a few thought that authorities ought to move cautiously, the majority favored steady programs that benefited at-risk youngsters. Indeed, the successful exercise was a tangible illustration of how best to tackle long-term needs and to further consolidate national unity. It must be emphasized that few observers concluded that this first dialogue would be repeated, as several argued authorities could not tolerate such transparency, and would surely find the necessary excuses to shut the entire process down.

Second national meeting: fighting fanaticism and extremism

Although the technical theme of the second meeting, held between December 27, 2003 and January 1, 2004 in Makkah, was, "Hyperbole and Moderation: A Comprehensive Methodological Perspective," this gathering wished to address religious fanaticism and extremism head on. Naturally, the choice of these topics was not accidental, and while Sa'udis – like all nationalities – confronted this scourge throughout their history, fanaticism and extremism had reached unprecedented levels in the kingdom during the past few decades. In fact, Riyadh confronted significant losses of lives, as well as sustained damage to private as well as public property as a direct result of extremist violence. Broaching such topics, therefore, was no longer restricted, and could not be confined to highly regulated academic exchanges.

Once again, a large number of *'Ulamah* and specialists in various fields, including psychologists, sociologists, educators, and economists, gathered for the meetings, where 15 working papers were presented. Unlike the first dialogue sessions, this one included the participation of several businessmen and journalists, not only to comment and report, but to also add their own ideas and perspectives. This time around, a new pattern was devised, which proceeded with formal presentations of the working papers followed by open comments. Carefully moderated by KACND officials, discussions were conducted freely, as speakers were granted ample time to develop their views. Given the objectives of the meeting, to study hyperbole, its intellectual and material reasons, and analyze those factors that engendered it from the standpoint of *Shari'ah*, the agenda was full. Several speakers concentrated on the psychological, sociological, educational, political, economic and media-related reasons affecting this phenomenon, with specific goals in mind: namely, to arrive at suggestions and mechanisms to counter manifestations of hyperbole in society and to suggest appropriate solutions to confront it.

Judging by the eight public recommendations made by participants, attendees took on some of the most difficult topics that confronted Sa'udi society, which was often easily assuaged by romanticism and idealism and did not confront stark realities. The recommendations called for:

1 The pace of political reform to be accelerated and popular participation expanded through the election of the members of the *Majlis al-Shurah* and the regional councils, followed by encouragement to establish unions, volunteer organizations, and other civil society institutions;
2 Emphasis to be placed on the economy so as to preserve public funds, with the priority in all expenditures given to the basic needs of citizens, in accordance with balanced and comprehensive development programs. At the same time, reducing public debt in accordance with a strict schedule must be emphasized, with full transparency and accountability;
3 The renewal of religious discourse, in accordance with changing times, accompanied by awareness and understanding of conditions in the world at large and an openness in interaction with them;
4 Emphasis to be given to the rejection of fatwahs issued on an individual basis, which deal with general questions affecting the welfare and future of the nation, such as issues of war and peace. The right to rule in such instances must only be granted to organizations qualified to issue fatwahs, and the standard of those bodies and their methods of operation must be improved;
5 The concepts underlying dialogue to be planted in Sa'udi society, and youth in schools and universities to be raised to benefit from such exposures, accordingly. At the same time, authorities ought to encourage responsible freedom of expression in accord with the needs of public welfare;
6 Curricula in all fields to be modernized by specialists, in a manner that would guarantee the dissemination of the spirit of tolerance, along with a commensurate growth of all knowledge skills, so as to contribute to the realization of comprehensive development;
7 Those who renounce violence and admit their errors to be rehabilitated. Such persons should not be marginalized nor should they be dealt with severely. Rather, they should be reintegrated into society;
8 Persons accused of crimes of violence and terror must be guaranteed a fair trial, granted the right to choose their own lawyers, and be allowed to meet with them whenever they desire.[50]

By raising such super-sensitive topics as the creation of unions, the need to establish civil society institutions, and calling for a full evaluation of how those accused as extremists were treated by both authorities and society at large, dialogue leaders highlighted the lengths to which they were ready to go to address national concerns. In fact, the mere suggestion that leaders reevaluate the phenomenon of extremism in Saʻudi society, and acknowledge the right to a fair trial in the presence of a defense attorney, was truly historical. Although critics perceived these calls as basic and long overdue, their inclusion could not be dismissed as mere exercises in wishful thinking. By addressing issues openly, and with relative transparency, Riyadh was genuinely embarked on the kind of long-term reforms that every nation-state emphasized as it formulated a working governance system. Irrespective of the pace with which these transformations were introduced, the mere fact that they were under consideration could not be ignored and, more important, their eventual implementation could not be avoided.

Participants also called for speeding up the process of political reforms in the country with the aim of widening popular participation in the affairs of the nation. Among the substantive recommendations were several dealing with elections, presumably to *Shurah* and/or regional assemblies, while encouraging the creation of trade unions that would also organize citizens. These measures were meant to improve channels of communication between the Al Saʻud and the general public. Remarkably, without denying the rights of the ruling family, the second dialogue proposals specifically invited the latter to introduce a separation of powers between the executive branches of government and the judiciary. Indeed, by insisting that fatwahs dealing with national security affairs only be handed down by qualified individuals from official bodies, dialogue leaders telegraphed their support to the Al Saʻud, even if they also requested strong discipline against usurpers. While it would take another six years before King ʻAbdallah would finally introduce the required regulations, the calls did not fall on deaf ears, for the very idea of free-lance Shaykhs issuing edicts on a helter-skelter basis did more damage than good to the country.[51]

Equally important was the attention devoted to the country's educational system, and sorely needed efforts to overhaul it under the supervision of qualified experts, who would emphasize the spirit of tolerance and moderation. Dialogue participants recommended that additional efforts be exerted to provide advanced professional training to young students, with the aim of ensuring comprehensive socio-economic growth all over the country. Inasmuch as these suggestions were forward-looking, there was also the customary warning to monitor negative tendencies, as well as the requirements by authorities to draw up contingency plans for dealing with deviant elements. In the event, senior officials wished to set the example for strong tolerance and, towards that end, welcomed those who decided to give up violence and return to peaceful normal life. Those who repented, officials argued, should be shown sympathy and re-admitted into society.

Finally, the Makkah meeting also called for boosting the role of women in society in all fields of human endeavor, and proposed the establishment of a specialized national organization that would be entrusted with the task of looking after their needs.

Third national meeting: women's rights

Women's rights and their roles within society formed the main theme of the third national dialogue meeting, which was held between June 12 and 14, 2004 in Madinah, the capital of the first Islamic state. Opening the three-day gathering, Shaykh Salih bin 'Abdul Rahman al-Husayn, the chairman of the third national dialogue meeting, underlined the need for mutual understanding between men and women. Each must understand the other and their role in life, he stressed, noting that relations between the two should be characterized by complementarity rather than competition. Shaykh Salih underscored the basic notion that women were men's natural partners, and that women who performed their roles properly, determined the fate of entire nations. He added that society was obliged to treat women justly, in line with *Shari'ah* obligations, regardless of local customs. He further stated that, in the field of education at least, Sa'udi women must receive the same opportunities as men.[52]

When the women's turn came to speak, Dr. Salihah al-Hulays, who taught at Umm Al-Qurah University, promptly dismissed calls for equality between men and women. Other women participants insisted that women faced genuine challenges and that these should be addressed candidly. "How come we see all these injustices being committed against women [as] if women are facing no real problems?" asked Dr. Hanan al-Ahmadi, from the Institute of Public Administration in Riyadh. In an attempt to defuse growing tensions, several participants fell back on time-tested conspiracy theories, which was in poor taste. Dr. Marqouk bin Tunbak, a professor of literature at King Sa'ud University, declared that people should focus on the real problems facing society instead of blaming others, although this was yet another illustration on how not to address social concerns. To bring the discussions to an orderly pace, Faysal bin 'Abdul Rahman bin Mu'ammar, the secretary general of the KACND, interjected: "I am pleased by the wholehearted support given to the center by *'Ulamah* and intellectuals. This meeting followed in the footsteps of the second meeting in Makkah, which supported the role played by women in Sa'udi society, as well as the establishment of a specialized organization that promoted their causes." He concluded by stating: "The importance of this meeting emanates from the fact that today Sa'udi women play a vital role in the on-going development process all over the country. They occupy a prominent place in society that was bestowed on them by Islam. Today Sa'udi women are participating in various fields of economic activities along with their men folk." Even if this was an optimistic assessment, the dialogue finally tackled the "rights and obligations" issue, which was a significant change in attitude towards women, especially with respect to potential employment regulations that prevented women from registering gains. Equally valuable were the exchanges of views on social problems facing women, including domestic violence, and how best to prevent it in the first place.

Participants agreed on a set of nine recommendations to alert decision makers to basic needs, as well as strengthen the position of women in society, precisely to overcome some of the many ingrained prejudices held against them in what was still a quintessentially patriarchal environment. The nine bold proposals concentrated on:

1 The need to emphasize the supreme importance of the role that women play within the family, which is their primary responsibility, without neglecting the right to work and earn decent wages, objectives that were fully compatible with *Shari'ah*;
2 Relations between a husband and wife should be founded on piety, guardianship, obedience, and consultation. Guardianship must not be interpreted to mean control, nor does it negate a woman's jurisdiction over herself. Furthermore, obedience is only within the limits of what is good, and not that akin to slavery;
3 A specialized national organization should be set up to deal with issues related to women and the family. It should also be responsible for coordinating the efforts of governmental and private agencies;
4 The position of women involved in litigation before the courts must be reviewed in light of the following:

- Plans for establishing family affairs courts must be implemented in a manner that takes into consideration the special circumstances of women;
- More departments of women's affairs must be set up in law courts, in order to receive female litigants and record their complaints;

5 Vocational institutes appropriate for women must be established on a larger scale. These institutes should be integrated within development programs;
6 Employment opportunities and positions must be made available for women in order to accommodate graduates of education and training programs. This must be accomplished in such a manner as to achieve a respectable life for the family and, at the same time, participate in achieving the comprehensive goals of development. Technological developments and means of electronic communications should be employed to develop work opportunities for women toiling outside of their homes;
7 Opportunities for women to express their opinions and to play a part in issues of general concern must be expanded, in accordance with the principles of *Shari'ah*, and in a manner consistent with the social, economic and cultural variables of society;
8 Legislation derived from *Shari'ah* must be developed and promulgated to prohibit all forms of violence directed against women. The steps necessary for enforcement of this legislation must also be taken. Moreover, research into the issue of violence directed against women should be carried out, and conferences and symposia devoted to this topic should also be organized;
9 The mass media should be called upon to publicize issues concerning women, and to make their rights and obligations better known, in addition

to their role in building the family and society according to the guidance of Islam and its fundamental principles.[53]

With about 70 participants, divided equally between men and women, the third dialogue was deemed the most successful, as it dealt with the sensitive topic of segregation in Sa'udi society. Remarkably, all present agreed that Islam granted women the right to work and earn a living, which was an eye opener to otherwise devout attendees who usually let traditions overcome religious obligations. By calling for the establishment of a specialized organization that purposefully looked after the need of women, in coordination with pertinent government agencies and private organizations, participants telegraphed a specific message to Riyadh: the time was right to draw up a national blueprint, which would clarify the rights of women, their obligations to society, and their roles within the family in line with Islamic teachings.

It was also interesting to note that the KACND took the initiative to define terms used in connection with women's rights and to make necessary inroads to improve textbooks that would expose boys and girls to the rights and obligations of the other gender. No longer were easy answers sufficient as dialogue participants called for taking more steps to prepare women for better employment opportunities as new fields of specializations were opened up. Indeed, there was a realization that the large number of female university graduates ought to be absorbed in the workforce to better serve the nation, as well as reduce an excessive dependence on foreign labor. For most, there were no contradictions between assuming specific roles within the family while assuring that their families received decent quality of life opportunities, if women were allowed to engage in economic activities. By making this fundamental linkage, dialogue participants focused on the problems facing poorer women, and called on Riyadh to provide them with material assistance as they enhanced their productive roles. There was, underneath all of the discussions, a plea for the Sa'udi mass media to pay more attention to concerns facing women, rather than be seduced by sensationalist stories. Sa'udi women, by and large, were better off than most women throughout the developing world, but that did not mean that their roles ought not expand. Few observers of the kingdom expected rapid changes but even fewer could dismiss the level of internal awareness that was devoted to this critical question. As part of Riyadh's reform initiatives, a dialogue on women's affairs was a valuable addition to the country's socio-economic discussions, even if the pace of change was painfully slow.

Fourth national meeting: young people's expectations

If a dialogue on women's rights required care and sensitivity, the problems and expectations of young Sa'udis were even more difficult to handle, as the generation gap had widened significantly during the past few decades. Notwithstanding the many challenges that young people faced, dialogue organizers convened their fourth meeting in Dhahran between December 7 and 9, 2004, where an estimated 650 young citizens, both males and females drawn from throughout the country, joined a large number of *'Ulamah* and experts to address pertinent preoccupations. Inasmuch as the meeting was devoted to specific issues of interest to, and expectations of, young people, one wondered whether this exercise, like its predecessors, was not geared to tutor decision-makers on ailing questions that the country confronted.

Unlike for the first three dialogues, starting with the fourth one, the KACND held preliminary meetings in each of the kingdom's thirteen administrative regions before convening a national assembly where participants could finetune global points of reference that necessitated national attention. This effort was also made to ensure that recommendations and ideas laid before relevant committees, at the Center, or the *Majlis al-Shurah*, were properly vetted. Preliminary gatherings eliminated excessive repetitions and narrowed the field to critical aspects of any given topic that required concentration and resolution. Finally, preparatory meetings in all thirteen regions allowed many more Sa'udis to have a say in ongoing dialogues, rather than for these media-driven events to be perceived as serving elites in a more or less exclusive fashion.

As in the past, organizers set specific objectives, which included the needs to identify and discuss youth-related predicaments, clarify their roles in the nation's development, activate and disseminate the principle of national dialogue to better instill the very idea among youngsters, and to reach sound conclusions and recommendations that would then be forwarded to relevant agencies concerned with youth affairs.

At the conclusion of the Dhahran gathering, participants settled on seven recommendations, which focused on:

1 The subject of unemployment needs, including clarification of the extent and seriousness of the problem. Programs capable of dealing with the problem must be designed, including the establishment of a Supreme Commission for Human Resources. The process of employment in both the public and private sectors needs to be organized and the efforts of the relevant agencies in this regard need to be coordinated;
2 Engagement in positive exchanges with other cultures to benefit from the positive outputs of globalization, while strengthening the natural defenses of our youth;
3 Granting youth a role in the leadership of the institutions of civil society and facilitating their participation in issues of general importance;
4 Encouraging communication between the youth of the kingdom with all their different orientations; they must be encouraged to adopt the culture of dialogue and to respect the opinions of others. Organizations pertaining to youth must be called upon to devote greater attention to the academic, cultural, social and sports-related needs of youth, and programs for those with special talents must be established;

National and international dialogues 85

5 Attention to those with special needs, orphans, and those having special circumstances; legislation and programs concerned with them must be reviewed;
6 Encouraging youth to undertake all sorts of volunteer activities. A national center for volunteer work should be set up to organize the activities of volunteers and attract participation by all categories of youth;
7 Addressing the problems of youth need more quickly. In this regard, a higher committee for youth affairs should be established which will be responsible for formulating general plans to deal with youth-related issues and strengthening their sense of belonging to the nation.[54]

Naturally, the three-day meeting homed in on the necessity to fully overhaul the country's educational system, with the aim of providing sorely needed skilled workers and to figure out how best to meet unskilled manpower requirements. Participants insisted that more efforts ought to be exerted to encourage inventiveness among students, as young minds cultivated the spirit of moderation and showed respect for others. Even if nothing else was debated, this was already a breakthrough, given the indifference displayed by many, perhaps the consequence of growing up surrounded with several maids serving their every whims.[55] Still, the fact that a call for dramatic improvements originated from within the ranks was a hopeful sign. For a change, students were quite aware that they needed to make greater use of modern teaching aids, including the reliance on laboratories and computers, to enable them to combine theory with practice. They drew attention to other needs, too. Some underlined the requirement for new admissions criteria, to allow wider acceptances into universities. Linkages were drawn between the quality of education youth received and expectations that they, their family members, and the private sector had for them. Towards that end, an emphasis was placed on science and technology to best meet local job market needs. How could they compete, many wondered, if the school system did not prepare them to conduct research? This was an appeal to distance young pupils from rote learning and the adoption of inquisitive methods that challenged them to think independently, and in the context of a curriculum dominated by rote memorization, especially of religious texts, the recommendation was truly revolutionary.

In the course of both preliminary and final discussions, participants referred to the important roles played by teachers in the educational process, and to sorely-lacking professionalism in academia. Periodic retraining for teachers was deemed essential, in conjunction with the necessity for continuous training programs. They requested that teacher performances be monitored regularly with appropriate rewards to outstanding instructors that shined. This was a practical demand, for young students drew a significant linkage between how well they were served in the school systems with future employment, since jobs were scarce and private sector employees strict in their descriptions. Consequently, every move that may be introduced ought to improve the lot of this age group, many of whom faced joblessness in adulthood. They even called on Riyadh to adopt contingency plans to deal with unemployment, perhaps with the creation of a higher commission for manpower resources. How the public sector and private organizations recruited, attendees concluded, was worthy of closer scrutiny.

In fact, this last point was especially pertinent, since Riyadh had pursued a poorly applied Sa'udization policy for years. Observers of the fourth dialogue concluded that a full transformation of this program was long overdue, since Sa'udization was not the shining model everyone hoped it would be.[56] They insisted that fresh regulations governing the process were necessary with the full participation of private sector leaders. Significant changes could no longer be decided by fiat, but ought to reflect market forces. Towards that end, a full overhaul of current employment regulations were deemed essential as well, with new regulations addressing such questions as minimum wages and complex working hours mechanisms that found a balance between the interests of the employer and those of workers who were still subject to traditional social norms. In fact, dialogue proceedings underlined the need to acquaint members of the general public with the virtues of work and one's responsibilities towards employers, which were overdue in a country where a majority of citizens were under the age of 15. They invited young people to take advantage of team spirit, assume self-discipline, reject corruption and nepotism, all to fulfill ethical values espoused by society. These were important approaches, they were told by older and presumably wiser officials, in need of renewed emphasis because Sa'udis distanced themselves from such practices in the aftermath of the 1970s oil boom, even if they were still worthy core values that existed before the discovery of oil and that altered normative behavior in the workplace. In the twenty-first century, the country's financial resources necessitated sound investments, primarily to ensure prosperity for future generations, which meant that current generations could not take their welfare system for granted. Therefore, while attendees called for setting up a special fund for the benefit of coming generations, it was essential to make useful contributions as quickly as possible. Still, and despite valiant efforts made by the erudite Ghazi Algosaibi when he was Minister of Labor, it was not until March 2011 that senior Sa'udi officials called on young nationals to seek any employment opportunities they could to improve employment prospects and secure a paying position.[57] In all of the discussions that led to the fourth assembly, a basic realization emerged that surprised decision-makers, many of whom assumed that young Sa'udis were ill-prepared to shoulder the immense burden required by nation-building. It was that young men and women could rise to the occasion if given a chance to display intrinsic capabilities. King 'Abdallah, who carefully followed these proceedings, was vindicated as he pushed for more reforms across the board.

Fifth national meeting: the national vision for dealing with world cultures

In a slight departure from previous gatherings, a group of male and female Sa'udi scholars, intellectuals, and specialists in literature and culture met between December 13 and 15, 2005 in the city of Abhah, to assess the results of thirteen meetings held under KACND auspices. Their mandate, summarized in the title "We and the Other: A National Vision for Dealing with World Cultures," digested over 700 interventions that shared a variety of perspectives. Conveners affirmed that Sa'udis, with all their rainbow colors, were part of the international human society, sharing with other civilized societies noble human values. They avowed that cooperation with other cultures was of utmost importance to spread prosperity on earth. Sa'udis, they declared, based their civilization on noble Islamic values and true Arab customs, which respected the "other" and his beliefs. Like individuals in many other traditions, Sa'udis expressed the desire to build and strengthen internal diversities in jurisprudence, intellect, culture, and mores, given that these were all universal laws that benefited from balance and openness. To better ascertain how society could make necessary adjustments as it competed with other civilizations, dialogue attendees addressed the focal questions of what common foundations existed upon which relations between different cultures could be built, and how best to disseminate awareness of world civilizations, while protecting religious and cultural parameters. Given the vastness of the topic and the many permutations that existed at several levels, recommendations issued by participants in the fifth dialogue could not comprise a simple set of items for Riyadh to digest and, whenever possible, amalgamate in its outlook and apply in its policies. Rather, the challenge was to offer something far more comprehensive and, according to several attendees, historical.[58] Towards that end, a series of general principles were issued, divided among humanistic and *Shari'ah*-based philosophies, along with specific cultural, social, political and economic interactions.

The attendees emphasized that general principles agreed upon by all of mankind, and affirmed by Islam, included: (1) the unity of the human race (since there was a fundamental belief that everyone was a descendent of Adam); (2) human dignity, which every human being deserved, to preserve life, honor, children, freedom of conscience, and possessions; (3) ethical standards, represented by justice, charity, kindness, faithfulness, mercy, and tolerance as well as the rejection of treachery, injustice, and aggression; (4) the pursuit of advantages and warding off of evils, provided that this was not done at the expense of others; and (5) becoming acquainted with other people, communicating with them, and cooperating with others in whatever was true and beneficial to humanity. These humanistic measures were supplemented by *Shari'ah*-based principles that covered the doctrines of faith and the rejection of that which contravened them, as well as the correct meanings of Islamic teachings related to interactions with the "other." This last point merited additional explanations – given centuries of interpretations that passed for dogma on the matter – including a focus on:

1 Fidelity, which was defined as a bond of love and mutual aid shared with other Muslims, regardless of their sectarian affiliations, in accordance with established principles of the *Shari'ah* derived from the Qur'an and *Sunnah*;

2 Disavowal, which was the need to distance oneself from whatever disagreed with Islam, and non-cooperation with whoever advocated the contravention of Islam in such matters. This, however, did not imply that the infringement of their rights was to be sanctioned, or that one should avoid cooperating with them in ordinary matters;
3 *Jihad*, meaning the exertion of efforts in the realization of good and the repulsion of evil. At the same time, it must be emphasized that relations between Muslims and non-Muslims were by their very nature peaceful, and that war was an extraordinary condition sanctioned by Islam for purposes of defense and to combat aggression and injustice;
4 Missionary work (*Da'wah*), which involved increasing Muslims' awareness of their own religion, and elucidating the lofty humanistic and faith-based values of Islam to non-Muslims;
5 Debating in the best possible manner, since dialogue in a soft-spoken and polite way was a better tool than that adopted by violent means;
6 Cooperation in good works and piety for the benefit of humankind through organizations or agreements involving other nations or peoples.[59]

Inasmuch as the question of fidelity, as described in this principle, called for a full acceptance of Shi'ah Muslims by the majority Sunni*s*, the declaration was nothing short of revolutionary given centuries-long confrontations between the two creeds. Likewise, cooperating with non-Muslims, even if it was reduced to the "ordinary matters" category, was another breakthrough for traditional believers who assumed that any interactions with non-Muslims could only be done under duress, since religious authorities indoctrinated – and literally denied others their faiths – by referring to non-Muslims as *kuffar* (sinners).[60] In fact, the state of war – *Dar al-Harb* – was not a permanent feature, since those who wished to create a wedge between Muslims and non-Muslims often misinterpreted it. Rather, it was to be understood as a defense mechanism, avowed attendees, after Muslims were assaulted for their faith.[61] With these principles established, participants of the fifth dialogue tackled a variety of mechanisms on how best to interact with others and, towards that end, concentrated on the following:

Cultural interactions

Given that culture included one's belief system, language, values, laws, customs, literature, and the arts, by means of which the personality of a society was given shape, Sa'udi Arabia's cultural interactions with "others," affirmed dialogue participants, consisted of:

1 Shouldering the cultural responsibility of Arab and Islamic states towards all humanity;
2 Profiting from the pioneering cultural experiences of diverse human societies, in a way that did not impinge on national identity;

National and international dialogues 89

3   Adoption of the principle of dialogue and participation with others, whether the subject related to religion, culture or civilization;
4   Positive interaction with international cultural organizations in accordance with religion and national interest;
5   Utilization of all channels of constructive cultural interaction, including: (a) exchanges of visits and meetings between public and private organizations and their counterparts around the world; (b) discussions among scholars, thinkers, fair-minded researchers; (c) encouraging cultural attachés in embassies abroad to become far more active; (d) supporting international organizations hosted by Arab and Islamic states, including the Muslim World League and the World Conference of Muslim Youth; (e) organizing cultural exhibitions and festivals, intellectual meetings, international gatherings and awards; (f) funding the translation of intellectual, artistic and innovative work in beneficial fields of thought; (g) creating scholarly centers and organizations, and jurisprudential institutes concerned with the study of interaction with others, particularly centers specialized in Islamic and Middle Eastern studies; (h) supporting the exchange of educational scholarships, visits of students, teachers, and researchers, and facilitation of their entry into Sa'udi Arabia; and (i) facilitating international media in a way which serves the goal of positive interaction with others.[62]

Social interactions

Equally important, attendees focused on how Arabs and Muslims, which they claimed were characterized by their enduring social and religious constants, were not living in closed environments shut off from the outside world. Rather, they insisted, social interaction with others was based upon the following criteria, which they wished to expand further:

1   Presentation of the Islamic social system as one that is comprehensive and just for humanity;
2   Cooperation with those who promoted noble humanistic values that preserve the rights, dignity, and freedom of man;
3   Participation in international charitable work, and cooperation with international associations dedicated to the service of humanity; taking advantage of the experiences of other people outside the nation;
4   Analysis of negative social manifestations that afflicted certain societies, and protection of Sa'udi society from them through the positive actions of educational and social associations;
5   Positive international interaction regarding social issues such as human rights, women's rights, children's rights, the rights of those with special needs, the issues of poverty and unemployment, and concern for environmental questions;
6   Cooperation with international organizations and associations concerned with women's affairs in a manner that preserved their dignity and the rights

granted to them by God; the removal of obstacles that interfered with that, and taking steps toward female representation in those organizations and associations; as well as the

7 Establishment of civil society institutions in accordance with the general welfare that promoted interaction with others.[63]

Political interactions

If cultural and social interactions encompassed a variety of principles, so did adherence in international relations to the methodology of Islam, which organizers maintained was founded upon justice as an absolute value, and on honoring covenants, contracts, and international agreements. In a traditional society like Sa'udi Arabia, such commitments were critical even if they are routinely and mistakenly dismissed, although one's word was literally worth gold and sufficient to conduct business. Consequently, dialogue attendees recommended that Riyadh reassess the methodology it relied upon to conduct its political interactions, and that ought to be based on the following criteria:

1 Contact and cooperation with others in a way that did not adversely affect national unity;
2 Emphasize the centrality of the Palestinian issue, the liberation of Jerusalem, and support for Arab peace initiatives;
3 Highlight positive interactions with guests living in Sa'udi Arabia and facilitate the implementation of laws that protected their rights;
4 Support the desire of Arab and Muslim countries to preserve their national unity, avoid the dangers of their fragmentation, preserve their human rights, and work towards integration among them;
5 Call on the nations of the world to abide by human rights and international laws pertaining to them, with respect both to their own citizens as well as those residing in their territories, and to deal with them in dignified ways that protected their humanity as well as their rights. Moreover, reject any racist actions or statements against Islam or Muslims, and authorize the Organization of the Islamic Cooperation to set up a legal entity for the protection of Muslim minorities around the world;
6 Propagate the culture of dialogue between societies and peoples, both at the regional and international levels;
7 Ensure an active role for embassies and representations abroad in a manner designed to promote positive contacts with others;
8 Affirm the roles of private and civil institutions in the realization of contacts with other societies;
9 Take advantage of strategic relations with the great powers so as to serve the national interest; form strategic partnerships with emerging powers around the world; and enlighten citizens as to the importance of these relations, all of which constituted critical aspects of what served the Sa'udi nation.[64]

Economic interactions

The last section of these carefully assessed recommendations focused on economic ties between Saʻudi Arabia and the rest of the world. Even if mercantilism was ingrained in local mentalities, and while most participants understood the power of the purse in the hands of the State, they nevertheless recommended that Riyadh employ the following means to improve the country's overall posture:

1 Affirm the role of an oil policy that strengthened global economic stability. Petroleum was a unique asset that truly empowered the kingdom, something that members of its elite, as well as ordinary citizens, understood all too well;
2 Confirm the role played by Arab development funds that offered financial assistance to other nations and peoples, and which strengthened contacts with others;
3 Invigorate the roles of various economic agencies, including the chambers of industry and commerce as well as joint economic committees, to promote contacts with others;
4 Work to attract foreign investment to Arab and Muslim states, and prepare suitable local investment environments that encouraged these investments to use the national workforce;
5 Accelerate the realization of economic integration among Arab and Muslim states;
6 Encourage commercial exchanges, including imports and exports, to realize the shared interests of all parties involved;
7 Benefit from the accessions of Arab and Muslim states to the World Trade Organization, in addition to their membership in other international economic organizations, in a manner designed to strengthen contacts with others; and
8 Participate in the creation of technology parks where serious scientific work would be undertaken alongside commercial and industrial partners.[65]

As these detailed recommendations confirmed, fifth dialogue participants provided one of the most comprehensive blueprints in contemporary Saʻudi memory, which dealt with globalization and the role of the kingdom within it. Ultimately, these suggestions were meant to acculturate Saʻudi society to the many changes under way elsewhere, and to those potential mechanisms that ought to be adopted by the government to better serve its citizens and expatriate workers who toiled there. Most of these programs would be channeled through either governmental and private institutions, including the ministries of Islamic Affairs, Endowments, Call and Guidance, Education, Culture and Information, as well as relevant universities and various civil institutions like the chambers of commerce, scholarly organizations, research centers and press establishments.

Conveners hoped that this "National Vision" might turn into a national document as they emphasized what it means to be Saʻudi citizens ("we"), bonded by Islam in a unified country, but with diversified opinions and orientations. They also underlined the necessity to interact with "others" since such contacts were both useful and mandatory for all of humanity. Even if the exercise was immensely ambitious, it was nonetheless successful, as it assembled a variety of issues linked through both the centrality of the nation and the primacy of faith. Riyadh was fortunate to receive such a blueprint, which reflected a host of serious concerns, which were carefully linked with each other and that illustrated that Sa'udi Arabia was indeed a developing nation-state in every sense of the word. The Abhah dialogue marked a maturation step in the long-term outlook for KACND activities, cloaked in a subtle application of legitimacy, which strengthened the Al Sa'ud. In a particularly satisfactory way, the sheer volume of analytic prowess presented at the gathering, distinguished this exercise from previous efforts, one that literally bode well for the country and its leadership. It was a true learning process that helped the Al Sa'ud in their bearings, one that relied on indigenous intellectual contributions that added value, and one that literally brought the ruling establishment so much closer to the country's increasingly alert and capable thinkers. In a way, the gathering was a discovery of sorts, as the Al Sa'ud gained a first-hand look at the indigenous pool of raw talent, which was a good omen for the kingdom.

Sixth national meeting: education – reality and ways of improvement

The topic selected for the sixth national dialogue, which was held in the Jouf region (located in the northern part of the country) between November 28 and 30, 2006, was "Education: Current Situation and Means of Development." KACND organizers aimed to diagnose the current situation of education in the country and study necessary ways and means to develop and improve its effectiveness. Once again, the writ was a tall order, given that Sa'udi education was not a stellar performer. Its emphasis on rote learning – which in reality was no learning – endured, while centuries of traditions ossified norms into abject mediocrity. Over the years, various attempts were made to introduce sorely needed changes, though religious objections and protestations based on custom almost always limited what could be done. Consequently, tackling one of the most complicated concerns in Sa'udi Arabia was a near herculean task, as various objective studies of the educational situation faced ingrained opposition. Recommendations that failed to take into account intrinsic constraints were not likely to be taken seriously by decision-makers who, nevertheless, desperately searched for serious reforms in this area, given the country's needs for an educated workforce that would ensure long-term prosperity.

Inasmuch as the topic was gargantuan, and following customary regional gatherings, Jouf Summiteers only offered three specific recommendations:

1 Given the current state of education in the kingdom, participants underscored the need to review and offer a comprehensive national strategy for the

development of all components of general, higher, and technical education. This strategy, they affirmed, ought to focus on new economic, social and political developments as well as local and international variables, and comprise a review of educational policy;
2 They also called for curricula and course materials to be reviewed and updated on an ongoing basis, while sorely needed improvements in the occupational level of teachers and faculty were identified as priorities;
3 Finally, they called for provisions to improve buildings along with the supply of technical equipment. In addition, it was deemed necessary to assess and offer accreditation programs through independent agencies, particularly with regard to the assessment of the performance of educational institutions and their output. Towards that end, a focus on higher standards of scholarly research were specified, with the tasks of carrying out some programs of university, technical and vocational education to be transferred to the private sector.[66]

The group of male and female intellectuals who met with the ministers both of Education and of Higher Education, along with the governor of the General Organization for Technical Education and Vocational Training, as well as several university rectors and other officials, could not be clearer. The state of education in Sa'udi Arabia was not good and needed a full reappraisal. Inasmuch as participants recognized the great transitions that occurred over the years, they called on King 'Abdallah to rethink his reform initiatives and, without disparaging the monarch's desire to establish several new universities in various regions of the kingdom along with a specialized university in the field of sciences and technology, they highlighted more fundamental needs. While participants affirmed the main principles on which education stood in Islam, they nevertheless noted that accelerating developments in all fields required reliance on modern technologies, which could only be acquired through scientific investigations. Furthermore, while they recognized past achievements, which introduced modernization to a tribal society, fresh education methods were now necessary to enhance the country's development. In various discussions held at the dialogue, attendees raised difficult issues, including the need for a healthy social adjustment to changes in economic, information, and demographic fields. How best to introduce modifications and mandate scholarly actions stemming from joint visions among intellectuals on one hand, and decision-makers on the other, was not easy to deal with. They beseeched the government to draw up appropriate policies, laws, and plans that homed in on useful curricula. They also insisted on quality rather than expedient admissions policies that accommodated the masses in fancy buildings, which were fully equipped, but where the methods for selecting educators and improving their performances were outdated. This was courageous, to say the least, as participants acknowledged that education and the fostering of a joint national strategy to develop all elements of the general, higher, and technical education sectors, would only produce solid results if a clear strategy was adopted by the "State." In short, no long-term economic, social, and political developments would produce desired results unless Riyadh reviewed its educational policies and improved the overall content to better serve Sa'udi Arabia. The sixth national dialogue concluded its work by asking relevant ministries to study recommendations assembled for their benefit since they contained opinions from intellectuals anxious to foster significant progress. The decisions were bold and, judging by the reception, effective.

Seventh national meeting: work and employment; dialogue between society and work related institutions

The seventh national dialogue convened in Qasim Province in the heart of the kingdom between April 22 and 23, 2008 to discuss "Work and Employment." Its aims were to study the reality of the workforce and employment problems, identify society's outlook on existing labor conditions, benefit from the expertise of pioneering business organizations and specialists in the field, all to devise new ideas to help develop a workforce that would fulfill local provisions. At first, participants gathered in Buraydah, the capital of the province, addressed the thorny question of unemployment in the kingdom, which took on bizarre features. Estimates varied as to what the real percentages of the unemployed were, and how Riyadh calculated these numbers. Few understood the roles played by educational and training institutes in arriving at accurate numbers. Even fewer Sa'udis could figure out the massive and largely intrusive roles played by expatriate laborers on the country's labor dilemma. It was a while ago when serious observers concluded that the Sa'udiazation program, which was supposed to invest locally to encourage indigenous citizens to work in all sectors, was a failure. Many believed that the efforts and finances devoted to such programs contributed to the unemployment crisis, rather than helped to alleviate it.[67]

Equally important, attendees discussed how best to employ women whose movements in the publicly segregated society were especially challenging. Naturally, religious conventions and a variety of unwritten public norms defined the vision under which women could find gainful employment both in the public as well as private sectors. During the discussions on women's employment, attendees focused on identifying the Islamic conditioning on working women and clarifying the meaning of *ikhtilat* (mixing of the sexes). Moreover, the public–private dichotomy generated heated debates, as certain realities were highlighted once again, just as they were during the 2004 Madinah dialogue. What employers demanded was quite different from what employees were comfortable with. In fact, because employers could fetch expatriate workers at relatively inexpensive rates, and employ them for longer hours – whereas Sa'udi employees requested high salaries and flexible working conditions – there were clear dichotomies between various positions. Riyadh was thus confronted with the impossible task of devising policies and strategies that increased indigenous employment, while it passed legislation that facilitated the import of a huge expatriate population that toiled to serve the kingdom, some of which was devised to serve the interests of unscrupulous merchants or high-ranking officials benefiting from legal loopholes.[68]

An estimated five thousand Sa'udis participated in the preparatory meetings that were held across the country in Dhahran, Abhah, Jiddah, Tabuk, and Riyadh. At the Buraydah, Qasim national dialogue, approximately 100 experts digested studies prepared by their peers, although leading businessmen and women, as well as officials from the Chamber of Commerce and Industry, added their perspectives in earnest. On the sidelines of the preparatory meetings, 7,216 Sa'udis signed up for 132 training courses, to better acquaint themselves with the intricacies of the job markets. Moreover, a series of communication training programs were also organized by the KACND in Qasim, which also facilitated the work of young people eager to benefit from existing opportunities. All agreed that Sa'udi society enjoyed an economic boom that changed work ethics and perceptions towards certain professions, though many lamented the transformations that occurred along the way. The government and the private sector now engaged self-employed Sa'udis who had earlier worked as herdsmen, in animal stock, or in agriculture and trade. While public jobs were limited, the sudden post-oil-boom demand for foreign labor further altered the country's economic stability, which was not necessarily a good omen for the indigenous population. As Sa'udis became more qualified and started to seek government jobs, employees saturated the public sector, whereas the private sector relied on cheap overseas labor to cover its needs.[69]

In turn, these steps created cultural and social challenges that worried Sa'udi nationals, and it was precisely to meet some of these trials that King 'Abdallah embarked on a systematic reform path. At the seventh national dialogue, concrete recommendations were made to improve work culture and ethics, encourage the private sector to assume a greater role in providing employment for nationals, devise standardized work hours as far as that was possible, potentially open new fields to female-only employment opportunities, provide incentives to pioneering companies that took risks on nationals, and improve the overall quality of graduates from educational and training institutes. These were neither easy tasks to accomplish, nor effortlessly implemented by the most flexible administrations, although few could ignore them. Above all else, dialogue conversations and the recommendations that ensued, were televised, which further sensitized decision-makers to the intricacies of tectonic changes among the population at large. While intransigent bureaucrats played for time, Riyadh could no longer bask in that luxury, as added demands on the government compelled it to act.

Eighth national meeting: health services – a dialogue between society and health institutions

The eight national meeting, on health services, was held in Najran Province (on the Yemeni border) between April 8 and 10, 2010. KACND organizers wished to examine the kingdom's health environment and, towards that end, invited health service providers to debate their economic, social, and psychological consequences. In this instance, participants aimed to identify the realities, qualities, geographical distribution, and the development of health services throughout the country. Moreover, they wished to have a clear idea of health plans, programs and projects currently in use, with the express desire to enhance that which could be, eliminate that which must be, and recommend that which policy makers ought to implement. Given the complexities of the topic, five preparatory meetings were conducted in Kharj, Khamis Mushayt, Qurayat, Yanbu', and Qatif.

Among the many issues explored were quality of services in the health sector, the geographical distribution of services (quality and quantity of services), medical errors, patient rights and work ethics in the healthcare sector, the roles of charitable institutions involved in wellbeing domains, education and awareness, medical insurance and privatization, integration among various sectors, rehabilitation and training of workers, and citizen expectations. Over the course of a long year, experts who attended the preparatory gatherings offered a slew of ideas to KACND observers, whose difficult task was to digest them all. Like other national dialogue meetings, these were broadcast live on the *Akhbariyyah Channel* – an up-and-coming national channel that employed uncovered anchorwomen who wore make-up and, more important, colored *abayas* that distinguished them from the generally black over-garments worn by the vast majority of Sa'udi women – which encouraged public transparency. Many vociferously complained of poor services, lack of emergency assistance programs, and deficiencies in qualified women specialized in the field. In fact, one of the chief complaints that emerged was the need for female security workers to document and follow up abuse cases both at home and hospitals. Not surprisingly, there were other concerns that preoccupied the public, including poorly qualified medical workers as well as increasing costs. In the course of the debates, it was pointed out that Sa'udi medical manpower consisted of 97% medical technicians while specialists stood at 3%, which illustrated the imbalance between professionals and assistants. As the preparatory meetings progressed, observers realized that the kingdom could no longer rely on expatriate medical personal to cater to its population's basic health requirements. The time was long overdue to activate a full-fledged education system whose primary goal was to assume responsibility to train indigenous nurses and doctors, and literally Sa'udize this vital and growing sector of the economy. This was easier said than done, of course, but most attendees understood that such decisions could no longer be postponed. Cooperation between the Ministry of Health, military and university hospitals, as well as clinics throughout the land, was not a luxury but a necessity in the full sense of the word. Unless and until these steps were urgently taken, existing weaknesses in the health services sectors would continue, which could only be resolved through training existing personnel and qualifying their replacements.

Participants noted that the 1998 Ministry of Health strategy to develop such programs was left in abeyance, which did not speak well of the bureaucracy or of officials entrusted with these concerns. While several specialized hospitals existed, a growing population required additional pediatric, emergency, gynecological, and geriatric care facilities, manned by properly trained personnel. One of the recommendations was to set forth ambitious plans for qualifying health workers and increasing continuous training. This was not unusual but what was new was making clear linkages with overall education starting in elementary schools. Simply stated, one did not pluck a nurse or physician off a tree. Such trained providers required years of schooling and specialized instruction to best serve the nation.[70]

Of course, as medical education was prohibitively expensive, dialogue attendees did not neglect the financial aspects of their recommendations. Towards that end, they stressed the role of the private sector to contribute by empowering hospital managers to operate within strict guidelines set by the State but with an outlook for semi-independence. Such methods, they deemed, promoted incentives that would encourage professionalism, as consumers would seek early checkups for common ailments instead of rushing to emergency rooms, which drained health budgets. They also considered the establishment of a government medical insurance system, which could support the creation of health endowments, and encouraged charities that volunteered their contributions to various facilities to pursue their critical work. Of course, the conference acculturated the public at large and, through various written suggestions, decision-makers on the health needs of the nation, which stood at the apex of national interests. From this standpoint, KACND officials digested opinions and thoughts on a critical topic, and they initiated long-term plans to foster genuine reforms.

The Sa'udi view of national dialogues

Because King 'Abdallah embarked on major reform initiatives, the KACND adopted a variety of programs to encourage dialogue among all of the groups that comprised the nation. Through eight major dialogue meetings between 2003 and 2010 – with the ninth dialogue under preparation as this book went to press in mid-2012 – as well as a great many preparatory gatherings, key subjects were debated with care and concern to better identify what ailed Sa'udi Arabia and how best to introduce effective reforms. Public opinion was taken into account and suggestions welcomed. Field studies supplemented commissioned research efforts to reflect as accurately as possible not only the views of participants in KACND activities but also those of the public at large. To verify whether the first few dialogues produced the desired effects, the KACND undertook a field survey of public opinion in 2006 to assess the opinion of Sa'udi society regarding the center and its activities, and thereby to gauge the extent to which residents were aware of the center's mission and objectives.[71]

Importantly, the large size and diversity of the study sample, at 1,970, represented a scientific breakthrough. Distributed according to a calibrated percentage and proportionally to the size of the respective populations in all thirteen provinces, the survey was deemed balanced. Moreover, the study sample was distributed to both males and females, with returns collected from males standing at 51% and females at 49%. It was observed that 74% of questionnaires retrieved were collected from external sources, while the remainder came from internal sources (26%), as individuals participating in the fifth dialogue were given preference. Most respondents had a college education (55.83%), with 23.96% being secondary school graduates. Higher education respondents stood at 15.31% while the percentage of those who had less than a secondary school education totaled 4.33%, with 0.56% of the sample lacking any formal schooling whatsoever. A majority of respondents were employed in the public sector (64.45%), followed by students (20.94%). Those employed in the private sector accounted for a small percentage of the sample, at 9.68%.[72]

The results of this survey were revealing. Approximately 78% confirmed that they knew of KACND and its activities. Likewise, a whopping 84% were aware that the Center's main goal was to "establish the principle and conduct of dialogue," reinforced "within the framework of the Islamic creed." Additional questions clarified how well KACND was disseminating the culture of dialogue, with 72% agreeing that its goals were clear. A very small percentage (5%) disagreed. Equally interesting was the confirmation that the number of Sa'udis who followed national meeting debates increased steadily from 17% (first dialogue), to 19% (second dialogue), 31% (third), and 33% (fourth). Although this first survey assessed the first four dialogues, interest in the following four sessions remained strong, especially after regional dialogue sessions before the national conventions.[73]

Survey samples corroborated that the subjects chosen for debates were very important.[74] Naturally, the fourth dialogue, on "Youth Issues … Reality and Aspirations," which garnered 50% of respondents, proved to be the most pertinent to real-life conditions. Attention to the third meeting, on "Women … Rights and Obligations, and their Relation to Education," stood at 40%, followed by the topic of the second meeting, "Hyperbole and Moderation: A Comprehensive Methodological Perspective" (39%). The subject of the first meeting, "International Relations and Treaties and the Effect of the Way They are Understood on National Unity," came in fourth at 32%.[75]

Many respondents approved of the media reporting devoted to various sessions and hoped that such coverage would alert senior decision-makers to popular concerns. Most participants concurred that recommendations issued by these dialogues ought to be taken very seriously and hoped that King 'Abdallah would rely on results as he accelerated his reforms. If his March 2011 decrees were any indication, King 'Abdallah paid attention, even if circumstances were not ideal to announce them upon his return from medical leave in the United States, as critics believed the latest decisions were driven by uprisings throughout the Arab world. Indeed, while epochal developments galvanized several Arab countries starting in late 2010 and well into 2011 when the monarch made his epochal announcements, and although these may well have affected his decision to move faster than was his preferred pace, the fact of the matter was that Sa'udis had held eight national dialogues over several years. These meetings accumulated a series of recommendations that, obviously, meant decision would need to be made on them sooner rather than later. In the event, perhaps the decrees that ushered in reforms were made sooner than anticipated, though there was no denying that the 2011 Arab Spring left an impact.

Nevertheless, 'Abdallah bin 'Abdul 'Aziz's major reforms were slowly gaining ground as a culture of dialogue became routine among what must still be considered one of the most conservative societies on earth. While it was easy for outsiders to offer generous criticisms of the kingdom for its serious socio-political shortcomings, what irked most observers and especially Sa'udi citizens was the slow pace of change, which could not be blamed on the government or the Al Sa'ud. By their very nature, Sa'udis were not eager to experiment, and proposals for dramatic transformations were often mitigated by traditional tribal customs. In short, 'Abdallah or any other ruler who wished to introduce genuine reforms because of a belief that such changes would benefit society at large, faced major cultural and political hurdles. Facing the ruler were a gaggle of traditionalists who forced a slow-down of the process and an equally vocal and effective throng of liberals who demanded a faster pace. Under such circumstances, any dialogue was bound to be contentious, although the king seldom backed down. His word was the law of the land. While every absolute monarch could assume that royal decisions were irrevocable, 'Abdallah was aware that his persuasive skills were his greatest assets, and his painstaking efforts to encourage national dialogues on thorny subjects paid off. To his credit, he enlarged the scope of dialogues to encompass interfaith initiatives, aware that Sa'udi Arabia could not survive in isolation, nor could it oppose extremism alone.

A meaningful Vatican summit

When the Custodian of the Two Holy Mosques, 'Abdallah bin 'Abdul 'Aziz, met Pope Benedict XVI at the Vatican on November 6, 2007, an immense taboo was eradicated between Islam and Catholicism.[76] Beyond its historic dimension, it was fair to ask whether the two men were harbingers of coexistence, or whether the meeting was an example of an impossible dialogue.

According to the Vatican, the monarch requested this first audience between the head of the Roman Catholic Church and a Sa'udi monarch, although the late Pope John Paul II received then Heir Apparent 'Abdallah in 1999 along with other senior Al Sa'ud family members. Earlier, the late King Faysal's foremost religious advisors initiated contacts with Catholic officials over thirty years ago, when Shaykh Muhammad Al Harakan, who became Faysal's Minister of Justice, Shaykh Rashid bin Khunayn, his Under-Secretary at the same ministry, Shaykh Muhammad bin Jubayr, the late head of the *Majlis al-Shurah*, and Shaykh 'Abdallah Al Musnad, who eventually chaired the Religious Studies Department at Imam Muhammad University and later became a member of the Board of Senior *'Ulamah*, visited Pope Paul VI on October 25, 1974.[77] At the time, the four Sa'udi religious scholars participated in the Catholic Church's dialogue between Christians and Muslims, part of a carefully laid out discourse between the two communities.[78] In fact, these dialogues were studied with utmost attention and, starting in February 1973, the organization MAE Medici signed a cultural, scientific, and technical exchange agreement in Riyadh. In June 1973, King Faysal visited Rome where the Islamic Cultural Center received approval for construction. At the time, and impressed by the progress achieved at the Center, Pope Paul VI approved an Italian Government request to allow the building of a mosque and a Centro Culturale Islamico in the Italian capital. The dialogue continued when, on April 24, 1974, Faysal received Cardinal Pignedoli, the President of the Vatican Office of Non-Christian Affairs, in Riyadh, who conveyed "the regards of His Holiness, moved by a profound belief in the unification of Islamic and Christian worlds in the worship of a single God, to His Majesty King Faisal as supreme head of the Islamic World."[79]

Like Faysal before him, 'Abdallah believed in acculturating the kingdom's Muslim scholars to other civilizations, to foster genuine harmony among them. Yet, 'Abdallah's task was more urgent, after the erudite and scholarly Pope Benedict XVI broadcast controversial views about non-Catholic beliefs. In fact, the pontiff's exceptionally controversial September 2006 speech at Regensburg University in his native Germany, when he quoted Emperor Manuel II Paleologos (r. 1391–1425) of the Byzantine Empire to offer judgments on the Prophet Muhammad, complicated and delayed whatever progress was made in the past.[80] The crusader ruler, who may have held some relevance in the 14th century, could not be perceived as a paragon of moral authority in the 21st. Still, by quoting him, Benedict XVI championed medieval scholarship with its own strain of convoluted purity. Of course, the Pope repeatedly stressed that the Byzantian emperor's words were not his own, and expressed regret for any offences his utterances caused throughout the Muslim world, though the damage was done in this age of instant communication and emotional reactions.[81]

Given this background, 'Abdallah's historic visit was even more impressive, as it concretely demonstrated that the Sa'udi monarch was a visionary, determined to pursue his multi-front reform programs no matter what. In fact, the ruler cajoled powerful religious scholars to extend a genuine hand in friendship, to develop strong interests in other cultures and religions, and to engage in a dialogue with the world's primary Christian institution. Remarkably, it was important for the king to listen to, understand, and assent to dialogue to better serve Islam, Sa'udi Arabia, and the Muslim world at large, and perhaps even to set an example for others in his country and throughout the Muslim world, especially if he, and they, insisted on reciprocity. In the event,

Vatican sources described to the press that the private summit between the two men was "warm" which, in diplomatic language, was quite positive. There were, to be sure, several contentions at play, especially since the two sides had no diplomatic ties. Without a doubt, the religious rights of an estimated 1.5m Christians who lived and worked in Sa'udi Arabia was probably discussed as well, although neither side acknowledged it. Bishop Paul Hinder, responsible for Catholics in Arabia and based in the UAE, confided to Reuters that the most important thing was "to get the possibility to gather in freedom and security for our worship, our masses and our activities."[82]

Because Benedict XVI greeted 'Abdallah bin 'Abd al-'Aziz warmly, affectionately grasping both of the king's hands, and because their private meeting covered a series of non-political topics, chances were good that spiritual and moral concerns would now be addressed in some detail. In Benedict, 'Abdallah found a compassionate interlocutor who underlined the need for a "just solution" to both the Israeli–Palestinian conflict and Lebanon – two subjects that concerned both the Catholic Holy See and the Kingdom of Sa'udi Arabia. Likewise, the Vatican uncovered in 'Abdallah a visionary who, in the footsteps of his predecessor and illustrious brother King Faysal, put the likes of Emperor Manuel II Paleologos to shame. Sometimes talking face-to-face helped clear up misunderstandings, but only noble men could take such initiatives.

Interfaith dialogues

Whether King 'Abdallah and Pope Benedict XVI discussed the issue was not revealed, although in June 2008, the Sa'udis invited several Muslim scholars led by Grand Mufti 'Abdul 'Aziz Al al-Shaykh, to endorse a call for opening a dialogue with people of other faiths at the start of a historic three-day summit at Al-Safah Palace. The monarch prayed for determination and strength to take up the Islamic mission of cordial dialogue with other faiths, even if the other side was "hostile," he posited.[83] He cited Chapter 16, Verse 125 of the Holy Qur'an: "Invite to the Way of the Lord with wisdom and beautiful preaching; and argue with them in ways that are best and most gracious." Inasmuch as the Sa'udi ruler acknowledged that Muslim extremists compounded the challenges faced by Islam, especially in Sa'udi Arabia, his purpose in this instance was nothing more than to seek the advice of the *'Ulamah* "to counter the challenges of isolation, ignorance, narrow vision and convey to the world the broad Islamic messages based on humanitarian principles and away from hostility and aggression."[84] The Grand Mufti endorsed the king's project and said the whole *Ummah* was looking up to the benevolent ruler to take the lead and bringing different communities of the world together. The 600 Muslim intellectuals and academics who attended the summit to work out the details and parameters of the interfaith dialogue were inspired, as the need for better understanding and cooperation between monotheistic religions was never this high. In the event, the monarch urged his audience to promote the true message of Islam, and declared that the Muslim world faced great difficulties as extremists targeted the basic tolerance of the faith. Few could argue with his premise, although neither the venue nor the attendance made the gathering an interfaith event.

Indeed, because of its sponsorship, within the biannual activities of the Muslim World League, as well as its Makkah location – that prevented non-Muslims from attending – the conference preached to the proverbial converted. To be sure, conference organizers heard from Shi'ah participants, including the former Iranian president 'Ali Akbar Hashemi Rafsanjani who shared the stage with the Sa'udi monarch, and others, though such attendance could not pass for interfaith dialogue in the strict sense of the word. More importantly, 'Abdallah wished to concentrate on religious values and not address political differences, although this proved to be a problem when Rafsanjani interjected: "Without Islam the world is nothing. We control 20% of the world's resources. We don't want to waste these and it is our duty not to hand over what we have. Muslims are authorized to defend themselves in a good manner."[85] Even if 'Abdallah listened politely, he disagreed with Rafsanjani since his aim was something entirely different. Indeed, the Sa'udi ruler wished to encourage scholars to promote dialogue with different religions, that is with non-Muslims precisely to break the vicious circle that galvanized Muslim as well as non-Muslim public opinion. His preferences were probably sharpened over the years, but gained specificity after his November 2007 talks with Pope Benedict XVI, as well as his March 2008 announcement that he planned to host a meeting between the three Abrahamic faiths: Judaism, Christianity, and Islam. These steps were not about natural resources and brinkmanship, but about greater unity among different Islamic schools of thought in the first place and, at a later stage, to enter into genuine dialogues with peoples who practiced other religions but shared similar divine inspirations. The monarch's vision differed significantly from what was understood by Muslim 'Ulamah, including the Grand Mufti of Sa'udi Arabia, for whom dialogue with other religions was a way to bring non-Muslims into Islam. Whether 'Abdallah shared the mufti's ultimate goal – to convert people to Islam – was difficult to tell. Suffice it to say that the Sa'udi ruler was probably thinking beyond such narrow interpretations, without denying a role to disseminate the principles of Islam. His writ was to put an end to the dangers of extremism.[86]

At the end of the important June 2008 gathering, 'Abdallah announced that he would convene a conference in Madrid, co-sponsored with the Spanish Government, to enlarge his outreach initiatives to defuse interfaith tensions, improve Islam's tarnished political image in the aftermath of 9/11, and restore respect for religious values. Critically, the Sa'udi announced that the three-day meeting would include Muslim, Christian, and Jewish clerics, as well as representatives of Eastern religions. This was as concrete an example as the kingdom could embark on, to stress Islam's tolerant expressions, as well as reject hard-liners. In fact, 'Abdallah was apparently "obsessed" by the idea for just such a conference for several years, and described to visiting Japanese scholars his wishes to invite monotheistic believers as well as those who professed other religions because, he asserted, "we all believe in the same God."[87] His goal was "to agree on something that would maintain humanity against those who tamper [with] religions, ethics, and family systems." He further told his guests that disintegrating family ties, a rise in atheism, and "an imbalance of reason, ethics, and humanity" in today's world, distressed him.[88]

Even if no one knew whether 'Abdallah shared his thoughts with Pope Benedict XVI when the two met at the Vatican in November 2007, the Sa'udi leader said he would "never forget" the moving encounter. Yet, less than a year later, the Sa'udi monarch joined his Spanish counterpart, King Juan Carlos de Bourbon, in welcoming nearly 300 delegates representing Islam, Judaism, Christianity, Buddhism, Hinduism, Sikhism, and Taoism, as well as a swami who said he did not belong to any organized faith and asserted that religion divides rather than unites people. It was a remarkable collection of participants, and while critics were not satisfied, few understood the gamble taken by the Sa'udi when so few of his countrymen shared his vision on this vital yet extremely complex concern. In Madrid, 'Abdallah met with all of the representatives, including those of the Jewish faith – while most were Americans or Europeans, one was Israeli, although he held dual nationality and registered at the conference as an American – which did not sit well with hard-core Muslims who considered such individuals as "nonbelievers." 'Abdallah instinctively knew that his interfaith conference allowed Sa'udi Arabia to embark on a pre-emptive engagement, since he understood that religions, including Islam, were used as sources for today's violence. If there were clashes of civilizations, he probably reasoned, surely one of the best remedies was to avoid the same mistakes committed by previous generations.[89]

The three-day international interfaith conference emphasized the need for promoting dialogue among religions and cultures to strengthen world peace and stability and, judging by the final declaration issued by the conference, rejected the notion of the so-called "clash of civilizations" (see Appendix 4 for the text of the final communiqué). They also warned against the danger of campaigns seeking to deepen conflicts and destabilize peace and security. As identified in his opening remarks, 'Abdallah underscored the absolute necessity to agree on a framework to combat terrorism, which required all nation-states to work for peace rather than conflict (see Appendix 3 for the text of his opening remarks). "Terrorism," declared the communiqué, was "a universal phenomenon that required unified international efforts to combat it in a serious, responsible and just way ... This demands an international agreement on defining terrorism, addressing its root causes and achieving justice and stability in the world." More important, every effort was necessary to distance such scourges from religions, since political problems were created by the behavior and practices of their followers, not the faiths themselves.[90]

Attendee reactions were interesting, with Rabbi Brad Hirschfield of the National Jewish Center for Learning and Leadership in New York concluding that the conference was like a baby taking its first steps: "On the one hand, it's the most ordinary moment," while "on the other, it's the most important.

But what matters is what the baby does next." "This will not be a one-off conference," declared Anthony Ball, an aide to the Archbishop of Canterbury Rowan Williams, who insisted: "I am sure the commitment of the king to engage in dialogue will continue." Rabbi Marc Schneier, North American chairman of the World Jewish Congress, said King 'Abdallah was reaching out to other faiths to counter extremists and fanatics: "What I heard from him is that 'I represent Islam, and I am the voice of moderation'," he added. These were valuable additions to the debate that aimed to enhance common human values. According to the final declaration, the gathering "emphasized the need to promote a culture of tolerance and understanding through dialogue by holding conferences and developing relevant cultural, educational and media programs," which certainly satisfied those who feared that this might be a single such event.[91]

Long before any follow-ups could be called, however, the Madrid Conference adopted specific principles that truly stood out.[92] Among these were various notions that presumably united all of mankind, including: divine messages aimed at realizing the obedience of humankind to the Creator (to achieve happiness, justice, security and peace); respect for heavenly religions, preserving their high status and condemning any insult to their symbols, as well as combating the exploitation of religion in the instigation of racial discrimination; observe genuine peace, honor agreements, and respect unique traditions of peoples and their right to security, freedom, and self-determination, as the basis for building good relations among everyone. While all of these offered soothing sentiments, the conference further emphasized the significance of religion and moral values and the need for humans to revert to God in their fight against crime, corruption, drugs, and terrorism. Naturally, it was up to men of good faith to apply these precepts, but preserving the institution of the family and protecting societies from deviant behaviors were not controversial objectives. All that was required was the will to fulfill both Man's and, presumably, the Creator's desires.

At the end of the Madrid conference, Muslim World League Secretary-General 'Abdallah al-Turki joined UAE representative 'Izaddin Ibrahim Mustapha to announce plans for a series of follow-up meetings around the world, at different levels. The first gathering brought more than 150 Muslim and Christian leaders, including some of the world's most eminent scholars and clerics, to Yale University in July 2008. Interestingly, the Yale gathering planned to respond to the call for dialogue issued in an open letter, *A Common Word Between Us and You*, written by major Islamic leaders. Yale scholars responded with a statement that garnered over 500 signatures.[93] On 30 September 2009, and under the sponsorship of the Muslim World League, a major follow-up meeting opened in Geneva, Switzerland. 'Abdallah al-Turki announced that the two-day event would discuss a number of papers under the banner "The Impact of King 'Abdallah's Initiative in Disseminating Human Values."[94] An estimated 166 religious leaders, academics, and other prominent personalities from around the world took part in the event, which further defined discussion parameters. Bava Jain, secretary-general of the World Council of Religious Leaders, confided that King 'Abdallah had "done his part in paving the foundation for this historic initiative by visiting the Vatican, meeting the Pope, organizing the Madrid conference and bringing together world leaders at the UN General Assembly to discuss the initiative." He continued: "Now it is our duty to build upon this initiative to make it a big success."[95]

Speaking on the eve of the two-day international interfaith conference in Geneva, which was to focus on the impact of King 'Abdallah's initiative in the dissemination of human values, Jain said the Geneva gathering should give a clear vision on implementation of the initiative and set a five-year time frame for the purpose. "King 'Abdallah deserves the Nobel Peace Prize for taking this extremely bold initiative to establish peace in the world," Jain said, as he hoped that the Nobel Foundation would consider him for the prize, adding that it would have great impact on the initiative, drawing popular support from Muslims as well as non-Muslims. That was not to be, although the monarch's initiative succeeded in challenging believers of all faiths to harness the skills and efforts of all those who supported the initiative. Moreover, the Geneva conference was meant to give a clear direction for future interfaith dialogues.

Delegates from 35 countries attended, including: William Baker, the president of Christians and Muslims for Peace in the US; David Rosen, the director of inter-religious affairs at the American Jewish Committee; Pramjeet Singh Sarna, the president of the Delhi Sikh Gurudwara Rakab Ganj Sahib; Kuniaki Kuni, president of the Association of Shinto Temples in Japan; and Xue Cheng, the vice chairman of the Buddhist Association of China. So was Professor M.D. Nalapat, UNESCO peace chair at Manipal University in India, who commended King 'Abdallah for taking this noble initiative. "Islam is a peaceful religion but the extremists have tarnished its image," he declared, requiring that one pass judgment only on the actions of others, because "when we attack or condemn others on the basis of their actions we are infringing on the authority of God." Nalapat, a Buddhist who learned a lot about Islam from his mother Kamala Suraiya, the famous Indian novelist and poetess, urged Muslims to show to the world that Islam was a religion of mercy and compassion through their actions. He criticized the world media for projecting the mischievous actions of a handful of extremist Muslims, ignoring the good works of the majority, which placed the onus on the Muslim World League (MWL) to hold international interfaith conferences in Southeast Asia, North America, Latin America and Africa as a means to address shortcomings.[96] In fact, the MWL chief expressed satisfaction over the global trend toward dialogue, referred to the speech by US President Barack Obama at the University of Cairo in June 2009 as a harbinger of greater understanding between the followers of different faiths and cultures, and pointed out that Obama had welcomed King 'Abdallah's interfaith initiative as the right vehicle to improve dialogue.[97]

Conclusion: another call for co-existence

A decade after the tragic attacks on the World Trade Center in New York City and the Pentagon in Washington, D.C., little progress was made on the all too critical "clash of civilizations" front, which set out to answer the poorly thought-out question, "why do they hate us."[98] To help alleviate this heavy burden, Sa'udi Arabia and Spain convened a significant interfaith conference to encourage genuine dialogue among the many cultures that encompass the world. The well-attended congress received strong coverage in the Middle East, limited reporting in Europe and Asia, and hardly any exposure in the United States. What did this tell us about the need to foster "coexistence between people" of differing ethnicities, religions, and cultures?[99]

As discussed above, nearly 300 delegates representing the world's major faiths – Judaism, Christianity, Islam, Buddhism, Hinduism, and others – gathered in Madrid to listen to the Sa'udi monarch set specific parameters. "We all believe in one God," declared 'Abdallah bin 'Abdul 'Aziz, "who sent messengers for the good of humanity in this world and the hereafter." In his carefully worded presentation, the ruler emphasized that "differences must not lead to conflict and confrontation," because whatever "tragedies that have occurred in human history were not attributable to religion, but were the result of extremism with which some adherents of every divinely revealed religion, and of every political ideology, have been afflicted."[100]

While no one could logically disagree that promoting dialogue among religions and cultures would strengthen world peace, one was tempted to ask whether such calls were the best avenues for understanding, or even worthy goals to pursue. It was critical to raise this concern because dialogue occurred best among equals or, more accurately, when all protagonists accepted their putative parities. Were there such perceptions in the 21st century among believers who gathered in Madrid? Did Jews, Christians, Muslims, along with many other non-monotheistic religions, accept that they were co-equals, if not in each other's eyes, at least in divine terms?

Optimists assumed such commonalities, whereas pessimists rejoiced that differences galore enhanced their cynicisms. In the spirit of moderation, nevertheless, one was tempted to state the obvious: while such sensitivities were not impossible to identify, they were rare indeed. It was ironic, therefore, that participants in Madrid were reminded of the 1994 UN Declaration for Tolerance, whereas many attendees knew that the 1998 Oslo Conference on Freedom of Religion or Belief – which celebrated the fiftieth anniversary of the Universal Declaration of Human Rights – reaffirmed that every person was privileged with such entitlements. These satisfactorily expressed sentiments in 1998, which sounded pleasant a decade later, were agreeable to hear even if they still remained hallow both in content as well as substance.

Still, what was presumably different this time around were the many links between laudatory objectives uttered in Madrid and the so-called "clash of civilizations," since the latter prospered on perpetual conflicts. Because contemporary realities were such that terrorism and counter-terrorism almost always took on independent lives and, more importantly, precedence over any and all dialogues, calls for moderation and the exchange of ideas were vital to limit instability. In fact, few "officials" could justify dialogue – serious or otherwise – when faced with life and death challenges, although 'Abdallah stepped up to the plate with gusto. While terrorism required unified international efforts to tackle this man-made scourge, competing and contradictory definitions demanded that nation-states engage in genuine dialogue, rather than plot to undermine each other's efforts.

Under the circumstances, it was not enough to have a universal vision that all believers upheld common values, because they did not. To be sure, everyone played a role in solving problems, but beyond the humanitarian perspective among isolated religious leaders and well-protected dignitaries, how were their messages conveyed to those in need of hearing them most? This is where Riyadh's efforts stood out, because 'Abdallah engaged his own nation in serious internal dialogues on a variety of topics that affected, directly or indirectly, domestic, regional and international stability. Critics of the kingdom's national dialogues disparaged the Sa'udi monarch for moving slowly, relying on inefficient committees to tackle very difficult problems, or for using money to placate opposition forces. Although the recommendations of the eight national dialogues covered a broad range of concerns, the care with which participants broached various subjects could not be ignored. Serious conversations based on carefully prepared discussion papers were held among scholars. While these were not *The Federalist Papers* that helped decipher the Constitution of the United States, they were nevertheless equally valuable as teaching and learning tools, in a society experimenting with modernizing institutions. Moreover, because the kingdom's constitution was the Holy Qur'an, it was vital to engage in social debates without contravening scriptures.

For true believers, therefore, religions faced specific puzzles, not dilemmas among themselves and with each other. In fact, the need was not only for a new era in interfaith relations, even if that could not but conceivably help. Rather, what was desirable was for religious figures to abandon cloistered rhetoric to stand with their flocks especially on domestic challenges that required serious planning rather than lofty but largely empty discourses. Likewise, it was essential for secular leaders to step back from moral pedestals, and work for common ground where the rights of ordinary people were respected, as eloquently promised in the Universal Declaration of Human Rights. So that policemen treated everyone with dignity, soldiers disobeyed orders to shoot a blindfolded prisoner's leg, or interrogation guards did not rely on water-boarding to torture.

Reaching out to other faiths to counter extremists and fanatics, as the Custodian of the Two Holy Mosques did, was certainly commendable, especially when that message conveyed the voice of moderation. In fact, the promotion of a culture of tolerance and understanding through dialogue was immensely valuable, though, it is worth repeating, clearly insufficient. What the community of nations required above all else were ethical principles, which meant that one reached out for dialogue first, before embarking on revenge. If history started at the last moment of every event, and every incident gained existential value, then everything that preceded that particular occurrence became meaningless, which could justify immoral responses each and every time. It was precisely to avoid such outcomes that 'Abdallah engaged his nation on the path of dialogue, internally as well as globally, for he at least understood that conversations among and with religious leaders ought to encompass what everyone craved: justice. 'Abdallah bin 'Abdul 'Aziz raised the bar high at home and set it even higher overseas. How he responded to his own people's demands, and how he secured internal and regional stability, were challenges that confronted him as they did his predecessors. To his credit, he was willing to take a few political risks, to secure his nation and improve the latter's ties with the rest of the world.

3 Political participation and municipal elections

Although King Fahd bin 'Abdul 'Aziz introduced major governance innovations on March 1, 1992, the first municipal elections in the kingdom's history were only held in 2005, when King 'Abdallah bin 'Abdul 'Aziz supervised the exercise. To be sure, the decision to hold these elections was reached by the Council of Ministers in 2003, which meant that Fahd technically authorized them, even if the late monarch was largely incapacitated at the time. While members of the military and women were excluded from the process, and the voting age was fixed at 21 – in a country where over 50% of the population was less than 15 years old – it was somewhat understandable that the voting did not raise great enthusiasm. It may be safe to argue that the electorate was unsure what municipal councils would presumably do, what kind of prerogatives they may have, and how they might cooperate with the ruling family. Consequently, participation was weak, with many voters falling back into time-tested tribal considerations. As discussed below, Riyadh skirted a key benefit of municipal elections, with many Al Sa'ud officials fearing that they would be perceived as a referendum. What both the Al Sa'ud and Sa'udi citizens agreed upon, however, was that the 2005 municipal elections were a first step in a long process of necessary reforms. Everyone understood that key obstacles remained, including the existing duality between elections and appointments, given that only half of 1,236 hopefuls, or 608 winners, served in 178 councils across the country. By 2009, when the next elections were scheduled, the kingdom's municipal councils reached 285, although the planned October 31, 2009 voting was postponed until September 22, 2011. The duality problem was not the only confusing matter. Voters were also bewildered by the putative prerogatives of municipal councils and the uncertain conditions associated with women, who could not cast ballots but, presumably, formed a key constituent of municipal activities. Even the rather high voting age posed a problem. As discussed below, voters were further worried about the prospects of broadening the participatory process to include the *Majlis al-Shurah*, which was the country's premier "legislative" outlet.

The purpose of this chapter is to assess the value of political participation through *Shurah* (Consultation), provide a detailed examination of the Consultative Council itself, discuss the first municipal elections held in 2005, scrutinize the reasons why the 2009 elections were postponed, and conclude with an evaluation of what may be the consequences of legislative changes for the monarchy.

Political participation in a tribal environment

Because the kingdom emerged within a tribal environment that was also influenced by Islam, the relationships between religion, tribal traditions, and the nascent institutions that were introduced in the monarchy after 1932, shaped political participation in the country. While it probably is a mistake to assume that whatever political life existed in the country was based on tribal or religious norms, customs associated with tribal affairs predominated societies on the Arabian Peninsula before the advent of Islam, and ever since.[1] Importantly, institutions that were painstakingly created under harsh desert conditions embodied not just survival characteristics, but embodied compacts between rulers and ruled that "provided" for both. Indeed, even if "tribalism" may no longer be a political constant, it formed an undercurrent of mentalities that only faced drastic changes about a generation ago, namely after the oil boom that followed the 1970s. What emerged over the centuries was a true balance of power between the institution of the tribe – through either confederations of tribes or individual groupings – and a central authority (the State), which came to embody the source of political loyalty. Riyadh thus absorbed tribal norms and shaped them to fit its needs, not to eliminate existing institutions, but to secure its authority. In the case of the Al Sa'ud, loyalty was sealed with the imprimatur of faith, best exemplified in the 1744 Compact that united the ruling family with the leading religious lineage of the Al al-Shaykh.[2]

Still, the founder's nation-building schemes were not meant to completely eliminate the tribe as a basic unit, but to incorporate the institution within the nascent state. Perhaps the best evidence for this phenomenon was the Al Sa'ud's reliance on loyal tribal levies to protect the ruling family through the National Guard and, eventually, through key military units to defend the monarchy. Although the founder relied on the *Ikhwan* (literally, the brethren of military – religious units that formed the ruler's private militia) to conquer much of Arabia before turning against them, the decision to incorporate *Ikhwan* fighters into state institutions was not haphazard, nor did they mean to eliminate an entire group of people. Rather, and this was worth underscoring, the ruler wanted to use loyal tribal members as one of the pillars of his monarchy.[3]

Naturally, with the development of a bureaucracy starting in the 1940s and 1950s, Riyadh also relied on technical expertise from a variety of educated subjects, as well as a slew of expatriate advisors, but these seldom replaced clerics and loyal tribal fighters. Of course, as state revenues increased, first through *Hajj* income and then petroleum exports, the state assumed the financial burdens of education – chiefly religious at the time – as well as various training institutions. In fact, the kingdom's leading clergymen benefited from Riyadh's financial largesse to propagate religious instruction, which enhanced their reputation. If senior 'Ulamah enjoyed access to the monarch, modernizing opportunities like radio and television, allowed the clergy to improve their direct access to the population at large. Of course, such prospects meant that clerics could, and they often did, discuss social matters, such as the role of women in society and the country's education programs. Whether by design or pure coincidence, 'Abdul 'Aziz bin 'Abdul Rahman conceded certain privileges to the clergy, even if his determination to muzzle the latter when they infringed on his authority was legendary.[4] Suffice it to say that this welcome mat, buttressed by oil wealth, combined to enlarge the religious bureaucracy to a far larger size and power than perhaps either intended or preferred.[5] Over the years, not only was the kingdom endowed with a Ministry of Justice that administered Shari'ah law and provided legal services to citizens, but it also created two additional ministers to administer purely religious needs: a Ministry of Islamic Endowments, Call (Da'wah) and Guidance Affairs, whose writ was to administer vast land holdings controlled by the religious trust (awqaf), along with a Ministry of Pilgrimage, whose exclusive task was to look after and provide facilities for the annual visit of pilgrims to Makkah, Madinah, and other holy places in the kingdom. Riyadh absorbed hundreds of thousands of graduates from religious educational institutions, guaranteed salaries to clerics, and enhanced their political importance. In fact, it may be accurate to state that the founder's objective was to link the ideological interests of the clergy to the political mechanisms he created for the country.

To some extent, the reason for this nascent marriage was because Riyadh believed, and circumstances confirmed, that clergymen were more likely to "administer" the state's policies. Tribal loyalties, while unwavering towards the Al Sa'ud, were nevertheless subject to internal challenges. At times, allegiances and rivalries created discipline problems and, in the 1930s and 1940s at least, posed certain disputes. It took Riyadh a few decades to professionalize the military forces, which meant that many tribal officers would simply pack and move away, rather than follow strict discipline. To be sure, tribal loyalty was cherished but so was consistency, which is where clergymen entered into the fray. As the country's finances improved, the state could thus mobilize several pillars to solidify its legitimacy, and gradually regularized political participation through unprecedented generosity. It was important to clarify that Riyadh provided for key segments of the population not to simply buy off everyone that mattered, but to create a multi-layered dependence mechanism that placed the state at the center. Leading merchants were important as were clergymen and tribal leaders, but only the state – in other words, the Al Sa'ud – could ensure steady employment to all. That, in turn, meant basic education, medical treatment, subsidized food programs, better housing facilities with modern amenities like water and electricity, all of which were in extremely short supply. Riyadh wished to provide such services and accomplished many of its stated objectives to assure loyalties, as urbanization created myriad opportunities to improve living conditions for the population at large, as well as to limit the extraordinary sufferings that nomadic lifestyles imposed. It is worth noting that severe desert conditions limited the average person's lifespan, which hovered between 30 and 40 years in 1932, with what passed for health care being provided by local healers. In fact, the first Western-trained physicians only arrived in the late 1920s to look after the ruler, and, to his credit, 'Abdul 'Aziz quickly introduced free health care, not just for citizens, but for pilgrims who visited holy cities. Within a relatively short period of time, once endemic diseases, such as malaria and smallpox, were virtually eradicated, life expectancy rose sharply. In 1970, the average Sa'udi lived to be 53.9 years, but could expect to live to 72.3 in 2005, and 73.87 in 2010 [71.93 years for males and 75.9 years for females].[6] Over time, health services, along with education programs, and other economic activities, essentially meant that urbanization gained ground. For the purposes of this investigation, such dramatic changes asserted the political prowess of the Al Sa'ud, who channeled existing authorities through the nascent prism of a state under their full control. While emerging social groups called for formal access to the decision-making progress, the genius of the Al Sa'ud was to channel such demands through key legitimizing institutions, both religious and secular, with Riyadh acting as the key nexus. The Al Sa'ud spoke of reforms and change, as in the *Majlis al-Shurah* phenomenon, but always through the central focus of the monarchy.

Still, despite this eclectic and highly effective institutionalization process, periodic impulses surfaced asking for representative and participatory organizations. When the state failed to follow up on its own promises, requests became demands, as members of the intelligentsia sought a role within the decision-making system. Towards that end, petitions were submitted to the monarch, ironically from both the secular and the religious establishments. Naturally, while each catered to their respective constituencies, reflecting class and ideological interests, in the absence of formal political parties in the country, rigidity or sanctimony by Riyadh only meant confrontation. It was not long before a *Salafi*, or *Sahwist* [from *Sahwah* or awakening], movement emerged as a serious political challenger. As discussed elsewhere in this volume, political groups and social institutions in Sa'udi Arabia became more vocal after 1979, but especially after the 1991 War for Kuwait, in what was an unprecedented level of political activism.

In response, Riyadh rekindled its *Shurah* promises, introduced a new Basic Law, and otherwise responded to growing demands to placate an increasingly educated and alert public. It was one thing to create institutions in the post-oil boom era that created a welfare state but something entirely different to share responsibilities with citizens. The vast majority of Sa'udis perceived decades of financial largesse, accompanied by undeniable benefits, as their "rights." Few conceived of any reciprocal obligations, and the ruling family was happy to accommodate such awareness, so long as the state reigned supreme. As times changed, and the economy floundered, many asked pertinent questions. Given the volatility in oil markets, coupled with several regional wars that mobilized even the most blasé, a growing number of Sa'udis concluded that the state was too important to simply leave to a single family, albeit a powerful one. Simply stated, citizens wished to participate in the affairs of the country, even if it was a monarchy. A majority continued to support the ruling family but increasingly voiced keen interest in transparency and accountability.

Whether this mobilization was a natural progression of nation building or whether it was encouraged by regional and international threats to the kingdom and the entire region were less important than the linkage with regional spillover effects. Indeed, the repercussions of the 1979 Iranian Revolution, the 1980–88 Iran–Iraq War, the 1990 Iraqi invasion and occupation of Kuwait, the 1991 liberation of the Shaykhdom, the post-2001 war for Afghanistan, along with the 2003 war for Iraq, all contributed to a mindset that valued political participation. Few Gulf citizens could simply stand idly by as they watched their countries, and systems of government, come under duress.

Ironically, the six conservative Arab Gulf monarchs accelerated this process when they created the Gulf Cooperation Council (GCC) in 1981, which called for the creation of supra-national institutions. How could Sa'udi Arabia add value to the GCC, many citizens reasoned, when similar coordination was not tolerated at home? Of course, and this must be acknowledged up front, domestic coordination was an on-going process, but mostly in the economic arena. For example, the Chamber of Commerce that represented the kingdom coordinated the activities of 19 regional chambers throughout the country, and lobbied local constituencies. Yet, on social and especially political matters, Riyadh seldom tolerated interference. Peripheral efforts were allowed to see light or expand, including the 1986 creation of the *Muntadah al-Tanmiyyah* [Development Forum] that sometimes addressed political concerns, even if most of its activities focused on economic matters. The small group of Gulf intellectuals started the *Muntadah* before the War for Kuwait but saw their ranks swell after the 1991 liberation of Kuwait. In May 1992, 90 Gulf intellectuals, academics, businessmen, and political figures established the *Multaqah al-Watani al-Khaliji* [Gulf National Forum], whose goal was to affirm democratic values and political participation. One of the Forum's objectives was to establish "civil society institutions" in GCC member-states, but that was not to be.[7] Gradually, the process gained popularity, and several monarchs, including King Fahd, responded. To be sure, Fahd often spoke of reforms throughout the 1980s – even funding the construction of a building to house a consultative body (which remained empty for years) – though no changes were introduced before 1992. Against a new trend of open challenges, however, the monarch hinted that he was ready to nominate 60 leading citizens to a *Majlis al-Shurah*, though even this minor pledge was delayed because of changing circumstances. In this endeavor, Fahd was supported by his heir apparent, who, true to Al Sa'ud traditions, rallied behind his monarch to ward off opposition that came, for the most part, from the kingdom's religious establishment.

On March 1, 1992, Fahd bin 'Abdul 'Aziz addressed his subjects on television and issued several key documents, including the *Basic Law of Government*, the statutes governing the newly created *Majlis al-Shurah*, and the *Law of the Provinces*.[8] This was, by any measure, a momentous step forward because an institutionalization process was clearly established. Even if the monarch's decision was propelled by the rising tide of internal opposition, as well as the repercussions of the War for Kuwait, significant and permanent changes were under way. The *majlis* came to be, engaged in relatively useful discussions and, in one of Fahd's last decisions, was expended from 120 to 150 members further indicating its growing popularity among Sa'udi elites.[9]

The Basic Law of Government was divided into nine main sections, dealing with the general principles of the state, the law of government, the values of Sa'udi society, the country's economic principles, the various rights and duties of citizens, the authority of the state, financial affairs, auditing authorities, and general provisions. In short, the revamped organization strengthened existing institutions and, perhaps, even modernized their outlook to better serve Crown and country.

Shurah *and the Sa'udi system*

Consultation was and is a key element of Muslim political affairs. According to the Holy Qur'an, Muslim leaders must practice it, even if specific methods were left unspecified, presumably to cater to local needs and circumstances. Over the centuries, Muslim rulers developed various political theories granting *Shurah* a vital role. The institution was ideally suited for the Arabian Peninsula where tribal confederations imposed law and order. Al Sa'ud leaders relied on *Shurah* during the first (1744–1818) and second (1822–91) monarchies, and 'Abdul 'Aziz bin 'Abdul Rahman ushered the mechanism for the third in 1902, almost three decades before the kingdom was reinstituted.[10] The most recent variation of the *Majlis al-Shurah* was its formalization in 1992, after King Fahd empowered the assembly to debate and enact certain laws even if the late ruler perceived the *Majlis* as a purely advisory body.[11]

It must also be emphasized that the very idea of *Shurah* was part and parcel of Arab traditions that predated Islam, since the definitive verb *Shawarah* (consulted) was part of the lexicon, with *Shawarahuh* (solicited consultation) a natural derivative. In the political context, *Shurah* called for the exchange of viewpoints and opinions to reach a mutually acceptable outcome that should not, indeed cannot, contradict scriptures. It must also serve the national interest, although how the latter was defined was not clear in all circumstances. In the norms followed on the Arabian Peninsula, and especially in Sa'udi Arabia, consultations focused, or at least were contemplated as converging, on the practical. In other words, Sa'udi society seldom encouraged obstinacy as a form of political engagement, which required a level of sophistication for those involved. Coupled with local norms that derived from both tribal and religious foundations, *Shurah* thus became an ideal vehicle to implement political principles within the judiciary (under *Shari'ah*), the executive (under the Al Sa'ud after 1744), and the nascent legislative after 1992. What distinguished

Shurah in the kingdom was its ingrained feature of unity that was the opposite of legislative mechanisms practically everywhere else. Simply stated, *Shurah* was enclosed in an envelope of harmony, and not just in periods of crisis. It may be worth repeating that *Shurah* predated Islam but that it gained vital support from the faith, since Islam granted a nation the right to participate in the affairs of state, while it imposed a level of consequential justice, even if details were murky. Technically speaking, *Shurah* was thought to prevent the abuse of power or the violation of laws, particularly since all decisions that served a nation would need to be achieved through consensus. Such a mechanism, when applied to the letter, kept distances between rulers and ruled to a minimum, which were interpreted as an ideal form of democratization even if several layers of uncertainty remained. For our purposes, what mattered most was the acceptance by the Al Sa'ud that *Shurah* was an obligation, and that the ruling family was entrusted with the duty to consult the nation on how best to conduct its affairs. It may be argued that the Al Sa'ud delayed this process until 1992 because, allegedly, education levels were minimal or tribal considerations prevented full implementation until then. Suffice it to say that devout Muslims accepted the veracity of *Shurah* and conceded its importance.

In the Muslim legal system, *Shurah* played a primary role, after the Prophet emphasized it. In fact, through his own practices, which were eventually enshrined in the *Sunnah* and some *Hadiths*, Muhammad set the example for his successors, both religious as well as secular. Naturally, not all of his heirs practiced the recommendations, although many did. Still, the Prophet encouraged Muslims to decide their affairs in consultation with those who would be affected by their decisions, which may be deduced from three Qur'anic references.

In the third Surah, Al-'Imran, verse 159, the Lord ordered Muhammad to consult with believers and forgive them after seeking the advice of the fallible. The verse reads:

> It was thanks to God's mercy that you dealt so leniently with them. Had you been cruel or hard-hearted, they would have surely deserted you. Therefore pardon them. Take counsel with them in the conduct of affairs; and when you are resolved, put your trust in God. God loves those who are trustful.[12]

In the 42nd Surah, which is named *Shurah*, a specific verse suggests that the practice was a praiseworthy lifestyle for a pious believer. It also declared that people who sought justice ought to be consulted since the matters concerned them.

> That which you have been given is but the fleeting pleasure of this life. Better and more enduring is God's recompense to those who believe and put their trust in Him, who avoid grievous sins and lewd acts and, when angered, are willing to forgive; who obey their Lord, attend to their prayers, and conduct their affairs by mutual consent; who give in alms from what We gave them and, when oppressed, seek to redress their wrongs.[13]

Although Arabian Peninsula norms contributed to various interpretations that defined *Shurah*, Muslims believed that the very idea of consultation was divinely inspired, not only because God determined that this was a praiseworthy activity, but also because it organized the affairs of believers, established righteousness, and erected stable societies. Muhammad organized society long before the idea of a parliament emerged, seeking advice from his companions, and when persuaded by the majority that he ought to make a certain decision, did so based on overall consent. Therefore, and in the footsteps of the Prophet who trusted consultation, Muslim rulers observed this Qur'anic principle attentively. In general, Sunni Muslims believed that *Shurah* was recommended in the Qur'an (with some classical jurists maintaining that it was obligatory), whereas Shi'ah Muslims trusted that Muhammad clearly indicated that 'Ali was his divinely appointed infallible successor, regardless of *Shurah*. Because the first three caliphs ignored the recommendation, Shi"ahs did not stress the role of *Shurah* in choosing leaders, but believed that God chose the divine vice-regent from the lineage of Muhammad (*Ahl al-Bayt*). In Sa'udi Arabia, and in the footsteps of Abu Bakr and 'Umar, the Prophet's first two successors, *Shurah* was carefully organized, which obligated both men to consult individuals who displayed expertise in *Shari'ah*. Both followed the Qur'an, the *Sunnah* and the *Hadiths*, but resorted to consultations when they could not find answers in the scriptures. In fact, 'Umar "went further by saying that the Muslim Caliph who [was] entrusted with ruling Muslims [had] no right to do so according to his own way of thinking."[14] In other words, a ruler ought to rely on expert opinion, which required consensus among a majority, if he wished to rule with justice.

The Consultative Council before 1992

Over the course of the twentieth century, *Shurah* passed through several stages, especially after 'Abdul 'Aziz bin 'Abdul Rahman entered Makkah in 1924, the year when he first called for its application.[15] Indeed, the monarch of the future kingdom made *Shurah* a foundation of his government, to fulfill the divine order by applying *Shari'ah*. Towards that end, he authorized the first "elected" council in 1924 to assemble under the chairmanship of Shaykh 'Abdul Qadir al-Shibbih, which included twelve members. At the time, when the state structure was not yet completed, the Consultative National Council – as it was formally known – was entrusted with drafting the basic laws for the administration of the nascent country. Besides the Holy Qur'an, there were no laws that specified what the functions of the Council ought to be, which clearly meant that the institution was a transitional body. In the event, the Council folded within six months, replaced by an expanded body in 1925. The new Council represented all 12 districts of Makkah, and included two religious scholars and a leading merchant among its twelve elected members. Three additional individuals were nominated by the ruler – who was then known as a Sultan who issued Sultanic decrees – from among the most distinguished citizens of Makkah. Remarkably, 'Abdul 'Aziz bin 'Abdul Rahman set the norm for a combination of elected and nominated officials in the formation of his 1925 Council, perhaps to cater to local needs but certainly to ensure internal stability. In another innovation, the ruler appointed Shaykh Muhammad Al-Marzuqi, with Shaykh al-Shibbih as vice president, to preside over fifteen members. As was expected, the 1925 Council was organized better, and set its first rules and regulations in six short articles. These instructions specified the qualifications for membership, the closing date for voting, and eligible voters. Parallel to its by-laws, the Council formulated its regulations in seven articles that addressed all affairs in courts, municipalities, endowments, education, security, and commerce, in addition to forming permanent committees to solve problems related to the social traditions that did not contradict *Shari'ah*.

By 1926, the ruler issued a Basic Law of Government, with a special section for councils, including the *Majlis al-Shurah*, for which six articles were devoted [28, 29, 30, 31, 36 and 37]. These clauses dealt with the Council's location, title (renamed *Majlis al-Shurah* instead of its previous title of National Council), membership, which stood at 12 individuals, specific considerations to convene sessions and who may be invited to attend them, and limiting membership terms to one year. All of these changes were introduced over a short time span that illustrated the ruler's due diligence.[16]

In 1927, the "Sultan" dissolved the outgoing Council and issued a decree that amended the fourth section of the Basic Law of Government, which dealt with the *Majlis*. Henceforth, the institution was allowed to work according to a revised system, whereby eight members served two-year terms. In yet another innovation, the *Majlis* was composed of four members elected by the government after consultation with eminent experts, and four members appointed by the government, two of whom hailed from the Najd region. Its 15 "constitutional" articles reflected previous experiences, but a fresh stipulation was incorporated, directing the reduced membership of eight full-time associates to meet under the chairmanship of the Viceroy of the Hijaz, His Highness Prince Faysal bin 'Abdul 'Aziz. Importantly, the 1927 *Majlis* convened twice a week, or more as Prince Faysal deemed it necessary.

Inasmuch as the tasks entrusted to the *Majlis* increased in volume, the public interest necessitated some amendments of its by-laws, which led to the 1928 emendations. In this instance, the updated version included 14 articles, including an increase in the number of members, from 8 to 12; the appointment of two vice presidents to assist Prince Faysal, one designated by the ruler while the other was elected by the *Majlis*; and the draconian new rule that called on a daily session instead of the established twice-a-week pattern. Over time, the *Majlis* developed and issued new by-laws (24 articles), which were reissued on September 18, 1932, when the ruler declared the restoration of the monarchy, and which remained in effect until the founding of the Council of Ministers in 1953.[17] It must be emphasized that the *Majlis al-Shurah* functioned more or less as a permanent government for several years, even if operated exclusively either under Prince Faysal's direction or one of his two deputies. As long as 'Abdul 'Aziz bin 'Abdul Rahman was king, that is until 1953, the *Majlis* operated as a government, advising the ruler as necessary and reaching decisions through consensus although the king remained *primus inter pares*. In 1953, many of the jurisdictions of the *Majlis al-Shurah* were distributed between the Council of Ministers and other departments of the government. Still, *Majlis* members continued to hold regular advisory sessions and to look into issues referred to them, albeit at a significantly reduced level of power. According to the record, between 1924 and 1982, the *Majlis* held a total of 6,222 sessions, and issued 9,349 decisions over the span of 51 terms.[18]

For reasons that were not entirely clear, but most probably the result of internal schisms that involved King Sa'ud and his Heir Apparent Prince Faysal, *Shurah* entered a period of abeyance in the country until November 6, 1962, when Riyadh adopted a ten-point reform program. At its outset, it declared:

> The time has arrived to issue a basic law of government ... setting precisely and clearly the basic principles of government and of the relationship between the ruler and the ruled; regulating the various state powers and their inter-relationships; and stating the basic rights of citizens, including the right to free expression within the limits of the Islamic faith and public order.[19]

At the time, such a program was considered revolutionary, as it called for a decentralized system of government and, more importantly, for the establishment of an independent judiciary. While observers focused, perhaps correctly, on the proposed ban on slavery, which was still legally permitted until that date, the real reform proposal was Faysal's preference for a separation of powers. The ten-point program skirted the idea of a *Majlis* and was, to some extent, a response to the overthrow of the monarchy in Yemen, which spread havoc within the ruling family that feared spillover effects into the kingdom. Inasmuch as both the revolutionary Yemeni government and its powerful Arab ally, the charismatic Nasir of Egypt, were embarked on a fierce campaign to topple the Sa'udi government, Faysal concluded that a reform program at home would strengthen his hand vis-à-vis the pro-Sa'ud faction. Once the power struggle was settled in 1964, and the danger from Yemen and Egypt was neutralized in the aftermath of the disastrous June 1967 Arab–Israeli war, King Faysal was too preoccupied with regional concerns to revisit his own reform proposals.[20] Critics concluded that, lofty expressions notwithstanding, "yet another declared attempt at constitutional reform went largely by the board."[21]

In the aftermath of the 1979 Makkah Mosque takeover, which literally shook the Al Sa'ud family, Heir Apparent Fahd bin 'Abdul 'Aziz, then serving an ailing King Khalid bin 'Abdul 'Aziz, revealed to the Kuwaiti daily *al-Siyassah* that a 209-article draft constitution was completed and that it would be issued without additional delays.[22] Outside his close circles, few believed that the commitment was genuine, with most observers asserting that the declaration was a response to very strong internal and regional pressures that threatened the monarchy. It was worth recalling that Riyadh weathered the repercussions of the February 1979 Iranian Revolution that overthrew a fellow monarch, the Shah of Iran, as well as the November 20, 1979 Makkah Mosque takeover, which was followed within days by Shi'ah uprisings in the Eastern Province, and the December 25, 1979 Soviet invasion and occupation of Afghanistan, all of which came as total surprises. The Islamic Revolution in Iran was particularly worrisome because it adopted faith as the source of its legitimacy, the same source upon which the Al Sa'ud family based its own authority. Whether the sum total of these dramatic events helped cajole King Khalid to move on the *Majlis* front ought not to come as a surprise. Still, despite the urgencies involved, Khalid and his putative heir were not in a hurry, as the draft constitution was left in abeyance.

It would take another cataclysmic development to finally nudge Riyadh to take action. A few months after the August 1, 1990 Iraqi invasion and occupation of Kuwait, which denied the Al Sabah their claims to rule, the Custodian of the Two Holy Mosques announced the formation of a long-awaited consultative assembly. The date was November 8, 1990. Even then he promised that the *Majlis* would be established "as soon as the final touches [were] made on a final draft of a basic law for the kingdom," ostensibly being fine-tuned by the Ministry of the Interior. This time, however, it was not possible to ignore his pledges, for at least two reasons. First, because Fahd acted as he hosted the recalcitrant Al Sabah in various Ta'if hotels, despite valiant Kuwaiti efforts to introduce democratization over the years. Second, because both liberal and conservative Sa'udi groups petitioned him to introduce reforms without further delays, which was an equally powerful nudge. Naturally, the presence of over half a million foreign troops in the kingdom prodded him, too, but that was a tangential factor. Simply stated, the monarch did not want his family to face consequences similar to those faced by the Al Sabah, even if he knew that members of the Kuwaiti ruling family had toyed with democratization ever since they declared their independence from Britain in 1961.

Perhaps more meaningful was the monarch's acquiescence to pleas issued by 43 leading Sa'udi intellectuals from all walks of life and political leanings, whose open letter for democratic reforms and the observance of basic liberties dotted i's and crossed t's. The petition – analyzed in Chapter 5 below – first circulated in the country during the first half of December 1990, and it focused on political participation and the necessity to finally set up a *Majlis al-Shurah*. If Fahd was once sympathetic, though his intuition led him to be dismissive, hoping to weather the current, this was no longer possible. In fact, when an estimated two hundred religious scholars, including the senior hierarchy of the religious establishment, circulated a similar petition, the monarch could no longer ignore such pleas and was literally obligated to pay attention. Once he vented his frustrations to the clergymen and several secularists who were close to the palace, Fahd understood that it was incumbent to reseal the shaken trust in his government, which he calibrated accordingly. On November 7, 1991, the ruler declared that an advisory council was about to see light, this time asserting that the felicitous event would occur "within a period of no more than a month or a month and a half." Finally, on 27 Sha'ban 1412H [March 1, 1992], i.e., nearly sixty years after 'Abdul 'Aziz's order and thirty years after Faysal's reform program to modernize the major laws of the country, King Fahd introduced three major laws: the Basic Law of Government, the Laws of the Provincial Councils, and the *Majlis Al-Shurah* itself.

The Consultative Council after 1992

Al Sa'ud rulers always insisted that the country's constitution was the Holy Qur'an, which meant that there was no need for a secular version, even if socio-economic circumstances changed dramatically during the past 1,430 years. Although the 1992 Basic Law of Government addressed key legal issues, including the all-too-important succession matter, it was not a constitution *per se*. In fact, according to the Basic Law's first article, the charter was defined as "God's Holy Book and His Prophet's Tradition," namely the Holy Qur'an and the *Sunnah*. Consequently, it was critical to understand what the Al Sa'ud actually meant to introduce with the new law, especially the evolving relationship towards *Shari'ah* that was inviolable.

For starters, Riyadh strengthened the 1744 alliance between the Al Sa'ud and the Al Shaykh, by emphasizing its commitment to the traditional role of the government-appointed clergy. The latter would be the nominal arbiters of constitutional matters, while the monarch would retain real authority in the affairs of state. By acquiescing to the ruler's orders on such issues, the religious establishment thus accepted that its authority, expressed through the Board of Senior *'Ulamah*, would fall under the king's full powers. Indeed, since the ruler appointed the clergymen to serve as senior *'Ulamah* on his council, it was a given that Al Sa'ud rule was preserved.

Moreover, even if the Council of Senior *'Ulamah* enjoyed a significant degree of autonomy in matters that were purely religious in nature, their acceptance of Al Sa'ud authority indicated that a clear separation of powers existed on all political matters. For as long as anyone cared to remember, religious and secular Sa'udis alike adhered to Al Sa'ud wishes and this was not about to change under the 1992 Basic Law. Likewise, and this was critical to underscore, Riyadh was absolutely clear that all "opinions," solicited or volunteered, were purely advisory, which signified that the monarch's powers could not be questioned by anyone. As discussed above, 'Abdul 'Aziz bin 'Abdul Rahman requested the advice of clergymen, but he was both the temporal as well as the spiritual leader of the community. In effect, he was the commander of the faithful, a tradition that his successors cherished and applied with gusto. Consequently, and "according to this long-standing interpretation, unless a royal decision openly contravene[d] Islamic principles or [was] clearly blasphemous (*kufr ba'wah*), all citizens [were] required to obey it even if they disagreed with it, lest they became guilty of *fitnah* or sedition."[23]

Still, what remained constant before and after 1992 was the religious basis of government, since the Qur'an underpinned all laws. Although religious extremists applauded this provision, concluding that it was a check on the absolute power of the state, in fact few searched for a separation of powers between religion and state. In the end, the final arbiter in all of these matters was the monarch himself, something that no one could even question. The Basic Law thus preserved the king's privileges along with those of his *'Ulamah*. Remarkably, this symbiotic relationship proved useful in the past, including when the ruler sought and received religious consent, as in the 1979 decree to storm the *Masjid al-Haram* in Makkah, or in 1990 when Riyadh sought and received a decree to invite Western forces to defend Sa'udi Arabia. It was hoped that the pattern would continue in the future, especially since under *Shari'ah*, constitutional rules were subjected to the interpretations of the *'Ulamah*, not any codified regulations. It must be emphasized that King 'Abdallah introduced minor changes to the 1992 Basic Law, by proposing that a constitutional court settle disputes between citizens and authorities, though his and the family's rights were further strengthened.

It may also be accurate to state that the 1992 modernization of the *Majlis Al-Shurah* updated what already existed by enhancing its frameworks, methods, and means. Through a better organization, and under a written law, the process injected a degree of efficiency that was not there earlier, even if each and every effort was made under duress. Needless to say, King Fahd faced a conundrum, as he realized that Sa'udi Arabia was confronted with dramatic socio-political changes and critical economic developments in practically every imaginable field. Under the weight of such pressures, and to simply keep pace with the demands and requirements of modern times, the time to open a new page in the long history of *Shurah* in Sa'udi Arabia was thus long overdue.

King Fahd launched the first four-year term of the Council with a speaker and 60 members, while an additional 30 members were added in the second term. By the time the third term rolled around, the council included a speaker and 120 members, which was raised to 150 members in the fourth term. As Article 13 stipulated that half of all members in every *Majlis* be renewed, a significant turnover occurred, with all appointees drawn from among the educated or leading members of the communities from which they hailed, bringing knowledge, experience, and competence to the assembly.[24] Though critics derided these appointments as little more than monarchical *takrims* [tributes], in reality the exercises allowed a bevy of trained minds to articulate ideas and thoughts, and raise key questions in a relatively safe environment. That too was part of the gradual reform efforts that the country entertained.

Majlis Al-*Shurah* under King 'Abdallah

With his accession to throne in 2005, the Custodian of the Two Holy Mosques 'Abdallah bin 'Abdul 'Aziz included the Council in his reform program, wishing to strengthen it even further. As a frequent participant in its annual opening sessions when he represented the ailing King Fahd, 'Abdallah delivered several speeches to set the agenda of the institution, especially during the third and fourth terms. He also surrounded himself with *Majlis* members, seeking their advice on every occasion, concluding that this elite group proved its worthiness to help set the state's long-term agenda on key areas. In short, 'Abdallah was not afraid of the *Majlis*, nor of its members organizing themselves into a separate government to challenge the Al Sa'ud. While such a conclusion may be obvious, it was not a given in the context of the conservative society, where the balance of powers was a delicate matter.

If the national dialogues set the tone for fundamental changes under King 'Abdallah, and several laws – but not the critical foreign policy concerns, budgetary questions, and sensitive legal matters – were debated within the *Majlis al-Shurah*, the concrete and natural next step was the introduction of electoral processes which was unhurriedly laid out starting in Riyadh on February 10, 2005, followed by the Eastern Province, as well as several southern provinces, in early March. Few expected these Municipal elections to produce the results they have, but when plebiscites were concluded in the West and North in April, key changes became rather obvious. Remarkably, but not surprisingly, the relatively well-attended elections (75% turnout for registered voters in Riyadh) proved far more popular than many anticipated. In fact, this was truly unprecedented for a conservative country like Sa'udi Arabia, where blasé attitudes dominated.

Nevertheless, conservative, pro-clerical candidates won most seats, illustrating the intricacies of democratization.[25] Although half of the 178 municipal posts would eventually be appointed by government subordinates, a significant precedent was established when ordinary Sa'udis flocked to polling stations, leading observers to foresee universal suffrage elections to the *Majlis al-Shurah* before long. Irrespective of future initiatives, Al Sa'ud leaders responded to public demands by accepting the idea of political participation, even if the process was not entirely transparent.[26]

It was also important to note that preparations for the municipal elections were not haphazard, as Riyadh managed a series of contradictory initiatives throughout 2004, which highlighted confusion in devising political, economic, and social reforms before 'Abdallah acceded to the throne. For example, the government authorized key dialogues, yet jailed a group of reformists in March 2004 without addressing any of their grievances. Strangely, reformists – not dissidents – called for the establishment of a constitutional monarchy that, at its very core, supported Al Sa'ud authority.[27] Whether the balancing act was necessary to maintain public order was debatable, although Riyadh was certainly emboldened by numerous arrests of *Jihadist* elements. In a clear message, the Cabinet issued a September 2004 ban on all State employees, including academics (given that all universities fell under State regulations), from questioning policies enunciated by the Al Sa'ud. Reforms would certainly be introduced, but only on a carefully laid out timetable, free of what certain officials perceived as foreign interferences. What these developments highlighted to then Heir Apparent 'Abdallah was the urgency to act as soon as it was practical. No wonder the new monarch embarked upon his multi-pronged reforms initiatives with a vengeance."[28]

The 2005 municipal elections

Two years before the first municipal elections were held in Sa'udi Arabia, the Council of Ministers decided "to broaden the participation of citizens in administrating local affairs by means of elections, and to revitalize Sa'udi Arabia's municipal councils in conformity with the ruling concerning municipalities and villages issued by Royal Decree in 1977, and to ensure that one half of the members of all municipal councils would henceforth be elected."[29] It took a few months to organize the actual procedures that would be followed, and municipal elections actually occurred in three stages beginning on February 10, 2005. By April 21, 2005, 608 candidates – out of a total of 9,330 hopefuls – were elected in 178 municipal councils, although not all of the 793,432 registered voters participated in the balloting. Inasmuch as women, all military personnel, as well as minors under the age of 21 were excluded from registration and voting, the actual pool of eligible voters was relatively small. Still, it would be a mistake to conclude that the limited number of voters hindered the overall legitimacy of the process, since the very idea of elections, municipal or otherwise, was a positive change for the kingdom. While domestic and regional developments pressed Riyadh to implement reform measures, including rapidly evolving dynamics within Sa'udi society, the primary impetus that accelerated the process was the monarch's desires to see increased participation. Al Sa'ud leaders, especially the ruler, were amply aware that socio-economic ties between the growing institutions of the state and the public needed urgent attention. They accepted the notion that Sa'udis were part of the global village and were clearly aware, even involved, in dramatic events that required the ruling family to respond in kind. No longer was it possible to wish for any political or even security breach to simply wither away. Just as security challenges necessitated specific responses, so did internal political dares, and the king for one was not shy about locking horns with the proverbial bull of confrontation. Therefore, Riyadh embarked on its multi-pronged reform initiatives, of which the municipal elections were one segment, alongside calls for national dialogues, the establishment of a journalists' association, the creation of a public organization for human rights, and several specific enhancements to the legal system. It was in this context that partial municipal elections were envisaged, whereby half of the members would be chosen by voters, while the other half would be appointed by Riyadh.

Registration process

Unaccustomed to voting, and given the limited authority and prerogatives that municipal councils held in their eyes, most Sa'udis were skeptical that elections were free or fair. Perhaps the exclusion of women, whose participation in *any* elections was not precluded *per se* by the 1977 electoral law, did not endear the public to these updated proposals. If there were apathy among the public, part of the reason was probably the result of the complex and largely unclear rationale for Riyadh's seeing to it that half of the municipal council members were duly appointed. Why have a two-tier system, many wondered, and would participation actually make a difference?[30] In the event, and even if most were reluctant to register and vote, not all of those who registered actually voted. In preparation for the February 10, 2005 balloting in Riyadh, for example, barely 65 percent of registered voters, or approximately two percent of the total population of Riyadh, actually participated.[31] Interestingly, this level of registration was not only visible in the capital, but throughout the country. In the governorates of the Riyadh area, where traditional family networks and tribal connections would mean higher registration percentages, less than 30 percent of eligible voters attended to their civic duties.[32] Observers focusing on confessional factors, specifically mining data from the Shi'ah communities in the Eastern Province, noticed a sharp difference. For example, the number of registered voters reached 46,600 in Al-Qatif, a small city inhabited by a Shi'ah majority. By contrast, the number of registered voters in Dammam, with a majority Sunni population, was noticeably lower: totaling only 45,400.[33] While similar statistics highlighted a strong mobilization and participation of Saudi Shi'ahs in the electoral process, with those in Qatif representing about 94 percent of all registered votes in the small city, the data from Dammam confirmed that Shi'ahs did not carry the day since they constitutes 4,600 of all registered voters, or less than 11 percent of the total. As in any elections, minority populations resorted to the ballot box to send as clear a message as was possible, in an entirely legal fashion. Given tensions throughout Hasah Province during the past few decades, it was normal to expect a solid political mobilization, even if electoral habits were poorly understood.

Electoral mobilization

Limited as they were, these first municipal elections were not only an important political step forward, but also an indication of future challenges to the monarchy. Indeed, educated candidates along with motivated religious contenders, as well as leading business leaders, were keenly interested in running for office. Al Sa'ud family members canvassed the scene and assessed the consequences of the experiment. Most concluded that citizens were anxious to add their voices to the process and could no longer be marginalized. In Riyadh, for example, 645 individuals competed for seven open seats, which meant that there were 92 candidates for each position. Even if some approached the exercise in jest, enjoying the trappings of colorful campaigns – election promotion tents were quite popular as were electoral posters vaunting their supposed merits – most candidates concluded that their drives were good opportunities to enhance reputations and acculturate the public on existing diversities. Perhaps some candidates appreciated the novelty and wished to enhance their social prestige although most were truly honored to run and took their initiatives seriously.

Not surprisingly, and despite the fact that an overwhelming majority of candidates running for office held university degrees, conservative religious candidates were victorious. Even in a large city like Riyadh, for example, traditional candidates gathered a majority of votes. Tribal and business candidates fared well too, but they conceded the majority to the pro-religious group.[34] This did not mean that clearly demarcated constituencies emerged that allowed for a categorization of the electorate, as inevitable overlaps emerged too, but it did emphasize that higher degrees, business skills, or other exceptional talents were all secondary considerations when it came to voters casting ballots for their preferred aspirants. Religious preferences were the dominant factors that assuaged concerns about untested and literally unknown personalities. When confronted with making critical choices on a person's capabilities or promises to serve his constituents, most voters fell back on what was unquestionably an unassailable credential: religious views. In other words, and no matter how serious, colorful, or entertaining many of the campaigns were, the results ushered in eclectic electoral alliances that were dominated by ideologically sound victors close to the religious community. In the words of a conservative voter: "What we finally decided upon, as a result of the Sheikhs' recommendations, was to vote for particular candidates because they are the best people to represent us. It is not as if the Sheikhs said, either vote for these seven candidates, or be disobedient to God and risk going to hell! We have based our votes on our own perceptions of our interests."[35] We listened to religious authorities, the vast majority seemed to say, and concluded that they represented the best interests of the nation. Although impossible to ascertain, it was also possible to surmise that Sa'udis viewed the religious establishment as a reliable balancer vis-à-vis the ruling family. Press reports alleged that leading clerics recommended specific candidates who, ostensibly, were not in cahoots with the establishment, which further indicated that participation in municipal elections was far more meaningful than the mere exercise to fill the 608 seats nationwide.[36] In fact, the Islamist victory surprised many, although not only because of the challenges associated with the *Sahwist* movement or because of foreign inspirations, but also because most voters were far more soothed by their programs than any businessman's platform or university professor's aggressive reform initiatives. While Sa'udis respected professionals and admired successful businessmen, few bought into unspecified ideological affiliations. Most considered religious affiliation to be far more valid, even as far as the Shi'ah constituents were concerned, because that "principle" fit in the political culture.

An assessment of the 2005 elections

If King 'Abdallah bin 'Abdul 'Aziz was vindicated that the citizens of Sa'udi Arabia viewed the first municipal elections as a significant step on his long reformist path, the 2005 voting identified six specific lessons both for authorities and the public at large.

First, despite the cacophony associated with nearly 10,000 candidates vying for 608 open seats – with an equal number of appointees to be designated by Riyadh – the campaigning and balloting process demonstrated that Sa'udi society was mature enough to undertake experiments in public political participation. It was no longer possible to opine that members of the conservative society were not able or ready to cast ballots. Likewise, authorities also demonstrated that they were capable to organize rather efficiently, the wherewithal associated with campaigning and balloting. The overwhelming majority of candidates took their participation seriously, while voters who bothered to register displayed awareness of, and avid involvement with, the process. Although women did not join in the voting, there were no legal reasons to deny their participation, even if Riyadh advanced several practical reasons to postpone their eventual involvement, including the dearth of segregated facilities that would help speed the process. Most registered voters wished to practice their political and civil rights in a proficient way. From the monarch on downward, everyone concluded that Sa'udis were at ease with electoral mechanisms, and wished to add their voices to the decision-making process. Just like the ruler exercised his "will to power" in so many areas, ordinary Sa'udis concluded that it was recommended that they too express their political will, albeit via the ballot box.

Second, the 2005 elections established the Sa'udi political consciousness as a sophisticated mechanism, away from classic hindrances like tribal influences.[37] While there was no denying that the "tribal vote" played a noticeable role in rural areas, this was a marginal phenomenon, given the highly urbanized environment that existed in the kingdom. Leading candidates who hailed from well-known tribes and who, by definition, were considered shoo-ins, sailed through if they vaunted their religious credentials. What this phenomenon underscored was the evolution of the kingdom's ideological nexus, which supplemented tribal influences in the rapidly changing political map, and which were no longer limited to narrow tribal interests. Most candidates understood that tribal affiliation alone was no longer sufficient to secure support.

The third lesson of the 2005 elections was the marginalization of the oldest and most widely practiced phenomenon in electoral politics: monetary inducements. To be sure, campaign tents that welcomed "constituents," glossy brochures that enticed voters and, perhaps, carefully solicited votes all required financial largesse, but Sa'udis separated votes from cash. Naturally, campaign expenditures played a role, and while several wealthy aspirants allocated significant sums to their respective drives, most of those candidates failed to secure victory. Whether this was further evidence of voters' maturity, or simply indicated that few of those who bothered to register needed financial inducements, was less important than the clear notion that there was little or no vote-buying. To their credit, Sa'udi voters recognized that candidates were, for the most part, wealthy and in no need for an office to accumulate wealth. Munificence, therefore, was not a consideration for candidates and even less for voters. Ironically, leading business candidates who failed to make the councils empathized with voters, since money alone was not sufficient to influence electoral campaigns that, in fact, were excellent lessons for future electoral experiments. The few businessmen who won secured seats when they aligned themselves with religious views, which received widespread support.

The fourth lesson was the major ideological divide that emerged in the kingdom between so-called conservatives and liberals. On the surface, the 2005 municipal elections highlighted the weakness of the liberal trend in society, especially when contrasted with inroads made by pro-religious conservative elements. Ironically, while liberal critics of the ruling family were at the forefront of reform advocacy for at least three decades – which was eminently understandable given the rapid modernization pace on which the country was embarked – ordinary Sa'udis were disillusioned with progressive rhetoric. More educated citizens were certainly perceived as being out of touch with the public at large and the latter's needs, whereas Islamists marketed their credentials as representatives of the downtrodden and marginalized. Clergymen in particular managed to dominate the public discourse, especially within the religious and educational spheres that, not surprisingly, were precisely where they held distinct advantages. Simply stated, so-called liberals could not successfully compete with Islamists outside of clerical and educational institutions, which altered the internal balance of power. Whether it was accurate to state that the 2005 results were an illustration of a liberal loss, or a conservative victory, were less important than an indication of a nascent trend, which hovered over the superior organizational skills displayed by religious candidates. Remarkably, so-called liberal candidates rested on their laurels, assuming that most voters would automatically support them because of their educational credentials. Their poor showing stemmed from overconfidence, perhaps even a degree of arrogance, which separated them from ordinary masses. Like all societies, Sa'udis were wary of elitist perspectives, even if an overwhelming majority respected those who gained advanced degrees.

The fifth lesson that stood out was the awareness that future municipal elections would further promote democratic values within society through increased participation of probable voters. Indeed, the 2005 municipal elections led to a dynamic political and social situation, and represented a true beginning for the reform process led by the monarch. Naturally, not all Sa'udis, including members of the ruling family, were keen on such progress. Still, Riyadh accepted that its reform programs developed the community to cope with new developments on both the national and international scenes. Riyadh took note that nearly one million people voted to elect half the members of various councils.

The sixth and final lesson of the 2005 municipal elections was the painstaking "democratization" process, although the use of the word did not indicate the advent of Jeffersonian democracy to Sa'udi Arabia. Still, these first "elections" were essential building blocks in the long-term creation of institutions that would be representative in every meaning of the term. Mere elections did not mean that the kingdom was now a democracy though the exercise fortified the legal definition. A new order was under way and this first step was a clear example of future activities as Riyadh enlarged the local and, perhaps, the national decision-making processes.

The 2009 (2011) municipal elections

The second municipal elections were technically scheduled for 2009, four years after the 2005 voting, when all citizens were expected to exercise their civic duties. Even women, who were excluded in 2005, anticipated the right to participate.[38] As it happened, and without fanfare, the 2009 balloting was postponed although no formal reasons were advanced. Speculation around the monarch's concerns with an even larger religious presence filled online pages although this could not be verified. Others opined that the semi-elected councils, which turned out to be less than stellar, disappointed the Al Sa'ud. According to these interpretations, members of the ruling family were keen to see active participation, but resigned themselves to accepting tangential initiatives that failed to add value. Conversely, some members of the 2005 class apparently resigned in disgust, after most concluded that state authorities were not interested in alternative perspectives.[39] By May 2009, authorities telegraphed their desires to postpone the elections for a few years, ostensibly to allow for an in-depth evaluation. Press reports insinuated that leading writers and political analysts agreed with the decision to postpone elections for at least two years, allegedly because a short delay would actually promote democratic values among members of society, and over time, encourage probable voters to step up to the proverbial plate. A few even suggested that a postponement would do away with the two-tier system. For Nayif Al Shammari, a professor of political science, after the deferment "there [was] no justification ... to elect half the members and appoint the other half."[40] "The price for this postponement must be convincing to the majority of the Sa'udi people and observers abroad through the election of all members of the next municipal councils," he noted. Others rejected the delay. Hatoon Al Fasi, an assistant professor of women's history at King Sa'ud University opined that the adjournment "in a reform process that we were supposed to believe really began when we started this process of elections," which raised doubts about the entire reform practices initiated by the monarch.[41]

In March 2011, 'Abdul Rahman al-Dahmash, the Electoral Commission Chairman, announced plans to hold municipal elections starting on April 23, 2011, after a two-year delay. Importantly, the Commission was set-up under the orders of the Municipal and Rural Affairs Minister, Prince Mansour bin Mit'ab, to supervise elections in all parts of the kingdom and remove obstacles without specifying what those were.[42] Still, the April balloting was postponed once again to September 22, 2011, but when officials realized that this date fell a day before the National Day, celebrated on September 23 to mark the kingdom's unification by 'Abdul 'Aziz, 'Abdul Rahman al-Dahmash postponed it by another week to September 29, 2011.[43] Whether irregularities

Political participation and municipal elections 129

were noticed to recommend a deferment from April to September, or whether the registration process was unsatisfactory, was impossible to determine. Suffice it to say that the voter registration stage was less than suitable, which prompted Riyadh to leave open the declaration of eligible candidacies beyond the originally planned May 28 through June 2 period by several weeks.

Interestingly, the updated process was set to incorporate some reforms to the previous electoral system, including the introduction of a single voting system, which would allow the electorate to cast their ballots for a single candidate from an electoral list; increase the number of municipal councils across the country from 179 to 258; and extend the term for municipal councilors from 4 to 6 years.[44] Moreover, because the municipality councils' mission and objectives were not clarified in 2005, which presumably disappointed many, Riyadh made an effort to explain what councilors were supposed to do. Sa'udi officials apparently got the message, and wished to provide voters with a deeper appreciation of the roles and tasks of the municipality councils, including councilors' responsibilities to set "forth a solid building regulation and [create] a future urban strategy."[45]

Noticeably, and despite the fact that article 1(6) of Ministerial Resolution 38396 on municipality elections entitled all citizens to cast their votes and run in municipal elections, authorities excluded female voters and candidates to exercise this right. Nevertheless, members of the *Majlis al-Shurah* voted 81 to 37 to grant suffrage to women of the kingdom, but not in the coming elections in September 2011.[46] Women were asked to wait at least another four years, for the next round of elections expected in 2015, though only if the monarch agreed to accept the *Shurah* Council recommendation.

When Sa'udi women were denied the right to vote in 2005, it was argued that only a few women had identity cards, which were essential for obtaining voting cards. This logical obstacle was supposed to be alleviated by 2009, as women were encouraged to apply for and receive, separate identity cards and/or passports. In fact, Riyadh pushed the issuance of separate papers for security reasons, and while this may have been one of the reasons (or explanations) to extend the term of the municipal councils by two years, it was difficult to understand why authorities were "not ready" for women to cast their votes in 2011. In the event, many Sa'udi women registered to vent their frustration with the system, while others got behind the wheel to further make their points. In June 2011, that is after the *Majlis al-Shurah* voted to grant suffrage to women, more than 60 Sa'udi intellectuals and activists – both men and women – called for a boycott of the September 29, 2011 ballot, partly because municipal council elections excluded women.[47]

Conclusion: consequences of legislative changes for the monarchy

Crucial steps were taken by the Al Sa'ud to enhance the first democratic institutions emerging in the kingdom. While these were in the making for several decades, King 'Abdallah bin 'Abdul 'Aziz set the tone for significant changes, after his accession to the throne in 2005. Given the nature of the monarchy, a conservative regime that believed in gradual reforms, the practices and values would not, indeed could not, be altered as fast as many wished. Still, dramatic transformations at all levels of society were noticeable, including at the *Majlis al-Shurah* stage and in terms of the first municipal elections, warts and all. What these transformations encompassed were nothing short of revolutionary, especially as a means to finally end inherent contradictions between what entrenched bureaucratic interests imposed on the country, and the inevitable democratization process that the monarch embarked upon. It was critical to stress that the democratization process was not intended, nor could it logically, replace the monarchy. Rather, for King 'Abdallah, it was meant to strengthen the monarchy and ensure Al Sa'ud rule. Therefore, *Majlis al-Shurah* debates and municipal elections filled key posts, which placed national and local administrations under the control and supervision of the ruling family. Although municipal elections enhanced voter rights, the fact that half of the councilmen were still appointed indicated that the process would be gradual and, perhaps, stretched over several years.

Still, what the monarch and senior members of the government wanted was to empower local authorities to assume additional decision-making burdens, especially as far as municipal budgets were concerned, to better serve local needs. If, for example, the 'Ar'ar Municipality wished to fund specific infrastructure projects, or allocate special services to its residents, or even negotiate land allotments, those decisions were best made at the local level. Neither the Ministry of the Interior nor the Ministry of Municipal and Rural Affairs were truly equipped to look after minute details across the vast country. Moreover, and while the Al Sa'ud managed as well as possible over the decades, growing demands necessitated a careful enhancement of the process. If the mechanism in place or its amended successors enhanced political participation and empowered citizens, the ruler was satisfied, as long as the institution of the monarchy was preserved. There was still the pesky problem of universal suffrage, although the *Majlis al-Shurah* recommendation was on the monarch's desk, and chances were good that 'Abdallah bin 'Abdul 'Aziz would eventually grant this right to Sa'udi women. It remained to be determined whether the sophisticated ruler would take the bold initiative soon, along an expansion of additional elections to encompass regional councils as well as the *Shurah* Council. Logic dictated that it was only a matter of time before local, regional, and national elected institutions would receive legislative and supervisory authorities to better serve the people of Sa'udi Arabia, when such a distance was already covered.

4 Political reforms and the succession dilemma

Modern Sa'udi Arabia exists because the ruling Al Sa'ud family forged together enduring tribal alliances that withstood the test of time.[1] Although this analysis is based on a corpus of contemporary works on the kingdom, a recent study by Toby Jones posits that Sa'udi Arabia "was founded on conquest and violence" and, even worse, while "Saudi leaders hoped and then subsequently claimed it was the case, Islam was not a unifying force ... [because] the kingdom was not culturally or religiously homogeneous."[2] For Jones, the kingdom was little more than a conglomerate of essentially incompatible tribes, which were tamed and held together by the sword. Regrettably, Jones saw nothing that united Sa'udis, although any visitor to the kingdom could easily attest to rising nationalism. Even worse, according to Jones, the founder allegedly displayed little understanding of what concerned or ailed the people he and his family ruled, which did not pass socio-political muster. Few readers will be satisfied with this thesis – that the application of violence as a form of coherent governance before the reign of oil or since – defined the kingdom. To be sure, *Shari'ah* is applied, but few ought to dismiss the Al Sa'ud's political shrewdness to unite the many divergent groups, secular and religious, which make up the country. The Al Sa'ud were and are not ignorant of the peninsula's wider realities, though it was Arabism and Islam – the twin pillars of Sa'udi ideology – that guaranteed their power and assured their longevity.

While ruling family politics in the kingdom shared many characteristics with other hereditary monarchies, Sa'udi Arabia stood alone in a number of aspects. First, the family's sheer size and complexity, in terms of its internal structure and composition as well as its connections to Sa'udi society, made the Sa'udi political system markedly different from other past and present monarchies.[3] In addition, family politics developed in the context of the vast wealth and profound transformations that have altered the face of Sa'udi Arabia, perhaps permanently. Thus, it was on such premises that family politics ought to be analyzed, with an emphasis on determining the interplay between politics and policy on the one hand, and the balance between alliances and opposition forces within the family on the other. These implications for Sa'udi behavior have a direct bearing on political stability and sensitive succession questions.

Nearly seven years into his reign, King 'Abdallah bin 'Abdul 'Aziz ushered in fundamental changes in the succession mechanism that defined Sa'udi political life, even if preferred procedures were still under development.[4] While a growing number of ordinary citizens resented that they had little or nothing no say in epochal family matters that clearly affected their lives, and while disgruntled elements called for a transformation of the kingdom into a constitutional monarchy, the vast majority of Sa'udis supported the ruling family. It would be a mistake to assume that Sa'udis extended their unabashed defense of the Al Sa'ud as nothing more than rewards for financial largesse. In fact, contemporary Sa'udi rulers earned their popular allegiances (*bay'ahs*), and continued to be accountable to key constituencies, by "modernizing" the system that aspired to be as transparent as a monarchy could be, while meeting tribal and customary obligations. In 2012, and despite the "family enterprise" epithet that presumably derives from old-fashioned ways in which they conducted their national business, the Al Sa'ud held the levers of power. Unlike their European counterparts, whose monarchical contributions were long exhausted, the agile if aging Sa'udi ruling family managed the actual workings of this system with relative gusto.[5] What distinguished the Al Sa'ud from any European counterpart family was the full and complete rejection of the notion that the monarch enjoyed divine privileges, or that he ruled in God's name, or even benefited from non-earthly rights. In fact, the Al Sa'ud knew that theirs was rule by consensus, a compact within traditional settings, tribal in its norms, and family oriented at its most detailed levels.[6]

Although the most senior princes around King 'Abdallah, like the monarch himself, were well advanced in age, seniority did not seem to slow the ruler down, who was eager to forge ahead with his reforms in the succession process, too. A pious and reserved man, the king deserves immense credit for how he tackled the many changes that have yet to be tested, but whose necessity could no longer be ignored. Though a monarch since 2005, 'Abdallah served as Heir Apparent for 23 years before ascending the throne, ten of which were marked by skillful management of Al Sa'ud affairs as regent, when Fahd bin 'Abdul 'Aziz was incapacitated.

Critics of the octogenarian monarch recognized his promotion of social reforms, but insisted that whatever political changes were introduced were cosmetic, and largely inconsequential.[7] Royal rule, many posited, remained as absolute as ever. Inasmuch as monarchical governance, by its very definition, could not be equivalent to any Jeffersonian style democratization process, such disparagement was nothing more than journalistic entertainment. It was more accurate to criticize the Al Sa'ud – and, for that matter, all modern monarchies – for being inefficient or unpredictable, though few ought to anticipate the kind of transparency that presumably existed in practicing or aspiring democracies. In the Sa'udi case, it may be more precise to conclude that the tested and relatively efficient succession mechanism, which functioned after 1953, was due a serious overhaul. That was precisely what King 'Abdallah's initiatives resembled even if – and it was important to highlight this point – its basic provisos were yet to be tested. Remarkably, many factors associated with the relatively smooth succession mechanism came into play once again in March 2009, when the ruler appointed his half-brother, Prince Nayif bin 'Abdul 'Aziz, as his Second Deputy Prime Minister. Both the appointment, as well as the candidate, came as something of a surprise, as few observers anticipated such a critical elevation for the ultra-conservative Minister of Interior. In fact, even if one pessimistic observer concluded that Nayif was bidding for the Sa'udi throne, most feared that the interior minister's updated status could potentially limit the many reforms introduced by the monarch since 2005.[8] Although few anticipated permanent schisms within the establishment, Nayif harbored a reputation for toughness, which may ironically have facilitated 'Abdallah's task with more conservative voices. Still, even that was pure speculation, since no outsider could authoritatively predict any particular outcome. What may be possible to anticipate, however, is the fact that Sa'udi Arabia was very much embarked on an accelerated pace for economic and social transformations, which would probably introduce epochal changes over the course of the next few years. As the country adapted to new domestic and regional dynamics, what were the most likely scenarios for succession in Sa'udi Arabia, and how could Nayif's appointment, and death in 2012, affect family stability? Was this latest selection a further 'Abdallah refinement of the system and would it add value to the Al Sa'ud?

This chapter proposes to assess the post-2005 reforms that may well alter the way future Sa'udi kings are chosen, by examining the key changes that were introduced after 2005. Was the political system in Riyadh anomalous in the modern world, even by monarchical standards, and were Sa'udis despondent that future successions would be as chaotic as several previous episodes? A corollary aim of what follows is to separate the wheat from the chaff when so many doomsday scenarios abound concerning the Al Sa'ud and their alleged demise.[9]

'Abdallah bin 'Abdul 'Aziz Al Sa'ud and the 1992 edict

'Abdallah bin 'Abdul 'Aziz became Heir Apparent in 1982 when Fahd bin 'Abdul 'Aziz acceded to the Sa'udi rulership. True to traditional arrangements, the two men were accepted by the majority, as 'Abdallah pledged his *bay'ah* (oath of allegiance) by declaring: "God has compensated [Sa'udi Arabia] well in His Majesty the great King Fahd," and called on Sa'udis to "unite [their] efforts and grow together, government and people, behind my lord, His Majesty King Fahd."[10] For the remainder of the 1980s, Fahd and 'Abdallah shared governing responsibilities, the former concentrating primarily on international concerns and the latter on regional, especially Arab, affairs. Agreements on broad international concerns notwithstanding, Fahd and 'Abdallah saw things differently, especially on critical family responsibilities as to who was to assume governance burdens. Towards that end, King Fahd's most important and lasting decree came on March 1, 1992, when the monarch issued several key documents, including the *Basic Law of Government*, the statutes governing the newly created *Majlis al-Shurah* [Consultative Council], and the *Law of the Provinces*.[11] While observers of the kingdom were surprised by the tone of these reforms, skepticism pervaded, allegedly because the Al Sa'ud could not possibly be serious in introducing such epochal changes.[12]

King Fahd's decrees ushered in a new period because an institutionalization process was clearly established. Even if the monarch's decisions were propelled by the rising tide of internal opposition, as well as the repercussions of the War for Kuwait that altered every political calculation in most regional capitals, significant and permanent changes were under way on the home front. Indeed, the second section of the Basic Law was of the greatest interest, "and proved to be a bombshell both within and outside the Al Saud."[13] In fact, just two sub-sections of the second chapter contained the most controversial, and undefined, lines. Article 5, Section b, states that "rulers of the country shall be from amongst the sons of the founder, King 'Abdul 'Aziz bin 'Abdul Rahman Al Sa'ud, and their descendants," and that "the most upright among them shall receive allegiance according to the Holy Qur'an and the Sunnah of the Prophet (Peace be upon him)" (see Appendix 5).[14] The last line, imposing a qualification – "the most upright" – was telling. One interpretation was that seniority was no longer the primary qualification for succession and that other considerations, including being upstanding, strengthened a candidate's eligibility. Another interpretation alluded to the fact that all direct descendants of the founder, that is grandsons as well as sons, were now eligible to rule the kingdom. Just as enigmatically, Article 5, Section c, further stated, "the King shall choose the Heir Apparent and relieve him by a Royal Decree." Without a doubt, this last line threatened the entire balance of power that existed in the country, foreshadowing the authority of then Heir Apparent 'Abdallah bin 'Abdul 'Aziz.

Fahd's bold decree – which was the law – that a Sa'udi monarch could name and remove his Heir Apparent, and that the latter would not automatically succeed, established several new criteria for succession. In fact, the 1992 edict granted a ruler the prerogative to choose and withdraw approval of an Heir Apparent, as an entirely legal proposition. Moreover, it further acknowledged that the more than sixty grandsons of 'Abdul 'Aziz were now legitimate claimants to the throne. By declaring that successors could be chosen from the most suitable of 'Abdul 'Aziz's progeny, Fahd implied that 'Abdallah was not necessarily the presumed heir to the throne. Finally, the decision to include grandsons into the process proved that some senior members were indeed committed to the younger generation. This was the turning point in the succession issue, for the decree clearly broke away from time-tested and tribally favored norms.

At the time these edicts were under preparation and about to be announced, 'Abdallah "was said to have been 'outraged,' that his position ... was defined as being at the whim of King Fahd, rather than as his right as the next in line."[15] Even if 'Abdallah was advanced in age, he was in good health and certainly considered himself to be eminently qualified for the post. Aware that such a posture might create a permanent wedge between him and his Heir Apparent, the monarch quickly issued another decree on March 1, 1992, confirming Heir Apparent 'Abdallah's safe position, including his command of the National Guard.[16] Defense Minister Sultan bin 'Abdul 'Aziz, for his part, was apparently equally concerned. After several years as Second Deputy Prime Minister, and presumed heir to the Heir Apparent, Sultan was placed in a position that would require him to lobby much harder within the family to step up the succession ladder. Moreover, he would have – at least theoretically – faced stiff competition from some of his younger brothers, sons, and nephews. Undeniably, after 1992, nothing prevented the ruling family from settling on a younger son or grandson of 'Abdul 'Aziz, to provide both continuity and change. Given that the succession line was not agreed to, and while it moved from brother to brother through the sons of the founder, the 1992 edict further ensured that fundamental political changes were indeed acceptable.[17]

As fate would dictate, and debilitated by disease, Fahd entrusted the Al Sa'ud as well as the kingdom's public custodianship to Heir Apparent 'Abdallah in 1995, who husbanded all of the country's needs with utmost care. Fahd bin 'Abdul 'Aziz passed away on August 1, 2005 at the age of 84 after a long illness. Senior family members held an urgent conclave and almost immediately appointed 'Abdallah to succeed his brother. In turn, the new ruler appointed the Second Deputy Prime Minister Sultan, as his designated heir. As expected, the fifth Al Sa'ud succession since the country's formal founding in 1932, was assured, even if critics opined that "this tribal way of succession [wa]s no way to run a modern country, let alone one with the largest known reserves of oil".[18] Within hours, senior Al Sa'ud leaders, followed by thousands of Sa'udis, pledged their oath of allegiance to 'Abdallah and Sultan. As discussed below, and though overtaken by a new deliberative body empowered to determine an Al Sa'ud successor, it would be a mistake to conclude that the 1992 edict was now obsolete. A more accurate assessment, developed below, may well be that this decree protected a specific royal authority even better than originally intended.

'Abdallah after 2005

When King Fahd passed away, his successor behaved according to a carefully choreographed script, earning oaths of allegiance galore. This *bay'ah* was not a foregone conclusion as many anticipated potential problems between the two senior most princes in the kingdom. In the event, it was duly delivered, probably because of the former ruler's 1992 edict, as well as 'Abdallah's demonstrated skills during his regency after 1995. 'Abdallah became king on August 1, 2005, but, as stated above, he was already, for all practical purposes, ruler since a stroke incapacitated the ailing monarch in 1995. Fahd reigned, but 'Abdallah governed the country with the full consent of senior family members who appreciated that disease prevented the king from making any lasting decisions. Sadly, King Fahd's carefully orchestrated public appearances confirmed what most could see for themselves, that the ruler was too sick to assume the mantle of power. To his immense credit, which illustrated a side of his character, 'Abdallah protected his brother's dignity by shielding Fahd from public ridicule, and avoiding inevitable gaffes that resulted from choreographed presentations where an inaudible monarch uttered his approval (or disapproval), even when few could understand him. These audiences were not the brightest moments in contemporary Sa'udi affairs, and 'Abdallah was furious when his ailing brother was used to make a futile point. Still, he respected traditions, and accepted his fate even if tensions within the ruling family ran high.

A week after acceding to the throne in 2005, 'Abdallah bin 'Abdul 'Aziz issued a blank pardon to 'Abdallah al-Hamed, Matruk al-Faleh and 'Ali al-Dumayni, who were earlier sentenced to jail terms.[19] It may be worth recalling that the three men were tried for seeking the establishment of a constitutional monarchy, and they were condemned to jail terms by a court that found them guilty of "stirring up sedition and disobeying the ruler." Yet, by issuing blanket pardons, 'Abdallah reflected both magnanimity as well as strength of character. The decision was as clear an expression of leadership as could be mustered especially after withholding his innermost sentiments for over a decade. Coming a week within his own accession, the choice spoke volumes, as the new ruler quickly stamped his political style that, presumably, was more transparent and less egregious. A reformist 'Abdallah could not do as he pleased when he was heir apparent. As an absolute monarch, however, he was no longer constrained by Article 5 of the Basic Law, which limited the Heir Apparent to "duties delegated to him by the King."[20] 'Abdallah could now *do as he pleased* and one of his first decrees sent a crystal clear message. He even received al-Dumayni and al-Faleh to accept their *bay'ah* and, perhaps, convey the notion that not all intellectual dissent was harmful to the Al Sa'ud.[21]

By acting the way he did, and as quickly as he did, he further set the tone for his preferences. It may thus be accurate to state that the ruler's decision to embark on a slew of changes pleased some and worried others. Moreover, and this is worth underlining, though the blanket pardons extended to several dissidents, everyone was surprised by the decision. Remarkably, these orders were quickly followed by an unprecedented decision to consult with intellectuals, several of whom had the audacity to call for the establishment of a constitutional monarchy. The king was on the march to further strengthen Sa'udi society. He was determined to introduce lasting reforms that would serve the family. By extension, and as important, 'Abdallah was resolute in his belief that the pool of intrinsic talent must be tapped to serve the kingdom. Of course, this did not mean that the new ruler was operating out of a carefully drafted blueprint that "crossed every t and dotted every i," but that 'Abdallah followed his instincts to act expeditiously.

'Abdallah bin 'Abdul 'Aziz and succession

In the few years since his accession, 'Abdallah made dramatic alterations to the way future monarchs would be chosen for Sa'udi Arabia, and which potentially threatened to upset the family's well-earned reputation for internal balance. In October 2006, he decreed that a committee of princes will vote on the eligibility of future generations of kings and heirs, to better formalize the succession process. Although the contemplated system was not stated to come into effect until the then Heir Apparent – Sultan bin 'Abdul 'Aziz – acceded to rulership, the mere fact that a formal committee was envisioned for the process was telling. It was King 'Abdallah's first major decision regarding succession and it was an epochal moment in the contemporary annals of Al Sa'ud affairs.

With the new committee named *Hay'at al-Bay'ah* [Allegiance Commission], 'Abdallah underscored the necessity to pledge allegiance to the Al Sa'ud, as the name clearly implied.[22] Although this new mechanism inspired observers to conclude that this was vintage 'Abdallah – that is, seeking allegiance to the Al Sa'ud – in reality the new law was nothing more than a new Succession Law.[23] In fact, the confusion arose because one pledged allegiance to something or someone, whereas this new law introduced 'Abdallah's long anticipated reforms to the kingdom's succession mechanism. With 25 articles defining its purposes, the "Allegiance Law of Succession" replaced the informal family gathering that selected and approved successors, though secret deliberations were not excluded.[24] The Commission, whose size was not initially announced, would be chaired by the oldest surviving son of the founder and include sons and grandsons of 'Abdul 'Aziz bin 'Abdul Rahman. This development was an innovation because it now included specific members of the second generation, even if the names of Commission members were not made public at first. Not surprisingly, the Commission was called to follow strict regulations contained in the Basic Law, which the new decree amended without canceling it.

Under the previous system, the monarch enjoyed a full prerogative to name and dismiss his Heir Apparent, although such decisions were almost always debated within inner family circles. Though the key provisions in the 1992 decree were not abolished, members of the Commission were empowered to have a say in the appointment of an heir in the new structure, even when recommended (or suggested) by the monarch. Though few appreciated its repercussions at the time, Prince Nayif's appointment as Second Deputy Prime Minister in March 2009 (see below), clarified what role(s) this commission may be called upon to play. If members rejected a nominated heir, or called for an alternative vote for one of three leaders designated by the ruler, all bets were off as far as an enthronement was concerned. Moreover, the appointment of a new heir was further placed within a strict timetable – within 30 days of the accession of a new monarch – even if few anticipated lengthy deliberations given the secret nature of all decision-making mechanisms.

To prevent nasty surprises, 'Abdallah foresaw the need for a *Transitory Ruling Council* composed of five members of the institution, which would assume responsibilities for state affairs for a maximum period of one week, if neither the monarch nor his heir were fit to rule. This idea was amply relevant given the advanced ages of the current leadership and the potential for disagreements within the Al Sa'ud. Importantly, the *Transitory Ruling Council* would not enjoy prerogatives affecting state institutions, such as dissolving the government or the country's self-styled Consultative Council, the *Majlis al-Shurah*, nor would it be allowed to amend the Basic Law or any laws that were linked to the system of rulership. In other words, 'Abdallah ensured that no one outside the family would contemplate recommending non-Al Sa'ud names for the post, which was a specifically defined and strictly protected entitlement. Moreover, by institutionalizing the process, the ruler etched in stone what was also largely guaranteed, namely that only sons and grandsons of 'Abdul 'Aziz would accede to the Sa'udi throne. Not only was this a turning point for Riyadh but, equally revelatory, it placed 'Abdallah's stamp on succession matters by actually strengthening the ruling family.

With this majestic imprimatur, 'Abdallah reaffirmed his will to power on October 8, 2007 when an 18-article decree provided by-laws to the 2006 Succession edict.[25] Although the 25-article "Allegiance Law of Succession" replaced the informal family gathering that selected and approved successors, it lacked critical operational features, which was probably intentional. In a surprise move, 'Abdullah addressed his brothers, sons, and nephews in a remarkable talk that centered on service to the nation and to Islam. He reiterated his belief that the Al Sa'ud ruling family was of the "nation and the people are from us, and we all share the honor of belonging to this country."[26] This theme was periodically strengthened by declarations that emphasized how the vast majority of tribes or families in the kingdom were founding partners of the Al Sa'ud or, at least, played critical roles in strengthening the family's legitimacy. Salman bin 'Abdul 'Aziz, the Governor of Riyadh and a leader well placed to offer such assessments, underscored this relationship as late as Spring 2011 in Madinah, at a time when the entire Arab world lived through an epochal revival that raised existential questions pertaining to authority.[27]

Still, the October 8, 2007 discourse was spontaneous, reminiscent of impromptu talks that the late King Faysal bin 'Abd al-'Aziz was famous for, as 'Abdallah called on the *'Ulamah* "of wisdom, thought and creed" to rally around the throne since the Al Sa'ud respected them. He further urged his brothers, sons and nephews "to become God fearing people and to enhance the pillars of justice, to close ranks, settle differences through discussion and dialogue, and never allow anyone to interfere in the family's affairs."[28] Most in attendance were stunned at this level of attention in preliminary remarks and anticipated a major declaration. 'Abdallah did not disappoint. Speaking to all surviving sons of the country's founder, 'Abdul 'Aziz bin 'Abd al-Rahman, who were led in the *Majlis* by Prince Mish'al, Heir Apparent Sultan, as well as dozens of grandsons, the monarch issued a breathtaking order that identified the membership of his Allegiance Commission. The official group encompassed every son of the founder or, in case of death, a single grandson chosen by the sub-branch. Remarkably, the royal decree placed 35 specific names around the decision-making table where the next ruler was to be chosen[29] [see Table 4.1].

Although the monarch and his Heir Apparent were naturally absent from this list, their respective eldest sons were part of the group, which was divided more or less evenly between sons (16) and grandsons (19) in 2007. After Fawwaz bin 'Abdul 'Aziz died on July 22, 2008 in Paris, France, the balance was 15 sons and 19 grandsons, although this number fluctuated with other changes too.[30] In late 2011, and because of adjustments, the balance stood at

Table 4.1 Original "Allegiance Commission" Membership (2007)

1	Mish'al bin 'Abdul 'Aziz Al Sa'ud
2	'Abdul Rahman bin 'Abdul 'Aziz Al Sa'ud
3	Mit'ab bin 'Abdul 'Aziz Al Sa'ud
4	Talal bin 'Abdul 'Aziz Al Sa'ud*
5	Badr bin 'Abdul 'Aziz Al Sa'ud
6	Turki bin 'Abdul 'Aziz Al Sa'ud
7	Nayif bin 'Abdul 'Aziz Al Sa'ud
8	Fawwaz bin 'Abdul 'Aziz Al Sa'ud
9	Salman bin 'Abdul 'Aziz Al Sa'ud
10	Mamduh bin Abdul 'Aziz Al Sa'ud
11	'Abdul-Ilah bin 'Abdul 'Aziz Al Sa'ud
12	Sattam bin 'Abdul 'Aziz Al Sa'ud
13	Ahmad bin 'Abdul 'Aziz Al Sa'ud
14	Mashhur bin 'Abdul 'Aziz Al Sa'ud
15	Hadhlul bin 'Abdul 'Aziz Al Sa'ud
16	Miqrin bin 'Abdul 'Aziz Al Sa'ud
17	*Muhammad bin Sa'ud bin 'Abdul 'Aziz Al Sa'ud*
18	*Khalid bin Faysal bin 'Abdul 'Aziz Al Sa'ud*
19	*Muhammad bin Sa'ad bin 'Abdul 'Aziz Al Sa'ud*
20	*Turki bin Faysal bin Turki (the first) bin 'Abdul 'Aziz Al Sa'ud*
21	*Muhammad bin Nasir bin 'Abdul 'Aziz Al Sa'ud*
22	*Faysal bin Bandar bin 'Abdul 'Aziz Al Sa'ud*
23	*Sa'ud bin 'Abdul-Muhsin bin 'Abdul 'Aziz Al Sa'ud*
24	*Muhammad bin Fahd bin 'Abdul 'Aziz Al Sa'ud*
25	*Khalid bin Sultan bin 'Abdul 'Aziz Al Sa'ud*
26	*Talal bin Mansur bin 'Abdul 'Aziz Al Sa'ud*
27	*Khalid bin 'Abdullah bin 'Abdul 'Aziz Al Sa'ud*
28	*Muhammad bin Mish'ari bin 'Abdul 'Aziz Al Sa'ud*
29	*Faysal bin Khalid bin 'Abdul 'Aziz Al Sa'ud*
30	*Badr bin Muhammad bin 'Abdul 'Aziz Al Sa'ud*
31	*Faysal bin Thamir bin 'Abdul 'Aziz Al Sa'ud*
32	*Mish'al bin Majid bin 'Abdul 'Aziz Al Sa'ud*
33	*'Abdallah bin Musa'id bin 'Abdul 'Aziz Al Sa'ud*
34	*Faysal bin 'Abdul-Majid bin 'Abdul 'Aziz Al Sa'ud*
35	*'Abdul 'Aziz bin Nawwaf bin 'Abdul 'Aziz Al Sa'ud*

Note: Grandsons are in italics; * Prince Talal resigned from the Commission on 16 November 2011.
Source: "King 'Abdallah Addresses Princes," Riyadh: Saudi Press Agency, 10 December 2007.

14 sons and 19 grandsons, for a total of 33 members.[31] All vowed before the ruler, pledging to God "Almighty to remain loyal to Religion, King and Country, not to divulge any of the state's secrets, to preserve its interests and systems, to work for the unity of the ruling family as well as the national unity, and to perform duties sincerely, honestly and justly."[32] The Sa'udi monarch named Mish'al bin 'Abdul 'Aziz, a former deputy Defense Minister and Governor of Makkah, chairman of the commission to select future kings and heirs apparent.[33] Gone was the closed-room conclave between a handful of senior men, and though it took more than a full year between the initial announcement on October 7, 2007 and when the body was in fact formed and its members appointed, it was nevertheless a major development as it regulated the super-sensitive succession question upon the death of every king. Interestingly, 'Abdallah issued the institution's by-laws, which explained how the process would actually work, before choosing its members, perhaps to allow for the idea to sink in.[34] Yet, the reliance on a growing number of grandsons confirmed that an institutionalization process was underway because members of this second generation lacked their predecessors' necessary experience.

Thereafter, upon the death of a monarch, the Commission was expected to quickly gather to chose a ruler and confirm the latter's Heir Apparent, who must be chosen within ten days of the ruler's accession to the throne. Failure to do so would mean accepting the Commission's alternative choice. Though the statute further confirmed that the king must approve Commission decisions, it was not clear what procedures would be followed if the sitting monarch contested Commission selections. This major stumbling block notwithstanding, King 'Abdallah was slowly placing his own mark on the Sa'udi monarchy through the refinement of the Allegiance Law. Although the powers of the monarch were not questioned in this regulation, they illustrated the ruler's meticulous approach and his intrinsic preferences, which were certainly different from those promulgated by his predecessor.

In fact, and this was worth underscoring, while secret deliberations were not excluded in this vision, the Commission was now equipped with clear regulations to rationalize the succession procedure. Interestingly, the king retained his 1992-granted right to dismiss his heir, but gently sidelined the family council that was amalgamated in the new Commission.

Composition of the Commission

As stated above, Article 1 of the Allegiance Commission limited membership to the sons of the founder, King 'Abdul 'Aziz bin 'Abdul Rahman Al Sa'ud or, in cases of death or incapacity, a chosen successor who would be appointed by the family of the son concerned. Because the ruler and his Heir Apparent were not part of the Commission, respective sons were designated, which was an unclear proposition in 2006. This lacuna in the nomination process was addressed when the 2007 Bylaws were published. According to the latest regulations [Article 1–1a],

> The King asks the sons of the deceased or unable, who have reached the age of 17, to nominate two or three among them for membership of the Commission. The sons of the deceased or unable would also nominate one of them to participate in designating the nominees for the Commission's membership, within 15 days from receiving the nomination request. If the deadline expires without any nominees designated, the King will have the right to appoint whomever he deems suitable for membership to the Commission.[35]

This was followed by further clarification in the same Article, as "The King will ask one of the sons of King 'Abdul 'Aziz, or sons of his sons, to nominate three of the sons of the deceased or unable, one of them [would be chosen] for membership in the Commission. The King has the right to charge one of the sons of the founder to designate one of the three nominees for the Commission's membership." There was even a provision for those who were unable to perform such duties. Section 2 of Article 2 explained that this appointee shall "notify the King in writing, and nominate one of his sons for membership of the Commission. If his notification does not include a nomination, or if the King does not approve of his choice, the appointment will be made according to the above-mentioned Section 1, of Article 1."[36] This provision was exercised by Nawwaf bin 'Abdul 'Aziz, who settled on 'Abdul 'Aziz bin Nawwaf to represent him on the Commission, passing over the eldest son, Muhammad bin Nawwaf, who served the kingdom as Ambassador to the Court of St. James.[37]

Articles 2 and 3 of the by-laws further stipulated that, in addition to being a son or grandson of the founder, Allegiance Commission members should be no less than 22 years of age, and be recognized for integrity and good conduct. The membership term, provided there was no violation of the Allegiance Commission's Law, was a non-renewable four-year stint, except in the case where the brothers agreed to an extension, subject to the ruler's approval.[38] Importantly, the by-laws covered potential violations of the Commission's provisions, stating:

> If a member fails to perform his duties and responsibilities, the matter will be investigated by a committee comprising of three Commission members, to be named by its chairman. The committee will submit the outcome of the investigation to the Commission. If the Commission, with the approval of two thirds of its members, decides to dismiss the member who fails to perform his duties and responsibilities, the matter will be submitted to the King to decide on what he views as the best course of action.[39]

Therefore, provisions were set by the law in cases of violations, which would be addressed through a resolution agreement reached *in camera*.

Allegiance Commission responsibilities

Significantly, when the Commission was created, the body's various responsibilities with respect to selecting a new Heir Apparent were clearly defined, with specific procedures for a full-range of eventualities outlined, including the king's or the Heir Apparent's sudden demise(s) or incapacitating illness(es). There was even a provision that anticipated the simultaneous death or illness of the king and his Heir Apparent. Article 6 of the by-laws stated, in language that was as precise as could be fathomed: "If the King passes away, the Allegiance Commission will pledge allegiance to the Heir Apparent in accordance with this Law and the Basic Law of Governance."[40] Likewise, Article 7 delineated the process through which the Allegiance Commission would select a successor Heir Apparent, through a process of nomination and election:

> After consultation with the members of the Allegiance Commission, the King will choose one, two or three candidates for the position of Heir Apparent. He will present his nominees to the Allegiance Commission, which will then designate one of them as Heir Apparent. In the event the Commission rejects all of the nominees, it will designate an Heir Apparent whom it considers to be suitable.[41]

This sensitive question was first addressed in the 2006 Allegiance Law. In fact, Article 7 further stipulated that the king may in turn reject the Commission's nomination, in which case, the Allegiance Commission would be called upon to vote and elect either the monarch's nominee or the Commission's own choice: "The nominee who secures a majority of votes will be named Heir Apparent," it specified, and, according to Article 9 (2006), must be appointed within 30 days of the new ruler's accession to the throne.[42] Under the law, and as discussed above, the Allegiance Commission was empowered to establish a *Transitional Ruling Council* composed of five members, which would temporarily run state affairs. Importantly, and as an interim governmental body, the *Transitional Ruling Council* did not have the right to amend any of the seminal laws of the Sa'udi constitution, such as the Basic Law of Governance, the Allegiance Commission Law, the Council of Ministers Law, the *Shurah* Council Law, the Law of the Provinces, the National Security Council Law, or any other laws relevant to issues of governance. Likewise, the *Transitional Ruling Council* was denied the right to dissolve or reshuffle the Cabinet or the *Majlis al-Shurah*, which fell under the exclusive prerogatives of the monarch. This effectively meant that the primary function of the *Transitional Ruling Council* was to protect the country's laws, Sa'udi Arabia's unity during periods of transition, as well as preserve well-established internal and external interests.

What was singularly crucial, nevertheless, was the importance allocated by the Law to preserve and protect the Al Sa'ud in the event of an emergency. According to Article 11 of the 2006 law, if the Allegiance Commission was persuaded that the monarch was too incapacitated to carry out his duties, this new mechanism allowed it to request a medical report on his health conditions prepared by a duly appointed medical committee. This was unprecedented and, in case such a report confirmed that the monarch was indeed unable to exercise his powers even temporarily, then the Allegiance Commission was

Political reforms and the succession dilemma 143

empowered to transfer rulership authority provisionally to the Heir Apparent until there was a full recovery. An equally crucial explanation was provided by the law, namely, how to respond to a written request from the monarch after he claimed that he was fully recovered. Under such circumstances, the Allegiance Commission was authorized to request a separate medical report prepared by the medical committee on very short notice (within 24 hours according to the law), before a decision could be made to restore suspended powers. Depending on the recommendations of the medical account, the monarch could either exercise his powers, or entrust the Heir Apparent to accede to the throne after receiving pledges of allegiance. It was worth noting, once again, that these procedures were not to stay in limbo but be carried out within a single day.[43]

If this foresight was not sufficient, the law further contemplated the simultaneous incapacitation of the top leadership, which meant that both the monarch and his Heir Apparent would not be able to exercise their powers for health reasons. Under such circumstances, the Allegiance Commission was tasked to request from the medical committee a statement and, based on its findings, sanction the *Transitional Ruling Council* to assume administrative powers and conduct the affairs of State until such time when a monarch was chosen. To say that this provision was revolutionary was truly an understatement. Even bolder, the law foresaw permanent incapacity for the top two positions, which not only meant that the *Transitional Ruling Council* would assume the temporary administration of the government, but be empowered to actually "select a suitable candidate from among the sons or grandsons of King 'Abdul 'Aziz Al Sa'ud within seven days, and call on him to take over as King of the country in accordance with this Law, and the Basic Law of Governance."[44] It may be worth repeating that this provision institutionalized the succession process to such a degree that it was literally impossible for a handful of senior family members to bypass it.[45] Only health-related reasons permitted the Allegiance Commission to assume an emergency role, to be thoroughly assessed by a medical team that included the supervisor of the "Royal Clinics"; the medical director of the "King Faisal Specialist Hospital," and three medical college deans to be selected by the Commission. Ominously, the team was even allowed to seek assistance from competent physicians, at its discretion, which was yet another illustration of how drastic these steps were.[46] Still, by addressing the mere possibility of simultaneous death of the monarch and his Heir Apparent, the Allegiance Commission adopted a rare public position on this most sensitive topic, which encouraged surviving sons and grandsons of King 'Abdul 'Aziz Al Sa'ud from engaging in the process with gusto. Without exaggeration, this was a healthy sign of reforms, contemplated by an octogenarian ruler with rare vision for the stability and survival of the ruling family.

Mode of operation

In introducing various reform mechanisms into the Allegiance Law of Succession, its authors outlined how the nascent institution ought to operate, hold meetings, and make critical decisions to better serve the Al Saʻud. Naturally, and under normal circumstances, all Commission meetings would only be held with the monarch's approval. The only exceptions to this rule involved his incapacitation or death along with the demise of the Heir Apparent. Without such guidance, it fell on the Commission's Chairman, a position held by the eldest surviving son of King ʻAbdul ʻAziz (other than the ruler or his heir), to summon members for urgent sessions. In case neither the Commission Chairman nor his Deputy were available, the eldest grandson of late King ʻAbdul ʻAziz would be empowered to chair Commission meetings.[47]

Given its relatively large membership, the law foresaw turnout problems and, to prevent many absences, set specific attendance rules.[48] It also mandated that meetings be limited to members of the Commission, its Secretary-General, and its *rapporteur*. With the king's approval, the Commission would be invited to provide explanations or information during a session, though availability excuses must be cleared through the Chairman who may grant an exemption at his discretion.[49] Consequently, it was easy to predict that the chairman, who was awarded comprehensive administrative powers, to exercise them generously. According to the law, the Chairman opened and closed meetings, moderated discussions, allowed members to speak, determined the agenda, ended discussions, and called for votes as necessary. The law further commanded a quorum for decision-making: "For any meeting to be valid it should have a quorum of two-thirds of the Commission's members, including its chairman or his deputy." "In accordance with Article 7," it further stipulated that, "the Commission [envisaged the approval of] its decisions with the consent of the majority of members present. In the event of a tie, the chairman [is the individual who would] cast the deciding vote. In the event where the quorum was not fulfilled, meetings with half of the members present [could be held], and decisions passed with the approval of two-thirds of the members present."[50]

Interestingly, documentation procedures were outlined in Article 21, which stated: "For each meeting there should be a record indicating the time and location of the meeting, and the names of its chairman, members present, absent members and the reasons for their absence, if any, and the name of the Secretary-General."[51] Despite years of bureaucratization that ushered in note-taking and record-keeping, the traditional tribal norms that were part and parcel of private family gatherings, where succession matters were settled in the past, were amended. Now the Allegiance Law of Succession spoke of official documents and the need to record "a summary of the discussions, the number of yes and no votes, the results of the voting process and the full text of the decisions taken." This was, to say the least, a perfect example of the institutionalization process under way. By providing such intricate details, and insisting that official records "show whether the meeting was postponed or adjourned, and, if so, the time when this took place, and any other matter that the chairman deem[ed] necessary," by requiring that "the record should be signed by the chairman, members present at the meeting and the Secretary-General," and by authorizing that all voting be "conducted by secret ballot," the law was crystal clear: Riyadh was no longer operating under a tribal mechanism but gradually modernizing its most sensitive institution. Critics often dismissed such developments, opining that the Al Saʻud were incapable of operating modernizing institutions, without, however, recognizing the gradual positive changes.

In an even more significant step, and according to Article 23, the Commission was directed to preserve the secrecy of its procedures. Members, consequently, would only be allowed to "review the agenda and all pertinent documents at the location in which the meeting [was] being convened, and [would] not be permitted to remove any documents from the meeting hall."[52] No longer were royal privileges assumed to override procedures introduced to protect the national interest. While this was a singular rule that applied to a particular case, its introduction was a giant step forward, as the government solidified its institutional prerogatives. Importantly, and while Riyadh was the headquarters of the Commission, the law allowed for meetings to be held wherever the Royal Court convened, which, obviously, required additional security measures.

Finally, Article 24 of the law called for the appointment of a Secretary-General to serve in a General Secretariat with the rank of a minister, and a deputy with the rank of Excellence, responsible for inviting members of the Commission, supervising the process of preparing the minutes and decisions, and announcing the results of meetings, as decided by the chairman. As royal appointees, the Secretary-General and his deputy served the ruler first and foremost, and were empowered to seek assistance as they saw fit, though Article 12 of the Commission's By-laws stipulated that holders of the position would "be responsible for all the financial and administrative affairs of the Commission."[53] An equally valuable aspect of the Secretariat were calls to establish a documentation facility "linked directly to the Secretary General," to keep "minutes, documents and reports pertaining to its activities, and preserve their confidentiality."[54] This was yet another feature of the professionalism that supported the institution that enjoyed a separate annual budget to cover routine expenses.[55]

In the words of an astute observer, the creation of the Allegiance Law of Succession illustrated the ways the Saʻudi ruling family began "to address complicated issues in heredity and governance, as the House of Saʻud prepare[d] to pass political power from the founder's sons to his grandsons."[56] Indeed, what the process did was to meet key challenges ahead and anticipate potential problems, all to ensure a smooth transmission of power to the next generation of Al Saʻud heirs. The major reform initiative undertaken by King ʻAbdallah, therefore, was to openly establish principles by which accession could be passed from brother to brother, or father to son, or even from father to grandson, based on family legitimacy. In other words, and without abandoning informal discussions that may still occur in traditional settings, the Allegiance Law of Succession provided a constitutional vehicle for the future selection of Saʻudi monarchs.[57] ʻAbdallah bin ʻAbdul ʻAziz's master plan also confirmed that the decreed mechanism would satisfy the kingdom's growing legal requirements. In fact, the very process through which the ruling family was called upon to select the most able individual to become Heir Apparent or monarch, even if chosen from among the founder's extensive lineage, was embedded in a legal framework. It was, in Professor Al-Badi's words "uncharacteristic of a monarchy," though "necessary to ... ensure the family's continued unity."[58] By reforming long-standing customary procedures, 'Abdallah wished, and seemed to have succeeded, in creating a smooth mechanism for the transfer of power from one generation to the next. This was, therefore, a legitimate constitutional change, in a body composed of various sections from the ruling Al Sa'ud family, which will now be subjected to strict rules rather than be at the mercy and whims of an individual, no matter how benign, transparent, or gifted that sovereign may be.

The Second Deputy Prime Minister

Because 'Abdallah left vacant the position of Second Deputy Prime Minister for almost five years after his accession to rulership, many concluded that the monarch was mulling over his various options, or that he was not ready to take the next step.[59] Among various interpretations was the option to defer that choice to his successor. For years, the non-choice fueled speculation that the ruler was ill at ease with tackling such a gargantuan topic, further illustrating existing family cleavages. In fact, 'Abdallah opted for internal stability by quickly designating his brother Prince Sultan as Heir Apparent, and seldom contemplated forcing a change to replace his heir with another Al Sa'ud, even if his predecessor's 1992 edict was available to make fundamental changes to the succession line. Nevertheless, Sultan's medical conditions and long absences from home necessitated an appointment for Second Deputy Prime Minister in case both the ruler and his heir were taken ill or became incapacitated.[60] Simply stated, 'Abdallah made a technical decision in March 2009, as he was neither keen to propel his offspring to the forefront, or enter into specific new alliances to encourage internal family divisions. Moreover, his preferences focused on the careful re-arrangements of the succession process, through an institutional mechanism discussed above. Yet, even that was in jeopardy because of Sultan's health conditions, which necessitated the urgent appointment of a Second Deputy Prime Minister.

Nayif bin 'Abdul 'Aziz[61]

As stated above, Nayif's nomination on March 27, 2009 came as something of a surprise, though Prince Sultan's treatment for colon cancer, and his extended absences from several demanding duties, necessitated a stop-gap selection. Because 'Abdallah was about to travel to Doha to attend the League of Arab States Summit before proceeding to London for the G20 Assembly, it was imperative to leave a senior official in charge, which added burdens to Nayif, who was 76 years old and suffered from leukemia.[62]

Born in Ta'if in either 1933 or 1934, Prince Nayif bin 'Abdul 'Aziz Al Sa'ud received basic religious education at the Palace, and held several government positions starting with a brief stint as Governor of Riyadh (1953–4). He was appointed Deputy Minister of Interior in 1954 by King Sa'ud bin 'Abdul 'Aziz and became Minister of State for Internal Affairs in 1970. Five years later, he was entrusted the interior ministry portfolio in full, a post he preserved in 2011. Over the years, and because of his most sensitive position, Nayif developed a rare reputation for being the most assertive Al Sa'ud. To his credit, he fulfilled his mandate with gusto, preserving and protecting family interests, which required a firm hand against tangible threats. On the other hand, he also attracted widespread scorn for implementing an iron-fist policy. So-called liberals and alleged conservatives criticized him in unison, maintaining that he relied on the sword more than the law, and that his methods backfired as the kingdom experienced a steady stream of opposition forces. Like other senior Al Sa'ud members, Nayif balanced his preferences, ostensibly to better gauge what would be tolerated. In 2006, he curbed the powers of the Commission for the Promotion of Virtue and Prevention of Vice, denying the *mutawa'in* the right to arrest suspects without the presence of police officers. This was certainly a difficult decision but in line with King 'Abdallah's sharp directives to abandon un-Islamic, disruptive, and questionable behavior by law-enforcement personnel. Nayif, who was not necessarily on the best of political terms with his monarch, applied his ruler's wishes both because he was a committed family player and, equally important, because he was the target of sustained denigration.[63] In the aftermath of the 9/11 bombing attacks in the United States, Nayif sustained a barrage of vilification from sources that identified with the fifteen Sa'udis involved in the attacks, since he gave specific orders to monitor their movements within the kingdom.[64] As part of the original "Sudayri Seven," Nayif was one of the most powerful members of the ruling family, technically third in line to the Sa'udi rulership. His essential role at the Ministry of Interior, to oversee public security, direct coast guard forces, supervise civil defense units, coordinate fire departments, instruct border police, control special security and investigative functions, including criminal inquiries, and administer the clergy within the kingdom, concentrated immense powers in his hands. By virtue of these responsibilities, he was a major power broker in internal family affairs, too, and cannot be dismissed for obtuse views. On the contrary, his opinions carried weight within various groups, including more moderate forces that wished to see him on their side in any deliberation. Likewise, conservative voices rallied to him as well, believing that he would represent their opinions best.[65]

To his credit, and while few would accord him the benefit of doubt, Prince Nayif was involved in landmark decisions that empowered women in the kingdom. Perhaps the most important decision was his insistence that women be issued separate identity cards starting in 2001, which freed them from the need to be listed in their husbands' and/or guardians' identity documents. This was no mean achievement in an ultra-conservative society, and Nayif deserved the accolade even if his chief concerns hovered around security issues.[66] As discussed earlier in this study, after 2003, Nayif's perceptions of how best to combat terrorism and extremist ideologies inside the kingdom changed dramatically, which he himself acknowledged. In a 2009 Arab Interior Ministers' gathering in Beirut, Nayif called on Arab media organizations to educate Arab citizens about the danger posed by deviant ideologies, all to prevent them from joining terrorist groups. "We in Saudi Arabia are more concerned with this issue and we don't allow our youth to follow such ideologies," he stressed.[67] Perhaps the change was evolutionary in his case too, but it was a marked departure from earlier positions that highlighted how pragmatic members of the ruling establishment could be. Above all else, the Al Sa'ud were an immensely cohesive group, and universally agreed on what mattered most, namely the survival and welfare of the family. Few outsiders accepted this interpretation, assuming that no group could possibly follow such a pattern. In reality, and a few exceptions notwithstanding, family unity was truly impeccable.

As chairman of the Supreme *Hajj* Committee, the annual pilgrimage to Makkah, the Sa'udi Interior Minister authorized breathtaking initiatives to improve overall services to pilgrims. This was duly noted by the ruler who commended his brother, declaring: "We thank you and all those who participated in this noble task. We express our immense satisfaction and pride at the coordinated efforts of all departments which enabled pilgrims to perform Hajj with utmost peace and safety." Even if such routine praise was customary among senior Al Sa'ud officials, observers added several clarifications to underscore Nayif's leadership qualities. Naif Al Shamri, a Sa'udi political analyst, opined that the royal decision was recognition of the statesmanship and administrative capabilities of Prince Nayif, who served in various capacities at the top hierarchy of the ruling dynasty for more than half a century. "He had served as deputy minister of interior and then state minister of interior before being elevated to the [full minister-ship]. All these positions have given him an opportunity to prove his efficiencies, capabilities, and talents as an administrator and head of the Kingdom's security apparatus," stated Al Shamri.[68] Jasim bin Muhammad Al-Yaqout praised Nayif in a laudatory essay, marking the prince's nationalist qualities, which all agreed were exceptional.[69] In a poignant open letter published in every Saudi newspaper, Prince Turki al-Faysal, praised his uncle, too. For the former intelligence chief-turned-diplomat, Nayif "radiates a sense of reassurance." "When he speaks to you," penned Turki al-Faysal,

> it is in a soft voice and with a smiling countenance, and he listens to you he does so attentively until you have conveyed all that you have to say. As for what he suggests to you, he is logical in his thoughts, and strings his words together in a way that draws you to reflect upon and analyze each word he says; he is a man who chooses his words carefully, and so one must confer full-weight to any conversation one conducts with him. He has great patience, and a big heart; he is rare to anger, and even when he is

angered he is not aggressive, and is keen to direct his anger towards the rapid elimination of its cause, adhering to orderliness no matter how complicated matters are, and always doing what is right no matter what.[70]

The equally self-confident Turki al-Faysal, hinted at Nayif's "deliberate nature with regards to decision-making," by which he meant to address his uncle's severity, but emphasized that this was due to "devotion," which he claimed was a characteristic "acknowledged by those near and far." He concluded his praise with a reference to the elder statesman's "generosity," acknowledging that "when crises intensify I would find him to be an impregnable rock, an invulnerable mountain, who would not become flustered, and would explore the issues with his great faith in God, and his belief in the people of Saudi Arabia;" in short, "the right man for the right job."[71]

For his part, Nayif pledged to "exert greater efforts in the service of the nation and religion," praying the Almighty to help him carry out his duties "in the best manner, matching the expectations of the country's leadership and people."[72] He welcomed his appointment with pride and committed himself to serve his nation. Importantly, Nayif received written or personal congratulations from Heir Apparent Sultan bin 'Abdul 'Aziz as well as other senior Al Sa'ud princes, including Bandar, Mit'ab, Badr, Salman, Ahmad and many others. Hail Governor Prince Sa'ud bin 'Abdul Muhsin acknowledged Prince Nayif's years of service, stating: "he became deputy governor of Riyadh when he was 18; and since then, he has to his credit innumerable achievements." Eastern Province Governor Prince Muhammad bin Fahd congratulated his uncle too and described him as a sincere leader: "Prince Nayif will be a support for the King and the Heir Apparent," he intoned.[73]

Others were equally generous with their comments as they expressed loyalty. The erudite Labor Minister and a genuine scholar in his own right, Ghazi Al-Gosaibi, described Nayif as a first-class statesman, enjoying vast experience, as someone who "contributed a great deal to the development of the country and to preserving its security and stability." Al-Gosaibi, who passed away on August 15, 2010, seldom engaged in fawning and uttered these words repeatedly to his visitors.[74] Former *Majlis al-Shurah* Chairman Salih bin Humayd described Nayif as a man of state and security, who "is known for his judiciousness, wisdom and worldly experience. He is one of the pillars of the country and the royal family," declared bin Humayd who was also chairman of the Supreme Judiciary Council.[75] Shortly after his appointment, Nayif met Grand Mufti Shaykh 'Abdul 'Aziz Al al-Shaykh to receive the latter's *bay'ah*, which further enhanced his credentials as the chief enforcer of law and order in the country.[76]

To be sure, while much of this praise was a natural function of promotion and the jockeying that was part and parcel of court politics, the outpouring highlighted a rare level of family harmony that often escaped observers. Not everyone was faking it for the sake of accommodation or to ingratiate himself with a potential king. Rather, what was on display were emotional backings that clarified certain aspects of the succession dilemma, which preoccupied family members. This view, however, was not universally shared, most notably because of controversial statements attributed to Prince Nayif in the aftermath of the 9/11 attacks in the United States.[77]

Talal bin 'Abdul 'Aziz questions the succession strategy

Although senior Al Sa'ud family members perceived Heir Apparent Sultan's safe return to the kingdom after an extended convalescence period as a good omen, a few were bewildered by Nayif's appointment to the second deputy premiership. Prince Talal bin 'Abdul 'Aziz, a noted liberal senior prince, issued a statement a day after the designation, questioning the very assumption of a Nayif election to the heirship. Unabashedly, Talal reflected the dissent that existed within the ruling family, releasing a statement to Reuters in which he asked the monarch to "clarify" the meaning of the selection. Without waiting for an answer, he further declared that Nayif's promotion should be subject to approval by the Allegiance Council, as he called on the court to confirm whether Nayif "will become crown prince."[78] Talal and many liberals were concerned that if Nayif were to eventually become Heir and Ruler, that Sa'udi Arabia's gradual steps toward political reforms would suffer severe setbacks. Moreover, because Talal remained a close ally of 'Abdallah, it was accurate to speculate that the ruler knew, or even approved, of this press release. In the event, Sa'udis close to the Palace confirmed that the ruler was aware of the Talal missive, but felt it necessary to go ahead with the appointment for technical reasons, knowing that members of the Allegiance Commission would intervene if need be. Accordingly, senior members gave their consent to Nayif's nomination, reserving the right to examine his credentials at the right time. Towards that end, and even if ill, it was critical to note that Sultan was still the Heir Apparent and, once elevated to rulership, could appoint whomever he chose.

Still, Nayif-bashing was added to the on-going Sa'udi-bashing repertoires in various regional and international media outlets, allegedly because Nayif was "perceived as one of the most conservative forces in the kingdom and an opponent of reforms that may reduce the clout of both the monarchy and the religious establishment in the kingdom."[79] A leading source informed its readers that when asked what he [Nayif] thought of women becoming members of the *Shurah* Council, he apparently declared that he did not "think it was necessary," further illustrating apparently how unqualified the new Second Deputy Prime Minister was. Ironically, Nayif's record was stellar on this as well as the key front of counter-terrorism, "and he is credited with Saudi Arabia's relative success at curbing radical Islamist terrorist groups."[80] Nevertheless, while it was facile to dismiss Talal's criticisms, those views represented a rare facet of internal debates, especially because so few senior leaders shared their views in public.

Talal spoke loudly, but he spoke for many who wanted reforms without necessarily attacking the unity of the family, and whereas equally powerful princes disagreed with his zeal for "constitutional modifications," few ignored him. In the event, he forcefully reopened the public debate over succession by questioning the very appointment of the Interior Minister as Second Deputy Prime Minister, declaring that "the monarch need[ed] to make sure the appointment served purely an 'administrative purpose'," which was problematic to say the least.[81] A few weeks after raising this most difficult question, which was interpreted in Palace circles as hurtful to Nayif, Talal bin 'Abdul 'Aziz granted a lengthy interview to the London *Financial Times*, to which he revealed that the time was right to introduce political and economic alterations. This was classic Talal. Not only was he addressing a super-sensitive topic, but he willfully enlarged the scope of his question by introducing an equally delicate topic, political parties, which bordered on the taboo.[82] Simply stated, raising the very idea of political parties in the kingdom was tantamount to a revolutionary call, which would alter the political system in place. According to the journalists who reported the story, Talal expressed fears that "the kingdom [was] not prepared to face the challenges of the 21st century" that, apparently, prompted him to speak out. He claimed that there was a desperate need for "dialogue within the ruling family and called for greater powers for the *Shurah* Council, an unelected consultative body, to pave the way for eventual elections."[83] He continued: "This region is roiling with turmoil and radicalism and the aspirations of a young population, and I am afraid we are not prepared for that. We cannot use the same tools we have been using to rule the country a century ago," remarks that appeared to solidify his opposition to Prince Nayif's elevation to the Second Prime Ministership. Interestingly, he underlined a concern that the appointment may bypass the Allegiance Commission from performing its assigned duties as decreed by King 'Abdallah, to select the next Heir Apparent. In his own words: "Bypassing the allegiance system would mean we do not respect our own rules or uphold our system," revealed Talal who, as a son of the founder, occupied a seat on the Commission. In his inimitable ways, he wondered what kind of a family bestowed with huge responsibilities failed to debate key questions, when the very future of the country depended on such dialogue.[84]

Sharp criticisms notwithstanding, Talal supported his ruler's efforts to reform the political system, rejecting any insinuations that he was being disloyal by airing dirty laundry in public. "Hypocrites claim our society is unprepared for change and blame religious institutions," he told the *Financial Times*, and while "certain people are pleased to hear that[,] we have to stop using them as an excuse. King 'Abdallah is the ruler. If he wills it, then it will be done."[85] For Talal, the time was long overdue to usher in the younger generation of royals, precisely to avoid a political vacuum. He was categorical in drawing differences between ruling and governing, opining that in Sa'udi Arabia, the family was the government that owned and ruled simultaneously. This, he concluded, was not a healthy phenomenon, and in light of developments throughout the region after late 2010 – when the Arab world experienced significant challenges to authority – his prescience was remarkable to say the least. To prevent potential hazards, Talal recommended that younger Al Sa'ud members become more involved to better participate in the decision-making process that, he insisted, was the reason why he embarked on his latest proposals.

A month after this major reportage, which was conducted on April 21, 2009, several media outlets published Talal's interview to the *Financial Times* in full. An edited version of the interview was posted on the newspaper's webpage with additional clarifications worthy of full quotations.

Six major questions and responses in particular were pertinent to this investigation.

First was Talal's views on the appointment of Prince Nayif as a Second Deputy Prime Minister, and why this was not necessarily in the kingdom's best interests. When queried by Abeer Allam and Andrew England whether the appointment left an impact on the future of Sa'udi Arabia, Talal responded:

> The Appointment of Prince Naif or any other individual is not the issue. We are protesting against the principle, not the person. This [the Second Deputy Prime Ministership] is more of an administrative, ministerial position, so we do not agree on the impression that he will automatically become crown prince because of the Biaa [*Bay'ah*] system (Allegiance Commission) established by King Abdullah, something that we all approved and abide by. The council nominates and elects the crown prince. Bypassing the allegiance system would mean we do not respect our own rules or uphold our system. For the past seven years I have called for preparing the next generation of leaders from among the most competent of our sons through the council. I think when the council chooses a crown prince, a deputy crown prince from the younger generation should be chosen simultaneously so that we do not face a political vacuum comparable to Kuwait. We can draw from historical precedent. King Faisal bypassed Prince Muhammad, the most senior member of the family, and chose Khalid as crown prince, after consulting all of his brothers. Prince Muhammad did not want to be a king, though it was his legitimate right. King Faisal asked all of us to vote. This was a very good approach which earned the approval of all his brothers.[86]

The second and equally pertinent question dealt with decision-making within the Al Sa'ud and whether such procedures followed consensus. The two journalists wondered whether the Nayif appointment was reached without consensus? Talal's answer spoke volumes. "There is no such thing as unanimity or global consensus. But there is dialogue and accord. For example what we have in Lebanon [*sic*] democracy is a kind of consensus democracy. We are a family here; we better have a dialogue that leads to consensus."[87] In other words, and this much was confirmed by other senior members of the Al Sa'ud ruling family, the monarch's decision to fill the second deputy premiership was not reached through the Allegiance Commission mechanism.[88]

As Prince Talal called for dialogue within the family throughout his interview, he was asked how he would usher in such discussions, when the ruler apparently made key decisions alone. This intriguing inquiry elicited the following response as Talal fell back to the legacy of the kingdom's founder:

> We have to have advisors who know what is going on in their countries and the entire world. King Abdelaziz ['Abdul 'Aziz bin 'Abdul Rahman] had 9 advisors from different Arab countries as well as his Sa'udi advisors. He started work at 7 a.m. My room was next to his in the palace and I remember advisors arriving at 7 a.m. to brief him on world affairs. They would have their breakfast between 8:30 and 9 a.m. and start working again. He met them three times a day. This region is roiling with turmoil and radicalism and the aspirations of a young population, and I am afraid we are not prepared for that. We cannot use the same tools we have been using to rule the country for a century. This is how this vast country was established despite the limited resources we had back then. We have to follow his lead, taking into consideration the current circumstances.

In his inimitable words, Talal hinted at the isolation that senior members of the ruling family may have unnecessarily placed themselves in, which did not bode well. Such conditions could only be remedied by a thorough engagement of able and highly educated young men, he recommended, who can add value to the decision-making process. In short, Talal was aware that King 'Abdallah was a futurist who intended to introduce, and was promoting, significant reforms, but that he alone was no longer capable of lifting an entire nation on his shoulders. The time was ripe to enlarge the framework and solicit serious contributions from those who were equipped to protect, defend and advance Sa'udi interests. This was visionary, even if very risky on his part, given local norms.

The fourth area of interest in the interview came in a series of short questions and answers that tackled those within the family who cared to encourage or, perhaps, influence the ruler to embark on Talal's much touted dialogue. Both journalists wondered whether Talal was the only one in the family who demanded such changes? His responses were telling as well: "If I said yes, then I am wrong. And I cannot say no. Ask them." A follow-up query delved in the oft-speculated topic regarding regular meetings held by senior family members and what kind of conversations occurred behind closed doors. Talal confirmed that exemplary meetings were held but refused "to talk about" them on the ground that "these [we]re family affairs."[89] Naturally, the *Financial Times* wished to know if the king was alone in wanting to push for change or whether others in the family, as well as senior members within the religious establishment, opposed him. Though Talal could not comment directly, he speculated as follows:

> The king is the decision maker, any king following Abdel-Aziz may rule as he pleases. If there are objections or obstacles as you say, then he is the

one who can remove the impediments. His word is final. If he wills it, then it will be done. We should not use this as an excuse. The man has the intention for reform. He has conducted some major reforms recently, did anyone object or stopped him?

When the journalists wondered why the prince was the only person in the ruling family who seemed concerned about these issues, and was willing to speak out, the affable Talal rejoined: "Did you meet all of them to judge them?" The follow-up exchanges were equally intriguing:

FT: Of course not. But you are most concerned?
PRINCE TALAL: I am concerned, I care.
FT: Do you see a bright future for the kingdom?
PRINCE TALAL: I am optimistic, despite my reservations.
FT: Will you be less optimistic if the situation does not change?
PRINCE TALAL: Well, I am as human as any other. I get frustrated.

If Talal addressed his concerns in a diplomatic way, Sa'udi activists felt emboldened to call for even more audacious reforms affecting the entire system of government. In May 2009, a group of advocates for change sent a petition for a sweeping reform of political institutions, which called for a sharp reduction in Al Sa'ud roles. The ultimate purpose of this petition was to move the kingdom towards a constitutional monarchy.[90] While the petition is examined in detail in the next chapter, the call to create an elected parliament, and for a commoner to serve as Prime Minister, shocked the Al Sa'ud. Among the many features of the petition were demands to limit "the terms of appointed royal family members in government posts," as well as allow "an elected parliament [to] have a role in deciding the succession to the throne." Here was one of the boldest challenges to the succession mechanism in place, including the emancipator Allegiance Commission, which presumably was deemed to be insufficient to address the country's needs. Talal highlighted many existing concerns in his latest interview with a respected Western newspaper, but he was also a mirror of serious internal contentions than could not, indeed, ought not be overlooked as the calls for participation multiplied.

Calls for the establishment of political parties

Talal's calls to form political parties, first made in 2007, posed something of a real challenge. Although his request was still awaiting approval by the ruler as this book went to press, it was a fact that all political parties were *illegal* in Sa'udi Arabia. Of course, Talal believed that the kingdom would be better served if it made gradual moves towards elections, starting with granting the *Majlis al-Shurah* greater powers, though he understood that such a process was a long-term proposition and could not be introduced by fiat. His arguments were sound, especially when he recalled that Sa'udis, especially young men and women, tuned in to developments elsewhere throughout the Arab world. All rejoiced as they followed elections in places like Lebanon or Iraq, among others, envious of the level of popular participation in Arab states – truncated as these were. Most aspired to emulate their brethren, wondering why they lacked the same opportunities. Talal recognized that "the political decision [was] in the hands of the king," and that he knew of 'Abdallah's "reformist penchants" even if the latter relied on numerous committees to avoid making rapid decisions. "We still believe in him," chimed Talal who expressed frustration as the slow pace of reforms, which he hoped could change to better serve the country and its citizens. Nevertheless, when asked whether Sa'udi Arabia was heading into the right direction economically, socially and politically, Talal was not circumspect. He affirmed that there was a need for the *Shurah* Council to be empowered through dialogue in the first instance, and over time, through elections because there was "no way around it," if the kingdom's numerous economic, social, and political concerns were to be resolved.

Still, while few observers of internal Sa'udi political affairs thought that members of the Al Sa'ud ruling family would ever publicly criticize the establishment, frequent calls for the potential adoption of political parties emerged in recent years. In addition to Talal bin 'Abdul 'Aziz, a number of younger Al Sa'ud family members voiced their opinion on this critical matter, couching their views tangentially by disparaging the kingdom's development plans. The goal was to strengthen internal stability, something Talal and several younger princes believed would occur more naturally, and of course better, if members of independent and functioning parties operated in the country.

In a widely read opinion piece in the London-based, Sa'udi-owned pan-Arab daily, *Al Hay'at*, Prince Fahad bin Sa'ad Al Sa'ud, a junior member of the ruling family, commented on an interview conducted with former deputy minister of finance Saleh Al Omair.[91] Fahad bin Sa'ad raised sensitive topics and referred to past problems regarding "the uneven distribution of the country's wealth and the government's failure to meet the objectives of several five-year plans that had been laid out by Mr. Al Omair between 1975 and 1996."[92] Though Fahad expressed his admiration for the work performed by Al Omair, he was more impressed by the latter's acknowledgment that many regions in Sa'udi Arabia lagged far behind others in economic development. This was the result of favoritism, the young prince suggested, with some regions receiving larger funds due to the presence of influential figures. Remarkably, this was not the first example of a member of the ruling family publicly questioning official policies, even if reformists clamored for more. Khalid bin Talal, a son of Talal bin 'Abdul 'Aziz and a brother of Al Walid bin Talal, openly disapproved of his brother's allegedly un-Islamic practices.[93] Speaking to a hard-line Islamist website, *Lujayniyyat*, Khalid bin Talal called for the freezing of his brother's significant assets, ostensibly to bring him back to the "righteous path."[94] While Khalid disparaged Al-Walid's glamorous media empire, which allegedly disseminated "vice," he also vociferously disapproved of plans to open a cinema in Saʻudi Arabia. In an ironic twist, Khalid bin Talal apologized to the government, his family, Saʻudi Arabia, and Muslims at large, for his brother's "misguided" practices, which reflected a sharp split between liberals and conservatives within the ruling family.[95]

Saʻudi reformists perceived such airings of major disputes in public as groundbreaking. Muhammad Al Qahtani, an assistant professor of economics at the Riyadh-based Institute of Diplomatic Studies, concluded: "Criticising the development strategy of the kingdom is no longer a taboo and young princes are trying to get involved in [discussing] the country's development" affairs.[96] Increasingly, educated voices were heard recommending bold new steps, including the adoption of political parties to articulate alternative opinions. This did not mean that the creation of political parties was imminent or that independent, non-Al Saʻud, voices would be allowed to have political platforms. It only meant, at least for now, that the seeds for political reforms were planted, and that senior Al Saʻud officials nurtured them on an ongoing basis.

Succession dilemma for Al Saʻud

Even before King ʻAbdallah's 2007 reform initiatives, leading Al Saʻud family members recognized that they had a succession problem, which required urgent attention. As recently as mid-2005, Prince Talal bin ʻAbdul ʻAziz, called on Riyadh to "start with political reform, that is introducing a new basic statute (of government), or what is known in the West as a constitution." Talal emphasized that the proposed constitution would be tantamount to "a social covenant between ruler and ruled, compatible with known constants in Saʻudi Arabia in terms of religion and genuine traditions."[97] Five years earlier Talal had cautioned that the Al Saʻud ought to "find a smooth way to pass the monarchy to the next generation, or face a power struggle after the era of old royals passes."[98] Prince Talal, who once was the leader of the "Free Princes" movement – that called for democratic changes in the early 1960s – drew the ire of senior Al Saʻud family members in the late 1950s and early 1960s and did so again in 1999, 2000, 2005, 2009, and 2011, as discussed above. Still, he was rehabilitated after several years in exile and, equally important, after pledging his undivided loyalty to the family.

More recently, Talal saw the need to further modernize the kingdom, "including giving women more rights to work and allowing them to drive, ... limit[ing] Riyadh's substantial military spending, and pass[ing] power to the next generation because," he further clarified, "our problems are with the grandsons," who will, presumably, require a new mechanism to ensure smooth successions. As stated earlier, in September 2007, Talal proposed to form a political party in Saʻudi Arabia, a proposal that could not have been made without the monarch's approval.[99] This was a calculated declaration by a trusted brother who no longer challenged family concord. In fact, Talal believed that political reforms were in the best interests of the ruling establishment, even if others preferred reform at a slower pace. ʻAbdallah for his part recognized that genuine sociopolitical reforms were long overdue and seemed to have worked in earnest with Talal to address them. Consequently, it would be safe to assume that should a political party be established, chances were excellent that it would be led by an Al Sa'ud steeped in established traditions. Although such an outcome was not imminent as this book was completed in early 2012, it is logical to assume that an Al Sa'ud-led political party would further guide whatever reforms were implemented, something that was bound to occur in due course.

The ultimate challenge for Riyadh, however, was whether the Al Sa'ud were able to keep up with the reformist ruler, since reorganizations by themselves were not enough. Rather, as societies equipped themselves with the wherewithal to self-govern, and trained legal minds to look after their interests – both those of the general public as well as of each individual – it behooved the ruling establishment to correctly interpret their "will to power." 'Abdallah's ultimate challenge was to affirm his own resolve and to acculturate putative successors to appreciate the limits of power. This was critical as he forged ahead with inclusive political institutions that added value to citizens at large – not easy propositions under the best of circumstances, but certainly within the realm of the possible in Riyadh because of the monarch's foresight, dedication, and impeccable credentials.

Although King 'Abdallah did not publicly respond to Talal's demands about modernization, social restructuring, and succession, these critical questions – certainly the most urgent and obvious facing the kingdom – were well known to him. As Prince Talal noted as early as June 1999, the ruling family faced certain inevitable challenges, to modernize and come to terms with the difficult succession question. Nonetheless, his frankness amply illustrated the dilemma for King 'Abdallah – as well as his successors – eager to maintain Sa'udi Arabia's traditions while engaging in a full-scale modernization program. Indeed, the monarch was amply aware of the delicate relationship between the kingdom's sustained development needs, and various legal and political reforms. How up and coming Al Sa'ud leaders positioned themselves and how their decisions affected Western security interests, mattered to political and economic leaders everywhere. How the Al Sa'ud defined and shaped their "will to power" (the determination to prevail against all odds), further affected long-term relationships between Sa'udi Arabia and a host of Western, Eastern, and Muslim countries.

If King 'Abdallah refrained from commenting in public on Talal's various prognostications or criticisms, he no doubt discussed his concerns with his brother, however. Presumably, the monarch raised some of these issues in his regular family *majlises*, which were held with more promptness than many assumed, a forum that was open to voice dissent within carefully drawn boundaries. The pragmatist ruler understood that his efforts were only the beginning steps and that the Allegiance Commission remained untested, even if his goal was to develop a functioning succession mechanism for his nation. Past succession patterns created something of a dilemma for the visionary, though neither 'Abdallah nor any other Al Sa'ud family member contemplated any changes that threatened the monarchy.

Nearly seven years into his rule, 'Abdallah bin 'Abdul 'Aziz thus demonstrated a knack for significant changes, first with his 2007 Allegiance Law of Succession and, more recently, with the appointment of a Second Deputy Prime Minister. Neither of these measures upset the 1744 alliance between the Al Sa'ud and the Al Shaykh, which formed the cornerstone of the kingdom's legitimacy, and which was seldom subjected to any cataclysmic tests. Rather, the Sa'udi monarch intended to strengthen that critical alliance by injecting fresh reforms, not to eliminate any party or group, but to open the doors for the gradual transformations required by time. These were clear signs of 'Abdallah's inherent skill at refining his "will to power," which required serious attention to political reforms, and which were nearly impossible to postpone.

5 Reforms and the petition industry

Although freedom of religion in Sa'udi Arabia was limited to Islam and freedom of the press was haphazard at best, the right to petition remained absolute, because God Almighty commanded in his Holy Scriptures that all righteous Muslim rulers seek advice. Consequently, devout officials, who took their responsibilities seriously, never flinched from the privilege to respond to petitions. Likewise, believers seldom shied away the right to approach administrators or, as necessary, from petitioning them for specific requests. In fact, the supplication tradition existed long before the nation-state system made its appearance in the Muslim world, and chances were excellent that it would continue to flourish for the foreseeable future.

As discussed throughout this chapter, political petitions – one this investigation focuses on – gained notoriety after the now-famous December 1990 draft that called for political reforms. A series of proposals followed throughout the decade and, in the aftermath of 9/11, increased in tempo and content as requests turned into demands. In 2003 alone, the ruling Al Sa'ud family received six major petitions, each signed by at least a hundred people asking for specific choices, including increased freedoms and political participation. One petition, signed by 300 women, asked for "new laws that would allow women to work in a wider variety of occupations, keep custody of their children after a divorce, and conduct business in public without a chaperone."[1] Another document, signed by approximately 450 Shi'ah citizens of the kingdom, asked for a declaration by the government that the Shi'ah creed is an accepted branch of Islam in the country.[2] It was as a partial response to this last petition that Riyadh relented and authorized Shi'ahs to publish their own religious books starting in 2005. along with several other rights. It was also after 2005 that Shi'ah men were allowed to celebrate *'Ashurah*, which mourned the martyrdom of Husayn, Muhammad's grandson, albeit only in the Eastern Province.[3] While Sunnis frowned on the self-flagellation that often transformed a simple march into a religious frenzy, Sa'udi Shi'ahs were allowed to demonstrate, beat their heads and chests with chains and whips, and otherwise expiate their sins for past failures.[4] These concessions notwithstanding, few senior level Sa'udi government positions were held by Shi'ahs, most of which were safely nestled within the appointed *Majlis al-Shurah*.[5]

While the petition production ebbed throughout the first decade of the 21st century, one of the key events that prompted action was the September 2007 petition to King 'Abdallah urging him to release nine advocates who had been held for at least seven months without trial, ostensibly because they had called for the establishment of a constitutional monarchy. At least 135 reformists, including 49 women, had signed the petition, according to Muhammad bin Hudayjan al-Harbi, one of the signatories. Ironically, this particular plea was mailed to the ruler rather than hand-delivered in an audience, as custom would require, because many of the signatories believed that they were not welcome at Court. Still, the petition was widely circulated in order to highlight the crackdown on reformists. It was difficult to determine whether these motivated petitioners were encouraged by the call to establish a political party, made a few weeks earlier by Prince Talal bin 'Abdul 'Aziz, and which would presumably be open to reformists. Suffice it to say that activists supported Talal's idea. Still, the nine detainees, all prominent lawyers who were first arrested in February 2007, faced serious charges.[6] According to Interior Ministry officials, they were allegedly involved in funding terrorist groups, or considering the formation of an Islamic political party.[7] It was not clear what the real motive was, and no one clarified specific goals. Since the nine did not appear in a court of law to answer charges, observers believed that they had been arrested for contemplating the creation of a political party, which was prohibited in Sa'udi Arabia under current regulations. The petition on their behalf confirmed this assertion as it read that all nine were "examining ideas pertaining to civil society mechanisms, such as an 'Islamic national charter' or an 'Islamic constitution party' and a 'committee for freedoms and basic rights' that would be proposed to a number of reformists." The guilt by association charge – funding terrorists – was rejected *in toto*, as the document contended that the real purpose of these detentions was to "tarnish (the image of) proponents of a civil society."[8] The petition urged King 'Abdallah to free all nine activists, or at least ensure that they get a public trial as stipulated by law. 'Abdallah surprised many when he ordered that 'Isam Basrawi, one of the nine advocates of a constitutional monarchy, be freed in late September 2007.[9]

These illustrations, which are discussed in some detail below, highlighted how Islamists, "nationalists, women, representatives of various regions, and courageous networks of social groups, presented their visions of a just state and a just society to the government in the form of petitions."[10] Regrettably, the absence of real expressions or popular elections, which allowed citizens to express themselves, meant that they would seek to articulate views in the form of advice and letters. Long before the late-2010 to early-2011 period, when the entire Arab world experienced epochal political uprisings euphemistically labeled the "Arab Spring," Sa'udi reformists seldom relented from long-term objectives to seek and implement meaningful changes in the kingdom's governance. Few questioned the right of the ruling family to be in charge, though some mistrusted the way the Al Sa'ud governed. The main purpose of the "petition," therefore, was to place a check on Al Sa'ud authority, with an important corollary: create an environment of accountability that gradually, but surely, introduced genuine socio-political reforms that did not threaten the country's delicate social fabric.[11] How the petition industry evolved is worthy of investigation to better ascertain whether it was an effective modernizing instrument.

Supplication to rulers

In the context of contemporary history on the Arabian Peninsula – that is, long before the creation of the modern Kingdom of Sa'udi Arabia – the very idea of supplication emerged within Islam. Muhammad Ibn 'Abdul Wahhab, who entered into the momentous 1744 political religious alliance with the Al Sa'ud, explained in his book *Kitab al-Tawhid* [The Book of Absolute Monotheism] that worship in Islam included a variety of prescriptions. In addition to five daily prayers, believers were called upon to fast; engage in *dua'* (supplication); seek *istia'dah* (request protection or refuge); ask for *isti'anah* (assistance), and search for *istiqatah* (benefits). All supplications, therefore, were to be made to God, as other searches would be acts of *shirk* (polytheism or associationism) and contradict *tawhid* (absolute monotheism). These *muwahhidun* – members of a reform movement started by Muhammad Ibn 'Abdul Wahhab (1703–92) and pejoratively known as Wahhabism – precepts were based on Qur'anic verses, which revealed the value of supplications and their meaning in Islam, where there were no ambiguities. The Holy Scriptures underscored God's words on supplication in these two verses that clarified basic meanings: "If My servants question you about Me, tell them that I am near. I answer the prayer of the suppliant when he calls on Me; therefore let them answer My call and put their trust in Me, that they may be rightly guided (2:186)"; and "Your Lord has said: 'Call on me and I will answer you. Those who disdain My service shall enter Hell with all humility' (40: 60)."[12]

Naturally, these verses treated the issue of supplication and their importance in terms of religion and/or spirituality. Concerns were about faith and beliefs, highlighting compassion, benevolence, and mercy, which allowed a believer to feel the divine care touching his soul and conscience. In turn, by opening one's heart to God, a *mu'min* found the Lord to be very close to him, listening to his call, perhaps understanding his needs, and soothing his sorrows. The ultimate purpose of such *dua'* were to alleviate burdens and earthly afflictions that denied one peace and tranquility. By beseeching God, a believer thus submitted to the will of the Almighty, which gave his life meaning. While supplications were not meant to alleviate temporal needs that arose in the course of ordinary challenges one faced, invoking God ensured that a profound spiritual quest could be tied with earthly needs, especially those of love and reassurance. It was critical to emphasize that the Prophet and members of his household set wonderful traditions by making supplications not only for themselves, but also for "others," neighbors, family members, or any number of strangers in desperate need for assistance. Their prayers asked the Lord to grant the wishes and desires of the "others," the same way they did for themselves, which was an extraordinary revelation that highlighted the necessity to look after one's neighbors or family members or even complete strangers, which was akin to what may be attributed to an individual becoming his brother's keeper. This fascinating aspect of Islam ought not simply be understood in terms of good deeds a believer might undertake, but must be perceived as a sign of profound spirituality and faith.

Still, the supplication tradition also carried a political message beyond religious prescriptions, which were relevant in various uses within reform programs. Those who took ordinary paths to pursue religious and political goals, including working to secure sustenance, assumed that all of their prayers would be answered. Over the centuries, such perceptions became ingrained in men and women throughout the Arabian Peninsula, in fact throughout the Muslim world, as many contemplated linkages between divine supplications and earthly outcomes.[13] Without making unsubstantiated leaps into the evolution of such views, it is indeed possible to assume that some believers came to understand the secular meanings of supplication, in terms of requests to their governors. This presupposition emerged from the undeniable reality that most rulers invoked their legitimacies from divine sources, claiming that they were good Muslims, and that their authorities were both inspired and implemented by celestial guidance.[14] Several Muslim dynasties, including the Hashemites in Jordan and 'Alawis in Morocco, prided themselves on such heavenly imprimaturs, claiming that their authority benefited from an association with the Prophet's extended family.[15] Muslim history was replete with such assertions, which generated their own controversies, but that seldom abated over time. Fourteen hundred years after its revelation, Islam was still used as a political instrument, both by ruling establishments as well as ordinary believers. A majority preferred to interpret God's words literally, which inevitably created controversies not in terms of faith, but in terms of socio-political discourses. Many difficulties associated with how a believer drew various linkages between the godly and the temporal surfaced, which arguably became worse after the rise of the nation-state system, especially in the Arab world. In fact, the gradual introduction of modern states to the Muslim world meant that the traditional systems in place – tribal, paternalistic, dynastic and others – were being phased out, while religious norms were open to interpretations.[16] Unforeseen clashes by so-called "Islamists," which often focused on demands made on those who exercised authority, neglecting to account for the massive destruction of tribal or patriarchal setups that functioned more or less untouched by innovation for a millennia. In the event, as the nation-state system gained a foothold on the Arabian Peninsula, especially in Sa'udi Arabia, a culturally significant tribal system was literally erased, only to be replaced with a contemporary apparatus that clarified how force would be used and by whom.[17] Even before the 1932 declaration that created the Kingdom of Sa'udi Arabia, the founder ruler painstakingly invoked the need to establish regular armed forces, a bureaucracy, and all of the trappings that accompanied a modernizing state. Religion – and not faith as it was mistakenly assumed – would be used to serve the righteous state and its rulers. To be sure, 'Abdul 'Aziz bin 'Abdul Rahman was a pious ruler, but he was a monarch nevertheless. Importantly, he made sure that everyone, including those learned men he was fond of welcoming in his *majlises*, understood where the seat of power in the nascent kingdom was.[18]

Unlike many Muslim ruling families, the Al Sa'ud did not claim divine privileges to rule the country, nor did they make any associations with the Quraysh tribe of the Prophet Muhammad. Their privileges for authority were chiefly based on innate capabilities that united the Peninsula's various tribes into confederations, which in turn were amalgamated into a nascent monarchy, under the control of a rising ruling family that wrestled power from competing hierarchies. At times, unification was violent and bloody through military conquests, whereas at other times it was relatively peaceful as tribal allegiances were sealed through marriage. Still, the founder monarch was a devout individual who was keenly aware of the power of the pulpit, and he did not shy away from exploiting that authority as necessary. His subjects could approach him to request favors and he would be predisposed to listen and comply to their wishes as circumstances allowed or warranted. It was a compact that was deeply rooted in tradition and religiosity, and the practice would be honed to tailor-fit his wishes, which imbued generosity while maintaining full power.

Petition traditions before 1979

'Abdul 'Aziz bin 'Abdul Rahman was a master at consulting. Early on, he fostered and retained good relations with his subjects, bestowing on as many as possible generous stipends. He also convened regular meetings of tribal, military, and religious leaders in Riyadh to discuss urgent matters. On June 4, 1924, for example, the founder gathered key tribal leaders to assess an *Ikhwan* – a religious and military brotherhood that helped the ruler to unite the Arabian Peninsula – petition that requested authorization to mount a campaign against Makkah and Madinah, where corruption was allegedly rampant. A few weeks after a debate on the matter in his *majlis*, which he led as was his custom, 'Abdul 'Aziz's minuscule staff managed to have a "Green Book" printed and circulated, that specifically explained his decision to authorize an assault. In July 1924, about 2,000 *Ikhwan* members raided the al-Turabah hamlet near Ta'if, where four thousand Ottoman soldiers and perhaps as many as 7,000 men from the Hijaz, were thoroughly defeated.[19] Ta'if was spared and the ruler threatened to authorize the execution of any soldier who murdered an unarmed civilian, as he promised the city's inhabitants full safety. Within two months, *Ikhwan* forces took Ta'if, after the Hijazi commander foolishly neglected the town's fortifications. As it turned out, what was important for this discussion was 'Abdul 'Aziz's responses to the petition, as well as his predisposition to inform friend and foe alike of his ultimate objectives.

Remarkably, 'Abdul 'Aziz relied on his daily *majlis* to settle the affairs of state wherever he was throughout the vast territory he conquered, and which he eventually united. The *majlis*, both the permanent version at his palaces along with its ambulatory variety during one of his numerous trips – essentially his large tent – acted as his office, where he received dignitaries and ordinary subjects. He would greet all those who wished to see him, even if the hour was late, especially when the Court was on the road. Every petition was received with utmost care and as was his habit, the founder monarch would give attendees a gift that he would "personally authorize, checking the ledger himself."[20] The ruler's generosity complicated matters financially. Amin Rihani, one of his contemporary chroniclers, reported that while "Every King in the world [was] supported by his people, the people of Najd [were] supported by their King."[21] Naturally, the gifts were bestowed according to status, though his early apprenticeship in Kuwait – where he probably attended his first power *majlis* in the 1890s – must have prompted him to be far more generous than his circumstances allowed. With rare exceptions, no one was turned away, and every petition received appropriate attention.

Sa'ud bin 'Abdul 'Aziz learned from his illustrious father, and while there were many reasons why the founder liked to keep his sons close, at least one may well have been related to his keen interest in teaching them how to lead. King Sa'ud equaled his predecessor in few areas, though he kept the *majlis* tradition alive. As conditions warranted, the monarch would receive ordinary citizens, entertain their petitions, and delegate one of a growing slew of assistants who specialized in the subject at hand to resolve the matter expeditiously. Most of the requests dealt with personal matters, ranging from financial assistance for dowry purposes to seeking advance medical care abroad, to the allocation of farmland or similar concerns.

Faysal bin 'Abdul 'Aziz followed his father's and his elder brother's examples of accessibility by maintaining a *majlis*, where his countrymen could discuss their problems or petition the monarch, and where ordinary citizens could have access to their ruler. Without exaggerating this last point, it was important to state that it was possible for a Sa'udi citizen to attend a royal *majlis* at the time, especially since King Faysal perceived the exercise as a legitimizing tool. Time and security concerns slowed down the frequency of these gatherings significantly in recent years but they were held nevertheless. Petitions were received, tabulated, and forwarded to appropriate ministries for action. Indeed, no matter how farfetched or long-winded the complaints presented were, Faysal would listen, confiding: "If anyone feels wrongly treated, he has only himself to blame for not telling me."[22] Both Faysal and his predecessor were keenly aware of how critical their responses were to citizen supplications, and both answered in the affirmative to most requests. It should be emphasized that few if any of these demands were political in nature. Most dealt with financial requests, which was understandable in a monarchical set-up, defining relationships between rulers and the ruled in a paternalistic society. Ironically, among the petitions that were political were Faysal's own pleas with the kingdom's *'Ulamah*, as the then heir apparent turned to religious authorities to settle his political differences with his brother.[23]

Juhayman 'Utaybi and his "Letters"

Direct confrontations with the regime diminished after the defeat of the *Ikhwan*, and while periodic occurrences throughout the 1950s and 1960s were not uncommon, it was King Faysal's assassination in 1975 that introduced a pivotal new marker within the body politic. Those who were anxious to challenge the legitimacy of the Al Sa'ud were significantly emboldened by this killing. Still, an equally cataclysmic rebellion occurred in 1979, when two quasi-simultaneous events rocked the kingdom's political establishment. On November 20, 1979, Juhayman bin Muhammad al-'Utaybi, the grandson of an *Ikhwan* warrior, challenged the guardianship of the ruling family over Islam's sacred space. Al-'Utaybi presented his followers with a *mahdi* – a guided one, who happened to be his brother-in-law, Muhammad bin 'Abdallah al-Qahtani – which illustrated, at least in the minds of militants, the existence of a linkage for rational Islamic Puritanism.[24]

Juhayman al-'Utaybi's uprising emerged from a movement called *al-Jam'ah al-Salafiyyah al-Muhtasibah*,[25] which rejected the legal schools of Islam and argued for literal readings of religious texts.[26] After the gates of the mosque were closed, when thousands of worshippers were trapped inside the Holy Haram, al-'Utaybi delivered a speech that called for the establishment of a true Islamic government in a country governed by a faithful believer. He showed contempt to the Al Sa'ud ruler and chastised the monarchy, insisting that the latter sever all ties with unbelievers, which chiefly meant the United States. 'Utaybi's warriors held a number of hostages for about three weeks, fiercely fighting security forces, which were seconded by Pakistani troops and French counter-terrorism experts from the Groupe d'Intervention de la Gendarmerie Nationale (GIGN), France's elite army commandos. Once defeated, 67 rebels were swiftly beheaded, several others imprisoned for various terms.[27] To be sure, the uprising shocked the Sa'udi population and its leaders, as Riyadh responded to this challenge with force. Once calm returned to Makkah, the government increased funding for religious endeavors and, reluctantly, bolstered additional powers to religious authorities. It was with this tragic episode in mind that Prince Fahd bin 'Abdul 'Aziz insisted on being called the "Custodian of the Two Holy Mosques," even if the change occurred in 1986, while the title "king" was periodically used, too.[28]

The second 1979 incident took place in the Eastern Province, where several thousand Sa'udi Shi'ahs, perhaps motivated by social and political frustration and energized by the then blossoming Islamic Revolution in Iran, celebrated *'Ashurah* on November 28. At the time, such a celebration was in clear violation of the official ban, which elicited a heavy-handed response that provoked local outrage. Authorities intended to restore law and order in a particularly sensitive part of the country that, not surprisingly, prompted security forces to respond with legendary severity.

These developments formed a turning point in Sa'udi domestic and international policy. As stated earlier, and partly to placate Juhayman's forcefully articulated frustration with what he considered to be moral depravity and deviation from strict religious tenets, the Al Sa'ud build new religious institutions and committed additional resources to the religious establishment. This pacification policy translated into beefed-up measures that encouraged thousands of Sa'udis eager to wage *jihad* against the Soviet Union, including 'Usamah bin Ladin, to move to Afghanistan. Even if bin Ladin's move was circuitous via Sudan and, perhaps, Yemen, Afghanistan turned out to be a solid outlet for the kingdom's reform-minded Islamists who were now supported by officials anxious for the militants to proselytize abroad. Likewise, the Shi'ah uprising in Qatif and other predominantly Shi'ah towns in the Eastern Province, prompted concern amongst the ruling family that the revolutionary message exported by Ayatollah Ruhollah Khomeini of Iran found fertile ground in the kingdom, which posed a genuine existential threat. Riyadh took some steps to address Shi'ah grievances without, however, acceding to any of their many political demands.[29]

For the purposes of this investigation, Juhayman's 'Letters' were especially important, as the supplication was delivered to the entire nation.[30] The militant's *Rasa'il* (Epistles or Letters) associated the kingdom's social, economic, religious and political disorders with the modern pace of change, and found fault in the 1744 Al Sa'ud-Al Shaykh alliance, which allegedly skirted traditions. There was no denying that Juhayman rejected this alliance and was willing to commit the ultimate act of defiance against the Al Sa'ud by desecrating the Holy Haram. In the event, theologically challenging arguments flowed with relative ease throughout his carefully drafted manuscripts, as the well-read man engaged in sound, even if objectionable, religious discourse. His political message was summarized in five main points that reverberated ever since, and that must be relevant to Sa'udi officials assessing the impact on more recent extremists.

First, Juhayman believed that indigenous values must supercede all else, and that Riyadh must reject Western emulations. Second, he called for the overthrow of the Al Sa'ud monarchy and the establishment of a just Islamic government. Third, the rebel demanded accountability from both the ruling family as well as the *'Ulamah*, ostensibly because the regime and its acolytes tolerated foreign exploitation of the country. Fourth, al-'Utaybi insisted that oil production should only meet internal needs and that no exports be allowed to the United States because of Washington's alleged rejection of Islam and of Muslims. Fifth, and finally, Juhayman demanded that all foreign civilian and military experts be expelled from the country, supposedly because they were dominating it.[31] Whether Juhayman believed that his epistles would mobilize a majority of Sa'udis against the ruling family was impossible to determine, though what was rather clear was the impact of his actions and words on a segment of the population. Rather than appeal to establishment figures for yet another ruling, the charismatic would-be preacher rejected the very idea of supplication, or even that of a petition to either the ruler or senior 'Ulamah who knew him rather well. Instead, he composed letters that inspired future militants, cognizant that entreaties were long-term propositions that necessitated gestation. This was, perhaps, the most dangerous aspect of Juhayman's outburst. Denial notwithstanding, his political impact was far greater than generally assumed, something that few anticipated before 9/11 in the United States and 5/12 in Sa'udi Arabia.[32]

Militant fundamentalism before 1991

What the 1979 siege of the Holy Haram revealed, above all else, was the existence of serious cleavages in Sa'udi Arabia. The state, which based its very legitimacy on Islam, as well as the ruling family's pledge to defend and uphold the faith throughout the world, generated opposition on these very premises. In retrospect, the occupation of the mosque would only represent "the 'the tip of the iceberg' with respect to the widespread revivalism that emerged in the 1970s."[33] Several factors defined the neo-fundamentalist protests that emerged in the 1980s and early 1990s, which grew into formidable political forces, but whose disunity helped the Al Sa'ud.

Before addressing the nascent movements, it is critical to briefly highlight a few pertinent concerns that materialized as the oil boom of the late 1970s and early 1980s galvanized the Sa'udi population, to better understand their repercussions on more recent events. In fact, the collapse of oil prices, which meant that oil production and exports diminished significantly, literally meant smaller revenues and a variety of economic problems. Budget deficits became the rule rather than the exception, as Riyadh drastically scaled back many of its cherished projects that marked the optimism of the late 1970s.[34] Gone were the days when every problem could be resolved by spending unlimited resources, especially as foreign powers added to the kingdom's financial burden, by insisting that Sa'udi Arabia pay for its physical protection.

Equally consequential was the 1990 Iraqi invasion and occupation of Kuwait, and the eventual war to liberate the Shaykhdom in 1991. Elated by the US-led, UN-mandated, and multi-national victory, Riyadh, perhaps much more than Kuwait, was nevertheless shocked by the financial bill presented by their ally, the United States.[35] Needless to say that the billions added up and created fresh economic pressures on an already overtaxed system. In the eyes of most Islamist opposition leaders, including 'Usamah bin Ladin, the financial commitments were exaggerated, many concluding that senior Al Sa'ud officials fattened their bank accounts throughout the period.[36] Corruption charges were nothing new in the kingdom with critics accusing members of the ruling establishment of living the high-life on the backs of the downtrodden. Even worse was the alleged infraction of welcoming hundreds of thousands of "heathen" Westerners that, in 1990–91 meant the presence of nearly 500,000 American troops, including women and Jews. There was no denying that members of the American armed forces incorporated many women soldiers who wore their uniforms rather than 'abayas. Likewise, a number of servicemen and women happened to profess Judaism, which upset fundamentalists who did not want to see Christians and Jews – believers in religions other than Islam, but "People of the Book" nonetheless – to even be in Sa'udi Arabia. That the very presence of American troops, with a complement of women, Jews, and other undesirable elements, was sanctioned by senior 'Ulamah further upset Islamists. Few appreciated the fatwah that declared Saddam Hussein of Iraq an "enemy of God," even if the latter's atrocities were widely known, as was that the Iraqi strongman nurtured an anti-Islamist reputation by routinely executing or torturing religious figures. All such considerations were brushed aside as Shaykh 'Abdul 'Aziz bin Baz's fatwah was targeted as the mother of all sellouts. Remarkably, the decree and, perhaps, news about how it was commissioned by the monarch and announced by the Palace, emboldened several opposition figures. This was when petitions to the king took on a particularly virulent form.

Al Sa'ud princes insisted that their visions of life went through the prism of Islam, arguing, nevertheless, that their interpretations were tolerant. Most were trenchant in their scrutiny of the country's conservative and new generation clerics, several of whom admonished the Al Sa'ud for tolerating corruption and for doing America's bidding in the Gulf region. The open confrontation between Riyadh and the Islamists occurred when six renowned individuals publicly announced the foundation of Saudi Arabia's first human rights organization, the *Committee for the Defense of Legitimate Rights* (CDLR).[37] Articulate and vocal committee members expeditiously became the voice of a genuine opposition movement, which was then, unsurprisingly and quickly, banned. Dr. Muhammad Al Mas'ari, a physicist with a doctorate from the University of California at Berkeley and married to an American, was one of the six original founders. He escaped through Yemen and reached London in 1994, where he sought asylum.[38] Fortuitously, the British capital proved an ideal spot for dissidents who relied on the city's vast pool of human rights defenders to present their cases on the airwaves. Shortly after Mas'ari settled down in London, a vast electronic system was put in place, with daily missives flying off facsimile machines, supplemented by monthly reports and various communiqués that were beamed in large quantities into the kingdom. In 1996, a schism occurred within the CDLR, when Muhammad al-Mas'ari disassociated himself from Sa'ad al-Faqih, who founded the Movement for Islamic Reform in Arabia (MIRA).[39] What these "outlawed" dissidents wanted above all else was to exert pressure on the regime for political reforms. Their examples encouraged others in the country to make similar calls, as both secularists, or so-called "liberalists," petitioned the monarch.

What passed for secularists in the kingdom urged the monarch to create new institutions and open up the political system. Presumably, the purpose of such steps would be to encourage greater public participation, perhaps even allow a degree of political as well as institutional liberalization. Not to be outdone by supposed liberalists, Sunni or *Salafi* religious reformers, certainly the most vocal of the regime's critics, jumped on the bandwagon, too. Unabashedly, they denounced what in their eyes constituted the country's Westernization, which was a misreading of the modernization that started under 'Abdul 'Aziz and continued ever since. Still, theirs was a political ploy par excellence, given that the primary objective was to take advantage of the opportunity to strengthen the weakened clergy's power. No Al Sa'ud ever dismissed the role of Islam in government policy and asking for such a restoration was comical at best. Yet, demands were made and fatwahs issued, which irritated senior members of the ruling family. Much like in 1979, the ruling family reacted to mounting pressure with several policies, including a suppression of vocal dissidents and the co-optation of different groups. These measures were, in large part, responses to the key petitions made in the early 1990s, which prompted King Fahd to finally issue his 1992 Basic Law, along with the creation of the advisory *Majlis al-Shurah* a year later. Although critics dismissed both as symbolic steps that ultimately changed little, both were significant responses to the petitions presented to the Al Sa'ud. Both initiatives deflated mounting internal pressures, which illustrated that the ruling family would entertain compromises as long as it retained its monopoly over political power.

Letters and memoranda

One of the most important developments associated with the 1990 Iraqi occupation of Kuwait was the heartening action of a few dozen women who got behind the wheel in the Sa'udi capital. On November 6, 1990, protesters defied the ban on women driving, but were quickly arrested, with several of the women reportedly being punished or denounced by powerful religious figures. Clergymen demanded that the government formally ban women from getting behind the wheels, even if *badu* women in the countryside availed themselves of such chores for decades.[40] Most were chastised for their abrasive actions, a few temporarily lost their jobs, while others saw their passports confiscated. Humiliated husbands, fathers, and brothers who took custody of their women from police headquarters, were sternly lectured by members of the *Commission for the Promotion of Virtue and the Prevention of Vice*, the *mutaw'ayyin*. Still, the joy rides emboldened at least forty-three businessmen and intellectuals to sign a petition to the monarch a month later, in which they demanded that the powers granted religious authorities be curtailed. They forcefully argued that all Qur'anic interpretation, even though the doors of *ijtihad* were long closed in Sunni Islam, were amendable. No one was questioning the authenticity of the Holy Scriptures, but all wondered why the *'Ulamah* were granted irrefutable clout. Without mincing their words, petitioners demanded the adoption of a new press law that would mimic progressive legislation in other countries, including Arab countries like Lebanon and

Kuwait, and insisted that women should not be ignored or neglected since they could play positive roles in the country's socio-economic activities.[41] Whether the petition prompted Riyadh to respond to these demands, or whether the presence of significant foreign media operations preparing to broadcast Operation Desert Storm acted as the catalyst to what occurred next, was impossible to determine. Still, as the war began, Sa'udi television offered its viewers live CNN feed. This measure stood in direct contrast to the news blackout on August 1, 1990 when Iraq invaded and occupied Kuwait. Liberal elements in society were pleased that real-time news was available on local airwaves, but conservative clerics perceived this action as an affront to their sensibilities. They posited that Sa'udi media should not assist images demonstrating Western military and technological superiority or, even worse, to feed the public Western perceptions of the war against a fellow Muslim state.[42]

At the end of the war, and as promised by King Fahd on the airwaves, a complete American withdrawal from Sa'udi soil started, though not as fast as younger motivated clergymen wished. The monarch was incensed that such demands would be made on a ruler who risked much to prevent an Iraqi invasion and occupation of the kingdom. Fahd was not amused by the brashness and, according to senior princes, voiced his displeasure in many private gatherings. In the event, several clerics openly criticized the ruler, which prompted the impetuous crowd to claim that they – the clerical class – and not the Al Sa'ud would better protect the country from what they perceived to be a Western cultural onslaught.[43] By February 1991, fifty-two religious figures, drafted a *Khitab al-Matalib* (Letter of Demands) petition, which made eleven specific demands, headed by a plea to establish an independent consultative council that would "decide on internal and external affairs" (see Appendix 10). They further stipulated that: (2) "all political, economic and administrative laws and regulations" conform to *Shari'ah*; (3) state officials and their representatives be competent, dedicated, upright and honest; (4) that everyone's rights be safeguarded "without any favoritism to the privileged or condescension towards the disadvantaged"; (5) public wealth be distributed "among all classes and factions of society"; (6) "strong and integrated armed forces" be built "to protect the country and its sacred values"; (7) media outlets be reconstructed to serve Islam; (8) that the country's foreign policy be directed to defend the interests of the nation "away from illegitimate alliances"; (9) religious and missionary institutions be provided "with all necessary human and material resources"; (10) judicial organs be unified with "real independence" to render justice; and (11) individual and collective rights be protected.[44]

In other words, the message was crystal clear: clergymen who would implement *Shari'ah* laws, and shun alliances like the Riyadh–Washington partnership, should be empowered.[45] Riyadh could not but take note of this petition, which may have garnered over 400 signatures from preachers, heads of Islamic organizations, judges, and leading religious scholars, especially from among younger clerics. Even the Mufti of the Kingdom, Shaykh 'Abdul 'Aziz bin

Baz, supported the petition by signing it, even adding a key sentence to the draft: "On the basis of Islamic Law," further legitimizing the petition. As expected, the draft was presented to the Palace, and thousands of copies were circulated throughout the country.

In July 1992, 107 religious scholars signed a still stronger petition under the title *Muzakarat al-Nasihah* (Memorandum of Advice) to King Fahd, who refused to receive the 46-page document.[46] It is possible to summarize the memorandum's complex and multifaceted contents into ten-major points.

1 Enhance the roles of the *'Ulamah* and support calls for *dua'*, as both were marginalized in public life. It was critical for secular authorities to submit to such authority uniformly across the country;
2 Apply *Shari'ah* law across the board to salvage what could be saved from the country's judiciary that, allegedly, was being "invaded by non-Muslim regulations;
3 Strengthen the authority of Muslim courts, which purportedly were significantly weakened over the years, and whose independence from secular powers was essential;
4 Stop the monarchy from continuing its supposed violations of human rights and human dignity which, to put it mildly, was both audacious and challenging;
5 End rampant corruption – ostensibly encouraged by Riyadh to serve its divide-and-rule preferences – throughout the bureaucracy, to allow for complete administrative reforms that would restore justice to people, and punish those who were responsible for hurting the national interest;
6 Introduce rational Islamic financial and economic practices so that public funds were expended to serve citizens. Because the Al Sa'ud supposedly financed corrupt regimes and dictatorships in various countries, and because it relied on international financial alliances, petitioners believed, Riyadh was neglecting internal concerns, ranging from education to health. The time had come for transparency and for instituting Islamic banking;
7 Maintain and empower the welfare system so that the current generation, as well as coming ones, benefited from oil wealth;
8 Equip the weak military with the latest available tools to avoid a repeat of the fiasco in the aftermath of the War for Kuwait, which highlighted intrinsic problems that needed urgent attention, especially since the country relied on external powers to defend itself. It was essential to protect the nation by enlarging the army and adding qualitatively to its arsenal. Moreover, military alliances that undermined the sovereignty of the nation should be cancelled, even if no foreign power launched an attack on the kingdom;
9 Propagate Islam since that was the most honorable duty that a Muslim state could embark on. Towards that end, equip the media to play a greater role in fulfilling this role, to promote Islam and the good deeds undertaken in its name, as well as defend against those who defamed the faith;

10 Practice a foreign policy that did not contravene the admonitions of the Holy Qur'an and the Prophet's *Hadiths*, which indicated that a Muslim state ought to have at its ultimate goal the propagation of the faith. All foreign policy initiatives, therefore, ought to advance Muslim objectives, and the monarchy, which apparently failed in this respect, was called upon to end its alliances with non-Muslim states whose goals were to dominate Muslims.[47]

Although King Fahd refused to accept this long petition, he nevertheless sought to diminish the challenges posed by its publication, by sharply increasing allocations for religious activities. At the height of an unending economic crisis, Riyadh authorized a significant manpower increase for employees toiling in a variety of religious establishments, including those affiliated with the Ministry of Pilgrimage and Religious Trusts from the *mu'uzins* (those who issue the call to prayer) to various imams working in mosques.[48]

In July 1993, the monarch elevated Shaykh 'Abdul 'Aziz bin Baz to the position of Grand Mufti of the kingdom, and established the Middle East Broadcasting Center (MBC) as an outreach to Muslims living overseas.[49] Parallel to these public steps, police and intelligence officials visited the homes of many of the individuals who had signed the petition to admonish them, even forbid a few from teaching or preaching, though it was not possible to ignore that several leading clergymen – the so-called "untouchables" – were among petition signatories. In addition to Shaykhs 'Abdul 'Aziz bin Baz and Muhammad bin Salih al-'Uthaymin, two important figures also gained notoriety: Shaykh Safar al-Hawali and Shaykh Salman al-Awdah. Hawali and Awdah were the two leading *Sahwists* ("awakening") Shaykhs who had publicly opposed the presence of American troops in the country. Though they temporarily froze criticisms of the ruling family after Iraq launched missiles at Riyadh and Dhahran in January 1991, both were vocal anti-Western advocates, fearing that American culture in particular would condemn Sa'udis to non-Islamic norms. Ironically, both eventually "repented," although few of their backers understood the transformation since consistency was a necessity for vocal preachers admonishing followers into action. More comically, Al-Awdah called for a boycott of American consumer goods, which was a nearly impossible task throughout the Arabian Peninsula that teemed with Western goods, and otherwise harped on his well-honed anti-American rhetoric. Even worse, he openly demanded that Riyadh expel all Shi'ahs, denying his fellow citizens a right that was well established after 1932, even if the Shi'ah were regularly discriminated against. For his part, Shaykh al-Hawali targeted Jews for corrupting the Middle East "through drugs, immorality, filthy films and filthy magazines" and opined that God would torment them until the end of time. "Hitler was a part of this promise," al-Hawali added, "and the [Palestine] liberation and *jihad* movements [we]re a part of this promise as well."[50]

Not only was it not possible to overlook this level of rhetoric, it was also dangerous, given the trickle-down phenomenon within the dissident community.

As a first reaction, the regime tried to co-opt some of the ideas posited by Awdah, Hawali, and others. In fact, after the first "religious" petition, King Fahd emphasized Muslim contributions to world civilizations, perhaps as a way to refute assertions that Western-materialism was replacing Muslim values. Several Sa'udi opinion columnists recommended that the kingdom formally launch a counterattack against Western denigrations that Sa'udi Arabia, and most Muslim states for that matter, were subjected to in more or less routine fashion. Indeed, to deny that Muslims made and were continuing to make major contributions to human civilization was infantile, though Islamophobia gained ground in the aftermath of 9/11, especially in the United States.[51] Still, a well-known academic contended that Riyadh "should exploit ties to Muslim diasporas in the West to transform the Christian crusade against Muslims into a crusade to Islamize the Christian world," even if no one acted upon this suggestion.[52]

It must be emphasized that King Fahd did not accede to *Sahwist* demands, either to abandon Riyadh's vital military alliances with Washington and other leading Western powers, nor to expel foreign troops. Nevertheless, the monarch's March 1992 announcements regarding the Basic Law of Government and the establishment of the Consultative Council were perceived as major concessions, which emboldened opposition figures. By granting the most important request made by nearly all petitioners, the ruler drew the proverbial "line in the sand" as far as dissent was concerned, though these were long promised items in the state's reforms agenda. Still, most petitioners could no longer complain, as opponents of the regime were forced to think about and propose fresh concerns. A few advocated a more pronounced Islamization of Sa'udi society, but this was akin to Catholics asking the Pope to convert to Christianity. The *Muzakarat al-Nasihah* irritated many but the tone was straightforward and its charges quite specific, which may be why the Al Sa'ud chose to respond to it. In that sense, at least, the "advice" was taken even if petitioners were made to settle for less than what they requested. As some of the demands made in these key petitions were similar in nature as well as substance, calling on the government to restore order in the economy, protect society from outside interferences, end widespread bribery, favoritism, and the extreme feebleness of the courts, Riyadh could not simply ignore everything at once. While senior ruling family members most probably stuck to their domestic and foreign policy planks, and while the Al Sa'ud remained faithful to a rigorous application of *Shari'ah*, they nevertheless relinquished to major demands. To be sure, they did not accept the fanciful notion of transferring political power to clergymen, but they did not wish to antagonize clerics either. In an important *tour de force*, Riyadh managed to muzzle Shaykh bin Baz and other senior clerics, insisting that the *Hay'at Kibar al-'Ulamah* [Board of Senior Scholars] condemn the Memorandum. Much like his father, 'Abdul 'Aziz bin 'Abdul Rahman, Fahd co-opted the clergy, drawing the boundaries of legitimate opposition. In a classic step, the monarch donned the opposition cloak, and insisted that liberal as well as conservative elements fall in. It may be worth repeating that he also recognized the value in making a few concessions.

Petitions after 1992

The 1992 creation of the *Majlis al-Shurah* did not mean the end of opposition criticisms or the circulation of petitions. Most targeted the United States and the Al Sa'ud's strong and growing alliance with Washington. A popular preacher, 'Ayad al-Qarni, released a cassette tape titled *America as I Saw It*, which criticized the ruling family for allying itself with a United States allegedly "overrun" by homosexuals, where children were frequently born out of wedlock, and where people were "beasts who fornicated" outside of marriage. On another cassette, a cleric who remained anonymous called the United States "the atheistic enemy of Islam," and insisted that "no allegiance is owed to the royal princes unless they follow Muslim law." One cleric even called for the execution of non-religious Muslims.[53] Such inflammatory rhetoric could not be ignored, which prompted Riyadh to adopt rather harsh methods to muzzle the opposition. In the summer of 1993, for example, *mabahith* (secret) police officers searched Shaykh Hawali's offices and froze Shaykh Awdah's bank accounts. As discussed earlier, Committee for the Defense of the Legitimate Rights (CDLR) founders were either arrested or allowed to escape via Yemen. Those who stayed in the country were apprehended, beaten, some were tortured, while others lost their university positions. A new chapter in the dissent war opened as facsimiles, television, e-mail and a variety of new electronic methods were used to flood the kingdom with "news" of the Al Sa'ud's suspected imminent collapse. Some clerics, including Hawali and Awdah were jailed, while a new crop of anti-Western free thinkers gained popularity. Among these was 'Usamah bin Ladin, who was energized by the Soviet defeat in Afghanistan, even if that victory was reached with the military cooperation of the United States, including to 'Usamah bin Ladin. Somehow, Riyadh managed to gradually regain control of the internal reforms debate and, no less important, further muzzled its religious opposition through minimal concessions.

Political petitions after 9/11

Two significant petitions in 2003 illustrated the gulf that existed between the Sa'udi intelligentsia and the pace of responses emanating from the Al Sa'ud. In January, the so-called "Vision for the Present and Future of the Nation" petition was signed by 104 professors, writers, businessmen, and retired officials, including both liberals and conservatives.[54] This was followed in September 2003 with an equally powerful petition, under the title "In "Defense of the Nation".[55]

Although the "Vision" petition began and ended with pledges of loyalty to the ruling family and never once used the words democracy, it forcefully called for absolute freedom of speech, assembly, and association. As will be discussed below, this comprehensive petition did not evade responsibility and did not mince its words, as it demanded equal rights for women, elections for legislatures with authority over the budget, an end to religious discrimination, amnesty for nonviolent political prisoners, and the promotion of "national dialogues" on critical issues. In fact, the petition invited the ruling family to begin moving toward a constitutional monarchy and, based on what King 'Abdallah embarked upon in sponsoring the country's comprehensive "National Dialogues," it may be safe to conclude that someone was paying attention.

At the time, of course, none of the concerns developed in the January 2003 petition were made public, although most members of the intelligentsia throughout the country knew about it, had seen a copy of it, read it, perhaps even digested it, or at the very least had heard snippets through highly effective rumor mills than oiled the monarchy's legitimizing engine. According to the generally well-informed London reporter writing for the *Guardian*, Brian Whitaker, Heir Apparent 'Abdallah invited 34 of the signatories to his Riyadh palace for a three-hour *majlis* on January 20, 2003.[56] News trickled out that the Regent informed those present: "Your demands are indeed my demands, and this is what I'm working on. And it's a matter of time. But we need time. Be patient, and rest assured that we are working on this."[57] An astute observer who spoke with elated attendees chimed in that the "precise meeting" – meaning one where specific concerns were aired and explicit answers provided – left many "jubilant and happy" that, finally, Sa'udi Arabia was entering a new era.[58]

Still, nothing occurred for several months, which led many to ponder whether 'Abdallah needed that much time to implement decisions. For reasons that are still murky, on September 24, 2003, 320 Sa'udis signed a new petition that repeated the demands of the January "Vision" supplication, this one under a rather provocative title "In Defense of the Nation," which implied that the ruling family may have been negligent on that front. Interior Minister Nayif was not amused and, according to Bassim Alim, the prince summoned several signers to ask them to discontinue their productions. "That meeting did not go very well," opined Alim, with Nayif chastising his guests to "stop these petitions. You should not write anymore. It's not going to be accepted anymore." When the minister was informed that petitions were the only available means to voice dissenting views, several were arrested, which added tensions to an already electrified environment. At yet another meeting, Alim confirmed that Nayif was even more adamant, as the minister vented his anger with severe admonitions:

> You know you should not have meetings, and you should not have congregations. And we are not going to condone the whole concept of reformation the way you think it should be. We are doing it the way we think it should be done. And it's not really reformation as in fixing things; it's reformation as in natural evolution. There is nothing wrong to be fixed. It's a matter of natural evolution.[59]

To say that the prospects for reforms in Sa'udi Arabia were not on a strong pedestal with such utterances, and that internal debates within the Al Sa'ud family were still unsettled, ought to surprise no one. In fact, the minister's reprimands stood in direct contradiction with utterances – and deeds – introduced by the monarch, which further highlighted existing differences. In the event, Muhammad Sa'id Tayyib, an elderly lawyer from Jiddah, reportedly told Prince Nayif: "If you want to stay 200 years more you must change to constitutional monarchy. The only way to save this country is through civil institutions. Otherwise the ceiling will fall on all of us." In response, according to one participant, Prince Nayif angrily accused the group of trying to "dismantle [the government] and turn the family into figureheads."[60] Even Heir Apparent 'Abdallah was unhappy with these clashes, and called the request for a written constitution an "arbitrary demand," which threatened "to destroy national unity."[61]

A few weeks after the meeting with Prince Nayif, several of the petitioners and other activists met in a Riyadh hotel to discuss what to do next, which telegraphed the gathering to the eyes and ears of internal security personnel. Senior Al Sa'ud leaders considered this a challenge to their authority and assumed that the effort was the genesis of an illegal political party. If few petition signers were arrested in the past for affixing their names to supplications made to a high-ranking official, the police could now apprehend and question men and women on the grounds that they made "statements that [did] not serve national unity or the cohesion of society."[62] Unlike previous raids, however, these fresh arrests were blatantly visible, which meant that internal security personnel had a public relations problem on their hands. Within days, ten of the thirteen men were released, after they were cajoled to sign a statement that committed them to refrain from future political activities. They were also banned from speaking with foreign media outlets. Three prominent men – a poet, a human rights activist, and a political science professor – refused to sign these declarations and remained confined. When several reformers met with Prince Nayif to ask for the release of the three prisoners, "over a dinner of chicken, lamb, rice and broccoli," the Minister of Interior warned the men to stay out of politics, lest their fate resemble those of his prisoners. "You're playing a game that's not yours," he apparently told his visitors, "You're getting into the business of the state, in which you don't belong."[63] After these arrests, there were no more petitions in 2004, and "newspapers stopped running articles about the need for reforms such as a more independent judiciary and a more detailed national budget." On May 15, 2004, after a trial that was closed to the public, "a Sa'udi court found the professor, the activist, and the poet guilty of sedition and sentenced them to six, seven and nine years in prison, respectively."[64] Behind the scenes American pressure finally influenced Riyadh to reconsider, as an appeals court scheduled to hear the cases, albeit a year later. On July 24, 2005, the Sa'udi Appeals Court upheld both the verdict and the long prison sentences, which were embarrassing to say the least.

When King Fahd bin 'Abdul 'Aziz died on August 1, 2005, barely a few days after the appeals court verdict was issued, it was up to 'Abdallah to respond. As if struck by lightening, one of 'Abdallah's first initiatives was to free the three dissidents. His order was executed on August 8, 2005, a week after he acceded to the throne, which signaled that the new monarch was keenly interested in genuine reforms and that he rejected some of the harsher methods used by the Ministry of the Interior under his predecessor's reign.

Political petitions under 'Abdallah

In the words of a leading historian, "political activism in Saudi Arabia manifests itself in the form of petitions," even if "the Saudi State is a post-modern pastiche in which several princes compete and co-operate and in which politics is dependent upon the subjective whims of princes who are at the centre of patronage networks that in recent years have spread across the globe."[65] After 2005, under the reign of King 'Abdallah, a series of new petitions made their way to the Palace, with various responses. A few deserve closer scrutiny, especially those concerned with women's emancipation, as well as several demanding the adoption of a constitutional monarchy.

It must be emphasized before proceeding that many of these petitions drew the ire of Al Sa'ud opponents, as was the case with the May 2006 statement posted on an Islamist website that condemned reformists in Sa'udi Arabia. That statement, which was signed by 61 conservative clerics, as well as university presidents, professors, attorneys, judges, educators and businessmen, warned that a "junta" had taken "hold of the Saudi media and was acting in the service of external enemies in order to 'Westernize' Saudi society – thus [allegedly] endangering society and its Islamic values."[66] It further demanded that Riyadh deny members of this "junta" positions of influence, and called on religious leaders to thwart its plans, without specifying how to proceed. Naturally, the proclamation provoked angry responses from many Sa'udi columnists for its extremism, as well as for its clear references to calls made by the likes of 'Usamah bin Ladin. Mashari Al-Dhaidi, for example, wrote in the London daily *Al-Sharq Al-Awsat*:

> The question is not whether [people] have or do not have the right to publish statements and to collect signatures, but rather whether the publication of such statements, using such language and with such incitement, is acceptable. We must take into account the fact that the accusations [made by the authors] of the statement, and their characterization of [the intellectuals] who disagree with them, amount to incitement to murder [intellectuals]. [Under the influence of this statement] the [public] might remain indifferent to the – hypothetical – possibility that some excitable youth might take the statement [literally], translating the words into deeds, and might think that it is his duty [according to] Shari'ah to grant the people and the country a respite from one of these "prophets of heresy".

Al-Dhaidi compared this statement to a April 23, 2006 'Usamah bin Ladin declaration, in which the invisible Afghani-resident incited his followers to fight the West. "There is some overlap between the imagery in bin Ladin's statement and [the imagery] used in the statement of the 61 [clerics]," wrote the reformer columnist, insisting that there was

> incitement against the same figures, but while bin Ladin mentions people by name and explicitly urges "to kill" them, the 61 [clerics], in insinuation that sounds very much like a pronouncement, describe them as being despicable hypocrites, and urge "to fight" them and to speak harshly against them, as was done to the hypocrites in Madinah in the Prophet's time. That is to say, the difference [between bin Ladin's statement and the clerics' statement] is one of tone, not of type.[67]

Regrettably, this statement was not the only one that directly challenged the monarch's reform initiatives. On April 9, 2006, over 130 Shaykhs and learned men issued a statement that opposed women's employment outside of the home, and generally opposed gender equality based on the claim that the *Shari'ah* designated men to be superior to women.[68] Earlier, a declaration in the name of 14 physicians called on heads of medical schools to ensure that only male students examined male patients and female students examined female patients, which was quite an idea, given the scarcity of experienced female medical personnel working in the country.[69] Other columnists expressed similar concerns, while a few were outraged to learn that signatories included learned individuals like physicians as well as presiding judges and Education Department officials.[70] The debate was heated to say the least, especially on the key concerns touching on gender equality and democratization.

Women petitioning to drive (2007)

In 2005, Muhammad al-Zulfah, a member of the *Majlis al-Shurah*, asked his colleagues to just entertain the idea of "studying the possibility of allowing women over the age of 35 or 40 to be allowed to drive un-chaperoned on city streets but accompanied by a male guardian on highways." A mere "suggestion," the question "touched off a fierce controversy that included calls for [the official's] removal from the council and stripping him of Sa'udi citizenship as well as accusations that he was encouraging women to commit the double sins of discarding their veils and mixing with men."[71] It was a futile effort, though the major test facing Sa'udi Arabia as a country was the challenge from Sa'udi women who insisted that modernization, often perceived by conservative elements as exposing oneself to immoral or outrageous behavior, was far from reality. The overwhelming majority of Sa'udi women were devout believers. Many were traditionalists who, nevertheless, trusted themselves to do the right thing, rather than be treated like incapacitated children. Driving was no longer a luxury for most, as urbanization, higher education, family duties, and business responsibilities imposed certain basic conditions on everyone. Above all else, the issue was economic, since it cost each family a significant sum of money to hire foreign drivers whose very presence became a necessity akin to a basic commodity that truly increased the burden on everyone in the household. Regrettably, and to date, this concern was not presented in the purely economic terms that may have persuaded authorities to introduce a gradual relaxation. Rather than present the issue in clinical terms that emphasized economics, a variety of social and religious angles were investigated over the years, which drew the ire of conservative elements steadfastly holding to age-old traditions.

On September 23, 2007, Sa'udi Arabia's National Day, over 1,100 Sa'udi activists, both men and women, petitioned King 'Abdallah to lift the ban on driving for women (See Appendix 15).[72] The petition, the brainchild of four activists – Fawziyyah al-'Ayouni, Wajihah al-Huwaydar, Ibtihal Mubarak, and Hayfah Usra – called for the establishment of a Committee for Women's Rights to Drive. Although the supplication did not succeed, it was not in vain either, since it raised a sensitive topic for public discussion. Interestingly, a few days before the petition was delivered, Wajihah al-Huwaydar declared that King 'Abdallah and Prince Nayif repeatedly stated this issue was "a social issue, not a religious one," and it was for this reason that members of the Committee for Women's Rights to Drive wished "to demonstrate to anyone who [thought] otherwise that there was a large swathe of society that was completely ready for [women] to exercise this right, and that it only took one stroke of the pen to issue the decision to allow women to drive cars – after which the entire world would see that Saudi women were completely ready to bear this responsibility."[73] She expressed the hope that influential men and women in positions of authority would support them, personalities like Her Highness Princess Lulwah Al-Faysal, the daughter of the late King Faysal, and Her Highness Princess 'Adilah bint 'Abdallah, the daughter of King 'Abdallah, among others. Naturally, if a few dozen princesses and businesswomen were to join such movements, chances were significantly better that solutions would be forthcoming. Such felicitous outcomes were not necessarily in the cards, however, especially when a putative natural ally like Dr. Turki al-Sudayri, the head of the Human Rights Authority in Sa'udi Arabia, apparently "expressed his indignation and anger at the campaign."[74] According to Wajihah al-Huwaydar, Dr. al-Sudayri was concerned that "the campaign would get in the way of a study that his institution was conducting to demonstrate that women driving was important because the [employment of] foreign drivers caused damage to families, and especially to children." This was certainly the case, although emotional attachments could not be so easily dismissed as to make room for yet another study. The encounter illustrated, however, that deeply ingrained sociological currents persisted in the paternalistic society.

Still, the 2007 petition marked the second major effort by women to break the ban on driving and came after the November 6, 1990 effort by a group of

47 educated women – a group that included university professors and physicians who, ironically, held valid foreign drivers' licenses from the time they spent in Western countries, Egypt and Lebanon – who defied the prohibition in Riyadh, only to be rounded up by police.[75] At the time, Shaykh 'Abdul 'Aziz bin Baz issued a fatwah that prohibited women from driving, even if no civil laws were ever issued for a prohibition. The issue then disappeared from the media for a few years only to return in 2007.

This time around, organizers presented their petition as a social, not a religious or political request, though a stronger case could have been made on economic grounds. For al-'Ayouni, the petition would at least highlight what many Sa'udi women, and some men, considered as a "stolen right," which was a financial burden as drivers were needed to go to work, school, shopping, or even to see one's physician. Paradoxically, and despite Shaykh bin Baz's decree, and this is critical to repeat, no laws explicitly declared that such a ban existed in the kingdom. The prohibition flowed from a strict interpretation of woman's need to be accompanied by a legal guardian in public. While Sa'udi religious scholars almost always argued that women who would get behind the wheel might come in contact with non-related men, this was exactly what occurred with foreign male drivers, who were total strangers to them.

As expected, nothing happened after the 2007 petition, although organizers forwarded a fresh follow-up appeal in early 2008. According to news reports, signatories hoped "that 2008 [would] be the year in which Saudi women obtained their natural right to drive a car," as Fawziyyah al-'Ayouni promised that the Committee for Women's Rights to Drive was prepared to send to the monarch an updated supplication each time they managed to secure 1,000 new signatures.[76] It was a new tactic that did not accomplish the desired results. That is until May 21, 2011 when Manal al-Sharif, a 32-year-old who uploaded a video of herself behind the wheel on YouTube (wearing a *hijab* but not a face-covering *niqab*), thereby becoming an Internet sensation, which promptly led to her arrest. Incredibly, she was held in police custody for ten days, a period of time that literally mobilized Sa'udi society, given her circumstances and family conditions.[77] To be sure, the "event" occurred in Al-Khobar, near Dammam, which was a relatively open city on account of its proximity to Bahrain. Nevertheless, and notwithstanding the generally more tolerant environment in the Eastern region of the kingdom, Ms. al-Sharif, an IT expert who worked for Aramco and was in need of basic transportation to reach her employer, lived with complicated male guardianship requirements. As a divorced woman living alone, she could neither depend on her former husband nor other male guardians to get to work. She was eventually released but detained once again the next day for violating public order. Importantly, however, when she was first arrested by members of the Commission for the Promotion of Virtue and Prevention of Vice, "she was asked to sign a mandatory paper stating that she would not break the kingdom's laws again." Al-Sharif announced that she planned to join a June 17 women's driving protest and, under very strong protests, tendered an apology for having violated driving laws.[78]

Figure 5.1 Manal al-Sharif – *Arab News*. Reproduced with permission.

Manal Al-Sharif's arrest and release was not the end of the story, as seven additional women were placed in custody for driving in June 2011. Over the course of several weeks, and leading up to a planned June 17 protest, about 30 or 40 Sa'udi women across the country took the wheel, determined to change the ban in place. Ironically, as revolutionary upheavals spread throughout the Arab world, the so-called March 11, 2011 "Day of Rage" in the kingdom was barely noticed, although the spark lit by Manal al-Sharif left a far greater impact. According to news reports, "police appeared to be under orders not to intervene," with one woman in Jiddah claiming that "she had been detained by soldiers and escorted home. Others reported being ignored." A few were stopped by traffic officers, issued a ticket for driving without a Sa'udi license, and sent home.[79] Wajihah al-Huwaydar, the activist who filmed Sharif's drive, insisted that the "big campaign" might make the government rethink.

Al-Huwaydar insisted that the 2007 petition was just a small element of committee members' plans, as she envisaged the creation of a Ministry of Women's Affairs, as well as an Association for the Protection and Defense of

Women's Rights in Sa'udi Arabia. To say that a few young Sa'udi women, albeit safe in their elite niches, were beginning to think big would be an understatement. In other words, and this much was certain, driving was a practical concern that was denied half the population of the kingdom, though some of these women were also interested in: improving their representation in *Shari'ah* courts, which was literally peripheral under current law; setting a minimum age for a girl to marry; allowing women to take care of their own affairs in government agencies; permitting them to enter government buildings; and protecting women from domestic violence, among other matters.[80] Though a few religious scholars devoted time to assessing whether women should work in lingerie shops or even attend sports matches – albeit in entirely segregated sections of popular volleyball or football stadiums, for example – others were carefully ushering in serious reforms on under-age marriage.[81] In fact, driving was an important matter, which necessitated a solution, and chances were good that the prohibition might be lifted before long. What were far more important, however, were the many other items on a long list of critical issues that affected women and their health, both physical and mental.

Democracy movement

In May 2009, a group of Sa'udi human rights and opposition activists drafted a new petition asking for additional political and judicial reforms, as well as fair trials for suspected al-Qa'idah militants. "We request his majesty," demanded the 77 predominantly academic signatories, "to implement his promised reform initiatives by establishing a modern state built on democracy, justice, dignity, equality, tolerance, pluralism and citizens' rights." This group, which included human rights activists, writers and academics, believed that long-promised trials against 991 suspected al-Qa'idah militants should be held without further delays in fair and public proceedings rather that the preferred secret variety.[82] Activists also appealed to the monarch to create an elected parliament with term limits on Al Sa'ud family members who were appointed to official posts. This was certainly a new wrinkle in the on-going debate as petitioners wished to see the post of prime minister, for example, to be assigned to "a commoner."[83] In language that was explicit, the petition "demand[ed] that the prime minister should be a commoner to ease accountability and to manifest the principle of circulations of authority."

If the attempt by this small but persistent group was to get its voice heard in an absolute monarchy that prohibited political parties, the effort was not in vain, given that none other than Prince Talal bin 'Abdul' Aziz raised the idea of a constitutional monarchy first, perhaps resembling the paradigm in Britain. Press reports quoted Fowzan Mohsin Al Harbi, a mechanical engineer at King 'Abdul 'Aziz City for Science and Technology in Riyadh, imploring that ordinary citizens "have to share in the decisions of our country." "We need an elected parliament and a prime minister from our people," he added, which would be "good for the royal family and ... good for the people." For Mohammed

Al Qahtani, a human rights activist who helped draft the petition, the effort was a "blueprint plan of what to do if [the Al Sa'ud] were serious about political reform."[84]

Whether the frequency with which these petitions were issued, or whether the confrontation between so-called liberal and conservative forces in the country irritated senior members of the ruling family, were impossible to know.[85] Rumors circulated that the monarch was displeased with the plethora of petitions on his desk just as much as he was irked by the bickering that such supplications engendered within the conservative society. More importantly, close associates of the ruler let it be known that the king was keenly aware of the progress that many were making within the national dialogues, and wished to strengthen that process. Petitions were welcomed as long as they stayed within established norms, as were fatwahs that senior clerics issued on key concerns that affected the nation as a whole. What upset 'Abdallah bin 'Abdul 'Aziz were the confrontations that resulted after clergymen refused to go along with his reform measures and wasted a good deal of time on tangential matters that bordered on the infantile. When Shaykh 'Abdul Muhsin al-Ubaykan, a former court advisor, issued a fatwah allowing unrelated men and women to mingle in public so long as a woman allows the male to drink her breast milk (albeit from a cup) in order to establish a maternal bond, or when an equally motivated cleric, Yusif al-Ahmad, issued another fatwah urging the faithful not to shop at the *Panda* supermarket chain because it employed women as cashiers, the ruler was not amused. On August 12, 2010, the king issued a royal decree, which stated that only officially approved religious scholars would henceforth be allowed to issue fatwahs.[86]

In the words of the editorialist Hussein Shobokshi, this epochal decree was a "pleasant surprise" since it imposed 'Abdallah's legendary "will to power." It was duly endorsed by the Grand Mufti of Sa'udi Arabia and presented in religious/legal language that stressed the necessity of confining the right to issue fatwahs to qualified scholars.[87] Shobokshi opined that the issuance of fatwahs was "held captive by a single religious viewpoint, weak interpretation, and a lack of doctrinal diversity, and it was therefore easy for the scene to be manipulated with opposing fatwahs being issued due to the huge number of issuers, which resulted in extremism giving rise to even greater extremism."[88] For many, the monarch's decision was a solid illustration of the kind of reforms Sa'udis desired, and fit nicely with ongoing initiatives through national dialogues and conferences where divergent views were openly discussed. If Riyadh recorded significant strides to rid mosques of extremist ideologies, and worked very hard to remove extremist sentiments from religious books, the decision to empower the Board of Senior *'Ulamah* was yet another marker on the ruler's reform path. It must be emphasized that the king's decision to limit authorization to the kingdom's Senior *'Ulamah* also meant that 'Abdallah was placing additional burdens on the Senior Board to reform itself, as well as on the entire clerical establishment to assume additional responsibilities. The monarch knew that strict restrictions were introduced in

2005, even if these were seldom enforced. After the August 2010 decree, few clerics in positions of responsibility could feign bureaucratization or institutional limitations. The monarch was no longer willing to settle for mediocre interpretations and, as he stated in the text of the decree delivered to Grand Mufti Shaykh 'Abdul 'Aziz Al Shaykh, the ruler underscored: "As part of our religious and national duty we want you to ensure that fatwahs are only issued by members of the Board of Senior *'Ulamah* and other permitted people." He continued, "individual fatwahs on personal matters such as matters of worship, dealings, personal matters are exempt from this ruling, but they should be between the questioner and the scholar. There should be a total ban on any topics involving strange or obsolete views." In other words, 'Abdullah was not asking the senior clerics to consider such perspectives, but to simply deny them. He went further by stating that it was a violation of *Shari'ah* to allow unqualified individuals to issue religious decrees, as such actions undermined state institutions and crossed into "state jurisdiction." The decree *instructed* the Grand Mufti to identify scholars qualified to issue fatwahs and, not surprisingly, several of the country's senior clerics, including Minister of Islamic Affairs Shaykh Salih bin 'Abdul 'Aziz Al al-Shaykh, and chairman of the Supreme Judicial Council Shaykh Salih bin Humayd, quickly voiced their unreserved support. In the event, the king's decree was a judicious use of an instrument – a royal decree – that was as effective as petitions forwarded to the monarch. The solid move to limit the chaotic opinions distributed in print or on unregulated Internet sites and some satellite television channels throughout the kingdom, essentially meant that the monarchy was no longer willing to allow every individual to interpret Islam as he or she pleased. Indeed, the ruler chose to use his power to impose order, but also to prevent extremists from misguiding younger adherents, preferably by encouraging excesses. One interpretation of the monarch's judicious use of the royal decree was akin to his own petition to clerics, although in his case the decree was the law of the land.

Conclusion

"If you could have read the letters that ['Abdallah bin 'Abdul 'Aziz] sent privately, brother to brother, to the king," confided 'Abdul 'Aziz Al-Tuwayjri, 'Abdallah's closest adviser, talking of the years before Fahd's illness, "you would have thought that the crown prince was leader of the opposition."[89] 'Abdallah's resort to letters was reminiscent of the petitions he was receiving, though little was known whether a largely debilitated King Fahd ever responded. The petition mechanism, whether private letters, political missives, decrees, or any number of private supplications presented to senior Al Sa'ud ruling family members were, to put it bluntly, the preferred communication method. Leading opponents of the government periodically highlighted how persistent their demands were, even if epochal developments throughout the Arab world changed the tone of the debate.

In early January 2011, an Associated Press report claimed that the Saʻudi Civil and Political Rights Association, a human rights group, petitioned King ʻAbdallah to remove Prince Nayif from his post as interior minister.[90] According to this *unpublished* petition, the monarch was asked to prosecute Nayif "for what it [allegedly claimed were] systematic human rights violations in the country." Even if true, such a tectonic shift in Saʻudi domestic discourse could not have come at a worst time, given the overall changes under way throughout the region. For it became clear that, in 2011, young men and women, mostly educated, secular, and unemployed, transferred their fear of authority to besieged governments throughout the Arab world who, in most cases, desperately held on to their seats. Although few could securely predict what the future would usher in, it seemed safe to assume that the Arab world would never again be what it looked like on December 17, 2010, the day when Tarek al-Tayyib Muhammad Bouazizi immolated himself in Tunisia. In less than six months, opposition forces in Tunisia, Egypt, Bahrain, Yemen, Syria, Libya, Morocco, Algeria, Oman, Jordan and Saʻudi Arabia, literally changed both the tone and the spirit of their long-standing demands for genuine political reforms. Bouazizi valiantly protested the confiscation of his meager possessions and rejected the humiliation that a poorly trained police officer baselessly inflicted on the 25-year-old. A moment of folly adjusted a regime and encouraged mobilized youths elsewhere in the region to fight for freedom and liberty. What Bouazizi did above all else, and for which he will long be remembered, was to free Arabs from the yoke of fear. In less than six months, most Arabs rejected their phobias, especially after the anxiety genie was let out of the proverbial bottle.

Few leaders seemed to have understood how fundamental these shifts were. Among those who recognized indispensable calls for political transformations was Sultan Qabus bin Saʻid of Oman, who shocked his subjects by acceding to popular demands, placing legislative authority in the hands of elected officials.[91] Likewise, Prince Turki Al-Faysal, the chairman of the King Faysal Center for Research and Islamic Studies in Riyadh and one of the kingdom's leading personalities, called for the election of members of the Saʻudi *Majlis al-Shurah*. Speaking at the Jiddah Economic Forum on a panel dealing with "Prosperous Citizenship," the erudite former chief of intelligence did not mince his words: "Participation in municipal elections and the election of members of the Shurah Council" will boost the country's intrinsic capabilities, he underlined.[92] Both of these men identified a key development in current makeovers, namely the critical role of increasingly educated masses with access to technology, rapid means of communication, and a desire to assume responsibilities. In fact, tribal, autocratic, or even military arrangements that guaranteed a semblance of stability were no longer applicable, because awakened and educated Arabs were finally willing to "step up to the plate." Most realized that economic prosperity would only come their way if they shouldered the burdens of a work ethic, put in minimum hours, and produced goods that their societies required. In a strange way, young Arabs rejected the *rentier* system, which had allowed current regimes to stay in power for so long, doling out cash as needed, but never doing more than what was required.[93]

Surprising many observers, both kings Muhammad VI of Morocco and 'Abdallah bin Husayn of Jordan, welcomed dramatic changes in their countries' respective constitutions, too. Rabat proposed constitutional reforms as it attempted to stave off democratic demands, with the monarch welcoming an enhanced role for an elected government that, allegedly, would strip him of some powers.[94] Muhammad VI foresaw the empowerment of an elected parliament, a strengthened prime ministership, a mandate to create an independent judiciary, guarantees to provide equality for women and, above all, efforts to reinforce the position of the monarch both as king and Commander of the Faithful. He was amply rewarded for his efforts although Moroccans clamored for more.[95] In Amman, King 'Abdallah II of Jordan, for his part, welcomed proposals for limited reforms of the constitution as a sign of political maturity among Jordanians. If approved, these changes would introduce a limited transfer of some powers to parliament, although the 42 proposals did not go far enough for most activists who were demanding the right to elect the Prime Minister. Whether the monarch would consent to forsake this privilege, which he promised to relinquish earlier, was impossible to determine as the wily ruler wished to avoid "chaos and unrest." Still, the Jordanian monarch confronted popular demands for greater government accountability and new economic policies, which were genuine and could no longer be addressed through simple gimmicks, given a steady stream of protests inspired by developments elsewhere in the Arab world.[96]

It was important to note that both Morocco and Jordan sought admission into the Gulf Cooperation Council, which posed a few serious problems precisely because of their rulers' desires to introduce changes – even of the cosmetic variety. Morocco and Jordan enjoyed healthy parliamentary lives that simply did not exist elsewhere in Arab monarchies, not even in Kuwait, where deputies were permanently locked in a catch-22 with the ruling Al Sabah family. To be sure, elected chambers may yet alter political lives in Oman and Bahrain, but few anticipated similar institutions in Sa'udi Arabia, the UAE and Qatar anytime soon.[97] Equally important were the active labor unions and political parties in Rabat and Amman, which made for interesting politics, even if the two monarchs retained veto power. Furthermore, and unlike the more conservative Gulf region, both Amman and Rabat displayed relatively open social structures, especially with respect to the roles of women, and which were not necessarily compatible with norms on the Arabian Peninsula.[98]

For most Arab leaders, the balance between ongoing programs and political adjustments was a delicate matter, and the kingdom was no exception. In his television address to the Sa'udi nation on March 18, 2011, King 'Abdallah declared that he was proud of his subjects, emphasizing that mere words could not describe them. He called on historians to note that after God, citizens were the "guarantors" of Sa'udi unity, especially since few bought into falsehoods. The vast majority of Sa'udis, the monarch accentuated, remained loyal and steadfast.[99] The most remarkable section in the short but carefully worded speech addressed religious scholars who were entrusted with the burden of explaining the word of God. While the monarch supported *'Ulamah* who confronted advocates of sedition, he reminded thinkers and *writers in general* to be vigilant on three fronts: religion, homeland, and the nation. Even if his words were couched in lofty praise, it was clear that the ruler was enthusiastic about every citizen who wished to support the truth, had nothing to fear, and, presumably, wanted to make useful contributions. In explicit terms, he underscored what one seldom heard from a Sa'udi monarch, indeed from most Arab leaders: namely, that citizens were at the heart of the nation and were its trustees to defend faith, provide for the country's security, and ensure its stability. 'Abdallah bin 'Abdul 'Aziz closed his presentation with a rare personal plea that touched all Sa'udis. He addressed his people saying, "God knows that I always hold you dear to my heart and that I derive determination, help and strength from God and then from you," and concluded with an even more private request: "Do not forget me in your prayers."[100]

Like most Arabs, Sa'udis were impressed and welcomed the monarch's generous financial packages, even if most were far more interested in learning how Riyadh planned to introduce solid reforms. They respected the king but demanded more. With a growing number of educated citizens, many wondered why the wheels of change were moving at a slow pace, when the need for frequent and meaningful updates was urgent. Many wondered why their petitions were ignored or, when acted upon, at a crawling pace. In fact, an overwhelming majority looked to Egypt, where voters approved a referendum on constitutional changes, as a useful paradigm. Countless Sa'udis demanded similar steps to be quickly adopted in their own society. In the Spring of 2011, Arabs everywhere, including in Sa'udi Arabia, rejected the stale debate between conservatism and liberalism. Few accepted fairytales that neatly categorized them as robotic creatures with pre-packaged views. Most screamed for comprehensive modifications to existing social contracts. A few worked hard to remake the entire region. A few more sacrificed their lives to give future generations a chance. Still more picked up the torches of freedom. In less than a year, young Arabs changed the entire Middle East, and in Sa'udi Arabia, their petitions called attention to significant changes in the political discourse.

6 Sa'udi Arabia and the United States

Although the Sa'udi–American alliance was literally etched in the stone of the Ghawar oil fields developed by American companies, it came under tremendous pressure in the aftermath of the September 11, 2001 terrorist attacks in New York and Washington, DC, as well as the thwarted attack that ended in a remote field in Pennsylvania. The kingdom, where fifteen of the nineteen alleged terrorists hailed from, was suspected of collusion, perhaps even conspiracy. In fact, senior Al Sa'ud officials failed to protect their own interests, when several advanced incredulous theories that pleaded innocence. Irrespective of what actually occurred, which was still murky as of this writing, Sa'udi Arabia lost a full two years arguing back and forth on minutiae, instead of focusing on the fundamentals. After the May 12, 2003 terrorist assaults in Sa'udi Arabia, however, the kingdom embarked on a widespread reappraisal of its responses, judged by Washington and others to have been mild in the past. Indeed, and beyond facile references to al-Qa'idah, there was a genuine homegrown threat in the kingdom, given the number of disaffected young men who were mostly idle. In the event, the May 2003 attacks solicited measured responses, which were nothing short of phenomenal. Not only were terrorists targeted in unison, but Riyadh also rounded up several thousand clerics for re-education programs, hoping to address this intrinsic challenge by focusing on religious teachers that may have – even if inadvertently – prepped putative Islamists to resort to violence. To be sure, while Washington lost its global compass after 9/11, perceiving everything through the terrorism prism, Riyadh was equally motivated to launch massive campaigns after 5/12. Remarkably, 5/12 gained notoriety in Sa'udi Arabia, nearly similar to 9/11 in the US, even if the casualties were far less. It was worth noting in this context that, parallel to this gigantic and unprecedented initiative to go after potential "terrorists" with gusto, the Sa'udi government created a brand new force to protect the Abqai'q oil facility, entrusting it to loyal Al Murrah tribesmen. One also noted the progress made by Deputy Interior Minister Muhammad bin Nayif, as he funded rehabilitation programs to salvage as many of the kingdom's Islamists as possible.

Given this fundamental transformation in the enduring but largely unwritten relationship between Riyadh and Washington, what were the prospects for long-term security cooperation, which defined ties that stretched over eight decades? Were there permanent issues that were threatened by 9/11, and could the two countries rethink perceptions that challenged this tested alliance?

If Sa'udi Arabia had once needed, and its leaders knew that they needed, a strategic defense partner to develop and protect the kingdom's oil industry, inevitable evolution snuck into the established relationship. To be sure, that partner was still the West in general, and the United States in particular, which literally guaranteed the kingdom's defenses.[1] Yet, because the Arab climate – hostility to Israel and its US backers, popular uprisings, conditions post-Afghanistan in 2001 and especially post-Iraq in 2003 – transformed the Sa'udi popular mood, many Sa'udis resented their government's friendship with Washington. There was a lot riding on the kingdom's strategic alliance with the US, with members of the intelligentsia rejecting what they perceived as a state of subservience. Even junior Al Sa'ud family members resented cavalier US attitudes, even if most understood that Washington was very close to them in terms of the economy. Periodically, Sa'udis applauded government officials who distanced themselves from Washington, more as an act of political satisfaction rather than any concrete anti-Americanism. In fact, this was due to the fact that Sa'udi rulers worried about several issues other than their exclusive relations with Washington, though the defense alliance was a critical item on their agenda. There were, of course, other critical challenges that faced the Al Sa'ud, who were called upon to deal with a plethora of concerns without making too many major mistakes. Though they managed rather well during the past decade, suspicions lingered. The purpose of this chapter is thus to provide as accurate a reading as possible on the direction of the Sa'udi–American divorce and whether there might be a renewed opportunity to settle on a mature and responsible course to better manage this inevitable alliance.

The Sa'udi–American divorce

Even before 9/11, leading analysts anticipated a significant split between Sa'udi Arabia and the United States.[2] One concluded that the divorce was unavoidable because, allegedly, the marriage was largely based on money and, absent any common values, could not endure.[3] Ironically, an objective reader could reach an entirely different conclusion, underscoring the shared values between American and Sa'udi societies, by reading the tale of an American woman who married into a leading Sa'udi family.[4] A motivated observer proposed that the West could not afford to remain on the sidelines, and needed to monitor and hold accountable Sa'udi officials – in the tradition of the 1975 Helsinki Act that aimed to modify Soviet and Eastern bloc states' behavior. The purpose of such monitoring, it was speculated, was to limit and, in time, eliminate incitement to violence. In short, the argument was made that Sa'udis needed to adhere to the same minimal standards of international behavior demanded of others and that, ultimately, Sa'udis must choose whether to oppose terrorists or to ally with them.[5]

That Riyadh needed to make such a choice was readily apparent, especially after a briefing presented to a Pentagon advisory board in 2002 identified the kingdom as an "enemy of the United States," and assigned the country such non-scholarly labels as, "the kernel of evil, the prime mover, the most dangerous opponent."[6] The George W. Bush Administration considered whether to aim at change within the ruling Al Sa'ud family or simply to limit or remove US dependence on Sa'udi oil (by relying on the Iraqi alternative), though it does not seem to have followed-up on its moments of anger after it turned its attention to the Iraq prize.[7] In the event, neither solution promoted American national interests, even if the danger survived the Bush presidency that the United States would unwittingly recast the war against terrorism as a struggle against Sa'udi Arabia or against Islam itself. Regrettably, some Christian fundamentalists, in particular, exacerbated this danger by identifying the Prophet Muhammad as a terrorist and by misrepresenting Islam as a vile, violent religion. Such spurious remarks were as harmful as they were humiliating, not least because they deflected attention from the dynamic and potentially beneficial process of self-examination underway in Sa'udi society, as in most of the Muslim world. Indeed, and even before the late 2010–early 2011 "Arab Spring" that shook the entire region, the Muslim world seemed to have entered a pre-Renaissance period wherein its adherents were deciphering normative questions that were of critical importance to the interrelationships between Islam and the West.

While uncharitable voices identified the kingdom's religious beliefs as being defective, one going so far as to declare that "Wahhabism has been a movement of total intolerance toward those who did not adopt its principles, including other Muslims," time healed the 9/11 wounds, even if those who suffered were, understandably, baffled.[8] For American policy-makers who considered Sa'udi Arabia as Washington's "anchor in the Arab Middle East [that] banked our oil under its sand," a frontal assault was necessary to tame Sa'udis who had strayed.[9] For years after 9/11, the primary focus centered on the kingdom's education system, which purportedly taught nothing but hatred, especially hatred of the United States.[10] When religion and education were discussed in tandem, the resulting assessments bordered on the highly subjective, a litany of emotional sermons.[11] The sum total of such negative publicity fundamentally altered American public opinion of the kingdom. On February 26, 2002, *The Washington Post* reported that 54 percent of Americans viewed Sa'udi Arabia as a state supporting terrorism, compared with a mere 35 percent who had a similar perception of Syria, a country long on the State Department's "Terrorism List."[12] Ironically, in 2007, fully 69 percent of Sa'udis surveyed supported strong and close relations between the United States and Sa'udi Arabia.[13]

These general views remained constant for the balance of the past decade and, after the spring 2003 American/British war on Iraq, anti-Sa'udi perceptions solidified.[14] A few years ago, a less charitable British commentator predicted a total collapse of the long-standing relationship between the United States and Sa'udi Arabia, as gloom and doom forecasts dominated media as well as scholarly outlets.[15] More recently, several analysts concluded that Riyadh was leading a "counter-revolution" against various "Arab Spring" upheavals, which shook the Arab World starting in late 2010.[16] Although leading Western observers and diplomats routinely forecast the collapse of the Sa'udi regime for more than sixty years, a few scholars asserted that the Sa'udi monarchy was not as fragile as many assumed. One concluded that Sa'udi Arabia was the Arab country least affected in its domestic politics by the Arab upheavals of 2011.[17] Mercifully, gloom and doom did not bring the monarchy down, but the damage was done.

The sum total of these changes ushered in permanent reforms both for the benefit of Sa'udi society and all of those who interacted with them. Still, the agenda was fully loaded, and there was a lot to be done. Critics concluded that Washington supported "ideologically" motivated Sa'udis – allegedly to spread their Unitarian [*Wahhabi*] creed to the rest of the Muslim world – and stood by Riyadh even if they disagreed with the Al Sa'ud because of the US dependence on oil. Somehow, according to this logic, American democracy preferred to embrace its "natural enemies," rather than stand by "natural allies," the so-called reform minded Muslims.[18] More recently, and in the aftermath of the political race between the kingdom and the Islamic Republic of Iran, Sa'udi Arabia was accused of peddling "the message of sectarian division," determined to be "a dangerously inaccurate misreading of what the Arab Spring [was] really about." Somehow, the otherwise astute observer concluded, if Washington wanted "stability in the Middle East, it [would not] bow to Sa'udi Arabia's opposition to Shiite Iran."[19] Still, this was a minority view, as both the George W. Bush and Barack H. Obama administrations stood by Riyadh, aware of the kingdom's intrinsic value to the global economy. Private misgivings notwithstanding, Washington understood that a G-20 member was not a banana republic, and though the US failed to articulate a public policy towards Sa'udi Arabia, it nevertheless accepted that Riyadh was a non-negotiable item on its global checkerboard.[20] What it desperately wished to see were genuine internal reforms that, presumably, would further enhance the kingdom's internal stability even if doing so threatened the very stability of the country that *owned* a quarter of the world's petroleum resources. That is why, and despite long-standing reservations that Washington minions harbored about 'Abdallah bin 'Abdul 'Aziz, the White House was satisfied with the monarch's gradual reform proposals.

American views of post-2005 Sa'udi reforms

Sa'udi Arabia and the United States shared common interests even when they were not always on the same side. For one astute observer, the time had come for US policymakers "to put aside the idea that they can go to the Saudis for help with issues as they arise and expect them to respond positively simply because the request ... [came] from Washington."[21] F. Gregory Gause III attributed to the former American ambassador to Sa'udi Arabia, Chas Freeman, a new characterization of the evolving relationship as "transactional," which presumably would allow each side to seek "specific benefits from the other through cooperation on various issues, but with no assumption that they will line up together on the next issue that comes up."

What were the key Sa'udi concerns that preoccupied Washington? Inasmuch as the United States conducts a global foreign policy and, consequently, monitors and assesses a variety of bilateral and multilateral issues, five specific concerns stood out in the US–Sa'udi equation: reforms within the judiciary (especially on sensitive religious matters); women's emancipation; scientific education; socio-political dialogues and elections; as well as the highly sensitive succession mechanism within the ruling family. All five of these topics have been analyzed in some detail throughout this study, but what follows are significant markers in American perceptions that, for better or worse, shaped US foreign policy towards the kingdom.

Legal and religious reforms

Given inherent contradictions between Jeffersonian democracy and *Shari'ah* law, chances were excellent that Washington and Riyadh spoke past each other, instead of to each other. Public declarations notwithstanding, American officials assessed the reforms introduced within the judiciary in the kingdom as positive steps, although few displayed any appetite to delve in Islamic jurisprudence. Not only was the subject mind-boggling to many Americans – it was also complicated for the Sa'udi legal community – but the separation of powers, especially the separation between state and church as practiced in the US, did not apply in the kingdom. Of course, that did not prevent legal activists in the US from making harsh generalizations, even when their value was questionable. The US State Department's annual report on *Religious Freedoms in the World*, for example, routinely listed the kingdom as being among the countries that violated religious freedoms, which was not appreciated by Muslim scholars and government officials who, despite cautionary views, understood the impact that these publications had.[22] Naturally, Sa'udis – and others – objected to such characterizations, voicing the strong opinion that Washington played the role of global policeman and intervened in the internal affairs of other countries by imposing US and Western values as if they were international norms. Some objected that the annual reports did not include listings for Israel that, according to this logic, demonstrated American bias in favor of Israel.[23]

The misreading of judiciary reforms, or commentary on religious characteristics that chose to overlook Islamic values, were significantly exacerbated after 9/11 as a slew of anti-Sa'udi and especially anti-Muslim commentaries flooded the airwaves and monopolized newsprints. Regrettably, criminal activities attributed to a few were elevated to existential levels, as an uncharacteristic view emerged that concentrated on a clash of civilization, while others practiced Islamophobia.

In the aftermath of 9/11 and the launch of the War for Afghanistan, the Institute for American Values prepared a 20-page paper entitled *What We're Fighting For* that raised several issues, including the moral explanations behind Washington's "War on Terrorism."[24] Unabashedly, *What We're Fighting For* called on Muslims to stand with America, perhaps even to adopt those universal values that they presented, and oppose radicalism – by which its authors meant Muslim radicalism. Sixty prominent thinkers signed the paper, including Amitai Etzioni [George Washington University], Francis Fukuyama [Johns Hopkins University], Samuel Huntington [Harvard University], Daniel Patrick Moynihan [a former US Senator then a professor at Syracuse University], and James Q. Wilson [UCLA].[25] Though they pledged to do all they could "to guard against the harmful temptations – especially those of arrogance and jingoism – to which nations at war so often seem[ed] to yield," they were persuaded that their war was just. Remarkably, the document's erudite signatories were determined to defend themselves, but were persuaded that they were also fighting "to defend those universal principles of human rights and human dignity that [represented] the best hope for humankind."

It was not long before a group of Muslim scholars responded in kind, issuing a rebuttal paper under the title *How We Can Coexist*.[26] The responders, all Sa'udi scholars, welcomed the exchange and expressed a desire to enter into a useful dialogue. At the outset, they rejected the language of power as the language of discourse, and called on their counterparts to engage in a process of dialogue "under the umbrella of justice, morality, and human rights, so we can give glad tidings to the world of a process that will bring about for it peace and tremendous good." Importantly, signatories acknowledged that they shared with the West "a number of concepts, moral values, rights, and ideas," and hoped that their interlocutors would respect everyone's governing principles and priorities that colored cultural assumptions. The authors then defined their values and guiding principles by quoting various Qur'anic verses, before addressing the events of September 11, 2011 and their implications. While they condemned the violence perpetrated that day against innocent civilians, they nevertheless highlighted the causative relationships that apparently existed between American foreign policy and what happened on that tragic day. In what was a bold step, the Sa'udi authors clarified their position on the United States, underscoring the disagreement that apparently existed between them and American society, which were not about values of justice or the choice of freedoms, they asserted. By addressing such a fundamental concern, the well-versed Sa'udi thinkers insisted that values were of two types: basic human values shared by all people, and values that were particular to a given society. They pointed out double and triple standards in US pronouncements and policies, and rejected the monopoly exercised by American thinkers as if these values were exclusive to them. On the contrary, many of the norms espoused by their American colleagues, the Sa'udis avowed, represented the contributions of other civilizations, among them Islamic civilization, which was why Muslims were flabbergasted when America effectively ignored them in its actions.[27] The document's most revelatory discussion centered around the ideal circumstances for cooperation and why these would "not be realized as long as American civilization remains in perpetual fear of growing weak or losing its hold on the world, and [was] perpetually concerned with keeping others from developing, especially the nations of the so-called third world." These were strong words, but signatories held to their principles, insisted on Islamic norms, and called on Washington to ponder whether "the use of military force or the power of the media [would always] provide ... real guarantee[s] for the future."[28]

There were a variety of similar exchanges throughout the decades but the two countries did not elevate the discussion to the State level. King 'Abdallah bin 'Abdul 'Aziz raised the issues with American presidents, even if the official conversations only occurred in Madrid in 2008. To be sure, American intellectuals, both secular and religious, attended the key conference co-sponsored by Sa'udi Arabia and Spain to engage in cross-religious dialogues, but the follow-ups were all at the non-governmental level. What was sorely needed were fresh avenues for dialogue and the exchange of ideas among decision-makers who needed to address issues of mutual interest, but also to devise social mechanisms that would prevent the language of violence and destruction to dominate every conversation held between officials representing the two countries, especially since long-term interactions were inevitable.

Muslim–Christian dialogues towards the end of the 20th century involved scholars that were part of the Muslim World League, the World Muslim Congress, and the Middle East Council of Churches (among the most notable examples), as a variety of non-governmental institutions developed formal and informal programs. Still, Muslim scholars were wary of such enterprises because of the long history of enmity and the more recent experiences of colonialism, while contemporary foreign policy considerations created problems for many would-be Muslim participants as described above.[29] In the aftermath of 9/11, it was safe to conclude that a major turning point in Muslim–Christian relations was reached, which created both opportunities and obstacles for Muslim–Christian dialogue. Regrettably, Washington and Riyadh failed to tame some of the most audible Christian and Muslim polemicists, with a few rejecting the other religion as "false," "demonic," or "evil." What emerged was a long litany of misunderstandings, mistrust, and animosities that shaped the attitudes of many people in both communities of faith. Still, extraordinary efforts were made by both sides, and by American and Sa'udi scholars in particular, even if the immense taboo was not eradicated between officials in both countries. The kingdom ushered in dramatic reforms at the legal and religious levels, empowered its nascent institutions with the wherewithal to oppose, even eradicate, extremism, though many deemed these to be insufficient. Whether Riyadh was ready to make additional concessions were impossible to know, although few in Washington should be under any illusions that Sa'udi Arabia would jeopardize its religious legitimacy to satisfy temporary foreign policy interests.

Women's emancipation

If 'Abdallah bin 'Abdul 'Aziz or his successors were not prepared to toy with their legitimizing institutions, concessions on women's issues were of the doable variety, which stood as a promising area of cooperation for the United States, especially when such emancipation was deemed to be in the best interests of the kingdom, too.[30] To be sure, the country harbored a segregation of the sexes and women were still not allowed to drive, travel without permission, or even undergo a surgical operation without the consent of their *mahrams* [a husband or, in the case of singles, an unmarriable relative]. Yet, it would be an error not to notice the many changes underway in the country, ranging from acts of defiance by young ladies literally attacking the *mutawa'in* [religious police], to posing for official photographs with the ruler and his Heir Apparent. There were those who objected vociferously to the mixing of genders in this most conservative society, but in Jiddah, as in most of the countryside throughout the vast country, significant changes on gender relations were noticed.

When King 'Abdallah decided to grant women more political rights, at least one senior cleric objected that he was not consulted, though the reform was not cancelled. In fact, in late September 2011, the Sa'udi monarch shocked many of his subjects when he announced that women would vote in, and run for, municipal council elections and even serve in the appointed *Shurah* Council to advise the king on policy matters. Although the ruler declared that he reached his decision after consultations with the country's senior clerics, Shaykh Salih al-Luhaydan, a member of the Board of Senior Religious Scholars, contradicted his ruler on the *al-Majd* television channel.[31] In Luhaydan's own words: "I wish the king did not say that he consulted senior clerics. When I heard the speech and what was said about consultation, without a doubt I had no knowledge of it before hearing the king's speech."[32] This was not mere griping by a marginalized figure, but a good illustration of the kind of hurdles that any Sa'udi monarch must overcome in the kingdom. Indeed, though women's emancipation in the United States and most Western countries was no longer the taboo subject it used to be at the beginning of the 20th century, such "rights" were still considered to be a super sensitive matter in the kingdom, as conservative doctors of law applied narrow *Shari'ah* interpretations. Any changes at this level provoked impassioned opposition from most clerics. Still, Shaykh Luhaydan was fairly careful in his remarks since he refrained from criticizing the monarch's decision directly, even if he camouflaged his disappointment in an Arabic proverb that cautioned that "the thread between a leader and his people" can snap if it was pulled too hard. Of course, King 'Abdallah was not only worried about Shaykh Luhaydan, who was removed from his position as chief of the kingdom's highest tribunal after he issued a fatwah that condoned the killing of television executives for programming unacceptable fare, but also the more conservative clerics who were not pleased with his reformist ideas. Although the monarch could still relieve from duty those who displayed the audacity to openly criticize their ruler, he could not dismiss everyone who disagreed with him. This was an aspect of his "will to power" that was poorly understood in Washington, especially among those who insisted that the king "wave his magic wand" and impose the kind of reforms they favored. It goes without saying that mixed-gender environments faced significant opposition, but steady and gradual reforms, ones that aimed to alter narrow views, were probably in the works. By acknowledging Riyadh's pace on this important topic, Washington decision-makers were actually in a good position to see significant progress on the matter, which leaders in both countries concluded were necessary and valuable.

Scientific education

One of the bright areas of change in Sa'udi Arabia and the best illustration of the evolving US–Sa'udi relationship, was the creation of the King 'Abdallah University of Science and Technology (KAUST) in 2009, a unique institution of higher learning in the entire Arab World.[33] It was useful to note that Sa'udi decision-makers compared KAUST, which received US technical assistance, to the Israel Institute of Technology [Technion] in Haifa, which was a formidable and peerless fortress of knowledge in the Middle East.[34] KAUST was where the real strength of the kingdom lay if and when Riyadh encouraged high standards and allowed its researchers and students to achieve competitive equality. Presumably, the significant financial as well as social investments in this university were good illustrations of what Sa'udi Arabia wished to accomplish and, towards that end, took the first steps to reach that goal. It will be a while for KAUST scientists to produce significant work, but chances were excellent that researchers there would make useful discoveries. Still, it was important to ask what would it take for KAUST to reach innovative heights.

With an initial focus on energy and the environment, as well as a concentration on the biosciences, bioengineering, applied mathematics, materials and computer sciences, KAUST promised to shine in areas that were critical for the kingdom and the Arab world in general. A first batch of slightly over 800 students entrusted to 67 faculty members hailing from over 30 countries were already at work, under the leadership of Choon Fong Shih, an American-trained professor of electrical engineering who worked for General Electric and taught at Brown University before returning to Singapore to found that country's Institute of Materials Research and Engineering. As the past deputy vice-chancellor of the National University of Singapore, Professor Shih's experiences were unique, and he thrust KAUST on the path of scientific investigations. Yet, and this much must be acknowledged truthfully, the gargantuan tasks assigned KAUST will only succeed if promises made to its students and faculty are kept.

To his credit, King 'Abdallah bin 'Abdul 'Aziz empowered the independent university with a multi-billion dollar endowment, and called on its Board of

Trustees to encourage merit-based admission. He authorized the university to welcome both men and women from around the world, and guaranteed that they would have the freedom to be creative in a relatively emancipated environment. This was challenging within conservative Sa'udi society, but it was an absolutely essential ingredient if the highest standards of scholarship and research were to be reached. Simply stated, it was next to impossible to unleash talent when one imposed strict behavioral conditions, given that freedom of thought cannot be divorced from the liberty to think and move outside the proverbial box.

One of the newest Sa'udi universities, KAUST promised to be different from all of its counterparts in the region not only because it is the first "international, graduate-level research university dedicated to inspiring a new age of scientific achievement in the Kingdom," but also because it challenged Sa'udi society. Even if it was located in the relatively open Hijaz region, along the Red Sea city of Thuwal, about 80 kilometers north of Jiddah, the key ingredient to its success surely was the unfettered access to information. This meant no more censorship – at least on KAUST premises. Again, while this was easy to accept theoretically, it was an entirely new concept for tradition-bound societies where norms were not based on individual creativity. 'Abdallah bin 'Abdul 'Aziz, along with the university establishment, understood that the type of knowledge Sa'udi society needed and now sought could not be accomplished by isolating great minds behind closed doors. In fact, KAUST stood as a testament to money well spent and, it was important to acknowledge, to close US–Sa'udi cooperation. By investing where it mattered most – by creating first-rate education systems that intended to help all of mankind – this university stood as a novel measurement of the nation's greatness.

A century from now, little of what happened after 2005 in the kingdom will be remembered, although KAUST may have earned the same reputation that Cambridge, Technion, Kharagpur, of any number of leading centers of learning around the world enjoy. By encouraging scientific investigations, Riyadh addressed internal needs that necessitated evolving social needs, while introducing gradual changes – both on religious as well as gender grounds. This was precisely what the United States appreciated, which was why Riyadh steadfastly welcomed American assistance. If thousands upon thousands of its sons and daughters received their higher education in American universities, Riyadh was amply conscious that the time was ripe to create the educational infrastructure at home, the kind that would allow for unfettered knowledge to be created in safe and free environments. On this score, close cooperation between Sa'udi Arabia and the United States was strong, and bound to grow even stronger.

Socio-political dialogues and elections

An equally important area of cooperation for the United States was the kingdom's efforts to foster dialogue among various citizens and groups, as well as its modest efforts to organize partial municipal elections. Naturally, because a great majority of senior Saʻudi decision-makers received their education in American universities, most were familiar with, and admired, those institutions that allowed free speech. Many experienced the cacophony of state and federal elections, including congressional and presidential contests that mobilized the US polity for years on end, and though they frequently voiced confusion, perhaps even bewilderment, most admired Jeffersonian democracy.

Yet, despite its convoluted nature, Saʻudis sought to take away from the American system only those features they deemed might serve their country. In addition to serious legal reforms, many concluded that the gradual introduction of national dialogues, followed by partial municipal elections, would in fact prove useful. In fact, at the height of the "Arab Spring" demonstrations in 2011, several important petitions called for an elected legislature to further bring the Saʻudi public into the decision-making process.[35] Although the monarch did not promise eventual political reforms in his March 2011 speech that accompanied his generous financial emoluments, he and his senior advisors took note of what intellectuals and activists demanded. Unanimously, most wished to see an elected parliament with full legislative powers serve the nation, along with a far more independent judiciary, as well as greater freedoms to establish civil society organizations, guarantees for freedom of expression, the release of political prisoners, and greater efforts to root out official corruption. As noted by an astute observer of the kingdom, liberal and Islamist thinkers more or less shared this objective, which meant "that, at least at the elite level, Saudi activists [we]re beginning to overcome differences of sect, region, and ideology" to articulate constructive political demands.[36]

In the aftermath of epochal changes that mobilized Arab and Muslim public opinion after 2011, Washington cannot but be pleased with *Salafi* calls for democratic reforms, which were nothing short of significant ideological shifts by Islamists who, for better or worse, concluded that democratization was a useful route to embark upon. Of course, as discussed earlier, this was not particularly unusual – as the case of Shaykh Salman al-Awdah illustrated – but, while Riyadh maintained certain reservations, it was amply clear that the message could no longer be ignored.[37] Though divided on many issues, Saʻudis coalesced around a demand for an elected parliament, which could no longer be neglected by the Al Saʻud leadership. Importantly, this was a key area of potential cooperation between Washington and Riyadh, to provide guidance in devising various mechanisms that would allow for every Saʻudi group to be brought onboard. Calls for elections gained momentum and there were no reasons either to oppose such a request, nor be concerned that open channels of communications would hinder the state's freedom to maneuver at will. On the contrary, by adopting inclusive methods, Riyadh would further institutionalize political demands and seal them into the national consciousness, something that a great power like the United States could easily encourage.

Succession concerns

Given the importance of this subject, as discussed in Chapter 4, how did Washington officialdom perceive the reforms introduced by King 'Abdallah bin 'Abdul 'Aziz after his accession to the throne in 2005?

King 'Abdallah's age, recent recuperations from back surgery, as well as Heir Apparent Nayif's own health problems, preoccupied senior American leaders. Well-connected journalists revealed that the possibility of a Soviet-style quick succession outcome loomed over the horizon, although this possibility was very exaggerated.[38] Alleged family disputes that apparently encouraged rival princes to mobilize support within Sa'udi society and, perhaps, to encourage outsiders to meddle, filled imaginations. Instant experts with convoluted understandings of Sa'udi Arabia opined, but most of this fare was pure entertainment. Without exception, more serious attention at the White House, the State Department, Departments of Treasury and Energy, and all of the intelligence community focused on the process by which inevitable changes would be introduced into the kingdom's leadership. Whatever transpired behind closed doors throughout Washington was impossible to know, although carefully placed leaks with favorite journalists reflected some of the apprehension that had built up over the years. It was nearly impossible to know what American officials knew of the process from open sources. The exception to this pattern, was the illegal publication of a secret cable from the US Ambassador to Sa'udi Arabia, General James B. Smith, which was leaked in the Wikileaks trove. Given its importance, and the rarity of actually seeing such classified documents long before they are made available to scholars, the key points analyzed by the ambassador deserve further scrutiny, as they influenced a slew of decision-makers at Foggy Bottom and perhaps elsewhere throughout the vast bureaucracy that contributes to the making of US foreign policy.

General Smith first summarized his views of the 2006 Allegiance Commission as an institution that codified the family's "traditional practices for choosing successors."[39] The cable reported that refinements addressed problems associated with the incapacitation of either the monarch or his Heir Apparent, and underscored that the ultimate purpose of the Commission was to "reflect the Al Saud consensus for managing the transition to the next generation." Smith was optimistic "that the mechanism would [not] be ignored, since its members constitute[d] the core of the kingdom's collective leadership, and it has the status of the kingdom's other constitutional laws." Quoting an unnamed correspondent, the Ambassador shared the characterization that the kingdom was "a country in transition" that nevertheless faced many questions regarding its political future. It was not clear whether the diplomat accepted the quoted opinion-maker's view, which posited that "there would be a new leader from the 'new generation' of princes" by 2020, even if no one could possibly know who that prince might be. He lamented that concerns over succession in Sa'udi Arabia had "given rise to an industry of royal-watchers and prognosticators," which presumably included independent researchers. Still, he wrote that "the appointment of Interior Minister Prince Nayif as Second Deputy Prime Minister in March 2009, ... which position[ed] him as a possible Crown Prince-in-waiting, had "not settled questions about the future."[40] He confirmed that the monarch was advanced in age, 86 in 2009, when the cable was actually written, that Heir Apparent Sultan was 84 years old and largely incapacitated by colon cancer, that Interior Minister Nayif was 75 and has had his own health problems, and that the youngest of the founder's surviving sons, Muqrin, was 64.

With this background, and to better acquaint his readers with how the embassy understood the Allegiance Commission, Smith then launched into a detailed analysis of the document, with the express goal of highlighting how the actual jump to the next generation of leaders would be managed. Citing only "some foreign observers" who have made the claim that the Commission was a 'Abdallah innovation "to make the succession process more transparent," and who even characterized "the law as decreeing that the next king would be 'elected' since members of the commission could vote to choose a candidate," Smith astutely answered his own question by stating that, for the ruling family, the Commission was nothing more that "a codification of the unwritten rules that have governed the selection of Saudi rulers since the passing of King Abdulaziz [sic] in 1953." Although there were no revelations in the avowal that 'Abdul 'Aziz bin 'Abdul Rahman's sons governed through consensus in what was "a unique system of collective rule," the mere fact that the diplomat saw fit to reiterate this point was revelatory – just in case folks in Washington assumed otherwise. What the Allegiance Commission Law did was to formalize the traditional practices of consultations and, in a judicious observation, Smith asserted that the very existence of this reform initiative may well have been a family decision rather than a unique 'Abdallah innovation. In other words, the ambassdor hinted that a consensus plan probably existed within the senior ranks of the ruling family to gradually transfer power from the sons of 'Abdul 'Aziz to his grandsons, which was precisely what Prince Talal bin 'Abdul 'Aziz had been clamoring about for years.

Five equally important points emerged from the diplomat's shrewd observations. First, there was the view that Interior Minister Nayif bin 'Abdul 'Aziz was well placed to be elevated to the heirship, long before the actual designation occurred. In fact, because King 'Abdallah survived his designated heir, and based on Article 7, subparagraph B, which stated that the ruler may ask the Allegiance Commission to nominate a suitable successor, the monarch submitted the name of his designee to the Commission for its approval. Although that is what occurred, the choice was a foregone conclusion, since 'Abdallah was not about to experiment by skipping over a generation in 2011. Yet, Nayif's appointment to the heirship essentially meant that princes 'Abdul Rahman (his elder full brother), Mit'ab (a full brother of the passed-over Mish'al), Talal, and Badr may all have agreed to relinquish their claims to succession, although no one knew for sure.

Second, the cable provided assessments of other candidates, including Riyadh Governor Salman (b. 1936), Royal Adviser 'Abdul Illah (b. 1935), Riyadh Vice Governor Sattam (b. 1943), Vice Interior Minister Ahmad (b. 1940), and the youngest, General Intelligence Presidency [GIP or *Mukhabarat* in Arabic] Head Muqrin (b. 1943).[41] These princes were eminently qualified, with Salman an almost automatic candidate despite being Nayif's full brother, and thus the third potential *Sudayri* king, should Nayif succeed 'Abdallah. Smith believed that although 'Abdul Illah was "next by virtue of seniority, his ill-starred government career (he was twice removed from governorships)" left serious questions about his competence. Likewise, the American diplomat concluded that Sattam was also "a dark-horse candidate," allegedly because of his low-profile as Vice-Governor of Riyadh, someone who operated in Salman's shadow. He further opined that Ahmad's potential candidacy was problematic on account of his *Sudayri* credentials, which would presumably raise additional objections from certain family quarters. Only Muqrin, the head of Sa'udi intelligence, received a relatively clean endorsement, ostensibly because the "enigmatic, constant companion of the King," was able to overcome his handicap – his mother's Yemeni roots – and assume added responsibilities.

Third, the diplomat introduced a cautionary tale, claiming that it was unclear who would emerge from among the next generation of princes to govern the kingdom. Nevertheless, he believed that the Allegiance Commission enjoyed the kind of institutional independence, perhaps by virtue of its composition, that suggested that the putative candidate would only be drawn from among princes already in senior government positions. Though several names were advanced in the report, including Al-Bahah Governor Muhammad bin Sa'ud (b. 1934), Makkah Region Governor Khalid al-Faysal (b. 1941), Khalid bin Sultan (b. 1949), Sa'ud al-Faysal (b. 1941), 'Abdul 'Aziz bin Fahd (b. 1973), Sultan bin Fahd (b. 1951), Mit'ab bin 'Abdallah (b. 1943), 'Abdul 'Aziz bin 'Abdallah (b. 1964), Sultan bin Salman (b. 1956), Muhammad bin Nayif (b. 1958), 'Abdul 'Aziz bin Salman (b. 1960), 'Abdul 'Aziz bin Bandar (b. 1952), and Mansur bin Mit'ab (b. 1950), one name was noticeably absent from the diplomat's list: Turki al-Faysal (b. 1945), the former head of intelligence and ambassador to both London and Washington.[42] A grave misreading in Ambassador Smith's cable is the assertion that the Al Sa'ud failed to produce "national figures," even if every single name on his list are very well known throughout Sa'udi Arabia. What truly stands out is the frequency with which senior members of the ruling family crisscross the country, attend weddings, funerals, conferences, *majlises*, and various other functions, which highlight their visibility far better than many assume.

Fourth, and irrespective of the names above, as well as their allegedly limited public exposure, Smith concluded that the selection process was well oiled, which ensured that it would not become susceptible to external influences. In fact, the diplomat correctly affirmed that no American or British officials – nor, for that matter, officials from any other country – stood the slightest chance of influencing eventual candidates.

Finally, and this was highly important, the former military officer believed that "whoever emerge[d would] likely have been educated in, and seek to advance Saudi interests by continuing the kingdom's critical partnership with the US." He believed that a next-generation candidate may be even more inclined to align with Washington, simply because "nearly all shared a common experience of having studied in, and therefore being favorably disposed towards, the United States." Given the current doldrums in US–Sa'udi ties, the affable officer-turned-diplomat recommended that the primary US concern in the short term ought to be to support "a process that ensure[d] stability and broad engagement rather than focusing on individual leaders." "Over the longer term," he maintained, "stability in Saudi Arabia [may well] depend on the Al Sa'ud's ability to meet and surmount social and economic challenges presented by a growing population and a dangerous neighbourhood," which, presumably, required closer American attention.

Another succession transition

Few were surprised when King 'Abdallah bin 'Abdul 'Aziz appointed Defense Minister Prince Salman bin 'Abdul 'Aziz as his third Heir Apparent, although many Sa'udis wondered why the Allegiance Commission was not convened in a timely fashion to make the choice. Of course, the swift designation – accompanied by the selection of the long-time Deputy Minister of the Interior, Prince Ahmad bin 'Abdul 'Aziz, to replace his predecessor, the late Prince Nayif – highlighted the monarch's concerns that a rapid transition was necessary given his own health problems. At 86, the king was generally in good health, although two recent operations slowed him down. Ever the pragmatist, 'Abdallah reasoned that regional instability required that he move fast, even if this decision reflected unnecessary anxiety.

Prince Nayif passed away in Geneva, Switzerland on June 16, 2012, after a long illness. His many critics, both Sa'udis and non-Sa'udis alike, lambasted his checkered record, concluding that the kingdom was not well-served by his tenure.[43] Although a controversial figure, Nayif was a strong leader who placed the interests of his country above all else, even when that earned him scorn. As fate would have it, he would not become a king, as the monarch entrusted his heirship to Prince Salman, a veteran statesman and administrator, someone who certainly knew internal family politics better than most. The monarch's short decree read: "We have selected Prince Salman as Heir Apparent and appointed him as deputy prime minister and minister of defense," which was uncharacteristic in its brevity, though meaningful in its content. A second decree appointed Prince Ahmad, the long-time Deputy Interior Minister, to replace Nayif in the latter's most sensitive post.

Indeed, the rapid announcements signaled that the ruling family wished to convey to Sa'udis and the rest of the world that the Al Sa'ud were fully united and that there would be no succession crises. What Riyadh intended was nothing short of a healthy display of solid continuity, a "smooth change" in the words of leading commentators, who believed that the confirmations highlighted the strength within the system.[44] In Salman, King ʻAbdallah designated another reformer, while stressing the importance of family harmony. By all accounts, Salman who was born in Riyadh on December 31, 1935, and who received his education at the Prince's School in the capital city, demonstrated his mettle in the thankless position of Deputy Governor of Riyadh from March 1954 to April 1955 before he was elevated to the Governorship in April 1955. He served the city, its inhabitants, and the ruling family in that position until December 1960, and again from February 1963 to November 5, 2011, when he was appointed Minister of Defense to replace Prince Sultan bin ʻAbdul ʻAziz. A pragmatic man, Salman assumed various duties, though none were as important as that of family arbiter. His reputation as a relatively transparent individual was well known, and while many wished to see him drive reforms more forcefully, he preferred to be respectful of local traditions. Like his ruler, Salman may be expected to introduce dramatic changes, even if he will probably not rush into hasty ones. Long anticipated, his designation introduced a level of cohesion to Saʻudi succession, placing the burden of family harmony squarely in his hands once he accedes to the throne.

Security ties with US

Apprehensive of change and accustomed to a privileged system, leading Al Saʻud rulers hesitated to introduce comprehensive reforms on a variety of concerns, with a group within the family arguing that the risks may not be worth taking. A small group of reformers, led by King ʻAbdallah bin ʻAbdul ʻAziz, displayed the necessary boldness to tackle gargantuan challenges that faced their nation. Remarkably, the irony was that a program of change offered the most likely path to stability, and the greatest risk to the kingdom's stability came from either doing nothing at all, or championing excruciatingly slow measures.

Still, the Saʻudi government's US ally was perturbed at the perceived complacency with Islamic extremism, while various domestic constituents increasingly resented Washington's alleged subservience to Riyadh.[45] American observers exaggerated both the Saʻudi domestic fragility and Saʻudi regional power, concluding that differences between the two countries led to a "crisis."[46] In fact, the resentment was so high after 9/11 that US officials routinely confronted their Saʻudi counterparts, demanding that Riyadh address internal and external pressures with force. Calls for gradual reforms – the kind that would be best received without alienating the conservative religious leadership, on which the country's very legitimacy rested – were somehow dismissed. Few wished to concentrate on the severe socio-economic problems that confronted the kingdom, including rising unemployment and poverty in a context of galloping population growth, assuming that these were far less important than the urgent threat of extremism. Of course, Riyadh was amply aware of the existence of militant groups that unleashed a wave of violence intended to shatter confidence in the regime, though Sa'udi leaders also understood that what truly threatened them were economic and social questions.

Under such trying circumstances, the Al Sa'ud concluded that the safest approach was to crack down on the more violent militants, while essentially clinging to the political status quo. This was not what Washington hoped for, but Sa'udi security forces recorded some success, arresting hundreds of suspected extremists, killing many others including the presumed leader of al-Qa'idah in the kingdom, and confiscating weapons and bomb-making materials. Most Sa'udis – even the few who opposed the Al Sa'ud – appeared repulsed by the militants' methods. Because of his impeccable "will to power," the Sa'udi monarch managed to gain full control and avoided prolonged confrontations at home, even when such dangers were never as serious as critics made them out to be. Riyadh was not on the brink of collapse, nor was the kingdom on the verge of civil war. In this context, the argument that a political opening unnecessarily risked giving voice and influence to extremist forces was appealing, though such considerations were balanced out with very complex internal affairs. Nevertheless, the monarch knew that the adoption of such a conservative approach would ultimately be a self-defeating strategy, which was what he shared with his American interlocutors.

Inasmuch as the rise of radical Islamism in Sa'udi Arabia had many complex causes – most recently including the US posture in the region, epitomized by the invasion of Iraq and neglect of the Israeli–Palestinian peace-process – the closed nature of the political system in Sa'udi Arabia limited the reform preferences that 'Abdallah pursued. Thus, the last thing he needed was additional prodding to force his hand, oblivious to the significant domestic pressures he contended with, ranging the gamut from the repercussions of the Israeli–Palestinian conflicts to criticisms on women's rights. Often the ruler confronted genuine dilemmas, as when President Bill Clinton approached then Heir Apparent 'Abdallah during the 1999 funeral of King Hussein of Jordan without any warning, asking if he would like to be introduced to Israeli leaders present at the ceremony, which drew a sharp reply: "I believe, Your Excellency Mr. President, that there are limits to friendship."[47] This was not the only time when such exchanges occurred. In August 2001, after President George W. Bush declared that Israel was under siege and that Prime Minister Ariel Sharon of Israel was "a man of peace," just as the latter moved tanks into parts of the West Bank, 'Abdallah was livid and reacted. The Sa'udi Ambassador to the United States, Prince Bandar bin Sultan, was then ordered to deliver a terse message to the White House through National Security Advisor, Condoleezza Rice. According to a *New York Times* correspondent – who paraphrased a Sa'udi official to give her readers the flavor of what was communicated and did not quote an actual document – the ruler's message read: "It is clear you made a strategic decision to support Sharon irrespective of what he does and regardless of the impact it has on your interests and your friends in the region. You leave us no alternative except to pursue policies based on our national interests regardless of their impact on you."[48] Whether this was what the message actually said was difficult to know, although serious diplomatic tensions existed at this time. Unsurprisingly, few improvements were detected after 9/11, a period dominated by raw emotional displays in the United States, which were reciprocated by equally emotional reactions to the killings in Palestine, Lebanon, Afghanistan, Iraq and, in the war on terrorism, pretty much everywhere else. Repeated meetings between Bush and 'Abdallah at the American President's Texas ranch in Crawford proved to be truly disastrous. Both in 2002 as well as in 2005, the two men did not mince words, with a particularly poignant exchange during the second visit when the monarch handed the president a videotape of Israeli atrocities committed in the Occupied Territories.[49] One image that infuriated 'Abdallah was a young Israeli soldier stepping on the head of an elderly Palestinian woman and holding her immobile. While Washington was not directly responsible for what an Israeli soldier did in Palestine, in the minds of the overwhelming majority of Arabs, an inseparable association existed between the US and Israel. Of course, these were not the best moments in the Sa'udi–American relationship, but they set the stage for additional divergences as Washington distanced itself from Riyadh, and vice versa.

From Riyadh's perspective, as the American presence in both Afghanistan and Iraq increased, the renewed militancy at home did not appear in a vacuum. Their roots were deep in contemporary Sa'udi history and a regional environment that stifled pluralism, prevented the organization of social and political interests, nurtured intolerance, and reacted to what its adherents concluded were humiliating policies. That these groups engaged in terrorist violence and expressed little interest in free elections or greater political participation for Sa'udi citizens was self-evident since they had identified enemies and were willing to sacrifice themselves to save what remained of their honor. But just as surely as militants capitalized on the erosion of regime legitimacy to recruit new volunteers, the Al Sa'ud adopted specific policies to help alleviate negative consequences, including earning genuine legitimacy at home by working with the United States in a progressive way.

Since the September 11, 2001 attacks in the United States, in which Sa'udi militants were heavily involved, Sa'udis debated the merits of their ties with the West in general and the US in particular. An informal reform lobby of liberals, progressive Islamists, nationalists, and *Shi'ahs* even began to press for change, offering a vision that was a non-violent alternative, consistent with Islam, home grown, and respectful of the Al Sa'ud's unifying role. In response, the government acknowledged the need for political, social, and educational reforms and began grappling with what those would entail. By sponsoring national dialogue, promising and holding partial municipal elections, easing (though far from lifting) press censorship, and establishing a committee to review school curricula, among other measures, the government signaled openness to at least some reforms. To date, however, the sum total of these steps has been limited by Western standards, but they were not ephemeral either. From the security perspective, it was important to note that, while the ruling family asserted its determination, the Al Sa'ud not only authorized the arrest of leading reformers, limited public debate and blocked initiatives it did not control, it also freed many intellectuals, accepted controversial petitions, encouraged discussions on gender questions, and finally granted women the right to vote and run for office. Even if the political reform agenda – initially triggered in some degree by the growing threat of extremism – appeared to have been at least temporarily set aside, since that threat took on a violent form, 'Abdallah bin 'Abdul 'Aziz did not cave in to the more extremist elements in his conservative society.

This was far-sighted, especially since security measures to curb extremist militancy required much more than an immediate line of defense, which Washington and others insisted upon. In fact, Riyadh was equally concerned with how best to deal with longer-term challenges and keep violent opposition marginalized, both of which required repair to a legitimacy that was battered by the closed and arbitrary nature of the political system, the concentrated power and wealth of the ruling family, and the record of financial corruption and profligacy of some of its members. Dealing with these dilemmas necessitated broadening the public space, granting citizens a voice and a stake in the system, allowing them to organize freely, strengthening political institutions such as the *Majlis al-Shurah*, creating a sense of accountability, and cracking down on corruption. 'Abdallah was certainly aware of these challenges and hoped that his necessary responses to recent violent attacks would not be used as a pretext to deviate from his reform agenda, but as an urgent reason to accelerate it. Regrettably, few outsiders acknowledged how significant many of these steps were, even if not all were quickly implemented.

The American–Sa'udi re-engagement

Towards that end, and though there were those who were persuaded that one of the most serious foreign policy crises facing the Administration of Barack Obama was Riyadh's inability to cope with the consequences – and spillover threats – of the "Arab Spring," King 'Abdallah bin 'Abdul 'Aziz wished to preserve and enhance Sa'udi–American ties by introducing long-lasting pillars. Regrettably, detractors colored the relationship, with a leading editorial page speaking of the nascent "rivalry that [apparently] erupted across the Middle East ... between Saudi Arabia and the United States, longtime allies that have been put on a collision course."[50] An influential commentator opined that "the ailing 87-year-old king of Saudi Arabia probably isn't getting much sleep," as "this Sunni monarch of monarchs, custodian of the holy mosques of Mecca and Medina," saw the "flames of instability" getting closer to his borders.[51] Presumably, an implosion in Yemen allowed al-Qa'idah to gain power, the Bahrain revolts necessitated a deployment of GCC military units, Baghdad's *Shi'ah*-dominated government strengthened Iran, while King 'Abdallah bin Hussein of Jordan was under pressure to become a constitutional monarch.

Of course, 'Abdallah bin 'Abdul 'Aziz grudgingly accepted the loss of Egypt's Husni Mubarak, even if the far greater threat was the collapse of the second and last Ba'ath stronghold in Syria. To be sure, the Sa'udi monarch was concerned by the many developments throughout the region but to assert that he perceived "President Obama as a threat to ... internal [Sa'udi] security," was bizarre.[52] This generally well-informed analyst, now perched on top of a Washington, DC think tank, delved into the comical when he wrote that the octogenarian monarch feared "that in the event of a widespread revolt, Obama will demand that he leave office, just as he did to Mubarak, that other longtime friend of the United States." Presumably, and to avoid Mubarak's fate, 'Abdallah reportedly made "arrangements for Pakistani troops to enter his kingdom should the need to suppress popular demonstrations arise," which of course was pure conjecture and did not occur. It was unclear whether the White House was oblivious to the Al Sa'ud's overwhelming popularity at home, or only considered the instability option that, presumably, would produce panic throughout oil importing countries that were dependent on Sa'udi stability.[53] Even worse, the assessment insisted that all the interventions and myriad reform initiatives could not possibly ensure the survival of Arab authoritarian regimes, which presumably the kingdom was, and that the United States ought to understand that the quest for political freedom was an immensely seductive idea that could not be "assuaged by economic bribes or police-state suppression."

In reality, the Sa'udi system was paternalistic but not authoritarian in the classic sense of the term, and while human rights violations were not unheard of in the kingdom, the far more serious dilemma facing the monarchy was its slow pace in addressing social needs, including transparency, women's emancipation, and religious tolerance. To thus conclude that "fragility" defined the Sa'udi system of government was inaccurate, given the kingdom's history since 1744. While there was no denying that power was concentrated in the hands of a few men, the Al Sa'ud's intrinsic abilities, as well as legitimacy, were not questioned by the overwhelming majority of Sa'udi citizens, which was what mattered in the end. Furthermore, claims that Riyadh was opposed to basic political reforms, including allowing political parties and trade unions, as well as guaranteeing basic human and equal rights for both men and women, were also imprecise. Indeed, assertions that the kingdom was mired in the 15th century were made so often that one wonders whether any additional evidence is necessary to describe the tunnel vision such analysts bring to the table. To be sure, there were extremist religious figures in the kingdom whose conservatism was from a different age, but to emphasize that such figures imposed their views on Sa'udi society *in toto* was not correct. In fact, the kingdom today was fully immersed in the 21st-century, with Western educated elites, not religious authorities, insisting that they ought to modernize rather than Westernize. Irrespective of how one felt about *Sunni* discrimination against *Shi'ahs* in the kingdom (and elsewhere), and though minority populations – not only *Shi'ahs* – were treated as less than full citizens, one ought not generalize about complex socio-religious or socio-political issues that evolved over centuries. To be sure, practicing discrimination was wrong and ought to be eliminated in all walks of life, but social norms usually took much longer to eradicate than a stroke of a pen or the issuance of a decree. Washington officials surely knew that King 'Abdullah would not renege on his multi-faceted reform programs, even if circumstances required that he fine-tune demands so as to maintain internal stability. Some analysts mistakenly concluded that the Sa'udi ruler abandoned many of his reform initiatives in 2011, preferring the safe cocoon of religious legitimacy. Allegedly, and in the aftermath of his March 2011 decrees when the monarch committed to spending nearly $130 billion over the next several years, the mere fact that a significant chunk of allocated commitments went to the religious establishment, was evidence of a retreat from putative reform initiatives.[54] Somehow, allocating financial resources to reinforce one of the country's legitimizing institutions was akin to abandoning reforms, a return to the Fahd era when the late monarch supposedly used a similar "playbook." In reality, the ruler recognized the critical contributions made by the clerical establishment as early as February 4, 2011, even before calls for demonstrations in Sa'udi Arabia emerged, when the Grand Mufti of the Kingdom, Shaykh 'Abdul 'Aziz Al al-Shaykh, condemned the marches and demonstrations occurring in Tunis and especially Egypt as "destructive acts of chaos" that were plotted by enemies of the *Ummah*.[55] Nothing in such financial arrangements indicated that the monarch was reneging on his long-term commitments to gradually reform all of the country's institutions, including the religious ones, since reneging would be nearly impossible. One does not authorize the re-education of hundreds of clerics and then simply abandon such plans. Rather, what the Palace chose to do was allocate a significant sum of money to various components of society, not only because it concluded this was in the best interests of the ruling family, but also because it determined that such investments were necessary to maintain internal stability.

Irrespective of such readjustments, Washington preferred to focus on security issues, which posed at least two dilemmas: first, because the US often declared that it did not wish to interfere in the internal affairs of another country – even if its status as a super-power and a permanent member of the Security Council granted it leeway denied many others – focusing on defense questions was eminently wise. Second, and despite numerous errors of judgment, Washington insisted that bilateral relations with the Kingdom of Sa'udi Arabia ought not, indeed must not, be subjected to the vagaries of the times. If and when President Obama, for example, determined that he needed to negotiate a new compact with the Sa'udi ruler, his advice – perhaps to empower 'Abdallah and the remaining seven Arab monarchs to transform their countries into constitutional monarchies – must be given in such a way as to not be interpreted as a blatant interference in the internal affairs of another country. Simply stated, because US–Sa'udi interests coincided on specific matters, like oil and defense issues, but diverged on others, Washington is well advised to focus on the doable instead of embracing what is beyond its writ. For like several of his counterparts on the Arabian Peninsula, King 'Abdallah was an innovator who chose the path of reforms which benefited from outside assistance, but that were devised at home, which meant that no one ought to expect him to be suicidal. The monarch remained persuaded that his internal compact, one devised in 1744 and that had endured both time and untold pressures, was his primary legitimizing instrument. Washington was an ally and provided a greatly appreciated safety net, especially in terms of defense questions but, like the best of allies, the US looked after its own interests, not necessarily those of the kingdom, and Riyadh reciprocated.

This was the crux of the matter, and the time was right to re-engage both American and Sa'udi officials to devise and adopt a new compact that would, this time around be based on trust. This White House, as indeed every administration, ought to look at this Sa'udi monarch, and certainly his successors, through the prism of the doable, instead of focusing on the impossible.

Conclusion

Because of its geo-strategic position, Sa'udi Arabia mattered to industrialized economies, emerging markets, regional foes, prospective acolytes, and internal consumers. As expected, King 'Abdallah bin 'Abdul 'Aziz focused on his country first and foremost, and though many assumed that he wished to reshape the Muslim world, such undertakings were alien to traditional power brokers on the Arabian Peninsula. Indeed, reshaping the Middle East was what Britain and France did at the end of World War One, through the infamous 1916 Sykes–Picot agreement, and that successive American administrations after Franklin Delano Roosevelt have tried, starting in the mid-20th century. Without exception, every White House occupant has looked at the Arab world through the Israeli prism and, throughout the Cold War with the Soviet Union, concluded that Israel was a strategic asset in various "Great Games." The most recent architect was President Barack Obama, whose design includes building bridges and displaying cooperation, most notably in his June 4, 2009 Cairo address to the Muslim world.[56]

Unlike his predecessor who excelled in wars that devastated the region – as well as the United States – Obama has relied on pragmatism to advance US interests. Gone were the catchy slogans of democracy and freedom, even if these were used to justify specific commitments. Rather, what Washington aimed for after 2009 was raw practicality, not idealism. It wanted to expand its military markets and continue to sell expensive hardware to Sa'udi Arabia and the other conservative Arab Gulf monarchies, which drove home the point that, at least on this score, there were no crises in the relationship. Towards that end, plans proceeded for Washington to sell the kingdom $60 billion in arms over the coming years, while American military "advisers" helped Prince Nayif's Interior Ministry build a 35,000-man "special facilities security force" to protect key oil installations in and around Abqai'q.[57]

In a way, the US assumed a classic British posture after 2009, one that displayed fewer ambiguities than previous American plans.[58] Like so many British prime ministers have done, the American president noted the many progressive steps embarked upon by King 'Abdallah – especially his rather successful efforts to curb the power of unapproved clerics and the religious police, the promotion of women in the health and education sectors, as well as the gradual liberalization of the kingdom's demanding economic policies – with satisfaction. The West in general, and the United States in particular, further noted that significant progress was made by the kingdom to tame the recruitment and fund-raising efforts by extremist elements that fed the imagination of the unemployed to fight unwinnable wars. Was this the adoption of new standards that, presumably, the American policy establishment seldom practiced? It is difficult to determine whether positive double-standards were now more prevalent, though what is clear is that Washington was far more pragmatic than at any other time in recent history. This was certainly a healthy development that articulated interests without preaching to the converted.

An equally important question that was now at the heart of American–Sa'udi relations was the two countries' shared perspectives on Iran. For some, Washington wished to take advantage of the fear that Tehran's *Shi'ah* revolutionary zeal inspired in Riyadh, even if the concern was not only political. Naturally, as Iran positioned itself as a leading power in the Gulf – by virtue of its geography and demographic weight in the region – Sa'udi Arabia took note of the rising influence of the Islamic Republic not only among *Shi'ahs* on the Arabian Peninsula, but also in Iraq, Syria, and Lebanon. Whether American interests required that Iran's growing power, especially its undeniable quest for nuclear power and, perhaps, its desire to eventually acquire a nuclear military capability, were certainly pertinent to American–Sa'udi ties. For it must be obvious to all concerned that Riyadh would not sit idly by if Tehran were to cross the nuclear threshold, a step that would almost certainly start a major arms race in the region. Whether such a scenario would enhance Sa'udi–American ties was impossible to know, although few ought to be surprised by its occurrence. In the larger scheme of things, Iran was not in a position to outspend Sa'udi Arabia to acquire sophisticated weapons – hence its logical desire to create a nuclear deterrent – and, in fact, Riyadh could not devote such a huge chunk of its resources to expensive hardware, which would mean that acquiring a nuclear deterrent was also in the cards. From Washington's perspective, sharing the foreign policy burden with regional allies was probably a necessity following the George W. Bush years that emaciated the American Treasury, though it is fair to ask whether, in the case of Sa'udi Arabia, relying on Washington made sense.[59] As stated above, pro-Israeli elements advising Obama warned that Washington must watch Riyadh carefully and insist on a new compact, concluding that the monarchy may not have what it takes to control the country.

For some reason, there is the belief, erroneous as it turns out, that Gulf rulers are truly beholden to Britain and now the United States for their very existence. Because great powers are deployed throughout the Persian Gulf region, the idea goes, and hence deny other hegemons predatory activities in an area they considered vital to their security, regional stability is somewhat assured. This is true of course, but only to a certain extent. Likewise, it is also true that after the first decade of the 21st century and perhaps for some time to come, Arab Gulf rulers would further need to rely on themselves, not only to preserve stability, but also to ensure that the region remains free from outside interference after 2020.

7 Conclusion

In the few years since he acceded to the throne on August 1, 2005, King 'Abdallah bin 'Abdul 'Aziz has instituted far-reaching reforms that, by general recognition, altered the face of the kingdom. Among the significant changes that were introduced were: fundamental reforms concerning the judiciary; launching a national dialogue mechanism that allowed Sa'udi citizens to engage each other in addressing issues that concerned society; holding interfaith dialogues that culminated in the July 2008 Madrid conference; establishing a brand new body to select the monarch and his Heir Apparent from among the sons and grandsons of the founder; introducing unprecedented bureaucratic transformations to manage the religious establishment, including the appointment of a new chairman for the Supreme Judicial Council, making changes within the Commission for the Promotion of Virtue and the Prevention of Vice; appointing a woman as Deputy Education Minister, and authorizing women to serve in the *Majlis al-Shurah*; along with a myriad additional alterations of a reformist nature in such areas as human rights, particularly women's rights, and in the ongoing struggle against extremism and terrorism. To say that 'Abdallah bin 'Abdul 'Aziz was a man in a hurry would indeed be an understatement, and it was likely that history will record his legacy as that of a reformer-monarch who sensed the time was long past for a fundamental socio-political evolution, in which his own yearnings matched those of his subjects.

This was not to say that the monarch was infallible, or that serious delays were not observed in implementing his orders, as discussed throughout this study. Rather, that among all of the kingdom's contemporary rulers, 'Abdallah understood best that Sa'udi citizens – and, for that matter, Arab and Muslim peoples – were on the march, which added an onus on officials to address core concerns before it was too late. In fact, the Sa'udi ruler spoke about serious shortcomings long before be assumed the burdens of power, calling on his fellow rulers attending the 22nd Gulf Cooperation Council Summit in Muscat, to tighten their belts. In his inimitably frank discourse, 'Abdallah underscored why he was not ashamed to say that [GCC States] have not been able to achieve the objectives [they] sought when [member-states] set up the Gulf Cooperation Council 20 years ago. ... We have not yet set up a unified military force that deters enemies and supports friends. We have not reached a common market, nor formulated a unified position on political crises. ... The painful events that have affected the Arab and Muslim society the world over dictate us to take our historical responsibility and demand that we make an introspection before accusing others. We admit we all, with no exception, have wronged the Ummah when we permitted ourselves to be vitiated by suspicion and misunderstanding instead of objectivity and frankness. While we sought the help of strangers, we forgot our kin and when we opened our countries and markets to foreign goods we closed our doors against the products of Muslim and Arab countries.[1]

As discussed in this volume, the reformist measures introduced since 2005 constituted a unique revolutionary process in the kingdom, which reflected the monarch's "will to power," and which echoed his own shortcomings in so many areas, including sensitive questions that dealt with succession, religious issues, economic matters, and political concerns. Shortcomings notwithstanding, the monarch tackled all of these topics with gusto. In fact, many of his thoughtful initiatives fulfilled progressive adjustments, rather than the full introduction of Jeffersonian democracy, best described as the practice of democratization that did not, perhaps even ought not, contravene local traditions. Though limited by Western standards, these transformations represented clear departures from policies introduced by previous Sa'udi monarchs, including the now famous 1992 Basic Law initiatives introduced by the late King Fahd bin 'Abdul 'Aziz.

Critics concluded that many, if not most, of these reforms were cosmetic and largely meaningless, highlighting the slow pace of change, the king's alleged indecision and, more often than not, his reluctance to impose his will. Many lamented the perception that the ruler did not issue stricter orders to see his objectives accomplished without further delays, deriding efforts that accommodated a variety of constituents, perhaps oblivious to the immense pressures exerted on the king by other members of the ruling family as well as the religious establishments. Indeed, while King 'Abdallah bin 'Abdul 'Aziz was in a hurry, he was not a dictator who exercised his absolute powers absolutely. Although his word was the law of the land, 'Abdallah stood out in several areas, including in the way he practiced his "will to power," something that was poorly understood even inside Sa'udi Arabia. Rather than legislate by fiat, the ruler prepared a generation of Al Sa'uds to appreciate the limits of power as much as its unmitigated application. Inasmuch as 'Abdallah's dual objective was to preserve the ruling family, as well as further legitimize the 1744 alliance that validated legitimacy in the kingdom, this was a foresightful goal, though neither the monarch nor his two Heir Apparents bothered to explain it. Often, and perhaps because the kingdom was mired in norms from a different era, especially with respect to gender and legal issues, the king and senior Al Sa'ud family members assumed that Sa'udis ought to simply trust Riyadh to make the right choices. Simply stated, such assumptions were not valid in the 21st century, and it was for that reason that 'Abdallah's reform initiatives were misinterpreted. What were the repercussions of King 'Abdallah's revolutionary measures in two of the most sensitive areas – gender matters and legal reforms – that illustrated this dilemma?

Key social changes affecting women

In late 2011, and true to his reformist traditions, the Custodian of the Two Holy Mosques, 'Abdallah bin 'Abdul 'Aziz Al Sa'ud, surprised everyone when he ordered that women be given the right to vote and run in municipal elections starting in 2015. He also empowered Sa'udi women to have the right to join the all-appointed *Majlis al-Shurah*. While no one expected that the monarch would use his opening address to the third year of the Council's fifth session with such a step, his short speech was almost exclusively devoted to the subject, closing with an admonition to those who might wish to challenge royal authority. "It is our right to seek your opinions and advice," underscored the ruler, warning that "those who stray from these guidelines" are nothing more than "arrogant persons" who would "have to bear the responsibility of their actions." These were strong words indeed, but highly illustrative of what the monarch intended to accomplish.

"We have decided that women will participate in the Majlis al-Shurah as members starting the next term," declared the king, emphasizing that such participation was compatible with *Shari'ah* and, equally important, with Islamic history. This last point was especially intriguing, as past efforts were limited to focusing on compatibility with Islamic law, especially since local norms and traditions were relegated to a secondary role. 'Abdallah rejected efforts to "marginalize the role of women in Sa'udi society," and underscored that his order was issued following extensive consultations with several religious scholars who, apparently, expressed the preference for this orientation and supported it. This too was vintage 'Abdallah, informing one and all that he consulted with leading scholars, but not all, and that he enlarged his circle of advisors by soliciting other views. In fact, because the king was not prone to emotional decisions, he placed yet another marker on a long list of epochal decisions that were gradually sealing the democratization process in the kingdom.

It may be worth recalling that over a single week in late 2007, King 'Abdallah authorized the establishment of a Supreme Court, issued by-laws for his 2006 succession edict that named its permanent members, and ordered his foreign minister to take necessary steps to counter the rise of the kingdom's regional hegemonic foe. 'Abdallah affirmed his will to power, husbanded new reforms that aimed to refurbish vital institutions, and strengthened the Al Sa'ud ruling family. Still, no subjects were as sensitive as those related to women, because segregation was still enforced in the country. Against all odds, the monarch was determined to address critical topics, not only in the aftermath of demands to allow women to drive or because of the repercussions of various uprisings throughout the Arab world, but also because of intrinsic Sa'udi developments that irritated him. As discussed above, the case that literally angered the ruler, and which probably colored his gender-related decisions, was the mid-2006 fate that befell the so-called "Qatif Girl" and mobilized the Palace. It was worth repeating that the monarch was furious when he heard of the case, and turned his wrath in private against clerics who appeared to take the law into their hands, blaming the two victims as much as the culprits. Remarkably, the monarch introduced his December 2011 changes in the presence of the Grand Mufti of the Kingdom Shaykh 'Abdul 'Aziz Al al-Shaykh, President of the Supreme Judiciary Council, Salih bin Humayd, as well as a number of religious scholars and Shaykhs. To his credit, 'Abdallah ensured that his "order," which was the law of the land, would be perceived in line with what his father and founder of the monarchy envisaged for the country. Towards that end, he expounded by stating: "The struggle of the father of the nation, the late King 'Abdul 'Aziz, and of your grandfathers (mercy be upon their souls), has resulted in the unity of hearts, land, and one destiny." "Today," he continued, "this destiny imposes on us to preserve this legacy, and not stop there but to develop it further in line with Islamic and moral values." In other words, 'Abdallah wished to re-seal the 1744 alliance between the Al Sa'ud and the Al Shaykh through this most sensitive topic, insisting that contemporary requirements obligated both groups to lead, rather than be led. In the event, the king's forward-looking initiative did not introduce full equality between men and women, although the latest royal order accelerated the process. It ensured that Sa'udi Arabia was not too far from the day when complete legal equality between genders would become reality, as Riyadh updated traditions, recognized the contribution that women can and ought to make to society, and, above all else, emphasized that Sa'udi men must welcome such changes by abolishing the huge anachronism which is segregation. 'Abdallah's latest accomplishment guaranteed that such an outcome was within the realm of the possible, and sooner than many assumed.

Whether Sa'udi women telegraphed this wish to the king through various interactions with members of the ruling family was impossible to determine, although a recent development probably reached the monarch's ears faster than anyone fathomed. In May 2011, Daliah al-Qurni, a student at King 'Abdul 'Aziz University pointedly asked HRH Prince Khalid al-Faysal, the Governor of Makkah, whether she should aspire to serve as a future Minister of Health. Although everyone in the Jiddah audience was utterly surprised, Prince Khalid did not discourage her, believing that prospective developments in the kingdom would open new doors to all citizens, perhaps aware that Sa'udi Arabia could not boast a healthy economy without the talent of all its citizens. Concurrent with this gathering, Sa'udi authorities detained Manal al-Sharif, after the female activist uploaded a video of herself behind the wheel of a car in Al-Khobar, which case was discussed earlier. An even more intriguing recent case, one of many that surfaced from time to time, was that of "Samia," a single woman in her 40s from Madinah who is a practicing surgeon. Samia lost two court cases when she sought a suspension of her father's guardianship to marry as she pleased. Sadly, her father and brothers, who insisted Samia marry a cousin, apparently abused her. Consequently, Samia has lived for the past five years in a shelter for battered women, which added additional hardships as she sought a hearing at the kingdom's Supreme Court. The latter was asked to either uphold previous court orders or grant her inalienable rights. Whether she will succeed remains to be determined, but in the words of Grand Mufti Shaykh 'Abdul 'Aziz Al al-Shaykh, the kingdom's highest ranking religious authority, "forcing a woman to marry someone she does not want and preventing her from wedding [the man] whom she chooses … is not permissible." Presumably a mild observation, this and many similar cases illustrated the large social gap that must be closed, even as Riyadh welcomed a recommendation from the United Nations Human Rights Council to abolish the guardianship system in 2009. Regrettably, it is still in place, though one of the consequences of King 'Abdallah's December 2011 reform initiatives was supposed to be to remove such barriers.

In the 21st century, and despite rigid social customs that made such a mundane necessity illegal, Sa'udi Arabia could no longer afford to neglect how it tackled gender questions. Truth be told, there was nothing to fear from Sa'udi women driving, since millions of other Muslim women sat behind the wheel without experiencing an erosion of moral values, including hundreds of thousands of Sa'udi women who drove overseas. Yet, beyond pledges to lift the social ban, the Custodian of the Two Holy Mosques refrained from issuing a blanket order that could legally explain why, according to Holy Scriptures – which guided Sa'udis in their socio-political outlooks – productivity was seldom forbidden. Clearly, Sa'udi women deserved an equal opportunity to flourish, and since the driving ban as well as a myriad other restrictions were social rather than religious issues, the king could easily separate religiosity from community norms. The point was not to create fresh controversies but to harness indigenous talent without enlarging the gulf that separated productivity and idleness. The king nevertheless preferred to work within his society's established norms, although everyone understood that the inevitable consequence of his initiatives would, in time, lead to lifting such peculiar bans.

Because Sa'udi Arabia remained the only country in the world that imposed strict guardianship conditions and prohibited women from driving and exercising various personal freedoms, many believed that the time was long overdue to let the kingdom's Manals drive kids to school or shop in peace, her Samias to operate on patients to save lives, and, more importantly, for Riyadh to let Daliah al-Qurni be educated enough to serve as a future Minister of Health. This was the inevitable consequence of King 'Abdallah's gender-related reforms, which intended to give the majority of Sa'udi women the chance to assume their full responsibilities. If for no other reason than to allow the kingdom to transform itself into a world-class economic power and, in doing so, fulfill Qur'anic calls for complete productivity.

Legal challenges and reforms

The second major area of change was in the kingdom's legal environment, although a full codification of significant developments was painstakingly slow. After his 2007 and 2009 legal reforms, the king embarked on a full-fledged reorganization of the judiciary that, technically, was supposed to be capped with the introduction of new codifications, which would be uniform across the country. Regrettably, the process was not implemented *in toto*, leading many to wonder whether the monarch was incapable of seeing it through. The ruler's initial steps focused on new procedure laws that encouraged judges to welcome attorneys into their courtrooms and, generally speaking, to make the whole experience friendlier to the legal profession. Naturally, the more drastic changes were made at the very top of the "profession," which removed various adjudication functions from the Supreme Judicial Council and handed them over to a newly created Supreme Court, along with key personnel changes discussed in Chapter 1. By all accounts, these alterations were epochal, which literally stunned the kingdom's religious establishment. Most clerics resented the monarch's interference in their lives and, more important, refused to budge from established traditions. *Shari'ah* law was not politics, many argued, and Sa'udi judges preferred to rule on the basis of their own understandings of relevant texts in the *Hanbali* school of thought. Although Islamic jurisprudence produced copious texts that were widely available, Sa'udi judges opted to rely on their own "training," which were often of an *ad hoc* nature, to render judgments. Their primary argument was that the ultimate legal text was the Qur'an, which was infallible and did not require further elucidation. This was the context that confronted the reformer-oriented monarch who could make laws but who needed to tread carefully on an area of absolute truths. Consequently, he avoided pushing the proverbial envelope, opting to encourage clerics to assume additional responsibilities and explain how the *nizam* (system) in place could gradually add certain *qanuns* (laws) that would never contradict the Holy Scriptures but that would help define better what were individual believers' rights and responsibilities. In other words, the king placed the burden of this codification process on the same clergy he chastised for being too rigid, and who were now called upon to humanize the law. Whatever contradictions existed between *Shari'ah* law and rules and regulations that needed elaboration were the writ of scholars to elucidate and clarify. Inasmuch as divine law was the only one with any merit in Sa'udi Arabia, any codification was subjected to a series of tough tests, including the justification to erect a parallel *nizam* that ought not transform God's law into man-made legislation.

Of course, neither the ruler nor any of his more enlightened advisors, advocated a full-fledged codification that contravened Islamic jurisprudence.

For the king's goal was not only to habituate the clergy to adapt to changing circumstances, but to also welcome the very idea of uniformity in the law, something that was rejected by staunchly individualistic clerics whose privilege to interpret at will would be significantly altered. That was the logical consequence of 'Abdallah bin 'Abdul 'Aziz's legal reforms, and that was what truly bothered entrenched clerics who rejected such compromises, preferring to live in their well-oiled cocoons. Which judge was ready to rule on the basis of a universally accepted text – even by Sa'udi standards – when so much of his influence came from personal training and avowedly impeccable knowledge of jurisprudence? Religious scholars in the kingdom were genuinely persuaded that no single jurist, or even a panel of senior clergymen no matter how qualified their credentials, ought to have final authority on how to interpret *Shari'ah* law. Equally important, and unlike many other Muslim societies, Sa'udi clergymen relied on their intellects, not necessarily past authorities, to rule with justice. In other words, their system may be said to be far less rigid, because every generation automatically adapted to changing circumstances, even if the *nizam* relied on the cleric to actually take his work seriously and delve in the sacred texts.

This was the context into which the Sa'udi monarch wished to make reforms without, it is important to re-emphasize, questioning the authority of clergymen to adjudicate. Yet, by insisting on legal reforms, the king called on the religious establishment to accept the executive branch's rights to legislate, albeit carefully, in an area that was heretofore reserved to clerics. Even if the Sa'udi king did not claim to exercise such authority, in fact, he was signaling that a monarch was also a spiritual leader who could encourage "scholars" to agree on what the nation required and to codify what they presumably agreed upon for use as a "guide" by fellow judges serving throughout the kingdom. The late King Fahd failed to nudge the *Hay'at Kibar al-'Ulamah* (Board of Senior Religious Scholars) to accept such a mechanism, and it remains to be determined whether his successor – or perhaps a future monarch – will succeed in sealing such a *nizam*. At a time when the kingdom was increasingly connected to international commerce and finance, when the vast majority of citizens receive secondary and university education, and as many interact with other societies, the needs for sound and uniform legal institutions were essential. That was why King 'Abdallah took on this immense challenge. Above all else, he understood that his decisiveness on broaching this super-sensitive topic was probably the most critical challenge facing his conservative society, one that could no longer survive in isolation. Proposing legal reforms, including the preparation of codes, would still be undertaken within *Shari'ah* rules, which would respect the role of existing judiciary institutions, but that would be called upon to adapt Islamic jurisprudence to contemporary life. Whether the monarch's recommendations would be implemented in the near future were still unclear although such major initiatives were bound to require reflection, time, and, perhaps, more transparency. No dramatic breakthroughs were announced after 2009, although that was not unusual in and of itself, given that legal wheels turn slowly in every society.

Gradual reforms

In late February 2012, King 'Abdallah bin 'Abdul 'Aziz received members of the Presidential Committee of the King 'Abdul 'Aziz Center for National Dialogue, who reported on the Center's latest activities. The ruler approved of the progress achieved to date in this essential area and reiterated his support to encourage Sa'udis to engage in constructive conversations precisely to address grievances in a peaceful way. "My only goal," he declared, "is to serve the nation, people, and religion. This is my only goal. All what I feel is that it is my duty as well as every other Saudi citizen's duty."[2] Beyond the hyperbole, the monarch surprised his visitors when he launched into a heart-to-heart confession, stating:

> I have more ideas. If God wills, they will be achieved with your and my joint efforts. Without you I am nothing, without the Sa'udi people I am nothing. I am one of you and for you. I seek God's help first and then yours. ... There are two things I'll tell you. Sa'udi Arabia's position globally is excellent, and its economy is robust. But I wish for more, but what I tell you is that you help me and thus you'll help yourselves.

Audience members were stunned, for seldom anyone had heard a similarly frank comment. It was a rare moment in the kingdom's history, coming at the end of one of the most tumultuous years in contemporary Arab affairs, which witnessed dramatic regime changes in several countries. Although the ruler was amply satisfied that the so-called March 11, 2011 'Day of Rage' fizzled, as most Sa'udis reiterated their loyalties to king and country, 'Abdallah bin 'Abdul 'Aziz knew in his heart that discontent persisted. He was relieved that the vast majority of citizens welcomed his massive decrees that guaranteed unemployment benefits, allocated additional capital for housing lending projects, enhanced social benefits, encouraged debt forgiveness for the needy, as well as grant civil service wage increases – all of which were in the works long before he traveled to the United States for medical attention – he was, nevertheless, disappointed that tensions elsewhere in the Arab world forced his hand. That was the reason why his February 2012 confession was so poignant. Simply stated, the king's caution often meant that his "will to power" was subjected to internal vagaries that hamper his own preferences. Indeed, what distressed the leadership was a fundamental communication gap between a carefully thought-out vision – visionary in every sense of the word – that, nevertheless, was subject to norms dating from a bygone era. Whether in the economic field, legal and religious regulations, social traditions, or even concerning the sacrosanct succession matter, the king wished to accelerate the pace of his reforms, even if he preferred not to upset the proverbial apple cart. Inevitably, however, his initiatives upset far more than the entire system in place, which was why Sa'udi Arabia confronted a major dilemma: how to reform its institutions while holding to its well-tested norms.

Beyond its immediate challenges, Sa'udi Arabia was no longer in a position to remain isolated from the rest of its region, indeed separated from the rest of the world. Peculiar and anachronistic elements stood out, and while the kingdom was at a crossroads, the time was probably ripe to accelerate the kind of fundamental reforms King 'Abdallah bin 'Abdul 'Aziz harbored. His "I have more ideas" quest probably covered a variety of items, including the formulation of a serious political reform agenda, including the adoption of a written constitution, popular elections for the *Majlis al-Shurah* that may be transformed into a parliament, the appointment of a Prime Minister who would govern the country's increasingly complex affairs, and, most importantly, the strengthening of a separate and independent judiciary. Only such ideas may satisfy savvy Sa'udis disenchanted with the available fare. Still, only such ideas promised to fulfill the reformer monarch's complete aspirations for a reinvigorated society, which is no longer willing to bide for time. The king's burden, if not his dilemma, was to "serve his nation" well while he still had the time, to set the stage for the future so that his successors continued his many accomplishments, and to gradually eliminate the traditional roadblocks that prevented the nation from reaching new heights. A tall order indeed for a relatively young country, even if its roots were embedded in history.

Appendix 1: Interviews

Al Sa'ud Family Members (alphabetical)

HRH Prince Bandar al-Faysal, Retired Royal Saudi Air Force Lt. Colonel (in charge of Air Force Intelligence), Riyadh, March 28, 2011.

HRH Princess al-Bandari bint 'Abdul Rahman al-Faysal, Director General, King Khalid Foundation, Riyadh, March 29, 2011.

HRH Prince Muhammad bin Nayif bin 'Abdul 'Aziz, Deputy Minister of the Interior, Counter-Terrorism Chief, Riyadh, March 29, 2011.

HRH Turki al-Faysal bin 'Abdul 'Aziz Al Sa'ud, Chairman of the *King Faisal Center for Research and Islamic Studies*, Riyadh, March 30, 2011

HRH Prince Turki bin Talal bin 'Abdul 'Aziz, Personal Representative for HRH Prince Talal bin 'Abdul 'Aziz, and Colonel Pilot – Army Aviation within the Royal Saudi Land Forces, Jiddah, September 20, 2011.

HRH Prince Salman bin 'Abdul 'Aziz, Governor of Riyadh, Riyadh, October 17, 2010.

Other Sa'udi Interviewees (alphabetical)

'Abdul 'Aziz H. Al-Fahad, Principal of the Law Office of Abdulaziz H. Fahad, Riyadh, October 25, 2010.

HE Dr. Ghazi Al-Gosaibi, Minister of Labor, Manama, Bahrain, February 18, 2009.

Hassan Yassin, Advisor to Foreign Minister Sa'ud al-Faysal, Riyadh, March 29, 2011.

Khalid Al Maeena, Editor-in-Chief, *Arab News*, Jiddah, October 12, 2010, September 11, 2011.

Marianne Alireza, Author, Jiddah, September 14, 2011.

Mazin Salah Motabbagani, Professor at the Imam Muhammad bin Sa'ud Islamic University, Riyadh, March 15, 2010.

Dr. Saleh M. Al Namlah, Deputy Minister of Culture and Information, Riyadh, March 28, 2011.

HE Salih bin Humayd, Chairman, *Majlis al-Shurah*, Riyadh, October 16, 2010.

Shaykh Saleh Al Luhaydan, Riyadh, March 27, 2011.

Turki al-Hamad, Author and Academic, Riyadh, March 22, 2011.

Appendix 2: Consent to Establish the King 'Abdul 'Aziz Center for National Dialogue

Praise be to Almighty God who ordered us in the holy Qur'an to join forces with others in implementing worthy deeds. In the name of God, the most merciful and most gracious and in fear of God and peace be on the Prophet of Allah who guided us to be friendly toward every Muslim.

Dear brothers,

Recently we witnessed a very important development that found expression in the convening of the national dialogue forum, which brought together the elite of our society from different persuasions and schools of thought. They met under the umbrella of Islamic fraternity and exchanged views in the arena of national brotherhood.

Toward the end of their meeting they came up with some constructive recommendations that are expected to reinforce their adherence to their cherished faith and to further strengthen national unity. All citizens of this country owe these pioneers profuse thanks and appreciation.

These most esteemed brothers of ours realized the need for continuing the dialogue so that more people can take part in the exchange of views. They wanted to evolve the dialogue into a constructive way of life in the kingdom. I am happy to announce that the Custodian of the Two Holy Mosques, King Fahd bin 'Abdul 'Aziz, has given his consent to the establishment of the King 'Abdul 'Aziz Center for National Dialogue so that the new center will be in a position to realize the foregoing objectives. Preparations are being made to select the site of the new center, which will be located in Riyadh. To help the center begin operation as soon as possible, various facilities of the King 'Abdul 'Aziz Public Library will be placed at its disposal.

I have no doubt that the establishment of the center and the continuation of the dialogue will turn out to be a historic achievement, which could go a long way toward creating a new channel for responsible self-expression. In the long run, this will be very effective in fighting extremism and fanaticism and can create a healthy and clean environment, which promotes enlightened attitude and rejects terrorism and terrorist ideologies.

Appendix 2: Consent to Establish the King 'Abdul 'Aziz Center

Dear brothers,

In this beloved homeland of ours we were able to realize peace, security and prosperity, because we strictly adhered to the Islamic faith and because we equally adhered to the unity of our homeland and the equality of its children. To be assured of success any dialogue must be conducted in line with these two basic principles and be dedicated to further strengthening them. We will have no life without Islam and we will have no greatness without the unity of our motherland. We will not permit anyone, no matter who he is, to tamper with the principles of our faith and in same manner we will not let anyone undermine the unity of our homeland no matter whoever he may be.

The terms of reference of the national dialogue must be based on the practices and customs of early Muslims, which are embraced by the people of the Kingdom of Sa'udi Arabia. Early Muslims, may Allah be pleased with them, used to conduct the exchange of views with wisdom and with sound advice. Their activities are based on the guiding words of the Prophet, peace be upon him. The Prophet (pbuh) said "Anyone who believes in Allah and the Last Day should utter a nice word or remain silent." Early Muslims considered abusing a fellow Muslim an act of deviation and killing him outright apostasy. This is the right path that a dialogue should follow.

I am confident that the nation's *'Ulamah* and intellectuals are among those who follow this right path. They fully realize as I do that the Sa'udi government and people are not prepared to see the freedom to conduct dialogue to degenerate into the exchange of abuses or into waging attacks on the nation's shining symbols or against its leading *'Ulamah*.

This homeland, which has the honor of serving the two holy *Harams* and to which the hearts of Muslims from all over the world are attached, is not prepared to accommodate any idea even with slightest variation with the basic tenets of Islam. In the same manner, this homeland will not accept any ideology that is based on misinterpreting Islamic teachings and which use misleading emblems to justify its evil scheme of sowing terror and declaring practicing Muslims as apostates. The Sa'udi people will not accept any substitute for a moderate belief that rejects fanaticism as it rejects moral degeneration and permissiveness.

Source: " 'Abdallah bin 'Abdul 'Aziz Announces the Consent Given by King Fahd for the Establishment of the King 'Abdul 'Aziz Center for National Dialogue," Riyadh: KACND, August 4, 2003, at http://www.kacnd.org/eng/prince_word.asp.

Appendix 3: King 'Abdallah's opening speech in Madrid

July 17, 2008

"O mankind we have created you from a single (pair) of a male and a female, and made you into nations and tribes, that ye may know each other. Verily the most honored of you in the sight of Allah is (he who is) the most righteous of you."

Dear friends, I came to you from the place dearest to the hearts of all Muslims, the land of the Two Holy Mosques, bearing with me a message from the Islamic world (*Ummah*), representing its scholars and thinkers who recently met in the confines of the House of God. This message declares that Islam is a religion of moderation and tolerance, a message that calls for constructive dialogue among followers of religions, a message that promises to open a new page for humanity in which, God willing, concord will replace conflict.

Dear friends, we all believe in one God, who sent messengers for the good of humanity in this world and the hereafter. His will, praise be to Him, was that people should differ in their faiths. If the Almighty had so desired, all mankind would have shared the same religion. We are meeting today to affirm that the religions that God Almighty desired for the happiness of man should be a means to ensure that happiness.

It is therefore incumbent upon us to declare to the world that difference must not lead to conflict and confrontation, and to state that the tragedies that have occurred in human history were not due to religion, but were the result of extremism with which some adherents of every divinely revealed religion, and of every political ideology, have been afflicted.

Mankind is suffering today from a loss of values and conceptual confusion, and is passing through a critical phase which, in spite of all the scientific progress, is witnessing a proliferation of crime, an increase in terrorism, the disintegration of the family, subversion of the minds of the young by drug-abuse, exploitation of the poor by the strong, and odious racist tendencies. This is all a consequence of the spiritual void from which people suffer when they forget God, and God causes them to forget themselves. There is no solution for us other than to agree on a united approach, through dialogue among religions and civilizations.

Dear friends, most of the past dialogues have failed because they have deteriorated into mutual recrimination focusing on and exaggerating differences in a sterile endeavor that exacerbated rather than mitigated tensions, or because they attempted to fuse religions and creeds on the pretext of bringing them closer together. This is likewise a fruitless effort, since the adherents of every religion are deeply convinced in their faith, and will not accept any alternative thereto. If we wish this historic meeting to succeed, we must focus on the common denominators that unite us, namely, deep faith in God, noble principles, and lofty moral values, which constitute the essence of religion.

Dear friends, man could be the cause of the destruction of this planet and everything in it. He is also capable of turning it into an oasis of peace and tranquility in which adherents of religions, creeds and philosophies could co-exist, and in which people could cooperate with each other in a respectful manner, and address problems through dialogue rather than violence. Man is also capable, by the grace of God, of vanquishing hatred through love, and bigotry through tolerance, thereby enabling all mankind to enjoy the dignity that the Almighty has bestowed upon all of them.

Dear friends, let our dialogue be a triumph of belief over disbelief, of virtue over vice, of justice over iniquity, of peace over conflicts and wars, and of human brotherhood over racism. Thus, with God we began, and through Him we seek assistance. I offer you my sincere greetings and appreciation. Thank you and peace be upon you.

Source: "Text of King 'Abdallah bin 'Abdul 'Aziz Al Sa'ud Opening Speech in Madrid," *Saudi Gazette*, July 17, 2008, reproduced in Kingdom of Saudi Arabia, Ministry of Hajj, at http://www.hajinformation.com/display_news.php?id=934.

Appendix 4: The Madrid Declaration

July 19, 2008

In the Name of God, the Compassionate, the Merciful.

Praise be to God, Lord of the Universe, and may the peace and blessings of God be upon all His prophets and messengers.

In response to the invitation of the Custodian of the Two Holy Mosques King 'Abdallah bin 'Abdul 'Aziz Al Sa'ud, the Muslim World League organized the World Conference on Dialogue in Madrid, Spain, during the period 13–15 Rajab 1429, corresponding to July 16–18, 2008.

The participants in the conference and followers of the world religions and cultures express their profound gratitude for the Custodian of the Two Holy Mosques King 'Abdallah bin 'Abdul 'Aziz Al Sa'ud for his generous patronage and inauguration of the conference and for his speech to the participants, which they considered as a major document in the conference.

Furthermore, the participants extended their deep thanks and appreciation for His Majesty Juan Carlos I of Spain for his comprehensive welcome speech and for HE Mr. José Luis Rodríguez Zapatero, the prime minister of Spain, for his participation in the opening session and for his efforts in the dialogue of civilizations. The participants also thanked the Spanish government for having the conference in Spain. This great country is home to an historical heritage that belongs to the followers of different religions and has contributed to human civilization.

The participants also recall the objectives of the UN Charter, which calls for exerting collective efforts aiming at the enhancement of international relations, the creation of an exemplary human community and the promotion of dialogue as a civilized way for cooperation.

The participants further remind all people of the Declaration of UN General Assembly in 1994, which called for tolerance and the spread of the culture of peace, and also ask that they recall the declarations of 1995 as the Year of Tolerance and 2001 as the Year of Dialogue Among Civilizations.

The participants commend the Appeal of Makkah issued by the World Islamic Conference on Dialogue, which was called for by the Custodian of Two Holy Mosques King 'Abdallah bin 'Abdul 'Aziz Al Sa'ud and organized by the Muslim World League earlier this year (2008).

The participants build on the agreement among the followers of religions and prominent cultures regarding the value of dialogue as the best way for mutual understanding and cooperation in human relations as well as in peaceful coexistence among nations.

In light of the above, the participants affirm the following principles:

1 Unity of humankind in the original creation and the equality among human beings irrespective of their colors, ethnic backgrounds and cultures.
2 Purity of the nature of humans; as they were created liking good and disliking evil, inclining to justice and avoiding injustice. Such pure nature leads humans to show mercy and to seek certainty and belief.
3 Diversity of cultures and civilizations among people is a sign of God and a cause for human advancement and prosperity.
4 The heavenly messages aim at realizing the obedience of people to their Creator and achieving happiness, justice, security and peace for humankind. These messages seek to enhance ways of understanding and cooperation among people despite differences in their origins, colors and languages. They also call for spreading virtue through wisdom and politeness, and rejecting extremism and terrorism.
5 Respecting heavenly religions, preserving their high status, condemning any insult to their symbols, and combating the exploitation of religion in the instigation of racial discrimination.
6 Observing peace, honoring agreements and respecting unique traditions of peoples and their right to security, freedom and self-determination are the basis for building good relations among all people. Achieving this is a major objective of all religions and prominent cultures.
7 The significance of religion and moral values and the need for humans to revert to their Creator in their fight against crime, corruption, drugs, and terrorism, and in preserving the institution of the family and protecting societies from deviant behaviors.
8 The family is the basic unit of society and its nucleus. Protecting it from disintegration is a cornerstone for any secure and stable society.
9 Dialogue is one of the essentials of life. It is also one of the most important means for knowing each other, cooperation, exchange of interests and realizing the truth, which contributes to the happiness of humankind.
10 The preservation of the environment and its protection from pollution and other dangers are considered a major objective of all religions and cultures.

Mindful of accomplishing the above principles through dialogue, the conference has thoroughly reviewed the process of dialogue and its obstacles, as well as the catastrophes that afflicted humanity in the 20th century. The conference noted that terrorism is one of the most serious obstacles confronting dialogue and coexistence.

Terrorism is a universal phenomenon that requires unified international efforts to combat it in a serious, responsible and just way. This demands an international agreement on defining terrorism, addressing its root causes and achieving justice and stability in the world.

Based on the above, the conference has adopted the following recommendations:

- To reject theories that call for the clash of civilizations and cultures and to warn of the danger of campaigns seeking to deepen conflicts and destabilize peace and security.
- To enhance common human values, to cooperate in their dissemination within societies and to solve the problems that hinder their achievement.
- To disseminate the culture of tolerance and understanding through dialogue so as to be a framework for international relations through holding conferences and symposia, as well as developing relevant cultural, educational and media programs.
- To agree on international guidelines for dialogue among the followers of religions and cultures through which moral values and ethical principles, which are common denominators among such followers, so as to strengthen stability and achieve prosperity for all humans.
- To work on urging governmental and non-governmental organizations to issue a document that stipulates respect for religions and their symbols, the prohibition of their denigration and the repudiation of those who commit such acts.

To fulfill these desired objectives of dialogue by this conference, the participants have agreed on adopting the following:

1 Forming a working team to study the problems hindering dialogue and preventing it from realizing its desired results. Its task is also to prepare a study that provides visions for the solution of these problems and to coordinate among bodies promoting world dialogue.
2 Cooperation among religious, cultural, educational, and media establishments to deepen and consolidate ethical values, to encourage noble social practices and to confront sexual promiscuity, family disintegration and other vices.
3 Organizing inter-religious and inter-cultural meetings, conducting research, executing media programs and using the Internet and other media for the dissemination of a culture of peace, understanding and coexistence.
4 Promoting the issue of dialogue among the followers of religions, civilizations and cultures within youth, cultural, educational, and media activities.
5 Calling upon the UN General Assembly to support the results reached by this conference. It is strongly recommended to make use of these recommendations in enhancing dialogue among the followers of religions, civilizations and cultures through conducting a special UN session on dialogue. The participants express their hope that the Custodian of the Two Holy

Mosques King 'Abdallah bin 'Abdul 'Aziz Al Sa'ud will use his good offices with the concerned bodies in convening this session as soon as possible. It will be the pleasure of the members of this conference to take part in that session through a representative delegation, members of which are to be chosen by the Muslim World League.

In abiding with the agreed-upon principles and concepts, the participants do emphasize that it is essential for this world dialogue to be open and that its sessions be held periodically.

The participants have extended their profound gratitude to King 'Abdallah bin 'Abdul 'Aziz Al Sa'ud, the King of Sa'udi Arabia, for his kind initiation and invitation to this world dialogue. They also expressed their appreciation for the Muslim World League and other bodies that cooperated in organizing this conference. They have applauded the continued efforts made by the league in the fields of dialogue and cooperation among nations and peoples, hoping that the common objectives, for which humankind aspires, are accomplished.

Issued in Madrid, 15 Rajab 1429 (18 July 2008)

Source: "World Conference on Dialogue – The Madrid Declaration, July 19, 2008," http://www.SaudiEmbassy.net, also at http://www.saudi-us-relations.org/articles/2008/ioi/080719-madrid-declaration.html.

Appendix 5: Sa'udi Arabia: excerpts from the 1992 Basic Law

Article 5

(a) Monarchy is the system of rule in the Kingdom of Sa'udi Arabia.
(b) Rulers of the country shall be from amongst the sons of the founder, King 'Abdul 'Aziz bin 'Abdul Rahman al-Faysal Al Sa'ud, and their descendants. The most upright among them shall receive allegiance according to the Holy Qur'an and the *Sunnah* of the Prophet (Peace be upon Him).
(c) The King shall choose the Heir Apparent and relieve him by a Royal Decree.
(d) The Heir Apparent shall devote himself exclusively to his duties as Heir Apparent and shall perform any other duties delegated to him by the King.
(e) Upon the death of the King, the Heir Apparent shall assume all Royal powers until a pledge of allegiance (*bay'ah*) is given.

Article 6

In support of the Holy Qur'an and the *Sunnah* of His Messenger (Peace be upon Him), citizens shall give the pledge of allegiance (*bay'ah*) to the King, professing loyalty in times of hardship as well as ease.

Source: Kingdom of Sa'udi Arabia, *The Basic Law of Government*, Riyadh: Majlis al-Shurah, n.d. (translated and adapted from the Arabic), pp. 15–34.

Appendix 6: Sa'udi Arabia: Allegiance Law of Succession

The Allegiance Commission was created by decree in Makkah on 28 Ramadan 1427 H (October 20, 2006), and empowered with regulations that emended the 1995 Basic Law as well as the March 1, 1992 decree that allowed a monarch to dismiss his heir apparent.

Article 1

An Allegiance Commission is created by royal order, comprised of:

1. The sons of the founder King 'Abdul 'Aziz bin 'Abdul Rahman al-Faysal Al Sa'ud.
2. The grandsons of the founder King 'Abdul 'Aziz bin 'Abdul Rahman al-Faysal Al Sa'ud, whose fathers are deceased or incapacitated – as determined by a medical report – or are otherwise unwilling to assume the throne, if they are proven to be eligible and capable.
3. Two members appointed by the king, one of his own sons and one of the heir apparent's, if they are proven to be eligible and capable.

If any of the above relinquishes their post as part of the Allegiance Commission, the king will appoint a substitute, in accordance with sections 2 and 3 of this article.

Article 2

The Allegiance Commission shall exercise its duties in accordance with this Law, as well as with the Basic Law of Governance.

Article 3

The Allegiance Commission will abide by the teachings of the Qur'an and the *Sunnah* of the Prophet Muhammad (Peace be Upon Him), preserve the state, protect the Royal Family's unity, secure its cooperation, prevent its division, as well as promote national unity and the interests of the people.

Article 4

The Allegiance Commission will be based in Riyadh and will hold its meetings at the Royal Court. It may convene at any of the Royal Court's locations within the Kingdom, or any setting specified by the King, subject to the monarch's consent.

Article 5

Before assuming their duties, Commission members as well as the Secretary-General, will swear the following oath before the monarch:

> I swear by God Almighty to be loyal to my religion, monarch, and country, not to divulge any of the country's secrets, to preserve its interests and laws, to protect the Royal Family's unity and support, to safeguard the country's national unity, and to perform my duties truthfully, honestly, reliably and justly.

Article 6

When the King dies, the Commission will pledge allegiance to the heir apparent, in accordance with this Law, as well as the Basic Law of Governance.

Article 7

A Following consultations with members of the Commission, the King will choose one, or two or three candidates for the position of Heir Apparent. He will present his nominees to the Commission, which will be required to unanimously designate one as Heir Apparent. In the event the Commission rejects all nominees, it will be called upon to name a suitable heir apparent.

B The King may ask the Commission to nominate a suitable Heir Apparent at any time. In the event that the King rejects the Commission's nominee, the Commission will vote to choose between the King's contender and its own, in accordance with Sections A and B of this Article. The nominee who secures a majority of votes will be named Heir Apparent.

Article 8

A potential Heir Apparent nominee should satisfy the conditions set forth in Section B of Article 5 in the Basic Law of Governance.

Article 9

An Heir Apparent must be designated according to Article 7 within a period of 30 days after a King accedes to the throne.

Article 10

The Commission will set up a five-member Transitory Ruling Council which will temporarily assume governance responsibilities for all State affairs as provided for in this Law. The Transitory Ruling Council will not have the right to amend the Basic Law of Governance, this Law, the Council of Ministers Law, the *Shurah* Council Law, the Law of the Provinces, the National Security Council Law, or any other laws linked to governance. It will not have the right to dissolve or reshuffle either the Cabinet or the *Shurah* Council. During the replacement period, the Transitory Ruling Council should maintain national unity, in addition to protecting the country's foreign and domestic interests.

Article 11

In the event the Commission is persuaded that the King is incapacitated for medical reasons, it will request a report on his health conditions from a medical committee, in accordance with this Law. If the report determines that the King is temporarily unable to exercise his full powers, the Commission will certify this finding, and transfer governance authority to the Heir Apparent until a full recovery.

When the King issues a formal written notice to the Chairman of the Commission that he has recovered and is ready to resume his full authority, the Commission will seek a confirmation of the recuperation from the medical committee, in an updated report to be made available within 24 hours.

If the medical report determines that the King is capable to exercise his powers, the Commission will certify this finding, and the King will resume his rule.

If, however, the medical report concludes that the King is unable to exercise his powers on a permanent basis, the Commission will further certify that finding, and invite the Heir Apparent to accede the throne after receiving pledges of allegiance. These procedures must be carried out in accordance with this Law and with the Basic Law of Governance within 24 hours.

Article 12

If the Commission determines that both the King and his Heir Apparent can no longer exercise their powers due to health reasons, the Commission will call on its medical committee to prepare a report on their health conditions. If the medical report resolves that neither can resume their rule, even temporarily, the committee will empower the Transitory Ruling Council to assume governance responsibilities, and oversee the interests of the people until either the King or the Heir Apparent recovers.

After a written notice from either the King or the Heir Apparent is sent to the Commission stating that they have recovered from illness, and after the Commission is persuaded, it will request a health report from the aforementioned medical committee within 24 hours. If the report determines that either the King or the Heir Apparent is capable of exercising his powers then the Commission will certify that finding, and the individual in question will resume exercising his powers.

If, however, the report confirms that either the King or the Heir Apparent are medically unfit to rule, or are permanently incapacitated, the Commission will certify this finding, and call on the Transitory Ruling Council to assume governance responsibilities for a period not to exceed seven days. The Commission will, during this time, select a suitable candidate from among the sons and grandsons of the founding King 'Abdul 'Aziz bin 'Abdul Rahman al-Faysal Al Sa'ud. It will call on him to take over as King in accordance with this Law and the Basic Law of Governance.

Article 13

If the King and the Heir Apparent die simultaneously, the Commission will select within a period not to exceed seven days, a suitable candidate for governance from among the sons or grandsons of King 'Abdul 'Aziz bin 'Abdul Rahman al-Faysal Al Sa'ud. It will call for a pledge of allegiance to the new King in accordance with this Law and the Basic Law of Governance. The Transitory Ruling Council will assume governance responsibilities until new King ascends the throne.

Article 14

The medical committee will be comprised of:

1 The medical representative for the Royal Clinics.
2 The medical director of the King Faysal Specialist Hospital.
3 Three medical college deans selected by the Allegiance Commission.

The medical committee is empowered to issue the aforementioned medical reports in this Law and to consult physicians it deems appropriate.

Article 15

The eldest son of the founding King 'Abdul 'Aziz bin 'Abdul Rahman al-Faysal Al Sa'ud will chair the Commission with the second eldest acting as his deputy. In case neither is available, the eldest grandson will chair its gatherings.

Article 16

All Commission meetings will be held in camera with the King's approval. Commission members, the Secretary-General, and a rapporteur will only attend meetings. With the King's approval, the Commission may invite individuals to provide explanations or inform attendees, but those individuals will not have the right to vote.

Article 17

The Chairman of the Commission will call meetings in accordance with Articles 6, 11, 12 and 13 of this Law.

Article 18

All members should attend Commission gatherings and should not leave before the conclusion of any meeting without the permission of the chairman. If a member is unable to attend an assembly, he should inform the chairman as such, in writing.

Article 19

The chairman begins and ends all assemblies, moderates the debates, invites members to speak, determines the agenda, terminates discussions, and introduces resolutions for vote. A new item may be added to an agenda with the approval of ten members.

Article 20

Meetings will be considered valid when a quorum of two-thirds of the members is present, including the Chairman or his representative.

In accordance with Article 7, the Commission will approve its decisions with the consent of a majority of members present. In the event of a tie, the side on which the president of the Commission has voted, prevails. In emergency situations in which the quorum has not been met, meetings may be held with half of the members present, and decisions may be reached with the approval of two-thirds of those present.

Article 21

For each assembly, there should be a record that indicates the time and location of the meeting, the name of its chairman, the names of members present, along with the names of those who are absent and the reasons for their absence, if any, the name of the Secretary-General, a summary of all discussions, the number of yea and nay votes, the result of said votes, and the full text of all decisions.

The record should further indicate whether the gathering was postponed or adjourned, and if so, the time when this took place. Moreover, the record should include anything that the chairman deems necessary, and its minutes should be signed by the chairman, present members, as well as the Secretary-General.

Article 22

Commission votes will be cast by secret ballot in accordance with a model to be prepared for this purpose.

Article 23

Commission members may only review the agenda and all pertinent documents, at the location in which the assembly is convened, and will not be permitted to remove any documents from the meeting hall.

Article 24

The King appoints a Secretary-General who will assume the responsibility of inviting Commission members, supervising the process of preparing minutes and decisions, and announcing the results of its meetings as instructed by the Chairman. With the King's approval, the Secretary-General may seek assistance, as he deems necessary. The King will also appoint a deputy to the Secretary-General to preside during the Secretary-General's absence.

Article 25

A Royal Decree will amend the provisions of this Law after the approval of the Allegiance Commission.

Source: Translated from the Arabic version as published in *Al-Madinah*, Number 15886, October 21, 2006 at http://www.almadinapress.com/print.aspx?articleid=183874.

Appendix 7: Sa'udi Arabia: Bylaws of the Allegiance Commission

In the name of God the Merciful and Compassionate,
Number A/164
Dated 26/9/1428 [October 8, 2007]

With the help of God, We 'Abdallah bin 'Abdul 'Aziz Al Sa'ud, King of Saudi Arabia,

After examining the Basic System of Government issued by royal decree dated 27/8/1412,
And after examining the statutes of the Allegiance Commission issued by royal decree number A/135 dated 26/9/1427,
And after examining the draft executive bylaw of the Allegiance Commission,
And in order to meet the requirements of the public interest,
Order the following:
First: The draft executive law of the Allegiance Commission is issued as the text attached hereto.
Second: This decree shall be communicated to the parties concerned for endorsement and implementation.
'Abdallah bin 'Abdul 'Aziz Al Sa'ud

TEXT – BYLAWS OF THE ALLEGIANCE COMMISSION

Article 1

One of the sons of the deceased, who may be disinterested or who is unable in line with a medical report, from the sons of King 'Abdul 'Aziz bin 'Abdul Rahman al-Faysal Al Sa'ud – the Founder (of the Kingdom), to be appointed as a member at the Allegiance Commission in line with the following:

First:

a The King asks the sons of the deceased member of the Commission or who is unable from those who have reached the age of 17 to nominate two or three of them for the membership of the Commission. The sons of the deceased or who is unable from the sons of the sons nominate one of them to participate in naming the nominees for the Commission's membership. They should name the nominees within 15 days from receiving the nomination request. In case of the expiry of the deadline without naming one of the nominees, then, the King has the right to appoint whom he may view as suitable for the Commission's membership. The Commission's Secretary General will prepare a report in this respect.

b The King will ask one of the sons of King 'Abdul 'Aziz or sons of the sons to nominate three of the sons of the deceased or who is unable in line with a medical report to name one of them for the membership of the Commission. The King has the right to refer the nomination to one of the sons of the Founder to name one of the three nominees for the Commission's membership.

c In all cases, the King names one of the sons of the deceased, who is disinterested or who is unable for the membership of the Commission.

Second:

Whoever is disinterested from the sons of the Founder to be a member of the Allegiance Commission, he should notify the King in writing, and nominate one of his sons for membership of the Commission. If his notification does not include a nomination, or if the King does not approve of his choice, the appointment will be made according to the above-mentioned Section 1, of Article 1." These rules are valid for sons of sons and their successors.

Article 2

1 The age of the member of the Commission, who is appointed in line with paragraphs 2 and 3 of the first article of the system of the Allegiance Commission, should not be less than 22.
2 Nevertheless, he should be a man of a good reputation.

Article 3

Without violating what has been stipulated in the first article of the system of the Allegiance Commission, the period of the membership at the Commission is fixed at four years. This term, which cannot be renewed, starts from the date fixed in the Royal order about the appointment of the member. But, it will be possible to renew the term of the member if his brothers agree on that after the approval of the King.

Article 4

If a member fails to perform his duties and responsibilities, the matter will be investigated by a committee comprising of three Commission members, to be named by its chairman. The committee will submit the outcome of the investigation to the Commission. If the Commission, with the approval of two thirds of its members, decides to dismiss the member who fails to perform his duties and responsibilities, the matter will be submitted to the King to decide on what he views as the best course of action."

Article 5

If the place of one of the members of the Allegiance Commission becomes vacant, then, the King will replace him by another member in line with the First and Second articles of the statute.

Article 6

If the King passes away, the Allegiance Commission will pledge allegiance to the Heir Apparent in accordance with this Law and the Basic Law of Governance.

Article 7

After consultation with the members of the Allegiance Commission, the King will choose one, two or three candidates for the position of heir apparent. He will present his nominees to the Allegiance Commission, which will then designate one of them as Heir Apparent. In the event where the Commission rejects all of the nominees, it will designate an Heir Apparent whom it considers to be suitable.

Article 8

The meetings of the medical committee are confidential, and these meetings are to be attended by the Commission's Secretary General. Medical reports are to be prepared at the Commission's venue confidentially, and these are to be signed by all members of the committee.

Article 9

The medical reports prepared by the medical committee are to be delivered to the Chairman of the Allegiance Commission in a sealed envelope, and these reports should not be read except at the Commission's meeting.

Article 10

In case of the absence of the two members of the medical committee, stipulated in the paragraphs 1 and 2 of the 14th article of the system of the Allegiance Commission, or in case of the place of one of them becoming vacant, then, the acting person will replace him. But in case of absence of one of the deans of faculties of medicine mentioned in the paragraph 3, then the Commission should name who may replace him from the other deans of faculties of medicine.

Article 11

The Secretary General, under the supervision of the Commission, undertakes sorting of votes and announcing the results.

Article 12

The Secretary General is to be in contact with the King, and the Secretary General will be responsible for all financial and administrative affairs of the Commission.

Article 13

A documents' center is to be established at the Commission, and the center be associated with the Secretary General. The center will preserve the Commission's minutes (of the meetings) and all of its documents and reports pertaining to the Commission's activities. And these documents should remain confidential.

Article 14

The Commission will have an annual budget, and expenditures should be in line with the rules and instructions, approved by the King.

Article 15

The Commission's Secretary General is to be appointed at the rank of a minister, while his deputy is to be appointed at the excellent grade.

Article 16

The jobs at the Commission's General Secretariat are to be filled in line with the rules and procedures of the Royal Court.

Article 17

The employees of the Commission or those whom the Secretary General may seek their assistance should adhere to the confidentiality of all information and deliberations they may read during their works at the Commission. If they violate these regulations, then they will be liable for punishment in line with the systems and statutes.

Article 18

The rules of this statute can be amended in line with a Royal order after the approval of the Allegiance Commission.

Source: Information Office of the Royal Embassy of Sa'udi Arabia in Washington DC; at http://208.246.28.149/2007News/Statements/StateDetail.asp?cIndex=702.

Appendix 8: Partners in One Nation

29 April 2003
His Royal Highness Prince 'Abdallah bin 'Abdul 'Aziz Al Sa'ud
The Crown Prince, Deputy Prime Minister and Head
of the National Guards
Peace and the mercy of Allah upon you

Deriving from religious and national responsibilities, and from the duty of solidarity and advice, particularly at this crucial time, and because of our belief in the kingdom's dignity and that the protection of its unity is a shared responsibility between the leadership and the people, therefore, we present to Your Highness some of the nation's concerns and the hopes of its citizens. We fully trust your good understanding and eagerness to discover the sincere and true way of thinking, which intends to promote goodwill and reforms. We would like to take this opportunity to declare solidarity with our nation and its noble leadership in the face of threats and challenges.

We declare our appreciation of your generous gesture of meeting some of the intellectuals and informed elites from among the citizens of our country. We also consider that your welcome to their project, 'Focus for the Present and Future of the Nation,' which includes the views and seeks to promote the well-being of the citizens, is a good sign, which [fills our] hearts full of hope for a better future.

In this initial reading, we rely on deep and wide national awareness, which considers the treatment of the sectarian situation in our homeland as a significant sign in the path of reform and development. We look to solving this problem as a national and collective responsibility in which all the citizens of the country must participate.

First: The Enhancement of the Nation's (*Ummah*) Unity

At this stage, our Arab and Islamic nation faces the most dangerous challenges. There is a massive global hostile campaign intended to give a false image of Islam and Muslims. Additionally, the Zionist crimes were unleashed in the Palestinian Occupied Territories, at the time when the American and

British forces started their intensive attack against Iraq, with no consideration given to the Security Council and the United Nations and world opinion, and they are raising their threats to other Arab and Islamic countries.

The nation (*Ummah*) is targeted in its being, interests and its holy aspects; the threat surrounds all of us, no matter how different are the sects and directions. This requires that we stand collectively, shoulder to shoulder, before these severe challenges.

However, religious and sectarian conflict remains a tool to destroy the nation's unity. It will hinder national solidarity and cooperation. Additionally, it will keep major segments of the people involved in this conflict and divert their attention from the real issues.

The Kingdom of Sa'udi Arabia, with its distinguished role of leadership in the Arab and Islamic world, resulting from having and serving the two holy mosques and enjoying a leadership that is concerned about Islamic solidarity, is expected to play a major role in eliminating sectarian conflicts and in bridging the differences between religious sects.

Failure to achieve this task and allowing such unpleasant and fanatical tendencies to flourish make our country liable to earn a bad reputation and to look like a partner in this conflict.

Therefore, a moment of thought is required to erase the confusion and to enhance the shining face of our country, as a centre for the whole Muslim world and as a force for Islamic solidarity. That will prevent the followers of different religious sects from making a hostile stand against the country.

Accordingly, the following actions will help in attaining this objective:

Issuing a clear declaration indicating the Kingdom's respect for all Islamic sects, including the Shi'ah.
Opening up to all the various Islamic sects access and representation in all Islamic institutions supervised by the Kingdom, including the Muslim World League (*Rabitat al-'Alam al-Islami*), the World Association for Muslim Youth (WAMY), Higher Council for Mosques, World Muslim Charity Association and other organizations that are concerned with general Islamic and human affairs.
Encouraging communications between the Sa'udi religious bodies and the Muslim religious leaders from other sects, in order to achieve convergence and acquaintance between Islamic sects. This can be guided by the Islamic Union Covenant issued by the Islamic Jurisprudence Council – Resolution No. 98 (1/11) dated 25 Rajab, 1419 AH, and by the Strategy of Approximation between the Islamic Sects founded by experts in the Islamic Organization for Education, Sciences and Culture (ISESCO).

Second: National Unity

The dramatic changes taking place in the region and the world today are intensifying the pressure from world superpowers, which talk in no uncertain terms about changing the political map in the region, disassociation of entities and disintegration of countries. To face this pressure, it is necessary to ensure national unity and solidarity, to enhance and activate it practically with what may ensure protection and solidarity on the internal front, prevent enemies' penetration and frustrate their efforts to stimulate any misguided separatist tendencies.

Your Royal Highness,

The Shi'ah citizens in the Kingdom of Sa'udi Arabia are an original integrated part of the entity of this beloved nation. It is their final homeland; they have no alternative and they have no loyalty except to it. They have taken the initiative to join it without any hesitation or objection, since King 'Abdul 'Aziz, may Allah rest him in peace, founded this country and they put all their abilities and fortunes toward the building of the nation. They are looking forward to justice, security, equality and stability.

In these difficult circumstances, they give assurance of their loyalty to their nation. Out of their adherence to national unity and their concern for the development and future of their homeland arises their belief that these issues require quick treatment, and such issues have been repeatedly and frequently submitted to Your Highness and all the honorable officials.

1 The Shi'ah citizens look forward to being equal with the rest of the citizens and to having the opportunity to serve their homeland in all fields. Some levels and a number of governmental agencies and departments exclude Shi'ah citizens, such as the military, security and diplomatic arenas. Women are excluded from any administrative positions, even the Girls' Section of the Ministry of Education. This is a kind of sectarian discrimination that is admitted neither by Islamic *Shari'ah* (Islamic Laws) nor by international convention. It deprives the Shi'ah citizens of a natural right as well as depriving the homeland of the opportunity to benefit from their abilities and capabilities.

Educational programs provided by the government have developed the abilities and capabilities of their sons as all citizens. What leads to frustration and pain is that Shi'ah capabilities are not recognized equally and they have fewer opportunities than other nationals, who are advancing in different locations and positions in the government agencies. Shi'ahs are disregarded and marginalized because of sectarian policies.

To deal with this issue, we propose the following:

A The efforts of the officials to clearly ensure equality between all citizens regardless of their sects or areas.
B The urgent formation of an authorized national committee, including qualified Shi'ahs, to study the problem of sectarian discrimination and treat it by allowing Shi'ah representation in higher government positions,

such as the Council of Ministers, ministerial deputies, diplomatic posts, military and security fields, and by elevating their participation in the Consultative Council (*Majlis al-Shurah*).

C Incrimination and condemnation of the practice of sectarian discrimination that may be committed by the prejudiced and the privileged anywhere in the country, and making all necessary laws relevant to this measure, in addition to the cancellation of all previous circulars and discriminatory administrative procedures.

D Stopping all unlawful security procedures such as arrest, pursuance, interrogation, deprivation of travel, detention at the borders and intrusive personal frisking, and endeavoring to relieve the effects of previous arrests.

2 Our country is suffering from the existence of sectarian fanatical tendencies stimulating hatred and aversion against other Islamic sects and followers, particularly Shi'ahs. The religious educational curricula at schools and universities repeatedly describe the other Islamic sects and their opinions – Shi'ahs and others – as disbelievers, polytheists, deviants and heretics.

Religious programming and the official media are exclusive to one sect, propagating a culture of non-acceptance of the other Islamic sects and insulting their followers. This policy is applied in most of the religious bodies in the country such as the legal courts and in the institution of public morality and centers of mission and guidance.

Many instigative fatwahs (legal opinions) have been issued by some of these bodies against Shi'ah citizens. In addition, a large number of books of similar tendency have been – and still are being – printed and distributed, as well as numerous sermons and lectures.

This continuous instigation has educated generations in fanaticism and spite, and created an atmosphere of hatred and animosity between the citizens of the one nation, which creates anxiety for the future of national unity, social peace and security. External powers may benefit from feeding this atmosphere and utilize it against our country's interests. What happened in some other Muslim countries, which suffered civil wars and severe sectarian conflicts, must not happen here.

To confront this serious situation, we hope that the government will adopt the following measures:

A Put an end to these fanatical tendencies and practices, starting with the educational curricula, the media and official religious bodies.

B Adopt a cultural national policy announcing toleration, recognition and acknowledgment of the sectarian variety in the county, ensuring respect for human rights and the citizen's dignity and his religious and intellectual freedom.

C Confirm deterrent procedures to incriminate and condemn any form of instigation to hatred between citizens or to insult different Islamic sects.

D The leaders to make an official announcement assuring Shi'ah rights in the kingdom and equality with other citizens.

3   When the government recognizes the citizenship of its people, regardless of their different sects and areas, and bears the responsibility of taking care of them and protecting their interests, this means that they practice under state laws their right to worship according to their own teachings and to perform their religious rituals. Shi'ah citizens in the kingdom are still suffering from restrictions in performing their religious rites, they find difficulty in building mosques and *hussayniyyahs* (community halls) and they have no cultural freedom, as they are not allowed to print their books or bring them from outside or found any religious centre.

The powers and authorities of the judges of the two courts of endowments and inheritance in Qatif and al-Ahsah are greatly diminished by the interference of the *Shari'ah* Great Courts (the official government Sunni courts).

In some areas such as Madinah, Shi'ah citizens are suffering severe restrictions, which are not acceptable or justified.

These pressures and constraints contribute enormously to the infuriation and irritation Shi'ah citizens feel and to decreasing their human, religious and citizenship rights. This also gives the opportunity to our enemies to defame the image and reputation of our country.

For the treatment of these problems, we propose the following:

A Establishing an official body subordinated to the Ministry of Endowments and Islamic Affairs, similar to the Court of Religious Endowments and Inheritances subordinated to the Ministry of Justice, under the supervision of Shi'ah scholars, to organize their religious and cultural affairs under the care of the government.
B Cancellation of all restrictions on religious rites, and giving the freedom to print or publish Shi'ah books and printed matter, and admitting their freedom of opinion.
C Allowing Shi'ah citizens to exercise their right to religious education and to establish their institutions and colleges for religious education according to their sect.
D Application of the royal decrees calling for the Shi'ahs freedom to refer to their *Shari'ah* courts and to give these courts suitable legal executive power.

May God protect you and keep our country away from any adversity and perpetuate God, Grace of Security and Belief, under the shade of the Custodian of the Two Holy Mosques' care and Your Excellency Crown Prince and venerable Government.

Peace be upon you.

Copy with special regards to His Excellency Prince Sultan bin 'Abdul 'Aziz Al Sa'ud, Second Deputy of the Council of Ministers, the Minister of Defense and Aviation and General Inspector.

Copy with special regards to His Excellency Prince Talal bin 'Abdul 'Aziz Al Sa'ud, President of AGFUND.

Copy with special regards to His Excellency Prince Nawwaf bin 'Abdul 'Aziz Al Sa'ud, President of General Intelligence.

Copy with special regards to His Excellency Prince Nayif bin 'Abdul 'Aziz Al Sa'ud, Minister of the Interior.

Copy with special regards to His Excellency Prince Salman bin 'Abdul 'Aziz Al Sa'ud, Governor of Riyadh.

Copy with special regards to His Excellency Prince Ahmad bin 'Abdul 'Aziz Al Sa'ud, Deputy Minister of the Interior.

Copy with special regards to His Excellency Prince Muqrin bin 'Abdul 'Aziz Al Sa'ud, Governor of Madinah.

Copy with special regards to His Excellency Prince Sa'ud al-Faysal bin 'Abdul 'Aziz Al Sa'ud, Minister of Foreign Affairs.

Copy with special regards to His Excellency Prince Mohammad bin Fahd bin 'Abdul 'Aziz Al Sa'ud, Governor of the Eastern Province.

Copy with special regards to His Excellency Prince 'Abdul 'Aziz bin Fahd Al Sa'ud, State Minister, Member of the Council of Ministers and Head of Council of Ministers' Office.

Source: This petition was submitted to Heir Apparent 'Abdallah (the present king) on April 29, 2003 and was signed by 450 Shi'ahs, among whom were 151 businessmen, 42 academics, 50 religious scholars, 24 women and 31 journalists and writers. Adapted from Fouad Ibrahim, *The Shi'is of Saudi Arabia*, London and San Francisco: Saqi, 2006, pp. 257–62.

Appendix 9: "Secular" Petition to King Fahd December 1990

In the Name of God, the Merciful, the Compassionate.
The Guardian of the Two Holy Mosques, King Fahd
bin 'Abdul 'Aziz, may God support him.

Preamble

One of the favors bestowed by God upon you is that you held, during the past forty years, the most momentous and delicate responsibilities. That provided you an unadulterated acquaintance with the workings of the State as well as a fine knowledge of the various exigencies of state reforms. Your open-doors policy and your open-heartiness with regard to all people's appeals, your care and concern for the requests submitted to you, created truthfulness and encouraged your subjects to speak freely.

A number of your loyal subjects have prepared the enclosed memorandum about the ways of affecting certain reforms as they see them. They are concerned with the safety of the entity we are proud of. They address you out of their desire to enhance its safety and stability, progress and prosperity, out of their obligation to their rulers, and out of their obedience to God with regard to the religious duty of offering advice to God, His Messenger, the leaders of the community as well as all Muslims.

They put this memorandum before you, the Guardian of the Two Holy Mosques, in expression of their deep conviction that you are best qualified to turn their hopes to reality and sanction their loyalty.

May God preserve and support you in your search for the right path.

Proposed Landmarks of the Way of Reforms and Development

The critical conditions and painful events unfolding in this region for the Muslim Nation – with our country in the foreground – that emerged in the wake of the invasion of Kuwait and the scattering of its people, are in fact ominous forerunners which make the citizens duty-bound to give their advice to rulers. Citizens are obliged to share with their rulers, in words and deeds, what they deem to be advantageous to the country that belongs to all of them. All are responsible to build it and share in its benefits as well as losses.

The Holy Qur'an stresses this great religious duty in the following words: "And from amongst you there should be a party who invite to good and enjoin what is right and forbid the wrong, and these it is that shall be successful. And be not like those who became divided and disagreed after clear arguments had come to them, and these it is that shall have a grievous chastisement." This passage makes it quite clear that refraining from calling to good and keeping away from enjoining good and forbidding evil, inevitably leads to the emergence of rifts between people and spread confusion in their affairs, as well as scatter them in opposing fronts.

The Prophetic Holy *Sunnah* had explained the grades of this duty and identified the parties to whom Muslims should offer advice to. The Messenger of God (peace and the blessings of God be upon him) is reported to have said: "Faith is advice." Muslims who were present asked him: "To whom should we offer our advice." "To God (that means to be obedient to Him), to His Messenger, and to the leaders of the Community and to all Muslims," he replied.

Advice is then the soul of faith. It is obligatory on the Muslim to give his advice first to God and His Messenger, expressed in obeying them and abiding by their orders. Secondly, to the leaders of the Community, to emphasize his loyalty out of his duty to help them and bless their efforts. Thirdly, to the faithful out of his concern for their interests, care for their affairs and truthful desire in exhausting all means of serving them.

Thus, according to the holy traditions, there are three pillars on which the Muslim Nation is built:

1 The *Shari'ah* that governs people, regulates society's movement and is, in itself, the decisive word that settles all affairs.
2 The rulers who shoulder the responsibility of implementing the *Shari'ah*, do their utmost to secure the interests of the people, and serve the *Ummah*.
3 The believers who represent the whole Muslim Nation, the faithful party who are addressed by divine words.

Throughout Islamic history, Muslim communities progressed as long as these three pillars were in harmony. The power of the *Shari'ah* was extended and implemented as rulers did their duties and complied with God's orders. The whole *Ummah* were completely aware of their responsibilities and were forthcoming. But when these three pillars were shaken, the lives of all Muslims were thrown into chaos.

If the Holy *Shari'ah* had made it compulsory on rulers to advise their people, it had made it similarly obligatory on wise and fair-minded believers to advise their leaders as well. We are from this section of the faithful. If offering advice is an ordained duty observed at any time, it becomes more necessary during critical times of hardships and desperation, like those we are going through today. The momentous and horrid events we are witnessing, that make us stop at crossroads, are banging the doors of the region and the world violently and relentlessly. Out of our obedience by the *Shari'ah*, our love for the rulers and fidelity to this country and its citizens, we felt it was our duty to put before you this concise summary of opinions, views and frameworks, with the aim of solidifying the bases of this country, which lead it towards further achievements and keep it abreast of events. We have two prime goals in mind:

1 A full implementation of the blessed *Shari'ah*, as it has been the Kingdom's policy right down from its formation, for the purpose of fulfilling the sublime objectives of the *Shari'ah*, including establishing justice, achieving equality, carrying out reforms and restoring people's rights. That would make our society a noble image of the modern Islamic state and an example followed by others in implementing Islam.
2 Retaining the present rule and keeping the noble Royal family, the symbol of loyalty, the axis of unity and the just rule that serves the country and *Ummah*. It is the rule that keeps the interests of the country and *Ummah* above differences as well as criticisms, and prevents them from being a means of abandoning laws or ignoring them.

Accordingly, we propose the following:

First: Setting up an organized framework for the religious fatwah [decree], taking into consideration the Holy *Shari'ah* – that is never erroneous or immune from being changed – expressed in the texts from the Book as well as the *Sunnah*. Apart from these texts, we believe that all the *fiqh* [jurisprudence] presented by the *Fuqahah* [Islamic legal scholars], the religious schools of thought, the commentaries of Qur'anic exegetes and the fatwahs of the jurisprudent, are only human attempts at grasping the full meaning of the religious texts, likely to be affected by the grade of human power of understanding and the concerned people's knowledge. *Usul al-Fiqh* is also influenced by the times and surroundings. In other words, such interpretations are likely to be either flawless, or erroneous, and subject to lengthy discussions. That is why scholars unanimously agree that no one, no matter how high his status is, can monopolize the explanation of the true meaning of the words of God and His Messenger, nor can he impose his religious views as binding on the whole *Ummah*.

In our life, it is decisively necessary to draw a distinction between Divine Law, that is infallible and binding, and the views put forth by the *'Ulamah* that must be seriously examined beforehand. They are subject to boundless discussions. We must adopt the opinions of the *'Ulamah* and that of the prominent religious men, be they in the past or present, that may make our country the true image of the modern Islamic state and a good example adopted by other Muslims.

Second: Viewing the conditions of the main system of rule, and in light of the statements and addresses given by officials on various occasions, we call for:

Third: The immediate setting up of a consultative assembly comprising a group of competent, learned and fair-minded people, known to be honest and impartial, well-bred and hard-working, who perform in the interests of the country, and hail from different parts of the kingdom. One of the assembly's duties is to study, develop and approve the laws and regulations related to all economic, political, educational and other matters, as well as keep watch on the workings and duties of the executive.

Fourth: Reviving the municipal councils, implementing the system of provinces and opening trade chambers in the provinces.

Fifth: Examining the judiciary at all levels and powers, to modernize its working methods, re-examining the system of forming judges and their assistants, and taking all measures to secure their independence. These are necessary so that justice may be served in an effective way, and the judiciary power be solidified. Judicial institutions should open their doors to all citizens, without bias toward a certain section of the population, on the basis of granting equal chances to all. That is what the *Shari'ah* calls for.

Sixth: Establishing total equality between all citizens, in all domains, without discrimination against any group due to race, lineage, sect or social status, and implementing the principle of non-interference in any citizen's affairs without lawful and religious justification.

Seventh: Re-examining the media on the basis of a comprehensive and precise criterion that reflects the most modern technology and planning available in the world. The Sa'udi media is free to exercise its freedom in enjoining good and forbidding evil and enriching free discussions in an open society.

Eighth: Affecting a comprehensive reform of the *Bodies of Enjoining Good and Forbidding Evil* and laying down an exact system for their assignments, a religious framework for their duties, and stern standard with respect to the process of choosing their members and directors in a way that stresses the method of calling to Islam with wisdom and goodly exhortation, as well as achieving the outlined goals set for this important and sensitive apparatus.

Ninth: Notwithstanding our belief that caring for the new generations is the most sacred duty of the Muslim woman, we believe that there are various scopes for her participation in social activities. These spheres can be opened to the noble women within the limits of the *Shari'ah*, as a token acknowledging their role in building society and as a way of honoring them.

Tenth: All divine books and God's messengers had come to teach and nurture human beings. This fact emphasizes the great importance of teaching as an indispensable ground for the revival of the people and the progress of nations. We hold the opinion that teaching in our country is in need of deep and all-out reforms to prepare faithful, committed generations that can positively and effectively take part in building the present and future of the country, face contemporary challenges, and foster the *Ummah* to catch up with other nations that are quite ahead of us in every sphere.

These are broad lines that need detailed examination. You undoubtedly look at these demands as being pressing, exactly as we do, and take them into consideration, as we do. We made a covenant with God that we only tell you the truth and open our hearts to you as God had ordered us, and as a sign of our love and loyalty to you. We believe that the Arab and Islamic World and the whole World are entering a new era in which much of the old concepts have given way to new ones, where conditions changed and the equations of forces altered. This fact makes it necessary for us to review some of our affairs without bias, re-study the whole of our conditions actively and honestly, so that we are able to weather what events the future will bring and what troubles it may cause us.

It is worth mentioning that the signatories are the elite of your subjects, your brothers, and sons. You know very well that they are neither ill-meaning or spiteful, nor are they in pursuit of private interests or whims. Their sole motivation is, Insh'Allah, to seek the good and right and their goal is to secure the highest interests of the country. Their first and foremost objective is the preservation of this great entity, the continuation of its stability, security and safety.

Certainly God alone can grant us success.

Signatories:

1. Ahmad Salah Jamjun
2. Muhammad 'Abduh Yamani
3. 'Abdul Maqsud Khujah
4. Muhammad Salahuddin
5. Dr. Rashid al-Mubarak
6. Ahmad Muhammad Jamal
7. Salih Muhammad Jamal
8. 'Abdallah al-Dabbagh
9. Muhammad Hassan Faqi
10. Dr. 'Abdallah Manna'
11. Muhammad Sa'id Tayyib
12. Muhammad 'Ali Sa'id al-'Audi
13. 'Abdallah bin 'Abdul Rahman al-Ibrahim
14. Dr. 'Abdul Rahman al-Mari'i
15. Yusuf Muhammad al-Mubarak
16. Dr. Marzuq bin Manitan
17. Dr. Ibrahim bin 'Abdul Rahman al-Mudaybigh
18. 'Adil Jamal
19. Fahd 'Ali al-'Urayfi
20. Salih 'Abdul Rahman al-'Ali
21. 'Abdallah Hamad al-Sabkhan
22. Salih 'Abdallah al-Ashqar
23. 'Aql Rajih al-Bahili
24. Dr. Ahmad Mahdi al-Shuwaykhat
25. 'Ali Jawad al-Khurs

26 'Isa Fahd
27 Dr. Sa'ad al-'Abdallah al-Suyan
28 Dr. 'Abdul Khaliq 'Abdallah Al 'Abdul-Ha
29 'Abdul Karim Hamad al-'Awdah
30 'Abdallah Yusuf al-Kuwaylit
31 Hamad Ibrahim al-Bahili
32 'Abdul Jabbar 'Abdul Karim al-Yahyah
33 Ibrahim al-Hamdan
34 'Ishaq al-Shaykh Ya'qub
35 Muhammad 'Ubayd al-Harbi
36 Shakir 'Abdallah al-Shaykh
37 'Abdul Ra'uf al-Ghazal
38 'Ali al-Dumayni
39 Muhammad al-'Ali
40 'Abdul Rahman 'Abdul 'Aziz al-Husayn
41 Ibrahim Fahid al-'Aql
42 Jam'an 'Abdallah al-Waqidi
43 'Abdallah Bukhayt al-'Abdul 'Aziz

Source: "A Memorandum to the King," translated from the original Arabic. According to *Middle East Watch*, this so-called "secular" petition, believed to have been first written in October 1990 and presented to the monarch in December of that same year, was written by Dr. 'Abdallah Manna', a physician and writer known for voicing critical views of the government.

Appendix 10: "Religious" Petition to King Fahd February 1991

In the Name of God, the Merciful, the Compassionate.
To the Custodian of the Two Holy Mosques: May God help you. May the peace and blessings of God be upon you.

This state has distinguished itself by announcing its adherence to Islamic *Shari'ah*, and the *'Ulamah* and those capable of offering guidance have always fulfilled their divine obligation in offering sound advice to those in power. We therefore find that the most pressing task, at this critical juncture and at a time when all have realized the necessity of change, is to direct our energies to reforming the situation, which put us in our present predicament. For this reason, we request the ruler to look into the matters, which need to be addressed by reform in the following areas:

1 The establishment of a consultative council to decide on internal and external affairs. The members of this body should be selected so as to include individuals of diverse specialization, and who must be known for their sincerity and upright conduct. The council must be fully independent and free from any pressures that could affect the discharging of its full responsibilities.
2 Examining all political, economic and administrative laws and regulations to ascertain their conformity to *Shari'ah*. This task should be conducted by fully-mandated, competent and trustworthy *Shari'ah* committees. All laws not conforming to the *Shari'ah* should then be abrogated.
3 Ensuring that all state officials and their representatives internally and abroad must be competent and suitably specialized. They must also be dedicated, upright and honest. Failure to fulfill any of these requirements must be deemed as betrayal of trust and a major threat to the country's interest and its reputation.
4 Granting justice and equality for all members of society to safeguard full rights and exacting duties without any favoritism to the privileged or condescension towards the disadvantaged. It should also be realized that taking advantage of one's influence to shirk one's duties or usurp the rights of others could cause the disintegration of society and lead

to the dire fate against which the Prophet (peace be upon him) had warned.
5 Establishing justice in distributing the public wealth among all classes and factions of society. Taxes must be abolished and government fees must be decreased as they have overburdened people. The financial assets of the state must be safeguarded against waste and exploitation, and priority must be given to the dire needs of the country. All forms of monopoly and illegitimate types of ownership must be removed. The ban on Islamic banks must be lifted, and all public and private financial institutions must be cleaned of usury (interest), which is an assault against God and His Messenger and a reason for the vanishing of God's bounties and blessings.
6 Building strong and integrated armed forces fully equipped from diverse sources. Special attention should be paid to the development of military industries. The aim of the army should be to protect the country and its sacred values.
7 Reconstructing the media to bring them in line with the Kingdom's policy of serving Islam. The media should reflect the values of society and enhance and advance its culture, and they must be purified from all that contradicts the above goals. Freedom of the media to educate and inform, through the propagation of true stories and constructive criticism, must be safeguarded in accordance with legitimate safeguards.
8 Directing foreign policy to safeguard the interests of the nation, away from illegitimate alliances. The state must champion Muslim causes, while the status of our embassies abroad must be rectified to reflect the Islamic character of this country.
9 The development of religious and missionary institutions in this country, and providing them with all the necessary human and material resources. All obstacles preventing them from fulfilling their tasks properly must be removed.
10 Unifying judicial organs, according them full and real independence, and ensuring that the authority of the judiciary extends to all. An independent body must be set up to follow the implementation of all judicial decisions.
11 Safeguarding the individual and collective rights, and lifting all traces of pressures against the will and rights of people in a way that preserves human dignity and that accord with the acceptable legal rules and regulations.

Signatories [partial list]:

Shaykh 'Abdul 'Aziz bin Baz
Shaykh Muhammad bin Salih al-'Uthaymin
Shaykh Hamudah bin 'Abdallah al-Tuwayjiri
Shaykh 'Abdallah bin Jibrin
Shaykh 'Abdul Muhsin al-'Ubaykan

Shaykh Safar al-Hawali
Shaykh Sa'id al-Qahtani
Shaykh Salman al-'Awdah
Shaykh 'Abdallah al-Jalali
Shaykh Muhammad al-Shihah
Dr. Ahmad al-Tuwayjiri
Dr. Tawfiq al-Qasir
Shaykh Sa'id bin Zuayr

Note and Sources: Known as the "Shawwal Document," or more commonly, the "Letter of Demands" (sometimes also referred to as the "Letter of the *'Ulamah*"), this petition was probably written in February 1991, although various sources give an April 1991 date as well. This so-called "religious" petition may well have been a response to the December 1990 "secular" petition or, as claimed by opposition groups, was in the making long before the latter surfaced. See Sa'ad al-Faqih, *The Rise and Evolution of the Modern Islamic Reform Movement in Saudi Arabia*, London: The Movement for Islamic Reform in Arabia (MIRA), 1996 [on-line at http://www.miraserve.com/HistoryOfDissent.htm]. MIRA maintains that an estimated 400 individuals signed this petition, although it does not reproduce any names. The facsimile copy I have reproduces 52 signatures although most are illegible [the 13 signatures above are the names that are relatively legible]. Shaykh 'Abdul 'Aziz bin Baz added this phrase: "On the basis of Islamic Law," before giving his support to the demands. Shaykh Muhammad bin Salih Al-'Uthaymin also gave his support to this memorandum. Together, the support of these two senior religious scholars must have caught King Fahd and other Al Sa'ud officials by surprise. Signatories included religious scholars, judges, university professors, and members of the intelligentsia. Translated from the original Arabic, in author's hands, and adapted to the MIRA text (reproduced as an appendix on the home page edition). Reproduced from Joseph A. Kéchichian, *Succession in Saudi Arabia*, New York: Palgrave, 2001, pp. 199–201.

Appendix 11: A Vision for the Present and Future of the Nation

In the Name of Allah, the Most Merciful, the Most Beneficent

His Royal Highness Prince 'Abdallah bin 'Abdul 'Aziz, Heir Apparent, Deputy Prime Minister and Commander of the National Guards, May God's peace and blessing be upon you:

We convey to you the admiration of intellectuals in this kind country, from your brothers and sons from different visions and regions, and their appreciation for your call for public participation.

They send you their utmost regards for this initiative, and they consider it as a step in the right direction the country was waiting for, and they see that it is the greatest evidence for the deep relationship between the society and their leadership. They address their standing with the leadership in facing all the dangers and conspiracies against our country.

Since September 2002, your brothers and sons started to form a strategic view for the present and the future of our country. They hope it will help you, along with other efforts, in reaching the desired goals, the unity, stability and strength for this country.

They have tried to deliver this document directly to your Highness' hand in different ways but they failed, so mail was the only way left to deliver it, wishing it will help you in reaching the noble goals. Please accept our best regards.

View for the Present and Future of Our Homeland.

His Royal Highness Prince 'Abdallah bin 'Abdul 'Aziz, Heir Apparent, Deputy Prime Minister and Commander of the National Guards:

Citizens were pleased with the transparent way you took in dealing with our country's problems and solving them, through your open meetings with different sections of the society and the intellectuals, and your public declaration of your wish to hear the people's voice. It is a commendable course that generated support among a score of your citizen brothers and sons, who are worried about the dangers facing their country since 11 September 2001. For instance, international and regional conditions, which preoccupy our country, threatened us with military action, intervention in our internal affairs and redrawing the whole regional map.

While the signatories of this document have different views, they nevertheless believe in the unity of their country, "The Kingdom of Sa'udi Arabia," and its leadership, and they announce their standing with their leaders in facing all dangers that threaten our country's present and future. And they see that facing those dangers require serious reforms to strengthen relations between the leadership and the community.

Standing from the Prophet's ["May God's prayers be upon him"] saying (The religion is to advise … for the Muslim leaders and the community), signers of this document are vying to participate in a comprehensive national dialogue. They hope their document will help both the government and public to focus their efforts towards solving problems.

The First Concern: Constitutional Reforms

More Steps in Building a Country of Constitutional Institutions

The legality of government in the Qur'an and the *Sunnah*, which are the base of the nation's constitution, comes from two sources. First, to do what Islam has ordered in matter of rituals and conduct with people. Second, leaders represent the community to ensure their rights and do their duties, to satisfy citizens with the way their leaders rule them.

Since justice is the base of ruling, God ordered social justice and considered it one of the foundations of the faith. And since justice cannot be achieved without obligatory *Shurah*, God obliged his Prophet Muhammad to rely on *Shurah* in political matters. He said in His holy book "and consult them in affairs."

At the same time, *Shurah* cannot materialize unless serious steps are made toward institutional and constitutional systems. And this reasserts the importance of developing the basic law system to strengthen constitutional concepts, which rely on the Qur'an and the *Sunnah*, depend on the separation of the executive, judiciary and legislative authorities, and ensure basic rights in justice, equality, and uniform opportunities.

Moreover, applying the parliamentary *Shurah*, which reflects the public's participation, invokes the social contract between leaders and members of the community. It also builds the national unity on a relationship of acceptance, choice and cooperation, which will be the base of stability and progress.

Elected Parliament (elected Shurah council)

The signatories form their strategic view in this primary concerns as follows:

1. The formation of the *Shurah* council through direct elections by all eligible citizens, to reflect the power of the legislators, to whom the affairs of state are referred after God's book and His Prophet's way. These officials represent the agreement and trust of the nation in their decisions, which

enables the council to carry on its legislative and monitoring duties toward other branches of the government.
2. Forming regional legislators through direct elections, to manage regional affairs, and ensure the citizen's supervision over executive authority.
3. Insisting on the concept of an independent judiciary, which is theoretically set, but that cannot materialize unless all safeguards are made to apply the concept. The judiciary ought to expand its authority to exercise its influence on matters that are currently under the control of several ministries, including the prerogatives to investigate prisoner conditions. The General Persecuting Authority ought to be placed under the High Council of Justice or under its supervision. Moreover, all interferences that limit the independence and effectiveness of the judiciary, or reduce a judge's immunity, ought to be removed. Establishing a mechanism to enforce judicial rulings by the executive branch in a manner to ensure the judiciary's respect and status must be accepted. Recording judicial rulings and unifying them to develop a written national judicial code to ensure consistency in judicial sentences must also be initiated. Expanding the authority of the high court and develop training institutions for judges, to give them the ability to reach better solutions to growing and complicated problems, ought to be introduced.
4. Royal announcements that ensure citizens' rights, especially in the area of freedom of expression, assembly, election's rights and all human rights. Islam approved most of these long before they became codified by international resolutions, which were ratified by many countries, including our own.
5. Announcing the right to establish civil institutions such as clubs, committees, and educational, economical, social and labor unions to play their roles in encouraging experts and opinion leaders to guide public participation in making decisions. Allow civil society and human rights activists to function, because these activities will spread the culture of dialogue and peaceful debates instead of the culture of elimination and exclusion, in addition to violent struggles that threaten our future.

The Second Concern: A Way to Solve Economic Problems

Signatories' perspectives on how best to address the country's economic challenges are as follows:

1. Insist on the concept of fairness in economic plans and the distribution of wealth between different regions.
2. Place required restrictions to control public spending after setting spending priorities. Simultaneously, fight corruption and prevent the spread of bribery, as well as arbitrary expropriations of public land.
3. Strengthen and empower oversight and accountability institutions, such as the Public Supervision Directorate, and connect it with the *Shurah* Council.

4 Consider the national debt a national concern and a major responsibility that requires an effective solution to pay it off following a strict timetable. Also, allocate part of the country's income to a next-generations fund, to prevent an onslaught as alternative sources of energy are developed.
5 Decrease the single source of income nature of the economy, by developing other sources of income, and encourage national and international investments. Develop legal provisions to control future activities and protect economic rights.

The Third Concern: Encouraging Interaction between Society and the Leadership

To strengthen our internal front in the face of external threats and to ensure our national unity, we propose the following:

1 Insist on the role of the government and of society to spread the culture of human rights, which our religion has ordered, including tolerance, fairness, justice, respecting the right of different views. Encourage national unity and remove all elements of discrimination, be it sectarian, ethnic, regional or social.
2 Reform the public services system to satisfy the minimum needs of each citizen, in employment, housing, education, healthcare and fair trials.
3 Form programs to solve increasing unemployment problems. Set a minimum wage for workers and retirement pensions to allow them a decent life and establish assistance programs for the unemployed.
4 Women represent half of society and are a primary element in its structure. Consequently, women should be given all the rights that Islam has approved, to do her duties and activate her role in public affairs, according to the rules of Islam.

The Fourth Concern: Reform Initiatives

For the government to ensure its intentions to introduce serious reforms and avoid future threats, the signatories propose that the government take key steps that send positive indications, strengthen patriotism, infuse public trust, and indicate the will to address internal problems, by adopting the following steps:

1 Announce a general amnesty for political prisoners or give them a fair and open trial.
2 Restore the civil rights of reformers who are concerned with the country's situation such as university professors and judges, and reinstate them to their jobs from which some were expelled.
3 Provide the legal freedoms for all social elements, specially scholars and intellectuals, to discuss public affairs in various fora. Lift all restrictions on freedom of expression in matters of public affairs, including travel bans,

threats with prison sentences, expulsion from work, and eliminate imposed signatures on statements that call on them to stop writing or express an opinion.

The Fifth Concern: Invitation to a National Dialogue Convention

Signatories perceive that the best achievement for these initiatives is for the government to call for a national dialogue convention, to discus the main concerns raised here, which would be attended by representatives from all regions, cultural and social parties. In addition to a group of intellectuals interested in public affairs to discus challenges and the problems identified here, we call on the government to lay the foundations of a constitutional framework that focuses on a nation built on institutions.

Finally, while we repeat our solidarity with the leadership in facing impending dangers surrounding our country, we trust it realizes that addressing challenges cannot be achieved without serious reforms, which reflect the public's participation.

God is behind the effort. He is the Guide to the right path. May God's peace and blessing be upon you.

103 SIGNATORIES

Source: Adapted from the "Saudi National Reform Document" available at the Al-Bab web-page, http://www.al-bab.com/arab/docs/saudi/reform2003.htm.

Appendix 12: In Defense of the Nation

Riyadh, on 27 Rajab 1424 (September 24, 2003)
In the name of Allah most Gracious Most Merciful

Our country is witnessing increasing violent acts that use weapons and bloodshed as a means to prove its existence and impose its points of view instead of words and dialogue, which will generate a lot of damage on national security and social stability and civil peace. And in such hard circumstances, in which our country faces the hardest internal and external challenges, expressing refusal and condemnation to all kinds of extremism and violence becomes a national, political, moral, and cultural necessity.

And based upon our faith that we are partners – both people and government – in preserving the stability, security, and unity of our country, we are all invited to take our responsibility and review our steps and admit that being late in adopting radical reforms and ignoring popular participation in decision-making have been the main reasons that helped the fact that our country reached this dangerous turn, and this is why we believe that denying the natural rights of the political, cultural, and intellectual society to express its opinions has led to the dominance of a certain way of thinking that is unable to dialogue with others because of its inherent structure, and which does not reflect the greatness of Islam nor does it reflect its enlightened trends, which is what helped create the terrorist and judgmental mind that our country is still plagued with.

Confronting terrorism cannot only be done through security means and solutions, but with a thorough diagnosis of the political, social, economical, and cultural factors that have led to it, and by starting to implement the political and economic reforms, developed through many suggestions, opinions, and demands that were expressed in the writings and speeches of those interested in the public affairs of our country, one of them being a report of a vision "to the present and future of our country," which was submitted to his Royal Highness (May God Preserve him) last January, and which included a demand to empower the constitutional governmental institutions, and make room to achieve popular participation in decision-making and electing the *Shurah* Council, and enable this council to enact all its legislative and observational missions, and implement the notion of separation of powers, and reinforce the independence of the judicial branch, and respect Human Rights, and permit the work of civil society institutions, and work on elaborating on a religious, informative, cultural, and educational speech that refuses unilateral and judgmental thinking and pretending to hold and monopolize the truth, but instead works on nurturing a pluralistic atmosphere and paves the way towards strengthening cultural values such as compassion and the acceptance of the different Other, whether it is on the national Islamic level or the humanistic one, and these ideas and demands express the expectations of the different groups within the Sa'udi people, and convey mostly a vision shared by the political leadership and different national figures.

We also see that eliminating all aspects of administrative corruption and mismanagement of public funds, as well as widening the productive bases, and applying the principle of fair redistribution of wealth among all social classes and regions, in addition to addressing the problems of poverty, education, healthcare, and housing, and enabling women of practicing their social and economic duties, and other recurrent problems, will not be addressed properly unless they come through implementing the general reform demands.

And as we proclaim our condemnation to all kinds of extremism and symbolic or material violence that seeks to kidnap society and destroy the foundations of government, we demand from those who participate and instigate these actions to reject all kinds of extremism and violence and terrorism, in words and actions, hoping that this will be taken into account by the officials in government, and that they be treated according to fair judicial laws and systems, we also emphasize on the other hand the need for the political leadership to announce an encompassing national initiative – that has been long awaited – and to found an independent national organization made up of all national figures that shows the cultural, regional, and religious plurality in our country, and this to achieve the execution of the mechanisms that will put forth the demands of a constitutional, economic, social and political reform, and move to a phase of executing and implementing the reform according to a publicized timetable.

May God preserve our country from any harm and May He direct its footsteps towards good.

Signatories to Letter to Heir Apparent 'Abdallah

1	Muhammad Sa'id Tayyeb	Legal consultant and writer
2	Dr. 'Abdul 'Aziz Al-Dakheel	Economic consultant and writer
3	Jamil Farsi	Businessman and writer
4	Dr. Turki Al Hamad	Writer and novelist
5	'Ali Al Damini	Businessman and writer
6	Najib Al Khuwaynzi	Writer
7	Dr. Khalid Al-Dakheel	Academic and writer
8	Dr. 'Abdul Muhsin Hilal	Academic and writer
9	Dr. Ahmad Al 'Uways	Academic
10	'Akl Al Bahili	Businessman
11	'Abid Khazindar	Writer and critic

12	Kinan Al Ghamdi	Journalist and writer
13	Ja'afar Al Shayib	Businessman
14	Dr. Yusif Makki	Writer and researcher
15	Dr. Sa'ad 'Abdallah Al Zahrani	Academic
16	Dr. Bakr Hassan	Academic
17	Dr. Muhammad Al Harfi	Academic and researcher
18	'Abdul Muhsin 'Ali Al Khuwaynzi	Writer
19	Dr. Nasser Al Juhani	Academic and writer
20	Dr. Hamad Al Kanhal	Academic
21	Dr. 'Abdul Khaliq 'Abdul Hayy	Academic
22	Dr. 'Abdallah Mannah	Physician and writer
23	Muhammad Al Fayidi	Writer
24	'Abduh Khal	Writer and novelist
25	Sultan Muhammad Al Suhayl	Businessman
26	'Abdul Rahman 'Abdul Latif Al 'Issa	Businessman
27	'Abdallah Mansur Al Saghir	Businessman
28	'Abdallah Ibrahim Al Habib	Businessman
29	Dr. Fawziyyah Abu Khalid	Academic and writer
30	Dr. Yusif Al 'Ajaji	Academic
31	Dr. 'Adnan Al Shakhss	Academic
32	Sa'ad Al Kanhal	Retired
33	Dr. Fawziyyah Al Bakr	Academic and writer
34	Dr. 'Abdul Rahman Al Habib	Researcher and writer
35	Dr. 'Abdallah Al Mu'akil	Academic and critic
36	Dr. 'Aali Al Kourshi	Academic and critic
37	Dr. Amirah Al Kashghari	Academic and writer
38	Dr. Fa'ikah Muhammad Badr	Academic
39	Dr. Fahd Al Dawsari	Academic
40	Dr. Hassan Al Na'ami	Academic and critic
41	Dr. Munirah Al Nahid	Academic
42	Dr. Su'ad Jabir	Academic
43	Hamad Al Bahili	Writer
44	'Abdallah Al Faran	Social Activist
45	Ahmad 'Abdallah Al 'Ajaji	Consultant
46	Khalid Salih Al Shatri	Writer and businessman
47	Dr. 'Abdallah Dahlan	Writer
48	'Abdallah Abu Al Samah	Writer
49	Dr. Fatimah Al Khariji	Educational supervision director
50	Dr. Jasir Al Harbash	Physician and writer
51	Dr. 'Ali Al Khoshayban	Academic and writer
52	Dr. Salih Al 'Ajaji	Academic
53	Muhammad Al Muhaysin	Writer
54	Dr. Muhammad Al Rassiss	Academic
55	Dr. 'Aishah Al Manah	Hospital Director
56	Dr. 'Abdul Rahman Al Suwaynih	Scientist and researcher

Appendix 12: In Defense of the Nation 265

57	Dr. Hamad Al 'Ajrush	Academic
58	Dr. Ma'amun Al Munif	Academic and writer
59	Dr. Shukri Hassan Al Sinan	Academic
60	Dr. 'Abdul Wahab Abu Khudayr	Academic
61	Dr. 'Abdallah Al Makushi	Academic
62	Dr. Ibrahim 'Abbass Nitto	Writer and researcher
63	Dr. Falih Al 'Ajami	Academic
64	Dr. 'Abdul Rahman Al Shamlan	Academic
65	Dr. Hazab Al Sa'adun	Academic
66	Dr. Amir Muhammad Al Alwan	Academic
67	Dr. 'Ali Al Sultan	Academic
68	Dr. Ibrahim Al Bayz	Academic
69	Dr. Muhammad Mahdi Al Khuwaynzi	Academic
70	Sayf Al Sayf	Academic
71	Dr. Hassan Al Bariki	Physician and writer
72	Muhammad Zayed Al 'Almai	Writer and poet
73	Dr. Taysir Al Khuwaynzi	Economist and researcher
74	'Abdul 'Aziz Al Sunayd	Writer
75	Muhammad Al Haraz	Critic
76	Zakir Al Hubayl	Researcher and writer
77	Dr. Ghaleb 'Abdul Muhsin Al Faraj	Physician
78	Ishak Ya'akub Al Shaykh	Writer
79	'Issam Hassan Bassrawi	Attorney
80	Rabih 'Issa Al Sa'adun	Attorney
81	Mansur Al Bakr	Engineer
82	'Abdul Rahman Al Hassan	Employee
83	Hashim Murtadah Al Hassan	Social Activist
84	'Abdallah Hassan 'Abdul Baki	Social activist
85	'Abdul Rahman Al Hamad	Composer and dramaturge
86	'Abdallah Ja'afar al Murshidi	Dramaturge
87	Salih Abu Hinah	Culture and Arts organization
88	Dr. Kamil 'Ali Al 'Awami	Physician
89	Dr. Muhammad Hassan Al Sinan	Physician
90	Dr. 'Adil Al 'Ali	Physician
91	Muhammad Bakir Al Nimr	Businessman
92	Dr. 'Adil Sa'id Al Naji	Physician
93	'Adnan Al 'Awami	Researcher and poet
94	Sa'ad Al Dawssari	Writer and narrator
95	Salih 'Abdul Rahman Al Salih	Poet and writer
96	Dr. Ghazi Mahdi Al Qatari	Physician
97	Muhammad al-Fal A. Al Sayyid 'Atif	Former editor-in-chief and poet
98	Ahmad Thabit 'Assiri	Attorney
99	Ahmad Buqari	Writer and Critic
100	Ghassan Al 'Ajaji	Businessman
101	'Abdallah bin Bakhit	Writer

102	'Abdul Karim Al 'Awdah	Writer and poet
103	Salih 'Abdallah Al Ashkar	Narrator and writer
104	'Ali Bafkih	Poet
105	Muhammad Al Damini	Poet and writer
106	Hassan Al Mustafa	Writer
107	'Abdallah Yussif Al Kuwaylit	Journalist
108	Sadiq Al Jubran	Legal consultant
109	Muhammad Al Rutyan	Poet and writer
110	'Abdul Rahman al Duran	Narrator and writer
111	Yahiyah Muhammad Al Amir	Writer and poet
112	Wajihah Al Huwaydir	Writer
113	'Abdul Rahman Al Lahim	Writer
114	'Abdallah Al Qa'id	Writer
115	Salih Al Shahwan	Writer
116	Ahmad Al Sha'dawi	Critic
117	'Adil Ahmad Al Sadiq	Journalist
118	Mahdi 'Usfur	Aramco employee
119	Muhammad Al Kashmay	Writer
120	Muznah Al 'Amari	Social Activist
121	Ahmad Al Mullah	Poet
122	Nahid Bashtih	Writer
123	Ghassan Al Khuwaynzi	Poet and writer
124	'Abdallah Safar Al Safar	Critic
125	Fawziyyah Al Jar Allah	Writer and narrator
126	'Abdallah Al Tazi	Novelist
127	Ahmad Al Buq	Poet
128	'Abdul Rahman Al Shahri	Poet
130	Mahah Al Jahni	Poet
131	'Abdul 'Aziz Al Khozam	Poet
132	Iman Ibrahim	Businesswoman
133	Hayah Muhammad Al Sharif	Journalist – "People's Lives"
134	Hamidah Al Sinan	Artist
135	'Abdul Majid Al Ghamidi	Journalist
136	Zahra'a Al Damin	Artist
137	Yahiyah Sabi	Narrator and writer
138	Hussayn Al 'Awami	Journalist
139	Nasir Al Hazimi	Writer
140	Masfar Al Ghamidi	Poet
141	'Abdul Wahhab Al 'Arid	Journalist
142	Amirah Radi Al Khuwaynzi	Analyst
143	Yasir Ahmad Al 'Uways	Employee
144	Fu'ad Al Mushaykhiss	Journalist
145	Fawziyyah Al 'Uyuni	Education
146	'Ubayd 'Ali Al Suhaymi	Journalist
147	Mamduh 'Isa Al Muhayni	Journalist

Appendix 12: In Defense of the Nation 267

148	Hamad Muhammad Al Salimi	Writer
149	Laylah 'Abdallah Al Kazim	Psychiatrist
150	Sa'ud 'Abdallah Al Sayari	Retired
151	Muhammad 'Abdallah Al 'Ali	Employee
152	Nasser Sulayman Al 'Issa	Employee
153	Muhammad Al Hanaki	Employee
154	Ahmad Al Shakhss	Employee
155	Mudi Al Mita'ab	Housewife
156	Sa'id Al Ahmad	Narrator
157	Muhammad Ahmad Abu 'Ali	Banker
158	Intissar 'Akl Al Baheli	Laboratory specialist
159	Fa'ik Muhammad Al Hani	Writer
160	Faris Huzam Al Dawssari	Journalist
161	Ja'afar Ahmad Al Jashi	Narrator
162	Masha'il Al Bakr	Educational development
163	Muhammad 'Abdul 'Aziz Al Sama'il	Writer
164	Walid Yusif Al Hilal	Journalist
165	'Adnan Hashim Al Sada	Poet
166	Habib Ahmad Mahmoud	Poet and journalist
167	Yusif Ahmad Al Hassan	Writer
168	'Alia Farid Makki	Writer
169	Hanah 'Abdallah Al Amir	Lecturer
170	Nadah Radi Al Khuwaynzi	Teacher
171	Nawal Salih Al Malik	Educational supervisor
172	Fatimah Hassan Al 'Awami	Petroleum engineer
173	Mudi Al Ghanem	Teacher
174	Rkia Al 'Unayzan	Employee
175	Amal 'Ali Al 'Awami	Petroleum engineer
176	Iftikhar Hilal	Teacher and narrator
177	Duniyah Salih Al Salih	Artist
178	Najibah Al Sayyid	Writer
179	Nawal Al Yusif	Writer
180	Daliah Ahmad Al 'Awami	Education
181	Hussah Al Ghanim	Employee
182	Hanadi Al Salih	Student
183	Fida'ah Zaki Al Faraj	Breathing specialist
184	Nuhah 'Abdul Ghani Al Shihab	Bank employee
185	Mahah Al Ghanem	Student advisor
186	Hiyam Hassan Al Sinan	Nurse
187	Hayfah Mansur Abul Sa'ud	Teacher
188	'Urubah 'Abdallah Al Munif	Housewife
189	Azra'a Hashim Al Hashimi	Design and Marketing
190	Salwah Mansur Abul Sa'ud	Teacher
191	Hussah 'Abdallah Al Azaz	Social worker
192	Hussah Muhammad Al Shaykh	Educational supervisor

193	'Abdul Rahman 'Ali Al Kharaz	Civil employee
194	Wafa'a Al Munif	Housewife
195	Salah Al 'Umari	Employee
196	Muhammad Al Zamel	Engineer
197	Nasir Sulayman Al 'Issa	Employee
198	Fawzi Sa'ud Al Tanab	Attorney
199	'Abdallah Muhammad Al Shamassi	Employee
200	Muhammad 'Abdallah Al 'Ali	Employee
201	'Abdul Rahman Al Madini	Retired
202	May Al Salih	University student
203	'Ali Fahad Al Sufyan	Employee
204	Asma'a Muhammad Al 'Abudi	Employee
205	Al 'Unud Muhammad Al Shamassi	Employee
206	Zaki Hassan 'Abdul Jabbar	Project consultant
207	'Abdallah Al 'Akil	Employee
208	'Adil 'Abdallah Al Muhsin	Computer engineer
209	Khalid Sa'id Al Naji	Mechanic engineer
210	'Abdul 'Aziz Al Suwaylim	Employee
211	Kamel Ahmad Al Shamassi	Rights activist
212	Fahd Al Hanaki	Employee
213	'Abdallah Ibrahim Al Habib	Businessman
214	Mujahud 'Abd Al Muta'ali	Journalist
215	'Adil Mahdi Al Jashi	Poet analyst
216	'Abdallah Ahmad Al 'Akil	Engineer
217	Munir 'Abdallah Al Shaykh Mubarak	Engineer
218	'Abdul 'Aziz Sa'ad Al Ghoneim	Civil employee
219	'Abdallah 'Abdul Rahman Al Shahwan	Architect
220	Amin 'Ali Al 'Awami	Analyst
221	Tamir Al Habudil	Civil employee
222	Mufid Hassan Al 'Awami	Engineer
223	Madini Mubarak Al Madini	Businessman
224	'Usamah 'Abdul Hayy Al Nahash	Analyst
225	Khalid Al Kuwaylit	Civil employee
226	Hani Nimih Al 'Awami	Analyst
227	Muhammad 'Abdul Majid Khamiss	Petroleum engineer
228	'Abdul Rahman Al 'Alulah	Employee
229	'Ali 'Abdul Jalil Al Qatari	Analyst
230	'Abdallah Al Yahyan	Employee
231	'Ali Hassan Al Khuwaynzi	Bank employee
232	'Abdul Rahman Al Yusif	Employee
233	'Abdul Ra'uf Sa'id Al Mahurzi	Businessman
234	Muhammad Al Sabi	Employee
235	Nazir 'Abdallah Al Hani	Businessman
236	Ibrahim Al 'Akl	Employee
237	Mahmud 'Ali Al 'Abdallah	Factory director

Appendix 12: In Defense of the Nation 269

238	Nabil Haydar Al Sada	Dentist
239	Bashar Al Bahili	Employee
240	'Abdul 'Aziz Al Kayss	Businessman
241	Muhammad 'Ali al Shakss	Employee
242	Muhammad Sa'id Al Khayyat	Businessman
243	Muhammad 'Abdul Latif 'Ababtin	Retired
244	'Abdul Muhsin Al Shibil	Aramco employee
245	Hamdan 'Abdul Rahman Al Kanhal	Businessman
246	Nizar Hussein Al 'Awami	Employee
247	'Ali Abdallah Al Sakit	Engineer
248	Khalid 'Ali Abu Al Sa'ud	Government employee
249	Muhammad Masfar Al 'Ajami	Employee
250	Hassan 'Abdul Majid Al Hajhuj	Employee
251	'Ali Salih Salim Al Shayban	Engineer
252	'Ali Abbass Al Matrud	Architect
253	Hamad Muhammad Al 'Abdali	Photographer
254	Fadi Rassul Sha'aban	Engineer
255	Muhammad bin Hussayn Al Askar	Employee
256	Hussayn 'Abdallah Al Qatari	Engineer
257	'Ali Al Faris	Free trade
258	Hisham 'Ali Al Sayf	Employee
259	Ahmad Musa Al Nashmi	Employee
260	Ja'afar 'Abdul Muhsin Al Nasr	Employee
261	Ibrahim Sulayman Al Tarif	Physicist
262	'Abdul Kadir Al Yusif	Telecommunication employee
263	Muhammad Yusif Al Mari	Employee
264	Sa'id 'Ali Al Jaruf	Employee
265	Khalid Muhammad Al Balihi	Businessman
266	Muhammad 'Ali Muhsin	Aramco employee
267	Sulayman Al Sayari	Businessman
268	Hussayn Ramadan Al Kharass	Social activist
269	Ibrahim Sa'ud Ju'yan	Merchant
270	Muhammad 'Ali Al Kharass	Businessman
271	Muhammad Muhannah Al Muhannah	Employee
272	'Ali Jawad Al Kharass	Businessman
273	Khalid 'Abdallah Al Furyan	Employee
274	Amir Musa Abu Khamsin	Writer and researcher
275	'Abdul Rahman Al Mullah	Social activist
276	'Abdallah Al Harakan	Legal accountant
277	'Ali Sulayman Al 'Ayid	Employee
278	Jawad Muhammad Bu Hlikah	Businessman
279	Zaki Abul Sa'ud	Rights activist and banker
280	Zaki Al Khuwaynzi	Businessman
281	Fathi Bakir Al Khuwaynzi	Education
282	'Abdul Rahman Ahmad Al Ghuriafi	Businessman

283	Ahmad Al 'Abdul Latif	Employee
284	Salmah Salman Al Nasir	Housewife
285	Muzid Al Muzid	Employee
286	Malik Ma'atuk Al Shibr	Aramco engineer
287	Makki 'Ali Al Hubayl	School director
288	Jawad Muhammad Al Safwani	Aramco employee
289	Hassan Ja'afar Al Hassan	Employee
290	Khudr 'Ali Al Ibrahim	Engineer
291	Sami Muhammad Abu Khamsin	Engineer
292	Ahmad Hassan Al Marhun	Businessman
293	'Abdul Ra'uf Quraysh	Employee
294	Muhammad 'Abdul Rahman Al Fahd	Employee
295	Hussayn Quraysh	Employee
296	Muhammad Al 'Abdul Jabbar	Businessman
297	Ahmad 'Abdul Rahim Al Tuli	Social activist
298	Ja'afar Jasim Tahifah	Employee
299	Sa'id Sayf Al Amani	Businessman
300	Muhammad Hassan Al 'Abdul Baki	Employee
301	Zaki Sa'id Al 'Awami	Social activist
302	Assad 'Ali Al Nimr	Writer
303	Jamal Jamil Abu 'Atik	Engineer
304	'Ali Nasir Al Sabah	Employee
305	Malik Muhammad Al Nasir	Social activist
306	'Abdul Wahid Ahmad Al Maqabi	Hospital director
307	Zaki 'Ali Al Salih	Businessman
308	Falah Muhammad Al Habil	Employee
309	Du'yah Sulayman Al Nasir	Employee
310	Sultan Batal Al Harbi	Aramco employee
311	Yahyah Muhammad Quraysh	Businessman
312	Ahmad 'Ali Al Nimr	Attorney
313	Yusif Ahmad Al Hassan	Writer
314	Ahmad Jasim Al Daud	Businessman
315	'Ali Ahmad Sulayman	Businessman
316	Hussayn Hashim Al Sada	Employee
317	Najib Sa'id Al Yusif	Banker
318	Sa'id Salih Al Shaykh	Employee
319	Hisham Sulayman Al Sada	Aramco employee
320	Zakariah Sa'id Al Shaykh	Businessman

Source: Translated by Gwen Okruhlik and Yara Yusif at the University of Texas at Austin for members of the Gulf 2000 website (http://gulf2000.columbia.edu/) managed by Gary Sick at Columbia University, in James A. Russell, "In Defense of the Nation: Terror and Reform in Saudi Arabia," *Strategic Insights*, Volume II, Issue 10 (October 2003), at http://www.nps.edu/Academics/centers/CCC/publications/OnlineJournal/2003/oct03/middleEast2.html.

Appendix 13: A Deviant Junta has Taken Hold of the Sa'udi Media and is Endangering Islamic Society and Its Values

[Excerpts]
May 23, 2006

... We warn the nation against the junta, known for its deviant Westernizing tendencies, that has managed to influence decisions and to take over some institutions that have great influence on [Sa'udi] society's identity and future. Our country is subject to pressures and foreign scheming, and this junta has become the eyes and ears of the foreign enemy and a tool in its hands, relying on its support and achieving its goals. This junta is a very great danger to [Sa'udi] society. It is waging a campaign against [our] morals, working to give a bad name to Islamic values, and [trying] to change [our] society's identity. In addition, it is making an accelerated effort to dry up the sources of good [in society], to drag it into various kinds of deviancy, and to take it away from religion by curtailing [the authority of] religious institutions and cutting down the religious curricula in state and popular educational institutions ...

The reform that is necessary, and through which [we] can mend both matters of religion and the matters of this world, can only be achieved through adherence to the dictates of *Shari'ah* and its principles on reform – and not through the false claims made by those who corrupt our society ...

It is a measure of Allah's grace that all society opposes [this junta's] Westernizing program ... This society has proven that it is aware [of the danger in] this program, no matter how much [the junta] has taken hold of the media platforms in the press and in the [media], no matter how many sick writers they have enlisted in favor of their patently Westernizing program, and no matter how much they have tried to impugn religious scholars, preachers, and judges in the eyes of the ruler in an attempt to keep them away from him and to keep him from hearing their message of reform. This junta is a small circle [of people], the majority of whom live in isolation and estrangement from their society; but in spite of this, they speak in the name of the majority and in the name of society ...

...

Since Women Have great influence on society, [the Junta] has craftily made efforts to Westernize them, using the patently fraudulent slogans of 'Women's

Rights,' 'Liberating [Women] From Their Shackles' and 'Progress' – all this in accordance with their deviant culture. They shed tears over women's current condition, and have not settled for just playing on their emotions, but have even dragged them into their [illusions] and deceit. Unfortunately, they have deceived some of the women, and used them as a tool in implementing their schemes ...

Since the media and its platforms [in Sa'udi Arabia] have considerable influence – whether constructive or destructive – they have tightened their control over it, and it has begun to express only their false opinions, with rare exceptions. Our media, at this stage, when it is in their hands, does not express the views of society, and does not reflect its identity; rather, it is directed towards undermining [Islamic] values and morals ...

They are acting like true hypocrites: They brandish deceptive slogans in order to market them via the media, yet act contrary to these slogans more than anyone else. They purport [to speak in the name of] patriotism, yet it is they who estrange themselves from the nation to the greatest degree, and act so much to lead its people astray. They maintain contacts with foreigners, and these contacts become known through these countries' embassies and through the Western media. It is they who write [for the Westerners] about the situation in the country, and write them reports on the school curricula and on [the status of] women. At the same time they [also] slander the *'Ulamah*, claiming that the *'Ulamah* support terror, and take advantage of the country's sensitivity to foreign criticism. Then they use these reports from the foreign media, to arouse fear in the country and among its leaders about the consequences of adhering to the Islamic way of life.

These transparent and ignominious methods are well known to all, and our society today is aware of the danger inherent in the actions of this junta. They purport to respect the opinion of the other and to call for dialogue, but none are more extreme than they ... Some of them say heretical things, stand by them, and do not retract them, and [others] promote abominations in their poems, stories, and writings. The writings of some of them are rife with heresy and atheism, and openly call for secularism, without hiding it. Some of them have established a satellite [television] station for the purpose of corrupting society's morals. Most of them were educated by atheist, communist, and pan-Arab parties. Some of them are senior [journalists] who hold managerial positions in some newspapers, and slander every *Shari'ah* institution in the country and every other positive aspect in society ...

...

The nation as a whole, and in particular those promoting [true] reform [i.e. the religious conservatives], expect the rulers to stand as an impenetrable bulwark against these corrupting currents of thought, which aim to spread vice in the country and among the people. They must repulse everyone whose [dedication to] religion and loyalty are in question ... and keep them away from positions of authority, media platforms, and platforms of instruction.

The responsibility that lies with the *'Ulamah* of Islam is great, and it includes the obligation to make value judgments, to express opinions, to

Appendix 13: A Deviant Junta in Sa'udi Media 273

warn, [and] to command good and to forbid evil. Both those who hold official positions and those who do not [hold such positions] have equal responsibility, and they must fulfill it. [They should] advise the rulers and call on the entire public [to do] what is good for the country and for the people, and warn them about the surrounding dangers and the [heretical] tendencies that lead [people] astray, for the *'Ulamah*'s statements, sermons, and fatwahs have already had great influence in thwarting the scheme of these hypocrites.

We call on the general public to expose the disgrace of this scheme, to warn against this Westernizing program and against being deceived by it ... Finally, we call on this deviant junta to [return] to the right path, and likewise [we call on] all those who followed them or were deluded by them to make sincere repentance ... "

Source: http://www.islamlight.net/index.php?option=content&task=view&id=2640&Itemid=25, at L. Azuri, "Debate on Reform in Saudi Arabia," Washington, D. C.: The Middle East Media Research Institute, September 21, 2006 [Inquiry & Analysis Series Report No. 294].

Appendix 14: 2007 Sa'udi Women Petition for Driving Right

In the Name of God the Compassionate, the Merciful,
    We the League of Demanders of Women's Right to Drive Cars in Saudi Arabia.
    Peace be upon you [women], and the grace and blessings of God:
    On the occasion of the passage of two years since the accession of the Servant of the Two Holy Mosques, King 'Abdallah bin 'Abdul 'Aziz Al Sa'ud, and on the occasion of the National Day on 23 September, we the League of Demanders of Women's Right to Drive Cars in Sa'udi Arabia announce that we are submitting a letter in which we demand that King 'Abdallah – may God preserve him – give back to women the right to movement by use of the automobile, the means of movement today that was stolen from women. That right was enjoyed by our mothers and grandmothers in full freedom, to use the means of transportation available in their time.

Source: AAFAQ [Horizons] Arab Reform Website, "Campaign to Grant Women's Right to Drive Cars in Sa'udi Arabia," AAFAQ, September 19, 2007 at http://www.aafaq.org/english/aafaq_today.aspx?id_news=55.

Appendix 15: Sa'udi Activists Petition King for Reforms

May 13, 2009
To the Custodian of the Two Holy Mosques, King 'Abdallah
bin 'Abdul 'Aziz Al Sa'ud

In the past few weeks, several media outlets reported the beginning of secret tribunals for hundreds of alleged Sa'udi terrorists (991 defendants). Several ad hoc security courts are in place under the auspices of the Sa'udi judicial system. The names of the accused, the charges against them, names of judges, the exact dates, and timing of the hearing should be matter of public discourse; however, that did not happen and the judges unfortunately went on with absolute secret-court proceedings. The presiding judges should not have been under the illusion that justice will be best served under secrecy and they thought that it is within their good judgment to try the accused citizens behind closed doors.

We have waited for a long time hoping that some other human-rights groups would blow the whistle and bring the case to the world's attention; to be only disappointed by the complete lack of oversight of Sa'udi organizations and intellectuals. It seems to us as if the Ministry of Interior decided that those allegedly involved in violent acts or terrorism have no rights and anyone who defends them is as guilty as they are: hence their attorneys can easily be accused of being accomplices or traitors.

For these reasons we are calling for fair and public trials, otherwise it is impossible to mete out justice, especially whenever such an authoritarian government is strongly involved in the cases; in addition, a clout of secrecy will grant the government carte blanche to pass tough verdicts against helpless and powerless defendants. Based on such legal rulings, which might result in the innocent being victimized, we assert that secret tribunals are unfair but also deprive the basic rights of the accused. Hence we contest the legal basis of any rendered judgments that resulted out of these "Security Courts." Moreover, we also take this opportunity to remind everyone that violence and terrorism can only be rooted out by applying justice, and by respecting the rule of law and closely following legal procedures.

We, furthermore, take this opportunity to remind everyone that fair trials have certain measures and procedures that guarantee justice and protect rights of every individual. There are more than twenty justifications that prove our case. The strongest among these justifications is that: these secret proceedings have violated the fundamental principle of transparency, but have also denied defendants their basic rights as granted by the Islamic jurisprudence, and as prescribed by international conventions particularly the standards for judiciary independence and human rights. The Sa'udi statute (i.e., Criminal Procedure Law) states that accused individuals have seven basic rights that must be maintained:

1 "During the investigation, the accused shall have the right to seek the assistance of a representative or an attorney" (Article 64);
2 "Any accused person shall have the right to seek the assistance of a lawyer or a representative to defend him during the investigation and trial stages" (Article 4);
3 "The Bureau of Investigation and Prosecution shall conduct its investigation and prosecution in accordance with its Law and the implementing regulations thereof" (Article 14);
4 "In cases that require detention for a longer period, the matter shall be referred to the Director of the Bureau of Investigation and Prosecution to issue an order that the arrest be extended for a period or successive periods none of which shall exceed thirty days and their aggregate shall not exceed six months from the date of arrest of the accused. Thereafter, the accused shall be directly transferred to the competent court, or be released" (Article 114);
5 "An arrested person shall not be subjected to any bodily or moral harm. Similarly, he shall not be subjected to any torture or degrading treatment" (Article 2);
6 "No penal punishment shall be imposed on any person except in connection with a forbidden and punishable act, whether under *Shari'ah* principles or under the statutory laws, and after he has been convicted pursuant to a final judgment rendered after a trial conducted in accordance with *Shari'ah* principles" (Article 3);
7 "Court hearings shall be public. The court may exceptionally consider the action or any part thereof in closed hearings, or may prohibit certain classes of people from attending those hearings for security reasons, or maintenance of public morality, if it is deemed necessary for determining the truth" (Article 155).

Open court trials' is one of the international standards for judiciary independence because it helps impartial judges to withstand pressures and resist possible interventions during court hearings of the accused. Transparency also protects judges and exposes transgressors.

Because political prisoners, in general, should have more rights rather than be subjected to more harassments, or more tortures, the transparency of court hearings would protect political defendant's basic rights against a totalitarian government that they oppose. Moreover, and because the Sa'udi judiciary does not stem from general role of popular oversight of rulers by citizens, which means that it lacks independent authority, that it has no written laws, legal precedent for political case, that it constantly abuses human rights and severely punishes activists, that secret tribunals are pretexts for confiscating and abusing prisoners' rights to cloak tortures, that there is no guarantee against extracting confessions through coercion in secret trials, that the Bureau of Investigation and Public Prosecution falls under the jurisdiction of the Interior Ministry – which is evidence enough to demonstrate to the world community that the Sa'udi Judiciary is neither fair nor just – and that, the system accepts or justifies tortures, secret trials will definitely cover up courts' admittance and ratifications of coerced confessions. [It must also be noted that] since justice is not going to be served if it is not all inclusive of the principles by which courts should reach an independent decision, justice will not be guaranteed unless the judiciary system has oversights of prisons, that lack of transparency of court hearings limit arbitrary false criminal accusations, and that the Ministry of Interior has the ultimate discretions vis-à-vis the accused as it wishes to try him/her in courts of law or let the defendants languish in prisons without verdicts., that the secret tribunals, in addition to being flagrant violation of the principles of popular oversight and justice, also hamper people's understanding of the root causes of violence; which are lack of democratic values and political oppressions.

The authority has resorted to security solutions that deal with the symptoms rather than the root causes. Although deep inside, they know that obliterating violence requires well-balanced political solutions.

These justifications prove beyond reasonable doubts that it is not within a judge's discretion to turn political trials into security tribunals.

Unfortunately, as the Sa'udi legal system engages in flagrant human-right abuses it violates the principles of Islamic jurisprudence as well.

Recommendations and Demands:

First: We request the Custodian of the Two Holy Mosques to put his words ["will smash the head of transgression by the sword of justice"] into action by establishing a practical and institutional due process that guarantees fair court trials for all prisoners, especially the aforementioned seven basic rights. The state must adhere to clear and specific standards of principles – as prescribed in Islamic jurisprudence, practiced in other constitutional countries, and defined by scholars of political sociology – to reach a clear definition of political crimes, anti-state rebellious warfare, and a judicial and practical due process for punishments.

Second: We would like to take this opportunity to remind his Majesty that there is an increasing relationship between extremism and official and societal violence meted out by the authority. The advocates of human rights and civic society denounce violence as means to reach or continue a tight grip on power, and would like to emphasize two points:

1 The root cause of terrorism has political reasons: despotism, injustice, human-right abuses, and oppression; and resorting to a religious discourse to sugarcoat politically motivated and ill-intended decisions has driven society toward extremism and violence. This mindset and such practices only flourish in dictatorial states.
2 Our emphasis on the denunciation of violence and extremism does not mean they will end by issuing of religious edicts because when people become deeply frustrated then society as a whole starts boiling and congesting like a volcano that is going to erupt with no need for any further impetus. Sometimes due to naïveté, people may believe that violence is going to cease but that will never happen unless the state roots out the real causes of violence: oppression, injustice, and absence of liberty and freedom. We believe that the carpet would not be pulled from underneath the feet of violence unless the state adopts a constitution that nurture the growth of civic-society institutions, as the only way that leads toward the establishment of a modern and democratic state. The statement by the late American president John F. Kennedy, who warned in the early 1960s that "those who make peaceful revolutions impossible will make violent revolutions inevitable" is applicable to our state of affairs. Therefore, we remind everyone that using police brutality only results in neglecting other components of violence, hence exaggerating security solutions – without political reforms – will distort people's awareness and ultimately result in swallowing the bitter medicine.

Third: For these reasons, we remind everyone that political reform is the only solution for eliminating extremism and violence and we look forward to the establishment of, what advocates called, "the fourth Sa'udi State" as a beacon for democracy and human rights. We therefore request his majesty to implement his promised-reform initiatives by establishing a modern state built on democracy, justice, dignity, equality, tolerance, pluralism, and citizens' rights. Furthermore, we request that the following constitutional reforms be implemented:

1 Ensuring judiciary independence, as called for by advocates of democracy and human rights, especially the seven criteria of fair court trails namely transparency as effective solutions to limiting violence and counter violence because they are two faces of the same coin.
2 Permission to establish unions, non-government organizations, and other forms of assembly; people must have the rights to engage in cultural, social, economic, scientific, legal, and political associations. This requires a speedy promulgation of NGOs' regulations.
3 We emphasize Islamic tolerance, equality, and equal opportunity as the only cure of violence; in order to establish the principle of tolerance we must ascertain cultural and political pluralisms.
4 Establishing an elected parliament that ensures people's oversight over the government.

5 Democratically elected parliament that will run with checks and balances from the public.
 6 Separating the three authorities, i.e., the executive, judiciary, and legislative branches.
 7 Amending the Allegiance Committee's law by adding a critical article that stresses the rule of the elected body (the parliament) in the process, hence, the choice of the future heir apparent will be up to the choice of both the Allegiance Committee and the elected parliament. As for the benefits of such a procedure:

   A It limits unhealthy competitions and blocks venues that may lead to overt and covert conflicts.
   B It manifests legitimacy so we would have a practical and workable concept of democratization.
   C It combines choices of both the people and the ruling family, which will result in political stability and durability of the regime; because alienating the people from the political process would turn the country into a family business. It will be in the best interest of the monarchy if the public is allowed to participate in the election process and is given a choice, and a voice. This in turn will lead to healthy competition and will allow democracy to prevail. This will also increase and validate public's interests as well as that of the officials and the ruling bodies.
   D It will make sure the principle of "who is best fit" as stated in Sa'udi Arabia's Basic System of Governance with accordance to specific standards and applicable procedures, otherwise the "best-fit" concept would be meaningless.

 8 Limiting the terms of appointed royal family's members in government posts. Moreover, we demand designing new laws that would ensure equal opportunity, transparency, monitoring, and accountability.
 9 We demand that the prime minister should be a commoner to ease accountability and to manifest the principle of circulations of authority similar to what happened in King Sa'ud's reign and what is being implemented in some other constitutional monarchies like the United Kingdom, Jordan, and Morocco.
10 Written constitutional laws must be promulgated to ensure and protect basic human rights for an individual and groups; especially political rights, rights to demonstrations and public sit-ins to express their personal sentiments and to publicly protest injustice.

Fourth: We ask his Majesty to grant necessary permission to human-right activists to see and monitor prisons. Not to jail and torture the ones who expose such practices, like what had happened to Professor Matruk Al-Faleh or others. The establishment of an independent commission to allow the hearings of human-right abuse cases, which can also investigate claims and allegations. According to reports, the latest of which is a statement issued by a protesting group of women in Qasim (a province located 300 km north of Sa'udi capital, Riyadh) who demanded restitutions for the victims and taking those alleged defendants to courts of law in very transparent and public hearings.

Fifth: We say to the judges you must respect the rule of law, and you must reject secret tribunals. The judges should stand up against blatant violations of law. The judges should see what independent judges in France, former Yugoslavia, and recently in Pakistan had done to contest injustice? Why are the judges so afraid of transparency in their courts? Have not they rendered unjust and tough punishments against peaceful advocates of constitution and human rights? Then, why are they so afraid of trying alleged terrorists in open courts?

Sixth: We ask those who are concerned with political reform from every background in our society, human rights advocates, and attorneys to unite their efforts to defend human rights, the allegedly accused, and prisoners regardless of their backgrounds. We demand various government agencies to adhere to international benchmarks of fair trials and imprisonments for any human being, expose those responsible in abuses, and ensure publicity of court hearings. This is the only savior that would ensure perseverance of the society vis-à-vis violence and extremism and counter aggression (i.e., official).

Seventh: To the Custodian of the Two Holy Mosques:

Once more, we would request his Majesty to ensure cessation of hostilities by the Ministry of Interior. In addition, we condemn the Ministry's attempt to engage in character assassination of the advocates of constitutional reforms and human rights, by falsely accusing them of justifying and inciting violence. We would also like to emphasize and encourage our adherence to peaceful means in all our discourse and deeds. Certainly, we are not in any possible way justifying violence when we elaborate on its causes; rather we present some reasons for the occurrences of violence and solutions for its elimination. We can comfortably declare, that no solution to violence and extremism is practical unless we, first and foremost, establish a new constitutional hierarchy. Second, we must allow, encourage, and respect dialogue in society in order to end political debacle.

Signed by the following advocates of Constitutional Reforms, Civic Society and human rights:

1 Professor 'Abdul Kareem Yusuf al-Khathar, Professor of Islamic Jurisprudence in Qasim University and Human Rights Activist.
2 Dr. 'Abdul Rahman Hamid al-Hamid, Assistant professor of Islamic Economics and a Human Rights Activist.
3 'Abdul Rahman Musah Al-Qarni, Human Rights Activist.
4 Professor 'Abdallah H. al-Hamid, former Professor of Comparative Literature and Founding member in the Defunct and Banned Committee of Defense of the Legitimate Rights (CDLR).

Appendix 15: Activists Petition King for Reforms

5 'Abdallah Musah al-Qarni, Human Rights Activist.
6 Asmah Muhammad al-Saqabi.
7 Ayman Muhammad al-Rashid, Human Rights Activist.
8 'Ayshah Muhammad al-Qarni, Human Rights Activist.
9 'Abdul Majid Sa'ud al-Bulawi, Writer and Human Rights Activist.
10 'Abdul Muhsin 'Ali al-'Ayash, Human Rights Activist.
11 'Abdul 'Aziz Ahmad al-Fuqahah, Human Rights Activist.
12 Ahmad Khalaf al-Rashid, Lawyer.
13 Ahmad Musah al-Qarni, Human Rights Activist.
14 Ahmad Muhammad Al Hijri, Human Rights Activist.
15 'Ali Ahmad al-Bahrani, Human Rights Activist.
16 'Ali Hamid al-Hamid, Interested in public affairs.
17 Aljawharah Sulayman al-Bradi, Interested in public affairs.
18 Asmah 'Abdul Karim al-Mutiq, Interested in public affairs.
19 Ibrahim 'Abdallah al-Mubarak, Lawyer.
20 Ibrahim Mugaytib al-Mugaytib, Human Rights Activist.
21 Fadhilah Muhammad al-Qarni, Human Rights Activist.
22 Fahd 'Abdul 'Aziz 'Ali al-'Urani, Human Rights Activist.
23 Fatimah 'Abdul Karim al-Qaba'ah.
24 Fatimah Muhammad al-Qarni, Human Rights Activist.
25 Fatimah Muhammad 'Ali al-Humayd, Interested in public affairs.
26 Fatimah Rabi' al-Madkhaly, Human Rights Activist.
27 Fawzan Muhsin al-Harbi, Human Rights Activist.
28 'Isah Hamid al-Hamid, Human Rights Activist.
29 Jalilah Ahmad al-'Ayashi, Human Rights Activist.
30 Hafsah Muhammad al-Saqabi.
31 Hagir 'Ali al-Qaba'ah.
32 Halimah 'Abdul Karim al-Qaba'ah.
33 Hashim 'Abdallah al-Rifa'i, Human Rights Activist.
34 Hissah Muhammad 'Ali al-Humayd, Interested in public affairs.
35 Iman 'Abdul Rahman al-Shumayri, Human Rights Activist.
36 Iman Jamil al-Dik, Interested in public affairs.
37 Khadijah Muhammad Dahiqi, Human Rights Activist.
38 Khalaf Farhan al-Bulawi, Human Rights Activist.
39 Latifah Sulayman al-'Abudi.
40 Lynah 'Abdul Rahman al-Shumayri, Human Rights Activist.
41 Mahah 'Abdul Raham al-Qahtani, Human Rights Activist.
42 Mahah 'Ali al-Bradi, Interested in public affairs.
43 May al-Talaq, Interested in public affairs.
44 Maymunah Muhammad al-Mudayfir, Interested in public affairs.
45 Mhanah Muhammad Al-Falih, Human Rights Activist.
46 Mish'ari 'Ali al-Gamdi, Human Rights Activist.
47 Miznah Muhammad al-Saqabi.
48 Muhammad 'Abdallah Bursays, Interested in public affairs.
49 Muhammad Hudijan al-Harbi, Human Rights Activist.

50 Dr. Muhammad Fahd al-Qahtani, Academic and Writer.
51 Muhammad Hamad al-Muhaysin, Human Rights Activist
52 Muhammad Salih al-Bigadi, Human Rights Activist.
53 Muhammad Musah al-Qarni, Human Rights Activist.
54 Munah Hamad al-Shwayir, Human Rights Activist.
55 Nadah Muhammad al-'Umran, Interested in public affairs.
56 Najlah 'Abdul Rahman al-Shumayri, Human Rights Activist.
57 Nathir al-Majid, Writer and Human Rights Activist.
58 Nurah Sulayman al-Talaq, Interested in public affairs.
59 Nusaybah Musah al-Qarni, Human Rights Activist.
60 'Umar 'Abdul Rahman al-Shumayri, Human Rights Activist.
61 'Umaymah Musah al-Qarni, Human Rights Activist.
62 Rimah al-Jiraysh, Interested in public affairs.
63 Ruqayyah Musah al-Qarni, Human Rights Activist.
64 Ruqayyah Muhammad al-Qarni, Human Rights Activist.
65 Sa'ad 'Abdul 'Aziz al-Mubarak, Human Rights Activist.
66 Sa'id 'Abdallah al-Wahabi, Human Rights Activist.
67 Safa'ah 'Abdul Rahman al-Shumayri, Human Rights Activist.
68 Safi'ah 'Abdul Karim al-Qaba'ah.
69 Salahhidin 'Abdul Rahman al-Shumayri, Human Rights Activist.
70 Salih 'Ali al-Qaba'ah.
71 Salmah Muhammad al-Qarni, Human Rights Activist.
72 Sa'ud Ahmad al-Dughaythir, Human Rights Activist.
73 Dr. Sha'im Lafi al-Hamazzani, Professor of Social Sciences, Al-Imam University.
74 Sharifah Muhammad al-Saqabi.
75 Sultanah 'Ali al-Jurissi.
76 Dr. Wajnaat 'Abdul Rahom al-Maymani, Professor of Islamic Jurisprudence.
77 Walid Sami Abulkayr, Writer and Legal Researcher.

(A 25-page legal memorandum was attached with the Arabic version of this petition that documented secret-court trials.)

Source: "Establishing Secret Tribunals is an Attempt to Obscure Oppression and Thwart Any Possible Political Reform in Sa'udi Arabia," May 17, 2009, at http://en.alkarama.org/index.php?option=com_content&view=article&id=235:saudi-arabia-77-human-right-activists-send-a-petition-to-king-abdullah-condemning-secret-tribunals& catid = 159:communiques-other-ongs&Itemid=181.

Appendix 16: A Declaration of National Reform

January 23, 2011

It is no secret that the revolutions of Tunisia and Egypt, and their aftermath of crises and changing political discourse in many Arab countries, have created circumstances in which we need to reevaluate our situation and do our best to reform before it is too late, and before we are confronted with developments whose consequences we cannot prevent nor predict.

A group of Sa'udi intellectuals have previously presented the Custodian of the Two Holy Mosques in January 2003 with a set of specific suggestions in a statement titled "A Vision for the Nation's Present and the Future." His Majesty has welcomed it then, and promised to consider it. Moreover, a number of senior officials announced later that the government is determined to adopt a wide range of reform policies in the state apparatus, and in its relationship with the Sa'udi society.

After a decade of those promises, very little of the promised reforms has been achieved. We believe that the delay in political reform has aggravated the problems which were referred to in the "Vision" document and the other statements that followed it.

The status quo is full of risks and causes for concern. We are witnessing with the rest of the Sa'udi people the decline of our country's regional role, the stagnation of the government, the deterioration in the efficiency of the management, the prevalence of corruption and nepotism, fanaticism, and the increasingly widening gap between the state and society, especially the new generation of youth. This could lead to disastrous consequences on the country and the people, and it is something we cannot accept for our homeland and our children.

Addressing this situation requires a serious review and an immediate adoption of large-scale reforms by both the state and society, focusing on fixing the fundamental flaws in our political system, and leading the country to a well-grounded constitutional monarchy.

The people's acceptance is the basis for legitimacy of the authority, and it is the only guarantee for unity, stability, the efficiency of governance, and protecting the country against foreign interference. This requires a reformulation of the relationship between society and the state, in which the people are the source of power, a full partner in deciding public policy through their elected representatives in the *Shurah Council*, and that the purpose of the state is to serve society, protect its interests, enhance the standard of living, and guarantee the dignity and honor of individuals and the future of their children.

Thus, we look forward to a royal declaration that clearly underlines the commitment of the state to become a "constitutional monarchy," and to set a timetable that specifies a date for the beginning of desired reforms, the initiation of applying them, and the date of concluding them. The declaration has to confirm adopting the great objectives of reform, namely: the rule of law, full equality for members of the public, legal guarantees for individual and civil freedoms, popular participation in decision making, balanced development, uprooting poverty, and the optimum use of national resources.

In this regard, we see that the reform program should include the following:

First: The development of the Basic Law into a comprehensive constitution that serves as a social contract between the people and the state stating that the people are the source of power. The separation of the three branches of government: the executive, judicial and legislative; defining authorities, and tying them with responsibility and accountability; the equality of all citizens, the legal protection of individual and civil freedoms, ensure justice, equality of opportunity. Reaffirming the responsibility of the state in guaranteeing human rights, protecting the right to peaceful expression of opinion, and reinforce public freedoms, including the right to form political and professional associations.

Second: To emphasize the principle of the rule of law, and that everyone – statesmen and citizens – are under the law equally and without discrimination; and to incriminate improper handling of national resources or using them outside the framework of the law.

Third: The adoption of general election as a way to form municipal, provincial, and the *Shurah Council*; and the participation of women in nomination and election.

Fourth: The adoption of the principle of administrative decentralization, and granting local administrations in regions and governorates the necessary powers to establish effective, local government that can interact with the demands of citizens in each region.

Fifth: To activate the principle of the independence of the judiciary, by canceling all the bodies that play parallel roles outside the framework of the judicial system, and to have the courts presiding over the investigation with the accused and the conditions of prisoners, and public prosecution; and to cancel all the instructions and regulations that limit the independence of the judiciary and its effectiveness or limit the immunity of judges, or open the door to the interference in judiciary. The codification and standardization of provisions must be accelerated. *'Ta'zir'* [corporal punishment] must be regulated. The international charters on Human Rights that our government has signed must become part of the judicial system. All of this to ensure justice, equality and discipline in the application of the provisions. The system of criminal procedures and legal defense system must be activated, preventing any action or conduct outside their framework or a breach of their limits.

Sixth: Accelerating the issuance of the non-governmental organizations law, which was approved by the *Shurah Council*, and opening the door to establishing civil society institutions in all forms and for all purposes, as a channel to rationalize and shape public opinion, and increase popular participation in decision-making.

Seventh: Despite widespread debate on women's rights in Sa'udi Arabia, the government had failed to take adequate action to fulfill the requirements of this pressing issue. Ignoring or postponing the rights of women contributes to deepening the problems of poverty and violence, and undermines the contribution of the family in improving the quality of education. What is required is to take legal and institutional measures to empowering women to attain their rights to empower women in order to gain their rights in education, ownership, work and participation in public affairs without discrimination.

Eighth: The issuance of legislation banning discrimination between citizens, for any reason and under any justification. The legislation must criminalize any practice that involves sectarian, tribal, regional, racial, ethnic or any other type of discrimination. The law must also criminalize hate speech for any reasons, religious or otherwise. Implementing a strategy for national integration that explicitly recognizes the social and cultural diversity of the Sa'udi society, and affirms respect for this diversity and considers it a source of enrichment for national unity and social peace. We need an effective strategy for national integration that can rectify the situation of groups that suffer from exclusion, marginalization and denial of rights due to any of the above reasons, and to compensate them for what they have undergone.

Ninth: King 'Abdallah's decision to set up the Human Rights Commission and the National Society of Human Rights was a promising step. But we find now that both HRC and NSHR have turned into what looks like a bureaucracy with a limited role in the defending the rights of citizens. One of the reasons for this decline is the government's interference in the appointment of these bodies members, as well as the refusal of many government agencies to deal with them. Guarding the rights of citizens and residents, and protecting them against injustice, must be at the top of the priorities for the government and society. Therefore, we demand the removal of restrictions imposed on HRC and NSHR, and to ensure their independence within the framework of the law. We also call for legalizing the right to form other non-governmental organizations for the defense of human rights.

Tenth: There is no dignity without decent living. Our country has been blessed, but a large segment of our citizens complain of poverty and neediness. We have witnessed the slowness of the government in addressing the problem of unemployment and housing, and improving the quality of life, particularly in rural areas and suburbs, and among the retired and the elderly. There is no justification for the failure to develop solutions to these problems. We believe that not raising these issues for general debate, ignoring the role of the private sector and civil society when thinking about such problems, and to see it from a purely commercial perspective, had turned these problems into dilemmas, and it has become one of the reasons and to humiliate citizens and restricting them.

Eleventh: The past years revealed the aggravation of tampering with public funds, which requires the elected *Shurah Council* to use its powers to monitor government agencies and keep them accountable. The Council can establish structures and independent bodies capable of carrying out monitoring functions, the declare their findings to the people, especially those related to the administrative corruption, misuse of power, and mismanagement of public funds by government agencies. We reaffirm the need for the adoption of the principle of transparency and accountability, and the establishment of an institutional framework to ensure these principles by a) establishing a national center for integrity that enjoys independence and declares the results of its investigations to public opinion; b) enabling the citizens to obtain access to the use of public funds by government agencies, and abolishing restrictions that prevent the press from exposing transactions suspected of being involved in corruption.

Twelfth: Oil revenues have jumped over the past five years to high levels, providing the government with huge funds that should have been used and spent wisely, rather than squander them in expensive, cost-ineffective projects. We call for a review of the foundations used as basis for the five-year development plans, and to adopt a long-term strategy for overall development, focusing on expanding the base of national production, building the base for alternative economic sources, creating jobs, and including the private sector in deciding economic policies.

In conclusion, we reiterate our call for the political leaders to adopt the reform proposals.

In order to show the goodwill and determination to reform, four steps must be taken immediately:

1 A royal declaration that confirms the government's intention to introduce political reform, and to set a timetable to initiate and apply it.
2 The immediate release of political prisoners, and to present those who committed crimes to trial without delay, while ensuring the necessary judicial guarantees for each of the accused.
3 Lifting the travel ban orders that have been imposed on a large number of people who expressed their opinions.
4 Removing the restrictions imposed on the freedom of publishing and expression, and to enable the citizens to express their opinions publicly and peacefully. And to stop prosecuting those who express their opinion in a peaceful manner.

As we make this declaration to our political leaders and the citizens of our country, we reaffirm the solidarity of all, the people and the government, in the face of the dangers facing us, and to avoid any unexpected surprises. We

Appendix 16: Declaration of National Reform 287

trust that all of us have learned the lessons from what happened in brotherly Arab countries.

Facing challenges can only be achieved through serious, comprehensive and immediate reform that embodies popular participation in decision-making, enhances national cohesion, and meets the people's aspirations in a glorious homeland

Source: Translated by [Saudijeans.org]. The document, both in Arabic and English, at http://www.saudireform.com/?p=english.

Notes

Introduction

1 Joseph A. Kéchichian, "Testing the Sa'udi Arabia 'Will to Power': Challenges Confronting Prince 'Abdallah," *Middle East Policy* 10:4, Winter 2003, pp. 100–115; and *idem*, "Sa'udi Arabia's Will to Power," *Middle East Policy* 7:2, February 2000, pp. 47–60.
2 Joseph A. Kéchichian, *Faysal: Saudi Arabia's King for All Seasons*, Gainesville, Florida: University Press of Florida, 2008, especially pp. 105–44 [Hereafter Kéchichian-Faysal].
3 This theme is developed in some detail in Kéchichian – Faysal, *Ibid.*, chapter 1; see also Joseph A. Kéchichian, "Refining the Saudi 'Will to Power'," *Perspectives*, Number 3, Singapore: National University of Singapore–Middle East Institute, June 2009, at https://docs.google.com/fileview?id=0B35LxaKpjlgIMjA3NDc5Mz ctN2M2Ni00OWRjLThiNWUtZTE5MWVlYmQ2YTI0& hl=en_GB&safe=on.
4 This study will primarily examine internal Sa'udi concerns, although additional regional and international challenges that weigh in the decision-making process may be analyzed for clarification purposes.
5 This key petition is analyzed in Chapter 5. For further details, see Agence France-Presse, "Saudi Activists Take Case of Jailed Reformists to King: Detainees had been Considering Foundation of an Islamic Constitution Party, August 31, 2007 at http:// www.middleeasttransparent.com/spip.php?page=article&id_article=1975&-lang=en; for the integral text in Arabic see, http://www.middleeasttransparent.com/spip.php?page=article&id_article=1972& lang = ar.
6 The nine lawyers were: 'Isam Basrawi, Sa'ud al-Hashemi, 'Abdul Rahman Khan, 'Abdul 'Aziz al-Khirayji, Musa al-Qarni, Fahd al-Qarshi, Sayfiddin Faysal al-Sharif, 'Abdul Rahman al-Shemayri, and Sulayman al-Rushdi.
7 Agence France-Presse, "Sa'udi Activists Urge King to Free Jailed Reformists," September 14, 2007.
8 Agence France-Presse, "Sa'udis Free One of Nine Reformists," September 22, 2007.
9 See, Robert Lacey, *Inside the Kingdom: Kings, Clerics, Modernists, Terrorists, and the Struggle for Saudi Arabia*, New York: Viking, 2009, p. 69. In turn, Lacey credits Madawi Al-Rasheed, *A History of Saudi Arabia*, Cambridge University Press, 2002, p. 91, for this information, which also appears on page 87 of Rasheed's second edition, published in 2010.
10 Turki Al-Saheil, "Mufti 'Am al-Sa'udiyyah Yahziru al-Shabab min al-Zihab ilal-Khatij Biqasad al-Jihad" [Sa'udi Arabia: Calls Against Imams Politicizing Prayer], *Al-Sharq al-Awsat*, October 2, 2007, p. 1.
11 This was confirmed by an astute observer of the kingdom. Interview with Professor Mazin Salah Motabbagani, Department of Orientalism, Faculty of Da'wah, Imam Muhammad bin Sa'ud Islamic University (Madinah), in Riyadh, March 28, 2010.

12 Khaled Al-Awadh, "Oudah Denounces Bin Laden's Ideology," *Arab News*, September 17, 2007, at http://archive.arabnews.com/?page=1&section=0&article=101271&d=17&m=9&y=2007.
13 For a solid assessment of Al-Awdah's views, see Mansoor Jassem Alshamsi, *Islam and Political Reform in Saudi Arabia: The Quest for Political Change and Reform*, New York and London: Routledge, 2011.
14 Khaled Al-Awadh, "Oudah Denounces bin Laden's Ideology," *Islam Daily*, September 18, 2007, at http://www.islamdaily.org/en/islam/5983.oudah-denounces-bin-ladens-ideology.htm/.
15 A detailed description of the violence is beyond the scope of this study, although fairly accurate summaries, which border on strict police work, are available in Thomas Hegghammer, *Jihad in Saudi Arabia: Violence and Pan-Islamism since 1979*, Cambridge, UK: Cambridge University Press, 2010.
16 "Over 1,500 Extremists Freed After Repenting," *Arab News*, November 26, 2007, p. 1.
17 *Ibid.*
18 *Ibid.* Critics of the system referred to the late Shaykh 'Abdul 'Aziz bin Baz, and the many fancy fatwahs he issued over the years, to highlight that establishment clerics almost always supported the center of power. See Riad Najib El-Rayyes, *Riyah al-Shamal: Al Sa'udiyyah wal-Khalij wal-'Arab fi 'Alam al-Tis'inat*, [Northern Wind: Saudi Arabia, the Gulf and the Arabs in the Nineties], London and Beirut: Riad El-Rayyes Books Limited, 1997, pp. 174–78.
19 "Woman Attacks Vice Cops With Pepper Spray," *Arab News*, September 25, 2007, at http://arabnews.com/?page=1& section=0&article=101656&d=25&m=9&y=2007.
20 Between 2007 and late-2011, I visited the kingdom on twelve separate occasions, for periods lasting between 2 and 8 weeks for each trip to research this book. Needless to say that a myriad opportunities existed to observe a rapidly changing society, especially when contrasted with earlier stays starting in 1983. Over the years, and after countless discussions with ordinary people as well as members of the ruling family, it may be safe to affirm with little hesitation what I witnessed, which are discussed in some detail throughout this book.
21 It was indeed possible to witness such debates in several settings, including majlises, which confirmed that serious questions were often discussed in private quarters.
22 This is, needless to say, a complex case with a variety of perspectives worthy of the utmost care in any assessment. For the official version, see "Explanatory Statement by the Ministry of Justice about Qatif Girl," November 21, 2007 at http://www.mofa.gov.sa/detail.asp?InNewsItemID=71849&InTemplateKey=print. See also Ibn al-Hashimi, "The Hidden Truth About the Qatif Case: Response to "Rape Victim Gets Lashes," n.d., www.calltoislam.com. See also Vicky Baker, "Rape Victim Sentenced to 200 Lashes and Six Months in Jail," *Guardian*, November 17, 2007, at http://www.guardian.co.uk/world/2007/nov/17/saudiarabia.international.
23 Ebtihal Mubarak, "'Qatif Girl' Subjected to Brutal Crime: King," *Arab News*, December 19, 2007, p. 1.
24 Joseph A. Kéchichian, "Reforming the Fatwa Process: Saudi King Abdullah has Taken Steps to Ensure that Unauthorised People do not Issue Embarrassing Religious Edicts," *Gulf News*, August 19, 2010, p. 10.
25 Mariam Al Hakeem, "Saudis Approve Independent Judiciary," *Gulf News*, October 2, 2007, at http://archive.gulfnews.com/region/Sa'udi_Arabia/10157753.html.
26 Agence France-Presse, "Sa'udi Court Imprisons Anti-Western Cleric," January 1, 2008.
27 As discussed below, law students were eager to introduce additional changes. See "Female Law Students Demand Opportunities for Court Practice," *Arab News*, March 16, 2011, p. 3.
28 "Saudi Arabia: Law of God versus Law of Man," *The Economist*, October 13, 2007, pp. 50–51 at http://www.economist.com/world/mideast-africa/displaystory.cfm?story_id=9954500.

29 Samar Fatany, "Let Us Codify Shariah Laws," *Arab News*, January 30, 2008, at http://www.Sa'udi-us-relations.org/articles/2008/ioi/080130-fatany-laws.html.
30 Such requirements were certainly novel and seldom applied in the past, when the major concentration was on religious education.
31 Many of these reports were only available in Arabic, and few scholars have consulted them in recent years. Several are available online at http://www.nshrsa.org/articles.php?ID=64.
32 Fatany, January 30, 2008, *op. cit.*
33 While it is beyond the scope of this study to address in any detail, competing scholarly interpretations of *Shari'ah* law dominated the Muslim world for centuries, which was confusing rather than elucidating. For example, during the Arab Cold War between 1957 and 1967, religious outreach work to exhort people to embrace Islam [*da'wah*] attained greater recognition in Sa'udi Arabia after several leaders realized the possibility of broadening their political and cultural influence by "promulgating the word of God, promoting the message of Islam and bringing the Moslems back to the orbit of Islam." Consequently, Sa'udi Arabia established the Imam Muhammad bin Sa'ud Islamic University in Medina in 1961, for the education and training of *da'wah* workers. In 1962 the Muslim World League (*Rabitat al-'Alam al-Islami*) was founded to organize various transnational *da'wah* activities. While it succeeded in bringing together various reformist *da'wah* groups in India, Pakistan, Morocco, and Sa'udi Arabia itself, results were mixed. In 1970, the institution extended its activities within the nascent Organization of the Islamic Cooperation, which proved to be an effective body on all five continents. In the early 1970s, when Islamic politics became a major expression of political and cultural struggle, the *da'wah* of the transnational organizations gained greater attention from Muslim believers. By December 1972, Riyadh organized an International Youth Conference for Islamic Da'wah, which became the foundation stone of the new Sa'udi-sponsored World Assembly of Muslim Youth (*al-Nadwah al-'Islamiyyah lil-Shabab al-Islami*). Regrettably, in May 1972, the Libyan Government inaugurated a new transnational *da'wah* organization, the Islamic Call Society (*Jami'yyat al-Da'wah al-Islamiyyah*), which hardly exercised any influence, since its *raison d'être* was to act as a competitor to the Sa'udi-based Muslim World League and a mouthpiece for Mu'ammar al-Qaddafi's "Third Theory." Another interesting case is that of the Al-Azhar University in Cairo, whose degrees are prized throughout Sunni Islam, though its monopoly on authoritative pronouncements is increasingly challenged. Sa'udi Arabia invested heavily in, and continues to perceive, the education of religious students as a top priority. Professors and preachers on missions abroad with degrees from the Imam Muhammad bin Sa'ud Islamic University in Madinah are in high demand. They have helped establish and improve Islamic schools and communal institutions everywhere, although these outreach efforts have also drawn sharp criticisms from Western powers that deem such activities unhelpful to promoting tolerance for other faiths.
34 This insight was confirmed by HRH Prince Bandar al-Faysal, a retired Air Force officer with a keen interest in his country's internal affairs. Interview in Riyadh on October 15, 2010.
35 Joseph A. Kéchichian, *Power and Succession in Arab Monarchies*, Boulder, Colorado: Lynne Rienner Publishers, 2008, pp. 240–43 [Hereafter Kéchichian-Power and Succession].
36 Yousuf Al-Qablan, "Al-Hiwar al-Watani wal-Taghyir" [National Dialogue and Change], *Al-Riyadh*, December 9, 2007, p. 1.
37 Preparations for the ninth national dialogue, to be held in Hail, were under way in late-2011 with an anticipated convention in Spring 2012. Its announced theme was "The Media and Society: Reality and Paths to Development—Dialogue between Society and Media Organizations."

38 Salah Nasrawi, "Islamists Make Strong Showing in Saudi Election," *Independent*, April 24, 2005, at http://www.independent.co.uk/news/world/middle-east/islamists-make-strong-showing-in-saudi-election-503559.html; see also Brian Whitaker, "Clerics' Choices Clean Up in Saudi Election," *Guardian*, April 25, 2005, at http://www.guardian.co.uk/world/2005/apr/25/saudiarabia.brianwhitaker.
39 Neil MacFarquhar, "Saudi Reformers: Seeking Rights, Paying a Price," *The New York Times*, June 9, 2005, pp. A1, A8; see also *idem*, "Some Saudi Candidates Claim Election Violations," *The New York Times*, February 14, 2005, p. A6; and M. Ghazanfar Ali Khan, "Government Intensifies Efforts to Constitute Municipal Councils," *Arab News*, August 11, 2005, p. 1.
40 Joseph A. Kéchichian, "Democratization in Gulf Monarchies: A New Challenge to the GCC," *Middle East Policy* 11:4, Winter 2004, pp. 37–57 especially, 46–49.
41 Kéchichian-Power and Succession, *op. cit.*, pp. 245–59 463–69.
42 According to a high-ranking official who attended this meeting, it was both rare and electric, especially when so many of the younger princes were in attendance.
43 P. K. Abdul Ghafour, "Mishaal Named Allegiance Commission Chairman," *Arab News*, December 11, 2007, p. 1.
44 *Ibid.*
45 Nathan J. Citino, *From Arab Nationalism to OPEC: Eisenhower, King Sa'ud, and the Making of U.S.–Sa'udi Relations*, Bloomington and Indianapolis, IN: Indiana University Press, 2002, p. 162.
46 Rachel Bronson, *Thicker than Oil: America's Uneasy Partnership with Saudi Arabia*, New York: Oxford University Press, 2006, pp. 168–77 183–88; see also Robert Vitalis, *America's Kingdom: Mythmaking on the Saudi Oil Frontier*, Stanford, California: Stanford University Press, 2007.
47 J. E. Peterson, *Sa'udi Arabia and the Illusion of Security*, London, UK: Oxford University Press (for the International Institute for Strategic Studies, 2002 [Adelphi Paper 348]).
48 Anthony H. Cordesman, *Sa'udi Arabia Enters the Twenty-First Century: The Political, Foreign Policy, Economic, and Energy Dimensions*, Westport, CT and London, UK: Praeger (published in cooperation with the Center for Strategic and International Studies, Washington, DC), 2003, pp. 116–22.
49 Cordesman's numerous publications over the years, which quantified in countless charts, figures, and tables the many permutations he detected in Sa'udi affairs, have provided invaluable assistance to researchers.
50 Anthony Cave Brown, *Oil, God, and Gold: The Story of Aramco and the Saudi Kings*, Boston and New York: Houghton Mifflin Company, 1999.
51 Nawaf E. Obaid, *The Oil Kingdom at 100: Petroleum Policymaking in Saudi Arabia*, Policy Papers No. 55, Washington, D.C.: The Washington Institute for Near East Policy, 2000.
52 See the many essays, written predominantly by Sa'udis, in Joshua Craze and Mark Huband, eds., *The Kingdom: Saudi Arabia and the Challenge of the 21st Century*, New York: Columbia University Press, 2009.
53 Roger Hardy, "Whatever happened to Sa'udi reform?," *BBC News*, June 6, 2008, at http://news.bbc.co.uk/go/pr/fr/-/2/hi/middle_east/7230083.stm.
54 The following are a sample of the post 9/11 books on the kingdom that took the Al Sa'ud to task. There are, of course, many recent additions that focus on 9/11 and terrorism – a corpus of prose that is both bewildering and selectively entertaining, even if devoid of hard facts. The books listed here do not fall under this category as they are written by individuals familiar with the kingdom, even if few can muster anything positive to say about the country or the ruling family. See, Stephen Schwartz, *The Two Faces of Islam: The House of Sa'ud from Tradition to Terror*, New York: Doubleday, 2002; Dore Gold, *Hatred's Kingdom: How Saudi Arabia Supports the New Global Terrorism*, Washington, DC: Regnery Publishing, Inc.,

2003; As'ad AbuKhalil, *The Battle for Saudi Arabia: Royalty, Fundamentalism, and Global Power*, New York: Seven Stories Press, 2004; Craig Unger, *House of Bush, House of Saud: The Secret Relationship Between the World's Two Most Powerful Dynasties*, New York: Scribner, 2004; Mark Hollingsworth, *Saudi Babylon: Torture, Corruption and Cover-Up Inside the House of Saud*, Edinburgh, U.K.: Mainstream Publishing, 2005; Laurent Murawiec, *Princes of Darkness: The Saudi Assault on the West*, Lanham, Maryland: Rowman & Littlefield Publishers, 2005; Gerald Posner, *Secrets of the Kingdom: The Inside Story of the Saudi–U.S. Connection*, New York: Random House, 2005; Kristin Decker, *The Unveiling: An American Teacher in a Saudi Palace*, College Station, Texas: Virtualbookworm. com Publishing, 2006; John R. Bradley, *Saudi Arabia Exposed: Inside a Kingdom in Crisis*, New York: Palgrave Macmillan, 2006; David B. Ottaway, *The King's Messenger: Prince Bandar bin Sultan and America's Tangled Relationship With Saudi Arabia*, New York: Walker & Company, 2008; Yaroslav Trofimov, *The Siege of Mecca: The 1979 Uprising at Islam's Holiest Shrine*, New York: Anchor, 2008; and Sami Alrabaa, *Veiled Atrocities: True Stories of Oppression in Saudi Arabia*, Amherst, New York: Prometheus Books, 2010.
55 For serious treatments of the subject, see Paul Aarts and Gerd Nonneman, *Saudi Arabia in the Balance: Political Economic, Society, Foreign Affairs*, London: Hurst and Company, 2005; Tim Niblock, *Saudi Arabia: Power, Legitimacy and Survival*, London and New York: Routledge, 2006; and Madawi Al-Rasheed, *Contesting the Saudi State: Islamic Voices from a New Generation*, Cambridge, U.K.: Cambridge University Press, 2007.
56 For the perspectives of a prominent academic, see Bernard Lewis, *What Went Wrong?: Western Impact and Middle Eastern Response*, New York: Oxford University Press, 2002; see also Bernard Lewis, *The Crisis of Islam: Holy War and Unholy Terror*, New York: Random House, 2004; for other treatments in the genre, see John R. Bradley, *Saudi Arabia Exposed: Inside a Kingdom in Crisis*, New York: Palgrave Macmillan, 2005; and Mark Hollingsworth with Sandy Mitchell, *Saudi Babylon: Torture, Corruption and Cover-Up Inside the House of Saud*, Edinburgh and London: Mainstream Publishing, 2005.
57 An important exception to this trend must be noted here. Mansoor Jassem Alshamsi has composed a critical new study that provides rare insights into Sunni Fiqh (jurisprudence), intellectual interactions in the kingdom, political struggles since 1979, and various other significant initiatives. Originally scheduled for publication in 2008, it finally became available in the Fall of 2010 when the bulk of this book was already drafted. Still, I benefited from this valuable addition to the literature. See, Mansoor Jassem Alshamsi, *Islam and Political Reform in Sa'udi Arabia: The Quest for Political Change and Reform*, London: Routledge, 2010. A forthcoming title might also shed light on the Sa'udi judiciary when Ibrahim Ibn Abdul Aziz Al-Bishr's small volume is finally released. See Ibrahim Ibn Abdul Aziz Al-Bishr, *Judicial Systems and Safeguards of Human Rights in the Kingdom of Saudi Arabia*, Reading, UK: Garnet Publishing, January 2013.
58 A partial list of interviewees is available in Appendix 1.

1 Reforms within the judiciary

1 Ziad A. Al-Sudairy, "The Constitutional Appeal of Shari'a in a Modernizing Saudi State," *Middle East Law and Governance* 2:1 (2010), pp. 1–16.
2 For a discussion of the alliance, as well the epochal changes that occurred in the early 1990s, see Abdullah F. Ansary, "Succession Process in Saudi Arabia: A Brief Overview of the Historical, Religious, Legal and Royal Family Traditions," *World Law Bulletin* (Library of Congress), Volume 7, July 2005, pp. 31–37; see also

Joseph A. Kéchichian, *Succession in Saudi Arabia*, New York: Palgrave, 2001, pp. 23–89 [hereafter Kéchichian-Succession]; Joseph Kostiner, *The Making of Saudi Arabia 1916–1936: From Chieftancy to Monarchical State*, New York and Oxford: Oxford University Press, 1993; Madawi Al Rasheed, *A History of Saudi Arabia*, 2nd edition, Cambridge: Cambridge University Press, 2010; Gary Samuel Samore, *Royal Family Politics in Saudi Arabia (1953 – 1982)*, doctoral dissertation, Cambridge, Massachusetts: Harvard University, 1983; Alexei Vassiliev, *The History of Saudi Arabia*, London: Saqi Books, 1998. This section also draws on Abdullah F. Ansary, "A Brief Overview of the Saudi Arabian Legal System," July 2008, published online at the Hauser Global Law School Program, http://www.nyulawglobal.org/globalex/saudi_arabia.htm.
3 Kéchichian-Succession, *Ibid.*, pp. 25–26, 72, 202–7; see also Joseph A. Kéchichian, *Power and Succession in Arab Monarchies: A Reference Guide*, Boulder and London: Lynne Rienner Publishers, 2008, pp. 225–77 [hereafter Kéchichian-Power]; see also Mahmoud al-Khalidi, *Ma'alim al-Khilafah fil-Fikr al-Siyasi al-Islami* [Features of Succession in Islamic Political Thought], Beirut: Dar al-Jil, 1984, pp. 87, 293–311; and Stig Stenslie, *Regime Stability in Saudi Arabia: The Challenge of Succession*, London: Routledge, 2011.
4 Abdullah F. Ansary, *op. cit.*, at http://www.nyulawglobal.org/globalex/saudi_arabia.htm.
5 Shmuel Bachar, Shmuel Bar, Rachel Machtiger, and Yair Minzili, *Establishment Ulama and Radicalism in Egypt, Saudi Arabia, and Jordan*, Washington, D.C.: Hudson Institute [Center on Islam, Democracy, and the Future of the Muslim World], Research Monographs on the Muslim World, Series No. 1, Paper No. 4, December 2006, p. 12.
6 *Ibid.*, pp. 12–13.
7 John Wensick, "Khadim" in Martijn Theodoor Houtsma, ed., *E.J. Brill's First Encyclopedia of Islam, 1913–1936*, Volume 4, Leiden, The Netherlands: E. J. Brill, 1993, p. 861.
8 Joseph A. Kéchichian, *Faysal: Saudi Arabia's King for All Seasons*, Gainesville: University Press of Florida, 2008, p. 27.
9 Joseph A. Kéchichian, "The Role of the Ulama in the Politics of an Islamic State: The Case of Saudi Arabia," *International Journal of Middle East Studies* 18:1, February 1986, pp. 53–71. See also *Idem.*, "Islamic Revivalism and Change in Saudi Arabia: Juhayman Al-Utaybi's 'Letters' to the Saudi People," *The Muslim World* 70:1, January 1990, pp. 1–16; Thomas Hegghammer and Stephane Lacroix, "Rejectionist Islamism in Saudi Arabia: The Story of Juhayman al-'Utaybi Revisited," *International Journal of Middle East Studies* 39:1 February 2007, pp. 103–22, and Yaroslav Trofimov, *The Siege of Mecca: The Forgotten Uprising in Islam's Holiest Shrine and the Birth of Al Qaeda*, New York: Doubleday; London: Penguin Books, 2007.
10 "Ulamah Council Supports Actions of King Fahd," *Foreign Broadcast Information Service-Middle East* [FBIS-MEA], 90–157, August 14, 1990, p. 26.
11 Toby Craig Jones, "The Clerics, the Sahwa and the Saudi State," *Strategic Insights* 4:3, March 2005, at http://www.ccc.nps.navy.mil/si/2005/Mar/jonesMar05.pdf.
12 The Basic Law of Government, Royal Decree A/90, 27/8/1412, *Umma Al-Qura*, Number 3397, March 6, 1992, reproduced in Kéchichian-Succession, *op. cit.*, pp. 209–18; see also Joseph Kostiner, "State, Islam and Opposition in Saudi Arabia: The Post Desert-Storm Phase," *MERIA: Middle East Review of International Affairs* 1:2, July 1997, at http://meria.idc.ac.il/JOURNAL/1997/issue2/jv1n2a8.html.
13 Larbi Sadiki, "Saudi Arabia: Re-reading Politics and Religion in the Wake of September 11," in *Islam and Political Legitimacy*, ed. Shahram Akbarzadeh and Abdullah Saeed, London: Routledge Curzon, 2003, pp. 37,88; see also Joshua Teitelbaum, *Holier than Thou: Saudi Arabia's Islamic Opposition*, Washington, D.C.: Washington Institute for Near East Policy, 2000, Policy Paper Number 52, p. 33.

14 Minbar al-Tawheed wal-Jihad, at http://www.tawhed.ws/r?i=1377&PHPSESSID=7 b78e15030b4c75c0764cb3da41e560.
15 Teitelbaum, *op. cit.*, pp. 37–38.
16 Teitelbaum, *op. cit.*, pp. 38–40.
17 This fatwah was highly criticized by many. For a full analysis, see Riad Najib El-Rayyes, *Riyah al-Shamal: Al Sa'udiyyah wal-Khalij wal-'Arab fi 'Alam al-Tis'inat*, [Northern Wind: Saudi Arabia, the Gulf and the Arabs in the Nineties], London and Beirut: Riad El-Rayyes Books Limited, 1997, pp. 56–59.
18 F. Gregory Gause, III, *Oil Monarchies: Domestic and Security Challenges in the Arab Gulf States*, New York: Council on Foreign Relations Press, 1994, p. 106.
19 The Basic Law of Government, articles 45 and 55, in Kéchichian-Succession, *op. cit.*, pp. 214 and 215.
20 Ayoub M. al-Jarbou, *Judicial Review of Administrative Actions: A Comparative Study between the United States and Saudi Arabia*, Charlottesville: University of Virginia [S.J.D. dissertation], 2002, pp. 129–30.
21 Ansary, Succession Process in Saudi Arabia, *op. cit.*, footnote 46; see also The Basic Law of Government, articles 44 and 67–70 in Kéchichian-Succession, *op. cit.*, pp. 214, 216–17; The Shurah Council Law, article 18 in Kéchichian-Succession, *op. cit.*, p. 222.
22 Ibn Qayyim al-Jawziyah, *al-Turuq al-Hukmiyyah fil-Siyasah al-Shari'yyah* [Legal Administration in Divine Law], 13 (1986); see also Frank E. Vogel, *Islamic Law and Legal System: Studies of Saudi Arabia*, Leiden, The Netherlands: E. J. Brill, 2000, pp. 142–43, 370–73; and Muhammad Farouq al-Nabhan, "The Islamic View of the Legislative Role of the State," *Al-'Arabi Magazine* (Kuwait), Number 296, July 1983, translated by Kathryne Lydiatt and published in *Arab Law Quarterly* 1:5, November, 1986, pp. 557–61.
23 Ansary, *op. cit.*, p. 52; see also al-Jarbou, *op. cit.*, pp. 137–38.
24 Al-Sudairy, *op. cit.*, p. 5.
25 For thorough discussions of existing judiciary institutions, see Sa'ud al-Darayb, *Al-Tanzim al-Qada'i fil-Mamlakah al-'Arabiyyah al-Sa'udiyyah fi Da'wah al-Shari'ah al-Islamiyyah wa Nizam al-Sulta al-Qada'iyyah* [The Judiciary in the Kingdom of Sau'di Arabia in Shari'ah and the Rules of its Authorities], Riyadh: King Muhammad bin Sa'ud University Press, 1999; see also Hamid Muhammad Abu Talib, *Al-Nizam al-Qada'i fil-Mamlakah al-'Arabiyyah al-Sa'udiyyah* [The Judiciary in the Kingdom of Sau'di Arabia], Beirut: Dar al-Fikr al-'Arabi, 1984.
26 The Basic Law of Government, Article 45, in Kéchichian-Succession, *op. cit.*, p. 214.
27 Al-Sudairy, *op. cit.*, pp. 9–10.
28 Al-Darayb, *op. cit.*, pp. 45–80.
29 Interview with Abdulaziz H. Al-Fahad, Riyadh, October 25, 2010. This leading attorney shared many of his insights during an extended conversation.
30 For additional insights on the codification dilemmas, see Al-Sudairy, *op. cit.*, pp. 5–11.
31 Teitelbaum, *op. cit.*, pp. 99–113.
32 Fouad Al-Farsy, *Modernity and Tradition: The Saudi Equation*, London: Knight Communications, 1994, pp. 40–44, 63–104.
33 Diligent inquiries on this subject revealed few details. In repeated conversations with clerics and members of the intelligentsia, various figures were advanced, the composites presented here. Al Sa'ud family members who answered my questions on this sensitive topic were hesitant, either because they themselves did not know or, if they did, most considered that information to be truly privileged. Suffice it to say that the figure of 1,000 *'Ulamah* was generally accepted to be accurate, and while there were thousands of mosques throughout Sa'udi Arabia, not all were staffed by imams. Remarkably, while many self-appointed clerics elevated themselves to the level of an *'alim*, in reality the total number of *'Ulamah* is accurately

known to senior members of the clergy as well as the Al Sa'ud. In short, not everyone who claimed to be an *'alim*, was one.

34 Glen Carey, "Saudi King Counters Dissent With $36 Billion as Clerics Scold Protesters," *Bloomberg*, March 11, 2011, http://www.bloomberg.com/news/2011-03-11/saudi-king-counters-protests-with-36-billion-as-tension-mounts.html. See also "Al-Malik 'Abdallah li-'Ulama' al-Muslimin: Antum al-Qaduat, fa-shamiru 'an aydikum" [King 'Abdallah to Muslim *'Ulamah*: You are the Example, So Roll Up Your Sleeves], *Al-Watan* (Sa'udi Arabia), Number 3952, July 26, 2011, p. 8.

35 "Amr Malaki bi 'Ifa' al-Huma'yn wa Ta'yin Al Shaykh Ra'isan li Hay'at al-Amr bil Ma'ruf wal-Nahi 'an al-Munkar" [Royal Order to Excuse al-Huma'yn and the appointment of Al Shaykh Head of the Committee for the Promotion of Virtue and the Prevention of Vice], *Al Hay'at*, January 14, 2012, p. 1, at http://lsa.daralhayat.com/ksaarticle/350183.

36 "King Tells New HAIA Chief to be Lenient with People," *Arab News*, January 20, 2012, p. 1, at http://arabnews.com/saudiarabia/article565532.ece.

37 Thomas Hegghammer, *Jihad in Saudi Arabia: Violence and Pan-Islamism Since 1979*, Cambridge: Cambridge University Press, 2010, pp. 59–69, 130–33.

38 For the June 20, 2004 video, with English subtitles, see "Saudi Arabia's *Jihad* TV," at http://archive.frontpagemag.com/readArticle.aspx?ARTID=12467 [The Middle East Media Research Institute-MEMRI], June 26, 2004. Interestingly, on June 4, 2008, Shaykh Muhammad bin Suleiman Al-Mani'i delivered an equally powerful interview. See "Dr. Muhammad bin Suleiman Al-Mani'i Forbids Killing Jews and Christians on Saudi TV," at http://videos.wittysparks.com/id/3582529 388, MEMRI.org.

39 "Saudi Sheik Saleh Al-Sidlan: The Terrorists Distorted the Religion of Islam," June 23, 2004, at http://memritv.org/Search.asp?ACT=S9&p1=131.

40 "In Response to a Fatwah calling for the Islamisation of Games ... Judicial Advisor Condemns Saudi Prohibition of Football or Change their Laws," *Al-Watan*, June 16, 2005, at http://www.alwatanvoice.com/arabic/news/2005/08/26/27225.html.

41 Hegghammer, *op. cit.*, pp. 99–129.

42 Alshamsi, op. cit., pp. 65–77; see also Mahmud al-Rifa'i, *Al-Mashru' al-Islahi fil-Sa'udiyyah: Qisatul-Hawali wal-Awdah* [The Reformist Project in Sa'udi Arabia: The Story of al-Hawali and Al-Awdah], Washington, D.C.: n.p. 1995.

43 Alshamsi, *op. cit.*, pp. 1–16; see also Mamoun Fandy, *Saudi Arabia and the Politics of Dissent*, New York: St. Martin's Press, 1999.

44 For a detailed discussion of this period and the roles leading actors played, see Madawi Al-Rasheed, *Contesting the Saudi State: Islamic Voices from a New Generation*, Cambridge: Cambridge University Press, 2007.

45 Al-Rasheed, *Ibid.*, pp. 223–30, 237–40; see also Alshamsi, *op. cit.*, pp. 42–44, who provides a detailed list of the ten principles espoused by Shaykh al-Hamid.

46 Stéphane Lacroix, "Between Islamist and Liberals: Saudi Arabia's New 'Islamo-Liberal' Reformists," *The Middle East Journal* 58: 3, Summer 2004, pp. 345–65.

47 Al-Rasheed, *op. cit.*, pp. 134–74.

48 Hegghammer, *op. cit.*, pp. 186–226.

49 Dore Gold, *Hatred's Kingdom: How Saudi Arabia Supports the New Global Terrorism*, Washington, DC: Regnery Publishing, Inc., 2003. See also Stephen Schwartz, *The Two Faces of Islam: The House of Sa'ud from Tradition to Terror*, New York: Doubleday, 2002.

50 Eleanor Abdella Doumato, "Manning the Barricades: Islam According to Sa'udi Arabia's School Texts," *The Middle East Journal* 57:2, Spring 2003, pp. 230–47.

51 This is a hugely controversial issue, though a solid analysis of Muhammad 'Abdul Wahhab and his relevance to today affirms the merits of his teachings. See Natana J. Delong-Bas, *Wahhabi Islam: From Revival and Reform to Global Jihad*, New York: Oxford University Press, 2004

52 Gold, *op. cit.*, pp. 225–28.
53 Antoine Basbous, *L'Arabie Saoudite En Question: Du wahhabisme à Bin Laden, aux origines de la tourmente*, Paris: Perrin, 2002; and Stéphane Marchand, *Arabie Saoudite: La Menace*, Paris: Fayard, 2003.
54 Gold, *op. cit.*, p. 182.
55 Most of these texts are only available in Arabic, although a few were recently translated into English. For an overview, see, Oussama Arabi, *Studies in Modern Islamic Law and Jurisprudence*, Leiden, The Netherlands: Brill Academic Publishers, Inc., 2001. See also Imam Abul Husayn Ahmad Ibn Muhammad Ibn Ahmad Ibn Ja'far Ibn Hamdan al Baghdadi, *The Mukhtasar Al-Quduri: A Manual of Islamic Law According to the Hanafi School*, translated by Tahir Mahmood Kiani, London: Taha Publishers, 2010; Muhammad Al Kharshi Al Maliki, *Hashiyah 'ala Mukhtasar Khalil* [Commentary on Khalil's Mukhtasar], 8 volumes, 1997; and Musa Furber, *Ghayat Al-Taqrib* by Abu-Shujah available at http://www.shafiifiqh.com/?p=172.
56 Aaidh al-Qarni, "Our Religious Education: A Critical Look," *Asharq Al-Awsat*, February 2, 2008, at http://www.asharq-e.com/news.asp?section=2&id=11653.
57 *Ibid.*
58 *Ibid.*
59 For a good exposure to this critical subject, see Noel J. Coulson, *Conflicts and Tensions in Islamic Jurisprudence*, Chicago: University of Chicago Press, 1969.
60 It must be emphasized that 'Abdallah seldom spoke of these subjects in public, although several high-ranking officials confirmed that he hinted at the topics in his contemporaneous allocutions in his *majlises*.
61 Al-Qarni, *op. cit.*, at http://www.asharq-e.com/news.asp?section=2&id=11653.
62 Samar Fatany, "Let Us Codify Shariah Laws," *Arab News*, January 31, 2008, at http://archive.arabnews.com/?page=7&section=0&article=106293&d=31&m=1&y=2008.
63 *Ibid.*
64 *Ibid.*
65 It is important to note that the absence of a single source of authority in the Muslim world prevented such uniform codification. Al-Azhar in Cairo was, for all practical purposes, the seat of Sunni Islam for centuries, even if recent changes meant that competing sources emerged. The Royal Aal al-Bayt Institute for Islamic Thought, which was an independent non-governmental institute headquartered in Amman, Jordan, whose ultimate purpose was to serve Islam and humanity at large, was one such pole of authority. Sa'udi sources were equally valid interlocutors for leadership positions, while Iran and Iraq competed for authority within the *Shi'ah* world.
66 Quoted in Fatany, *op. cit.*, at http://archive.arabnews.com/?page=7&section=0&article=106293&d=31&m=1&y=2008.
67 Angel M. Rabasa, et al., *The Muslim World after 9/11*, MG-246, Santa Monica, California: RAND [Project AIR FORCE], p. 111, at http://www.rand.org/pubs/monographs/2004/RAND_MG246.pdf.
68 Mordechai Abir, "Saudi Arabia, Stability, and International Islamic Terror," *Jerusalem Letter/Viewpoints*, Number 481, July 1, 2002, Jerusalem Center for Public Affairs, at http://www.jcpa.org/jl/vp481.htm.
69 *Saudi Publications on Hate Ideology Invade American Mosques, Washington: Center for Religious Freedom*, Freedom House, 2005, at www.freedomhouse.org/religion. See also Rabasa, *op. cit.*
70 "Riyadh: Al-Islah al-Tarbawi Yu'amiqu al-Khilaf al-Dakhilih wa Yuthiru Makhawuf Inshiqaqat Wasi'at" [Riyadh: Education Reforms Deepen the Internal Dispute and Raise Fears of Wide Splits], *Majalat al-'Asr*, June 4, 2003, at www.alasr.ws/index.cfm?method=home.con& contentID=4123.

71 Samar Fatany, "Let Us Codify Shariah Laws," *Arab News*, January 31, 2008, at http://archive.arabnews.com/?page=7&section=0&article=106293&d=31&m=1&y=2008.
72 *The First Report on Human Rights Conditions in the Kingdom of Saudi Arabia*, Riyadh: The National Society for Human Rights, 1427H/2006G, at http://nshr.org.sa/english/aRightMenuCMS.aspx?mid=30.
73 Fahd al-Dughaythar, "Limaza Nahtaj ila Tanzim 'amal Hay'at al-Amr bil Ma'ruf?" [Why We Need to Reorganize the Committee for the Promotion of Virtue and the Prevention of Vice], *Al-Watan* [Sa'udi Arabia], Number 4126, January 16, 2012, p. 21.
74 Raouf Ebeid, "The King Was not Amused," *Political Islam Online*, March 29, 2010, at http://www.politicalislam.org/index_categoryfilter.php?CategoryName=Women%20issues&CategoryID=43. See also *Reuters*, "Saudi Cleric Backs Gender Segregation with Fatwa," February 24, 2010, at *Al Arabiya News*, http://www.alarabiya.net/articles/2010/02/24/101355.html. For a copy of the fatwah in Arabic, dated 03/08/1431H, is available at http://albarrak.islamlight.net/index.php?option=content&task=view&id=17426. The reaction of the ruler was confirmed by a high-ranking female member of the ruling family, on condition of anonymity, but which was verified by additional sources as discussed above.
75 Ian Black, "Saudi King's Photo Brings Women's Rights Into Focus," *Guardian*, May 6, 2010, at http://www.guardian.co.uk/world/2010/may/06/saudi-king-abdullah-women-photo.
76 Maureen Dowd, "Loosey Goosey Saudi," *The New York Times*, March 3, 2010, p. A31, at http://www.nytimes.com/2010/03/03/opinion/03dowd.html.
77 KAUST is discussed below and at http://www.kaust.edu.sa/.
78 Black, *op. cit.*, at http://www.guardian.co.uk/world/2010/may/06/saudi-king-abdullah-women-photo.
79 This reaction was confirmed by a young female member of the ruling family (in her early thirties), on condition of anonymity, but which was verified by additional sources as discussed above.
80 Ebeid., *op. cit.*, at http://www.politicalislam.org/index_categoryfilter.php?CategoryName=Women%20issues&CategoryID=43.
81 Siraj Wahad, "A Picture Worth More than a Thousand Words," *Arab News*, May 3, 2010, at http://arabnews.com/saudiarabia/article49472.ece.
82 Black, *op. cit*, at http://www.guardian.co.uk/world/2010/may/06/saudi-king-abdullah-women-photo. Importantly, the photograph was prominently published – often occupying half of the page – in leading pan-Arab newspapers on May 2 and 3, 2010, and shown on most satellite television programs. For an essay on the coverage, see Siraj Wahad, "A Picture Worth More than a Thousand Words," *Arab News*, May 3, 2010, at http://arabnews.com/saudiarabia/article49472.ece.
83 *Ibid*.
84 "Urahibu bil-Ikhtilat al-Abiad wa Niqabi la Yamna' al-liqa' al-Qasa'id: Sha'irat Sa'udiyyah tatasadah li-fatwah al-Barrak 'ala Masrah "Sha'ir al-Maliun" [I Welcome Transparent Mixing and my Head Cover does not Prevent My Poetry: Sa'udi Poet Identifies Barrak's Advisory Opinion on the Stage of "Millionaire Poet"], *Isharah: Shabakah Ikhbariyyah Thaqafiyyah*, March 8, 2010, at http://www.esharh.net/index.php?act=artc&id=3221, which includes a complete version of the poem in Arabic that propelled her to fame.
85 *Ibid*.
86 Ebeid, *op. cit.*, p. 2.
87 "Al-Islamiyyun wal-Libiralliyyah fil-Sa'udiyyah" [Islamists and Liberalism in Sa'udi Arabia], *Al-Jazeera*, March 18, 2010, at http://www.aljazeera.net/NR/exeres/59F96660-CFF9-4211-9242-C8C52CB5E3DB.htm.
88 Tariq Ramadan, *In the Footsteps of the Prophet: Lessons from the Life of Muhammad*, New York: Oxford University Press, 2009. See also Shamima Sheikh,

"Denying Women Access to the Mosque: A Betrayal of the Prophet," 1995, at http://www.ilaam.net/Articles/DenyingAccess.html and "Does Islam Discourage Women from Attending the Masjid?," at http://www.tamilislam.com/english/human_rights/Islamdiscouragewomen.htm.

89 Qays al-Mubarak, a respected Professor of Islamic Jurisprudence at King Faysal University in Riyadh, earned a reputation for highly original analytical studies that focused on social problems confronting the Muslim world. 'Abdul Rahman al-Zunaydih was a Professor of Islamic Law at Al Imam Muhammad bin Sa'ud Islamic University in Riyadh. Both men served on the Board of Senior *'Ulamah*.

90 The 20-page long "What We're Fighting For: A Letter from America," which was a response drafted after 9/11 and the War for Afghanistan, first circulated in late 2001 but was dated February 2002. It was available at http://www.americanvalues.org/html/what_we_re_fighting_for.html. "How We Can Coexist," the Muslim response, was dated January 1, 2002, and first appeared on www.islamtoday.net at http://en.islamtoday.net/artshow-417-2952.htm. Both were key documents that are analyzed in Chapter 6.

91 See Asma Barlas, *Believing Women in Islam: Unreading Patriarchal Interpretations of the Qur'an*, Austin: University of Texas Press, 2002.

92 Yaser Ba 'Amer, "Council of 'supreme Scholars' Rejects the Appointment of Women," *Islam Online*, March 15, 2008, at http://www.islamonline.net/servlet/Satellite?c=ArticleA_C&cid=1203758052409& pagename = Zone-Arabic-News/NWALayout.

93 See, Sahih al-Bukharih, Volume 5, Book 59, Number 709, at http://mukto-mona.com/women/women_in_islam2.htm.

94 The Sahih al-Bukharih were collected by the Persian Muslim scholar Muhammad Ibn Isma'il al-Bukharih (810–70 AD), while the Jami' al-Tirmidhih were collected by Abu 'Isa Muhammad Ibn 'Isa al-Tirmidhih (824–92 AD); and the Sunan al-Nassa'ih were collected by Ahmed Ibn Shu'ayb Ibn 'Ali Ibn Sinan Abu 'Abdul Rahman al-Nassa'ih (829–915 AD).

95 On the Imamah al-Kubrah, see Muhammad Hasan Qazwini, et al., *Al-Imamah Al-Kubrah Wal-Khilafah Al-'Uzmah*, Tehran, Iran: Dar al-Mujtabah, 2006.

96 Alshamsi, *op. cit.*, pp. 137–52.

97 Al-Rasheed, Contesting the Saudi State, *op. cit.*, pp. 134–74.

98 "Saudi Arabia: Saudi al-Qaida 'chief' May Surrender, *Al Jazeera*, July 22, 2004, at http://aljazeera.co.uk/archive/2004/07/200849161826130350.html.

99 "Saudi Exile Urges Regime Change," *BBC NEWS*, December 15, 2004, at http://news.bbc.co.uk/2/hi/middle_east/4098277.stm.

100 This was a hugely controversial topic and repeated attempts to seek clarification resulted in total objections to the very question. Nevertheless, in dozens of conversations with younger members of the family, one could not but reach the conclusion that frustrations existed, and that many believed the time for reforms was not too distant. Whether such transformations would touch fundamentals was impossible to determine.

101 Juan Cole, *Engaging the Muslim World*, New York: Palgrave Macmillan, 2009, pp. 83–113, especially pp. 90–92.

102 "Shaykh Salih al-Fawzaan on the Khawaarij, the Bombings (in Riyadh) and the Sanctioning of the Hypocrites," at www.Salafipublications.com/sps/downloads/pdf/CAF020017.pdf.

103 Lafif Lakhdar, "Is There A Response to a Fatwah Inciting to Crime?," *Al-Hayat*, with excerpts translated in "The Role of Fatwas in Incitement to Terrorism," *MEMRI Special Dispatch*, Number 333, January 18, 2002, at http://memri.org/bin/articles.cgi?Page=archives& Area = sd& id = SP33302.

104 Yoni Fighel and Moshe Marzouk, "Saudi Cleric Issues Fatwah on the Use of Weapons of Mass Destruction," IDC Herzliya–International Institute for

Counter-Terrorism, July 5, 2003, at http://www.ict.org.il/Articles/tabid/66/Articlsid/580/currentpage/21/Default.aspx.
105 The November 6, 2004 open letter was posted on the Internet and stressed that armed attacks launched by Iraqi groups on US troops and their allies in Iraq were legitimate resistance. Signatories issued an additional fatwah that prohibited Iraqis from offering any support for military operations carried out by US forces against anti-US fighting strongholds. For additional details, see "Majmu'at min al-'Ulamah al-Sa'udiyyun Yuwajjihunah Khitaban Maftuhan li-Sha'b al-'Iraqi" [Group of Saudi Scholars Direct Open Letter to the Iraqi People], November 5, 2004, as cited in Toby Craig Jones, "The Clerics, the Sahwa and the Saudi State," *Strategic Insights* 4:3, March 2005 [Center for Contemporary Conflict, Naval Postgraduate School, Monterey, California], at http://www.nps.edu/Academics/centers/ccc/publications/OnlineJournal/2005/Mar/jonesMar05.html.
106 Gregory Gause, "Be Careful What You Wish For: The Future of U.S.–Saudi Relations," *World Policy Journal* 19:1, Spring 2002, pp. 37–50.
107 For a reportage on statements issued by leading Muslim Shaykhs, including Shaykh 'Abdul 'Aziz Al al-Shaykh, the Grand Mufti of Sa'udi Arabia and Chairman of the Senior *'Ulamah* (September 15, 2001), see "Statements from Leading Muslim Leaders, Condemning the Terrorist Attacks of September 11th," at http://groups.colgate.edu/aarislam/response.htm.
108 The Kingdom of Saudi Arabia, *Public Statements by Senior Officials and Religious Scholars Condemning Extremism and Promoting Moderation*, Washington, DC: Royal Embassy of Saudi Arabia, November 2008, p. 15, at www.saudiembassy.net.
109 "In Comprehensive Interviews on the Current Issues: Prince Naif Ibn Abdul Aziz: The Constitution of the Kingdom of Saudi Arabia is Based on the Rules of the Islamic Faith and Rumours Around the Leadership Are Far From the Truth. The Kingdom is Not Affected by the Campaign Lead Against It. Islam is a Religion of Peace, Love, Tolerance and Friendly Relations with the Worlds' Nations and a Religion of Security and Stability Inside the Country," *Ayn Al Yaqeen*, November 29, 2002 at http://www.ainalyaqeen.com/issues/20021129/feat6en.htm
110 "Bomber Struck as Prince Spoke by Phone," *A1Saudiarabia.com*, at http://www.a1saudiarabia.com/Bomber-struck-as-Prince-spoke-by-phone/
111 "Saudi Arabia: Transcript of Call from Bomber to Prince Reveals Tangled History," *The Los Angeles Times*, September 2, 2009, at http://latimesblogs.latimes.com/babylonbeyond/2009/09/saudi-arabia-phone-call-from-suicide-bomber-to-prince-reveals-tangled-history.html.
112 Christopher Boucek, "Clearing a Path for Guantanamo Returnees: Rehabilitation and Risk-Assessment," Carnegie Endowment for International Peace, January 28, 2009, at http://www.carnegieendowment.org/2009/01/28/clearing-path-for-guantanamo-returnees-rehabilitation-and-risk-assessment/34l. See also Tawfik Hamid, "Saudi Rehabilitation Program for Terrorists Needs Re-evaluation," *Islam Daily: Observing Media*, August 30, 2009, at http://www.islamdaily.org/en/saudi-arabia/7725.saudi-rehabilitation-program-for-terrorists-needs-.htm/.
113 As quoted in Bachar, *op. cit.*, p. 21.
114 Abeed al Suhaimy, "Munasaha Program: An essential Tool in Saudi Arabia's War on Terror," *Asharq Al-Awsat*, July 12, 2009, at http://www.asharq-e.com/news.asp?section=1&id=17397.
115 *Ibid.*
116 "Amnesty: Saudi terror Law 'Would Strangle Protest'," *BBC Middle East*, July 22, 2011, at http://www.bbc.co.uk/news/world-middle-east-14239259 [with an embedded link for the Arabic text of the draft law].
117 Reuters, "Saudi Says Draft Anti-Terrorism Law Being Amended," August 6, 2011, at http://www.nytimes.com/reuters/2011/08/06/world/middleeast/international-us-saudi-terror.html.

118 *Ibid.*
119 The ruling that sparked international concern involved judge Shaykh Sa'ud al-Yusuf, who ordered a man to be paralyzed in retribution for injuries he allegedly caused with a meat cleaver during a fight two years before the verdict. Applying the principle of "an eye for an eye, a tooth for a tooth," the judge ruled that the man should be injured at the same place on his spinal cord to cause identical crippling damage to what he inflicted on his victim, 22-year-old 'Abdul 'Aziz al-Mitayry. Earlier, al-Mitayry had petitioned the court in Tabuk to replace its sentencing of his attacker to seven months in prison with an equivalent punishment, in accordance with the Muslim principle of *qisas*, or retribution. Two Sa'udi hospitals, including Riyadh's prestigious King Faysal Specialist Hospital and Research Center, rejected the judge's request that they implement his ruling. In a statement condemning the ruling, Amnesty International said another hospital advised the judge that it was medically possible to inflict on the perpetrator an injury identical to the one that he caused. "Under international human rights law, the use of this sentence would constitute a violation of the absolute prohibition of torture and other cruel, inhuman or degrading treatment or punishment," the Amnesty statement read, suggesting that the court instead imprison, fine, or flog the condemned man. In response, the monarch met with al-Yusuf to persuade him to change his ruling. Naturally, an embarrassed judge denied that he had seriously considered ordering the mutilation, although the damage was done. *Al-Riyadh* newspaper quoted the judge saying: "the proceedings in this case are still pending and no verdict had been issued in that regard." Regardless of his declaration, the cleric/judge opined in court that he had queried hospitals and other authorities about surgical paralysis, precisely to convince the plaintiff that it would be impossible to carry out such a medical procedure. "The plaintiff was demanding punishment of the attacker, and the judicial ruling in this case only includes the plaintiff's eligibility for blood money," al-Yusuf concluded. See Amnesty International, "Saudi Arabia Urged not to Deliberately Paralyse Man as Retribution Punishment," August 20, 2010, at http://www.amnesty.org/en/news-and-updates/saudi-arabia-urged-not-deliberately-paralyse-man-retribution-punishment-2010-08-20.
120 Labelled "the hot and curious issue of gender mixing," authorities pulled the plug on the daily radio program of Shaykh 'Abdul Muhsin al-Ubaykan, a cleric and royal court adviser, who earned notoriety by decreeing that women could give men breast milk to avoid illicit gender mixing. "The man should take the milk, but not directly from the breast of the woman," al-Ubaykan was quoted in this bizarre rendering. "He should drink it," he continued, "and then become a relative of the family, a fact that allows him to come in contact with the women without breaking Islam's rules about mixing." Since Muslim traditions stipulated that breastfeeding established a degree of maternal bond, even if a woman breast-fed a child who was not hers, the clever switch was taken seriously by idle minds. King 'Abdallah was not amused. See Habib Toumi, "Saudi Scholar's Fatwa Wades Into Controversy (Men Should Drink Breast Milk Before Contact w/ Women)," *Gulf News*, May 22, 2010, at http://www.habibtoumi.com/2010/05/22/saudi-scholar-wades-into-controversy-following-adult-breastfeeing-fatwa/.
121 In this incident, the kingdom's most senior religious scholar, Grand Mufti Shaykh 'Abdul 'Aziz Al al-Shaykh, ordered a preacher to be silent after he issued a fatwah calling for a boycott of the Panda supermarket chain, because the stores employed women as cashiers. The fatwah forced the chain, owned by Prince Al-Walid bin Talal bin 'Abdul 'Aziz Al Sa'ud, to reassign 11 of its 16 female cashiers who were part of a pilot project to employ unemployed Sa'udi women. Because of the kingdom's segregation laws, women were prevented from working in gender mixed environments, and the preacher, Shaykh Yusuf Ahmad (known for his strident opposition

Notes 301

to gender mixing), was anxious to issue his opinion on the matter. Earlier, the cleric suggested that only Muslim maids could work in Sa'udi homes, which created a set of unimaginable problems for the conservative society. He also called for the Grand Mosque in Makkah, Islam's holiest site and the world's largest mosque, to be demolished and rebuilt to ensure segregation between the sexes at the shrine. See James M. Dorsey, "Judicial Reform in Saudi Arabia: A Battle of the Fatwas," *Qantara.de*, December 8, 2010, at http://en.qantara.de/A-Battle-of-the-Fatwas/8414c8483i1p471/.

122 'Azam Shuwayr, a ministry official, warned clerics they would face punishment if they didn't trim their speeches, including the potential forced training or, an even worse, punishment, to have their paychecks docked. Shuwayr declared that clergymen needed to keep in mind that elderly or sick worshipers may not be able to sit and listen to hour-long speeches filled with their words of wisdom. A debate on the ministerial edict in the *Saudi Gazette* suggested a generational divide among religious scholars, with older clerics displaying contempt for their younger colleagues whom they dismissed as uneducated. "The impact of the sermon is not measured by its length but by the eloquent, concise and precise wording," said Salih Humayd, a ranking cleric. "Imams should refrain from flowery and bombastic language and delve directly into the core of their sermon," he reiterated. Another scholar accused some clergymen of copying and pasting Friday sermons from books or the Internet and reading them aloud without even understanding what they're saying. Yet others suggested that clerics needed to improve their writing skills. "Some of them elaborate on the topic by repeating themselves and going around in circles," Ahmad Mawra'i, a Saudi professor, told the *Gazette*. "In many cases they jump from one topic to another. This is why their sermons are tedious and boring." As quoted in Dorsey, Judicial Reform in Saudi Arabia, *op. cit.*, at http://en.qantara.de/A-Battle-of-the-Fatwas/8414c8483i1p471/.

123 Joseph A. Kéchichian, "Prelude to More Reforms in Saudi Arabia," *Gulf News*, February 18, 2009, p. 10, at http://gulfnews.com/opinions/columnists/prelude-to-more-reforms-in-saudi-arabia-1.52217.

124 "King Tells New Haia Chief to be Lenient with People," *Arab News*, January 20, 2012, at http://arabnews.com/saudiarabia/article565532.ece.

125 *Ibid.*

2 National and international dialogues

1 "Consent to Establish the King 'Abdul 'Aziz Center for National Dialogue," Riyadh: KACND, August 4, 2003; See Appendix 2 for full text.

2 On June 17, 2006, "Al-Riyadh newspaper reported that the King gave a speech in Buraida in which he said that labeling citizens as secular, liberal, hypocrite, or extremist was divisive and contrary to the country's two key principles, Shari'a and national unity." See U.S. Department of State, *2006 Country Reports on Human Rights Practices – Saudi Arabia*, Washington, D.C., March 6, 2007, at http://www.state.gov/g/drl/rls/hrrpt/2006/78862.htm.

3 "Consent to Establish the King 'Abdul 'Aziz Center for National Dialogue," *op. cit.*, [Appendix 2].

4 Caryle Murphy, "Saudi King Set to Lead Rare Interfaith Talks in Spain," *The Christian Science Monitor*, 8, 2008, at http://www.csmonitor.com/2008/0708/p01s03-wome.html.

5 Muhammad 'Ali al-Jawwad Muhammad, *Al-Tatawwur al-Tashri'i fil-Mamlakah al-'Arabiyyah al-Sa'udiyyah* [Legislative Development in the Kingdom of Sa'udi Arabia], Alexandria, Egypt: Munsha'at al-Ma'arif, 1977, pp. 39–42; for the text of the 1926 Constitution, see Helen Miller Davis, *Constitutions, Electoral Laws,*

Treaties of States in the Near and Middle East, Durham: Duke University Press, 1947, pp. 248–58.
6 For a discussion of the first nine meetings of the Majlis al-Shurah, see Fuad Hamzah, Al-Bilad al-'Arabiyyah al-Sa'udiyyah [The Kingdom of Saudi Arabia], 2nd edition, Cairo: Maktabat al-Nasr al-Hadithat, 1968, pp. 98–111.
7 H. St. John Philby, Sa'udi Arabia, London: Ernest Benn Limited, 1955, pp. 8–32.
8 For a history of the Ministries and the growth of their functions, see Ibid., pp. 157–78 (Finance), pp. 113–56 (Foreign Affairs), and pp. 248–60 (Defense). See also Hisham B. Sharabi, Governments and Politics of the Middle East in the Twentieth Century, Princeton: D. Van Nostran Co., Inc., 1962, p. 231.
9 Gaafar 'Abdul Salam 'Ali, Al-Nizam al-Idari al-Sa'udi [The Administrative Law in Sa'udi Arabia], Cairo: Al-Salfiyat, 1977, pp. 24–31.
10 The audit office was headed by a controller-general appointed by the king and was directly responsible to him. His extensive powers included a right to lodge complaints against officials and dignitaries. The office was not filled until June 1957 when Sa'ud trusted it to his uncle Prince Musa'id bin 'Abdul 'Aziz bin 'Abdul Rahman Al Sa'ud [whose son assassinated King Faysal in 1975] who was, simultaneously, head of the Grievances Office. Arguably, since the audit office was supposed to monitor state funds, and since the king was its largest spender, the authority of the audit office was sharply limited so as not to reveal the monarch's extravagant spending habits.
11 Abdulmunim Shakir, "Saudi Arabia," in A. P. Blaustein and G. H. Flanz, eds., Constitutions of the Countries of the World, Dobbs Ferry, March 1976, p. 5.
12 For the text of Royal Decree number 380, dated 22 Shawwal 1377 (May 11, 1958), and translated by H. St. J.B. Philby, see The Middle East Journal 12:3, Summer 1958, pp. 320–3.
13 David Holden and Richard Johns, The House of Saud: The Rise and Rule of the Most Powerful Dynasty in the Arab World, New York: Holt, Rinehart and Winston, 1981, pp. 198–222.
14 Joseph A. Kéchichian, Succession in Saudi Arabia, New York: Palgrave, 2001, pp. 93–6 [Hereafter Kéchichian-Succession].
15 Holden and Johns, op. cit., p. 210.
16 "Document: Transfer of Powers from HM King Sa'ud to HRH Amir Faysal," The Middle East Journal, 18:3, Summer 1964, pp. 351–4. The fatwah issued by the 'Ulamah was signed by 12 leading clerics; in turn, the religious decree was ratified by 68 senior Al Sa'ud family members.
17 Joseph A. Kéchichian, Faysal: Saudi Arabia's King for All Seasons, Gainesville: University Press of Florida, 2008, pp. 76–8, and passim [Hereafter Kéchichian – Faysal].
18 Gerald De Gaury, Faisal: King of Saudi Arabia, New York: Praeger, 1967, pp. 130–40; Faysal's own views on the engineered coup are reproduced from his first interview to the Beirut newspaper Al-Hayat in Idem, pp. 136–8.
19 Holden and Johns, op. cit., pp. 379–83.
20 Steven Rattner, "Saudis Widen Rule After Mosque Raid," The New York Times, February 17, 1980, p. 33; see also, James Dorsey, "After Mecca, Saudi Rulers provide a channel for dissent," The Christian Science Monitor, March 14, 1980, p. 7.
21 Joseph A. Kéchichian, "The Role of the 'Ulama in the Politics of an Islamic State: The Case of Saudi Arabia," International Journal of Middle East Studies 18:1, February 1986, p. 53–71. See also Joseph A. Kéchichian, "Islamic Revivalism and Change in Saudi Arabia: Juhayman Al-Utaybi's 'Letters' to the Saudi People," The Muslim World 70:1, January 1990, pp. 1–16.
22 The reputation of the Sa'udi military establishment diminished somewhat after the Makkah incident. First, the National Guard (headed by 'Abdallah) failed to rapidly put down the takeover, and second, the Army (under the authority of

Fahd) took a long time to defeat the rebels. Both of these military institutions required the assistance of Jordanian and French officers to overcome the 1979 Makkah siege. See Yaroslav Trofimov, *The Siege of Mecca: The Forgotten Uprising in Islam's Holiest Shrine and the Birth of Al Qaeda*, New York: Doubleday; London: Penguin Books, 2007.
23 John M. Goshko, "Saudi King Seen Seeking Wider Base," *The Washington Post*, December 20, 1982, p. A1; see also David B. Ottaway, "Saudi King Seeks Islamic Law Review," *The Washington Post*, June 16, 1983, p. A1; and *Idem*, "New Saudi Monarch Wields Slack Reins," *The Washington Post*, May 31, 1983, p. A1.
24 Peter W. Wilson and Douglas F. Graham, *Saudi Arabia: The Coming Storm*, Armonk, New York: M. E. Sharpe, 1994, pp. 102–6.
25 Graham and Wilson report that staffers at the American embassy in Riyadh told them the recall was likely tied to Horan's meeting with the monarch concerning the Sa'udi purchase of Chinese missiles. "When Horan protested, Fahd reportedly told him that every country had a right to defend itself. Later in the conversation, Fahd asked for American assurances that Israel would not attack its rockets. Horan infuriated the King by then repeating Fahd's own words that every country including Israel had a right to defend itself." See Graham and Wilson, *Ibid.*, pp. 106, 137 (footnote 43).
26 R. Hrair Dekmejian, "Saudi Arabia's Consultative Council," *The Middle East Journal* 52:2, Spring 1998, pp. 204–18.
27 As later developments would confirm, delays in drafting a Basic Law for the kingdom indeed centered on this key question. See the interview with Prince Talal bin 'Abdul 'Aziz in "Change Is Inevitable in Saudi Arabia," *Al-Quds Al-Arabi*, April 16, 1998, reproduced in *Mideast Mirror*, April 17, 1998.
28 Kéchichian – Succession, *op. cit.*, pp. 71–73, 209–42.
29 P. K. Abdul Ghafour, "Shoura Council Strength Increased to 150," *Arab News*, April 12, 2005, p. 1.
30 Joseph A. Kéchichian, "Testing the Saudi 'Will to Power': Challenges Confronting Prince Abdallah," *Middle East Policy* 10:4, Winter 2003, pp. 100–15.
31 "Saudi Arabia: The Limits of Reform," *The Economist*, 370:6368, p. 47.
32 "Foreword," *Prologue – King 'Abdul 'Aziz Center for National Dialogue*, Riyadh: KACND, 2008(?), p. 3.
33 *Ibid.*, p. 15.
34 Yahyah bin Muhammad Zamzami, *Al-Hiwar wa Adabuhu wa Dhawabituhu fi dhaw al-Kitab wal-Sunnah* [Dialogue and its Linguistic Roots in Scriptures and the Sunnah], 2nd ed, Amman, Jordan: Dar al-'Alami, 2002, p. 22.
35 Jamaluddin Muhammad bin Mukaram bin Manzur, *Lisan al-'Arab* [The Arab Tongue], Beirut: Dar Sadir, 1997, volume 2, pp. 182–3. Ibn Manzur (1233–1312 AD) moved to Tripoli, Libya though he was born in Tunis, became an *'alim* then a *qadi* (judge), and devoted his life to correspondence, archiving, and copying of key manuscripts. His opus was reprinted several times over the years and remains a major linguistic reference source today.
36 Disputation was intense argument or controversy; according to a Prophetic *Hadith*, "Any people who have given themselves over to disputation have gone astray." Disputation, according to Ibn Manzur was defined as countering an argument with another argument, and disputation was seen as akin to debate and argument. See Ibn Manzur, *op. cit.*, vol. 1, p, 391.
37 As defined is another classical Arabic text, argumentation was a discussion or form of verbal competition in which each participant brought forward what was arrived at through discernment. See Abul Husayn Ahmad Ibn Faris, *Mu'jam Maqayis al-Lughah* [Glossary of Standards in Language], Beirut: Dar al-Fikr, 1997, p. 1034.

38 Variations of the Arabic equivalent of this word occur twenty times in the Holy Qur'an; on some of these occasions the meaning was to dispute or argue, as in the following verse: "Ah, Ye are those who fell to disputing (even) in matters of which ye had some Knowledge! But why dispute ye in matters of which ye have no knowledge? It is Allah Who Knows, and ye who know not!" See Holy Qur'an, 3:66.
39 This was defined in the ancient Arab texts as "going to the furthest point in reckoning until nothing at all remained." Ibn Manzur, *op. cit.*, vol. 6, p. 244.
40 Abdallah U. al-Saqhan and Muhammad A. al-Shuwaier, *Rules and Principles of Effective Dialogue*, Riyadh: King 'Abdul 'Aziz Center for National Dialogue, 2008, p. 4.
41 *Ibid.*, pp. 10–1.
42 F. Gregory Gause III, "The FP Memo: How to Save Saudi Arabia," *Foreign Policy*, Number 144, September/October 2004, pp. 66–70.
43 "Special Report: Arab Women – Out of the Shadows, into the World," *The Economist*, 371:8380, June 19, 2004, pp. 26–8.
44 "Riyadh Professor Objects to Woman Pilot," *Arab News*, July 3, 2005, p. 1.
45 Lubna Hussain, "This is not a Saudi Soap Oprah," *Arab News*, July 1, 2005, p. 8. See also Rania Al-Baz, *Défigurée: Quand un crime passionnel devient affaire d'Etat*, Paris: Michel Lafon, 2005; *Idem.*, translated by Catherine Spencer as *Disfigured: A Saudi Woman's Story of Triumph over Violence*, New York: Interlink Publishing Group, 2008.
46 Judy Al-Bakr, "Preparations in Full Swing for 5th National Forum for Dialogue," *Arab News*, April 25, 2005, p. 3.
47 "Editorial: Dialogue Forum," *Arab News*, December 17, 2005, p. 6.
48 Ebtihal Mubarak, "Dialogue Participants Meet King, Review Results," *Arab News*, December 18, 2005, p. 1.
49 "The First National Meeting for Intellectual Dialogue," *Prologue – King 'Abdul 'Aziz Center for National Dialogue*, Riyadh: KACND, 2008(?), pp. 18–9.
50 "The Second National Meeting for Intellectual Dialogue," *Prologue – King 'Abdul 'Aziz Center for National Dialogue*, Riyadh: KACND, 2008(?), pp. 20–1.
51 "Amr Malaki Yaqsaru al-Fatwah 'ala 'Qibar ul-'Ulamah' and Yahzaru min al-tadaful 'ala Mawa'id al-Shari'ah" [Royal Decree Limiting the Fatwah to Supreme Judicial Council with a Warning Not to Disparage *Shari'ah*], *Al Hayat*, August 13, 2010, p. 2.
52 Abdul Wahab Bashir, "Madinah Forum on Women Calls for Respecting Tradition," *Arab News*, June 14, 2004 at http://archive.arabnews.com/?page=1&section=0&article=46787&d=14&m=6&y=2004.
53 "The Third National Meeting for Intellectual Dialogue," *Prologue – King 'Abdul 'Aziz Center for National Dialogue*, Riyadh: KACND, 2008(?), pp. 22–3.
54 "The Fourth National Meeting for Intellectual Dialogue," *Prologue – King 'Abdul 'Aziz Center for National Dialogue*, Riyadh: KACND, 2008(?), pp. 24–5.
55 Pei-Chia Lan, *Global Cinderellas: Migrant Domestics and Newly Rich Employers in Taiwan*, Durham, North Carolina: Duke University Press, 2006 [with extensive references to Sa'udi Arabia]. See also Laura Bashraheel, "Coping with culture shock," *Arab News*, July 3, 2009 at http://archive.arabnews.com/?page=1&section=0&article=124239&d=3&m=7&y=2009.
56 Robert E. Looney, "Saudization and Sound Economic Reforms: Are the Two Compatible?," *Strategic Insights*, Vol. III, Issue 2, February 2004, at http://www.nps.edu/Academics/centers/ccc/publications/OnlineJournal/2004/feb/looneyFeb04.html.
57 Dr. Algosaibi urged unemployed young men to take jobs they traditionally scorned or left to expatriates, who mostly hailed from the Indian subcontinent, asserting that there was no shame in doing so. To drive his point home, he served hamburgers for nearly three hours at a fast food restaurant in Jiddah in June

2008, to set a good example. See Mariam Al Hakeem, "Saudi Arabian Minister Serves Burgers to Get Nationals to Work," *Gulf News*, June 24, 2008, at http://gulfnews.com/news/gulf/saudi-arabia/saudi-arabian-minister-serves-burgers-to-get-nationals-to-work-1.113477.
58 Alain Gresh, "Amorce de changements, pression des conservateurs: Kaléidoscope saoudien," *Le Monde Diplomatique*, February 2006, pp. 8–9; an English translation of this essay, published under the title "Between Tradition and Demands for Change: Saudi Arabia: Reality Check," was posted online at http://mondediplo.com/2006/02/02saudi.
59 "The Fifth National Meeting for Intellectual Dialogue," *Prologue – King 'Abdul 'Aziz Center for National Dialogue*, Riyadh: KACND, 2008(?), pp. 26–33.
60 For a useful critique see, "Mafhum al-Wala' wal-bara' wal-Takfir hawla Masa'il 'Iqadiyyah Sha'ikat Zata Sabghah Siyasiyyah ila Shi'arat Baraqat" [The Concept of 'Loyalty and Enmity' and 'Atonement' about Thorny Ideological Questions of a Political Nature to Glamorous Slogans], *Al Hayat*, August 21, 2010, p. 14.
61 Several contemporary authors who perceived the Muslim World on a permanent war footing developed this theme. See, for example, Bernard Lewis, *The Crisis of Islam: Holy War and Unholy Terror*, New York: The Modern Library, 2003; Idem, *What Went Wrong?: Western Impact and Middle Eastern Response*, New York: Oxford University Press, 2001. See also Andrew G Bostom, *The Legacy of Jihad: Islamic Holy War and the Fate of Non-Muslims*, Amherst, New York: Prometheus Books, 2005.
62 "The Fifth National Meeting for Intellectual Dialogue," *Prologue – King 'Abdul 'Aziz Center for National Dialogue*, Riyadh: KACND, 2008(?), p. 29.
63 *Ibid.*, p. 31.
64 *Ibid.*, p. 32.
65 *Ibid.*, p. 33.
66 "The Sixth National Meeting for Intellectual Dialogue," *Prologue – King 'Abdul 'Aziz Center for National Dialogue*, Riyadh: KACND, 2008(?), p. 35.
67 Officially, unemployment was estimated at 10.8% in 2010 (10.5% in 2009), whereas in reality a more accurate percentage was nearer 25%. See Ellen Knickmeyer, "Idle Kingdom: Saudi Arabia's Youth Unemployment Woes go far Deeper than Most Realize," *Foreign Policy*, July 19, 2011, at http://www.foreignpolicy.com/articles/2011/07/19/all_play_no_work?page=0,0. See also Central Intelligence Agency, "Unemployment Rate – Saudi Arabia," *The World Factbook*, at https://www.cia.gov/library/publications/the-world-factbook/geos/sa.html.
68 This was one of those rare taboo subjects that raised eyebrows each and every time someone brought it up. Accusations flew that authorities "granted" a well-connected member of the ruling family or an influential merchant the privilege of, say, 200,000 visas. In turn, these employment visas were sold to brokers at fixed rates, who then engaged in further trade with potential employees. In the absence of solid evidence to corroborate such hearsay, it was important to exercise caution in assessing such claims, although on the surface, the potential for abuse was clearly there.
69 It remained to be determined how the March 2011 decrees, which were geared to provide the indigenous population with employment priorities, would alter the current labor balance.
70 In March 2011, King 'Abdallah issued a decree that mandated the creation of new hospitals, whose objectives were to cater to those with limited access. See P. K. Adbul Ghaffour, "King Abdullah's Six Glorious Years of Achievements," *Arab News*, May 29, 2011, at http://arabnews.com/saudiarabia/article437699.ece.
71 Kingdom of Saudi Arabia, *From the Point of View of Saudi Society: An Analytical Field Study*, Riyadh: King 'Abdul 'Aziz Center for National Dialogue, 2006. The study distributed a questionnaire that was composed of 14 detailed questions

(reproduced on pages 36–43) that wished to ascertain whether Sa'udi society was aware of the center's goals, and to what extent Sa'udis followed the proceedings of the mational meetings for intellectual dialogue [Hereafter From the Point of View].
72 Ibid., pp. 12–21.
73 Leigh Nolan, *Managing Reform?: Saudi Arabia and the King's Dilemma*, Doha, Qatar: Brookings Doha Center, May 2011, p. 4.
74 Although surveys were quite common in the kingdom, few were on this scale, which spoke well of its sponsors.
75 From the Point of View, *op. cit.*, pp. 22–30.
76 "Khadim al-Haramayn wa-Baba al-Vatican fi liqa' Tarikhi: Hiwar al-Adyan Tariq al-Tasamuh wal-Amn wal-Salam" [The Custodian of the Two Holy Mosques and the Pope in a Historic Meeting: Dialogue Among Religions is the Road for Tolerance, Security, and Peace], *Al-Sharq al-Awsat*, November 7, 2007, at http://www.asharqalawsat.com/details.asp?section=1&issue=10571&article=444661.
77 Kéchichian – Faysal, *op. cit.*, p. 118.
78 Benoist-Méchin, *Fayçal, Roi d'Arabie: L'Homme, Le Souverain, Sa Place dans le Monde 1906–1975*, Paris: Albin Michel, 1975, p. 111.
79 As cited in the newspaper *Le Monde* and quoted in Maurice Bucaille, *The Bible, the Qur'an, and Science: The Holy Scriptures Examined in the Light of Modern Knowledge*, Chicago: Illinois: Kazi Publications, Incorporated, 2002, p. 15.
80 Andrew G. Bostom, "The Pope, *Jihad*, and 'Dialogue'," *The American Thinker*, September 17, 2006 at, http://www.americanthinker.com/2006/09/the_pope_jihad_and_dialogue.html.
81 For the text of the Catholic Pontiff's Regensburg address, see, "Lecture of the Holy Father Aula Magna of The University Of Regensburg," September 12, 2006, at http://www.vatican.va/holy_father/benedict_xvi/speeches/2006/september/documents/hf_ben-xvi_spe_20060912_university-regensburg_en.html.
82 "Historic Saudi visit to Vatican," *BBC News*, November 6, 2007 at http://news.bbc.co.uk/2/hi/europe/7080327.stm.
83 Siraj Wahab and Badea Abu Al-Naja, "King Abdullah Inspires Scholars," *Arab News*, June 5, 2008, at http://archive.arabnews.com/?page=1&section=0&article=110609&d=5&m=6&y=2008&pix=kingdom.jpg& category=Kingdom.
84 Ibid.
85 Riazat Butt, "King Abdullah calls for better interfaith relations: Saudi highlights dangers of Islamist extremism," *Guardian*, June 5, 2008, at http://www.guardian.co.uk/world/2008/jun/05/religion.islam.
86 "Islam 'must do away with dangers of extremism'," *Gulf News*, June 5, 2008, at http://archive.gulfnews.com/articles/08/06/05/10218531.html.
87 Caryle Murphy, "Saudi king set to lead rare interfaith talks in Spain; The three-day conference of religious leaders will start July 16 in Madrid," *The Christian Science Monitor*, July 8, 2008, at http://www.csmonitor.com/2008/0708/p01s03-wome.html.
88 Ibid.
89 Claude Salhani, "King Abdullah's Experiment," *International Herald Tribune*, July 29, 2008, at http://www.iht.com/articles/2008/07/29/opinion/edsalhani.php.
90 Badea Abu Al-Naja, "Dialogue is Essential for Peace," *Arab News*, July 19, 2008, p. 6.
91 Ibid.
92 See Appendix 4.
93 For the text of "A Common Word Between Us and You," see http://www.acommonword.com/downloads/CW-Booklet-Final-v6_8-1-09.pdf. The response, along with various documents associated with the conference, were posted at the Yale Divinity School web-page at http://www.yale.edu/divinity/commonword/. See also "Yale to Host Interfaith Meeting," *Arab News*, July 19, 2008, p. 1; and "Muslim

Notes 307

and Christian Leaders Meet at Yale for Historic 'Common Word' Conference," July 15, 2008, at http://opac.yale.edu/news/article.aspx?id=5900.
94 See "Final Statement," Conference on the Initiative of the Custodian of the Two Holy Mosques on Dialogue and its Impact in Disseminating Human Values, Organized by the Muslim World League, 12–12 Shawwal 1430H, September 30-October 1, 2009, Geneva, Switzerland, at www.world-dialogue.org/Geneva/English/final%20statement.pdf.
95 P. K. Abdul Ghafour, "Interfaith Dialogue Now Needs Clear Direction," *Arab News*, September 30, 2009, p. 1, at http://archive.arabnews.com/?page=1&section=0&article=126869&d=30&m=9&y=2009.
96 P. K. Abdul Ghafour, "MWL to Organize Interfaith Forums Around the World," *Arab News*, September 30, 2009, at http://archive.arabnews.com/?page=1&section=0&article=126876&d=30&m=9&y=2009.
97 P. K. Abdul Ghafour, "Geneva Meeting Seeks Greater Understanding Among Religions," *Arab News*, October 1, 2009, at http://archive.arabnews.com/?page=1&section=0&article=126934&d=1&m=10&y=2009. For Obama's Cairo Speech, in which he envisioned the children of Abraham mingling peacefully together, see The White House, Office of the Press Secretary (Cairo, Egypt), "Remarks by the President on 'A New Beginning,'" Cairo University, Cairo, Egypt, at http://www.whitehouse.gov/the-press-office/remarks-president-cairo-university-6-04-09.
98 Popularized by US President George W. Bush, who goaded Americans to repeat his question endlessly after 9/11 and for which he telegraphed a universal answer – "They hate us for our freedoms" – an entire cottage industry emerged around the query and the non-convincing argumentations that resulted. See, for example, Brigitte Gabriel, *Because They Hate: A Survivor of Islamic Terror Warns America*, New York: St. Martin's Griffin, 2008; Ziauddin Sardar and Merryl Wyn Davies, *Why Do People Hate America?*, New York: The Disinformation Company, 2003; Gabriel Weimann, *Terror on the Internet: The New Arena, the New Challenges*, Washington, D.C.: United States Institute of Peace Press, 2006; Steven Emerson, *American Jihad: The Terrorists Living Among Us*, New York: Free Press, 2002. For a poignant reply to these pretentious essays see Mark Levine, *Why They Don't Hate Us: Lifting the Veil on the Axis of Evil*, New York: Oneworld, 2005.
99 See Appendix 4.
100 See Appendix 3.

3 Political participation and municipal elections

1 For insights on the founder's view of this key question, see Leslie McLoughlin, *Ibn Saud: Founder of a Kingdom*, Houndmills and London: Macmillan Press, Ltd., 1993, pp. 40–71.
2 For one of the best studies on tribal affairs, see Donald Powell Cole, *Nomads of the Nomads: The Al Murrah Bedouin of the Empty Quarter*, Arlington Heights, Illinois: Harlan Davidson, Inc., 1975. See also Toby Craig Jones, *Desert Kingdom: How Oil and Water Forged Modern Saudi Arabia*, Cambridge, Massachusetts and London, England: Harvard University Press, 2010.
3 Joseph Kostiner, *The Making of Saudi Arabia 1916–1936: From Chieftancy to Monarchical State*, New York: Oxford University Press, 1993, pp. 71–140.
4 Madawi Al-Rasheed, *A History of Saudi Arabia*, 2nd edition, Cambridge: Cambridge University Press, 2010, pp. 59–62.
5 Summer Scott Huyette, *Political Adaptation in Sa'udi Arabia: A Study of the Council of Ministers*, Boulder and London: Westview Press, 1985.
6 Information Office, "Education and Healthcare in Saudi Arabia," Royal Embassy of Saudi Arabia, Washington, DC at www.saudiembassy.net. See also United

308 Notes

Nations Development Program, *The Real Wealth of Nations: Pathways to Human Development* [Human Development Report 2010], New York: Palgrave Macmillan, 2010; and "Explanation note on 2010 HDR composite indices: Saudi Arabia," at www.hdrstats.undp.org/images/explanations/SAU.pdf.

7 Over the years, the *Muntadah al-Tanmiyyah* published several annual reports, which covered much of the intellectual debates held among its members, mostly edited by 'Abdul-Khaliq 'Abdallah. See, for example, Muntadah al-Tanmiyyah, *Qadayah wa Humum al Mutjama'ah al Madani fi Duwal Majlis al Ta'awun* [Civil Society Issues and Concerns in the Gulf Cooperation Council States], Kuwait: Dar Qurtas, 1998; *Al-Khalij 'Arabi wa Farisi wa-Tahadiyyat al-Qarn al-Wahid wal-'Ushrun* [The Arabian and Persian Gulf and the Challenges of the Twenty-First Century], Kuwait: Dar Qurtas, 1990; Muntadah al-Tanmiyyah, *Duwal al Khalij wal 'Awlamah* [GCC States and Globalization], Kuwait: Dar Qurtas, 2000; Muntadah al-Tanmiyyah, *Mutatalabat wa Tahadiyat al-Tahawal al-Democrati fi Duwal Majlis al-Ta'awun* [Demands and Challenges of the Democratic Transformations in the Gulf Cooperation Council States], Kuwait: Dar Qurtas, 2001; Muntadah al-Tanmiyyah, *Al-Khalij al-'Arabi wal Muhit al-Asyawih* [The Arab Gulf Region and the Asian Continent], Kuwait: Dar Qurtas, 2002; Muntadah al-Tanmiyyah, *Al-Tanmiyyah al-Bashariyyah fi Dawal Majlis al-Ta'awun* [Human Development in the Gulf Cooperation Council States], Kuwait: Dar Qurtas, 2003; Muntadah al-Tanmiyyah, *Al-Wulayat al-Mutahidah al-Amerikiyyah wal-Khalij* [The United States of America and the Gulf], Kuwait: Dar Qurtas, 2005; Muntadah al-Tanmiyyah, *Ittijahat al-Shabab fi Dawal Majlis al-Ta'awun* [Prospects for Youths in the Gulf Cooperation Council States], Kuwait: Dar Qurtas, 2006; Muntadah al-Tanmiyyah, *Al-'Alam fi Dawal al-Khalij* [The World in the Gulf States], Kuwait: Dar Qurtas, 2007; see also F. Gregory Gause, *Oil Monarchies: Domestic and Security Challenges in the Arab Gulf States*, New York: Council on Foreign Relations Press, 1994, p. 88.

8 Joseph A. Kéchichian, *Succession in Saudi Arabia*, New York: Palgrave, 2001, pp. 71–3 [the documents are reproduced as Appendices 13 (pp. 203–7), 14 (pp. 209–18), 15 (pp. 219–31), and 16 (pp. 233–40)] [Hereafter Kéchichian – Succession].

9 P. K. Abdul Ghafour, "Shoura Council Strength Increased to 150," *Arab News*, April 12, 2005, p. 1.

10 For an analysis on the founder's views on this subject, see McLoughlin, op. cit., pp. 81–2.

11 Faisal bin Misha'al al-Saud, "Political Development in the Kingdom of Saudi Arabia: An Assessment of the Majlis Ash-Shura," Doctoral Dissertation, University of Durham, UK, 2000.

12 *The Koran*, translated with notes by N. J. Dawood, London: Penguin Books, 1999, p. 56 [3:159].

13 *Ibid.*, p. 342 [42:38]. There was another Qur'anic reference to *Shurah*, in the 2nd Surah, Al-Baqarah, where a collective family decision regarding weaning the child from a mother's milk is discussed, and which encouraged that both parents decide by mutual consultation about the timing, pp. 34–5 [2:233].

14 Faisal bin Mishaal bin Saud Al-Saud, *Decision Making and the Role of Ash-Shura in Saudi Arabia: Majlis Ash-Shura (Consultative Council): Concept, Theory and Practice*, New York: Vantage Press, 2003 and 2004, p. 78.

15 This section draws on several ideas developed in E. M. Al Johany, *Consultation and the Art of Government in the Kingdom of Saudi Arabia*, Riyadh: King Saud University Press, 1992.

16 Kingdom of Sa'udi Arabia, "Shura in the Kingdom of Saudi Arabia: A Historical Background," at the *Majlis al-Shurah* web-page, http://www.shura.gov.sa/wps/wcm/connect/ShuraEn/internet/Historical+BG/.

17 The September 18, 1932 "Royal Order," number 2716, was one of the first issued that day, which ushered in the independent monarchy, and which solidified Al Sa'ud rule.
18 Kingdom of Sa'udi Arabia, "Shura in the Kingdom of Saudi Arabia: A Historical Background," at the *Majlis al-Shurah* web-page, http://www.shura.gov.sa/wps/wcm/connect/ShuraEn/internet/Historical+BG/.
19 Quoted in Ahmad bin Ibrahim al-Ghazawi, "Al-Faysal wa Majlis al-Shurah" [Faysal and the Consultative Council], *Al Darah* 1:3, September 1975, reproduced in Fahd bin 'Abdallah Al Samari, *Al Malik Faysal bin 'Abdul 'Aziz Al Sa'ud: Ru'yah wa Zikriyyat*, Riyadh: Darah al-Malik 'Abdul 'Aziz, Number 225, 1429H [2008], pp. 71–80.
20 Joseph A. Kéchichian, *Faysal: Saudi Arabia's King for All Seasons*, Gainesville: University Press of Florida, 2008, pp. 57–88.
21 Middle East Watch, *Empty Reforms: Saudi Arabia's New Basic Laws*, New York: Human Rights Watch, May 1992, p. 6 [Hereafter Middle East Watch – Empty Reforms].
22 The interview was reproduced in *al-Siyassah*, March 19, 1980.
23 Middle East Watch – Empty Reforms, *op. cit.*, p. 9.
24 Faisal bin Mishaal bin Saud Al-Saud, *op. cit.*, pp. 90–144.
25 Salah Nasrawi, "Islamists Make Strong Showing in Saudi Election," *Independent*, 24, 2005; see also Brian Whitaker, "Clerics' Choices Clean Up in Saudi Election," *Guardian*, April 25, 2005.
26 Neil MacFarquhar, "Saudi Reformers: Seeking Rights, Paying a Price," *The New York Times*, June 9, 2005, pp. A1, A8; see also *Idem*, "Some Saudi Candidates Claim Election Violations," *The New York Times*, February 14, 2005, p. A6; and M. Ghazanfar Ali Khan, "Government Intensifies Efforts to Constitute Municipal Councils," *Arab News*, August 11, 2005, p. 1.
27 Joseph A. Kéchichian, "Democratization in Gulf Monarchies: A New Challenge to the GCC," *Middle East Policy* 11:4, Winter 2004, pp. 37–57, especially, 46–49.
28 This point is worth repeating because the monarch was often caught between competing currents within the family. I thank Professor Mazin Salah Motabbagani, a professor at the Imam Muhammad bin Sa'ud Islamic University who follows these questions closely, for elucidating them. Interview in Riyadh, March 15, 2010.
29 United Nations Development Program, "Programme on Governance in the Arab Region, Local Government: Saudi Arabia," at http://www.pogar.org/countries/theme.aspx?t=6&cid=16.
30 "Saudi Law Unclear on Women's Vote," *BBC News*, August 10, 2004, at http://news.bbc.co.uk/2/hi/middle_east/3552336.stm.
31 In Riyadh, the capital city and then home to 2,692,780 citizens, registered voters did not exceed 18% of those eligible, i.e., 86,462 voters out of a potential electorate of approximately 470,000 persons. Regrettably, this represented just two percent of the total population, which was troubling even if every effort was made to encourage registration and participation. See Pascal Ménoret, "The Municipal Elections in Saudi Arabia 2005," December 27, 2005, at http://arab-reform.net/spip.php?article1. This section draws on Ménoret's important essay.
32 *Ibid*. See also John Duke Anthony, "The Elections in Saudi Arabia," *Saudi–US Relations Information Service* (SUSRIS), February 10, 2005, at http://www.susris.com/articles/2005/ioi/050210-saudi-elections-anthony.html.
33 Mishal Fahm Al-Sulami, "Reform in Saudi Arabia: The Case of Municipal Elections," *JKAU: Arts & Humanities* [Journal of the King 'Abdul 'Aziz University] 16:2, 2008, pp. 113–35.
34 "Islamist Win in Key Saudi Poll," *BBC News*, February 11, 2005, at http://news.bbc.co.uk/2/hi/middle_east/4252079.stm.
35 Ménoret, *op. cit.*, at http://arab-reform.net/spip.php?article1.

36 Brian Whitaker, "Clerics' Choices Clean Up in Saudi Election," *Guardian*, April 25, 2005, at http://www.guardian.co.uk/world/2005/apr/25/saudiarabia.brianwhitaker.
37 J. E. Peterson, "Tribes and Politics in Eastern Arabia," *Middle East Journal* 31:3, Summer 1977, pp. 297–312.
38 Ghada Aboud, "Saudi Women Will Be Allowed To Vote In '09," *Arab News*, January 4, 2005, at http://archive.arabnews.com/?page=1&section=0&article=57051&d=4&m=1&y=2005.
39 Brian Whitaker, "Hello, Democracy – and Goodbye: Saudi Arabia has Quietly Abandoned the Municipal Elections that were Due to Take Place this Year," *Guardian*, February 24, 2009, at http://www.guardian.co.uk/commentisfree/2009/feb/24/saudiarabia.
40 Abdul Rahman Shaheen, "Saudi Election Delay Gives Room for Evaluation," *Gulf News*, May 20, 2009, at http://archive.gulfnews.com/articles/09/05/21/10315420.html.
41 *Ibid*.
42 "Municipal Elections Set for April 23," *Arab News*, March 22, 2011, at http://arabnews.com/saudiarabia/article326296.ece.
43 Reuters, "Saudi Arabia Delays Municipal Elections by One week," *Gulf News*, May 21, 2011, at http://gulfnews.com/news/gulf/saudi-arabia/saudi-arabia-delays-municipal-elections-by-one-week-1.810877.
44 Kelly Buchanan, "Saudi Arabia: The Second Municipality Election in the Kingdom's History," *Library of Congress* [guest post by George Sadek, Senior Legal Information Analyst], April 21, 2011, http://blogs.loc.gov/law/2011/04/saudi-arabia-the-second-municipality-election-in-the-kingdoms-history/.
45 *Ibid*.
46 Stephen Kohutiak, "Women of Saudi Arabia will Provide the Right to Vote in Local Elections," June 7, 2011, at http://chuiko.com/world/5064-women-of-saudi-arabia-will-provide-the-right-to-vote-in-local-elections.html.
47 Nathalie Morin, "Saudi Women May Be Able To Vote In Municipal Council Elections in 2015," http://www.abigmessage.com/saudi-women-may-be-able-to-vote-in-municipal-council-elections-in-2015.html.

4 Political reforms and the succession dilemma

1 See Joseph A. Kéchichian, "Affirming the Saudi Will to Power: Domestic Challenges to King 'Abdullah," *Middle East Institute Policy Brief*, Number 16 (June 2008), pp. 1–9 at http://www.mideasti.org/policy-brief/affirming-saudi-will-power-domestic-challenges-king-%E2%80%98abdullah; *Idem*, "Testing the Saudi Arabia 'Will to Power': Challenges Confronting Prince Abdullah," *Middle East Policy*, Vol. 10, No. 4 (Winter 2003), pp. 100–115; *Idem*, "Saudi Arabia's Will to Power," *Middle East Policy*, Vol. 7, No. 2 (February 2000), pp. 47–60; for historical background on the Al Sa'ud family, see Joseph A. Kéchichian, *Succession in Saudi Arabia*, New York: Palgrave, 2001, especially pp. 1–65 [Hereafter Kéchichian – Succession].
2 Toby Craig Jones, *Desert Kingdom: How Oil and Water Forged Modern Saudi Arabia*, Cambridge, Massachusetts and London, England: Harvard University Press, 2010, pp. 7 and 15. For a few leading studies that argue the opposite, see David E. Long, *The Kingdom of Saudi Arabia*, Gainesville, Florida: University Press of Florida, 1997; Anthony Cave Brown, *Oil, God, and Gold: The Story of Aramco and the Saudi Kings*, New York: Houghton Mifflin, 1999; and Madawi Al-Rasheed, *A History of Saudi Arabia*, 2nd edition, Cambridge, UK and New York: Cambridge University Press, 2010.
3 For a good discussion of the Al Sa'ud ruling family, see David Holden and Richard Johns, *The House of Saud: The Rise and Rule of the Most Powerful*

Dynasty in the Arab World, New York: Holt, Rinehart and Winston, 1981. See also Anthony Cave Brown, *Ibid*; As'ad AbuKhalil, *The Battle for Saudi Arabia: Royalty, Fundamentalism, and Global Power*, New York: Steven Stories Press, 2004; and Stig Stenslie, *Regime Stability in Saudi Arabia: The Challenge of Succession*, London and New York: Routledge, 2012. For useful non-scholarly sources, see, Robert Lacey, *The Kingdom: Arabia and the House of Saud*, London: Hutchinson, 1981, and *Idem.*, *Inside the Kingdom: Kings, Clerics, Modernists, Terrorists, and the Struggle for Saudi Arabia*, New York: Viking, 2009.

4 "Exciting Five Years" (editorial), *Arab News*, June 8, 2010, at http://arabnews.com/opinion/editorial/article62849.ece.

5 For a fair but slightly magnified recent assessment, see "Briefing: The Saudi Succession; When Kings and Princes Grow Old," *The Economist*, 396:8691, July 17, 2010, pp. 29–30.

6 These insights were gathered in conversations with a retired member of the ruling family who was still very well attuned to internal discussions. Interview with HRH Prince Bandar al-Faysal, Retired Royal Saudi Air Force Lt. Colonel (in charge of Air Force Intelligence), Riyadh, March 28, 2011.

7 Simon Henderson, *After King Abdullah: Succession in Saudi Arabia*, Washington, D.C.: The Washington Institute for Near East Policy, *Policy Focus* Number 96, August 2009 [Hereafter Henderson – Abdullah].

8 Simon Henderson, "Desert Schism: Prince Nayef Bids for Saudi Throne," Washington, D.C.: The Washington Institute for Near East Policy, *Policy Watch* Number 1501, 31 March 2009; see also "Saudi Arabia's Prince Nayef: A rising but enigmatic prince," *The Economist*, 391:8625, April 4, 2009, p. 51. For a different perspective, see Turki al-Faisal, "He is My Uncle Naif Bin Abdulaziz," *Al-Sharq Al-Awsat*, April 2, 2009, at http://www.asharq-e.com/news.asp?section=2&id=16267.

9 Joseph A. Kéchichian, "Saudi Arabia: 'Heir to the Heir' Gets an Upgrade," *Newsweek*, November 14, 2011, p. 12.

10 For the text of Heir Apparent 'Abdallah's speech, see *Foreign Broadcast Information Service – Middle East and Africa FBIS-MEA-V-82-115*, 15 June 1982, pp. C2–C3.

11 Kéchichian – Succession, *op. cit.*, pp. 71–73; for the texts of these laws, see *Idem.*, pages 209–18 [*Basic Law of Government*], 219–31 [*Majlis al-Shurah*], and 233–40 [*Law of the Provinces*].

12 John Bulloch, *Reforms of the Saudi Arabian Constitution*, London: Gulf Centre for Strategic Studies, 1992; see also Rashed Aba-Namay, "The Recent Constitutional Reforms in Saudi Arabia," *The International and Comparative Law Quarterly* 42:2, April 1993, pp. 295–331.

13 Simon Henderson, *After King Fahd: Succession in Saudi Arabia*, Washington, D.C.: The Washington Institute for Near East Policy, 1994, 1995, p. 21 [Hereafter Henderson – Fahd].

14 Basic Law of Government, Article 5, Section b, in Kéchichian – Succession, *op. cit.*, p. 210.

15 Henderson – Fahd, *op. cit.*, p. 22.

16 Henderson – Fahd, *op. cit.*, p. 22, footnote 2.

17 Of 21 successions in Al Sa'ud reigns to date, a monarch's rule went to a son seven times, and to a cousin four times. The total for brother-to-brother succession stands at ten.

18 "Saudis Need Better Successions," *The Christian Science Monitor*, August 4, 2005, p. 8. For details on the late King's life, see Douglas Martin, "Saudi Arabia's King Fahd Dies; Abdullah Named New Leader," *The New York Times*, 1, 2005, at http://www.nytimes.com/2005/08/01/international/middleeast/01cnd-fahd.html.

19 "Reformists' Trial Set to Resume Today," *Arab News*, April 2, 2005, p. 1; see also "3 Saudi Reform Advocates Sentenced," *The Los Angeles Times*, May 16, 2005, p. A5.

20 Basic Law of Government, Article 5, Section d.
21 "Abdullah Receives Al-Damini [Dumayni], Al-Faleh," *Arab News*, August 14, 2005, p. 1.
22 "Al-Malik Yaqur al-Nizam al-Asasi li-Hay'at al-Bay'ah … wa-Yu'ainu al-Tuwayjari Aminan 'Aman," [The King Issues Basic Laws for the Allegiance Institution and Appoints Al-Tuwayjiri as Secretary-General], *Al Jazirah*, Number 12441, October 21, 2006, p. 1.
23 Though the literal translation for *Hay'at al-Bay'ah* is indeed "Allegiance Commission," a more accurate translation may be "Allegiance Law of Succession."
24 The text of this decree is reproduced in Joseph A. Kéchichian, *Power and Succession in Arab Monarchies: A Reference Guide*, Boulder, Colorado: Lynne Rienner Publishers, 2008, appendix 16, pp. 463–69 [Hereafter Kéchichian – Power and Succession]; it is reproduced in this volume as appendix 6.
25 "Khadim al-Haramayn Ya'tamidu al-La'ihat al-Tanfiziyyah li-Nizam Hay'at al-Bay'ah" [The Custodian of the Two Holy Mosques Adopts Bylaws for the Allegiance Commission], *Al-Sharq Al-Awsat*, October 9, 2009, at http://www.asharqalawsat.com/details.asp?section=3&article=440516&issue=10542. The Bylaws are reproduced in appendix 7.
26 Kéchichian – Affirming the Saudi Will to Power, *op. cit.*, p. 1.
27 'Ali Shirayah and Muhammad Al-Qa'abi, "Al-Amir Salman: La Tujad Usrah Aw Qabilah fil-Sa'udiyyah ila wa li-Abnauhah wa-Ajdaduhah Musharakah Fa'ilah fi Tawhid al-Bilad" [Prince Salman: The are no Families or Tribes in Sa'udi Arabia whose Sons or Grandfathers did not Play Effective Roles to Unite the Country], *Al-Sharq Al-Awsat*, Number 11810, 30 March 2011, pp. 38–39.
28 Kéchichian – Affirming the Saudi Will to Power, *op. cit.*, p. 1; see also P. K. Abdul Ghafour, "Mishaal Named Allegiance Commission Chairman," *Arab News*, 11 December 2007, p. 1.
29 "Al-Sa'udiyyah: Tasmiyat Ra'is wa A'da' 'Hay'at al-Bay'ah'," [Saudi Arabia: Appointed of Chairman and Members of Allegiance Commission], *Al-Sharq Al-Awsat*, 11 December 2007, at http://www.asharqalawsat.com/details.asp?section=3&article=449311&issue=10605.
30 Fawwaz bin 'Abdul 'Aziz, who was born in 1934 to a Moroccan concubine named Bazzah, died on July 22, 2008 in Paris, France; a past governor of Riyadh, Fawwaz was part of the Talal Free Princes movement (1962–64) but was rehabilitated by King Faysal and served as governor of Makkah from 1971 to 1979. He resigned after the 1979 Makkah Mosque takeover. His adopted son was not elevated to the Allegiance Commission. See "Wafat Amir Mantakat Makkah al-Sabiq Al-Amir Fawwaz bin 'Abdul 'Aziz" [Death of Former Makkah Governor Fawwaz bin 'Abdul 'Aziz], *Al Hayat*, July 23, 2008, p. 2. Turki bin Faysal bin Turki bin 'Abdul 'Aziz Al Sa'ud died on 28 February 2009. 'Abdul 'Aziz bin Nawwaf bin 'Abdul-'Aziz Al Sa'ud has an older brother, Muhammad bin Nawwaf, who is Ambassador to London; 'Abdul 'Aziz was chosen by his father, a decision accepted by the monarch, to serve on the commission.
31 For yet another interesting, albeit puzzling, evaluation of the Allegiance Commission from the perspective of the US Ambassador in Saudi Arabia, see, Ambassador James B. Smith, "Saudi Succession: Can The Allegiance Commission Work?," [Secret Riyadh 001434-E.O. 12958: DECL: 10/25/2019 Tags: PGOV, PREL, PINR, Ref: A. Riyadh 1402 B. 08 Riyadh 1757], leaked on April 18, 2011 by Wikileaks and posted at http://www.aftenposten.no/spesial/wikileaksdokumenter/article4094994.ece.
32 "King 'Abdallah Addresses Princes," Riyadh: Saudi Press Agency, December 10, 2007.
33 P. K. Abdul Ghafour, "Mishaal Named Allegiance Commission Chairman," *Arab News*, 11 December 2007, p. 1; see also Mariam Al Hakeem, "Mesha'al to

Notes 313

Head Saudi Allegiance Commission," *Gulf News*, 11 December 2007, at http://archive.gulfnews.com/articles/07/12/11/10174017.html.
34 I owe this insight to HRH Prince Turki bin Talal bin 'Abdul 'Aziz who kindly discussed the issue in Jiddah on September 20, 2011.
35 Bylaws to the Allegiance Commission, Article 1–1a; see appendix 7.
36 Bylaws to the Allegiance Commission, Article 2–2; see appendix 7.
37 Simon Henderson, *After King Abdullah: Succession in Saudi Arabia*, Policy Focus Number 96, Washington, D.C.: The Washington Institute for Near East Policy, 2009, p. 34.
38 The four-years public service rule, which was also valid for the Council of Ministers, could be overridden by royal decree.
39 Bylaws to the Allegiance Commission, Article 4; see appendix 7.
40 Bylaws to the Allegiance Commission, Article 6; see appendix 7.
41 Bylaws to the Allegiance Commission, Article 7; see appendix 7.
42 Saudi Arabia: Allegiance Law of Succession, Articles 7 and 9; see appendix 6.
43 Saudi Arabia: Allegiance Law of Succession, Article 11; see appendix 6.
44 Saudi Arabia: Allegiance Law of Succession, Article 12; see appendix 6.
45 Needless to say that this highly sensitive issue was seldom discussed outside of family circles. In the event, I am truly grateful to two well-placed Al Sa'ud members who clarified the issue, while a third preferred anonymity. Interviews with HRH Prince Bandar al-Faysal, Riyadh, 28, 2011; and HRH Prince Ahmad bin Nayif, a deputy to the Minister of the Interior, Riyadh, March 29, 2011.
46 Saudi Arabia: Allegiance Law of Succession, Article 14; see appendix 6.
47 Saudi Arabia: Allegiance Law of Succession, Article 15; see appendix 6.
48 This too was a novel development as the ruler telegraphed Commission members that they ought to take their responsibilities seriously.
49 Thereby granting the chairman unprecedented powers.
50 Saudi Arabia: Allegiance Law of Succession, Article 20; see appendix 6.
51 Saudi Arabia: Allegiance Law of Succession, Article 21; see appendix 6.
52 Saudi Arabia: Allegiance Law of Succession, Article 23; see appendix 6.
53 Bylaws to the Allegiance Commission, Article 12; see appendix 7.
54 Bylaws to the Allegiance Commission, Article 13; see appendix 7.
55 Bylaws to the Allegiance Commission, Article 14; see appendix 7.
56 Awadh Al-Badi, "Institutionalising Hereditary Succession in Saudi Arabia's Political Governance System: The Allegiance Commission," Paris: Arab Reform Initiative, February 14, 2008, at http://arab-reform.net/spip.php?article1232.
57 Kéchichian – Power and Succession, *op. cit.*, pages 253–57.
58 Awadh Al-Badi, *op. cit.*, at http://arab-reform.net/spip.php?article1232.
59 See, for example, Henderson – After Abdullah, *op. cit.*, p. 8.
60 "Crown Prince Sultan Medical Update: Surgery in U.S. Said to be Success," *Arab News*, February 25, 2009, p. 1.
61 Prince Nayif bin 'Abdul 'Aziz passed away on June 16, 2012 in Geneva, Switzerland. He was succeeded by Salman bin 'Abdul 'Aziz Al Sa'ud who, in addition to assuming the heirship, kept his Ministry of Defense portfolio.
62 Simon Henderson, "Desert Schism: Prince Nayef Bids for Saudi Throne," *op. cit.*, March 31, 2009; see also "Talaqa al-Tahni'at min Wali al-'Ahd wa Mas'ulin … al-Amir Nayif: Ashkuru Khadim al-Haramayn Kathiran … wa Arju An Aqun 'Ind Hasan al-Thun" [Received Congratulations from Heir Apparent and Officials … Prince Nayif: I Thank the Custodian of the Two Holy Mosques … and Hope to Measure Up to his Right Expectations], *Al Hayat*, March 29, 2009, p. 2. It must also be emphasized that while Prince Nayif was ill, he was under treatment, and the leukemia he fought was brought under control.
63 Critics routinely highlighted political disagreements between these two officials, which was entirely logical as political differences existed within all governments

everywhere, and the Kingdom is no exception. On the personal level, however, 'Abdallah and Nayif were close, and circumstances brought them even closer to each other. To claim otherwise is facile.
64 Regrettably, hasty comments by Prince Nayif were used against him, though the Minister of Interior's opposition to terrorism was undaunted. For an illustration, see Thomas Hegghammer, *Jihad in Saudi Arabia: Violence and Pan-Islamism since 1979*, Cambridge: Cambridge University Press, 2010, p. 156 and passim.
65 Badr Mahfouz, "Khabir Amni wa 'Mukhmid Fatn' 'ala Mada 35 'Aman" [A Security Expert and a Secession Smasher for over 35 Years], *Al Hayat*, March 29, 2009, p. 2; see also Jamil al-Ziabi, "Jidar al-Ma' – Nayif … al-Amn wal-Watan" [A Water Barrier – Nayif … Security and the Nation], *Al Hayat*, March 29, 2009. p. 3.
66 "Naif named second deputy premier," *Arab News*, March 28, 2009, p. 1; see also Mahmoud Ahmad, "Prince Naif Curbs Power of Virtue Commission," *Arab News*, May 25, 2006, at http://www.arabnews.com/?page=1&section=0&article=82705&d=25&m=5&y=2006; and, Michael Scott Doran, "The Saudi Paradox," *Foreign Affairs* 83:1, January/February 2004, pp. 35–51.
67 "Naif named second deputy premier," *Arab News*, March 28, 2009, p. 1.
68 Abul Rahman Shaheen, "Naif's Appointment Hailed as Recognition for his Leadership Qualities, *Gulf News*, at http://archive.gulfnews.com/articles/09/03/28/10299156.html.
69 Jasim bin Muhammad Al-Yaqout, "Nayif al-Watan … wal-Watan Nayif" [Nayif is the Nation … and the Nation is Nayif], *Al Hayat*, May 4, 2009, p. 26.
70 Turki al-Faisal, " Inahu 'Ammi Nayif bin 'Abdul 'Aziz" [He is My Uncle Nayif bin 'Abdul 'Aziz], *Al-Sharq Al-Awsat*, April 2, 2009 at http://www.aawsat.com/leader.asp?section=3&article=513503. The English version of the letter appeared on the same day at http://www.aawsat.com/english/print.asp?artid=id16267.
71 *Ibid.*
72 "Naif pledges greater efforts in the service of nation and religion," *Arab News*, March 29, 2009, p. 1; see also Ahmad Ghalib, "Fi Awal Hadith Ba'ad Ta'yinihi Na'iban Thaniyan li-Ra'is Majlis al-Wuzara' al-Sa'udi … al-Amir Nayif lil-Hayat: Sanasil ilal-Khiyalah al-Na'imah Qablah an Tastaqiz" [In His First Interview After his Appointment as Second Deputy Prime Minister to the Saudi Council of Ministers … Prince Nayif Tells Al Hayat: We Will Reach Dormant Cells Before they Awaken], *Al Hayat*, April 1, 2009, pp. 1, 13.
73 "Rafa'ah Shukrahuh lil-Malik 'Abdallah … wa Shakarah Muluk wa Zu'ama' al-Dual al-'Arabiyyah wal-Sadiqah … Al-Amir Sultan Yughadiru al-Mustashfa wa-Yahmi ba'ad al-Waqt lil-Istijmam" [Delivered his Appreciation to 'Abdallah … and Extended Thanks to Kings and Leaders of Arab and Friendly States … Prince Sultan Leaves Hospital and Will Spend Some Time Convalescing], *Al-Hayat*, 2 April 2009, pp. 1, 2.
74 Over the years, the late Minister granted me several interviews, entertaining my numerous questions. My last discussion was held a little over a year before he passed away. Interview with Labor Minister Ghazi Al-Gosaibi, in Manama, Bahrain, February 18, 2009.
75 Interview with Chairman Salih bin Humayd at the *Majlis al-Shurah* Headquarters, Riyadh, October 16, 2010.
76 "Nayef Moves Step Closer to Throne, Analysts Say," *Gulf News*, March 29, 2009, p. 19; see also Oxford Analytica, "Nayef Favourite to be Next Saudi Crown Prince," *Gulf News*, April 7, 2009. p. 12.
77 See, for example, Henderson – After Abdullah, *op. cit.*, p. 21.
78 "Prince Talal Bin Abdul Aziz Questions Saudi Succession Plan," *Gulf News*, April 3, 2009, at http://www.gulfnews.com/News/Gulf/saudi_arabia/10299544.html.

79 Souhail Karam, "Saudi Prince Questions King's Deputy Appointment," March 28, 2009, at http://www.forexfocusdaily.com/forum/commodity-news/12278-saudi-prince-questions-kings-deputy-appointment.html.
80 "Saudi Arabia's Prince Nayef: A Rising but Enigmatic Prince," *The Economist*, April 4, 2009, p. 51.
81 Reuters, "Prince Talal bin Abdul Aziz Questions Saudi Succession Plan," *Gulf News*, March 30, 2009, p. 10, at http://archive.gulfnews.com/articles/09/03/30/10299544.html.
82 No political parties were allowed in the kingdom as of mid-2012.
83 Abeer Allam and Andrew England, "Senior Saudi Calls for Political Reforms," *Financial Times*, April 28, 2009, at http://www.ft.com/cms/s/0/723d88b0-3412-11de-9eea-00144feabdc0.html.
84 Although Talal resigned from the Allegiance Commission in mid-November 2011 – after the Prince posted a notice on his website – this was not officially confirmed by the Palace. Press speculation oscillated around the "belief" that the resignation came three weeks after Prince Nayif was named heir to the throne, a promotion that Prince Talal allegedly rejected, though he could not oppose it because this was a royal decision that required full compliance. Interestingly, his website [http://www.princetalal.net/new/index.php] gave no reason for the resignation, contending itself with a single line making the announcement: "After informing King Abdallah, Prince Talal bin Abdul Aziz announced his resignation from the Allegiance Council." Presumably, Talal's resignation will now require that one of his sons take his position on the council, although no announcements were made as this book went to press. See "Saudi's Prince Talal resigns from Allegiance Council," *Arabian Business*, November 17, 2011, at http://www.arabianbusiness.com/saudi-s-prince-talal-resigns-from-allegiance-council-430306.html.
85 Abeer Allam and Andrew England, *op. cit.*
86 "Transcript of FT interview with Prince Talal," *Financial Times*, 31, 2009, at http://www.ft.com/cms/s/0/6fe89ec0-460e-11de-803f-00144feabdc0.html.
87 *Ibid.*
88 This point was confirmed by HRH Prince Salman bin 'Abdul 'Aziz, the Governor of Riyadh, who played a leading role in family affairs. Interview with Prince Salman, Riyadh, October 17, 2010.
89 "Transcript of FT interview with Prince Talal," *Financial Times*, 31, 2009, at http://www.ft.com/cms/s/0/6fe89ec0-460e-11de-803f-00144feabdc0.html.
90 "Saudi Activists Call For Reform of Monarchy," *An-Nahar* (Beirut), May 15, 2009, at http://www.naharnet.com/domino/tn/NewsDesk.nsf/getstory?openform&89C19FAB8F5C0BCBC22575B70044A864.
91 Fahad bin Sa'ad Al Sa'ud, "Awlawiyat al-Muwazanah wal-Tanmiyyah Ghayr al-Mutawazinah" [Not Prioritized Budgetary and Developmental Preferences], *Al Hayat*, June 26, 2009, p. 16; See also the rejoinder by 'Abdallah bin Rabi'an, "Al-Tanmiyyah Mutawazinah … wa Iqtirahat Fahad bin Sa'ad" [Developmental Preferences … and Fahad bin Sa'ad's Recommendations], *Al Hayat*, July 2, 2009, p. 15.
92 Wael Mahdi, "Younger royals find their voices," *The National* [Abu Dhabi, UAE], July 7, 2009, p. 12.
93 It must be emphasized that Prince Khalid bin Talal held controversial views, including the notion that 'Usamah bin Ladin was alive and being held by the United States. See "Saudi Prince Khaled Bin Talal: Bin Laden Is Alive and Being Held by the Americans; The Shiites in Saudi Arabia Are Loyal to Their Iranian Masters," *Al-Risala Television* (Kuwait), December 2, 2011, reproduced by the *Middle East Media Research Institute* (MEMRI), Number 3229, at http://www.memritv.org/clip/en/3229.htm. See also CBS News, " Saudi Royal Offers Bounty on Israeli Soldiers," October 30, 2011, at http://www.cbsnews.com/8301-202_162-20127668/saudi-royal-offers-bounty-on-israeli-soldiers/ for a bizarre story that

reportedly would see the prince add $900,000 to whomever abducted an Israeli soldier, to be exchanged for Palestinian prisoners, on top of the $100,000 that a Saudi cleric pledged.
94 The web page is accessible at http://www.lojainiat.com/.
95 Habib Trabelsi, "Prince Khaled calls for the freezing of the assets of his brother, Waleed bin Talal," 28, 2009, at http://www.saudiwave.com/index.php?option=com_content&view=article&id=1303:prince-khaled-calls-for-the-freezing-of-the-assets-of-his-brother-waleed-bin-talal. The actual interview conducted by Abu Lujayn Ibrahim, titled "Tafasil Hiwar al-Amir Khalid bin Talal bi-Sha'n Shaqiqihi al-Walid" [Details on the Debate between Prince Khalid bin Talal and his Brother Al Walid]," which include elaborate questions and several photographs showing the two brothers together, are available at http://www.lojainiat.com/index.cfm?do=cms.conPrint&contentid=3807. In early 2012, Prince Khalid "warned" his brother of unforeseen consequences if he did not "stop" his wife. See, "Saudi Prince AlWaleed warned over wife's media appearances," *Emirates 24/7*, January 18, 2012, at http://www.emirates247.com/news/region/saudi-prince-alwaleed-warned-over-wife-s-media-appearances-2012-01-18-1.438203?ot=ot.PrintPageLayout.
96 Wael Mahdi, "Younger Royals Find their Voices," *The National* [Abu Dhabi, UAE], July 7, 2009, p. 12.
97 "Prince Talal Calls for Reforms in Arab World," *Times of Oman*, August 27, 2005, p. 1; see also "Prince Talal Calls for Reform and a Saudi Constitution," *The Daily Star* (Lebanon), August 29, 2005, p. 1.
98 Salah Nasrawi, "Saudi Prince Urges Changes," *The Associated Press*, June 6, 1999.
99 BBC News, "Senior Saudi Royal Demands Reform," September 5, 2007, at http://news.bbc.co.uk/2/hi/middle_east/6980056.stm.

5 Reforms and the petition industry

1 Mark Weston, *Prophets and Princes: Saudi Arabia from Muhammad to the Present*, Hoboken, New Jersey: John Wiley & Sons, Inc., 2008, p. 432.
2 The "Partners in One Nation" petition is reproduced in Appendix 8 and analyzed in detail below.
3 With severe restrictions that, naturally, generated significant complaints to the Governor, HRH Prince Muhammad bin Fahd bin 'Abdul 'Aziz.
4 Fouad Ibrahim, *The Shi'is of Saudi Arabia*, London: Saqi, 2006, pp. 209–50.
5 Anthony H. Cordesman and Nawaf Obaid, *National Security in Saudi Arabia: Threats, Responses, and Challenges*, Westport, CT and London: Praeger Security International, 2005, p. 390.
6 The nine lawyers were: 'Isam Basrawi, Sa'ud al-Hashemi, 'Abdul Rahman Khan, 'Abdul 'Aziz al-Khirayji, Musa al-Qarni, Fahd al-Qarshi, Sayfiddin Faysal al-Sharif, 'Abdul Rahman al-Shemayri, and Sulayman al-Rushdi.
7 It was worth repeating that political parties were strictly banned.
8 "Saudi Activists Urge King to Free Jailed Reformists," *Agence France-Presse*, September 14, 2007.
9 "Saudis Free One of Nine Reformists," *Agence France-Presse*, September 22, 2007.
10 Gwenn Okruhlik, "The Irony of Islah (Reform)," *The Washington Quarterly* 28:4, Autumn, 2005, pp. 173–170 (quote on p. 167).
11 In other words, Sa'udi reformists did not intend to topple the Al Sa'ud ruling family, but wished to empower citizens with additional rights and, some hoped, responsibilities. Whether this was optimistic was far less important than what most hoped to accomplish. See, Madawi Al-Rasheed, *Contesting the Saudi State: Islamic Voices from a New Generation*, Cambridge, UK: Cambridge University Press, 2007.

12 *The Koran*, translated with notes by N.J. Dawood, London: Penguin Books, 1999, pp. 28 and 332. For background on Muhammad Ibn 'Abdul Wahhab, see Natana J. DeLong-Bas, *Wahhabi Islam: From Revival and Reform to Global Jihad*, New York: Oxford University Press, 2004.
13 It was impossible to address the emergence of such linkages here. The issue was covered in some detail in Jean-André Renoux, *L'Islam et la Conquête du Monde*, Carpentras, France: Édition CERDICIM, 1981, pp. 74–81 and 121–36.
14 For a sample of this rich literature, see Alexander S. Cudsi and Ali E. Hillal Dessouki, *Islam and Power*, Baltimore and London: The Johns Hopkins University Press, 1981; see also, Nazih Ayubi, *Political Islam: Religion and Politics in the Arab World*, London: Routledge, 1993; Patricia Crone, *God's Rule – Government and Islam: Six Centuries of Medieval Islamic Political Thought*, New York: Columbia University Press, 2005; and Sami Zubaida, *Islam, the People and the State: Political Ideas and Movements in the Middle East*, London: I. B. Tauris, 2009.
15 Joseph A. Kéchichian, *Power and Succession in Arab Monarchies: A Reference Guide*, Boulder and London: Lynne Rienner Publishers, 2008, pp. 349–78 and 383–404 [Hereafter Kéchichian – Power and Succession].
16 Ayubi, *op. cit.*, and Kéchichian – Power and Succession, *op. cit.*, pp. 25–59.
17 Madawi Al-Rasheed, *A History of Saudi Arabia*, 2nd ed. Cambridge, UK: Cambridge University Press, 2010, pp. 182–97.
18 *Ibid.*, pp. 66–68, and 69–101.
19 John S. Habib, *Ibn Sa'ud's Warriors of Islam: The Ikhwan of Najd and Thir Role in the Creation of the Sa'udi Kingdom, 1919–1930*, Leiden, The Netherlands: E.J. Brill, 1978, pp. 67–69.
20 Leslie McLoughlin, *Ibn Saud: Founder of a Kingdom*, London: Macmillan, 1993, p. 116.
21 Quoted in *Ibid*.
22 "King Faisal: Oil, Wealth And Power, *Time*, April 7, 1975, at http://www.time.com/time/magazine/article/0,9171,917226,00.html.
23 Joseph A. Kéchichian, *Faysal: Saudi Arabia's King for All Seasons*, Gainesville: University Press of Florida, 2008, pp. 55–59.
24 Joseph A. Kéchichian, "The Role of the Ulama in the Politics of an Islamic State: The Case of Saudi Arabia," *International Journal of Middle East Studies* 18:1, February 1986, pp. 53–71.
25 The "Salafi Group that Practices Hisbah," calling on society and individuals to account to eradicate social evils and improve public morality by promoting and enforcing that which "Commands Right and Forbids Wrong." *Muhtasibah* comes from a category of *Shari'ah* law, *hisbah*, whereby legal action in defense of the public interest may be taken, even though the individual making the charge has not personally suffered injury or harm.
26 Sherman A. Jackson, "Muhtasib," *The Oxford Encyclopedia of the Islamic World*, Volume 4, New York: Oxford University Press, pp. 127–28.
27 Kéchichian, Role of the Ulama, *op. cit.* For a more recent discussion of these events, see Yaroslav Trofimov, *The Siege of Mecca: The Forgotten Uprising in Islam's Holiest Shrine and the Birth of Al Qaeda*, New York: Doubleday, 2007. Trofimov assembled several anecdotal pieces of evidence, some of which is pure speculation, and relied heavily on published sources. A genuine novelty in his assessment, however, was the revelation that there were two American citizens among the rebels.
28 "Fidei Defensor," *The Economist* 301:7471, November 8, 1986, p. 49.
29 Fouad Ibrahim, *op. cit.*, pp. 178–208 and 222–50.
30 This paragraphs draws on Joseph A. Kéchichian, "Islamic Revivalism and Change in Saudi Arabia: Juhayman Al-Utaybi's 'Letters' to the Saudi People," *The Muslim World* 70:1, January 1990, pp. 1–16, which focused on the texts authored

by Juhayman. For a study on the impact of Juhayman on Islamist movements, see Thomas Hegghammer and Stephane Lacroix, "Rejectionist Islamism in Saudi Arabia: The Story of Juhayman al-'Utaybi Revisited," *International Journal of Middle East Studies* 39:1, February 2007, pp. 103–22.

31 Kéchichian, "Islamic Revivalism and Change in Saudi Arabia," *op. cit.*, p. 12.

32 The May 12, 2003 Riyadh compound terrorist attacks resulted in the deaths of 27 individuals of different nationalities, including nine Americans and seven Sa'udis, and wounded approximately 160 others. Reportedly, these attacks dramatically changed then Heir Apparent 'Abdallah's and Interior Minister Nayif's, outlooks. See Turki Al-Saheil, "Al Qaeda Sought to Replicate 9/11 Attack in 2003 Riyadh Bombings," *Al-Sharq Al-Awsat*, June 21, 2010 at http://www.aawsat.com/english/news.asp?section=1&id=21375.

33 R. Hrair Dekmejian, "The Rise of Political Islamism in Saudi Arabia," *The Middle East Journal* 48:4, Autumn 1994, pp. 627–43, quote from page 628.

34 Mordechai Abir, *Saudi Arabia in the Oil Era – Regime and Elites: Conflict and Collaboration*, Boulder, Colorado: Westview Press, 1988; See also Monica Malik and Tim Niblock, "Saudi Arabia's Economy: The Challenge of Reform," in Paul Aarts and Gerd Nonneman, eds., *Saudi Arabia in the Balance: Political Economy, Society, Foreign Affairs*, London: Hurst & Company, 2005, pp. 85–110.

35 According to the Pentagon's figures, the total cost of the war to the United States reached $61.1 billion, of which $52 billion was paid for by different countries around the world: $36 billion by Kuwait, Sa'udi Arabia, and other Persian Gulf States; $16 billion by Germany and Japan (which sent no combat forces due to their constitutions). Sa'udi Arabia may have disbursed a total of $32 billion and about 25% of its contributions were paid in the form of in-kind services to troops, including food and petroleum products. The US paid roughly $7 billion, less than 12% of the total US cost, and less than half what Sa'udi Arabia and Kuwait remunerated. See US Department of Defense, *Conduct of the Persian Gulf War: The Final Report to the US Congress*, Washington, D.C., April 1992; Appendix P, on pages 723–31 provides all of the data. For telling comments on how Sa'udi officials perceived the American requests for assistance, with sharp criticisms reserved for Commander of Allied Forces General Norman Schwarzkopf, see HRH General Khaled bin Sultan (written with Patrick Seale), *Desert Warrior: A Personal View of the Gulf War by the Joint Forces Commander*, New York: HarperCollins Publishers, 1995, pp. 290–94 and *passim*.

36 For a flavor, see Robert O. Marlin IV, *What Does Al-Qaeda Want?: Unedited Communiqués*, Berkeley, California: North Atlantic Books, 2004, especially pp. 1–30; and As'ad Abu Khalil, *Bin Laden, Islam, and America's New "War on Terrorism,"* New York: Seven Stories Press, 2002.

37 Mamoun Fandy, *Saudi Arabia and the Politics of Dissent*, New York: Palgrave, 1999, pp. 115–47.

38 Dr. Al Mas'ari shared details on his harrowing escape when we first met in London on March 25, 1995. His long saga to secure asylum is described in Gerald Butt, "Profile: Saudi political opposition," *BBC News*, February 10, 2005, at http://news.bbc.co.uk/2/hi/middle_east/3772583.stm.

39 Fandy, *op. cit.*, pp. 149–75.

40 Mahmud al-Rifa'i, *Al-Mashru' al-Islahi fil Sa'udiyyah: Qisat al-Hawali wal-'Awdah*, Washington: n.p., 1995, pp. 20–21.

41 "Secular Petitition to King Fahd," December 1990, Appendix 9.

42 Sa'ad Rashid al-Fakih, *Zalzal Al Sa'ud* [The Al Sa'ud Earthquake], London: Al-Harakah al-Islamiyyah lil-Islah, n.d, p. 49.

43 Mansoor Jassem Alshamsi, *Islam and Political Reform in Saudi Arabia: The Quest for Political Change and Reform*, New York and London: Routledge, 2011, pp. 78–116.

44 *Ibid.*, pp. 99–102. According to Alshamsi, a legal expert, 'Abdul' Aziz Al-Qasim, compiled the petition, though others participated in drafting it, too (p. 102).
45 Rif'ai, Al-Mashru' al-Islahi fil Sa'udiyyah, *op. cit.,* pp. 107–8.
46 Alshamsi, *op. cit.*, pp. 102–10. Alshami claims that 117 individuals signed the petition, which was published by the opposition newsletter *Al-Jazirah Al-Arabiyyah*, Number 21, October 1992, pp. 2–38
47 Based on my reading of the Memorandum. Alshamsi also provides a useful summary of several of these key points. See Alshamsi, *op. cit.*, pp. 103–94.
48 Joshua Teitelbaum, *Holier than Thou: Saudi Arabia's Islamic Opposition*, Washington, D.C.: The Washington Institute for Near East Policy, 2000, p. 101. It was useful to also point out that Riyadh instituted a uniform Friday sermon system in 2001.
49 "King Fahd Interview on MBC," *Foreign Broadcasting Information Service (FBIS)*, NES-223-91, November 19, 1991.
50 Quoted in Weston, *op. cit.*, p. 323. See also Teitelbaum, Holier than Thou, *op. cit.*, pp. 37–38; and Peter Molan, ed. and trans., *Arabic Religious Rhetoric: The Radical Saudi Sheikhs – A Reader*, Kensington, Maryland: Dunwoody, 1997, p. 128.
51 John L. Esposito, *The Future of Islam*, New York: Oxford University Press, 2010.
52 Salih Muhammad al-Namlah, "Hata la Yaqun 'Adaa'," *Al-Riyadh*, 28 May 1992, as cited in Uriya Shavit, "Al-Qaeda's Saudi Origins: Islamist Ideology," *Middle East Quarterly* 13:4, Fall 2006, pp. 3–13.
53 Weston, *op. cit.*, p. 323.
54 The "Vision for the Present and Future of the Nation" petition is reproduced in Appendix 11.
55 The "Defense of the Nation" petition is reproduced in Appendix 12.
56 Brian Whitaker, "Saudi National Reform Document," n.d., at http://www.al-bab.com/arab/docs/saudi/reform2003.htm.
57 National Public Radio, "The House of Saud: Martin Smith Interview with Bassim Alim," *Frontline*, December 6, 2004, at http://www.pbs.org/wgbh/pages/frontline/shows/saud/interviews/alim.html.
58 *Ibid.*
59 National Public Radio, "The House of Saud: Martin Smith Interview with Bassim Alim," *Frontline*, December 6, 2004, at http://www.pbs.org/wgbh/pages/frontline/shows/saud/interviews/alim.html.
60 Elizabeth Rubin, "A Saudi Response on Reform: Round Up the Usual Dissidents," *The New York Times*, March 21, 2004, at http://www.nytimes.com/2004/03/21/weekinreview/21rubi.html.
61 "Can Saudi Arabia Reform Itself?," *Middle East Report* Number 28, Cairo and Brussels: International Crisis Group, July 14, 2004, p. 18.
62 *Ibid.*
63 Anthony Shadid and Steve Coll, "At a Crossroads, Saudi King Tests the Winds of Reform," *The Washington Post*, August 18, 2005, p. A1+.
64 Weston, *op. cit.*, p. 434.
65 Madawi al-Rasheed, "Money Replaces Ideas as Petitioners' Silence Leaves Saudi Reform at an Impasse," April 8, 2006, in Joshua Craze and Mark Huband, eds., *The Kingdom: Saudi Arabia and the Challenge of 21st Century*, New York: Columbia University Press, 2009, pp. 19–24, the quotes are from pages 19 and 21, respectively.
66 L. Azuri, "Debate on Reform in Saudi Arabia," Washington, D. C.: The Middle East Media Research Institute, September 21, 2006 [Inquiry & Analysis Series Report No. 294]. [The statement is reproduced as Appendix 13].
67 Mashari Al-Dhaidi, "The Statement of the 61 Sheikhs is Reminiscent of bin Laden's Call to Murder Intellectuals," *Al-Sharq Al-Awsat*, May 30, 2006, p. 4.
68 "Statement on Women's Rights and Status in Islam," April 9, 2006, at http://www.islamlight.net/index.php?option=content&task=view&id=2519&Itemid=27.

69 "Statement of 14 Professors of Medicine," January 28, 2006, at http://www.islamlight.net/index.php?option=content&task=view&id=2627&Itemid=25, [Appendix 14].
70 See, for example, 'Abdul Rahman al-Lahim, "The Shaykhs' Statement is Part of the Continued Spread of Political Islam in Saudi Arabia," *Al-Watan* (Saudi Arabia), May 30, 2006, p. 14; Muhammad bin 'Abdul Latif Al al-Shaykh, "Presiding Judges Are Among the Signatories to the Statement," *Al-Jazirah* (Saudi Arabia), June 4, 2006, p. 8; and Hussein Shabukshi, "The State and the People Have Decided to Enter the 21st Century While Adhering to the 'Middle Way'," *Al-Sharq Al-Awsat*, June 6, 2006, p. 20.
71 "Saudi Arabian Women Petition King for Right to Drive," September 17, 2007, at http://www.breakingnews.ie/archives/2007/0917/world/saudi-arabian-women-petition-king-for-right-to-drive-328247.html#ixzz0hRkzOxCP.
72 The number of signatures on the actual document was far less but, adapting to the times, organizers circulated the petition online asking for additional endorsements.
73 "Wajeha Al-Huweidar: The Campaign for Women's Right to Drive in Saudi Arabia Is Just the Beginning," September 21, 2007, at http://memri.org/bin/articles.cgi?Page=subjects&Area=reform&id=sp172207. See also Ebtihal Mubarak, "Saudi Women Petitioning Govt for Driving Rights," *Arab News*, September 16, 2007, at http://www.arabnews.com/?page=1&section=0&article=101256&d=16&m=9&y=2007.
74 *Ibid* at http://memri.org/bin/articles.cgi?Page=subjects&Area=reform&id= SP172207.
75 Faiza Saleh Ambah, "Saudi Women Recall a Day of Driving: Women who Protested in 1990 Reunite as Debate over Women Drivers Returns," *The Christian Science Monitor*, December 7, 2005, at http://www.csmonitor.com/2005/1207/p06s02-wome.html.
76 "Saudi Women in Push for 2008 Driving Breakthrough," *Guardian*, January 2, 2008, at http://www.guardian.co.uk/world/2007/sep/19/saudiarabia.gender.
77 Fatima Sidiya, "Manal Al-Sharif: Testing Time," *Arab News*, May 25, 2011 at http://www.arabnews.com/saudiarabia/article427723.ece.
78 Siraj Wahab, "Manal Al-Sharif Released," *Arab News*, May 31, 2011, at http://www.arabnews.com/saudiarabia/article442275.ece.
79 Jason Burke, "Saudi Arabia Women Test Driving Ban," *Guardian*, June 17, 2011, at http://www.guardian.co.uk/world/2011/jun/17/saudi-arabia-women-drivers-protest.
80 "Wajeha Al-Huweidar: The Campaign for Women's Right to Drive in Saudi Arabia Is Just the Beginning," September 21, 2007, at http://memri.org/bin/articles.cgi?Page=subjects& Area=reform&id=SP172207.
81 Wafa' Ahmad and Samia al-'Isa, "Rasmiyyan ... Mahalat al-Nisa' lil-Nisa'," [Officially ... Women's Shops are Only for Women], *Al-Watan*, Number 4115, January 5, 2012, p. 1. See also Faysal al-Makhlafi, "Al-Mufti al-'Am: Tawzif al-Mar'at fi Bay' al-Lawazim al-Nisa'iyyah Jurmun wa Khata' wa Mukhaluf lil-Shara'," [The Grand Mufti: Women's Employment in Lingerie Shops is a Sin and an Error and Contravenes Shari'ah Law], *Al-Hayat*, December 31, 2011, pp. 1, 12; Arwah Khashifati, "'Adu Kibar al-'Ulamah: Hudur Nisa' fi Mudarajat Kurat al-Yad fi Jiddah ... La Yasuh," [Member of Senior Council of Learned Scholars: Female Attendance at Volleyball Matches in Jiddah ... Must Not be Allowed], *Al-Hayat*, January 29, 2012, pp. 1, 12; Faysal al-Makhlafi, "Hay'at Kibar al-'Ulamah Tukalif al-Jam'iyat Daris 'Zawaj al-Qasirat' wal 'Adil: Laysah 'Zahirah'," [Senior Council of Learned Scholars Designates Universities to Study Underage Marriages and (Ministry of) Justice: The Issue is Not Clear], *Al-Hayat*, January 28, 2012, pp. 1, 12; and Mustafa al-Ansari, "Al-Hayat Tanshiru 'Sijalan' bayna 'Adwayah 'Shurah' wa Kibar al-'Ulamah Hawlah Zawaj al-Qasirat," [*Al-Hayat* Publishes Transcript between Two Majlis al-Shurah Members and Senior Council of Learned Scholars Discussing Underage Marriages], *Al-Hayat*, February 3, 2012, pp. 1, 7 and 12.

82 "Saudi Activists Petition King for Reforms," *Reuters*, May 14, 2009 [Reporting by Ulf Laessing and Asma Alsharif; Editing by Andrew Hammond and Mark Trevelyan] at http://www.reuters.com/article/idUSLE922971. See Appendix 15.
83 Caryle Murphy, "Tiny Saudi Democracy Movement Sends King Blueprint for Reform," *The Christian Science Monitor*, May 14, 2009 at http://www.csmonitor.com/layout/set/print/content/view/print/246318. See also "Saudi Activists Petition Reform of Monarchy," May 16, 2009, at http://www.royaltyinthenews.com/tag/king-abdullah-bin-abdulaziz-al-saud/.
84 Murphy, *Ibid*.
85 A well-placed member of the ruling family dismissed my questions on the matter, but one could not but sense the frustration in his voice.
86 For the Arabic text recorded on the Banu 'Uqbah web page, see http://www.banioqbah.net/vb/showthread.php?p=15387.
87 Hussein Shobokshi, "A Wise Royal Decree," *Al-Sharq Al-Awsat*, August 18, 2010, at http://www.asharq-e.com/news.asp?section=2&id=22020.
88 *Ibid*.
89 Robert Lacey, *Inside the Kingdom: Kings, Clerics, Modernists, Terrorists, and the Struggle for Saudi Arabia*, New York: Viking, 2009, p. 188.
90 "Saudi Arabia: Rights Group Pans Prince," *The New York Times*, January 8, 2011, p. A9, and at http://www.nytimes.com/2011/01/08/world/middleeast/08briefs-SAUDI.html.
91 Joseph A. Kéchichian, "Fundamental New Reforms in Oman: Constitutional Amendments Highlight Sultan's Endeavour to Involve Ordinary Omanis in the Governance Process," *Gulf News*, November 3, 2011, p. 10, and at http://gulfnews.com/opinions/columnists/fundamental-new-reforms-in-oman-1.922951.
92 "Prince Turki Calls for Election of Saudi Shura Council Members," March 20, 2011, at http://www.kuna.net.kw/NewsAgenciesPublicSite/ArticleDetails.aspx?Language=en&id=2153792.
93 Eric Hendey, "Oil and Revolution," *Harvard Political Review*, May 19, 2011, at http://hpronline.org/covers/revolution/oil-and-revolution/.
94 Borzou Daragahi, "Morocco's King Proposes Constitutional Reforms, *Los Angeles Times* June 18, 2011, at http://articles.latimes.com/2011/jun/18/world/la-fg-morocco-king-reforms-20110618.
95 Joseph A. Kéchichian, "A New Constitution for Morocco," *Gulf News*, June 23, 2011, at http://gulfnews.com/mobile/opinions/columnists/a-new-constitution-for-morocco-1.825363. See also Nadim Audi, "Offering Slow, Small Changes, Morocco's King Stays in Power," *The New York Times*, July 10, 2011, p. A4, at http://www.nytimes.com/2011/07/11/world/africa/11morocco.html.
96 "Jordan's King Abdullah Welcomes Limited Reform Plans," *BBC News*, August 14, 2011, at http://www.bbc.co.uk/news/world-middle-east-14524634. See also "Constitutional Amendments Made to Ensure Balance between Powers, Wider Public Participation, *The Jordan Times*, August 15, 2011, at http://www.jordantimes.com/?news=40437. For the official translation of His Majesty King 'Abdallah's remarks on the suggested constitutional amendments by the Royal Committee on Constitutional Review, see "All Powers, Institutions should Engage, Invest in Reform Process," *The Jordan Times*, August 15, 2011, at http://www.jordantimes.com/?news=40415.
97 In early November 2011, Shaykh Hamad bin Khalifah Al Thani announced that municipal elections would be held in 2013. See "Qatar Elections to be Held in 2013 – Emir," *BBC News*, November 1, 2011, at http://www.bbc.co.uk/news/world-middle-east-15537725.
98 Joseph A. Kéchichian, "A Quest to Assert Authority," *Gulf News*, May 19, 2011, p. 10, at http://gulfnews.com/opinions/columnists/a-quest-to-assert-authority-1.809598.

99 "Saudi King Warns Against Unrest While Boosting Benefits," *BBC News*, March 18, 2011, at http://www.bbc.co.uk/news/world-middle-east-12781068.
100 "Custodian of the Two Holy Mosques Addresses Nation," *Ain-Al-Yaqeen* [Weekly Arab Political Magazine], March 19, 2011, at http://www.ainalyaqeen.com/arch_2011/mar-19/en1.php.

6 Sa'udi Arabia and the United States

1 For solid backgrounds on the US–Sa'udi relationship, see Rachel Bronson, *Thicker than Oil: America's Uneasy Partnership with Saudi Arabia*, New York: Oxford University Press, 2006; Robert Vitalis, *America's Kingdom: Mythmaking on the Saudi Oil Frontier*, Stanford, CA: Stanford University Press, 2006; and Mark Weston, *Prophets and Princes: Saudi Arabia from Muhammad to the Present*, New York: Wiley, 2008. It is not the purpose of this chapter to give a précis of US–Sa'udi ties, but to highlight how reforms in the kingdom affected existing and future relations.
2 The number of books dealing with putative problems between Sa'udi Arabia and the United States has reached gargantuan proportions in recent years. The following, listed alphabetically by author's names, is a random sampling: As'ad AbuKhalil, *The Battle for Saudi Arabia: Royalty, Fundamentalism, and Global Power*, New York: Seven Stories Press, 2004; Robert Baer, *Sleeping with the Devil: How Washington Sold Our Soul for Saudi Crude*, New York: Broadway, 2004; Dore Gold, *Hatred's Kingdom: How Saudi Arabia Supports the New Global Terrorism*, Washington, DC: Regnery Publishing, Inc., 2003; Bob Graham, *Intelligence Matters: The CIA, the FBI, Saudi Arabia, and the Failure of America's War on Terror*, New York: Random House, 2004; Thomas Hegghammer, *Jihad in Saudi Arabia: Violence and Pan-Islamism since 1979*, New York: Cambridge University Press, 2010; Steffen Hertog, *Princes, Brokers, and Bureaucrats: Oil and the State in Saudi Arabia*, Ithaca, New York: Cornell University Press, 2011; Stéphane Marchand, *Arabie Saoudite: La Menace*, Paris: Fayard, 2003; Laurent Murawiec, *Princes of Darkness: The Saudi Assault on the West*, New York: Rowman & Littlefield Publisher, 2005; David B. Ottaway, *The King's Messenger: Prince Bandar bin Sultan and America's Tangled Relationship With Saudi Arabia*, New York: Walker & Company, 2008; Gerald Posner, *Secrets of the Kingdom: The Inside Story of the Saudi–U.S. Connection*, New York: Random House, 2005; and Yaroslav Trofimov, *The Siege of Mecca: The Forgotten Uprising in Islam's Holiest Shrine and the Birth of al-Qaeda*, New York: Doubleday, 2007.
3 Antoine Basbous, *L'Arabie Saoudite en question: Du wahhabisme à Ben Laden, aux origines de la tourmente*, Paris: Perrin, 2002, p. 173.
4 Despite her many difficulties, Marianne Alireza's elegant prose is a reflection of how deep the Sa'udi affection is for family traditions that were no doubt harsh by American standards. Her book opens a fascinating window onto the ordinary lives of both the wealthy and relatively powerful, as well as the less well-off. Mazda Press reissued this marvelous essay, which was first published in 1971, because the times required an alert reader to dig deeper in what made the society tick. While some tried to decipher the Sa'udi mind set, others melted into Sa'udi life, growing closer than any politician could dream of doing. See Marianne Alireza, *At the Drop of a Veil: The True Story of an American Woman's Years in a Sa'udi Arabian Harem*, Costa Mesa, CA: Blind Owl Press, an imprint of Mazda Publishers, 2002 (first published in Boston by Houghton Mifflin Company in 1971).
5 Dore Gold, *op. cit.*, pp. 213–28.
6 The briefing was prepared by Laurent Murawiec for the Defense Policy Board, apparently on contract to the RAND Corporation, which denied any association

with the hapless author to cover its intellectual embarrassment. Murawiec reportedly argued in his briefing that the United States should demand Riyadh end all funding of fundamentalist groups, stop all anti-US and anti-Israeli statements in the kingdom, and "prosecute or isolate those involved in the terror chain," including in the Sa'udi intelligence services. If the Sa'udis refused to comply, the briefing emphasized, their oil fields and overseas financial assets should be "targeted," although specifics were not outlined. The Sa'udis, maintained the analyst, were active "at every level of the terror chain" and, clearly, needed to be reminded of their limitations. See Thomas E. Ricks, "Briefing Depicted Saudis as Enemies: Ultimatum Urged To Pentagon Board," *The Washington Post*, August 6, 2002, p. A1; and Jack Shafer, "The Power Point That Rocked the Pentagon: The La Rouche Defector who's Advising the Defense Establishment on Saudi Arabia," August 7, 2002, published online by *Slate* at http://slate.msn.com/id/2069119/.

7 One author added fire to the growing fuel with fantastic tales by asserting that the Al Sa'ud have a diabolical plan – identified as "Petro SE," for Petroleum Scorched Earth) – to sabotage the country's oil fields so as to deny them to any foe. See, Gerald Posner, *op cit.*, especially chapter 10. For a review of this bestseller, see Joseph A. Kéchichian, *The Middle East Journal* 59:4, Autumn 2005, pp. 683–85.

8 Gold, *op. cit.*, p. 12.

9 Baer, *op. cit.*, p. xxvii.

10 A carefully researched and analyzed study of the Sa'udi education system – that debunks most of arguments currently offered by "instant experts" – is available in Eleanor Abdella Doumato, "Manning the Barricades: Islam According to Saudi Arabia's School Texts," *The Middle East Journal*, Vol. 57, No. 2, Spring 2003, pp. 230–47. See also Neil MacFarquhar "Anti-Western and Extremist Views Pervade Saudi Schools," 19 October 2001, p. A1+; Michael Scott Doran, "The Saudi Paradox," *Foreign Affairs*, 83:1, January/February 2004, pp.35–51; Leon Watson, "The Arabic School Textbooks which Show Children How to Chop Off Hands and Feet Under Sharia Law," *Daily Mail*, 23 December 2011, at http://www.dailymail.co.uk/news/article-2077658/The-Arabic-textbooks-children-chop-hands-feet-Sharia-law.html.

11 Many anti-Saudi reports are widely available on the Internet. For a more serious assessment, but still in the same "genre," see Stephen Schwartz, *The Two Faces of Islam: The House of Saud from Tradition to Terror*, New York: Doubleday, 2002.

12 "Saudis Seen As Supporting Terror, Poll Shows," *The Washington Post*, February 26, 2002, p. 19. The poll, by the Institute for Jewish and Community Research, ranked Sa'udi Arabia ahead of both North Korea and Syria as a supporter of international terrorism.

13 See, "Saudi Arabians Overwhelmingly Reject Bin Laden, Al Qaeda, Saudi Fighters in Iraq, and Terrorism; Also among most pro-American in Muslim world: Results of a New Nationwide Public Opinion Survey of Saudi Arabia," Washington, D.C.: The Center for Public Opinion, 2007, at http://www.terrorfreetomorrow.org/upimagestft/TFT%20Saudi%20Arabia%20Survey.pdf.

14 Lisa Beyer with Scott MacLeod, "Saudi Arabia: Inside the Kingdom," *Time*, September 15, 2003, pp. 38–51; see also Juan Cole, *Engaging the Muslim World*, New York: Palgrave/Macmillan, 2009, pp. 83–113.

15 Paul Michael Wihbey, "The End of the Affair," *The Spectator*, September 6, 2003, pp. 20–21; see also Y. Admon and Y. Carmon, "Reforms in Saudi Arabia Under King Abdallah (Part I)," *The Middle East Media Research Institute-MEMRI*, 1 June 2009 [Inquiry & Analysis Series Report No. 519], at http://www.memri.org/report/en/0/0/0/0/0/254/3324.htm; and Daniel Pipes, "Is Saudi Arabia

Opening Up?," *National Review* [Online], January 4, 2011, at http://www.danielpipes. org/9274/saudi-arabia-opening-up.
16 Toby Jones, "Saudi Arabia's Regional Reaction," *The Nation*, September 12, 2011, at http://www.thenation.com/article/162962/saudi-arabias-regional-reaction. See also Bruce Riedel, "Brezhnev in the Hejaz," *The National Interest*, Number 115 (September/October 2011), pp. 27–32.
17 F. Gregory Gause III, *Saudi Arabia in the New Middle East*, New York: Council on Foreign Relations, Special Report Number 63, December 2011.
18 For an articulation of this viewpoint, see Fereydoun Hoveyda, "Saudi Arabia: Friend or Foe?," *American Foreign Policy Interests* 24: 491–505, 2002, especially p. 499.
19 Graham E. Fuller, "US Should Support Arab Spring, not Saudi Arabia's Dangerous Reaction," *The Christian Science Monitor*, June 7, 2011, at http://www.csmonitor. com/Commentary/Global-Viewpoint/2011/0607/US-should-support-Arab-Spring-not-Saudi-Arabia-s-dangerous-reaction.
20 According to a leaked State Department memo, Secretary of State Hilary R. Clinton complained that Sa'udi Arabia was "the world's largest source of funds for Islamist militant groups such as the Afghan Taliban and Lashkar-e-Taiba – but the Saudi government [was] reluctant to stem the flow of money." See Declan Walsh, "WikiLeaks Cables Portray Saudi Arabia as a Cash Machine for Terrorists," *Guardian*, December 5, 2010, at http://www.guardian.co.uk/world/2010/dec/05/ wikileaks-cables-saudi-terrorist-funding.
21 Gause, *op. cit.*, p. 23.
22 For the most recent report, see Bureau of Democracy, Human Rights, and Labor, "Saudi Arabia," *2010 International Religious Freedom, July–December*, Washington, D.C.: US Department of State, at http://www.state.gov/j/drl/rls/irf/2010_5/ 168275.htm.
23 Abdul Nabi Shaheen, "Saudi Legal Activists and Religious Scholars Slam US Report on Religious Freedom," *Gulf News*, September 15, 2011, at http://gulfnews.com/ news/gulf/saudi-arabia/saudi-legal-activists-and-religious-scholars-slam-us-report-on-religious-freedom-1.867302.
24 Institute for American Values, "What We're Fighting For: A Letter from America," which was a response drafted after 9/11 and the War for Afghanistan that first circulated in late 2001 but was dated February 2002. It was available, along with a full list of its signatories, at http://www.americanvalues.org/html/what_we_re_ fighting_for.html.
25 The majority were university professors.
26 "How We Can Coexist," was dated January 1, 2002, and first appeared on www. islamtoday.net at http://en.islamtoday.net/artshow-417-2952.htm.
27 The document provided a detailed list of alleged egregious American foreign policy faults that covered the gamut from Israel/Palestine to Afghanistan.
28 This was not an uncommon position held by leading Arab thinkers. For a unique analysis on Arab perceptions of the United States after for War for Kuwait, see, Mahdi Elmandjra, *Première Guerre Civilisationnelle*, Casablanca, Morocco: Toubkal, 1992. It is available, albeit in French, online at http://www.elmandjra. org/livre1/Tablematiere.html.
29 Many Muslims continued to refer to the thousand-year-old Crusades as determinant events that colored their views of the West.
30 Various US reports, official as well as academic, touched on this sensitive subject. For a sample, see the annual *Country Reports on Human Rights Practices: Saudi Arabia*, with the most recent covering 2010, Washington, D.C.: US Department of State, 2011, at http://www.state.gov/j/drl/rls/hrrpt/2010/nea/154472.htm. See also the equally valuable *Trafficking in Persons Report*, now in its 10th edition, Washington, D.C.: US Department of State, June 2010, at http://www.state.gov/ documents/organization/142979.pdf with critical data pertaining to women. For

further insights, see, Alfred B. Prados, *Saudi Arabia: Current Issues and U.S. Relations*, Congressional Research Service Issue Brief for Congress, IB93113, Washington, D.C.: The Library of Congress, February 24, 2006; Virginia N. Sherry, "Bad Dreams: Exploitation and Abuse of Migrant Workers in Saudi Arabia," in W. Brown and J. Saunders (eds.,), New York: Human Rights Watch, 2004, at http://www.unhcr.org/refworld/docid/412ef32a4.html; Amnesty International, "Saudi Arabia: Gross Human Rights Abuses Against Women," 2000, at http://www.amnestyusa.org/document.php?lang=e&id=D2C1FC0D-C59EC51C802569610071BFEC; A Report by the Office of Senator Frank R. Lautenberg, "In Whose Best Interest?: Top Ten Reasons to Change the Saudi–U.S. Relationship," Washington, D.C.: n.d (2006?), especially page 10; and The Freedom House, *Saudi Publications on Hate Ideology Fill American Mosques*, Washington, D. C.: Center for Religious Freedom, 2005, available at: http://www.freedomhouse.org/religion/publications/Saudi%20Report/FINAL%20FINAL.pdf.
31 Al-Majd operated four free air channels, including Almajd-Main (General), Almajd-Holy Qur'an, Almajd-Hadiths, and Almajd-'Ilmiyyah (Religious Sciences). An additional ten pay channels offered various religious programs.
32 Reuters, "Senior Saudi Cleric Gripes About Lack of Consultation by King Over Votes for Women," *The National* (Abu Dhabi, UAE), October 3, 2011, at http://www.thenational.ae/news/worldwide/middle-east/senior-saudi-cleric-gripes-about-lack-of-consultation-by-king-over-votes-for-women.
33 It is important to note that the US Department of State maintained a major Bureau of Educational and Cultural Affairs that is active throughout the world and that worked to foster mutual understanding between the people of the United States and others by offering scholarships and sponsoring a variety of educational programs. See http://exchanges.state.gov/.
34 Technion was established in 1924 as a science and technology center, even before Israel came into being in 1948. Its first class of 16 students enrolled in civil engineering and architecture classes, though the influx of Polish, German, and Austrian scientists throughout the 1930s quickly swelled its ranks. This is where members of the Jewish opposition to the British Mandate in Palestine learned how to rely on technology to engage the British as well as the Palestinians. At the time, the first President of the Technion Society, Albert Einstein, opined that "Israel can win the battle for survival only by developing expert knowledge in technology." After 1949, when a Department of Aeronautical Engineering was established that launched a successful aerospace industry, critical research areas were identified that encompassed several disciplines, ranging from chemistry to physics to medicine to computer sciences. Needless to say that Technion reached enviable levels and now competes with European, Asian, and American institutions of higher learning. To say that Technion is dedicated to serving Israel would be an understatement and, over the years, both the state as well as its thousands of alumni have generously contributed to its welfare. Today, its 15,000 faculty and students make important contributions, with several Nobel laureates adding value in various fields.
35 One petition, in particular, called on Riyadh to allow free elections for the *Majlis al-Shurah*. See, "A Declaration of National Reform," February 23, 2011, which is reproduced in Appendix 16. The petition was signed by 920 Sa'udis, whose names were published at http://www.saudireform.com/?p=names.
36 Gause, *op. cit.*, p. 9.
37 Riyadh was wary of the democratization wave and issued stringent regulations regarding political speech. Its security forces continued to arrest activists on a variety of grounds, though the writing was on the wall: political participation was no longer a taboo subject. See, "Saudi Arabia: Rights Activists, Bloggers Arrested," *Human Rights Watch*, May 3, 2011, at http://www.hrw.org/news/2011/05/03/saudi-arabia-rights-activist-bloggers-arrested.

38 Karen Elliott House, "From Tunis to Cairo to Riyadh?," *The Wall Street Journal*, February 15, 2011 at http://online.wsj.com/article/SB10001424052748704657104576142452195225530.html.
39 Ambassador James B. Smith, "Saudi Succession: Can the Allegiance Commission Work?," E.O. 12958: Decl: 10/25/2019, Ref: A. Riyadh 1402 B. 08 Riyadh 1757, Secret Section, Noforn Sipdis, October 28, 2009, available at Wikileaks, http://wikileaks.org/cable/2009/10/09RIYADH1434.html.
40 It was disquieting to read the use of the title "Crown Prince" for a kingdom that boasted no crown. The title, of course, was *wali al-'ahd*, which translates as "Heir Apparent."
41 The cable provides the following birthdates for the princes: Salman (b. 1935), Abdul Illah (b. 1938), Sattam (b. 1942), Ahmad (b. 1942), and Muqrin (b. 1945).
42 The cable provides the following birthdates for the princes: Muhammad bin Sa'ud (b. 1934), Khalid al-Faysal (b. 1940), Khalid bin Sultan (b. 1947), Sa'ud al-Faysal (b. 1940), 'Abdul 'Aziz bin Fahd (b. 1973), Sultan bin Fahd (b. 1952), Mit'ab bin 'Abdallah (b. 1953), 'Abdul 'Aziz bin 'Abdallah (b. 1962), Sultan bin Salman (b. 1956), Muhammad bin Nayif (b. 1958), 'Abdul 'Aziz bin Salman (b. 1960), 'Abdul 'Aziz bin Bandar (b. 1951), and Mansur bin Mit'ab (b. 1950).
43 Ali Alyami, "Saudi Arabia at a Crossroads," Washington, D.C.: Center for Democracy and Human Rights in Saudi Arabia, June 19, 2012, at http://www.cdhr.infor/. See also Simon Henderson, "Good Riddance: Saudi Arabia's Crown Prince Nayef was a menace. We should be happy he's gone, but worried about the aging House of Saud he leaves behind," *Foreign Policy* [online], June 18, 2012, at http://www.foreignpolicy.com/articles/2012/06/18/good_riddance
44 P. K. Abdul Ghaffour, "Strong and Smooth Transition," *Arab News*, June 18, 2012, at http://www.arabnews.com/saudi-arabia/strong-and-smooth-transition
45 American confusion arose once again in the spring of 2011 when the State Department criticized Sa'udi Arabia for its policy toward Bahrain, while the Secretary of Defense, in his April 2011 visit to Riyadh, did not even raise this particular issue. See Elisabeth Bumiller, "Defense Chief is on Mission to Mend Saudi Relations," *The New York Times*, April 7, 2011, http://www.nytimes.com/2011/04/07/world/middleeast/07military.html.
46 Simon Henderson, "Outraged in Riyadh," *ForeignPolicy.com*, April 14, 2011, at http://www.foreignpolicy.com/articles/2011/04/14/outraged_in_riyadh.
47 Elaine Sciolino, "Out Front: A Desert Kingdom Takes the Spotlight," *The New York Times*, March 3, 2002, at http://www.nytimes.com/2002/03/03/weekinreview/the-world-out-front-a-desert-kingdom-takes-the-spotlight.html.
48 *Ibid.*
49 For an interesting discussion of these visits, see David B. Ottaway, *op. cit.*, pp. 235–50.
50 Paul Richter and Neela Banerjee, "U.S.–Saudi Rivalry Intensifies," *The Los Angeles Times*, June 19, 2011, at http://articles.latimes.com/2011/jun/19/world/la-fg-us-saudis-20110619.
51 Martin Indyk, "Amid the Arab Spring, Obama's dilemma over Saudi Arabia," *The Washington Post*, April 7, 2011, p. 15, also at http://www.washingtonpost.com/opinions/amid-the-arab-spring-obamas-dilemma-over-saudi-arabia/2011/04/07/AFhILDxC_print.html.
52 *Ibid.*
53 For an interesting recent survey that documented the limited impact Arab revolutions have had on Sa'udi Arabia, see Sa'ud al-Sarhan, "Arab Reform Initiative: Arab Democracy Barometer," *The Rahmania Annual Seminar,* Riyadh: Saudi National Security Assessment Project Holdings, January 11–13, 2012.
54 See the comments made by Toby C. Jones, a Professor of History at Rutgers University, during the *Saudi Arabia in the New Middle East* seminar at the

Council on Foreign Relations in New York on January 26, 2012, at http://www.cfr.org/saudi-arabia/saudi-arabia-new-middle-east-video/p27175. For an interesting commentary on dissent in the kingdom, see Toby C. Jones, "The Price of Dissent in Saudi Arabia," *The Nation*, February 15, 2012, at http://www.thenation.com/print/article/166305/price-dissent-saudi-arabia.

55 'Abdul 'Aziz al-'Atar, "Mufti al-Mamlakah: al-Muzaharat Khutut li-Tafkik al-Ummah" [Mufti of the Kingdom: Demonstrations Are Plans to Dismember the Nation], *Al-Watan* [Sa'udi Arabia], February 5, 2011, at, http://www.alwatan.com.sa/Local/News_Detail.aspx?ArticleID=40472.

56 "Remarks by the President on A New Beginning," Cairo University, Cairo, Egypt, June 4, 2009, at http://www.whitehouse.gov/the-press-office/remarks-president-cairo-university-6-04-09; see also Martin Peretz, "Narrative Dissonance: What the Cairo Speech Got Wrong," *The New Republic*, July 1, 2009, at http://www.tnr.com/article/narrative-dissonance; and Joseph A. Kéchichian, "High Expectations for Obama in Cairo," *Gulf News*, June 4, 2009, at http://archive.gulfnews.com/articles/09/06/04/10319450.html.

57 Robert Burns, "US Quietly Expanding Defense Ties with Saudis," *Army Times*, May 19, 2011, at http://www.armytimes.com/news/2011/05/ap-us-quietly-expanding-defense-ties-with-saudis-051911.

58 Richard Spencer, "Saudi Arabia is safe for now. But what about in 2020?," September 22, 2010, at http://blogs.telegraph.co.uk/news/richardspencer/100054807/saudi-arabia-is-safe-for-now-but-what-about-in-2020/.

59 The contrary argument focuses on unsuccessful Sa'udi regional foreign policy efforts that, the logic goes, required Washington not to encourage Riyadh as it strengthened sectarian identities and sectarian confrontations. Although Sa'udis made a conscious decision to increase their support for allies and isolate Iran in the Arab world, and while they would, in all probability, support an American military strike against Iranian nuclear facilities, such strikes could stir up *Shi'ah* opposition that was presumably in neither country's interest.

7 Conclusion

1 Tajuddin Abdul Haq, "Abdullah Slams GCC Indecision," *Arab News*, December 31, 2001, at http://archive.arabnews.com/?page=4&section=0&article=11648&d=31&m=12&y=2001.

2 "Khadim al-Haramayn lil-Sha'ab al-Sa'udi: Ana bidunkum la-Shay'," [Custodian of the Two Holy Mosques: I am Nothing Without You], *Al Hayat*, February 25, 2012, pp. 1, 14, at http://www.ksa.daralhayat.com/ksaarticle/366955.

Bibliography

Additional materials, including newspaper citations and web links, are only included as footnotes to each chapter.

Aarts, Paul, and Gerd Nonneman. *Saudi Arabia in the Balance: Political Economic, Society, Foreign Affairs*, London: Hurst and Company, 2005.
'Abdallah, 'Abdul-Khaliq, ed., *Muntadah al-Tanmiyyah, Al 'Alam fi Dawal al-Khalij* [The World in the Gulf States], Kuwait: Dar Qurtas, 2007.
——. *Muntadah al-Tanmiyyah, Duwal al Khalij wal 'Awwlamah* [GCC States and Globalization], Kuwait: Dar Qurtas, 2000.
——. *Muntadah al-Tanmiyyah, Ittijahat al-Shabab fi Dawal Majlis al-Ta'awun* [Prospects for Youths in the Gulf Cooperation Council States], Kuwait: Dar Qurtas, 2006.
——. *Muntadah al-Tanmiyyah, Al-Khalij al-'Arabi wal Muhit al-Asyawih* [The Arab Gulf Region and the Asian Continent], Kuwait: Dar Qurtas, 2002.
——. *Muntadah al-Tanmiyyah, Al-Khalij 'Arabi wa Farisi wa-Tahadiyyat al-Qarn al-Wahid wal-'Ushrun* [The Arabian and Persian Gulf and the Challenges of the Twenty-First Century], Kuwait: Dar Qurtas, 1990.
——. *Muntadah al-Tanmiyyah, Mutatalabat wa Tahadiyat al-Tahawal al-Democrati fi Duwal Majlis al-Ta'awun* [Demands and Challenges of the Democratic Transformations in the Gulf Cooperation Council States], Kuwait: Dar Qurtas, 2001.
——. *Muntadah al-Tanmiyyah, Qadayah wa Humum al Mutjama'ah al Madani fi Duwal Majlis al Ta'awun* [Civil Society Issues and Concerns in the Gulf Cooperation Council States], Kuwait: Dar Qurtas, 1998.
——. *Muntadah al-Tanmiyyah, Al-Tanmiyyah al-Bashariyyah fi Dawal Majlis al-Ta'awun* [Human Development in the Gulf Cooperation Council States], Kuwait: Dar Qurtas, 2003.
——. *Muntadah al-Tanmiyyah, Al-Wulayat al-Mutahidah al-Amerikiyyah wal-Khalij* [The United States of America and the Gulf], Kuwait: Dar Qurtas, 2005.
Abir, Mordechai. *Saudi Arabia in the Oil Era: Regime and Elites; Conflict and Collaboration*, Boulder, Colorado: Westview Press, 1988.
AbuKhalil, As'ad. *The Battle for Saudi Arabia: Royalty, Fundamentalism, and Global Power*, New York: Steven Stories Press, 2004.
Aburish, Said. *The Rise, Corruption and Coming Fall of the House of Saud*, London: Bloomsbury Publishing, 1994.
Abu Talib, Hamid Muhammad. *Al-Nizam al-Qada'i fil-Mamlakah al-'Arabiyyah al-Sa'udiyyah* [The Judiciary in the Kingdom of Sa'udi Arabia], Beirut: Dar al-Fikr al-'Arabi, 1984.

Akbarzadeh, Shahram, and Abdullah Saeed (eds), *Islam and Political Legitimacy*, London: Routledge Curzon, 2003.

'Ali, Gaafar 'Abdul Salam. *Al-Nizam al-Idari al-Sa'udi* [The Administrative Law in Sa'udi Arabia], Cairo: Al-Salfiyat, 1977.

Alireza, Marianne. *At the Drop of a Veil: The True Story of an American Woman's Years in a Sa'udi Arabian Harem*, Costa Mesa, CA: Blind Owl Press, an imprint of Mazda Publishers, 2002 (first published in Boston by Houghton Mifflin Company in 1971).

Alrabaa, Sami. *Veiled Atrocities: True Stories of Oppression in Saudi Arabia*, Amherst, New York: Prometheus Books, 2010.

Arabi, Oussama. *Studies in Modern Islamic Law and Jurisprudence*, Leiden, The Netherlands: Brill Academic Publishers, Inc., 2001.

Armstrong, Harold C. *Lord of Arabia: Ibn Saud, An Intimate Study of a King*, London: Arthur Barker, Ltd., 1934.

Bachar, Shmuel, Shmuel Bar, Rachel Machtiger, and Yair Minzili, *Establishment Ulama and Radicalism in Egypt, Saudi Arabia, and Jordan*, Washington, D.C.: Hudson Institute [Center on Islam, Democracy, and the Future of the Muslim World], Research Monographs on the Muslim World, Series No. 1, Paper No. 4, December 2006.

Baer, Robert. *Sleeping with the Devil: How Washington Sold Our Soul for Saudi Crude*, New York: Broadway, 2004.

Al Baghdadi, Imam Abul Husayn Ahmad Ibn Muhammad Ibn Ahmad Ibn Ja'far Ibn Hamdan. *The Mukhtasar Al-Quduri: A Manual of Islamic Law According to the Hanafi School*, translated by Tahir Mahmood Kiani, London: Taha Publishers, 2010.

Barlas, Asma. *Believing Women in Islam: Unreading Patriarchal Interpretations of the Qur'an*, Austin: University of Texas Press, 2002.

Basbous, Antoine. *L'Arabie Saoudite En Question: Du wahhabisme à Bin Laden, aux origines de la tourmente*, Paris: Perrin, 2002.

Al-Baz, Rania. *Défigurée: Quand un crime passionnel devient affaire d'Etat*, Paris: Michal Lafont, 2005.

——. *Disfigured: A Saudi Woman's Story of Triumph over Violence*, translated by Catherine Spencer, New York: Interlink Publishing Group, 2008.

Belling, Willard A. *King Faisal and the Modernisation of Saudi Arabia*, London: Croom Helm, 1980.

Benoist-Mechin. *Fayçal, Roi d'Arabie: L'Homme, Le Souverain, Sa Place dans le Monde 1906–1975*, Paris: Albin Michel, 1975.

——. *Le Loup et le Leopard: Ibn-Seoud ou la naissance d'un royaume*, Paris: Albin Michel, 1955.

Al-Bishr, Ibrahim Ibn Abdul Aziz. *Judicial Systems and Safeguards of Human Rights in the Kingdom of Saudi Arabia*, Reading, UK: Garnet Publishing, January 2013.

Bligh, Alexander. *From Prince to King: Royal Succession in the House of Saud in the Twentieth Century*, New York and London: New York University Press, 1984.

Bostom, Andrew G. *The Legacy of Jihad: Islamic Holy War and the Fate of Non-Muslims*, Amherst, New York: Prometheus Books, 2005.

Bradley, John R. *Saudi Arabia Exposed: Inside a Kingdom in Crisis*, New York: Palgrave Macmillan, 2006.

Bronson, Rachel. *Thicker than Oil: America's Uneasy Partnership with Saudi Arabia*, New York: Oxford University Press, 2006.

Brown, Anthony Cave. *Oil, God, and Gold: The Story of Aramco and the Saudi Kings*, Boston and New York: Houghton Mifflin Company, 1999.

Bucaille, Maurice. *The Bible, the Qur'an, and Science: The Holy Scriptures Examined in the Light of Modern Knowledge*, Chicago: Illinois: Kazi Publications, Incorporated, 2002.

Bulloch, John. *Reforms of the Saudi Arabian Constitution*, London: Gulf Centre for Strategic Studies, 1992.

Citino, Nathan J. *From Arab Nationalism to OPEC: Eisenhower, King Sa'ud, and the Making of U.S.–Sa'udi Relations*, Bloomington and Indianapolis, IN: Indiana University Press, 2002.

Cole, Donald Powell. *Nomads of the Nomads: The Al Murrah Bedouin of the Empty Quarter*, Arlington Heights, Illinois: Harlan Davidson, Inc., 1975.

Cole, Juan. *Engaging the Muslim World*, New York: Palgrave Macmillan, 2009.

Cordesman, Anthony H. *Sa'udi Arabia Enters the Twenty-First Century: The Political, Foreign Policy, Economic, and Energy Dimensions*, Westport, CT and London, UK: Praeger (published in cooperation with the Center for Strategic and International Studies, Washington, DC), 2003.

Coulson, Noel J. *Conflicts and Tensions in Islamic Jurisprudence*, Chicago: University of Chicago Press, 1969.

Craze, Joshua, and Mark Huband, eds., *The Kingdom: Saudi Arabia and the Challenge of the 21st Century*, New York: Columbia University Press, 2009.

Al-Darayb, Sa'ud. *Al-Tanzim al-Qada'i fil-Mamlakah al-'Arabiyyah al-Sa'udiyyah fi Da'wah al-Shari'ah al-Islamiyyah wa Nizam al-Sulta al-Qada'iyyah* [The Judiciary in the Kingdom of Sau'di Arabia in *Shari'ah* and the Rules of its Authorities], Riyadh: King Muhammad bin Sa'ud University Press, 1999.

Davis, Helen Miller. *Constitutions, Electoral Laws, Treaties of States in the Near and Middle East*, Durham: Duke University Press, 1947.

Decker, Kristin. *The Unveiling: An American Teacher in a Saudi Palace*, College Station, Texas: Virtualbookworm.com Publishing, 2006.

De Gaury, Gerald. *Faisal: King of Saudi Arabia*, New York: Praeger, 1966.

Delong-Bas, Natana J. *Wahhabi Islam: From Revival and Reform to Global Jihad*, New York: Oxford University Press, 2004.

Elmandjra, Mahdi. *Première Guerre Civilisationnelle*, Casablanca, Morocco: Toubkal, 1992.

Emerson, Steven. *American Jihad: The Terrorists Living Among Us*, New York: Free Press, 2002.

Fandy, Mamoun. *Saudi Arabia and the Politics of Dissent*, New York: St. Martin's Press, 1999.

Ibn Faris, Abul Husayn Ahmad. *Mu'jam Maqayis al-Lughah* [Glossary of Standards in Language], Beirut: Dar al-Fikr, 1997.

Al-Farsy, Fouad. *Modernity and Tradition: The Saudi Equation*, London: Knight Communications, 1994.

Freedom House. *Saudi Publications on Hate Ideology Fill American Mosques*, Washington, D. C.: Center for Religious Freedom, 2005.

Fusul Min Tarikh al-'Arabiyyah Al-Sa'udiyyah [Chapters from the History of Saudi Arabia], Beirut?: Dar al-Fada' lil-Tibayat wal-Nashr wal-Tawzi', 1988.

Gabriel, Brigitte. *Because They Hate: A Survivor of Islamic Terror Warns America*, New York: St. Martin's Griffin, 2008.

Gause, F. Gregory, III. *Oil Monarchies: Domestic and Security Challenges in the Arab Gulf States*, New York: Council on Foreign Relations, 1994.

——. *Saudi Arabia in the New Middle East*, New York: Council on Foreign Relations, Special Report Number 63, December 2011.

——. *Saudi–Yemeni Relations: Domestic Structures and Foreign Influence*, New York: Columbia University Press, 1990.

Gold, Dore. *Hatred's Kingdom: How Saudi Arabia Supports the New Global Terrorism*, Washington, DC: Regnery Publishing, Inc., 2003.

Goldberg, Jacob. *The Foreign Policy of Sa'udi Arabia: The Formative Years 1902–1918*, Cambridge, Massachusetts: Harvard University Press, 1986.

Graham, Bob. *Intelligence Matters: The CIA, the FBI, Saudi Arabia, and the Failure of America's War on Terror*, New York: Random House, 2004.

Habib, John S. *Ibn Sa'ud's Warriors of Islam: The Ikhwan of Najd and Their Role in the Creation of the Saudi Kingdom, 1910–1930*, Leiden, The Netherlands: E. J. Brill, 1978.

Hamzah, Fuad. *Al-Bilad al-'Arabiyyah al-Sa'udiyyah* [The Kingdom of Saudi Arabia], 2nd edition, Cairo: Maktabat al-Nasr al-Hadithat, 1968.

Hegghammer, Thomas. *Jihad in Saudi Arabia: Violence and Pan-Islamism Since 1979*, Cambridge: Cambridge University Press, 2010.

Helms, Christine Moss. *The Cohesion of Saudi Arabia: Evolution of Political Identity*, Baltimore & London: The Johns Hopkins University Press, 1981.

Henderson, Simon. *After King Abdullah: Succession in Saudi Arabia*, Washington, D.C.: The Washington Institute for Near East Policy, *Policy Focus* Number 96, August 2009.

——. *After King Fahd: Succession in Saudi Arabia*, Washington, D.C.: The Washington Institute for Near East Policy, 1994, 1995.

Herb, Michael. *All in the Family: Absolutism, Revolution, and Democracy in the Middle Eastern Monarchies*, Albany: State University of New York Press, 1999.

Hertog, Steffen. *Princes, Brokers, and Bureaucrats: Oil and the State in Saudi Arabia*, Ithaca, New York: Cornell University Press, 2011.

Holden, David, and Richard Johns, *The House of Saud: The Rise and Rule of the Most Powerful Dynasty in the Arab World*, New York: Holt, Rinehart and Winston, 1981.

——. *Farewell to Arabia*, London: Faber and Faber, 1966.

Hollingsworth, Mark. *Saudi Babylon: Torture, Corruption and Cover-Up Inside the House of Saud*, Edinburgh, U.K.: Mainstream Publishing, 2005.

Hopwood, Derek. *The Arabian Peninsula: Society and Politics*, London: George Allen and Unwin Ltd., 1972.

Howarth, David. *The Desert King: The Life of Ibn Saud*, London: Quartet Books, 1965, 1980.

Huyette, Summer Scott. *Political Adaptation in Sa'udi Arabia: A Study of the Council of Minister*, Boulder and London: Westview Press, 1985.

Al-Jarbou, Ayoub M. *Judicial Review of Administrative Actions: A Comparative Study between the United States and Saudi Arabia*, Charlottesville: University of Virginia [S.J.D. dissertation], 2002.

Al-Jawziyah, Ibn Qayyim. *al-Turuq al-Hukmiyyah fil-Siyasah al-Shari'yyah* [Legal Administration in Divine Law], 1986.

Al Johany, E. M. *Consultation and the Art of Government in the Kingdom of Saudi Arabia*, Riyadh: King Saud University Press, 1992.

Jones, Toby Craig. *Desert Kingdom: How Oil and Water Forged Modern Saudi Arabia*, Cambridge, Massachusetts and London, England: Harvard University Press, 2010.

Bibliography

Kéchichian, Joseph A. *Succession in Saudi Arabia*, New York: Palgrave, 2001.

——. *Faysal: Saudi Arabia's King for All Seasons*, Gainesville: University Press of Florida, 2008.

——. *Power and Succession in Arab Monarchies: A Reference Guide*, Boulder and London: Lynne Rienner Publishers, 2008.

Al-Khalidi, Mahmoud. *Ma'alim al-Khilafah fil-Fikr al-Siyasi al-Islami* [Features of Succession in Islamic Political Thought], Beirut: Dar al-Jil, 1984.

Kishk, Muhammad Jalal. *Al-Saudiyyun Wal-Hal Al-Islami* [The Saudis and the Islamic Solution], Jeddah: The Saudi Publishing and Distribution House, 1982.

The Koran, translated with notes by N. J. Dawood, London: Penguin Books, 1999.

Kostiner, Joseph. *The Making of Saudi Arabia 1916–1936: From Chieftancy to Monarchical State*, New York and Oxford: Oxford University Press, 1993.

Lacey, Robert. *Inside the Kingdom: Kings, Clerics, Modernists, Terrorists, and the Struggle for Saudi Arabia*, New York: Viking, 2009.

——. *The Kingdom: Arabia and the House of Saud*, London: Hutchinson, 1981.

Lackner, Helen. *A House Built on Sand: A Political Economy of Saudi Arabia*, London: Ithaca Press, 1978.

Lan, Pei-Chia. *Global Cinderellas: Migrant Domestics and Newly Rich Employers in Taiwan*, Durham, North Carolina: Duke University Press, 2006.

Lees, Brian. *A Handbook of the Al Sa'ud Family of Saudi Arabia*, London: Royal Genealogies, 1980.

Levine, Mark. *Why They Don't Hate Us: Lifting the Veil on the Axis of Evil*, New York: Oneworld, 2005.

Lewis, Bernard. *The Crisis of Islam: Holy War and Unholy Terror*, New York: Random House, 2004.

——. *What Went Wrong: Western Impact and Middle Eastern Response*, New York: Oxford University Press, 2002.

Lippman, Thomas W. *Inside the Mirage: America's Fragile Partnership with Saudi Arabia*, Boulder: Westview Press, 2004.

Long, David E. *The Kingdom of Saudi Arabia*, Gainesville, Florida: University Press of Florida, 1997.

Al Maliki, Muhammad Al Kharshi. *Hashiyah 'ala Mukhtasar Khalil* [Commentary on Khalil's Mukhtasar], 8 volumes, 1997.

Bin Manzur, Jamaluddin Muhammad bin Mukaram. *Lisan al-'Arab* [The Arab Tongue], Beirut: Dar Sadir, 1997, volume 2.

Marchand, Stéphane. *Arabie Saoudite: La Menace*, Paris: Fayard, 2003.

McLoughlin, Leslie. *Ibn Saud: Founder of a Kingdom*, Houndmills and London: Macmillan Press, Ltd, 1993.

Middle East Watch, *Empty Reforms: Saudi Arabia's New Basic Laws*, New York: Human Rights Watch, May 1992.

Muhammad, Muhammad 'Ali al-Jawwad. *Al-Tatawwur al-Tashri'i fil-Mamlakah al-'Arabiyyah al-Su'udiyyah* [Legislative Development in the Kingdom of Saudi Arabia], Alexandria, Egypt: Munshaat al-Maarif, 1977.

Murawiec, Laurent. *Princes of Darkness: The Saudi Assault on the West*, Lanham, Maryland: Rowman & Littlefield Publishers, 2005.

Niblock, Tim. *Saudi Arabia: Power, Legitimacy and Survival*, London and New York: Routledge, 2006.

Nolan, Leigh. *Managing Reform?: Saudi Arabia and the King's Dilemma*, Doha, Qatar: Brookings Doha Center, May 2011.

Obaid, Nawaf E. *The Oil Kingdom at 100: Petroleum Policymaking in Saudi Arabia*, Policy Papers No. 55, Washington, D.C.: The Washington Institute for Near East Policy, 2000.

Ottaway, David B. *The King's Messenger: Prince Bandar bin Sultan and America's Tangled Relationship With Saudi Arabia*, New York: Walker & Company, 2008.

Peterson, J. E. *Sa'udi Arabia and the Illusion of Security*, London, UK: Oxford University Press (for the International Institute for Strategic Studies), 2002 [Adelphi Paper 348].

Philby, H. St. John B. *Sa'udi Arabia*, London: Ernest Benn Limited, 1955.

Posner, Gerald. *Secrets of the Kingdom: The Inside Story of the Saudi–U.S. Connection*, New York: Random House, 2005.

Powell, William. *Saudi Arabia and Its Royal Family*, Secaucus, New Jersey: Lyle Stuart, Inc., 1982.

Qazwini, Muhammad Hasan, et al. *Al-Imamah Al-Kubrah Wal-Khilafah Al-'Uzma*, Tehran, Iran: Dar al-Mujtabah, 2006.

Rabasa, Angel M. et al. *The Muslim World after 9/11*, MG-246, Santa Monica, California: RAND [Project AIR FORCE], 2004.

Ramadan, Tariq. *In the Footsteps of the Prophet: Lessons from the Life of Muhammad*, New York: Oxford University Press, 2009.

Al Rasheed, Madawi. *Contesting the Saudi State: Islamic Voices from a New Generation*, Cambridge: Cambridge University Press, 2007.

——. *A History of Saudi Arabia*, 2nd edition, Cambridge: Cambridge University Press, 2010.

——. *Politics in an Arabian Oasis: The Rashidi Tribal Dynasty*, London and New York: I. B. Tauris & Co. Limited, 1991.

Rashid, Ibrahim, ed. *Documents in the History of Saudi Arabia*, Salisbury, North Carolina: Documentary Publications, 1980.

al-Rashid, Zamil Muhammad. *Sa'udi Relations with Eastern Arabia and 'Uman (1800–1871)*, London: Luzac & Company Limited, 1981.

al-Rayyes, Riyad Najib. *Riyah al-Shamal: Al Sa'udiyyah wal-Khalij wal-'Arab fi 'Alam al-Tis'inat*, [Northern Wind: Saudi Arabia, the Gulf and the Arabs in the Nineties], London and Beirut: Riad El-Rayyes Books Limited, 1997.

——. *Sira al-Wahat wa-al-Naft: Humum al-Khalij al-Arabi Bayna 1968–1971* [The Struggle of Oases and Oil: Troubles of the Arabian Gulf, 1968–71], Beirut: al-Nahar, al-Khidmat al-Sihafiya, 1973.

Al-Rifa'i, Mahmud. *Al-Mashru' al-Islahi fil-Sa'udiyyah: Qisatul-Hawali wal-Awdah* [The Reformist Project in Sa'udi Arabia: The Story of al-Hawali and Al-Awdah], Washington, D.C.: n.p. 1995.

al-Sa'id, Nasir. *Tarikh Al Sa'ud* [*History of the Al Sa'ud*], 2 volumes, Beirut: Al-Ittihad Press, 1985.

Salamé, Ghassan. *Al-Siyasah al-Kharijiyyah al-Sa'udiyyah Munzu 'Am 1945: Dirasah fil-'Ilaqat al-Dawliyyah* [The Foreign Policy of Saudi Arabia Since 1945: A Study in International Relations], Beirut: Muassasat al-Rihani lil-Tiba'at wal-Nashr, 1980.

Al Samari, Fahd bin 'Abdallah. *Al Malik Faysal bin 'Abdul 'Aziz Al Sa'ud: Ru'yah wa Zikriyyat*, Riyadh: Darah al-Malik 'Abdul 'Aziz, Number 225, 1429H [2008].

Samore, Gary Samuel. *Royal Family Politics in Saudi Arabia (1953–1982)*, doctoral dissertation, Cambridge, Massachusetts: Harvard University, 1983.

Alshamsi, Mansoor Jassem. *Islam and Political Reform in Saudi Arabia: The Quest for Political Change and Reform*, New York and London: Routledge, 2011.

Al-Saqhan, Abdallah U., and Muhammad A. al-Shuwaier, *Rules and Principles of Effective Dialogue*, Riyadh: King 'Abdul 'Aziz Center for National Dialogue, 2008.

Sardar, Ziauddin, and Merryl Wyn Davies, *Why Do People Hate America?*, New York: The Disinformation Company, 2003.

Sharabi, Hisham B. *Governments and Politics of the Middle East in the Twentieth Century*, Princeton: D. Van Nostran Co., Inc., 1962.

Al Sa'ud, Faisal bin Misha'al. *Decision Making and the Role of Ash-Shura in Saudi Arabia: Majlis Ash-Shura (Consultative Council): Concept, Theory and Practice*, New York: Vantage Press, 2003 and 2004.

——. *Political Development in the Kingdom of Saudi Arabia: An Assessment of the Majlis Ash-Shura*, Doctoral Dissertation, University of Durham, UK, 2000.

Al Sa'ud, Khaled bin Sultan (with Patrick Seale). *Desert Warrior: A Personal View of the Gulf War by the Joint Forces Commander*, New York: HarperCollins Publishers, Inc., 1995.

Al Sa'ud, Talal bin 'Abdul 'Aziz, *Risalah ilal-Muwatin* [A Letter to the Citizen], Cairo?: n.p., 1962?

Sa'udi Arabia, Kingdom of. *From the Point of View of Saudi Society: An Analytical Field Study*, Riyadh: King 'Abdul 'Aziz Center for National Dialogue, 2006.

——. *The First Report on Human Rights Conditions in the Kingdom of Saudi Arabia*, Riyadh: The National Society for Human Rights, 1427H/2006G.

Sa'udi Arabia, Royal Embassy of. *Political and Economic Reform in the Kingdom of Saudi Arabia*, Washington, D.C.: May 2006.

Schwartz, Stephen. *The Two Faces of Islam: The House of Sa'ud from Tradition to Terror*, New York: Doubleday, 2002.

Stenslie, Stig. *Regime Stability in Saudi Arabia: The Challenge of Succession*, London: Routledge, 2011.

Teitelbaum, Joshua. *Holier than Thou: Saudi Arabia's Islamic Opposition*, Washington, D.C.: Washington Institute for Near East Policy, 2000.

Trofimov, Yaroslav. *The Siege of Mecca: The Forgotten Uprising in Islam's Holiest Shrine and the Birth of Al Qaeda*, New York: Doubleday; London: Penguin Books, 2007.

United Nations. Development Program, *The Real Wealth of Nations: Pathways to Human Development* [Human Development Report 2010], New York: Palgrave Macmillan, 2010.

United States. *International Religious Freedom, July–December 2010*, Washington, D.C.: US Department of State, Bureau of Democracy, Human Rights, and Labor, 2010.

——. *Country Reports on Human Rights Practices 2010*, Washington, D.C.: US Department of State, 2011.

——. *Trafficking in Persons Report*, 10th edition, Washington, D.C.: US Department of State, June 2010.

Unger, Craig. *House of Bush, House of Saud: The Secret Relationship Between the World's Two Most Powerful Dynasties*, New York: Scribner, 2004.

Al Uthaymin, A. *Nashat Imarat al Rashid* [Accomplishments of the Al Rashid Emirate], Riyadh: n.p., 1981.

Vassiliev, Alexei. *The History of Saudi Arabia*, London: Saqi Books, 1998.

Vitalis, Robert. *America's Kingdom: Mythmaking on the Saudi Oil Frontier*, Stanford, California: Stanford University Press, 2007.

Vogel, Frank E. *Islamic Law and Legal System: Studies of Saudi Arabia*, Leiden, The Netherlands: E. J. Brill, 2000.

Weimann, Gabriel. *Terror on the Internet: The New Arena, the New Challenges*, Washington, D.C.: United States Institute of Peace Press, 2006.

Weston, Mark. *Prophets and Princes: Saudi Arabia from Muhammad to the Present*, New York: Wiley, 2008.

Wilson, Peter W. and Douglas F. Graham. *Saudi Arabia: The Coming Storm*, Armonk, New York: M. E. Sharpe, 1994.

Winder, R. Bayly. *Saudi Arabia in the Nineteenth Century*, London: Macmillan, 1965; New York: St. Martin's Press, 1965.

Yizraeli, Sarah. *The Remaking of Saudi Arabia: The Struggle Between King Sa'ud and Crown Prince Faysal, 1953–1962*, Tel Aviv, Israel: The Moshe Dayan Center for Middle Eastern and African Studies, 1997.

Zamzami, Yahyah bin Muhammad. *Al-Hiwar wa Adabuhu wa Dhawabituhu fi dhaw al-Kitab wal-Sunna* [Dialogue and its Linguistic Roots in Scriptures and the Sunna], 2nd ed, Amman, Jordan: Dar al-'Alami, 2002.

Index

9/11 [September 11, 2001], 4, 14, 25, 54, 55, 102, 147, 150, 159, 167, 173, 174, 188, 189, 190, 192, 193, 194, 203, 205; and Clash of Civilizations, 106–7

abayas, 45, 96, 168
'Abdallah II of Jordan [King]. *See* Al Hashimi, 'Abdallah bin Hussein
'Abdallah, King. *See* Al Saud, 'Abdallah bin 'Abdul 'Aziz
'Abdul 'Aziz Ibn Baz. *See* Baz, (Shaykh) 'Abdul 'Aziz Ibn
'Abdul 'Aziz Al-Sa'ud. *See* Al Saud, 'Abdul 'Aziz ibn 'Abdul Rahman
'Abdul Wahhab, (Shaykh) Muhammad bin 22, 37, 161
'Abi Talib, (Caliph) 'Ali ibn 54
Abhah (Sa'udi Arabia), 5, 74, 86, 92, 95, passim
Abqai'q oil facility, 188, 209
Abu Bakr (Caliph 632–34), 116
Activists Petition King for Reforms, 275–82
Afghanistan 3, 113, 119, 166, 174, 189, 193, 205, 298 note 90, 324 note 27; and mujahhidin fighters, 14; and war for, 113
ahl al-Bayt (the Prophet's household), 116
al-Ahmadi, Hanan 81
Ahmad, Yusif al-, 183
Al-Akhbariyyah Channel, 96
'Alami, 'Abdallah al-, 46
'Alawis (Morocco), 162
Algeria, 3, 185
Al-Jazeera (television network in Qatar), 48, 52
'alim (religious scholar) (singular). *See* 'Ulamah
Alim, Bassim 175

Alireza, Marianne 221
Allam, Abeer 152
Allegiance Law of Succession, 11–12, 137, 199; and by-laws of, 237–41; and calls for constitutional monarchy, 154; and membership (2007), 139; and mode of operation, 143–46; and commission responsibilities 141–43; and composition, 140–41; and Talal bin 'Abdul 'Aziz, 150–54; and Text of, 231–36; and *Transitory Ruling Council*, 137–38, 142–43
Al-Sharq Al-Awsat, 177
American Empire, 13
American Jewish Committee, 105
Amnesty International, 58, 59
analogy. *See* qiyas
apostasy (*riddah*), 54
'aqlaniyyun (rationalists), 35
Arab League. *See* League of Arab States
Arab nationalism, 13, 131
Arabian American Oil Company. *See* ARAMCO (Arabian American Oil Company)
Arabian Peninsula, 4
'Ar'ar Municipality, 130
Archbishop of Canterbury, 104
ARAMCO (Arabian American Oil Company), 180
'Asiri, 'Abdallah Hasan Talih 56
Association for the Protection and Defense of Women's Rights in Sa'udi Arabia, 181–82
Association of Shinto Temples in Japan, 105
'Ashurah, 159, 165
Al-'Awdah, (Shaykh) Salman bin Fahd, 3, 4, 35, 52, 53, 54, 172, 198, 256, passim; rejected violence, 4

Index   337

'Ayouni, Fawziyyah al-, 179–80
Al-Azhar University (Cairo), 21

Ba'ath, 207
Badi, Awadh, al-, 146
Badr, Imam Muhammad (Yemen), 66
badu, 169
Baghdad (Iraq), 13, 208,
Bahrain, Kingdom of 180, 185, 186, 206, 326 note 45
Baker, William 105
Ball, Anthony 104
al-Barrak (Shaykh) 'Abdul Rahman bin Nasir 46, 47, 48
Basbous, Antoine 38
Basic Law of Government (al-Qanun al-Asasi): and national dialogues, 69–70
Basrawi, 'Isam, 3, 160, 288 note 6, 316 note 6
Bay'ah(s) (oath[es] of loyalty), 4, 21, 132–33, 135–37, 149, 152, 230
Baz, (Shaykh) 'Abdul 'Aziz bin 24, 25, 35, 51, 67, 74, 168, 170–71, 173, 180, 255, 256
Baz, Rania al-74
Bin Ladin, 'Usamah 3, 38, 55, 166, 167, 174, 177, 178
Board of Senior *'Ulamah* (BSU). *See Hay'at Kibar al-'Ulamah*
Bouazizi, Tarek al-Tayyib Muhammad 185
Bourbon, (King) Juan Carlos de 103, 226,
Buddhist Association of China, 105
Bukharih, Muhammad Ibn Isma'il Abu 'Abdallah al-Djufi al-, 50
Buraydah, 36, 52, 63, 94, 95
Bush, George W., 14, 190–91, 204–5, 210, 308 note 98

Catholic Church, dialogue with, 99–101, 173, 307 note 81
Cave Brown, Anthony 14
CDLR. *See* Committee for the Defence of Legitimate Rights in Sa'udi Arabia
Chartered Institute of Management Accountants, 42
Chechnya, 3
Cheng, Xue 105
Citino, Nathan, 13
Clinton, Bill, 204
"Clash of Civilizations," 106–7

Clerics, 2–6, 18, 21–23, 33–34, 41, 45, 47–48, 53–55, 170, 178, 195, 217, passim; and deprogramming, 4; and warnings to, 3, 43
Commission for the Promotion of Virtue and the Prevention of Vice, 8–9, 33, 42, 44, 59, 147, 169, 180; and terrorism, 5
Commission for the Settlement of Labor Disputes, 29
Committee for the Defence of Legitimate Rights in Saudi Arabia (CDLR). *See Lajnat al-Difa' 'an al-Huquq al-Shar'iyyah*
Committee for Women's Rights to Drive, 179
Council for Islamic Mission and Guidance (al-Majlis lil-Da'wah wal-Irshad), 24
consensus (*ijma'*), 19
Constitution: and Sa'udi Arabia (excerpts from the 1992 basic law), 20, 25, 28, 69, 109, 113–15, 120, 228; and Sa'udi Arabia (2006 Allegiance Law of Succession), 11–12, 137, 143–46, 199, 231–36, 237–41
Constitutional monarchy, 2, 154, 175–76, 208, passim
Consultative Council. *See* Majlis al-Shurah
Cooperation Council of the Arab States of the Gulf. *See* Gulf Cooperation Council
Cordesman, Anthony, 14
Crawford, Texas 205
Custodian of the Two Holy Mosques, 1, 19, 22, 46, 70, 99, 107, 119, 121, 165, 206, 214, 216, 222, 226, 228

Dahmash, 'Abdul Rahman al-, 128
Da'wah (propagation of faith), 23, 24, 32, 33, 88
Dammam (Sa'udi Arabia), 30, 124, 180, passim
Dar al-Harb (Land of the Other), 88
Declaration of National Reform, 283–87
Defense of the Nation, 174–75, 263–70
Delhi Sikh Gurudwara Rakab Ganj Sahib, 105
democracy movement, 182–84
Deviant Junta has Taken Hold of the Sa'udi Media and is Endangering Islamic Society and Its Values, 271–73

Dhahran (Saʻudi Arabia), 84, 95, 172, passim
Dhaidi, Mashari Al-, 177, 178
Dhimmi, 34, 57
dialogues, national and international 62–108; and Basic Law of Government, 69–70; and Eighth national meeting (health services – a dialogue between society and health institutions), 95–97; and Fifth national meeting (the national vision for dealing with world cultures), 86–92; and First national meeting (intellectual dialogue), 75–78; and Fourth national meeting (young people's expectations) 83–86; and interfaith dialogues, 101–6; and national meetings, 73–97; and Saʻudi view of, 97–99; and Second national meeting (fighting fanaticism and extremism), 78–80; and Seventh national meeting (work and employment; dialogue between society and work related institutions), 94–95; and Sixth national meeting (education – reality and ways of improvement), 92–94; and Third national meeting (women's rights), 81–83
Doumato, Eleanor Abdella, 37
Dowd, Maureen 45, 48
al-Dumayni, ʻAli 70, 136

Egypt, 1, 66, 68, 118, 180, 185, 187, 207, 208, 283
Eisenhower, Dwight D., 13
Electoral Commission Chairman, 128
Enforcer of Shariʻah Law, 25
England, Andrew 152
Etzioni, Amitai 193

Fahad, ʻAbdul ʻAziz H. Al-, 221
Fahad, Nasir al-, 36
Fahd, King. *See* Al Saʻud, Fahd bin ʻAbdul ʻAziz
Faleh, Matruk al-, 70, 136
Fallujah, 54
Fasi, Hatoon Al 128
Fatany, Samar 41, 43
fatwah (religious decree), 22–25, 31–35, 39, 44–49, 57, 168, 183, passim; and issuance of religious decrees by qualified members, 6
faqih (pl. *fuqahah* – experts in Muslim jurisprudence), 39–40

Faqih, Saʻad al-, 53, 168, 256
Fawzan, (Shaykh) Salih al-, 54, 57
Fayiz, Nura al-, 45
Faysal, King. *See* Al Saʻud, Faysal bin ʻAbdul ʻAziz
The Federalist Papers, 107
Financial Times, 151, 153
Fitnah (strife), 34, 59, 120
France, 139, 165, 199, 280, 312 note 30
Freeman, Chas 191
Fukuyama, Francis 193

G20 Group, 146
Gause, Gregory, III, 191
GCC. *See* Gulf Cooperation Council
General Electric, 196
General Organization for Technical Education and Vocational Training, 93
Ghamdi, (Shaykh) Ahmad al-, 45
Ghayth, (Shaykh) Ibrahim al-, 59
Ghayth, (Shaykh) ʻIsa al-, 45
Gold, Dore, 37
Gosaibi, Ghazi Al 149, 221
Grievances Board, 6, 7, 19
Gulf Cooperation Council (GCC), 113, 186, 206, 212, passim
Guardian, 175

Hadith(s), 39, 50, 115, 116, 172
Ha'il (Saʻudi Arabia), 7, 149, passim
Hamad, Turki al-, 221
Hamid (or al-Hamed), ʻAbdallah al-, 36, 70, 136
Hamrah Oasis Village, Al 55
Hanbali jurisprudence (Zaʻad al-Mustaqniʻ), 38, 39, 53, 217
Hanafi jurisprudence (*Mukhtasar al-Quduri*), 38, 39,
Harakan, (Shaykh) Muhammad Al 99
Harbi, Fowzan Mohsin al-, 182
Harbi, Muhammad bin Hudayjan al-, 2, 160
Hasah Province (Saʻudi Arabia), 124, passim
Hashimi, ʻAbdallah bin Husayn Al [ʻAbdallah II] (r. 1999–) 186, 206
Hashimi, Hussein bin Talal al- (Hussein I, king of Jordan), 204
Hashimites (Jordan), 162, 186
Hawali, Safar al-, 35, 52, 53, 54, 172, 173, 174, 256
Al-Hayat, 155
Hay'at al-Bayʻah [Allegiance Commission], 137, passim

Hay'at al-Amr bil Ma'ruf wal-Nahi 'an al-Munkar (Commission for the Promotion of Virtue and the Prevention of Vice), 8–9, 33, 42, 44, 59, 147, 169, 180
Hay'at Kibar al-'Ulamah, 23, 50, 54, 100, 120, 173, 183, 195, 218, passim; and potential women members, 49
Higher Committee for Administrative Reform, 26
Higher Council of *Qadis*, 23
Hilal, Hassah 47, 48
hijab, 180
Hijaz Province, 22, 34, 35, 64, 65, 117, 163, 197; and Al Sa'ud rulers in, 22
Hinder, (Bishop) Paul 101
Hindi, Hanadi 73
Hirschfield, Rabbi Brad 103
"How Can We Co-Exist", 49, 193
Hulays, Salihah al-, 81
Human Rights Authority in Sa'udi Arabia, 179
Humayd, (Shaykh) Salih bin 149, 184, 214, 221, 301 note 122
al-Huma'yn, (Shaykh) 'Abdul 'Aziz bin 33, 59, 60
Huntington, Samuel 193
Husayn, bin 'Ali 159
Husayn, (Shaykh) Salih bin 'Abdul Rahman al-, 81
Hussein, Saddam 168
Huwaydar, Wajihah al-, 179, 181

ifta' (opinion), 32, 51
ijma' (consensus), 19
ijtihad, 30, 169
Ikhwan (Muslim tribal military force), 110, 163, 165
ikhtilat (mixing in public places), 60, 94
Imam Muhammad bin Sa'ud Islamic University (Riyadh), 3
Imam Muhammad University (Buraydah), 52, 100
Imamah al-Kubrah (The Highest Imamate), 50
independent judiciary, 2
Institute for American Values, 49, 193
Institute of Diplomatic Studies (Riyadh), 156
Institute of Materials Research and Engineering (Singapore), 196
Institute of Public Administration (Riyadh), 81

interfaith dialogues, 101–6
Iran, 13, 14, 22, 23, 68, 102, 113, 119, 125, 126, 165, 191, 206, 210, passim; and Contra Rebellion, 14; and revolution in 1979, 13, 113
Iraq, 3, 13, 23, 24, 25, 34, 54, 70, 113, 119, 155, 167, 168, 169, 170, 172, 189, 190, 204, 205, 206, 210, 243; and 1991 liberation, 113; and invasion of Kuwait (1990), 13, 113
Iran–Iraq War (1980–88), 113
islahiyyun (reformers), 35
Islam, 4, 71, 87, 88, 90, 93, 100, 101, 103, 104, 106, 110, 114, 131, 161, 167, 168, 169, 205
Islamic Awakening. See *Sahwah al-Islamiyyah*
Islamic banking, 42
Islamic Fiqh Academy, 28
Islamic legal rulings. See fatwah(s)
Islamic University in Madinah, 52
Islamic World League (*Rabitat al-'Alam al-Islami*), 21
Israel, 24, 192, 205, passim
Israel Institute of Technology [Technion] (Haifa), 196, 197, 325 note 34
istia'dah (request protection or refuge), 161
isti'anah (assistance), 161
istiqatah (benefits), 161

Jain, Bava 105
al-Jam'ah al-Salafiyyah al-Muhtasibah, 165
Jericho, Palestine, 48
Jiddah (Sa'udi Arabia), 5, 28, 30, 43, 46, 195, 215, passim; and Wahhabism, 5
Jiddah Economic Forum, 185
Jihad, 166
Jizan Province (Sa'udi Arabia), 30
Jones, Toby 131
Jordan, 73, 162, 185, 186, 204, 206, 279
Jubayr, (Shaykh) Muhammad bin 100
Judiciary (Sa'udi), 27; and American views of, 192–94; and Administrative Courts of Appeals, 28; and Board of Appeal Circuits, 28; and Board of Grievances, 28, 29, 31; and Board of Senior *'Ulamah*, 27, 28, 31, 32; and Circuits of Appeals, 28; and Commission for the Settlement of Labor Disputes, 29; and First-Instance Courts (General Courts and Summary

340 *Index*

Courts), 27, 28; and Grievances Board, 6; and High Administrative Court, 28; and Higher Council of Qadis (judges), 33; and *Majlis al-A'lah lil-Shu'un al-Islamiyyah* (Supreme Council of Islamic Affairs), 32; and political concerns, 51–54; and the protection of victims, 6; and reforms within, 19–61; and religious establishment, 32–34; and Shari'ah Review Court (*mahkamat al-tamyiz*), 27; and *al-Siyasah al-Shari'yyah* (Islamic public policy), 26; and social concerns, 31–34; and Supreme Court, 6, 30–31; and Supreme Judiciary Council (SJC), 6, 27; and system reorganization, 28–30; and transformation of, 7–9
Justice, Ministry of 8
Justices and other senior personnel, 27–28

kafir (apostate), 36, 88
Khalid, King. *See* Al Sa'ud, Khalid bin 'Abdul 'Aziz
Khawarij, 54
Khitab al-Matalib (Letter of Demands), 170
Khobar, al- (Sa'udi Arabia), 5, 180, 215
Khomeini, (Ayatollah) Ruhollah 68, 166
al-Khudayr, 'Ali 36
Khunayn, (Shaykh) Rashid bin 99
Khutbah (sermon), 3
King 'Abdallah University of Science and Technology (KAUST), 45, 196
King 'Abdul 'Aziz Center for National Dialogue, 62, 71–73, 219; and consent to establish, 222–23
King 'Abdul 'Aziz City for Science and Technology (Riyadh), 182
King 'Abdul 'Aziz Public Library (Riyadh), 75, 222
King Fahd Security College, 4
King Faysal Center for Research and Islamic Studies (Riyadh), 185
King Sa'ud University, 24, 81, 128
Kitab al-Tawhid (The Book of Absolute Monotheism), 161
Koran. *See* Qur'an
kuffar (sinners), 88
Kuni, Kuniaki 105

Kuwait, 13, 22, 23, 24, 35, 69, 112, 113, 114, 118, 119, 134, 152, 164, 167, 169, 170, 171, 186, 248, passim; and 1990 Iraqi invasion of, 25

Ladin, 'Usamah bin, 3, 14, 38, 55, 166, 167, 174, 177, 178,
al-Lahidan, (Shaykh) 'Abdallah bin Muhammad, 23
Lajnah al-Da'imah lil-Buhuth al-'Ilmiyyah wal-Ifta', 32
Lajnat al-Difa' 'an al-Huquq al-Shar'iyyah, 32, 35, 168, 174, 280
Law of the Provinces, 69, 114, 134, 142, 233,
League of Arab States, 146
legal reforms in Sa'udi Arabia, 2–7,
legal system, 25–28
legislative branch, 26–27
Lebanon, 101, 152, 154, 169, 180, 205, 210, passim
Letter of Demands, 35
Luhaydan, (Shaykh) Salih Al, 3, 55, 195, 221
Lujayniyyat, 155

mabahith (secret police), 174
Madinah (Sa'udi Arabia), 22, 23, 30, 33, 50, 52, 70, 73, 81, 94, 111, 138, 163, 178, 216, passim
Madrid Declaration, 226–29
Madrid interfaiths conference, 104
Madrid Speech by King 'Abdallah (2008), 224–25
Madrid peace process, 24
MAE Medici, 100
Maeena, Khalid Al 221
Majlis al-Shurah, 10, 11, 24, 26, 27, 58, 69, 79, 84, 100, 109, 112–20, 130, 169, 178, 214, passim; and the Consultative Council after 1992, 120–21; and the Consultative Council before 1992, 116–20; and elections to, 80; and suffrage for women, 129; and succession strategy, 151; under King 'Abdallah, 121–25
Maliki jurisprudence (*Mukhtasar Khalil*), 38, 39
Maliki, Hasan al-, 36
Makkah (Sa'udi Arabia), 22, 78, 121, 163, passim; and 1979 mosque takeover, 22, 35; and malaria and smallpox, 112; and capture of (1924), 116

Mani', (Shaykh) 'Abdallah bin
  Sulayman bin 50
Al-Mani'i, Muhammad bin Suleiman 34
Manipal University in India, 105
Manzur, Ibn 72
al-Mas'ari, Muhammad, 35, 168
Marchand, Stéphane 38
Al-Marzuqi, (Shaykh) Muhammad 117
MBI International and Partners, 55
Mecca. See Makkah.
Medina. See Madinah.
Middle East Broadcasting Center
  (MBC), 172
Middle East Council of Churches,
  194
Millionaire Poetry Competition show, 47
Ministry of Commerce and Industry, 29
Ministry of Health, 96–97
Ministry of the Interior, 130, passim
Ministry of Islamic Affairs,
  Endowments, Call and Guidance, 4,
  32, 59, 111, 184
Ministry of Justice, 8, 19–61,
Ministry of Labor, 29
Ministry of Municipal and Rural
  Affairs, 130
Ministry of Pilgrimage (*Hajj*) and
  Endowments (*Awqaf*), 33, 111
Ministry of Women's Affairs, 181
MIRA. See Movement for Islamic
  Reform
Misnad, (Shaykhah) Mawzah bint Nasir
  Al 46–47
Morocco, 3, 162, 186, 290 note 33
Motabbagani, Mazin Salah 221
Movement for Islamic Reform in Arabia
  (MIRA), 53, 168
Moynihan, Daniel Patrick 193
Mu'ammar, Faysal bin 'Abdul Rahman
  bin, 81
Mubarak, Husni 207
Mubarak, Ibtihal 179
Mubarak, (Shaykh) Qays bin
  Muhammad bin 'Abdul Latif Al 49
Muftis (jurists), 22
Muhannah, Muhammad al-, 58
Muhammad (The Prophet), 50, 100,
  115, 163, 190
Muhammad VI, 186
Mukhtasar Khalil (Maliki
  jurisprudence), 38
Multaqah al-Watani al-Khaliji (Gulf
  National Forum), 113
munafiqun (hypocrites), 54

Municipal elections, 10–11, 109–30,
  122–23; and the 2005 elections,
  123–25; and the 2009 (2011)
  municipal elections, 128–29; and an
  assessment of the 2005 elections,
  125–29; and electoral mobilization,
  124–25; and political participation,
  10–11, 109–30; and registration
  process, 123–24
Muneef, Maha 46
Muntadah al-Tanmiyyah (Development
  Forum), 113
mushrikun (polytheists), 54
Musnad, (Shaykh) 'Abdallah Al 100
Muscat, 212
Muslim Brethren, 110, 154. See also
  Ikhwan
Muslim World League, 21, 24, 28, 29,
  33, 89, 102, 104, 105, 194, 226, 229,
  243, 290 note 33, passim
Mustapha, 'Izaddin Ibrahim 104
Mustaqni', Za'ad al- (Hanbali
  jurisprudence), 38
muti'ah (woman jurist), 51
mutawa'in ("morals" security forces), 5,
  33, 59, 60, 61, 147, 195
Muwahiddun (Wahhabis), 14, 16,
  21, 22–25, 33, 36, 43, 46, 161, 190,
  191
Muzakarat al-Nasihah (Memorandum
  of Advice), 171, 173

Najd Province (of central Arabia), 34,
  35, 117, 164, passim
Najimi, (Shaykh) Muhammad al-, 58
Najran Province (Sa'udi Arabia), 45, 56,
  95
Nalapat, M.D. 105
Namlah, Saleh M. Al 221
Al-Nassa'ih, 50
nasihah (advice), 24, 171, 173
Nasir, Gamal 'Abdul, 66, 118, passim;
  and the Arab–Israeli war (1967), 118
National Dialogues, 9–10, 62–108
National Guard (Sa'udi Arabian), 68, 110
National Jewish Center for Learning
  and Leadership, 103
National Meeting for Intellectual
  Dialogue, 62
National Security Council, 25
Nawwab, Nimah 46
Nayif, Prince. See Al Sa'ud, Nayif bin
  'Abdul 'Aziz
New York Times, 45

Nimr, Shaykh Ibn 3
Niqab, 180
Nizam, 217–18
Nujaimi, Muhammad al-, 4

Obama, Barack Hussein, 105, 191, 208, 209
Omair, Saleh Al, 155
OPEC. *See* Organization of Petroleum Exporting Countries.
Organization of the Islamic Coperation (OIC), 28, 90
Organization of Petroleum Exporting Countries, 13, 66
Osamah bin Laden. *See* Ladin, 'Usamah bin
Oslo Conference on Freedom of Religion or Belief (1998), 106

Paleologos, (Emperor) Manuel II (r. 1391–1425), 100–101
Palestine/Palestinians, 48, 54, 172, 205, 324 note 27, 325 note 34
Partners in One Nation, 242–47
Penal Law for Terrorism Crimes and Financing Terrorism, 58
Permanent Committee for Scientific Research and Legal Opinion. *See* Lajnah al-Da'imah lil-Buhuth al-'Ilmiyyah wal-Ifta'
Peterson, John E., 14
petitions, 112, 159; after 9/11, 174–77; after 1992, 174; and 2003 production, 159; and *Activists Petition King for Reforms*, 275–82; and constitutional monarchy, 175; and *A Declaration of National Reform*, 283–87; and *Defense of the Nation*, 174–75, 263–70; and democracy movement, 182–84; and *A Deviant Junta has Taken Hold of the Sa'udi Media and is Endangering Islamic Society and Its Values*, 271–73; and *dua'*, 161, 171; and Juhayman 'Utaybi's Letters, 165–67; and *Khitab al-Matalib* (Letter of Demands), 170; and letters and memoranda, 169–74; and *Muzakarat al-Nasihah* (Memorandum of Advice), 171, 173; and traditions before 1979, 163–65; and *Partners in One Nation*, 242–47; and *Religious Petition to King Fahd February 1991*, 254–56; and *Sa'udi Women Petition for Driving Right* (2007), 274; and *Secular Petition to King Fahd December 1990*, 248–53; and Shiah drafts, 159; and supplication to rulers, 161–63; and *Vision for the Present and Future of the Nation*, 174, 257–61; and women driving, 169, 178–82; under 'Abdallah, 177–84
petition industry: and reforms 159–87
Pignedoli, Cardinal 100
political participation: and municipal elections, 10–11, 109–30; and tribal environment, 110–21
political reforms and the succession dilemma, 131–58
Pope Benedict XVI, 99–101, 102, 103
Pope John Paul II, 99

Qaboos, Sultan. *See* Sa'id, Qaboos bin Sa'id Al
Qaeda, al-. *See* Qa'idah, Al-
Qahtani, Muhammad bin 'Abdallah al-, 36, 165
Qa'idah, al-, 4, 35, 38, 53, 54, 56, 58, 182, 188, 204, 206
Qanuns, 217
Qarni, Shaykh 'Awad al-, 38, 174
Qahtani, Muhammad Al 156, 182–83
Qasim, (Shaykh) 'Abdul 'Aziz (Shaykh) al-, 35
Qasim, (Sa'udi Arabia) 94, 95, 280
Qatar, 46, 186
Qatar Foundation for Education, Science and Community Development, 46
Qatif (Sa'udi Arabia), al-, 124, passim
"Qatif Girl" (case of), 5–6, 8, 44, 61, 215
qiyas (analogy), 19, 72
Quduri, Mukhtasar al- (in Hanafi jurisprudence), 38
Qur'an, Qur'anic, 28, 39, 76, 107, 120, 169, 172, passim
Quraysh (tribe), 163
Qurni, Daliah al-, 215, 216

Rafsanjani 'Ali Akbar Hashemi 102
Reagan, Ronald, 14
reforms and the petition industry, 159–87
reforming the judiciary in Sa'udi Arabia, 20–31
Regensburg University, 100
religious education in the kingdom, 37–42
religious fanaticism and extremism, 78

Religious Freedoms in the World, 192
Religious Petition to King Fahd February 1991, 254–56
Reuters, 150
Rice, Condoleezza, 204
Rihani, Amin 164
Riyadh, 5, 15, 23, 24, 107, 127, 191, passim
Role of the Sa'udi Islamic establishment in education, 42–43
Roosevelt, Franklin Delano, 209
Rosen, David, 105
Russia, 166

Sabah, Al (Rulers of Kuwait) 119, 186
Sadlan, (Shaykh) Salih Al 3
Safah Palace, Al-, 101
Sahwah al-Islamiyyah, 35, 52, 53, 112
Sahwah 'Ulamah, 23
Sa'id, Qaboos bin Sa'id Al [Sultan of Oman], 185
Salafi Shaykhs, 112, 169
Salman, Prince. *See* Al Sa'ud, Salman bin 'Abdul 'Aziz
Sarna, Pramjeet Singh 105
Sa'ud, Al: and 1744 alliance with Al Shaykh, 19, 20, 22–25, 37, 51, 52, 53, 61, 110, 113, 120, 158, 161, 166, 207, 209, 213, 215; and constitutional monarchy, 136; and divine privileges, 132; and funding terrorist groups, 2; and Sudayri branch, 147; and Supreme Hajj Committee, 148
Sa'ud, 'Abdallah bin 'Abdul 'Aziz Al (r. 2005–), 1, 6, 11, 21, 52, 108, 130, 132, 191, 209, 220, passim; and accession, 135; and intellectuals, 136; and Madrid Conference Speech (2008), 224–25; and Madrid Declaration, 226–29; and Muslim–Christian dialogues, 99–101; and pleas for prayers, 187; and political petitions under his rule, 177–84; and Pope Benedict XVI, 99–101; and reform efforts to succession mechanisms, 137–40; and reign after 2005, 135–36; and succession, 137–40; and succession dilemma, 156–58; and Supreme Court, 1; and views of reforms, 99; and warnings to clerics, 3; and "will to power," 1, 4, 6, 9, 15, 61, 126, 157–58, 183, 196, 213, 219, passim

Sa'ud, 'Abdul 'Aziz bin 'Abdul Rahman Al (r. 1932–54), 1, 11, 21, 38, 64, 118, 140, 199–200, passim; and clergy, 111; and Shari'ah Law, 111; and Shurah before 1992, 116
Sa'ud, 'Abdul 'Aziz bin 'Abdallah bin 'Abdul 'Aziz Al, 201
Sa'ud, 'Abdul 'Aziz bin Fahd bin 'Abdul 'Aziz Al, 201
Sa'ud, 'Abdul 'Aziz bin Nawwaf bin 'Abdul 'Aziz Al, 141
Sa'ud, 'Abdul Illah bin 'Abdul 'Aziz Al, 201
Sa'ud, 'Abdul Rahman bin 'Abdul 'Aziz Al, 200
Sa'ud, 'Adilah bint 'Abdallah bin 'Abdul 'Aziz Al, 179
Sa'ud, Ahmad bin 'Abdul 'Aziz Al, 202, 247
Sa'ud, al-Bandari bint 'Abdul Rahman al-Faysal bin 'Abdul 'Aziz Al, 221
Sa'ud, Badr bin 'Abdul 'Aziz Al, 200
Sa'ud, Bandar al-Faysal bin 'Abdul 'Aziz Al, 221
Sa'ud, Bandar bin Sultan bin 'Abdul 'Aziz Al, 204
Sa'ud, Fahd bin 'Abdul 'Aziz Al (r. 1982–2005), 22, 23, 24, 26, 35, 62, 67, 68, 69, 70, 121, 132, 133, 173, 246, passim; and death, 135; and petitions, 119–20, 171; and US withdrawal from Arabia, 170
Sa'ud, Fahad bin Sa'ad Al, 155
Sa'ud, Faysal bin 'Abdul 'Aziz Al (r. 1964–75), 1, 11, 21, 65, 164, passim; and assassination, 67; and Egyptian intervention in Yemen, 118; and first contacts with Vatican, 99–101; and separation of powers, 118; and viceroy of Hijaz, 117
Sa'ud, Faysal bin Musa'id bin 'Abdul 'Aziz Al, 67
Sa'ud, Khalid bin 'Abdul 'Aziz Al (r. 1975–82), 21, 66 passim
Sa'ud, Khalid al-Faysal bin 'Abdul 'Aziz Al, 201, 215
Sa'ud, Khalid Sultan bin 'Abdul 'Aziz Al, 201
Sa'ud, Khalid bin Talal bin 'Abdul 'Aziz Al, 155–56
Sa'ud, Lulwah al-Faysal bin 'Abdul 'Aziz Al, 179
Sa'ud, Mansur bin Mit'ab Al, 128, 201

Sa'ud, Mit'ab bin 'Abdallah bin 'Abdul 'Aziz Al, 201, 326 note 42
Sa'ud, Mit'ab bin 'Abdul 'Aziz Al, 200
Sa'ud, Mish'al bin 'Abdul 'Aziz Al, 12, 140, 200, passim
Sa'ud, Muhammad bin Sa'ud Al, 22, 37, 201
Sa'ud, Muhammad bin Nawwaf bin 'Abdul 'Aziz Al, 141
Sa'ud, Muhammad bin Nayif bin 'Abdul 'Aziz Al, 4, 55, 57, 188, 201, 221, passim
Sa'ud, Muhammad bin Fahd bin 'Abdul 'Aziz Al, 149, passim
Sa'ud, Muqrin bin 'Abdul Aziz Al, 201
Sa'ud, Nawwaf bin 'Abdul 'Aziz Al, 141
Sa'ud, Nayif bin 'Abdul 'Aziz Al, 55, 133, 199–200, passim; and death in 2012, 133, 202–3; and ideological deviancy, 148; and second deputy prime minister, 146–50; and Turki al-Faysal, 148–49; and views on 9/11, 147; and women's rights, 147–48
Sa'ud, Salman bin 'Abdul 'Aziz Al, 200, 202, 221, passim
Sa'ud, Sattam bin 'Abdul 'Aziz Al, 201
Sa'ud, Sa'ud bin 'Abdul 'Aziz bin 'Abdul Rahman Al, (r. 1953–64), 164, passim
Sa'ud, Sa'ud al-Faysal bin 'Abdul 'Aziz Al, 201, passim
Sa'ud, Sultan bin 'Abdul 'Aziz Al (Heir Apparent and Defense Minister), 12, 45, 135, 203, passim
Sa'ud, Sultan bin Salman bin 'Abdul 'Aziz Al, 201
Sa'ud, Talal bin 'Abdul 'Aziz Al, 2, 15, 66, 155, 200, 221, passim; and Allegiance Commission, 315 note 84; and views of succession, 150–54
Sa'ud, Turki bin Faysal 'bin Abdul 'Aziz Al, 148–49, 185, 201, 221, passim
Sa'ud, Turki bin Talal 'bin Abdul 'Aziz Al, 221
Sa'ud, al-Walid bin Talal bin 'Abdul 'Aziz Al, 73, 155
Sa'udi Arabia, 2, 3, 103, 114, passim; and 1992 Basic Law, 25; and 2006 Allegiance Law of Succession, 11–12, 137, 199, 231–36, 237–41; and 2010–11 Arab uprisings, 184–87; and 5/12 terrorist attacks, 167; and the American divorce, 189–91; and anti-Americanism, 16; and Association for the Protection and Defense of Women's Rights in, 181–82; and cabinet (Council of Ministers), 63; and clerics, 3, 21–22; and constitutional continuum, 64–69; and constitutional monarchy, 132, 175–76, 208; and democracy movement, 182–84; and dialogues, 62–108; and enforcer of Shari'ah Law, 25; and existential challenges, 15–16; and fundamentalism before 1991, 167–69; and Hajj, 110; and *Hay'at Kibar al-'Ulamah*, 23; and Human Rights Authority in, 179; and ideology, 131; and Ikhwan, 110; and interfaith dialogues, 101–6; and issuance of religious decrees, 6; and interfaith discussions held in July 2008 (Madrid), 63; and legal counseling, 4; and legal system, 25–28; and the Majlis al Shurah, 10, 11, 24, 26, 27, 58, 69, 79, 84, 100, 109, 112–20, 130, 169, 178, 214, passim; and Makkah Mosque takeover, 22, 23, 35; and March 11, 2011 "Day of Rage," 181, 219; and March 11 decrees, 208; and May 2003 terrorist attacks in Riyadh, 53, 54, 55–57; and Ministry of Women's Affairs, 181; and National Dialogues, 9–10; and National Guard, 110; and political participation and municipal elections, 10–11; and political parties, 15, 154–56; and political violence, 57–58; and reengagement with US, 206–9; and reforms within the judiciary, 19–61; and rehabilitation program 57–58; and *Sahwah 'Ulamah*, 23–24; and Salafi Shaykhs, 44; and second deputy prime ministerships, 146; and security ties with US, 203–6; and Shurah, 114–16; and succession, 131–58; and Supreme Court, 6, 7, 19, 30–31, 51, 214, 216; and Supreme Judiciary Council (SJC), 6, 19, 30, 55, 150, 184, 212, 215; and *takrims* (tributes), 121; and trials, 2; and tribal rule, 145; and unemployment, 94; and Unitarian (Wahhabism), 14, 16, 21, 22–25, 33, 36, 43, 46, 161, 190, 191; and view of national dialogues, 97–99; and the United States 13–15, 188–211; and Vatican summit, 99–101
Sa'udi Civil and Political Rights Association, 185

Sa'udi National Society for Human Rights, 8, 44
Sa'udi Women's Association, 6
Sa'udization (policy), 86, 94
Schneier, (Rabbi) Marc, 104
Secular Petition to King Fahd December 1990, 248–53
Shammari, Nayif, Al, 128
Shamsi, Kamel Ahmad Al, 9, 41
Shafi'i jurisprudence (*Al-Taqrib* by Abu-Shujah), 38
Shamri, Naif, 148
Shari'ah (Islamic) Law, 4, 6, 7, 21, 33, 40, 51, 171, passim
Shari'ah education, 41
Shari'ah Review Court (*mahkamat al-tamyiz*), 27, 33
Sharif, Manal Faysal Al 46, 180–81, 215
Sharon, Ariel 204
Shaykh, Al al- (family alliance), 22
Shaykh, 'Abdallah Al al- (Minister of Justice), 5
Shaykh, (Grand Mufti) 'Abdul 'Aziz Al al-, 101, 149, 184, 208, 216
Shaykh, 'Abdul Latif bin 'Abdul 'Aziz bin 'Abdul Rahman Al, 33, 52, 60
Shaykh, Muhammad bin Ibrahim Al, 36
Shaykh, Salih bin 'Abdul 'Aziz Al, 184
Shaykh, Tarfah bint Al, 22
Shi'ah(s), 23, 39, 42, 43, 54, 62, 67, 72, 88, 102, 116, 119, 124, 125, 159, 165, 166, 172, 205–7, 210, 243–46, passim; and riots (1979–80), 119, 165–66; and uprisings in Qatif, 166
Shibbih, (Shaykh) 'Abdul Qadir al-, 116–17
Shih, Choon Fong 196
shirk (polytheism or associationism), 161, 254
Shobokshi, Hussein 183
Shu'aybi, Humud bin 'Uqlah al-, 36
Shurah and the Sa'udi system, 114–16
Shurah and the holy Qur'an, 115
Sidlan, (Shaykh) Salih al-, 34
Singapore, 196
Smith, James B., 199
Somalia, 3
Soviet Union. *See* Russia.
Spain, 63, 75, 106, 194, 226
status of women, 43–51
struggle for Islamic primacy in Sa'udi Arabia, 52–54
succession (*khilafah*), 131–58,; and 1992 Basic Law (excerpts) 230; and 2006

Allegiance Law in Sa'udi Arabia, 11–12; and Allegiance Commission membership (2007), 139; and Allegiance Commission mode of operation, 143–46; and dilemma for Al Sa'ud, 156–58; and political reforms in the kingdom, 131–58; and Talal bin 'Abdul 'Aziz, 150–54; and strategy questions. 150–54; and *Transitory Ruling Council*, 137–38, 142
Sudayri, Al 67, 179, 201
Sudayri, Turki Al 179
"Sudayri Seven," 147
Sudan, 166
Sudays, (Shaykh) 'Abd al-Rahman al-57
Sultan, Prince. *See* Al Sa'ud, Sultan bin 'Abdul 'Aziz
Sunnah, 27, 39, 77, 87, 115, 116, 120, 134, 231, 232, 249, 250, 258, passim
Sunni, 39, 62, 70, 88, 116, 124, 159, 169, 206, 207, 246, 290 note 33, 296 note 65, passim
supplication (*dua'*). *See* petitions.
Supreme Council of Higher Education, 26
Supreme Council of Islamic Affairs (*al-Majlis al-A'lah li-Shu'un al-Islamiyyah*), 24, 26
Supreme Court, 6, 7, 19, 27, 31, 214, 217
Supreme Judiciary Council (SJC), 6, 7, 18, 19, 30, 31, 49, 149, 184, passim
Suraiya, Kamala 105
Suwaidan, Tarek al-, 8, 40
Sykes-Picot Agreement (1916), 209
Syria, 168, 185, 190, 207, 210

Ta'azir ruling, 6
Tabuk (Sa'udi Arabia), 300 note 119
Ta'if (Sa'udi Arabia), 5, 163
Takfir, Takfiris (ideology, ideologies), 4, 36, 53, 56
Takrims (tributes), 121
Talal, Prince. *See* Al Sa'ud, Talal bin 'Abdul 'Aziz
tanawiriyyun (enlighteners), 35
Al-Taqrib (Abu-Shujah in Shafi'i jurisprudence), 38
Tariqi, 'Abdallah, 66
Tawhid, doctrine of, 161
Taymiyyah, Taqi al-Din Ibn 39
Tayyib, Muhammad Sa'id 176
Terrorism, 33, 78; and the war on, 55–58
Thani, (Shaykh) Hamad bin Khalifah (r. 1995–) Al, 46
Tirmidhih, al-, 50

tribal environment, 110–21
Tunbak, Marqouk bin, 81
Tunisian uprising (2010), 185
Turabah hamlet, al-, 163
Turki, 'Abdallah al-, 104
Tuwayjri, 'Abdul 'Aziz Al-, 184

al-'Ubaykan, (Shaykh) 'Abdul-Muhsin, 34, 51, 183, 255, 300 note 120
'Ulamah (plural of 'alim – religious scholar), 21, 23, 35, 51, 54, 75, 84, 111, 121, 165, 168, 169, 187, 272, passim; and non-establishment scholars, 34–37; and numbers of Imams in country, 33; and Sahwah, 23
'Umar (Caliph 634–44), 116
Umm Al-Qurah University, 81
Ummah, 101, 208, 213, 224, 242, 243, 249, 250, 251
UN Declaration for Tolerance (1994), 106
Unitarian faith (Wahhabism), 14, 16, 21, 22–25, 33, 36, 43, 46, 161, 190, 191
United Arab Emirates (UAE), 101, 104, 186,
United Kingdom, 69, 162, passim; and High Court of Justice, 31
United Nations, 147; and Universal Declaration of Human Rights, 106
United Nations Human Rights Council, 216
United States of America, 188–211, passim; and 9/11, 188; and the 1998 US Embassy bombings in Kenya and Tanzania, 54; and concerns over succession, 199–202; and Constitution of, 107; and Ghawar oil fields, 188; and Islamophobia, 192; and misrepresentation of Islam, 190; and Pentagon advisory board, 190; and reengagement with Sa'udi Arabia, 206–9; and *Religious Freedoms in the World*, 192; and Sa'udi Arabia, 13–15, 188–211; and Sa'udi divorce, 189–91; and security ties with Sa'udi Arabia, 203–6; and Supreme Court, 31; and views of legal reforms in Sa'udi Arabia, 192–94; and views of post-2005 Sa'udi reforms, 191–203; and views on scientific education in Sa'udi Arabia, 196–97; and views on socio-political dialogues and elections, 197–98; and views of women's emancipation in Sa'udi Arabia, 195–96
University of Cairo, 105

Usra, Hayfah 179
USSR. *See* Russia.
'Utaybi, Juhayman al-, 23, 34, 165–67
'Uthaymin, (Shaykh) Muhammad al-, 24, 172

Vatican Office of Non-Christian affairs, 100
Vatican summit, 99–101
Vinnell Corporation Compound, 55
Vision for the Present and Future of the Nation, 174, 257–61

Wahhabis. *See* Muwahiddun
Wahhabism. *See* Unitarian faith
wali al-'ahd (heir apparent), 29, 326 note 40
wali al-'amr (ruler), 22, 34
War for Kuwait (1991), 22
Wasatiyyun (modernizing intellectuals), 35, 53
Washington Post, 190
What We're Fighting For, 49, 193
Whitaker, Brian 175
White House, 191, 199, 204, 207, 209
"Will to Power." *See* Al Sa'ud, 'Abdallah bin 'Abdul 'Aziz
Williams, Rowan (Archbishop of Canterbury), 104
Wilson, James Q. 193
women: and Committee for Women's Rights to Drive, 179; and driving demonstration in Riyadh, 169; and key social changes affecting women, 214–17; and petitioning to drive (2007), 178–82; and Sa'udi Women Petition for Driving Right (2007), 274
World Association of Mosques, 21
World Association of Muslim Youth, 21
World Council of Religious Leaders, 105
World Jewish Congress, 104
World Muslim Congress, 194

Yanbu' (Sa'udi Arabia), 96
Yaqout, Jasim bin Muhammad Al-, 148
Yaquby, (Shaykh Nizam), 42
Yassin, Hassan, 221
Yemen, Republic of, 56, 66, 74, 95, 166, 118, 166, 168, 174, 185, 201, 206

al-Za'atrah, Yasir, 48
Zapatero, José Luis Rodríguez, 226
Zulfah, Muhammad al-, 178
Zunaydih, 'Abdul Rahman Al-, 49

www.routledge.com/middleeaststudies

Related titles from Routledge

State Reform and Development in the Middle East

Turkey and Egypt in the Post-Liberalization Era

By **Amr Adly**

Series: Routledge Studies in Middle Eastern Economies

The economies of Turkey and Egypt, remarkably similar until the early 1980s, have since taken divergent paths. Turkey has successfully implemented a policy of export led industrialisation whilst Egypt's manufacturing industry and exports have stagnated.

In this book, Amr Adly uses extensive primary research to present detailed comparisons of Turkey's and Egypt's state administrative and private sector capacities and links between the two. The conclusion the author draws is that the external contexts for both were so alike that this cannot account for their diverging paths. Instead, the author suggests a counterintuitive yet compelling explanation; that a democratic polity is far more likely than an authoritarian one to engender a successful developmental state.

Emerging in the wake of the January revolution in Egypt, when hopes for democratisation were raised, this book provides a fresh perspective on the topical subject of state reform and development in the Middle East and will be of interest to students and scholar alike.

November 2012: 234x156: 272pp
Hb: 978-0-415-62419-0
Eb: 978-0-203-10017-2

For more information and to order a copy visit
www.routledge.com/9780415624190/

Available from all good bookshops

www.routledge.com/middleeaststudies

Related titles from Routledge

The Middle East Today
Political, Geographical and Cultural Perspectives, 2nd Edition
By **Dona Stewart**

The new edition of The Middle East Today provides an accessible and comprehensive introductory textbook for undergraduate students of Middle East Studies, Middle East politics and geography. This updated and revised edition features a host of pedagogical features to assist students with their learning, including; detailed maps and images, case studies on key issues, boxed sections and suggestions for further reading.

The book highlights the current issues facing the Middle East, linking them to the rich political, geographical and cultural history of the region. The author examines the crises and conflicts, both current and potential, likely to dominate the region in coming years.

The second edition has been fully updated and revised to include discussion of such recent events as:
- the effects of the Arab Spring
- Turkey's growing influence in the region
- the dramatic increase in Iran's nuclear capabilities
- Usama bin Laden's death and declining support for violent extremist movements in the Middle East.

Further supplemented by a companion website containing sample chapters, a selection of maps formatted for use in presentations, and annotated links to online resources and websites, The Middle East Today is an essential resource for all students of Middle East Studies, Middle East politics and geography.

November 2012: 234x156: 304pp
Pb: 978-0-415-78244-9
Hb: 978-0-415-78243-2
Eb: 978-0-203-82896-0

For more information and to order a copy visit
www.routledge.com/9780415782449/

Available from all good bookshops

www.routledge.com/middleeaststudies

Related titles from Routledge

The Transformation of the Gulf

Politics, Economics and the Global Order

Edited By **David Held, Kristian Ulrichsen**

This book examines the political, economic and social transformation of the six member-states of the Gulf Cooperation Council (GCC) and the ways in which these states are both shaping, and being reshaped by, the processes of globalisation. Adopting a multidisciplinary approach, the volume combines thematic chapters focusing on issues such as globalisation, nationalism and identity, political thinking, and economic diversification and redistributive policymaking with empirical chapters studying specific aspects of reform and change.

Contributions from experts in the field provide cutting-edge snapshots of a region in flux and collectively offer a roadmap of its repositioning in the global order, examining the interaction between global processes and internal dynamics of change and resistance that inject new dimensions into debates over the loci of local and global transformations and the manner in which each plays off the other.

Situating the Gulf States firmly within their global twenty-first century context, this book will hold particular appeal to theorists of globalisation as well as to scholars of comparative politics, international political economy and area studies.

October 2011: 234x156: 376pp
Pb: 978-0-415-57452-5
Hb: 978-0-415-57451-8
Eb: 978-0-203-81321-8

For more information and to order a copy visit
www.routledge.com/9780415574525/

Available from all good bookshops